INTERNATIONAL DIRECTORY OF HOME PLANS

A Letter from the Editor,

If you're interested in a fresh approach to home design, you'll enjoy this special collection of plans. Many are being published for the first time. Discover them right here.

Exciting architects and designers from many countries are attracted to the world's largest home market and are designing first-rate plans for North American tastes and building conditions. The result is that you have more choices than ever before.

Compare for yourself. No matter what your family size, budget, or preferences, you're sure to find a home that suits you. And, you'll save thousands of dollars on the construction blueprints for one of these homes compared to the cost of custom plans.

Today, more than ever, it pays to build "smart". If you're seriously interested in the best home for your lifestyle . . . if you're seriously interested in the most home for your money. . . if you're seriously interested in maximizing the investment in your home . . . take a look at this remarkable collection of plans.

Best wishes for a wonderful home,

Ed

Ed Rothwell
Editor in Chief

P.S. To order complete construction blueprints for any design, see pages 316-317.

Library of Congress Number: 87-83318

ISBN: 0-938708-19-8

Canadian orders should be submitted to:

MacMillan of Canada
(a division of Canada Publishing Corporation)
164 Commander Blvd.
Agincourt, Ontario M1S 3C7

Traditional Plan Has an Added Bonus

No. 91012

If you like traditional styling, you'll love this bright, compact home with an ingenious plan that groups rooms according to their use. Lead guests right into the living room from the central foyer. The formal living and dining rooms unite, but remain separate from the kitchen and family living areas. Enjoy your family meals in the nook off the kitchen. There are no walls to keep you from the kids while you're cooking dinner. With its toasty fireplace and glass wall to the back yard, the family room is a great place for informal gatherings. All the bedrooms are upstairs, away from the action.

Total area — 2,634 sq. ft.

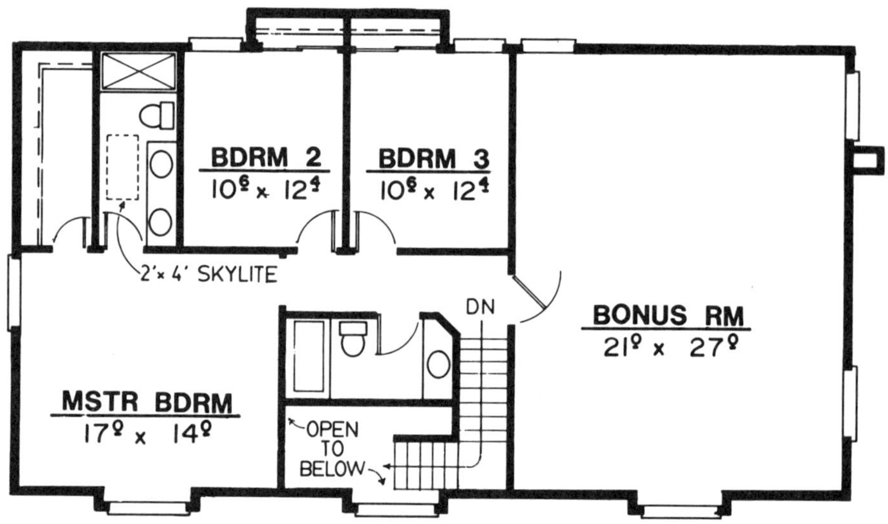

UPPER LEVEL

No. 91012

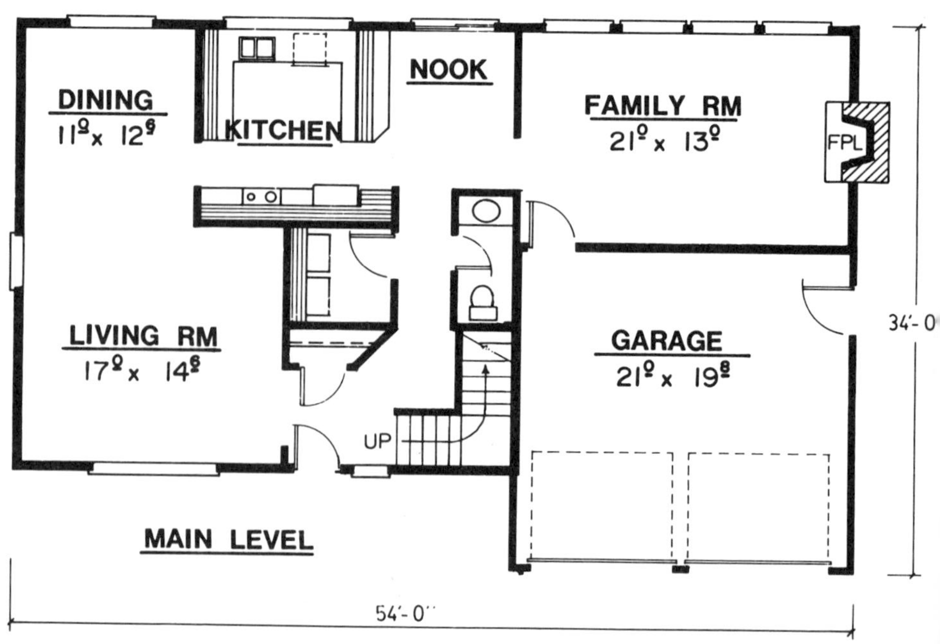

MAIN LEVEL

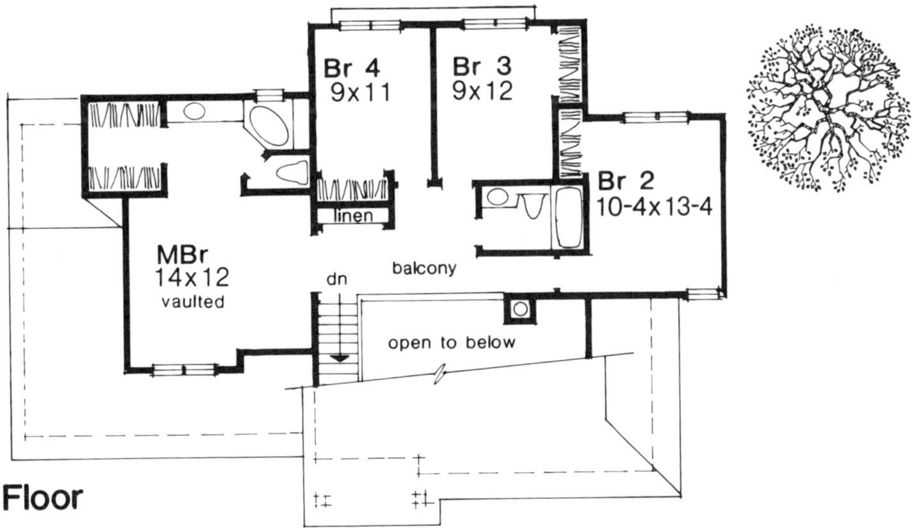

Upper Floor

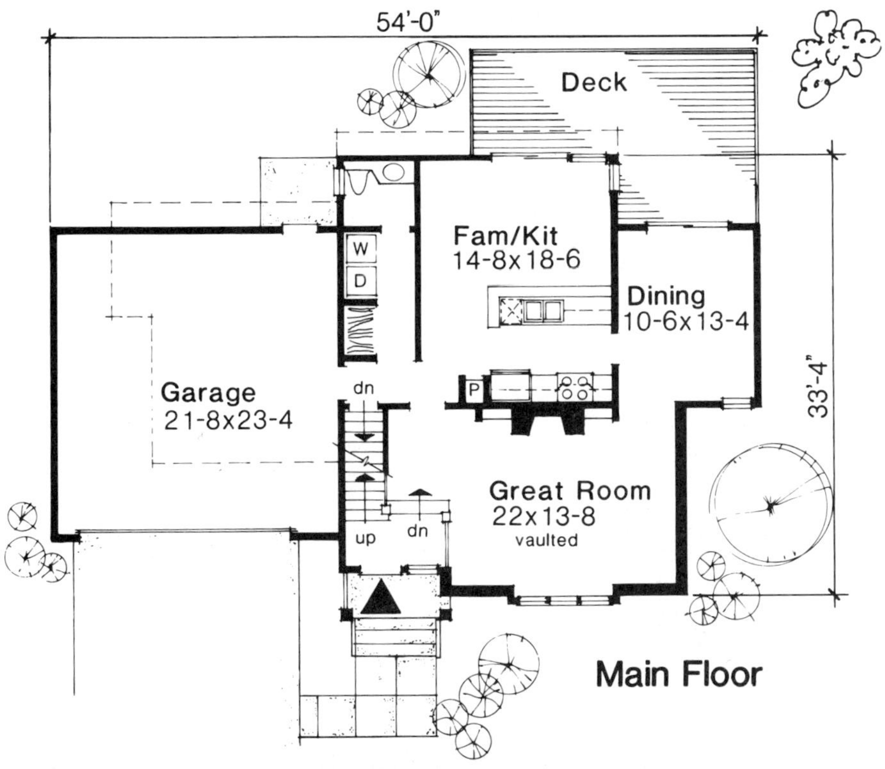

Main Floor

Master Bedroom Has a Vaulted Ceiling

No. 90371

Young families and the move up market are looking for lots of liveable space in a good looking package that combines a look of substance with sophistication. This kind of house has that design character with an exterior that uses masonry and rough siding under a sweeping roof line, an interior that lets space flow and accepts high impact views. The entry and great room vault up to the hall balcony above, the country kitchen is great for family doings, the master bedroom suite emphasizes good walk in closet space and a luxurious bathroom. And note how well the house hugs the ground line for a two story home, a look that makes the house one of the 80's generation.

First floor — 952 sq. ft.
Second floor — 915 sq. ft.

Sun-Washed Entry Hints at Airy Ambiance

No. 91013

Are you a sun worshipper? You won't have to go outside to benefit from the sun's cheerful warmth in this three-bedroom beauty. Cheerful views envelope the fireplaced living room, which opens to a formal dining room with glass on three sides. Sharing the rear view with the nook and family room, the kitchen is adjacent to both dining areas for mealtime convenience. Upstairs, behind double doors, the master bedroom is brightened by an elegant palladium window. High window placement in the connecting bath means your privacy will be assured.

First floor — 1,034 sq. ft.
Second floor — 795 sq. ft.

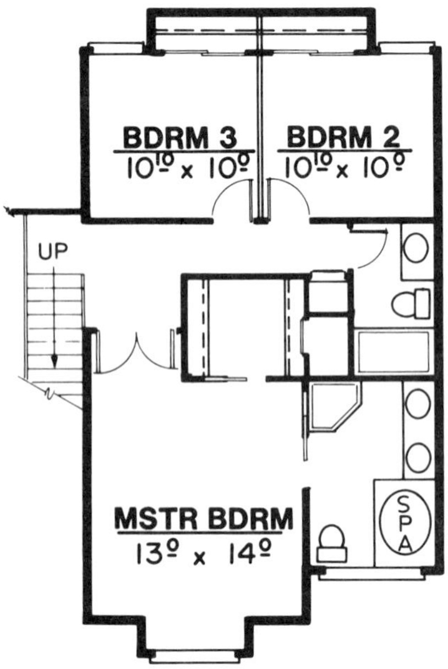

UPPER LEVEL
795 SQ. FT.

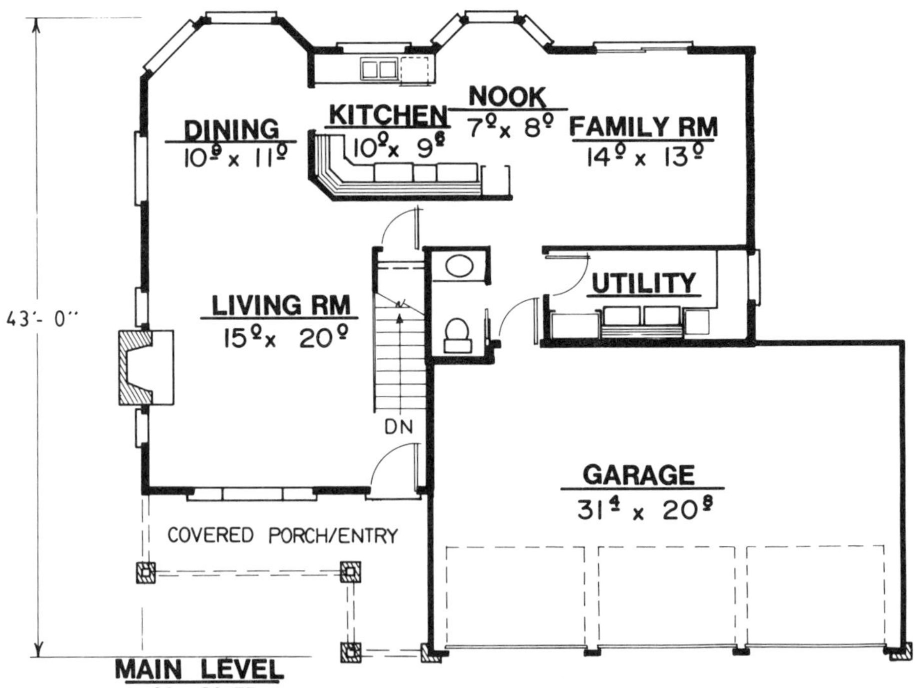

MAIN LEVEL
1034 SQ. FT.

51'- 0"

No. 91013

Lots of Living in a Small Space

No. 91015

Here's a compact multi-level that will be at home on your hillside lot. And, with four bedrooms, everyone can enjoy a plenty of room. You'll appreciate the privacy of the bedroom wing, a few steps up from main living areas. Oversized windows and french doors make the wide-open design of the formal dining and living rooms seem even larger. For informal meals, the bay nook in the kitchen is cheerful and convenient. A large family room, powder room, and a fourth bedroom provide even more living space downstairs.

Main level — 1,320 sq. ft.
Lower level — 556 sq. ft.

1876 SQ. FT.

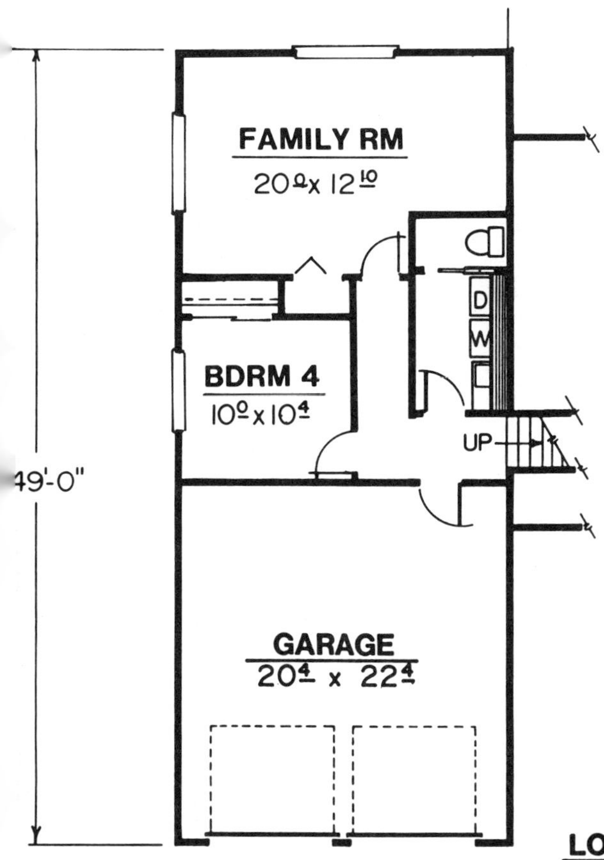

LOWER LEVEL
556 SQ.FT.

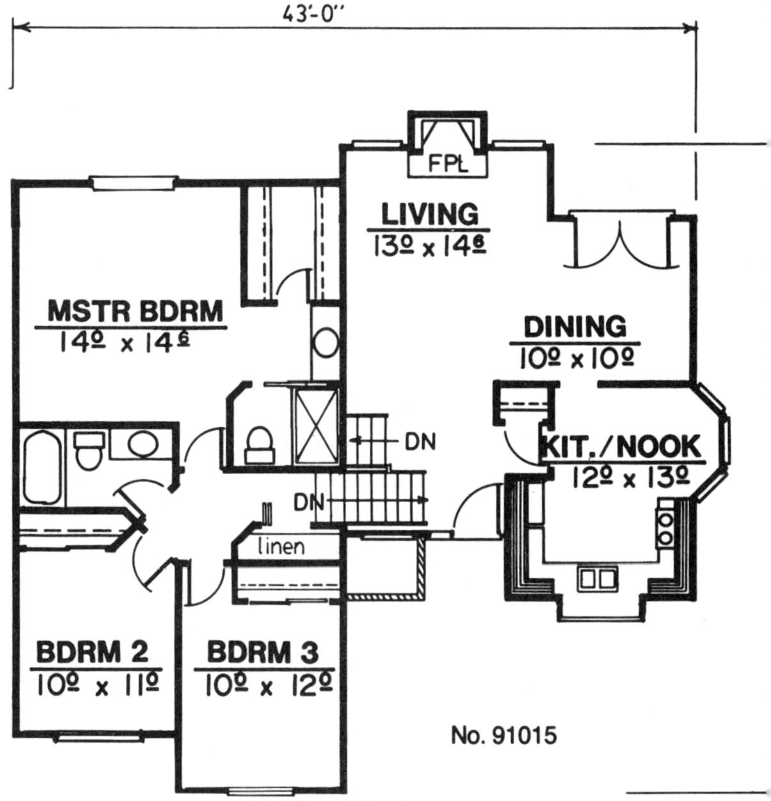

MAIN LEVEL
1320 SQ. FT.

Arched Window Graces Formal Living Room

No. 90910

Lots of attention to fine detail sets this family jewel apart from the average house. An unusual, attractive porch shelters your arrival. Inside, open spaces, soaring ceilings, and a well-placed skylight provide a wonderful feeling of spaciousness. The excellent traffic pattern and zoning of this design will make living here a delight. Up the open staircase you will find three large bedrooms with many other special features. A whirlpool and make-up vanity in the master suite, double sinks in the family bath, and a knock-out window perfect for curling up with a favorite book will add to your enjoyment.

Main floor — 1,099 sq. ft.
Second floor — 846 sq. ft.
Garage — 483 sq. ft.
Width — 42 ft.
Depth — 44 ft.

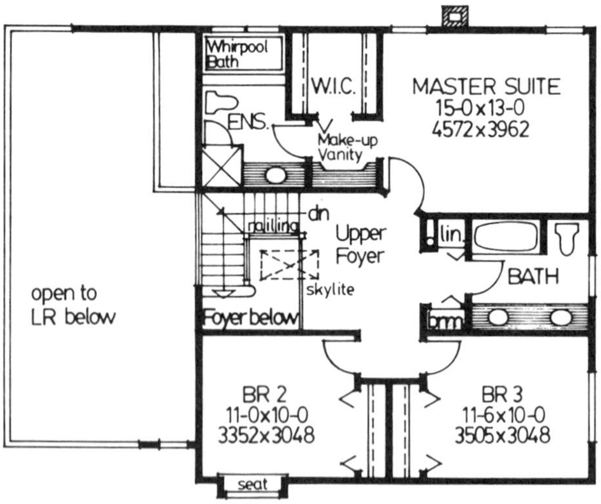

SECOND FLOOR PLAN

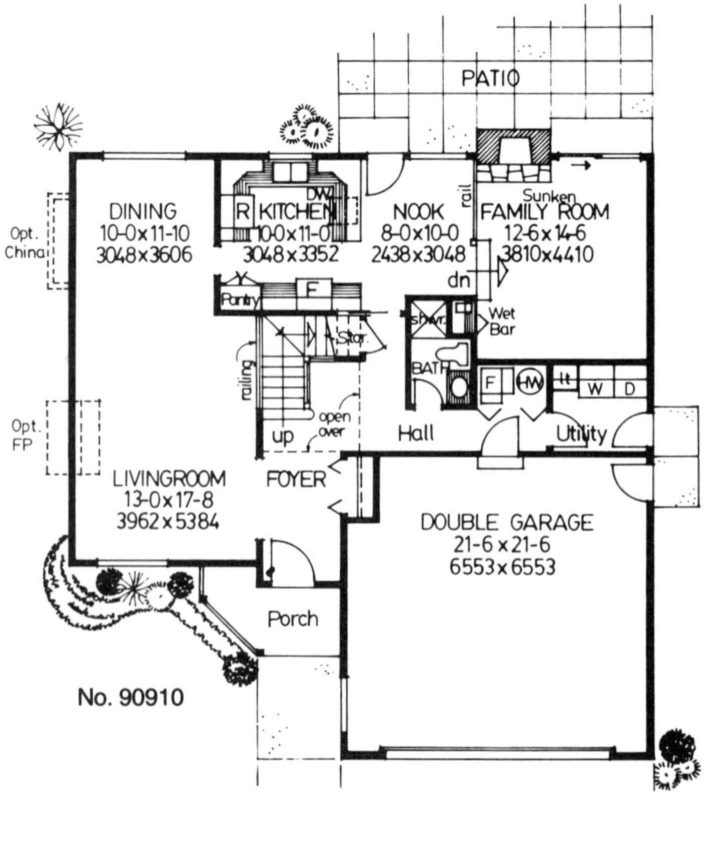

No. 90910

Two-Story Solarium Warms Lavish Master Suite

No. 90602

Sophistication abounds in this passive solar split-level. The excellent layout begins with the front-to-back central foyer. To the right are the living and dining areas, featuring a heat-circulating fireplace and a stunning bayed window wall. Large glass doors lead to the south terrace, allowing direct gain heat. Down a half-flight, the recreation room is separated from the solarium by a glass wall. Three bedrooms and two full baths share the upper level.

Upper level — 1,505 sq. ft.
Lower level — 478 sq. ft.
(optional slab construction available)

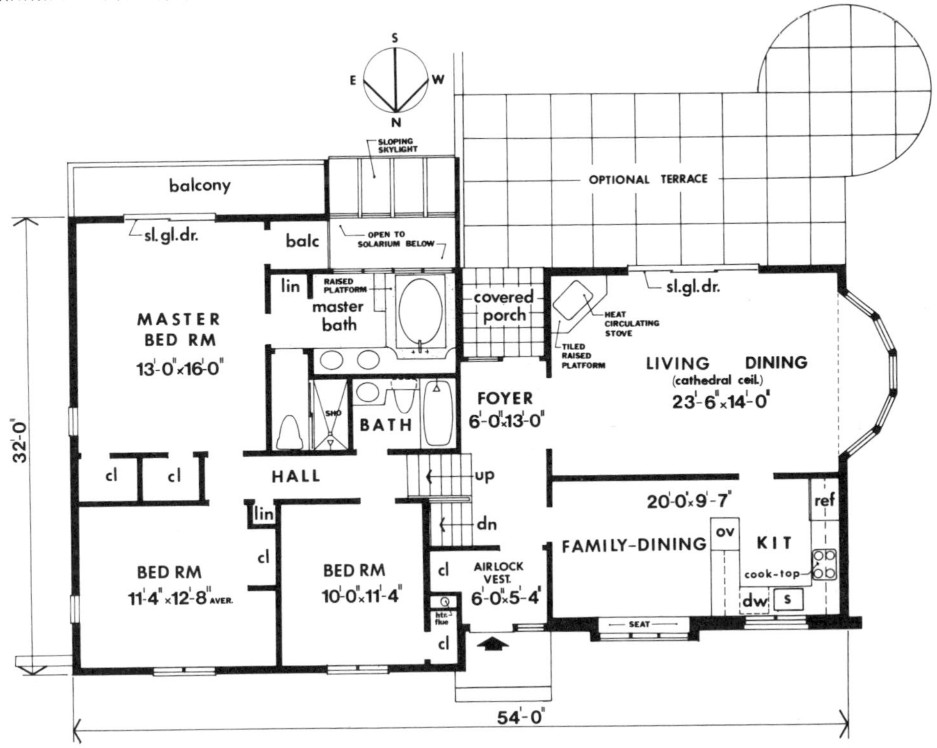

No. 90602

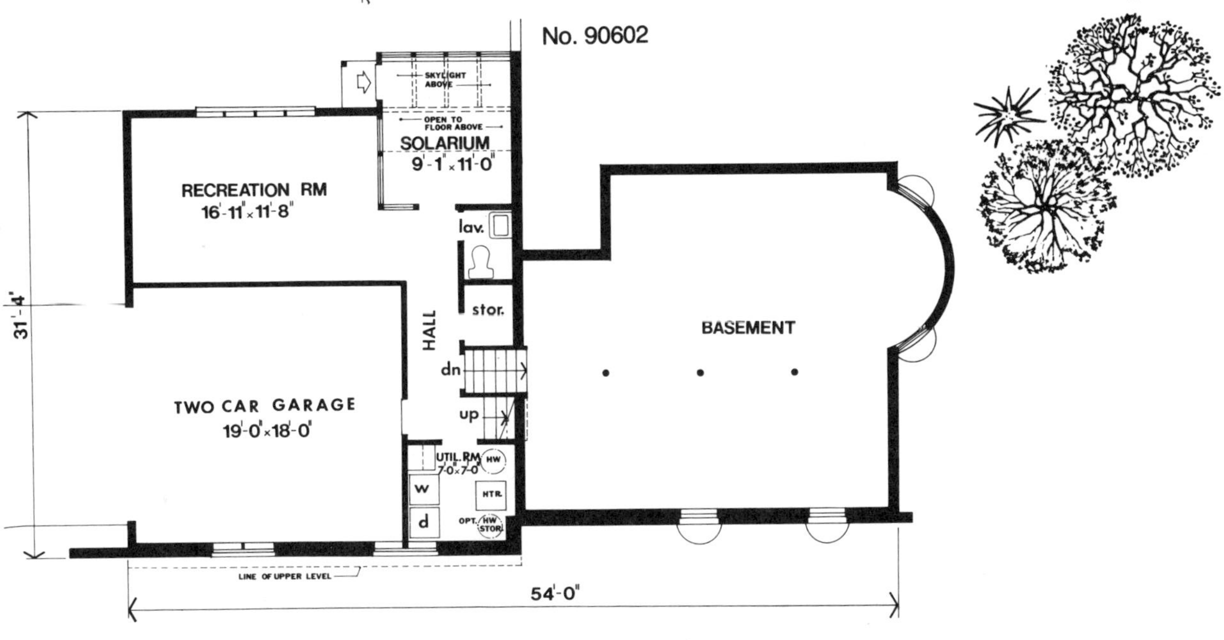

Plenty of Room for Plants

No. 90907

This beautiful Victorian-styled 2-story design presents all of the desired amenities in a neat, efficient package. Both entrances to this home offer many practical features. A large covered porch welcomes your guests and leads them into a spacious foyer with a large coat closet. And, the side entrance off the garage doubles as a mud room and utility area. Living areas surround the open, central staircase, providing excellent traffic flow for busy families or easy entertaining. Notice how the powder room serves two purposes: as a guest powder room, and as a washroom for the kids returning home from play.

Main floor — 1,006 sq. ft.
Second floor — 772 sq. ft.
Unfinished basement — 1,006 sq. ft.
Garage — 451 sq. ft.

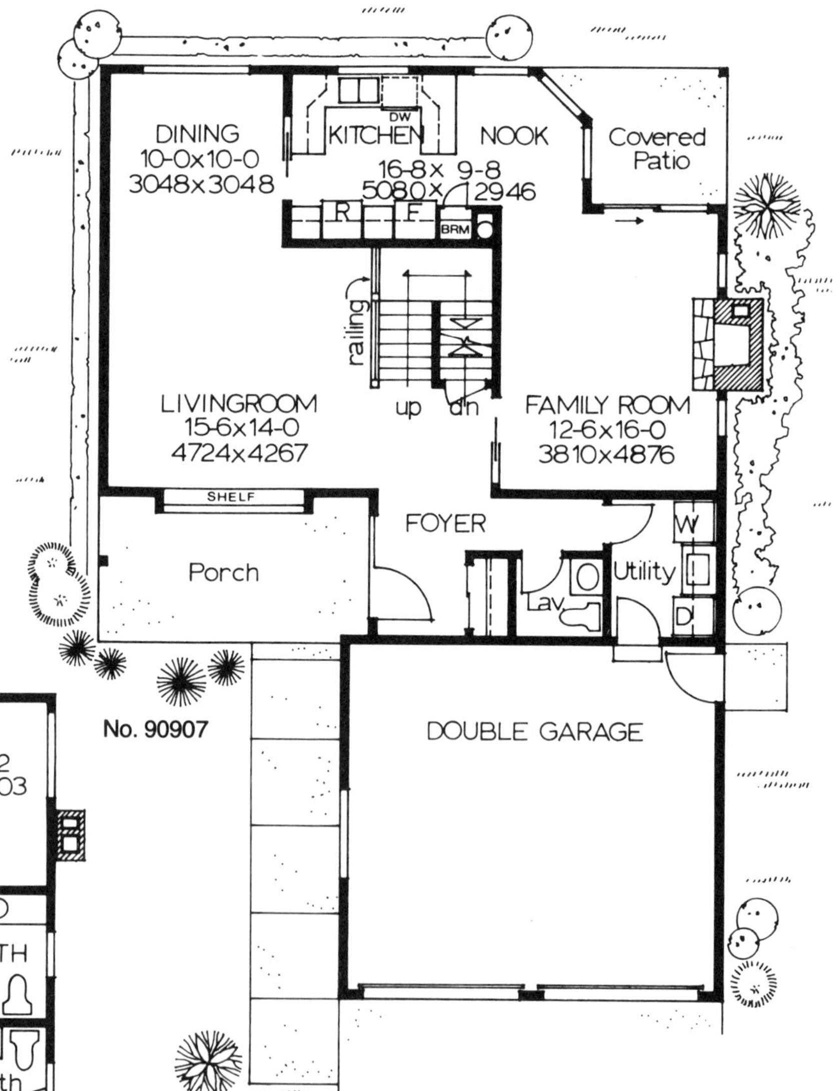

No. 90907

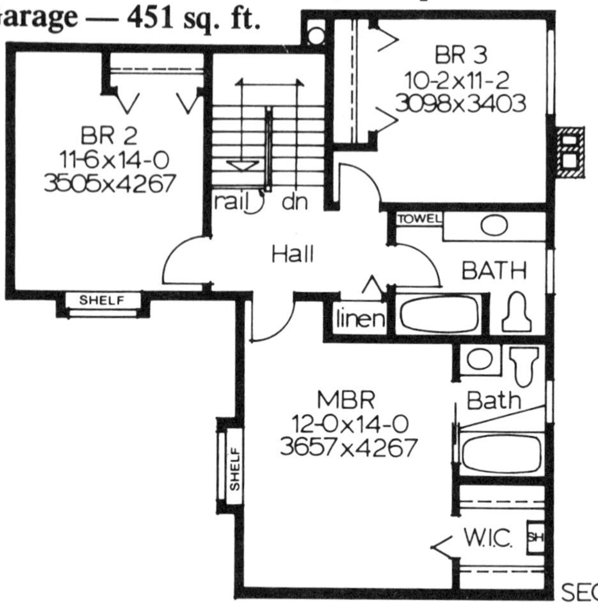

SECOND FLOOR

Width — 36 ft.
Depth — 54 ft.

Family Living on One Level

No. 91027

Arches adorn exterior and interior spaces in this four-bedroom beauty. Look at the graceful openings between the sunken living and dining rooms just off the foyer and the massive half-round window and curved entryway facing the street. Walk past the den to family areas at the rear of the house, centering around the convenient island kitchen. An open plan keeps the cook from getting lonely while the kids are gathered around the fireplace or doing homework at the handy desk. And, the master suite is a special retreat. French doors unite the room with the back yard. At the end of a long day, the private spa is a plus you'll really appreciate.

Living area — 2,174 sq. ft.

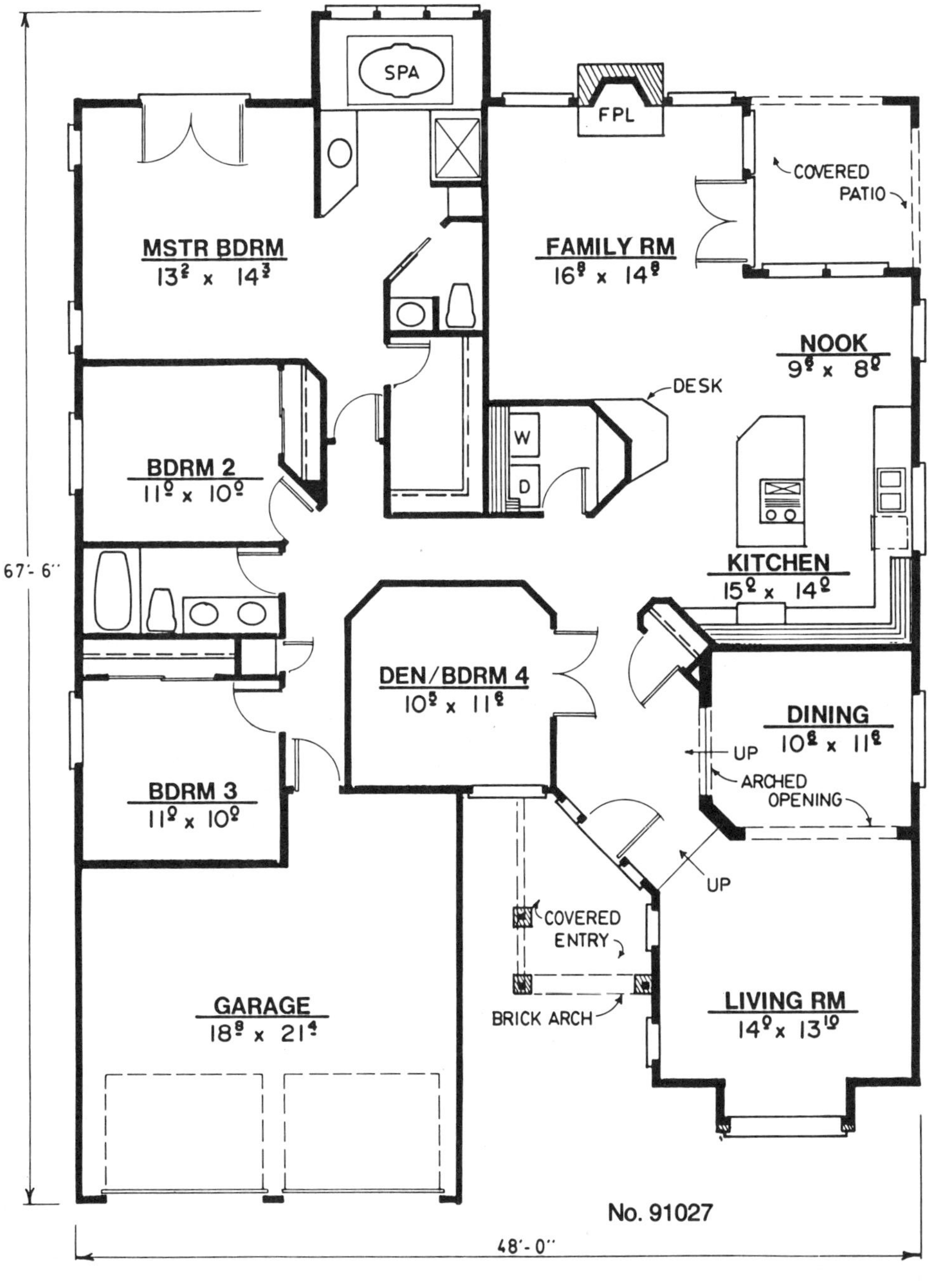

Indoor/Outdoor Unity

No. 91011

One-level living has never been more interesting than in this three-bedroom home with attached three-car garage. From the protected entry, the central foyer leads down the hall to the bedroom wing, into the formal living areas, or into the sun-washed library. At the end of the bedroom hall, you'll find a luxurious master suite, complete with spa and a private deck. Straight ahead, glass walls and an open plan unite the formal dining and sunken living rooms with the back yard. The adjoining island kitchen, nook, and family room continue the outdoor feeling with expansive windows and sliders to the surrounding covered patio.

Total area — 2,242 sq. ft.

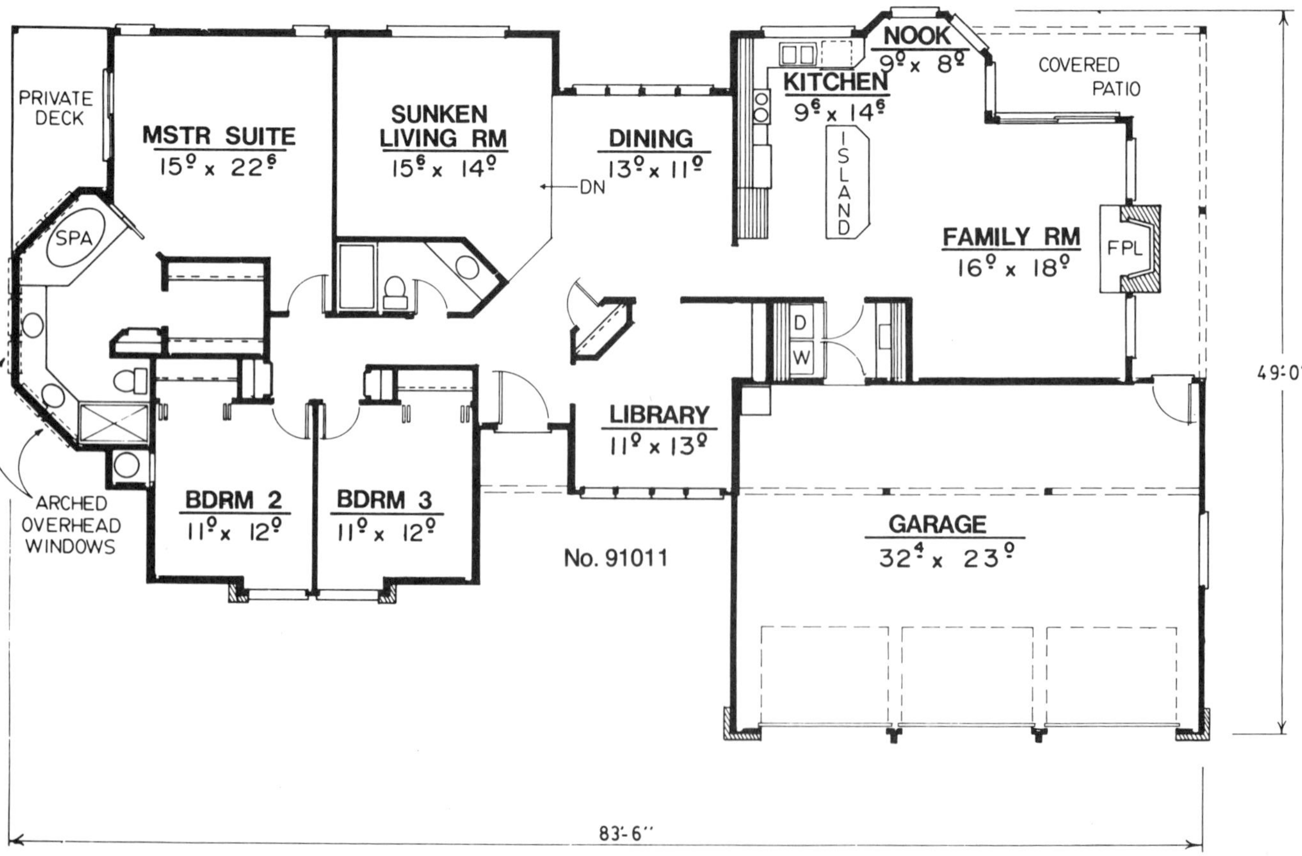

Compact Design Provides for Family

No. 90300

This well organized design provides a separate half story for the three bedrooms plus two baths and plenty of closet space. The main floor employs the garage to buffer street noise. The front living room provides easy access to the rear dining room and the more informal areas of the home. Roomy closets are placed near the front entrance and at the family entrance through the garage. The half bath is located just off the kitchen which shares a counter with the adjacent family room. A fireplace plus sliding glass doors which open onto the rear deck make this a prime candidate for many cozy evenings.

Total area — 1,630 sq. ft.

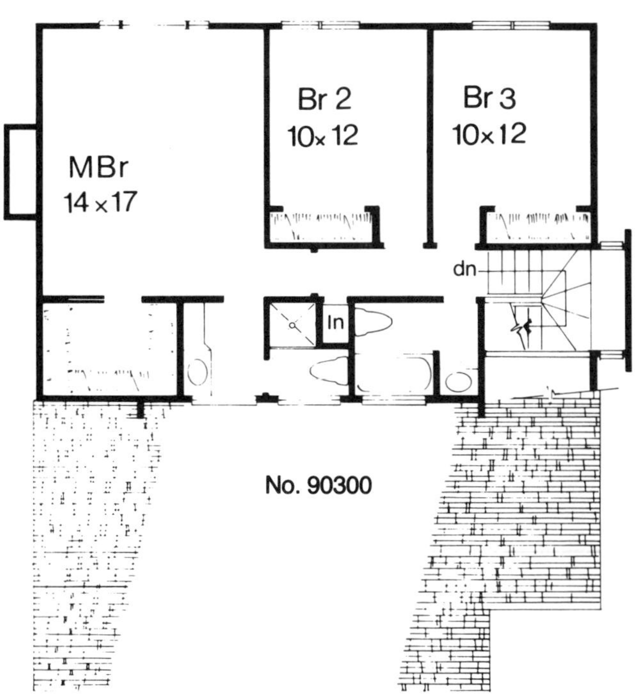

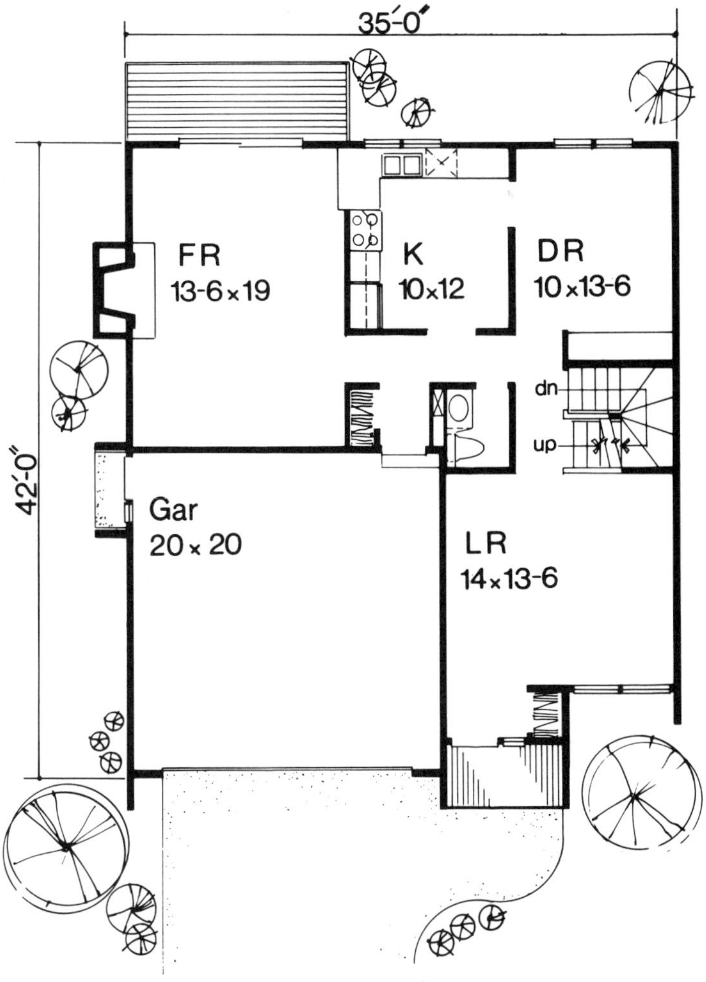

Sunny and Warm

No. 91029

Here's a home unlike any you've ever seen. The multi-level plan unfolds as you walk through the foyer. You'll find a handy den on this floor. Four steps up, active areas revolve around a hexagonal hallway, giving every room a distinctive shape. Mealtimes are a breeze with the pass-through between the island kitchen and dining room. Fireplaces keep formal and family living areas toasty even on the coldest days. And, when the weather's nice, the rear deck is a great place to relax. The other staircase off the foyer winds its way up to four spacious bedrooms. Look at the raised spa and double vanities in the master suite. A home this special is hard to resist.

First floor — 1,638 sq. ft.
Second floor — 1,210 sq. ft.

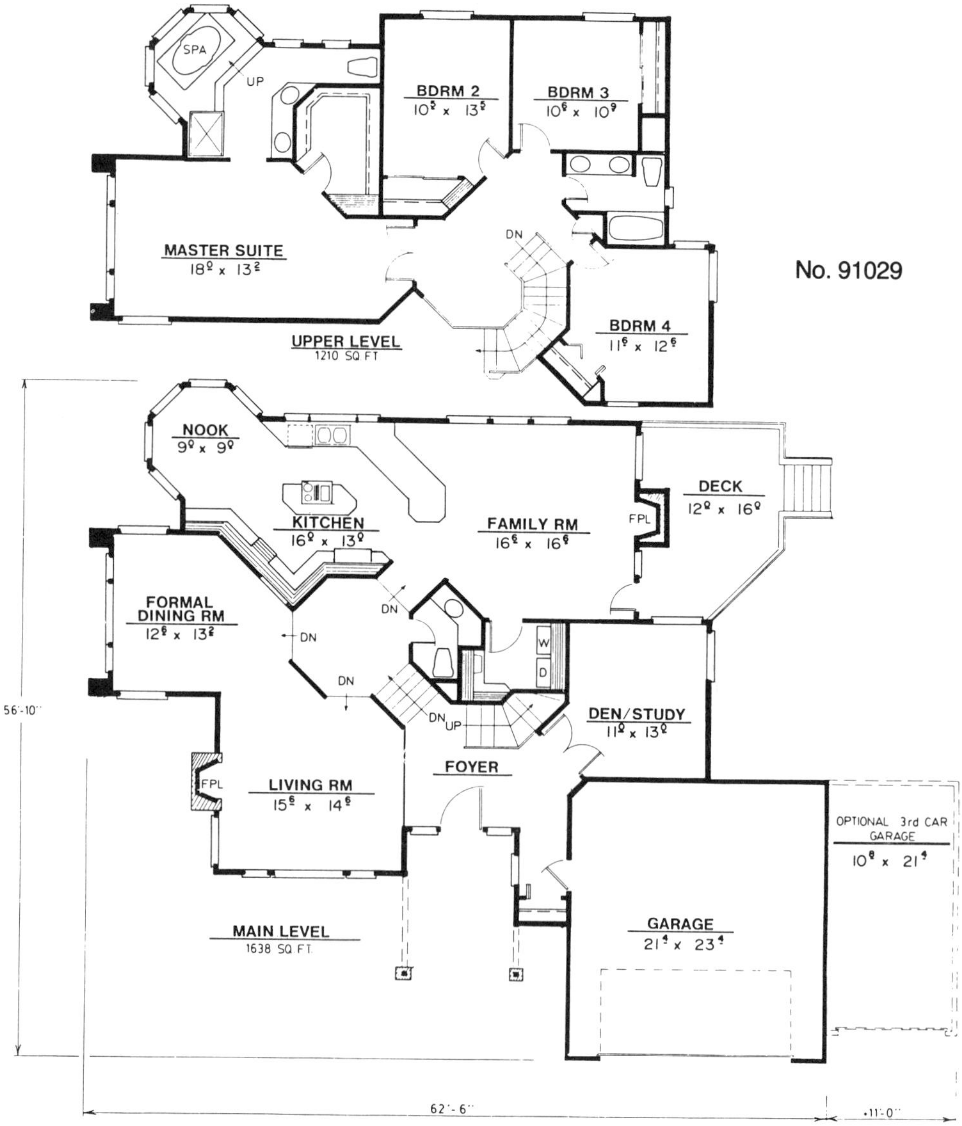

No. 91029

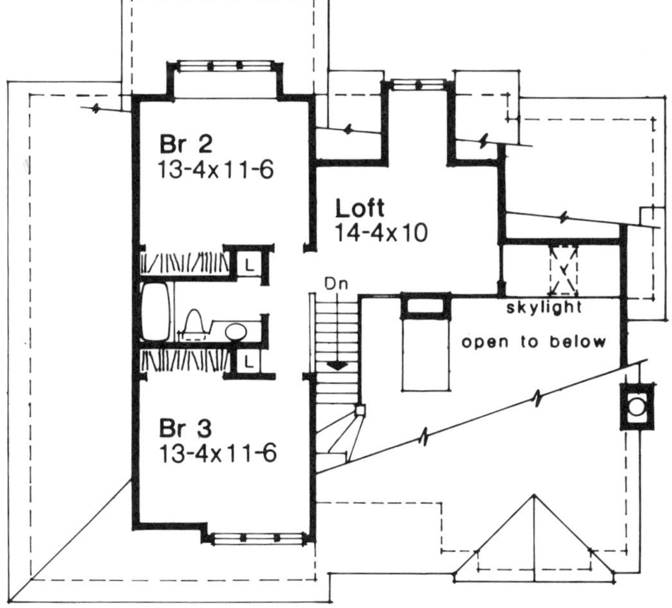

Upper Floor

Design Offers Customized Features

No. 90362

Family homes today need all the luxury features of a custom home to capture the buyer's attention. This home is full of those fcatures; walk-in, pass-thru wet bar; vaulted great room with featured fireplace; deluxe master bedroom/bath suite; convenient laundry with counter space; dormered loft; etc. Plus, the exterior looks importantly large, with variegated roof line interest, transom glass great room bay window, and protective front entry porch.

First floor — 1,290 sq. ft.
Second floor — 664 sq. ft.

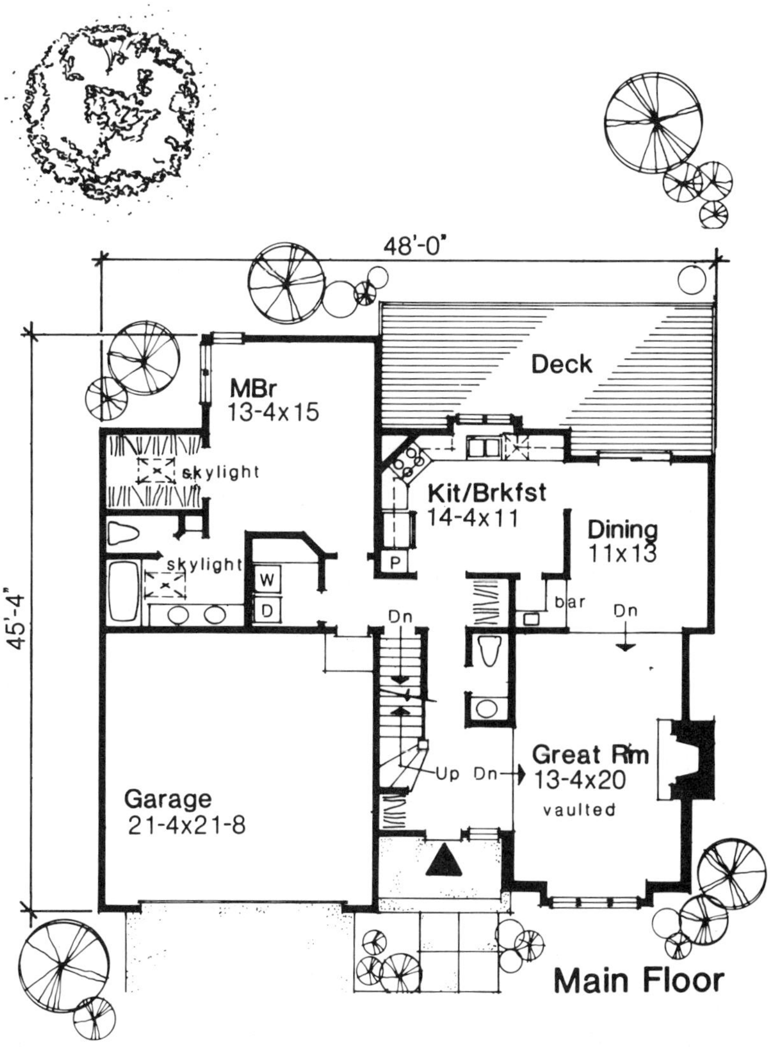

Main Floor

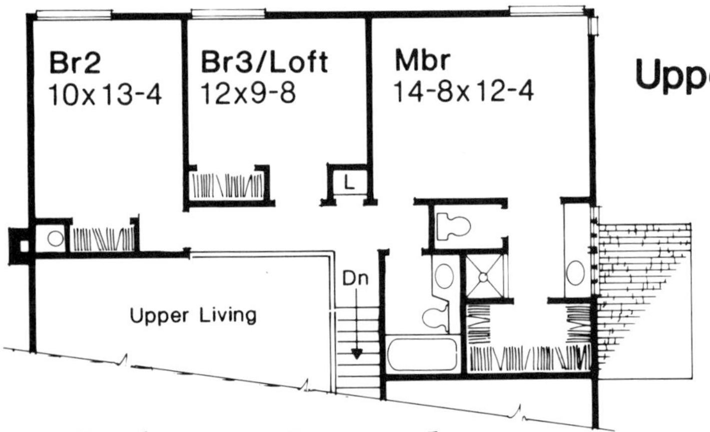

Upper Floor

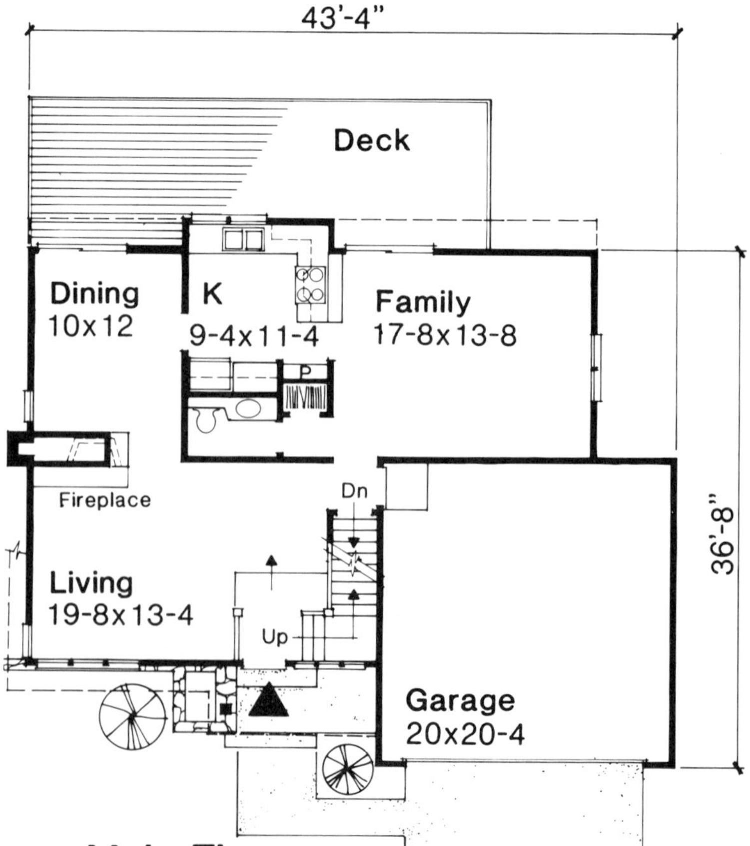

Main Floor

Bedrooms Located on Second Level

No. 90369

Today's houses of modest size are being designed with the impact of formerly much larger designs. This two story is just such a concept with a vaulted ceiling in its living room up to the hall balcony above, the triple room accommodation of living room, dining room, and family room, the luxurious master bath and closet, the long low sweep of roof lines. Note, too, the design importance centered around the front porch and entry, and the carefully proportioned sash on all four elevations to make this house look good from every angle. Masonry accent helps further tie the house to its site.

First floor — 888 sq. ft.
Second floor — 776 sq. ft.

UPPER LEVEL

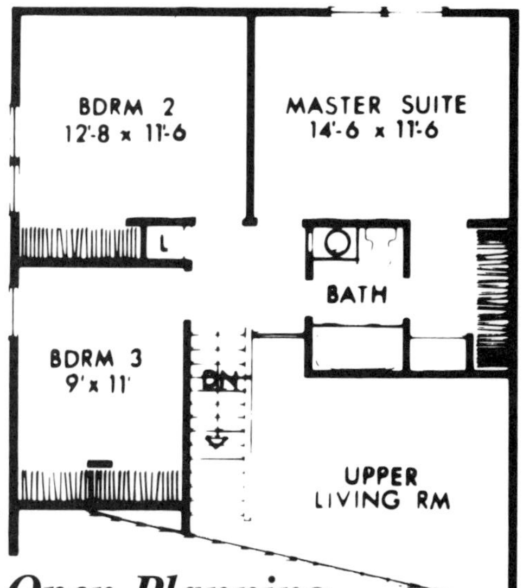

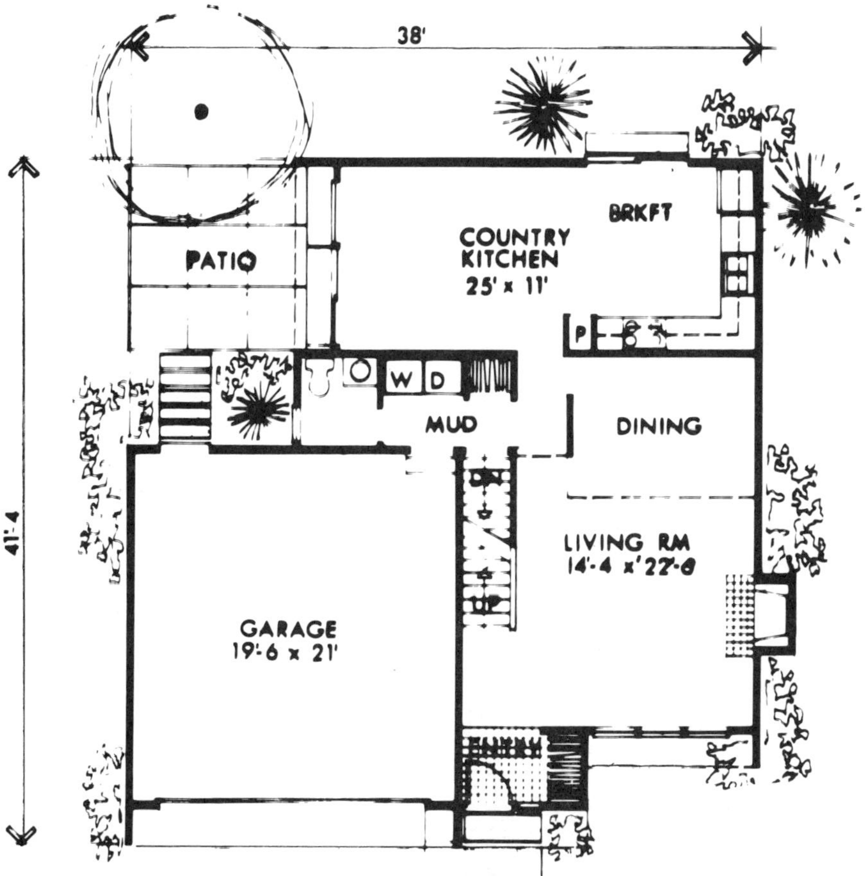

MAIN LEVEL

Open Planning Maximizes Space

No. 90346

Togetherness, the key to today's life styles, is a consideration when a family selects a home. Most couples don't want walled-off living, dining and kitchen spaces. They prefer rooms that combine functions. For example, in this two-story home, space is maximized by merging rooms. At front, living and dining areas are combined; the living section, with a dramatic ceiling that slopes up to a second-floor balcony; the dining area more intimate with an eight-foot ceiling.

Lower & Upper levels — 1,462 sq. ft.

Special Features Enhances Plan

No. 90365

Character is derived from the warmth of saw-textured redwood siding with natural stain and earth colored brick. Entrance features double doors and clerestory glass. Triple garage doors are sided and stained to match the siding. Central entrance gives immediate impact indoors with a two-story, open stair wall. Living room also has vaulted ceiling up to the stair landing overlook. Generous family room is stepped down for another change of spatial character. Garden kitchen and breakfast area extend indoor space to deck outside, as does greenhouse window box in dining room. Convenience and luxury features are highlighted. Note pantry and broom closets, the microwave oven, trash compactor, five-foot wet bar and first-floor laundry-mud room. Upstairs note the optional fourth bedroom or master suite retreat, attic for extra storage, oversized master bathing pool-tub and the large master closet.

Area — 2,360 sq. ft.

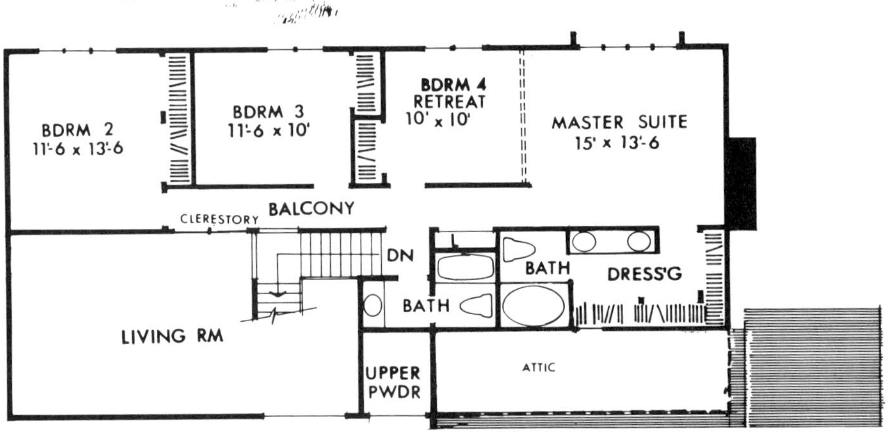

Upper Floor

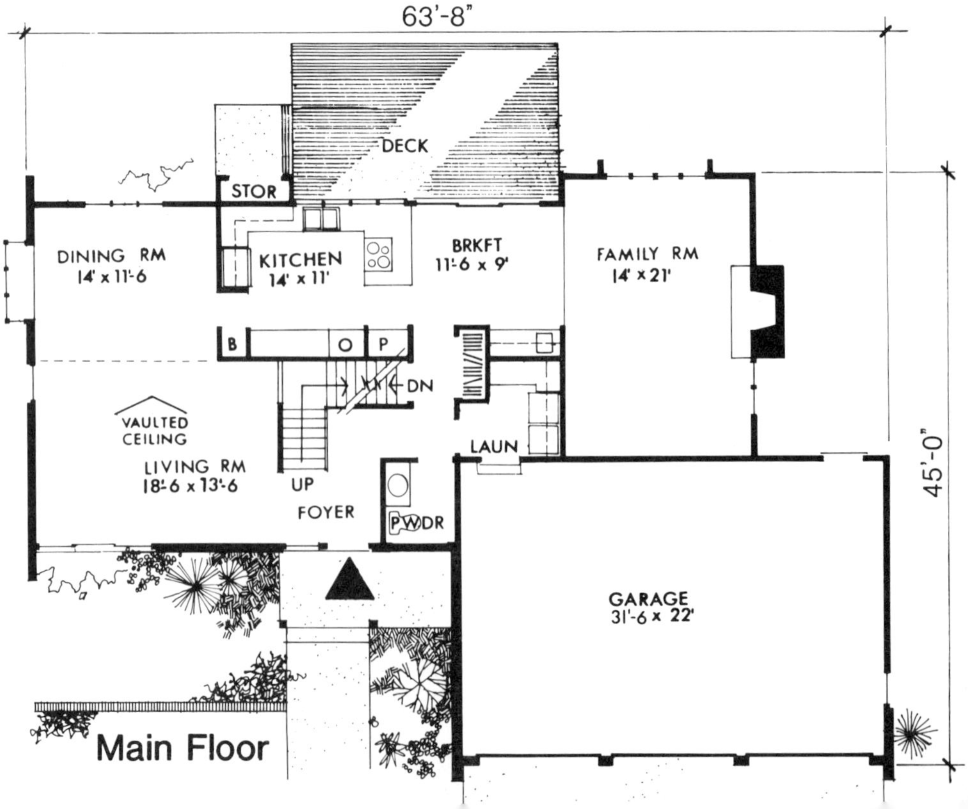

Main Floor

Victorian Touches Disguise Modern Design

No. 90616

Indulge in the romance of Victorian styling without sacrificing up-to-date living. Out of the past come porches with turned wood posts, exterior walls of round shingles, wonderful bay windows, and decorative scroll work. But the present is evident in the kitchen and family room, with a skylit entertainment area for today's electronic pleasures. The stairs begins its rise with a turned post and rail. The master suite features a high ceiling with an arched window, private bath, and tower sitting room with adjoining roof deck.

Basic house - 1,956 sq. ft.
Laundry — 36 sq. ft.
Garage — 440 sq. ft.
Basement — 967 sq. ft.

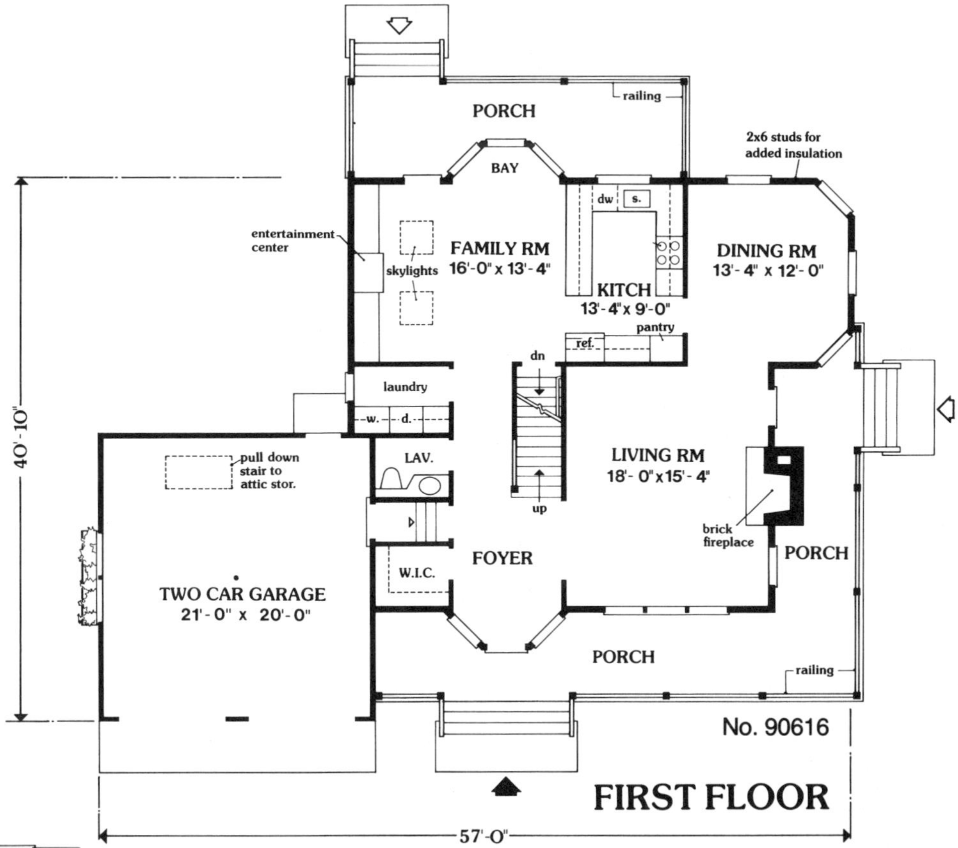

FIRST FLOOR

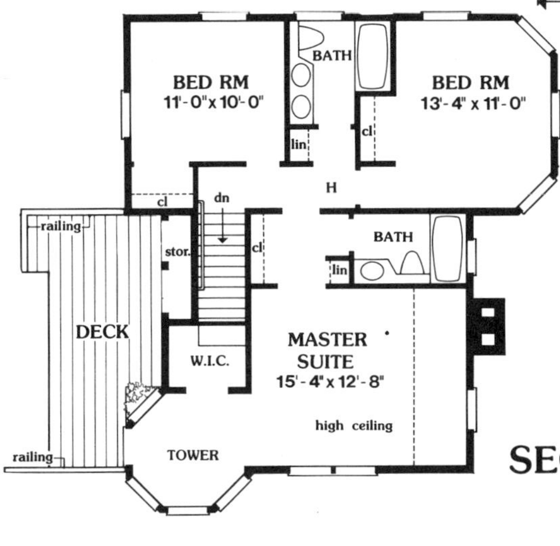

SECOND FLOOR

Old American Saltbox Design

No. 90123

A sloping living room ceiling creates a sense of spaciousness to the modest square footage. You can relax in front of the centrally located fireplace in cool weather or move through triple sliding glass doors to the roomy deck when the weather is warmer. Behind the living room lies a bedroom, full bath and kitchen/dining area which has a window seat. Laundry facilities are conveniently placed off the kitchen. On the left of the living room a quiet corner has been tucked under the stairs leading to the second floor. The second level affords two equal sized bedrooms (one with its own private deck), joined by a full bath. A balcony skirts the entire level and overlooks the living room below.

First floor-840 sq. ft.
Second floor-440 sq. ft.

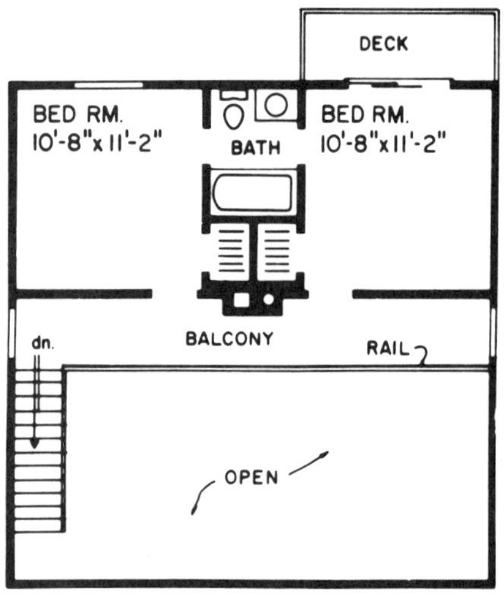

SECOND FLOOR

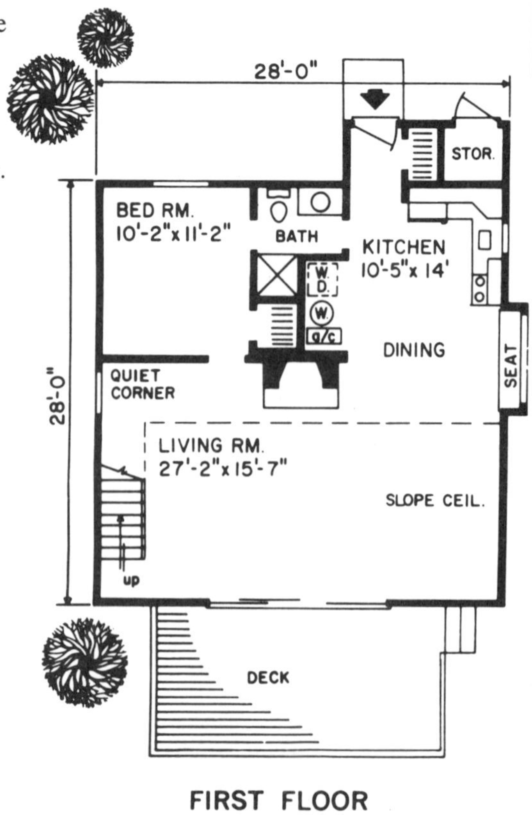

FIRST FLOOR

Simple Lines Enhanced By Elegant Window

No. 10503

An arched window in the front den, a sloped ceiling in the living room, and a wall of windows overlooking the rear deck provide a feeling of spaciousness in this elegantly designed home. The dining room opens directly onto the efficiently arranged kitchen. A master suite is appointed with a walk-in closet, double vanities, and a bath.

First floor — 1,486 sq. ft.
Garage — 462 sq. ft.

To order blueprints only for any design, see pgs. 108-109

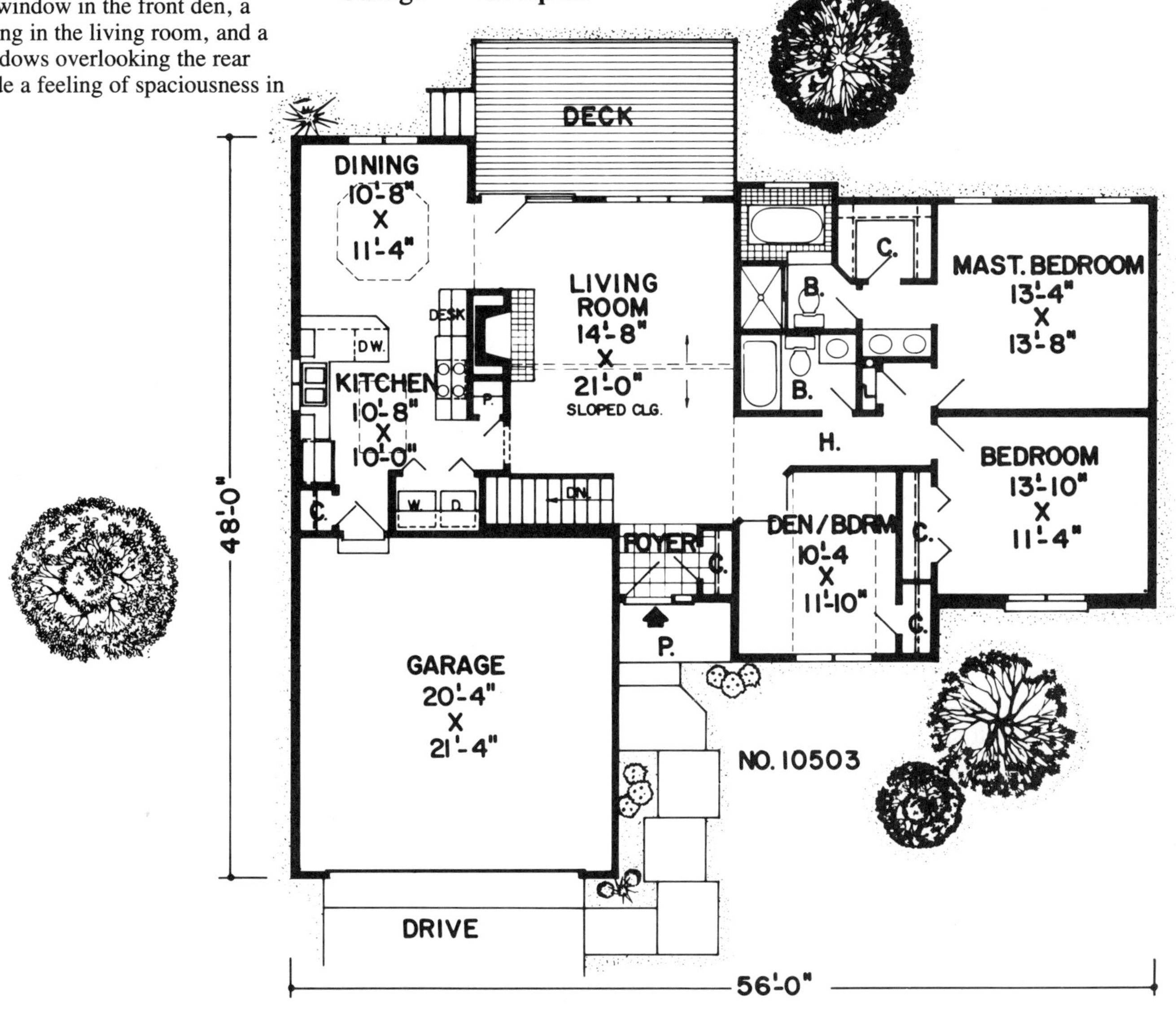

Perfect for a Hillside

No. 10595

From the road, the appearance of this two level home is deceiving. A central staircase directs traffic from the front entry to the den and master bedroom suite, to the living room, with its sloping ceiling and fireplace, or to the half bath, laundry and garage. Enter the island kitchen and formal dining room from either the breakfast or the living rooms. Two screened porches make outdoor living easy, rain or shine. Downstairs, the huge recreation room features a kitchenette and fireplace for entertaining. Two more bedrooms and a full bath complete this level, which could even be used for in-law quarters.

Upper floor — 1,643 sq. ft.
Lower floor — 1,297 sq. ft.
Garage — 528 sq. ft.

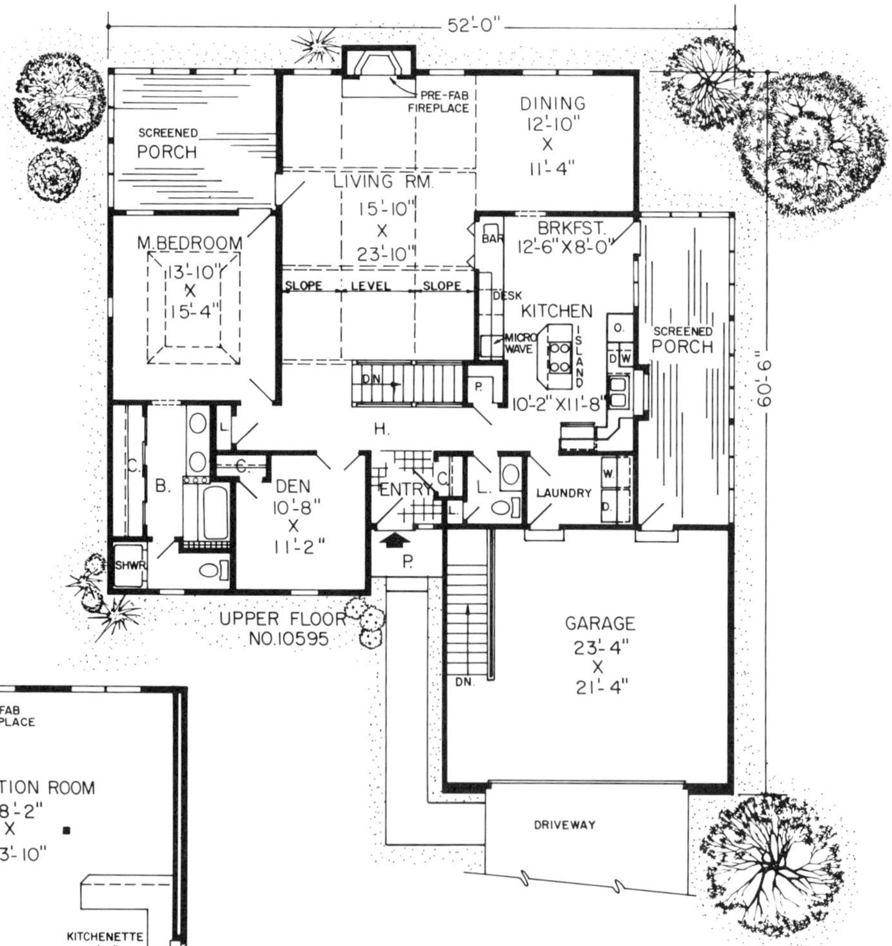

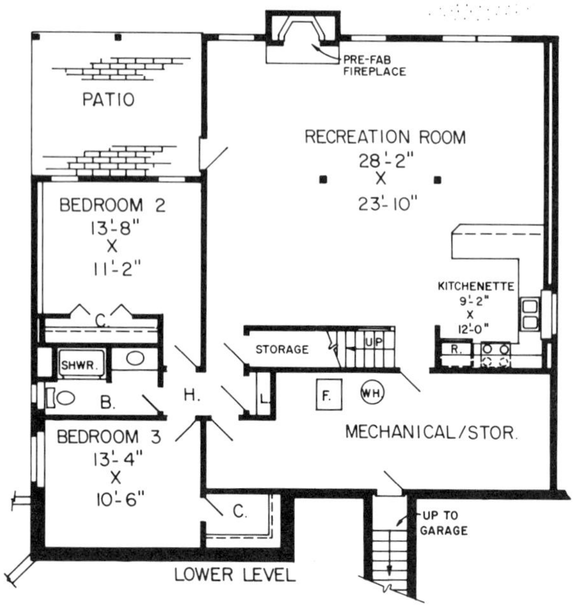

Upper Floor

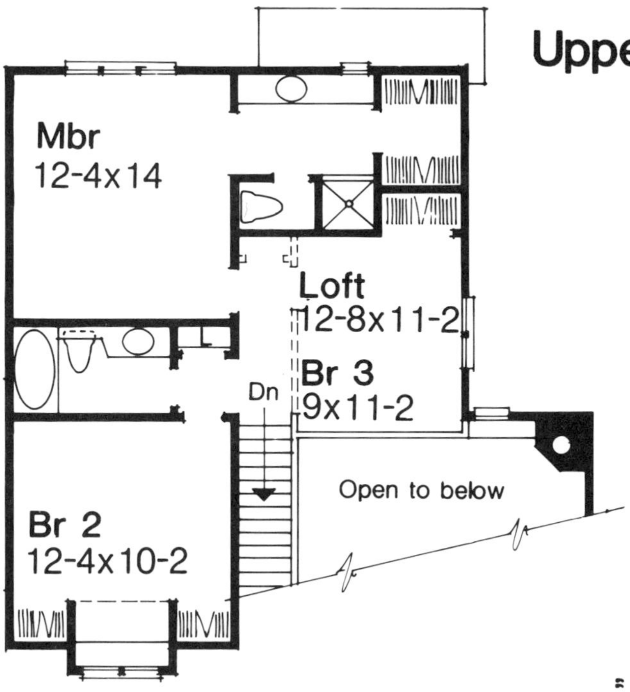

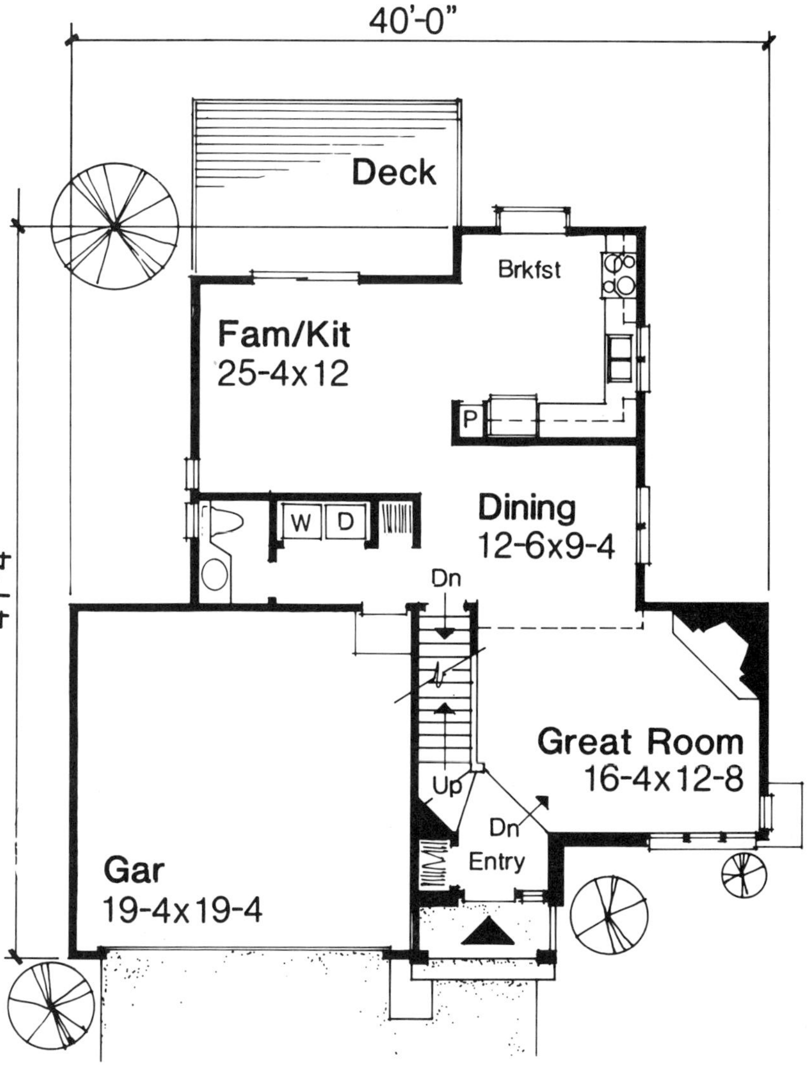

Compact Design Images Bigger House Look

No. 90370

The move up market is demanding more than the basics, more in appearance, more in space, more in quality equipment. This plan is designed to appeal with the look of a bigger house with "establishment" traditional details within a contemporary form.

First floor — 817 sq. ft.
Second floor — 699 sq. ft.

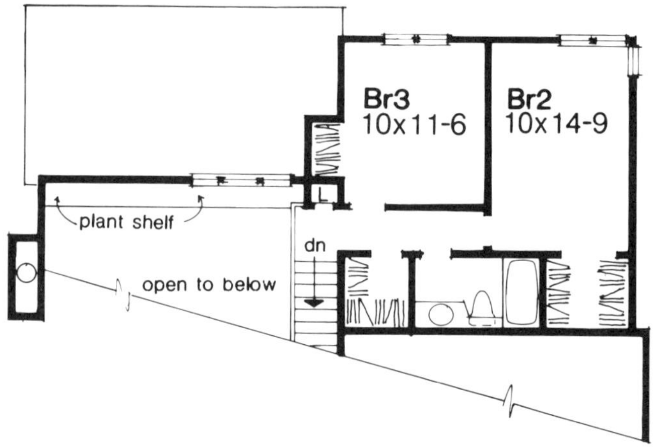

Upper Floor

Four Bedroom 1 1/2 Story Design

No. 90358

Many of todays single family markets are looking for a flexible plan that grows and adapts to their families changing needs. This is such a house with its master bedroom and den/4th bedroom down, double bedrooms up, stacked baths and well working open and flowing living areas. The exterior impact is of hi-style, hi-value; the interior impact is highlighted by the vaulted living room and thru views to the rear deck and yard. This house belongs in a neighborhood where the custom exterior look will make for a surprising space/value combination to the move up young family market.

Main floor — 1,062 sq. ft.
Upper floor — 469 sq. ft.

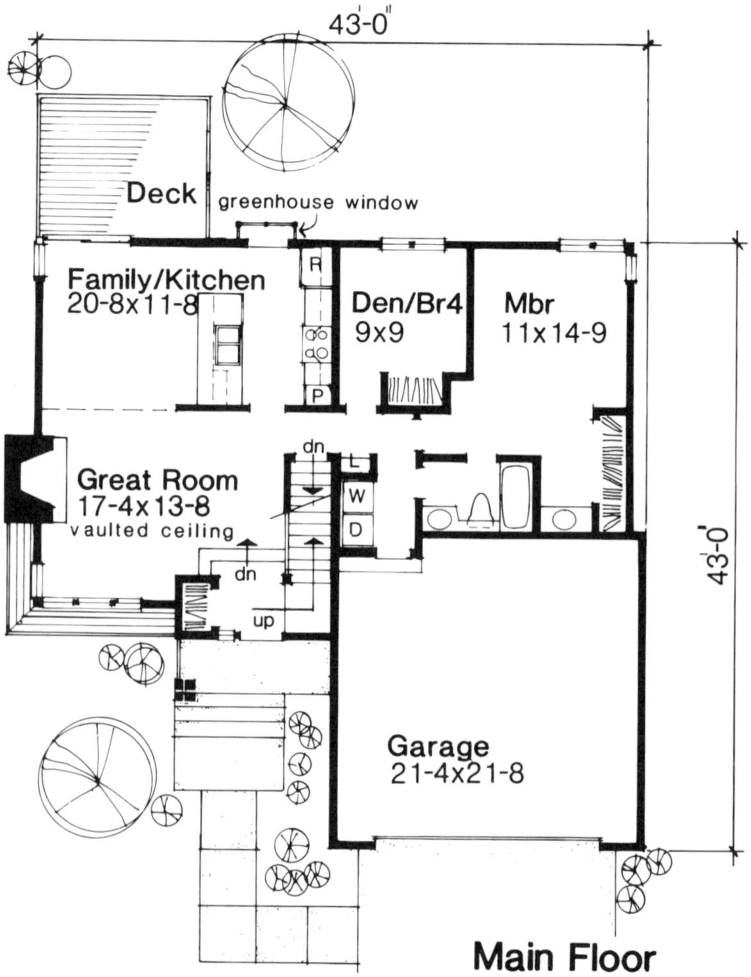

Main Floor

Above Reproach

No. 91002

Perched above an uneven lot, this house transforms an awkward site to greet and impress your family and guests. The welcome continues inside where the firedrum fireplace warms both entryway and living room. Both living and dining rooms open out onto a deck that surrounds the house on three sides. The downstairs bedroom has its own bath, and the enclosed sleeping room with two bunk beds is adjacent to a loft large enough to be divided. The second full bath provides for a large group of guests. If you don't love company, watch out. Your company will love your home.

Main Level — 744 sq. ft.
Upper Level — 288 sq. ft.

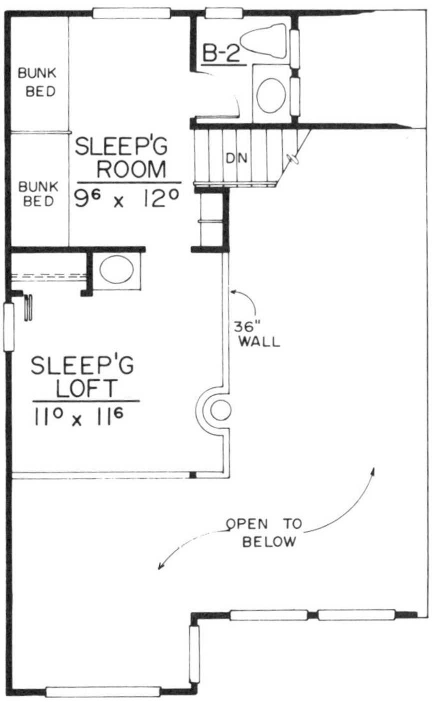

UPPER LEVEL PLAN
288 SQ.FT.

No. 91002

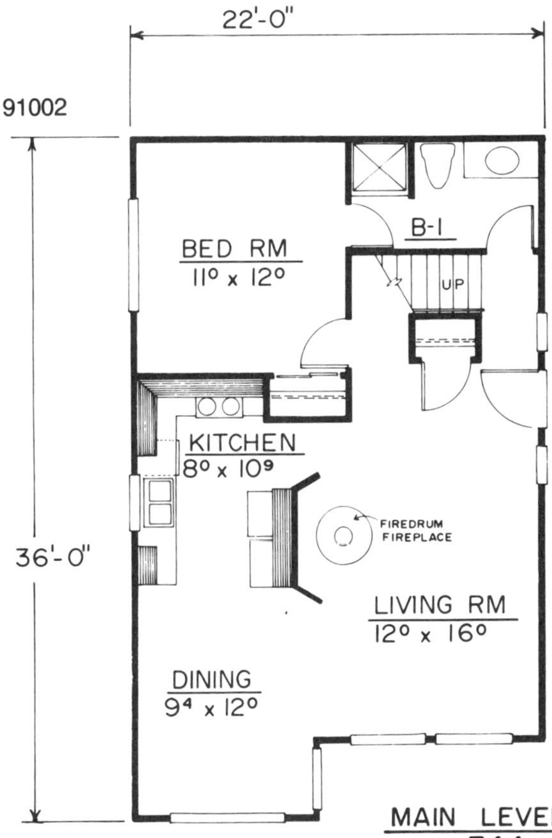

MAIN LEVEL PLAN
744 SQ.FT.

Bay Window Brightens Dining Room

No. 90703

Don't worry about getting wet on a rainy day. You're protected from the car to the kitchen by the three car garage and laundry wing. The front entry, flanked by a cheerful dining room and cozy living room, is sheltered by a columned porch. Four bedrooms and two baths at the top of the central staircase allow lots of space for a growing family.

First floor — 1,171 sq. ft.
Second floor — 965 sq. ft.

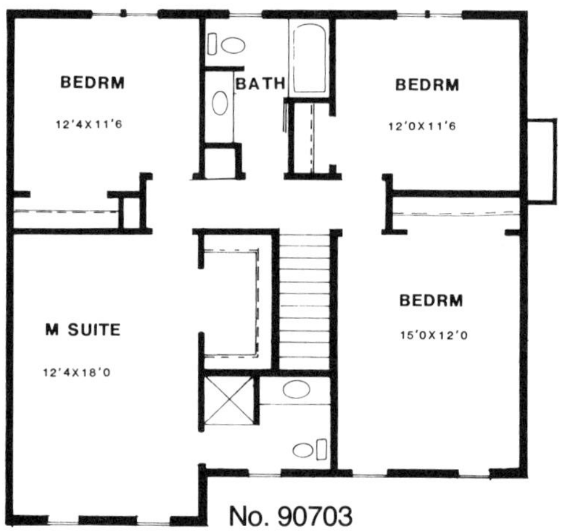

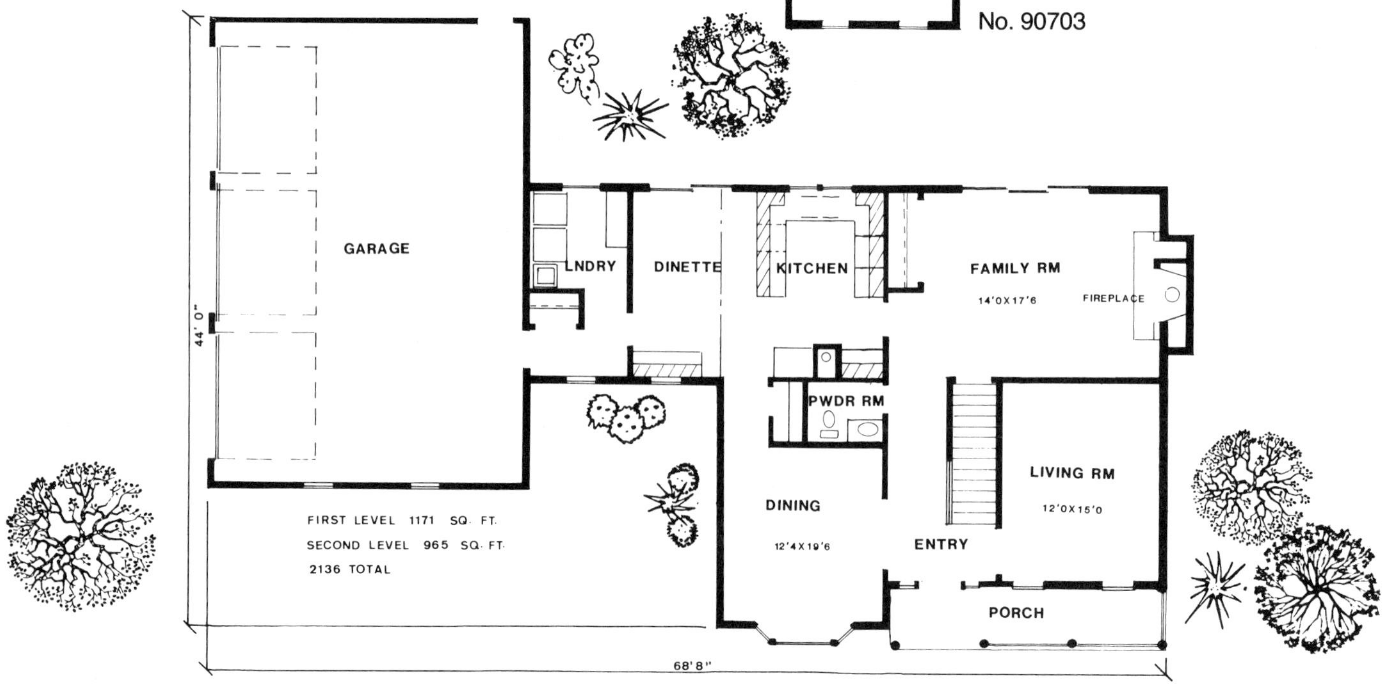

Open Plan Brightens Compact Dwelling

No. 90506

Open to the balcony above and the entry and dining room below, the vaulted great room is the highlight of this home. A central staircase winds its way up to three bedrooms, two baths, and a play room that doubles as storage. The master bedroom and breakfast nook feature bay windows that give both rooms a distinctive shape and cheerful atmosphere.

First floor — 996 sq. ft.
Second floor — 942 sq. ft.

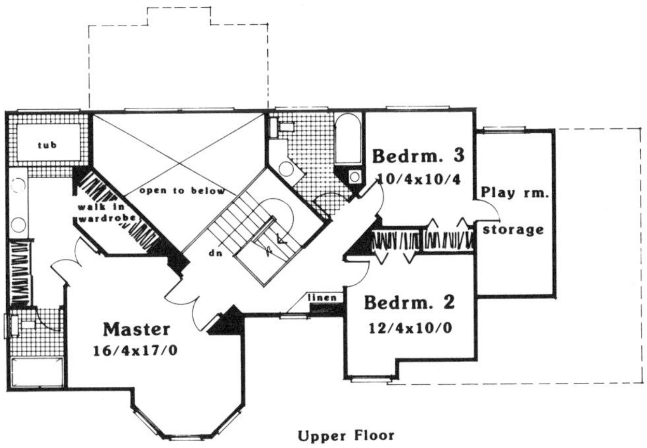

Upper Floor

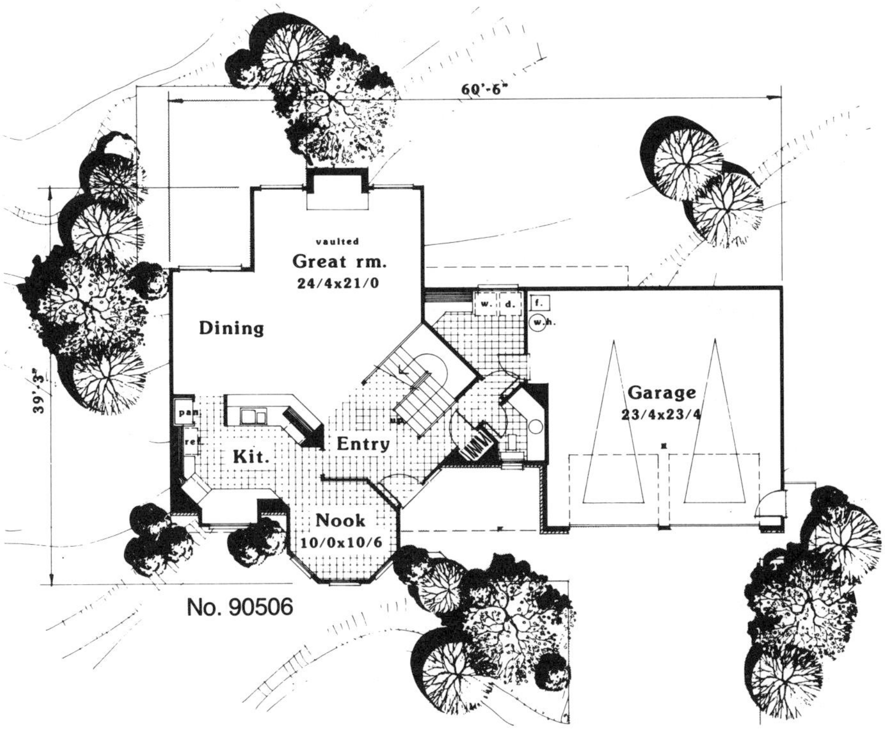

Arches Adorn Windows and Porches

No. 90702

Multiple peaks decorate the Victorian facade of this attractive three bedroom dwelling. A covered porch shelters the front entry. For meals, choose the bay-windowed breakfast nook or formal dining room. Windows over the kitchen sink look out over another porch, accessible to both breakfast and fireplaced family rooms. Upstairs, a second fireplace makes the master suite a cozy retreat. Two bedrooms and a full bath lie just across the hall.

First floor — 1,172 sq. ft.
Second floor — 995 sq. ft.

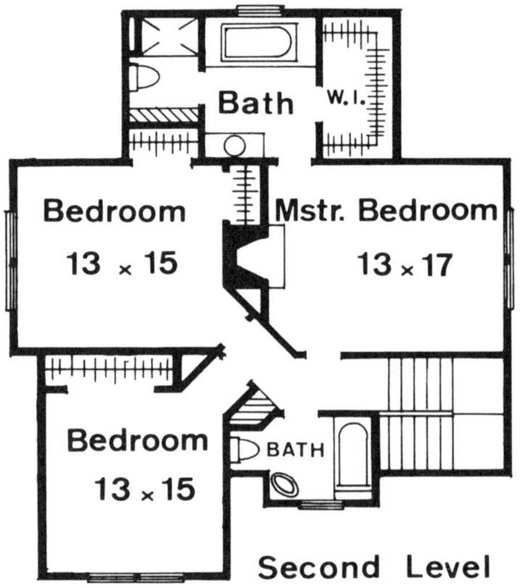

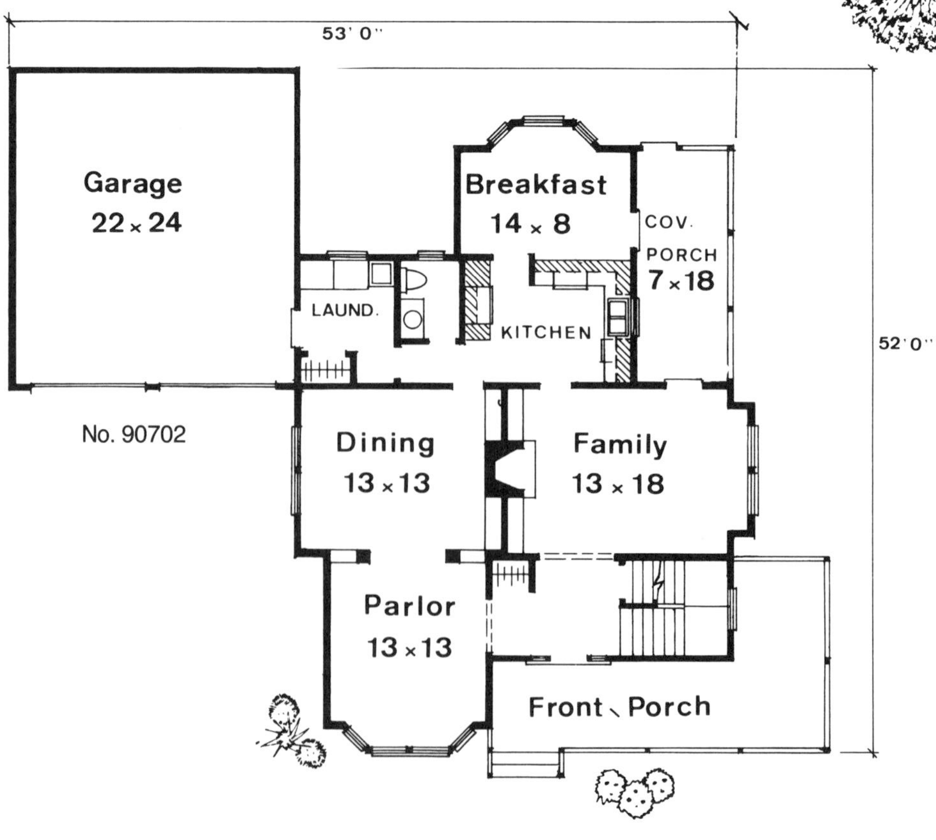

Vaulted Ceiling and Balcony

No. 90308

The hallway leading between the bedrooms on the upper floor opens onto the floor below dramatizing the vaulted ceiling of the living room. Adjoining the living room is the dining room with its direct access to the centrally located kitchen. The breakfast nook along one side of the kitchen looks out over the deck. The family room, with its hearty fireplace and wet bar, completes the main floor of the home. The upper floor encompasses four bedrooms or three bedrooms and a den. The large master bedroom includes a five-piece bath, optional fireplace and a complete wall of closet space. Another bath is located just off the landing.

Total area — 2,460 sq. ft.

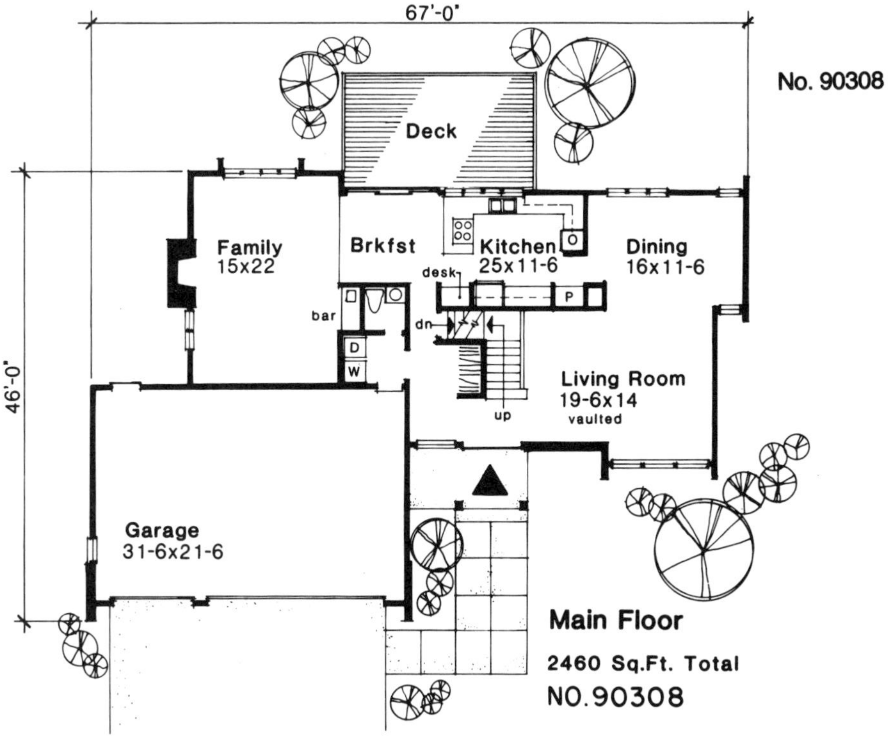

Main Floor
2460 Sq.Ft. Total
NO.90308

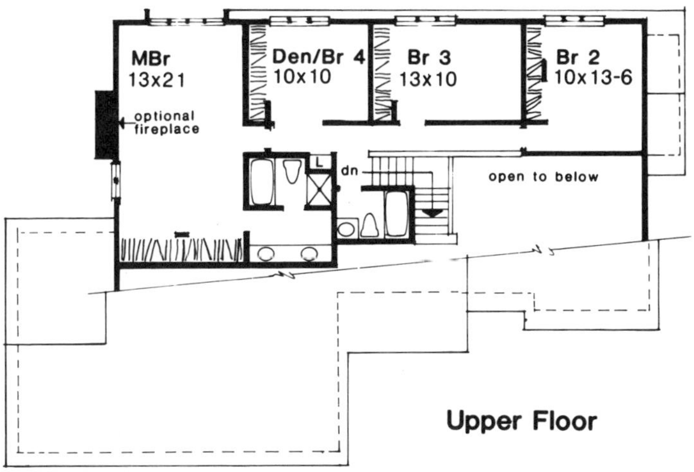

Upper Floor

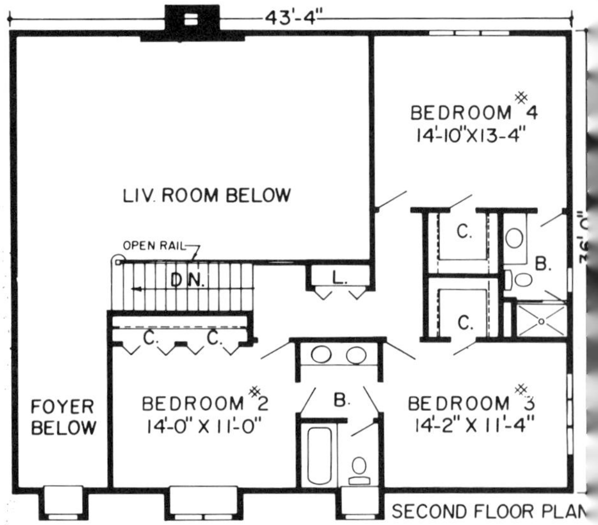

SECOND FLOOR PLAN

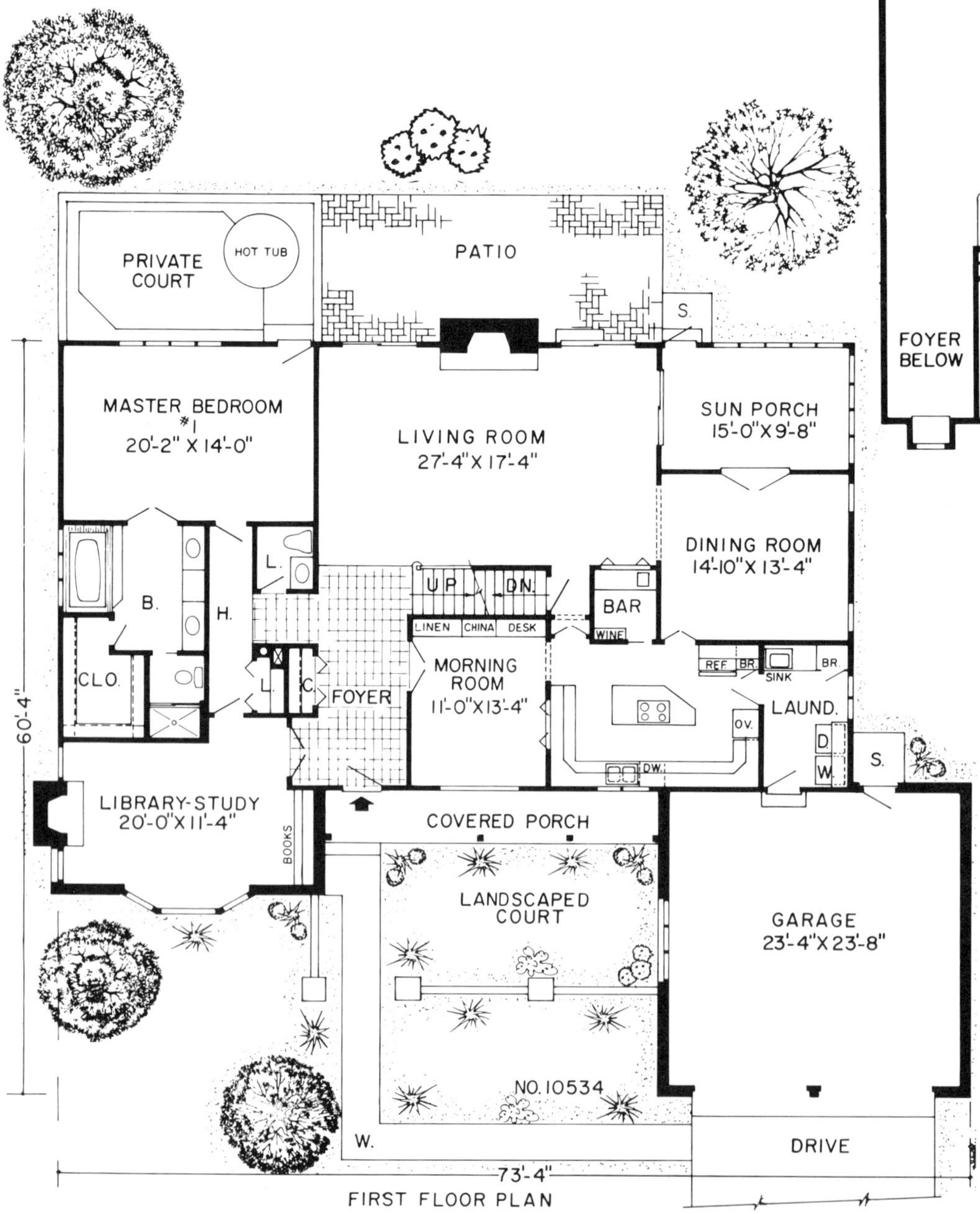

FIRST FLOOR PLAN

Private Court With Hot Tub Outside Master Bedroom

No. 10534

Adjoining the luxurious master suite of this stately home is a private court complete with hot tub. Secluded from the rest of the first floor this suite is comprised of a spacious bedroom, oversized walk-in closet and five-piece bath. Just down the hall is the cozy library which opens onto the two-story foyer through French doors. Other elegant touches on the first floor include a morning room with built-ins, a bar with wine storage, and a sun porch with French doors into the dining room. The living room and foyer rise to the second floor which encompasses three large bedrooms and two full baths.

First floor—2,486 sq. ft.
Second floor—892 sq. ft.
Basement—2,486 sq. ft.
Garage—576 sq. ft.

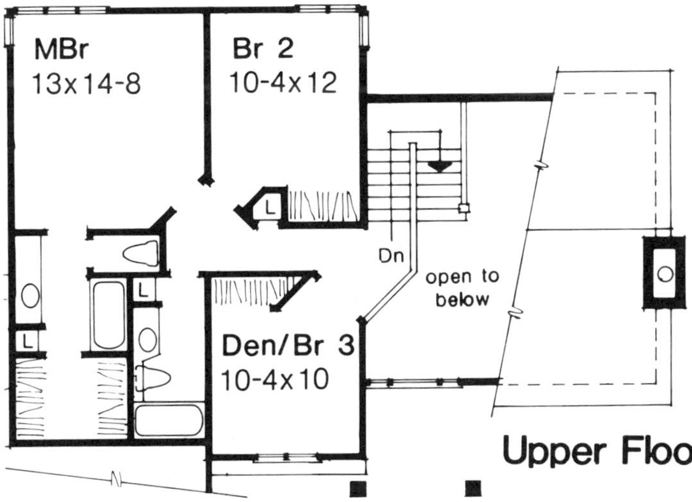

Upper Floor

Roomy 1 1/2 Story Design

No. 90355

This striking home features an exterior design with lots of roof importance, plus an interior with impact volumetrics, a terrific kitchen and a luxurious master bedroom suite with full bath and walk-in closet. Interior spacial flow maximizes the roominess of the formal and informal living areas, through views take in rear yard outdoor living decks, and exterior enhances perceived value. Masonry veneer could be added around the great room sash to highlight this impact window wall.

Main floor — 1,022 sq. ft.
Upper floor — 741 sq. ft.

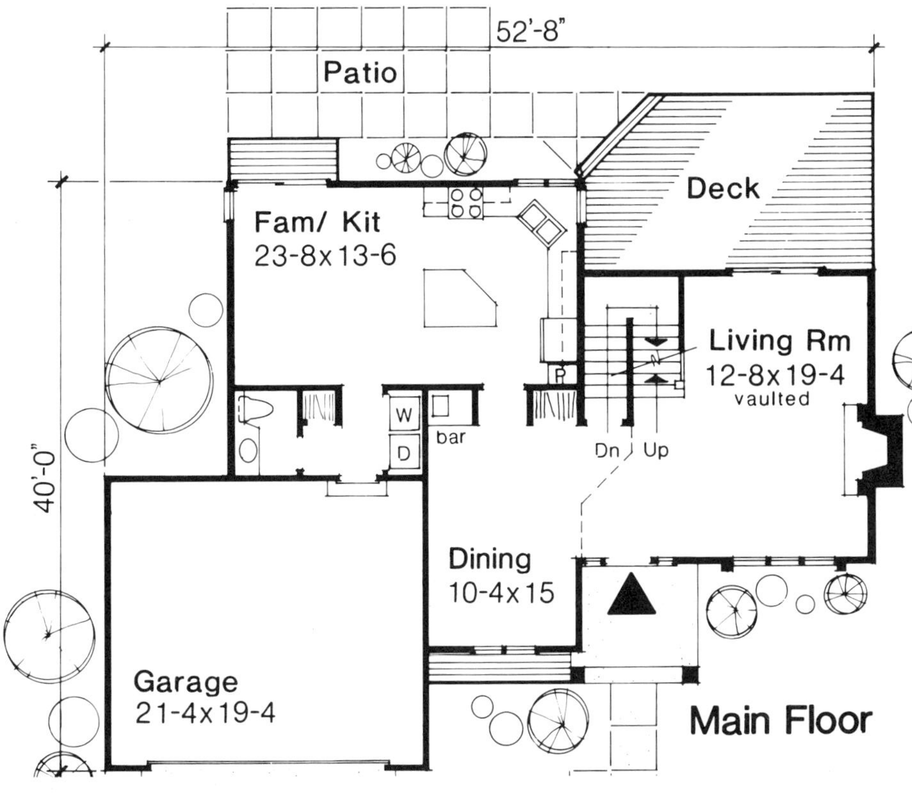

Main Floor

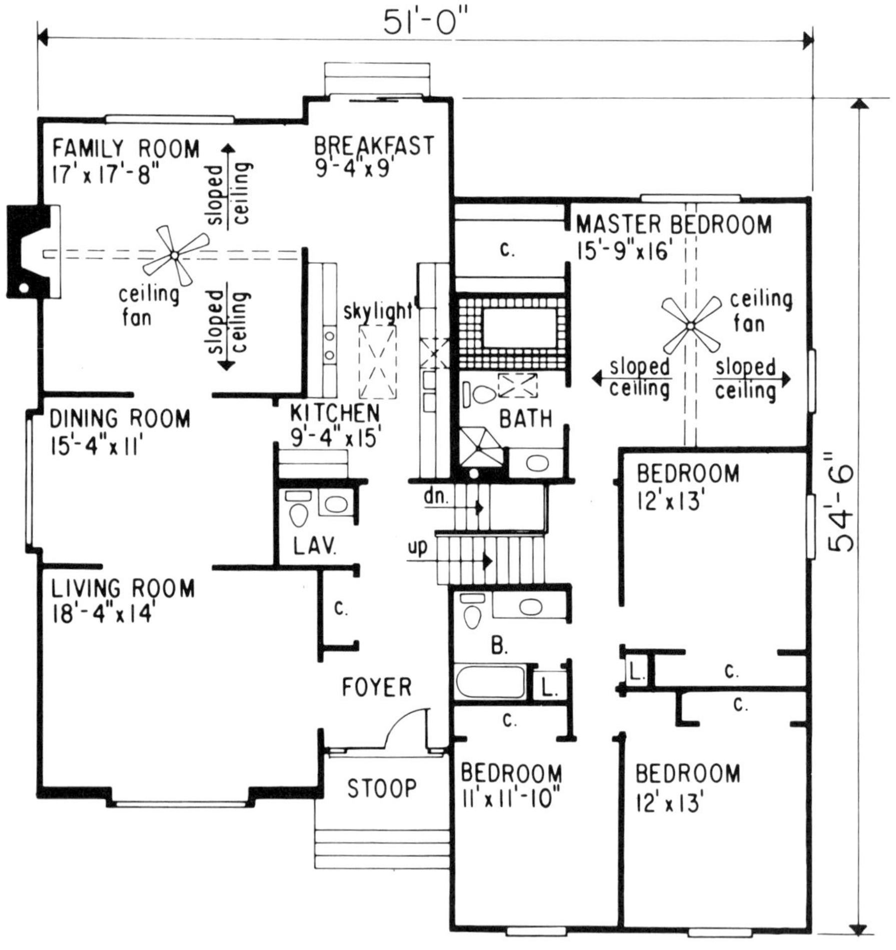

MAIN AND UPPER LEVEL

LOWER LEVEL

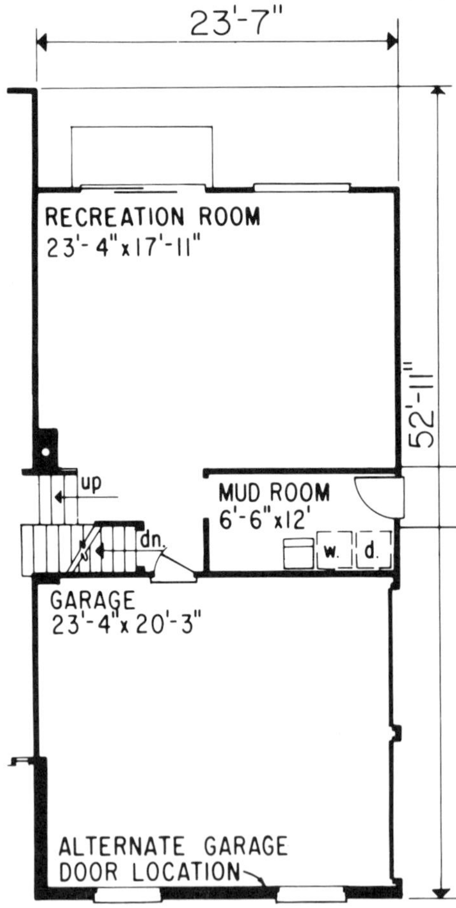

English Tudor With Three Levels Plus Basement

No. 90160

The delightful tudor exterior is enhanced by the massive support posts and beam at the recessed entrance. Box bays and diamond lite windows add to the exterior charm. Flow from room to room in this well laid-out plan. The large living and dining rooms each have box bay windows. The family room features cathedral ceilings, and the spacious kitchen has a skylight and breakfast area with sloped ceiling and patio doors. The upper level features four bedrooms, including the master suite with deluxe bath and walk-in closet. A two-car garage, mud room and oversized recreation room on the lower level help make this a home the entire family will enjoy.

Main & upper level—2,320 sq. ft.
Lower level—600 sq. ft.

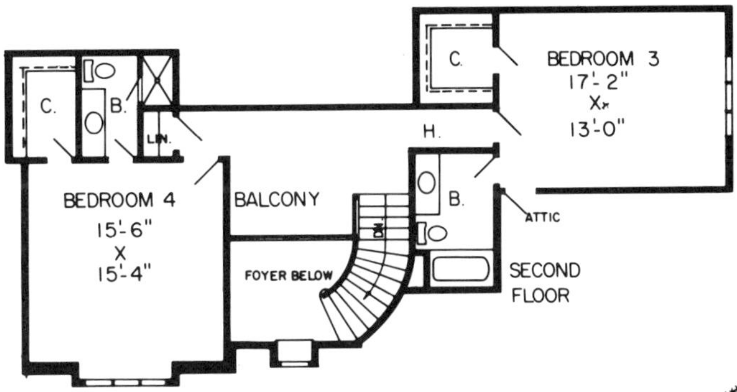

Balcony And Spiral Staircase Accent Traditional Four-bedroom

No. 10537

The elegant curve of the staircase leads upward from the foyer to the second floor balcony. Two roomy bedrooms, each with a walk-in closet and full bath comprise the second floor. The master bedroom and a guest bedroom are on the first floor. On either side of the entry foyer are the formal dining room and the parlor. Just off the spacious great room is the inviting kitchen, complete with a spacious pantry and lots of cabinet space. The unique morning room features a large fireplace and entry onto the patio for year 'round enjoyment. A three-car garage completes this handsome design.

First floor—3,114 sq. ft.
Second floor—924 sq. ft.
Basement—3,092 sq. ft.
Garage—917 sq. ft.

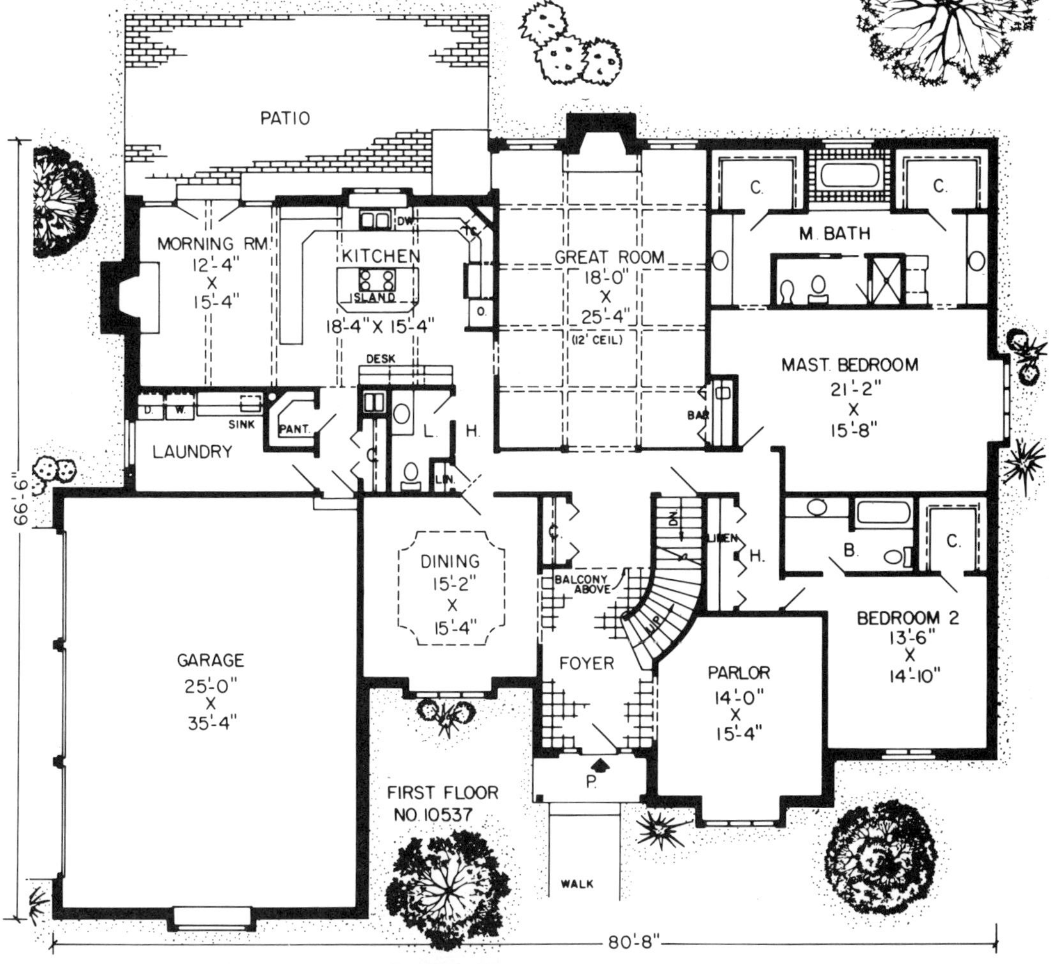

Compact Plan Allows For Gracious Living

No. 90158

A great room, accessible from the foyer, offers a cathedral ceiling with exposed beams, brick fireplace and access to the rear patio. The kitchen-breakfast area with center island and cathedral ceiling is accented by the round top window. The master bedroom has a full bath and walk-in closet. Two additional bedrooms and bath help make this an ideal plan for any growing family.

First floor—1,540 sq. ft.
Basement—1,540 sq. ft.

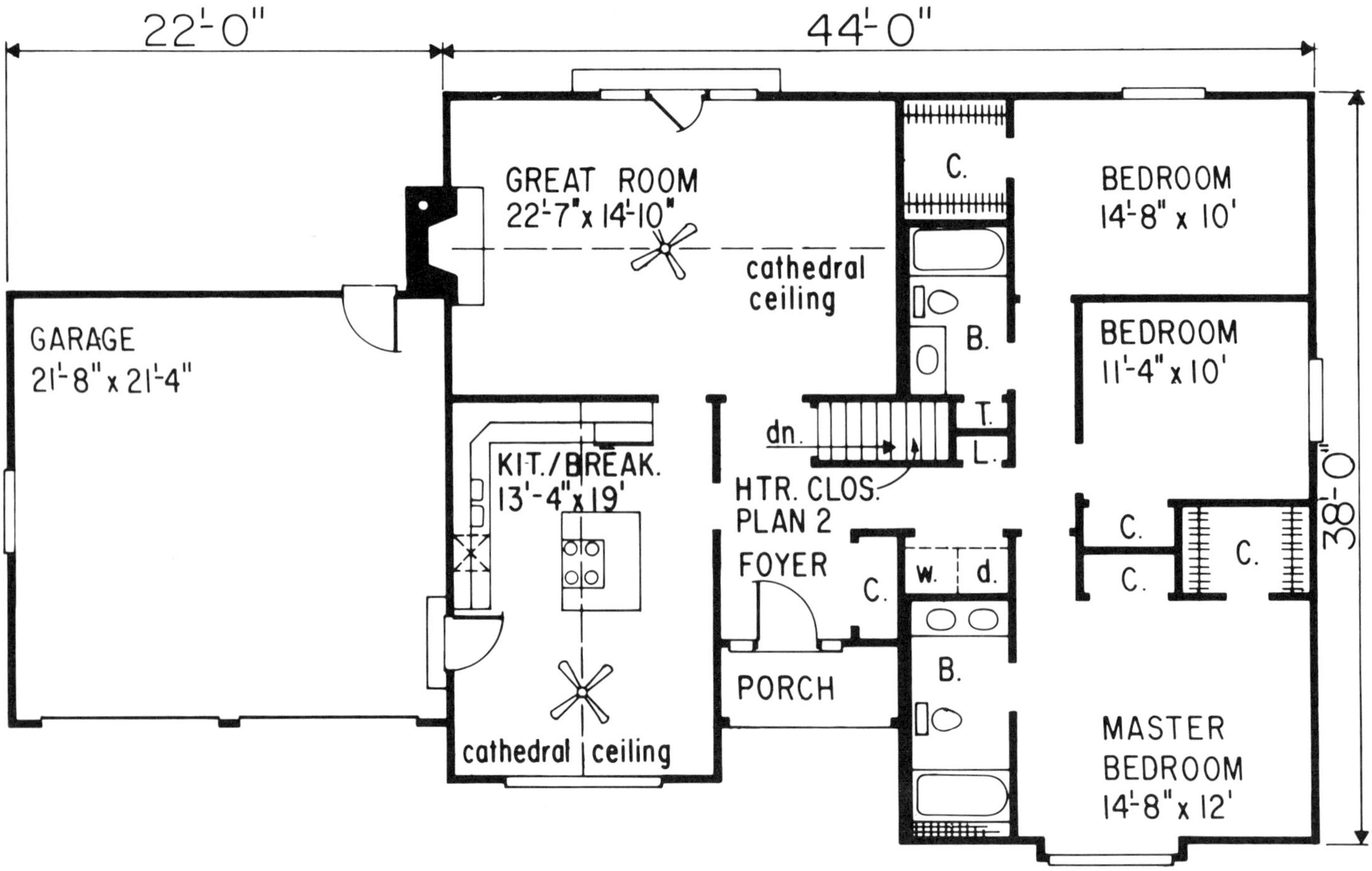

Victorian Details Enhance Facade

No. 10593

A charming porch shelters the entrance of this four bedroom home with country kitchen. In colder climates, the closed vestibule cuts heat loss. Off the central foyer, the cozy living room shares a fireplace with the family room, which contains a bar and access to the patio and screened porch for entertaining. The bay windowed breakfast room is handy for quick meals. Or, use the formal dining room with octagonal recessed ceiling. All the bedrooms, located on the second floor, have walk-in closets.

First floor — 1,450 sq. ft.
Second floor — 1,341 sq. ft.
Basement — 1,450 sq. ft.
Garage — 629 sq. ft.
Covered porch — 144 sq. ft.

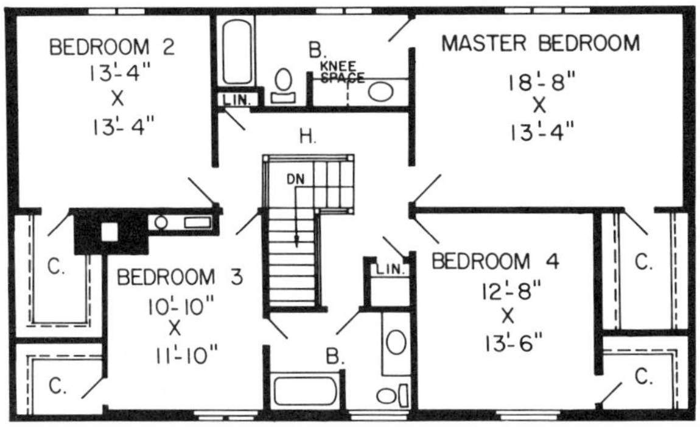

SECOND FLOOR

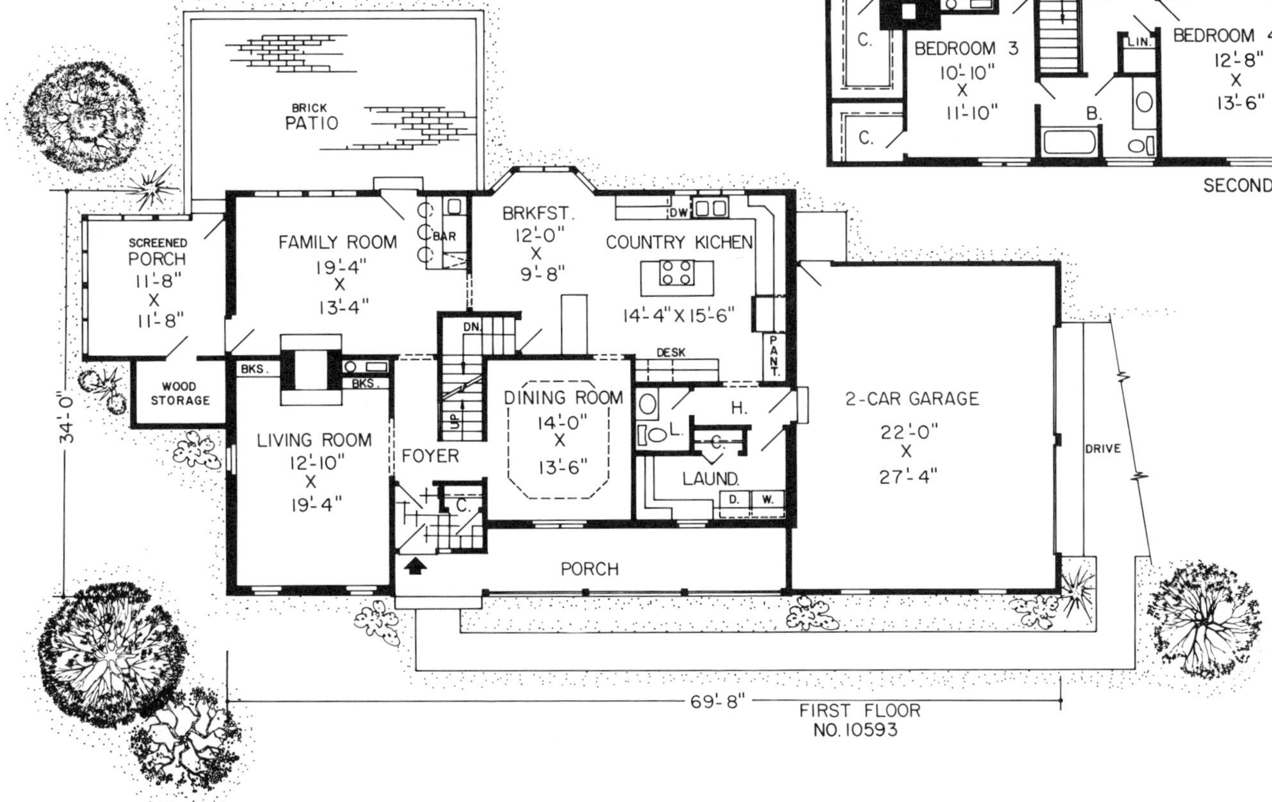

FIRST FLOOR
NO. 10593

L-Shaped Bungalow With Two Porches

No. 90407

Pleasing L-shaped design indicates a smooth flowing floor plan. Master suite includes garden tub, shower, his and her vanities and separate walk-in closets. Two other bedrooms and a full bath complete the sleeping wing. A large family room, separate foyer, living and dining combine to form the center section. U-shaped kitchen, breakfast nook with bay window and separate utility complete the plan. Specify basement, crawlspace or slab foundation when ordering.

Area — 1,950 sq. ft.

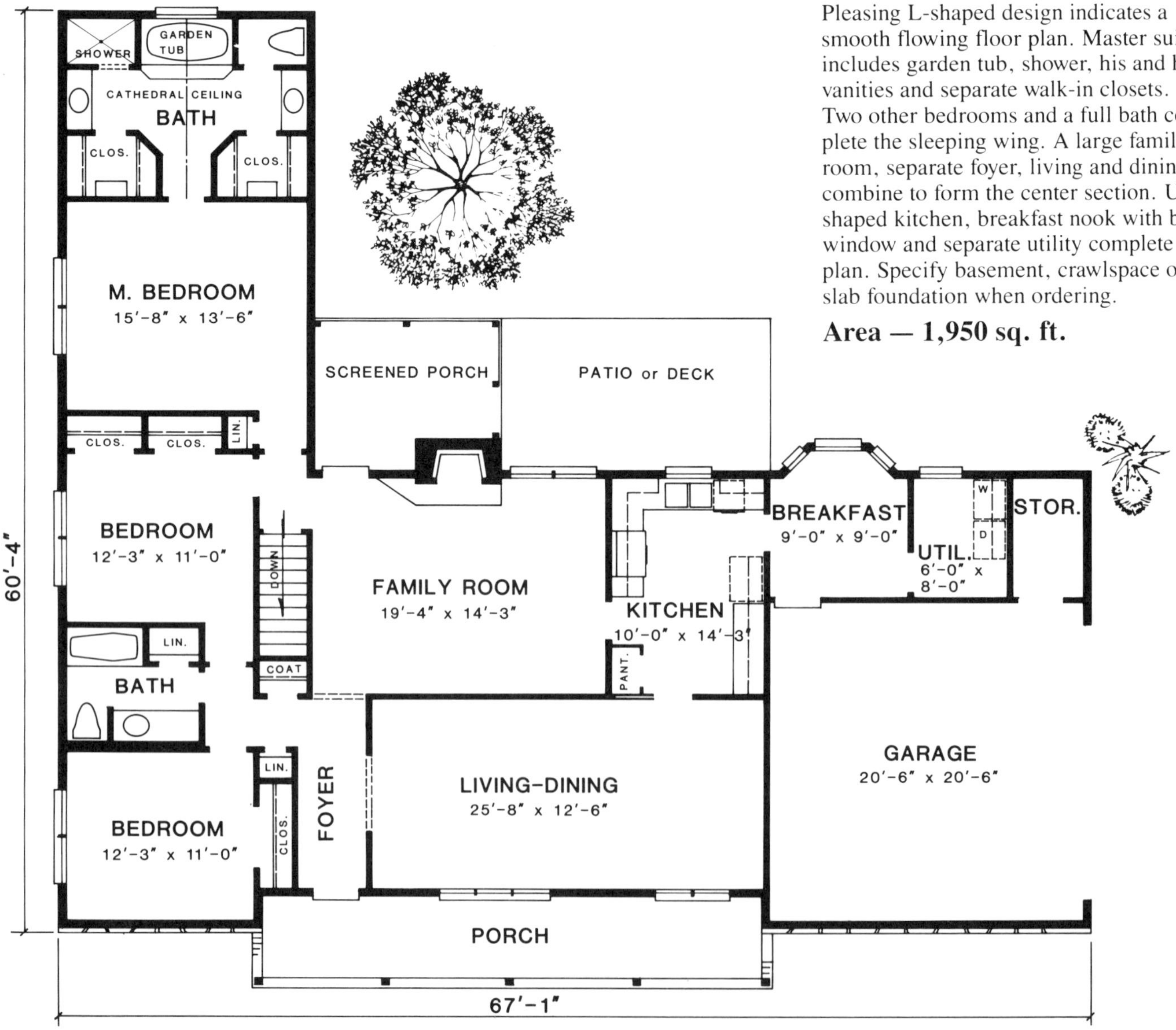

Open Design Creates Spacious Feeling

No. 90925

Looking for just the right plan for that hillside lot? Here's a design that will fit a smaller lot with a front to back or a side to side slope. Vaulted ceilings and lots of glass brighten the living areas, arranged to afford a view to the street. The large kitchen and breakfast nook overlook a cozy family room, which opens out onto an attractive patio. Up a short flight of stairs are three roomy bedrooms and family bath. The master suite has its own bathroom, a wall of mirrored closets for dressing and a beautiful vaulted ceiling with clerestory windows overhead.

Lower floor — 1,118 sq. ft.
Upper floor — 688 sq. ft.
Basement — 380 sq. ft.
Garage — 430 sq. ft.
Width — 40 ft.
Depth — 37 ft.

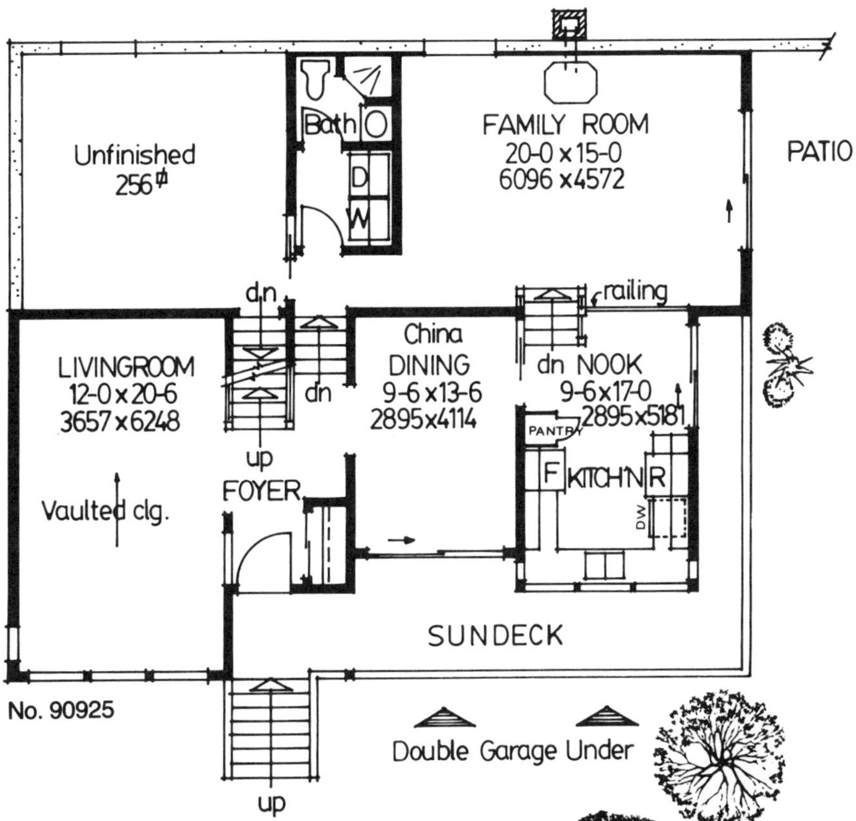

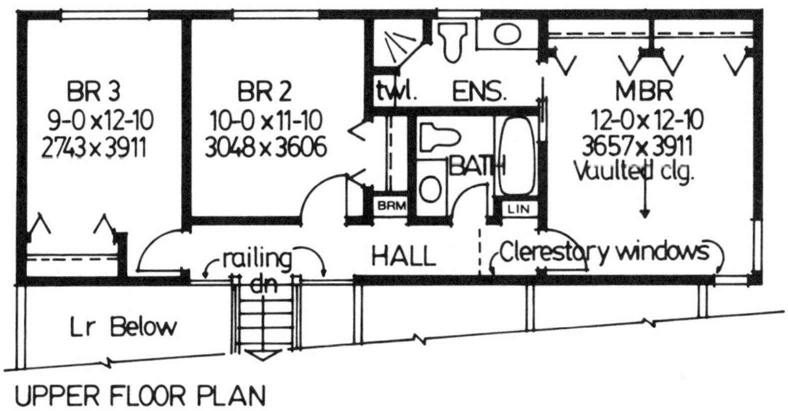

UPPER FLOOR PLAN

Country Charm Designed For Modern Living

No. 90157

The central two-story foyer with wrap-around balcony has access to a second floor front porch. The 22-foot family room with fireplace opens onto the rear patio. A country-sized kitchen features an adjacent breakfast area. The large master bedroom includes a deluxe bath with corner platform tub, angled vanity and separate shower. A spacious walk-in closet completes the master suite. A vaulted ceiling and half-circle window add to the charm of the front bedroom. Also featured is a two-car garage with plenty of storage space.

First floor—1,428 sq. ft.
Second floor—1,369 sq. ft.

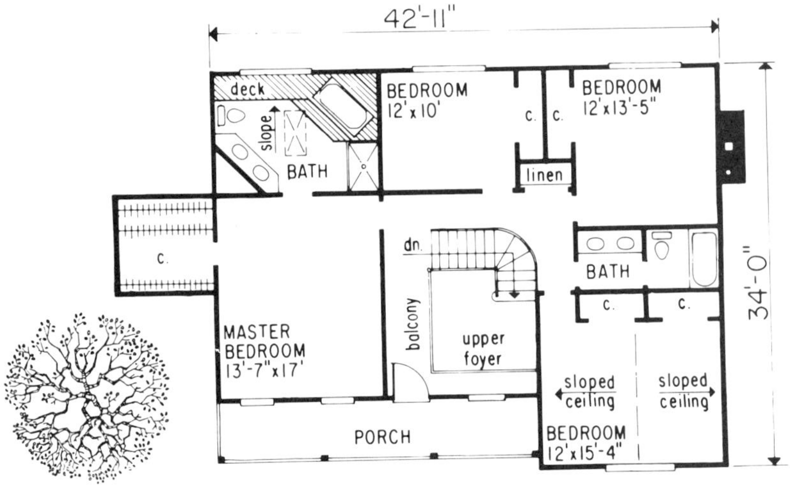

SECOND FLOOR

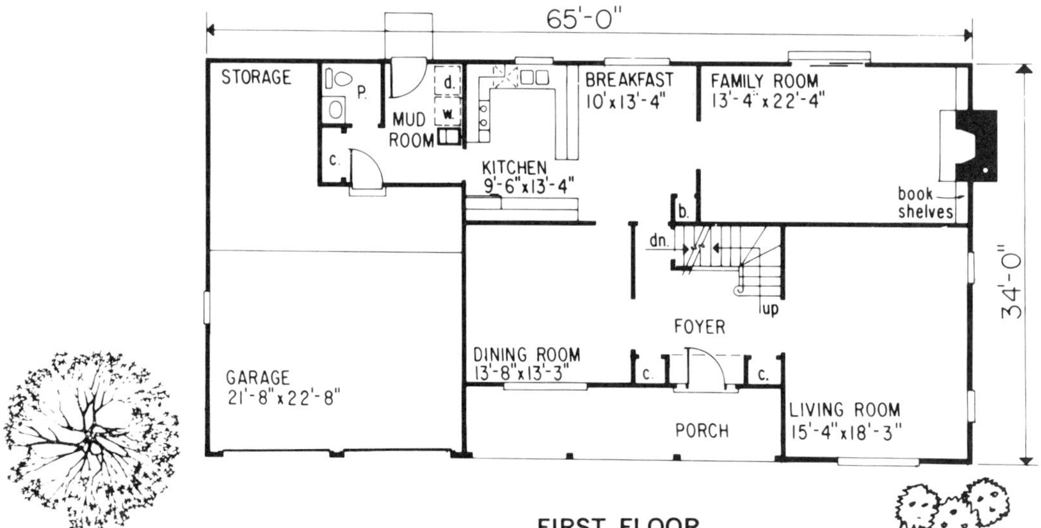

FIRST FLOOR

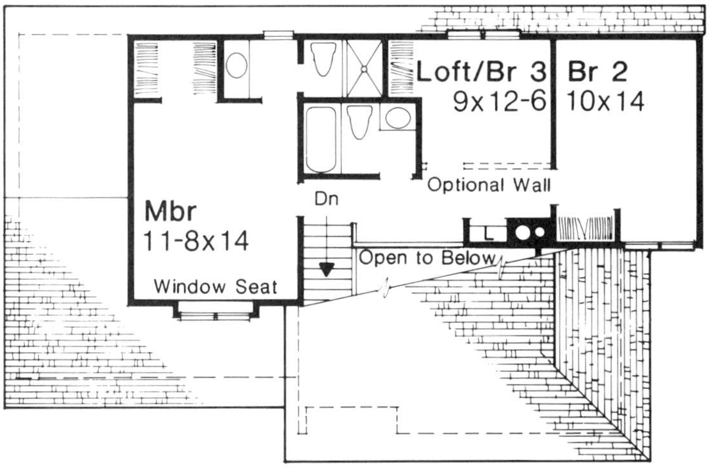

UPPER FLOOR PLAN

Balcony Overlooks Living Room Below

No. 90356

Smaller houses are getting better all the time, not only in their exterior character and scale, but in their use of spacial volumes and interior finish materials. Here a modest two story gains importance, impact, and perceived value from the sweeping roof lines that make it look larger than it really is, the impact of vaulted ceiling in living room up to balcony hall above, the easy flow of traffic and space in the kitchen and dining areas, plus convenience of family garage entry, powder room, coat closet, and basement stair. Note too, the luxurious master bedroom suite with window seat bay, walk-in closet, dressing area, and private shower.

Main floor — 688 sq. ft.
Upper floor — 691 sq. ft.

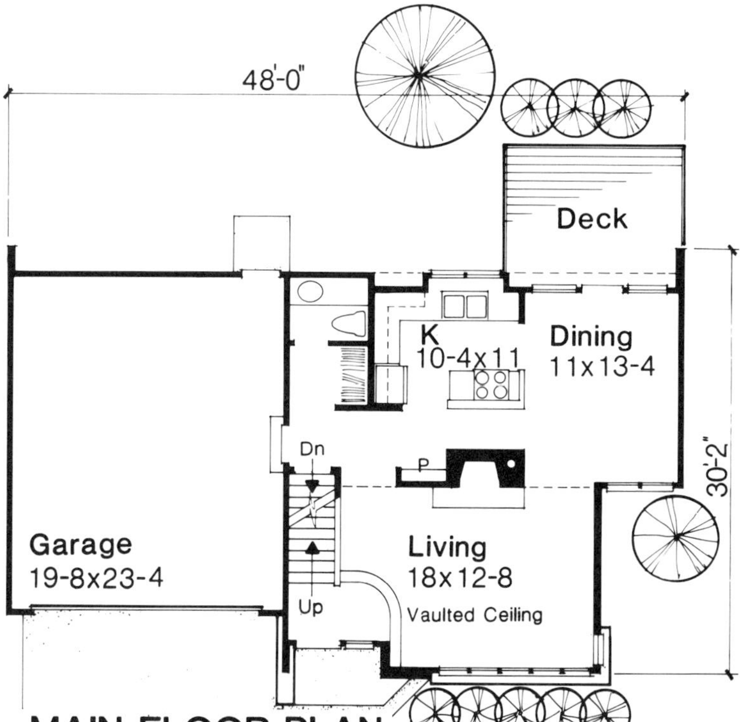

MAIN FLOOR PLAN

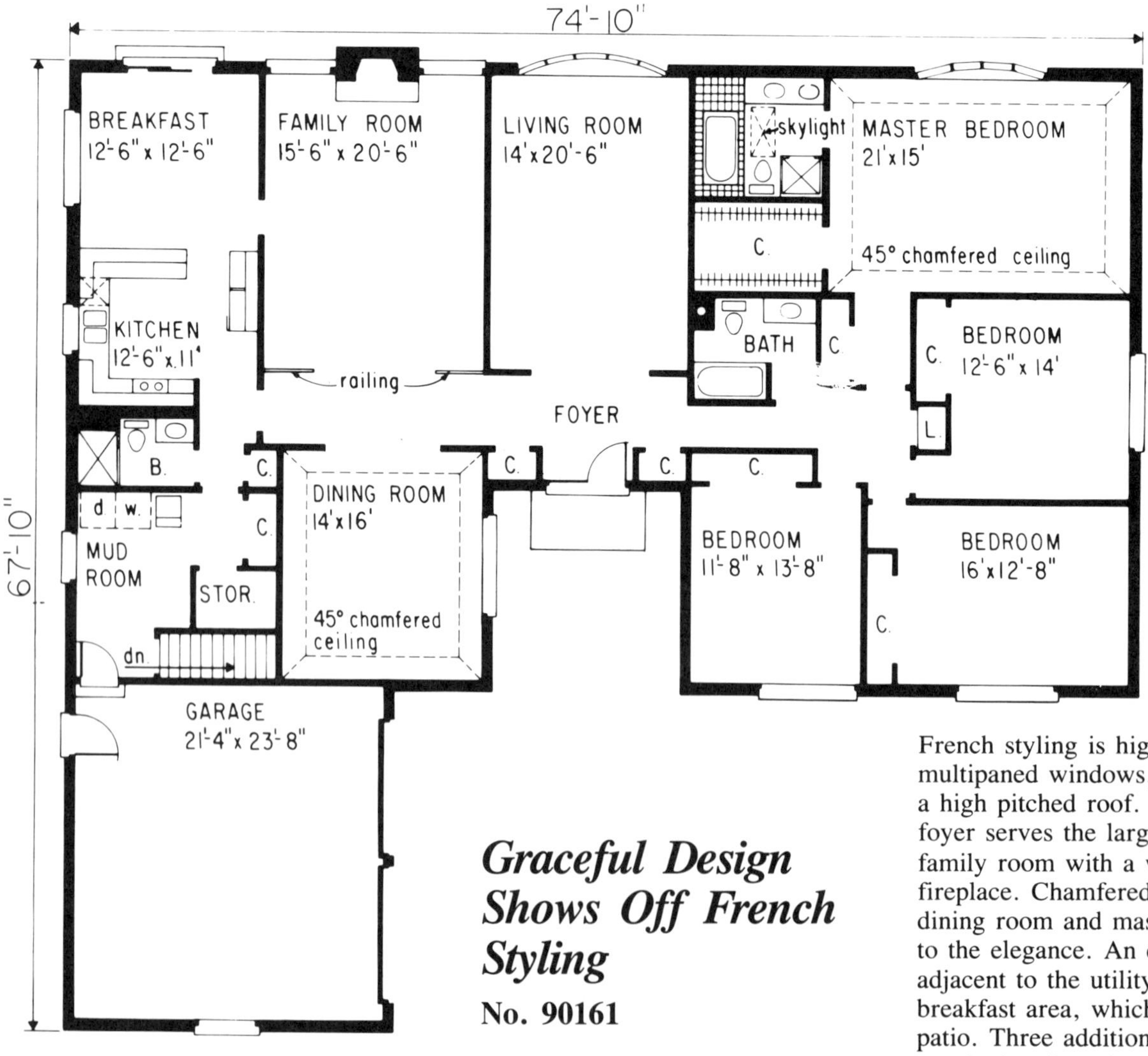

Graceful Design Shows Off French Styling

No. 90161

French styling is highlighted by brick, multipaned windows, bay windows and a high pitched roof. The elegant central foyer serves the large living room and family room with a wood-burning fireplace. Chamfered ceilings in the dining room and master bedroom add to the elegance. An efficient kitchen is adjacent to the utility room and breakfast area, which opens to the patio. Three additional bedrooms and two baths allow for a large family.

First floor—3,108 sq. ft.
Basement—3,108 sq. ft.

Three Fireplaces Will Keep You Warm

No. 91030

Have you always wanted your own private getaway, where you could just kick off your shoes and relax? You'll find it in the luxurious master suite in this distinctive four-bedroom home. The built-in spa is a feature you'll welcome at the end of your day. And the fireplace, glass blocks, and skylights make this a sunny, warm retreat. On the main level, bay windows brighten the living room and nook. The kitchen, which features a cooktop island, is centrally located for convenient meal service to formal and informal dining rooms.

First floor — 1,207 sq. ft.
Second floor — 1,341 sq. ft.

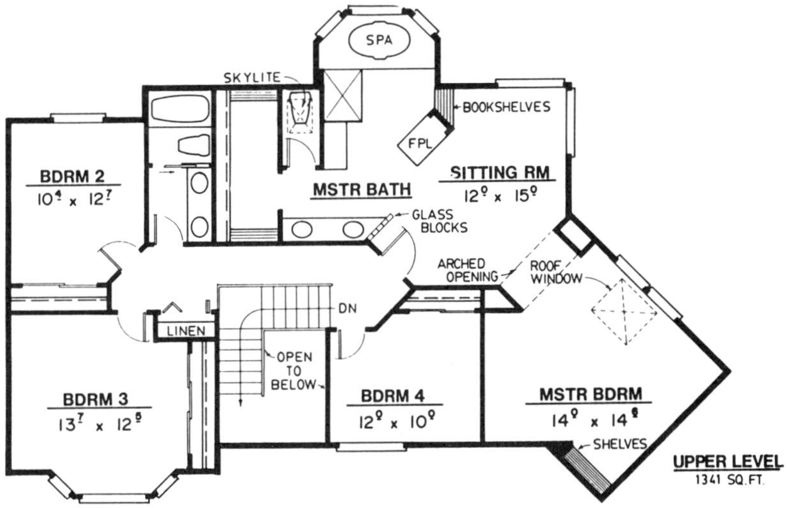

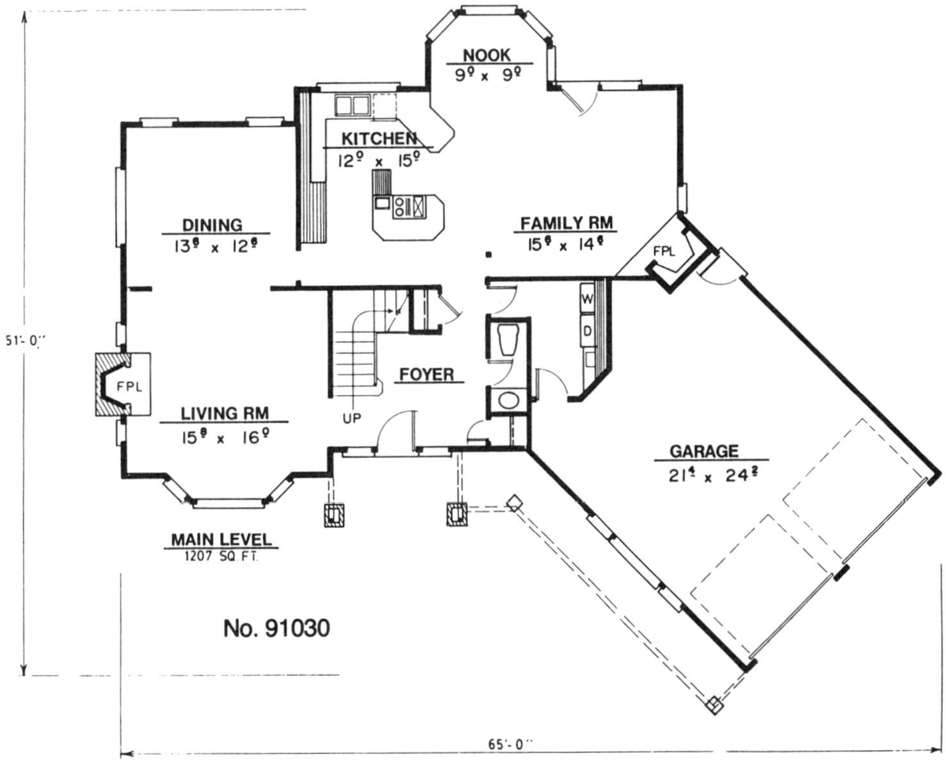

Family Living at its Best

No. 90904

Here's a rear-view variation on a popular Tudor theme. This family-oriented plan boasts lots of practical features. Convenient access through the mudroom and utility area makes returning from shopping or playtime easy. The island kitchen with bay-windowed nook enhances the spacious family room, a cheery gathering point for the family at the end of a busy day. Off the vaulted foyer, the large dining and living rooms provide an atmosphere of quiet elegance. An attractive open staircase leads to three bedrooms off a well-lit hall with loft-style atrium sitting area.

Main floor — 1,246 sq. ft.
Second floor — 940 sq. ft.
Garage — 584 sq. ft.
Unfinished basement — 1,228 sq. ft.
Width — 46 ft.
Depth — 61 ft.

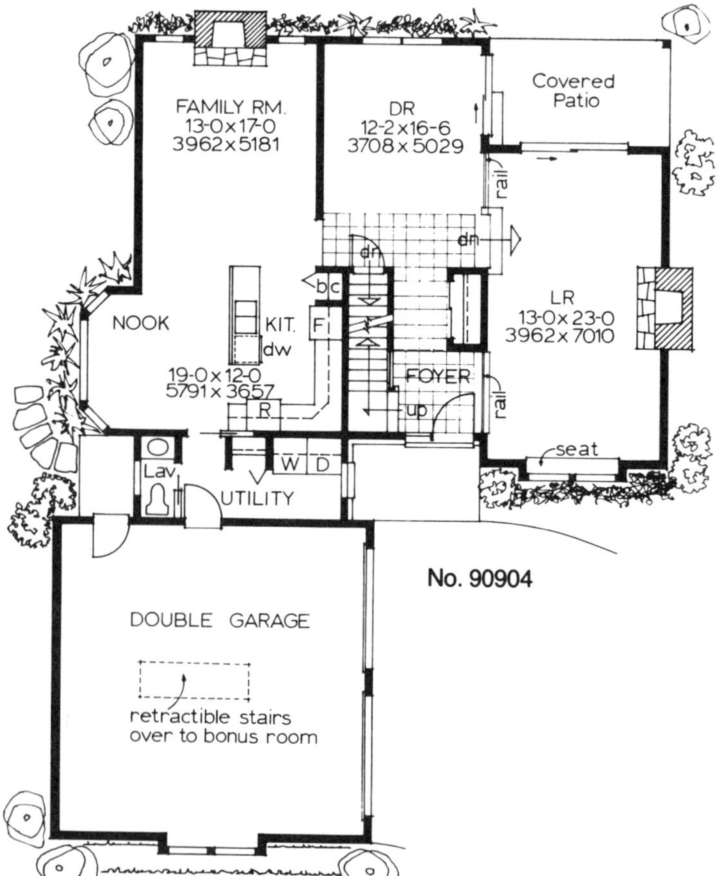

No. 90904

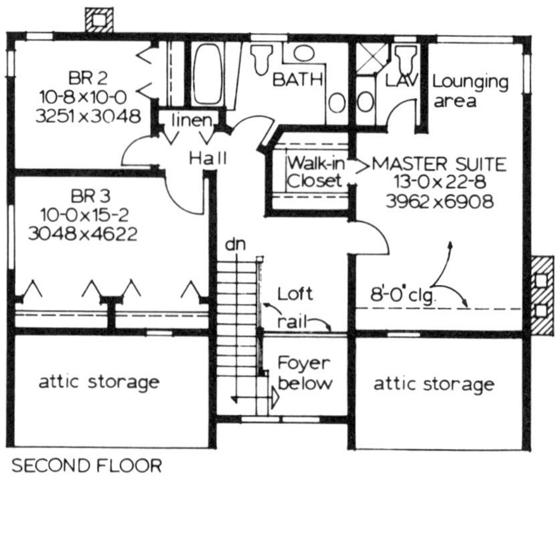

Hill House

No. 91026

Built into a hill, this vacation house takes advantage of your wonderful view. It features a Great Room that opens out on a deck and brings earth and sky into the home through sweeping panels of glass. The open plan draws the kitchen into the celebration of the outdoors and shares the warmth of the sturdy wood stove. Two bedrooms on the main level share a bath. Two large, upstairs lofts, one overlooking the Great Room, have a full bath all to themselves. This house feels as airy and delightful as a tree house.

Main Level — 988 sq. ft.
Upper Level — 366 sq. ft.
Basement — 988 sq. ft.

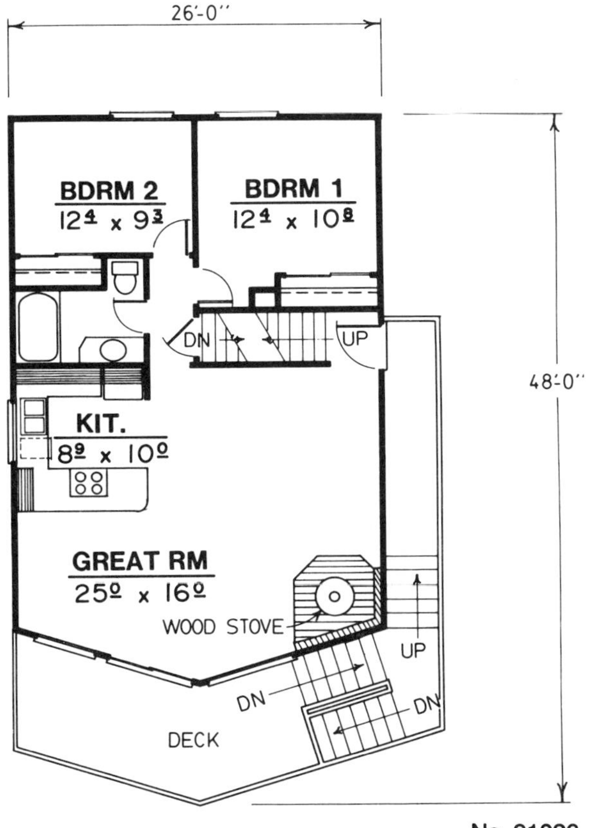

No. 91026

MAIN LEVEL
988 SQ.FT.

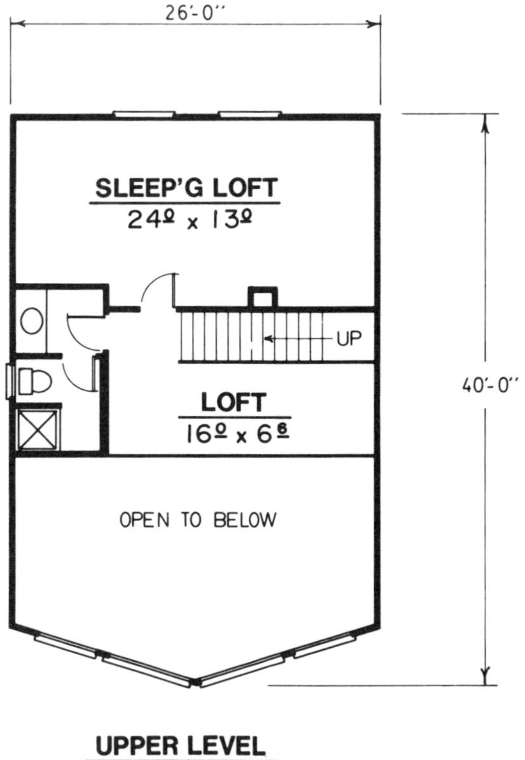

UPPER LEVEL
366 SQ.FT.

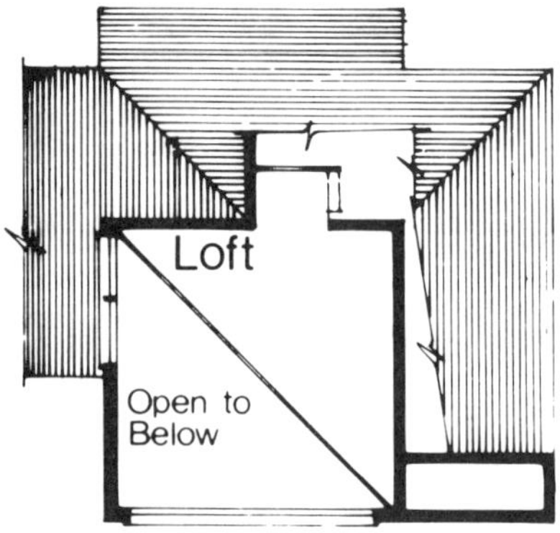

Loft

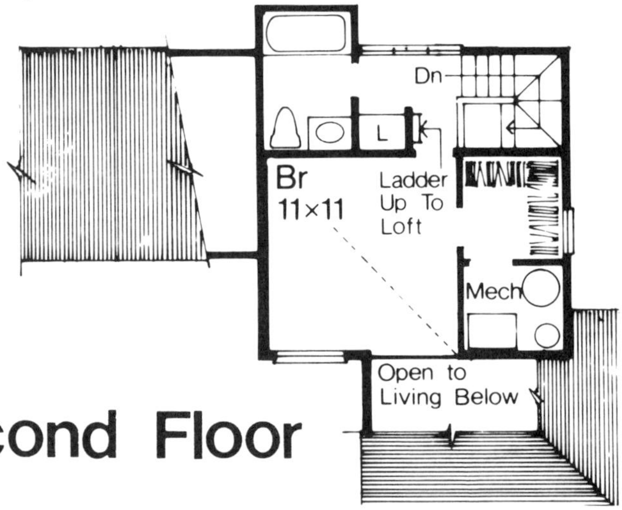

Second Floor

Window Design Highlights Plan

No. 90348

What's the one thing you absolutely must have in a vacation home? Windows that capture the view. This home has them all around. It also has a top-of-the-tower loft for sleeping, or for sightseeing through the huge fan-shaped-window. Loft's accessible via ladder from second floor bedroom, which has access to mechanical room and full bath. On main floor, living, dining and kitchen spaces open on each other. All have access to the deck as does the master bedroom.

Area — 1,097 sq. ft.

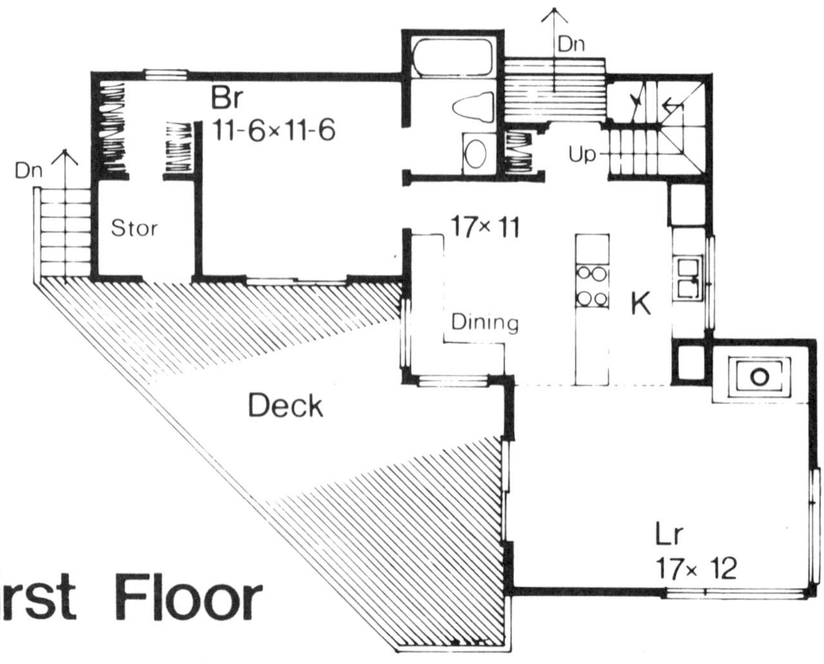

First Floor

Stacked Sleeping Rooms for Quiet Bedtimes

No. 20069

The kids can sleep in peace, away from the action, in this modern charmer with loft views of the living room and foyer below. Double windows give every room a cheery atmosphere. Soaring ceilings add drama to living and dining rooms, which conveniently flank the open kitchen and breakfast room. And, a deck off the breakfast room provides easy access to outdoor fun. Conveniently situated on the first floor, the master suite is a pleasant retreat.

First floor — 1,313 sq. ft.
Second floor — 588 sq. ft.
Basement — 1,299 sq. ft.

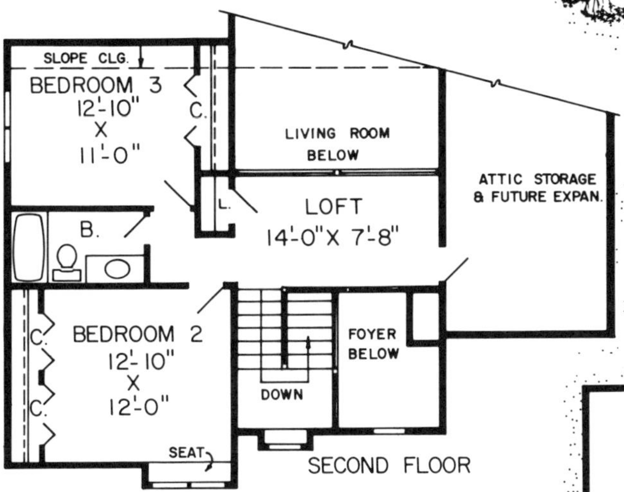

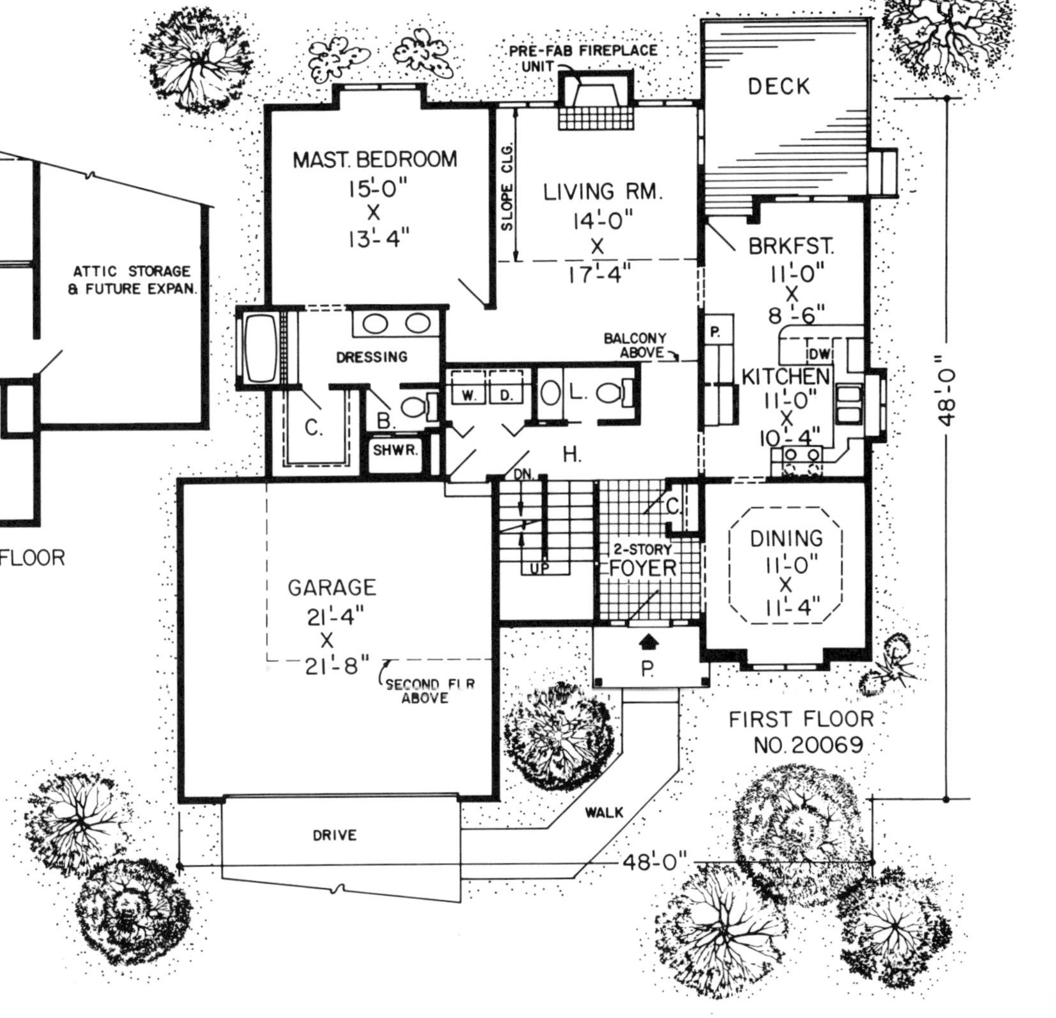

Unusual French Design

No. 90043

The glamour and serenity of French Provincial styling are on display throughout this unusual 1 1/2 story design. This is the perfect home for the family with a well developed feeling for traditional influence. Note the grand foyer with its circular staircase that flows up to the two second floor bedrooms; the sunken living room that is flanked with wrought iron rails and grilles; and the built-in wet bar and fireplace with French mantle in the family room. The master bedroom suite has two closets, a room-size walk-in, a dressing area vanity with full-length mirror, and a complete bath with double-basin vanity, sunken Roman tub, glass enclosed shower and sauna. Accessible to the rear sun-deck is the family room and the well equipped island kitchen.

First floor — 2,497 sq. ft.
Second floor — 527 sq. ft.
Garage — 550 sq. ft.

SECOND FLOOR PLAN

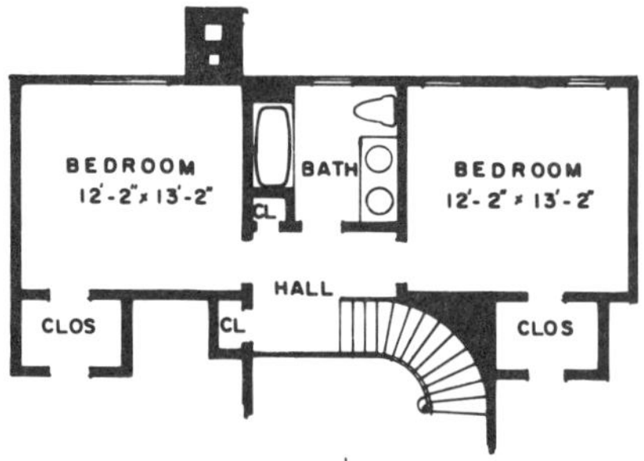

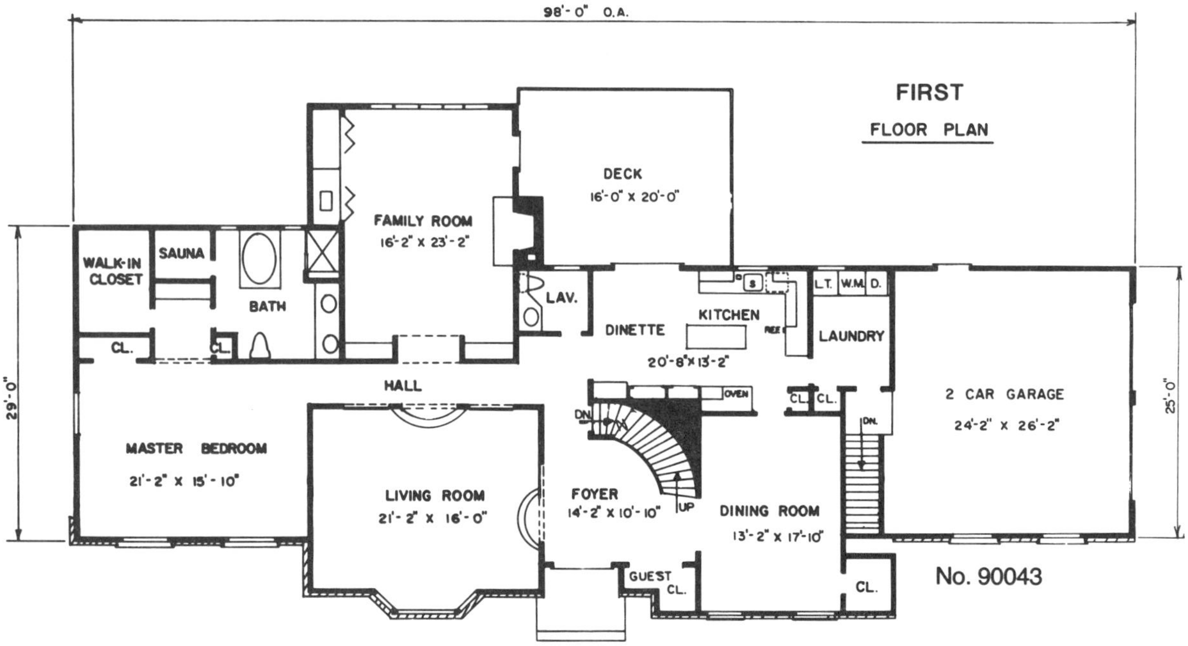

Enchanting Mediterranean Influenced Design

No. 90013

The charm of the Mediterranean can be seen in the massive stone facade, stucco walls, balconies, and arched entranceway. Walking through the archway is like walking through an ancient, thick wall —an illusion created by the wraparound design of the wall protecting the 12 x 18 ft. covered entrance court. Inside the wide, paneled doors, the foyer affords direct access to the expansive living room. The kitchen connects conveniently with both the dining room —which enjoys sliding doors to the patio— and the huge family room —which overlooks the private terrace to the rear. You'll also enjoy the two balconies on the second floor.

First floor — 1,048 sq. ft.
Second Floor — 922 sq. ft.

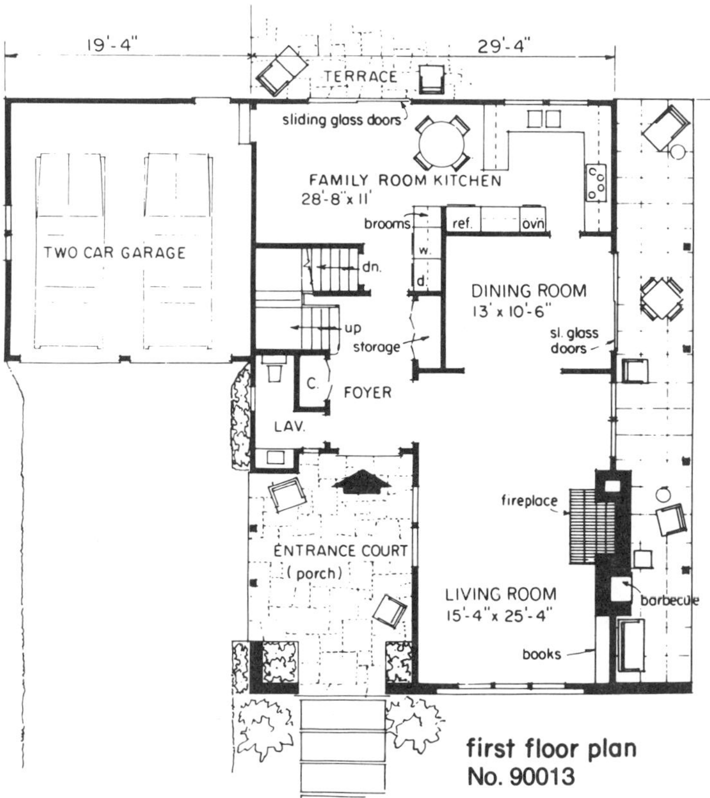

first floor plan
No. 90013

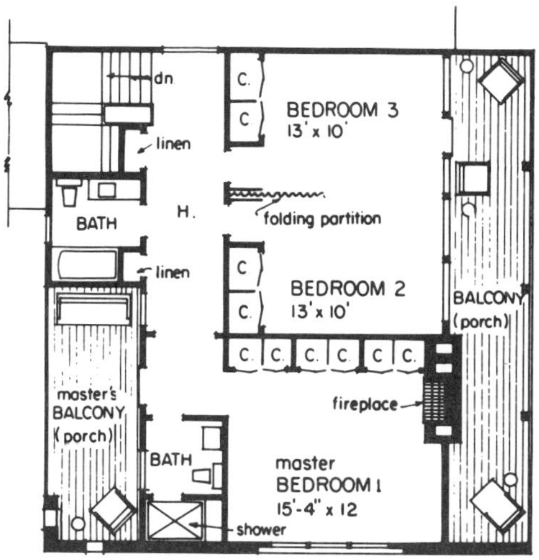

second floor plan

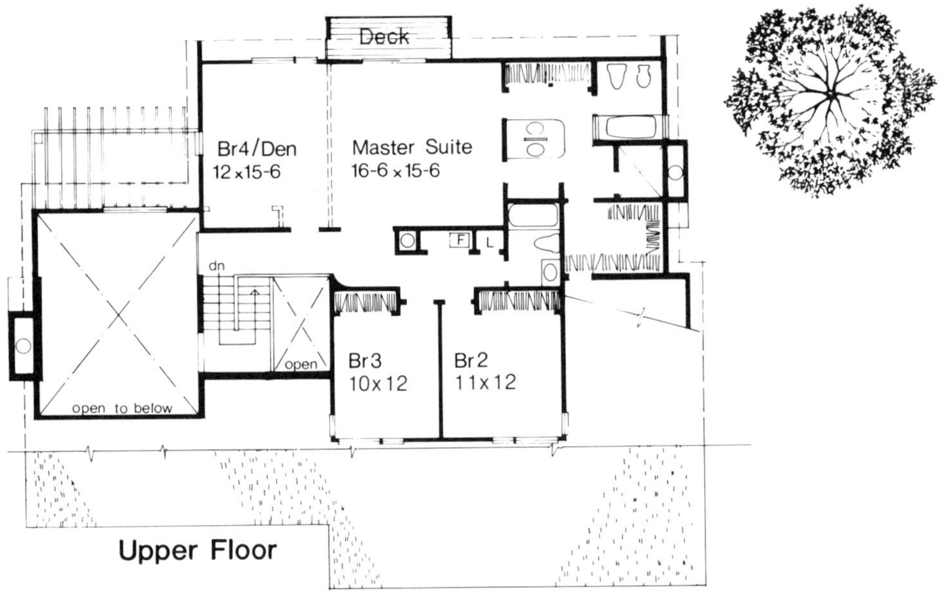

Unique 1 1/2 Story Design

No. 90350

The rooms of this modern home flow into other spaces, yet each area has its defined function. The island kitchen eat-in section blends with the step-down family room while the dining room opens into the great room with its vaulted ceiling. Master suite can be divided. The exterior is rough finish and stained.

Lower/
Upper levels — 2,758 sq. ft.

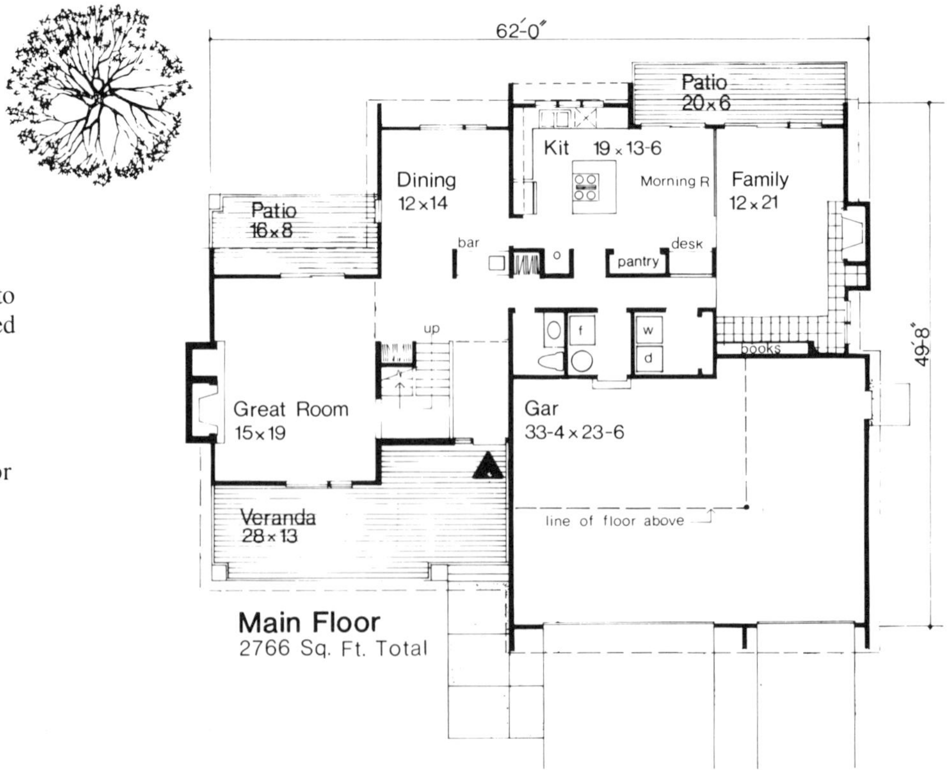

Zoned for Comfort

No. 90610

This ground-hugging ranch was designed for maximum use of three basic living areas. The informal area — fireplaced family room, kitchen, and breakfast room — adjoins a covered porch. The fully-equipped kitchen is easily accessible to the formal dining room, which flows into the living room for convenient entertaining. Well-situated closets and bathrooms set the bedrooms apart from more active areas. The spacious master suite includes plenty of closet space and its own bath. The other bedrooms are served by the lavish hall bath equipped with two basins.

Basic house — 1,771 sq. ft.

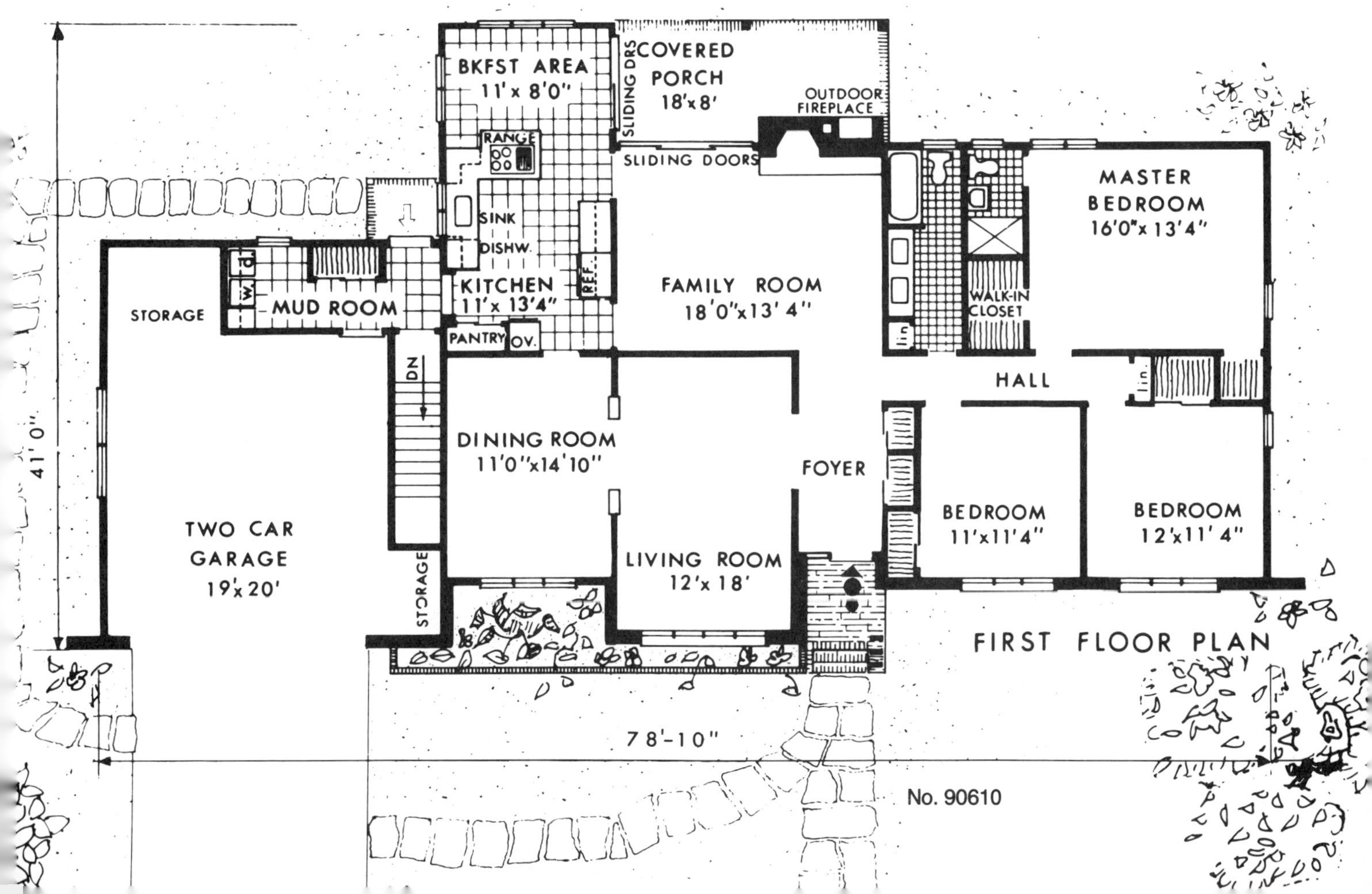

Suited to a Narrow Lot

No. 90814

If you need a compact home with room for all the kids, consider this traditional three bedroom plan. A large porch at the front door will provide ample protection from the weather. And, just inside the foyer the beautiful open stair will catch your eye. The island kitchen, nook and sunken family room create a spacious and comfortable family living and work space. A few short steps away, you'll find a convenient utility area with adjacent powder room.

Main floor — 1,080 sq. ft.
Second floor — 761 sq. ft.
Garage — 420 sq. ft.
Unfinished basement — 1,067 sq. ft.

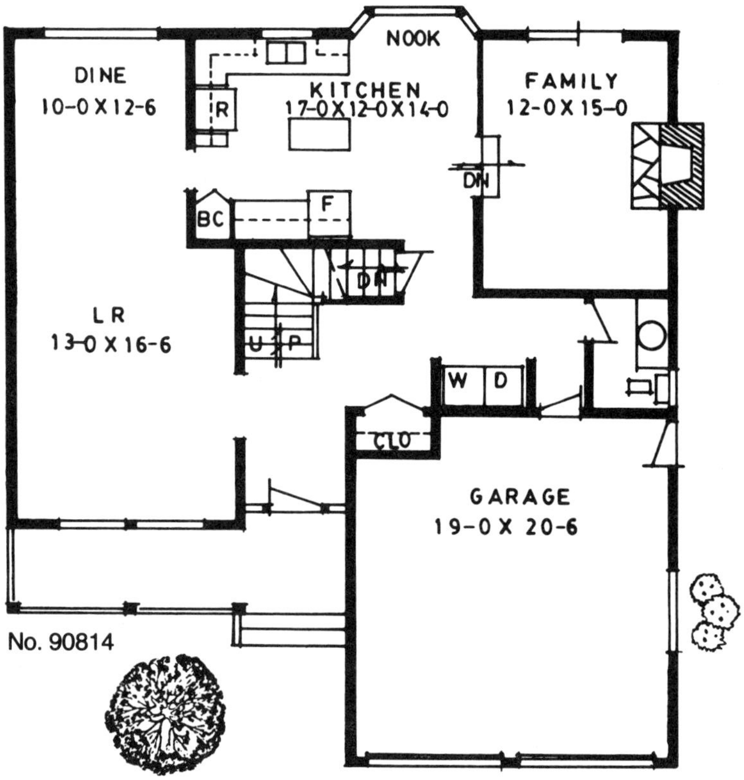

No. 90814

Width — 40 ft.
Depth — 46 ft.

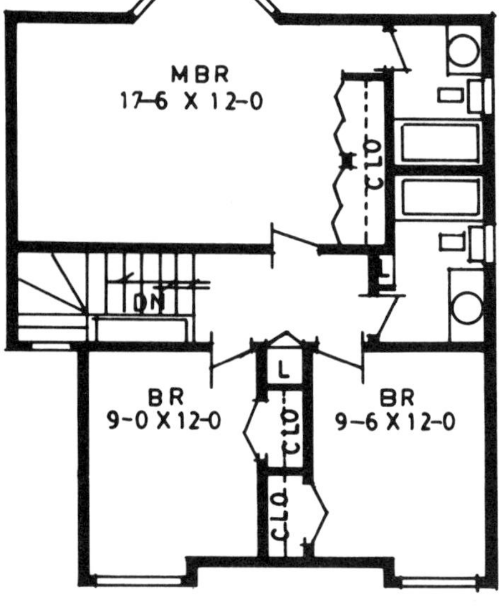

SECOND FLOOR

Overhang Provides Shade from the Noonday Sun

No. 90502

A sheltered entry opens to the airy, fireplaced living and dining room of this one-level, stucco home. Behind double doors, the family room shares a view of the deck with the kitchen and adjoining, bay windowed breakfast nook. The window of the front bedroom, framed by a graceful arch, looks out over its own, private garden. An angular hall leads to the laundry, two additional bedrooms and two full baths.

Floor area — 1,642 sq. ft.

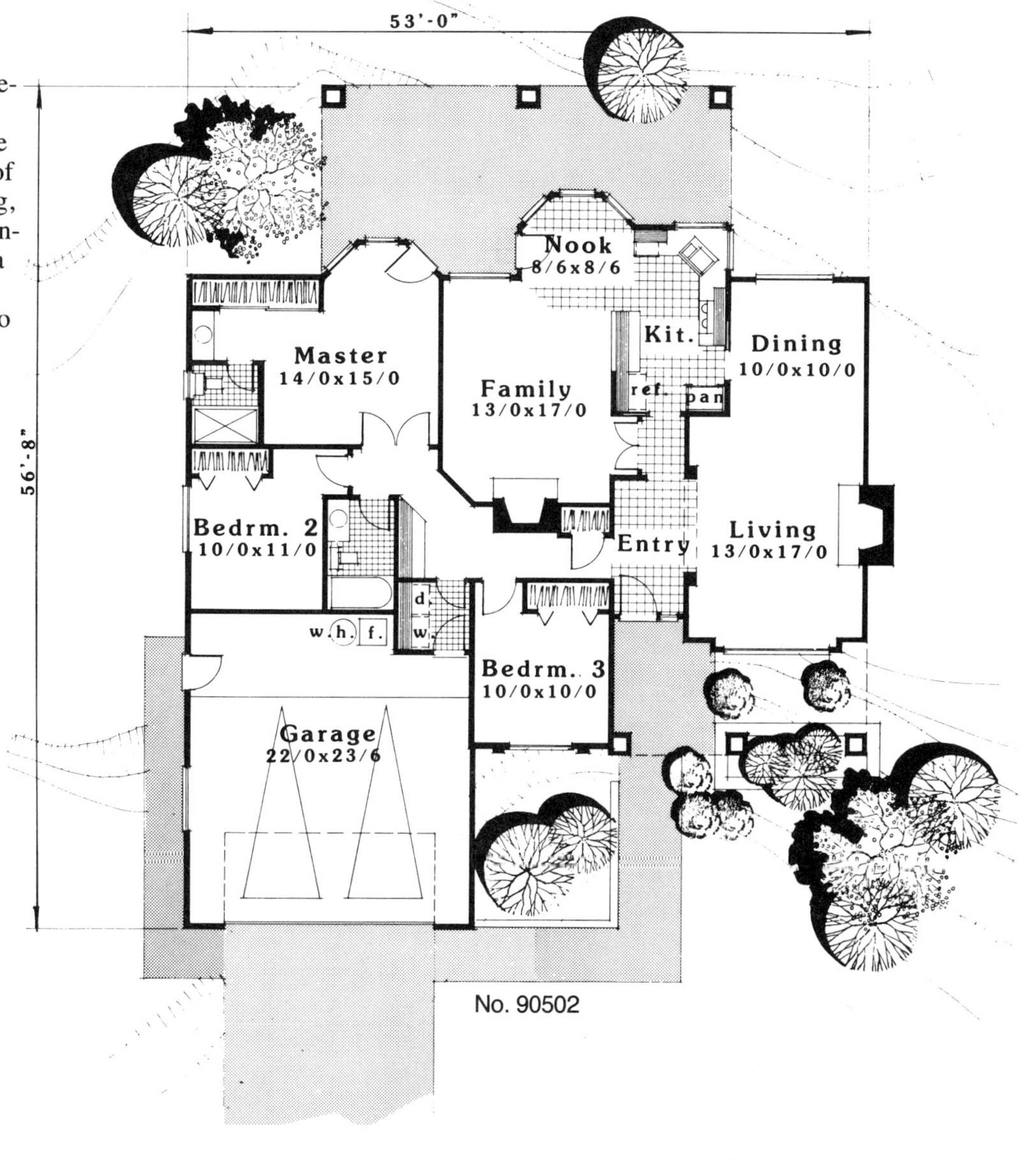

No. 90502

Beautiful Passive Solar Design

No. 90352

This very marketable house includes most of the most-wanted marketing features as well as impressive passive solar benefits. The major south facing to the rear opens up with the vaulted living room glass to highlight the great room and capture the sun's warmth with the trombe walls at rear and around fireplace/stove. The greenhouse is a further sun catch as well as a year 'round source of living pleasure. Kitchen overlooks the vaulted rear spaces and south yard and lets the cook become part of the family scene. Master suite has dressing area plus closet and private bath. Note the pleasing and inviting look of the house. It is neither experimental or engineered looking, but ready to site in your suburban area. Berming along east and west sides further protects these exposures and the north entrance is protected by the wing wall and garage projections.

First floor — 1,418 sq. ft.

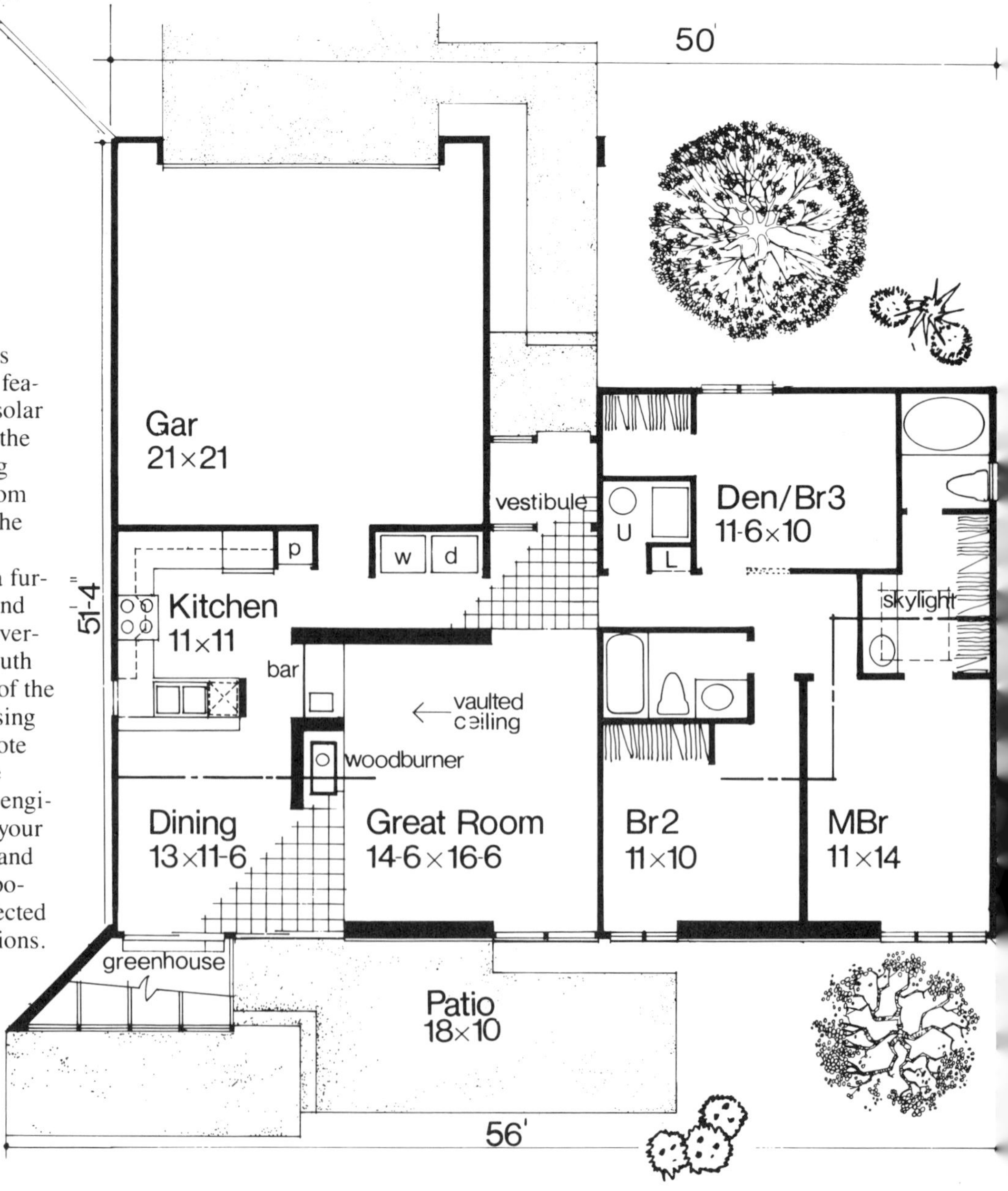

Bays Add Beauty and Living Space

No. 90607

The welcoming warmth that most Traditional houses seem to exude is especially evident in this center hall, four-bedroom residence. Just off the two-story foyer, the formal living room features a heat-circulating fireplace. Ionic columns and a semi-circular window wall give the dining room a classic grace. The U-shaped kitchen opens to the fireplaced family room. Off the foyer, there are two bedrooms and two baths. Two bedrooms upstairs share a bath.

First floor — 1,515 sq. ft.
Second floor — 530 sq. ft.

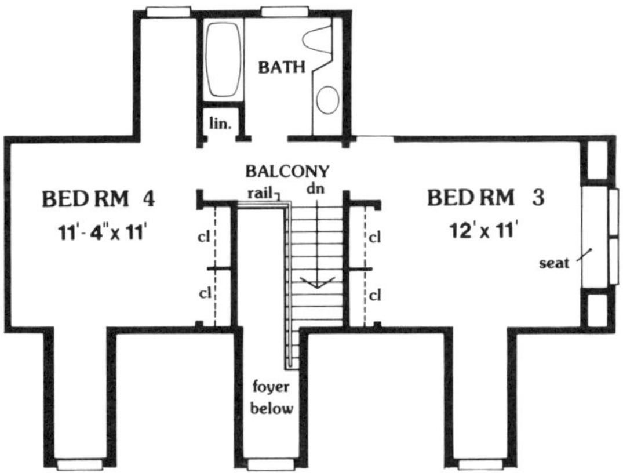

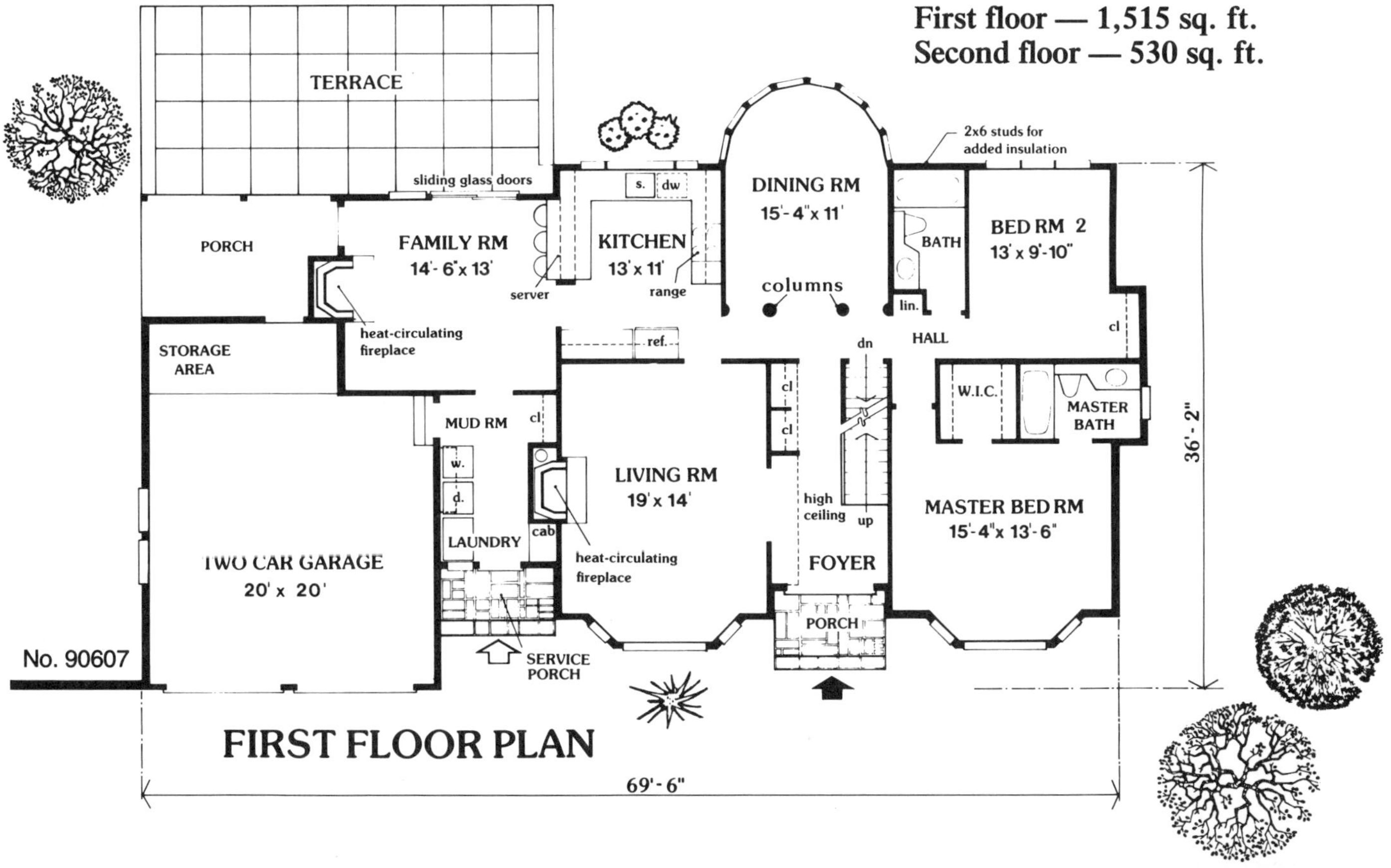

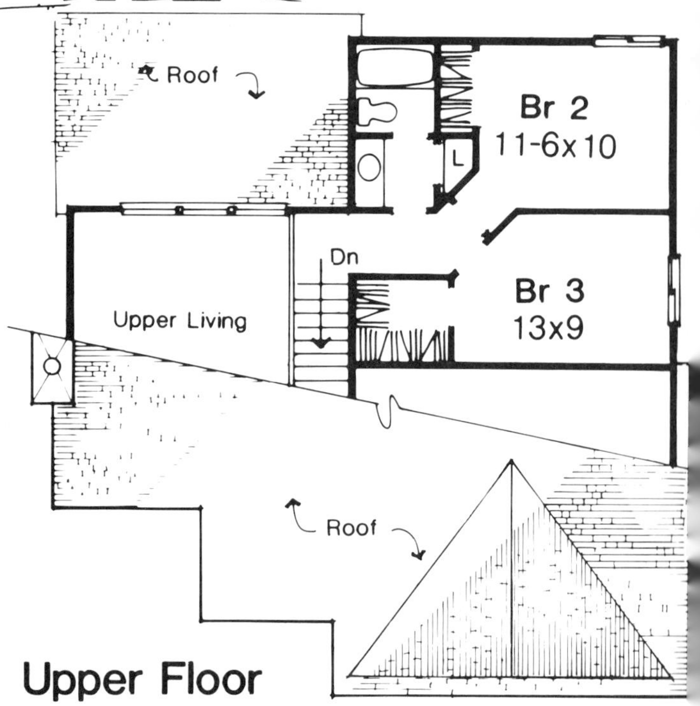

Upper Floor

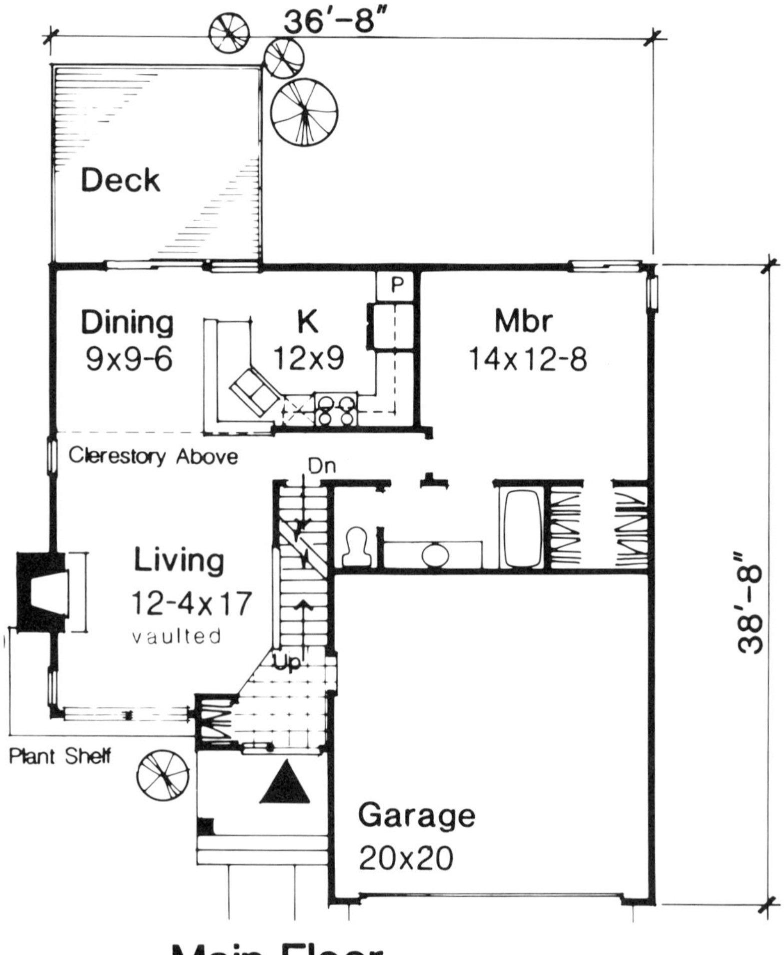

Main Floor

Living Room Features Vaulted Ceiling

No. 90353

This 3-bedroom home will appeal to today's style-sensitive buyer. The flowing roof lines and volumes of its design make the house seem larger than its real size and width. The living room features a vaulted ceiling and the dining room, with clerestory above, opens onto a backyard patio. The master bedroom has a full bath and walk-in closet. Two more bedrooms and another bath are located on the upper floor. Design features basement construction detailing and exterior wall construction.

Main floor — 846 sq. ft.
Upper floor — 400 sq. ft.

Rear Of Home As Attractive As Front

No. 90413

The rear of this rustic/contemporary home features a massive stone fireplace and a full length deck which make it ideal for mountain, golf course, lake or other locations where both the front and rear are visible. Sliding glass doors in the family room and breakfast nook open onto the deck. The modified A-Frame design combines a cathedral ceiling over the sunken living room with a large studio over the two front bedrooms. An isolated master suite features a walk-in closet and compartmentalized bath with double vanity and linen closet. The front bedrooms include ample closet space and share a unique bath-and-a-half arrangement. On one side of the U-shaped kitchen and breakfast nook is the formal dining room which opens onto the foyer. On the other side is a utility room which can be entered from either the kitchen or garage. The exterior features a massive stone fireplace, large glass areas and a combination of vertical wood siding and stone.

First floor — 2,192 sq. ft.
Second floor — 376 sq. ft.

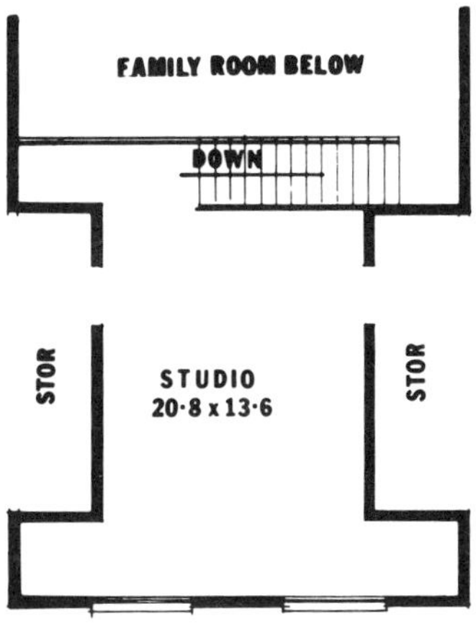

SECOND FLOOR

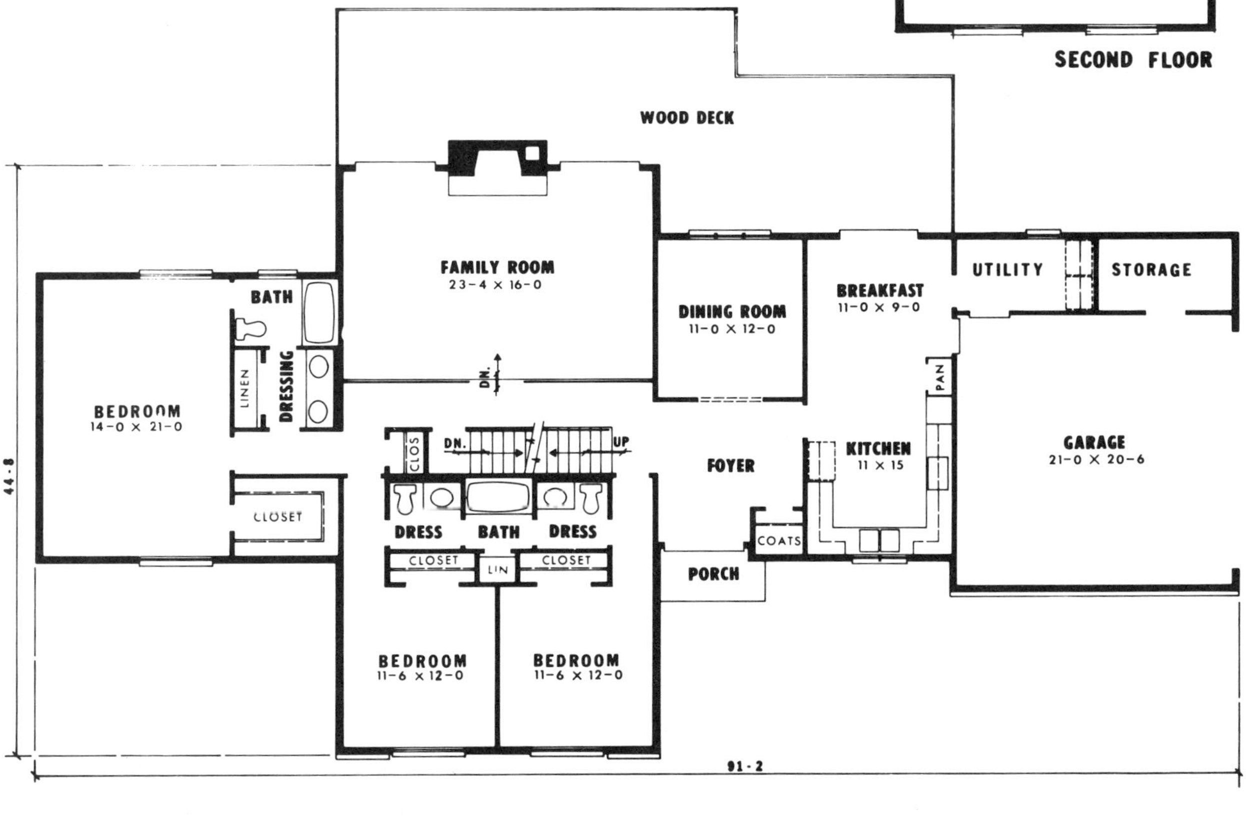

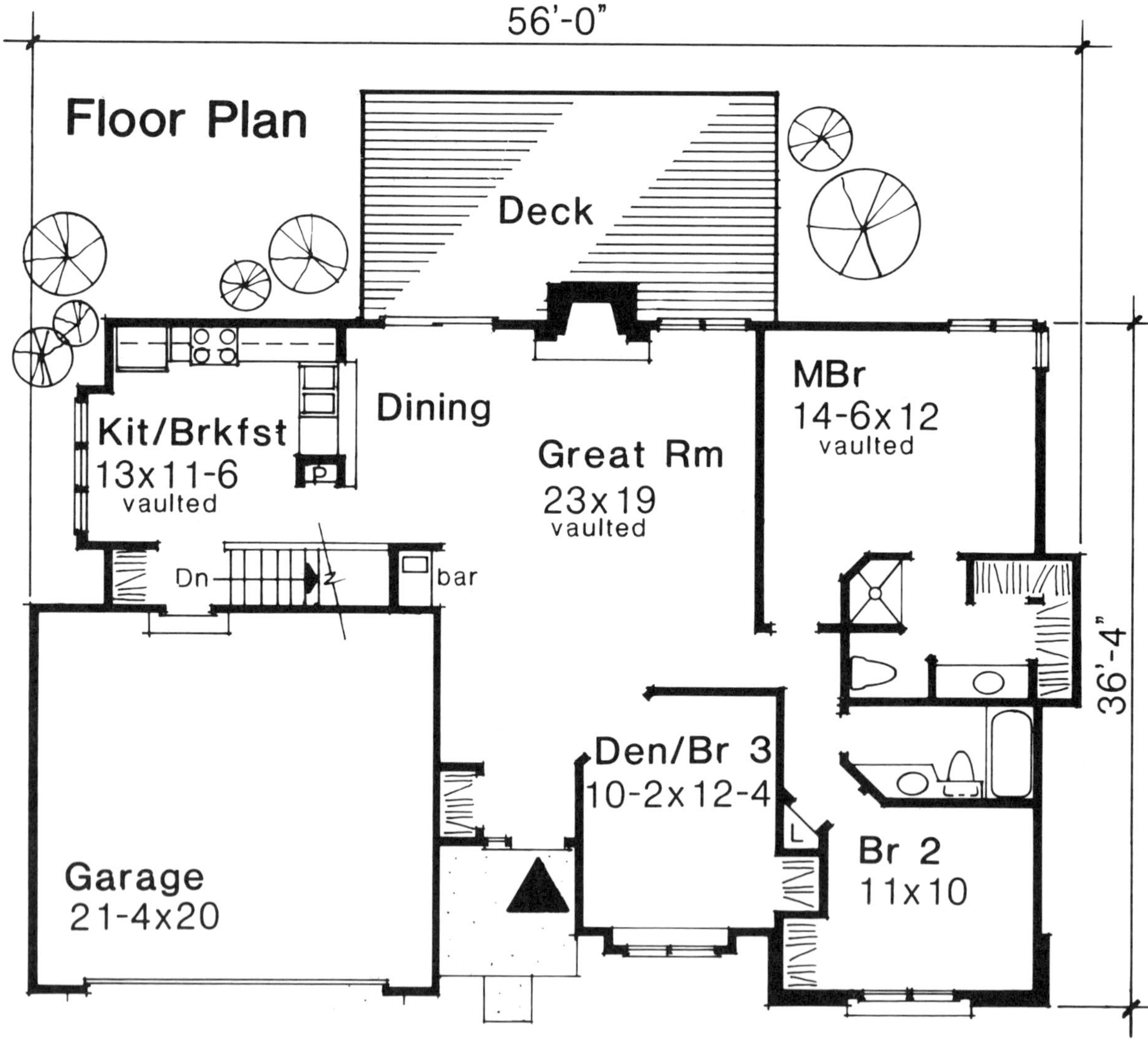

Another Nice Ranch Design

No. 90354

Small and move-up houses are looking much larger these days through their proportioning and roof massing as exemplified in this two-bedroom ranch. The inside space seems larger from the high-impact entrance with through-views to the vaulted great room, fireplace and the rear deck. The den (optional third bedroom) features double doors and the kitchen/breakfast area has a vaulted ceiling. the plan easily adapts to crawl or slab construction with utilities replacing stairs; laundry facing kitchen and air handler and water heater facing garage.

First floor — 1,360 sq. ft.

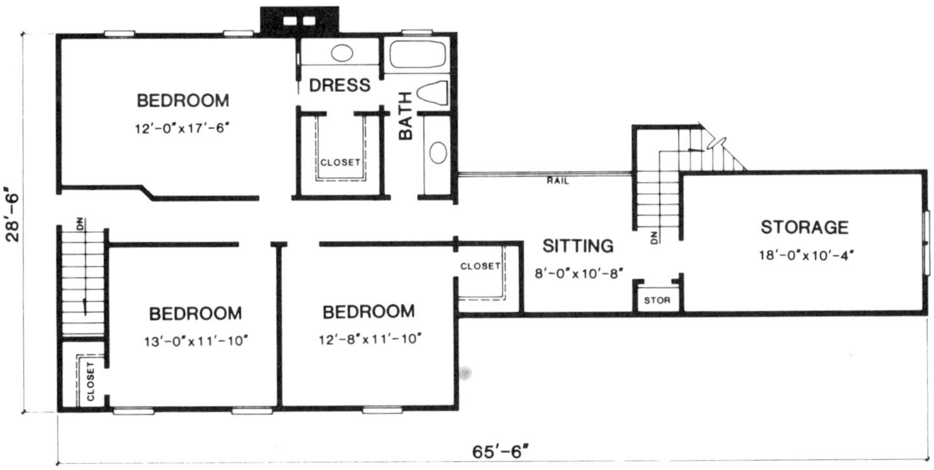

UPPER FLOOR PLAN

Bay Windows Enhance a Country Home

No. 90405

Large master bedroom suite includes deluxe bath with separate shower, garden tub, twin vanities and two large walk-in closets combine to form a super suite. Kitchen has direct access to both breakfast nook and dining room feature a large bay window. Three bedrooms, sitting area and storage or (bonus room) combine to form the second level.

First floor — 2,005 sq. ft.
Second floor — 1,063 sq. ft.

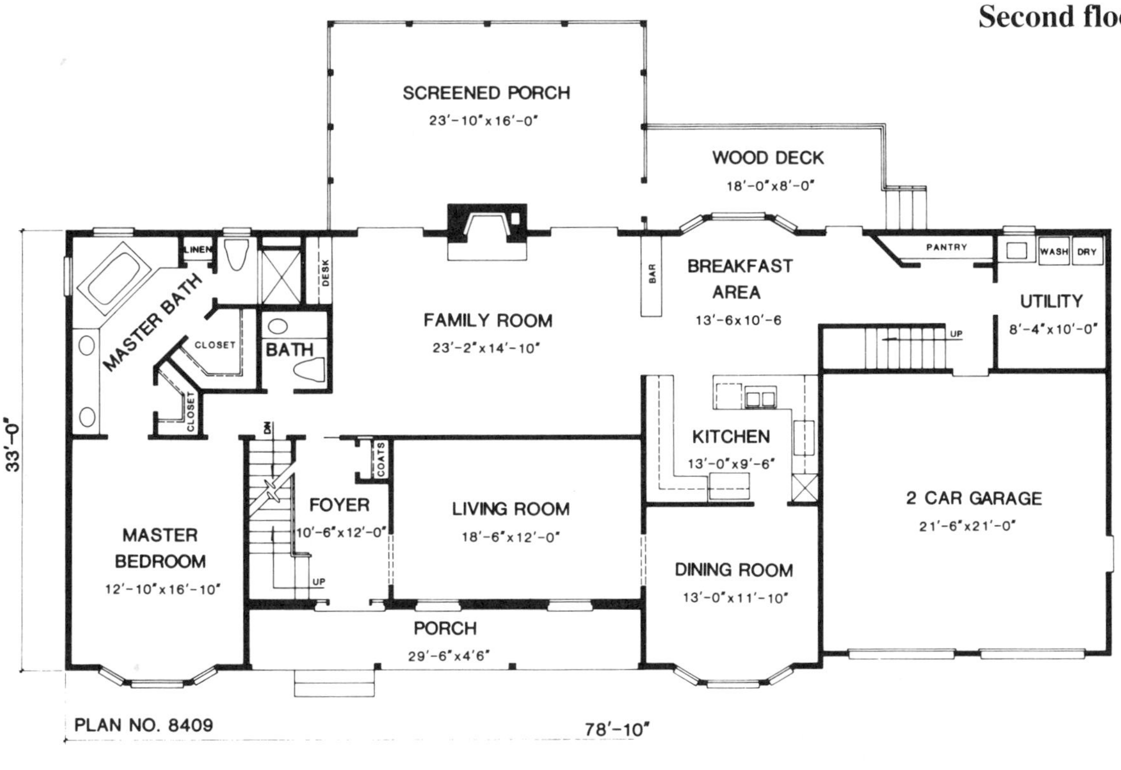

MAIN FLOOR PLAN

Clerestory Windows Let the Sun Shine In

No. 90926

A striking contemporary exterior compliments the exceptional floor plan in this attractive ranch home zoned for area function. Designed to sit on a level lot, it could be adapted to a hillside building site. Some of the amenities include a secluded, covered breakfast patio off the family room, a distinctive, angular kitchen, a fireplace complete with wood box, and a vaulted ceiling with clerestory windows in the sunken living room. The master suite features a 3/4 bath and a big walk-in closet.

Main floor — 1,589 sq. ft.
Basement — 1,534 sq. ft.
Garage — 474 sq. ft.
Width — 60 ft.
Depth — 56 ft.

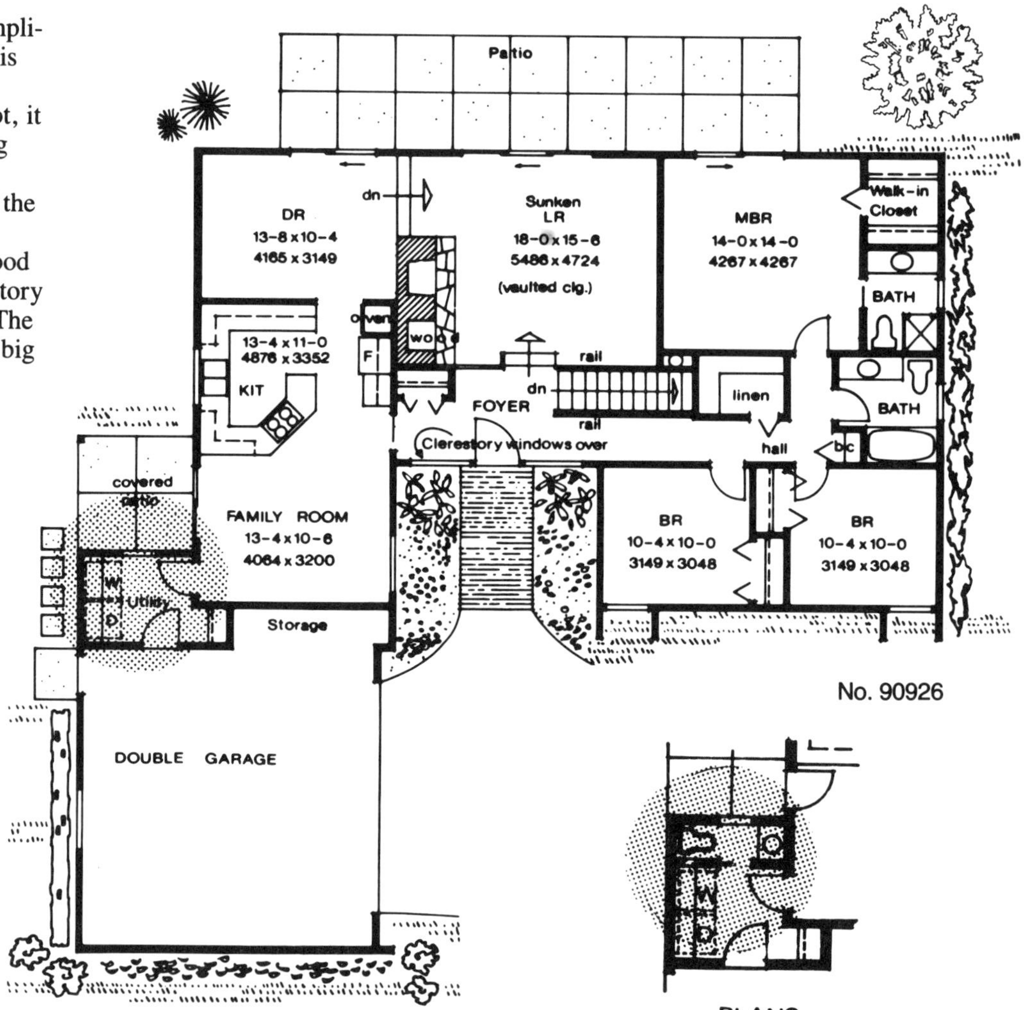

PLANS INCLUDE ALTERNATE OPT. WASHRM. LAYOUT OFF UTILITY

Deluxe Master Suite Includes Garden Tub

90400

This stately English Tudor design features a downstairs master suite with one walk-in plus two additional closets and a compartmentalized bath with double vanity, garden tub and separate shower. The formal foyer is flanked by a dining room on one side and a living room on the other. For more casual living, a sunken family room with a raised-hearth fireplace, wet bar and a half bath is included. The spacious kitchen with breakfast nook and a large utility room with a laundry chute from upstairs complete the main floor. An open stairwell leads to the upper level which includes your choice of a large study or a two story foyer. Also located on the upper level are three bedrooms with generous closet space including two walk-in closets, two more compartmentalized baths and a linen closet and laundry chute to the utility room. All or part of the basement can be used to supplement the main living area. Specify basement or crawlspace foundation when ordering.

First floor — 1,759 sq. ft.
Second floor — 1,269 sq. ft.

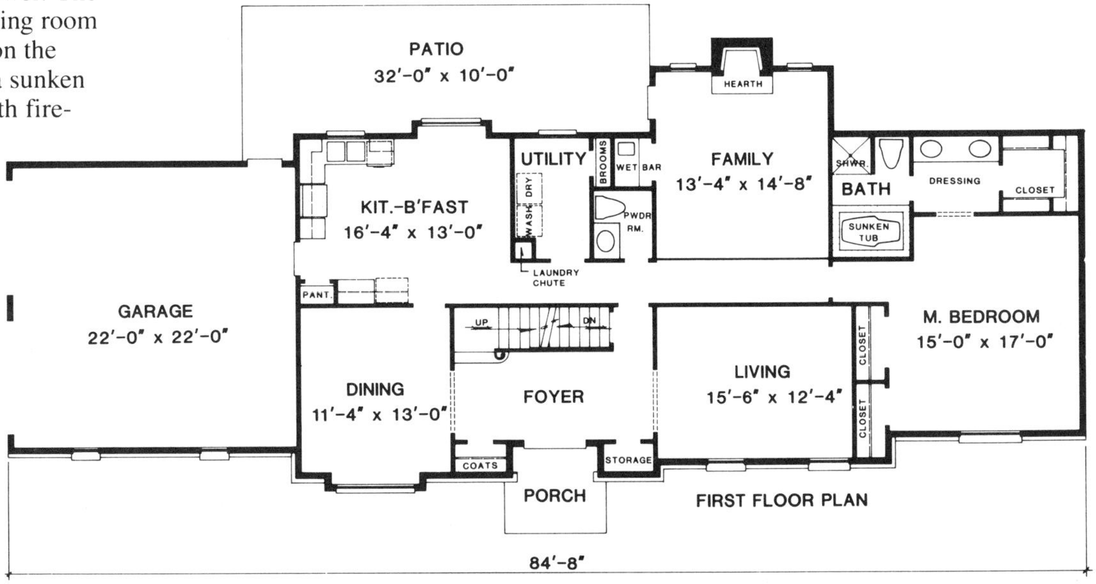

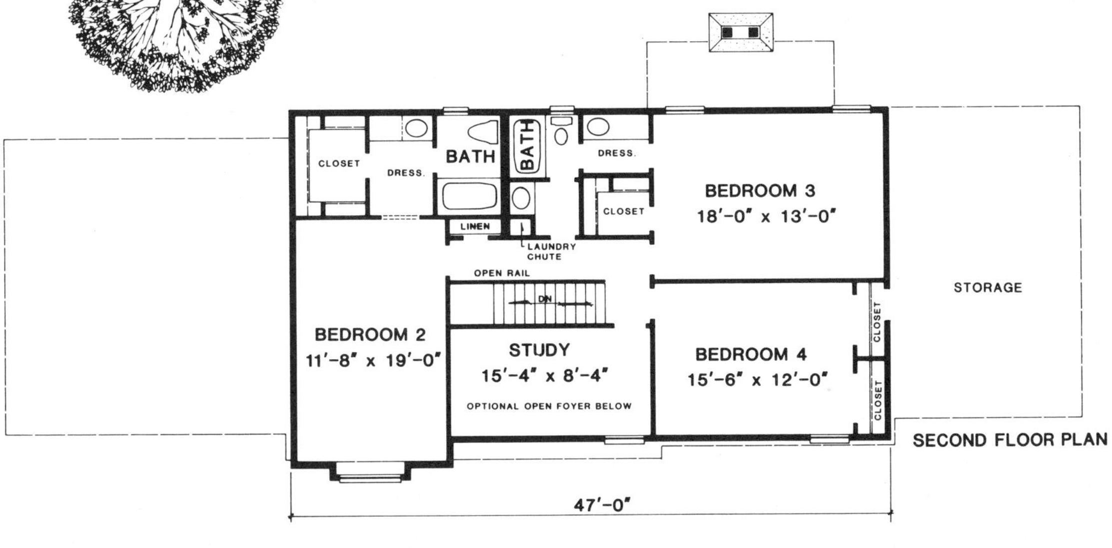

Brick Home Features Unified Floor Plan

No. 90103

From the sheltering porch, through the foyer and into the spacious living area, this home will make quite an impression. The central kitchen and dining areas separate the two smaller bedrooms from the master bedroom which is insulated from the street noise by the garage. The laundry area is conveniently located in the utility and storage area.

Living area — 1,494 sq. ft.

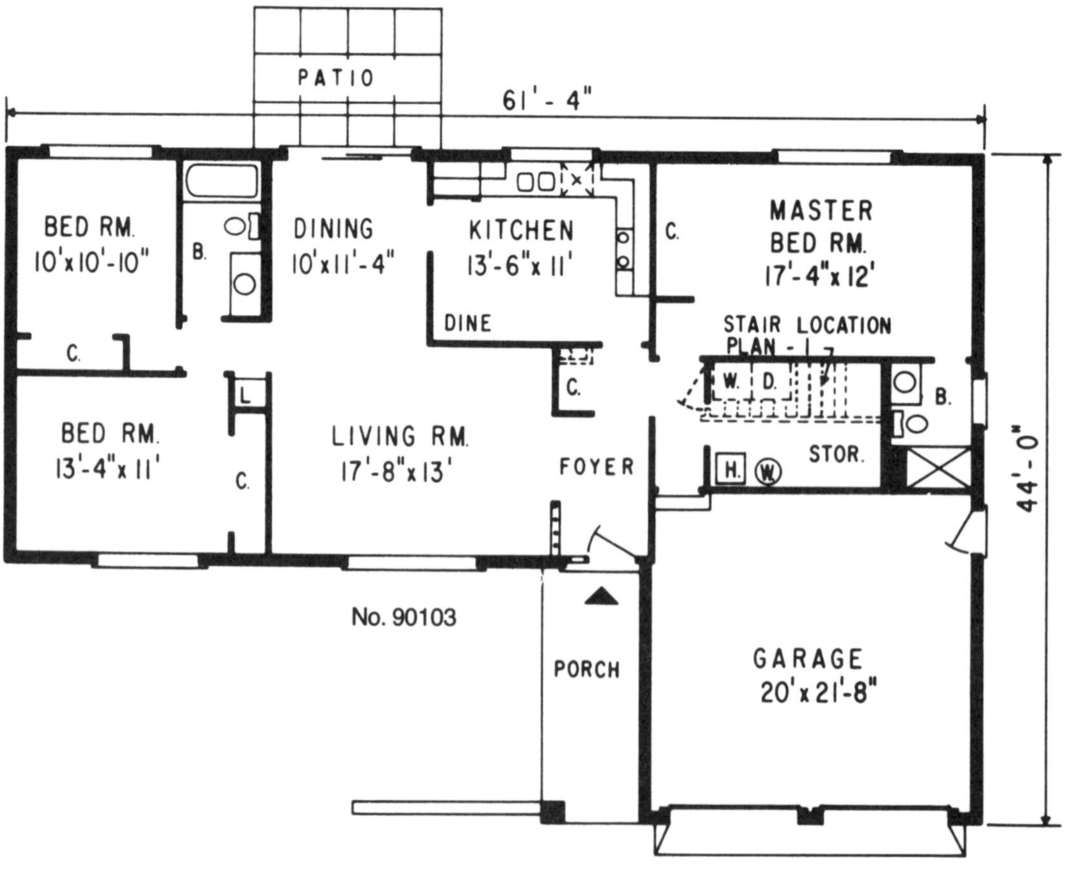

No. 90103

Focus on Family Activities

No. 90124

The whole family will enjoy the arrangement of this traditionally styled three bedroom home. Family and guests alike will be drawn to the cozy family room that opens onto the patio. The warm fireplace and beamed ceiling spread their charm to the adjacent kitchen, which easily serves the counter area and the formal dining room. The mudroom entrance is made even more practical by combining it with laundry facilities. A 3/4 bath complete the first floor. Each of the 3 roomy bedrooms on the second floor has ample closet space with the master suite enjoying a large walk-in.

First floor — 1,080 sq. ft.
Second floor — 868 sq. ft.

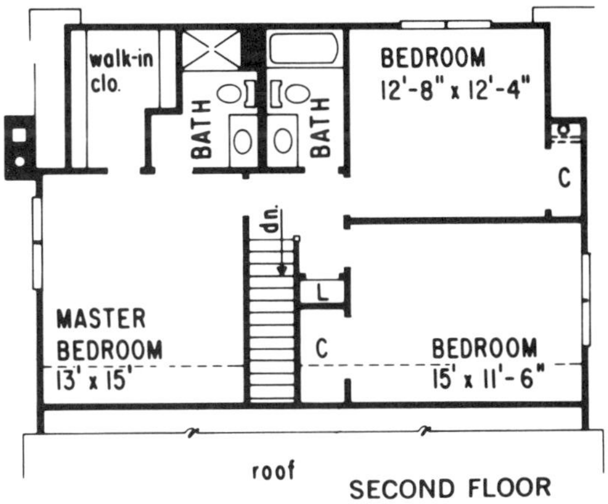

SECOND FLOOR

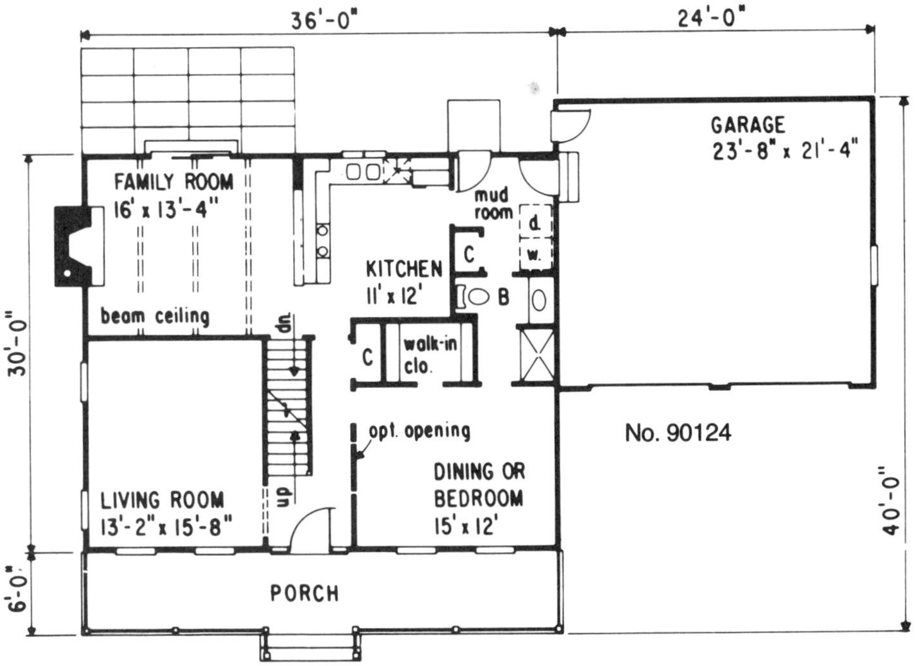

Year Round Retreat

No. 90613

This compact home is a bargain to build and designed to save on energy bills. Large glass areas face south, and the dramatic sloping ceiling of the living room allows heat from the wood-burning stove to rise into the upstairs bedrooms through high louvers on the inside wall. In hot weather, just open the windows on both floors for cooling air circulation. Sliding glass doors in the kitchen and living rooms open to the deck for outdoor dining or relaxation. One bedroom and a full bath complete the first floor. A stair off the foyer ends in a balcony with a commanding view of the living room. Two spacious bedrooms are separated by a full bath.

First floor — 917 sq. ft.
Second floor — 465 sq. ft.
(optional slab construction available)

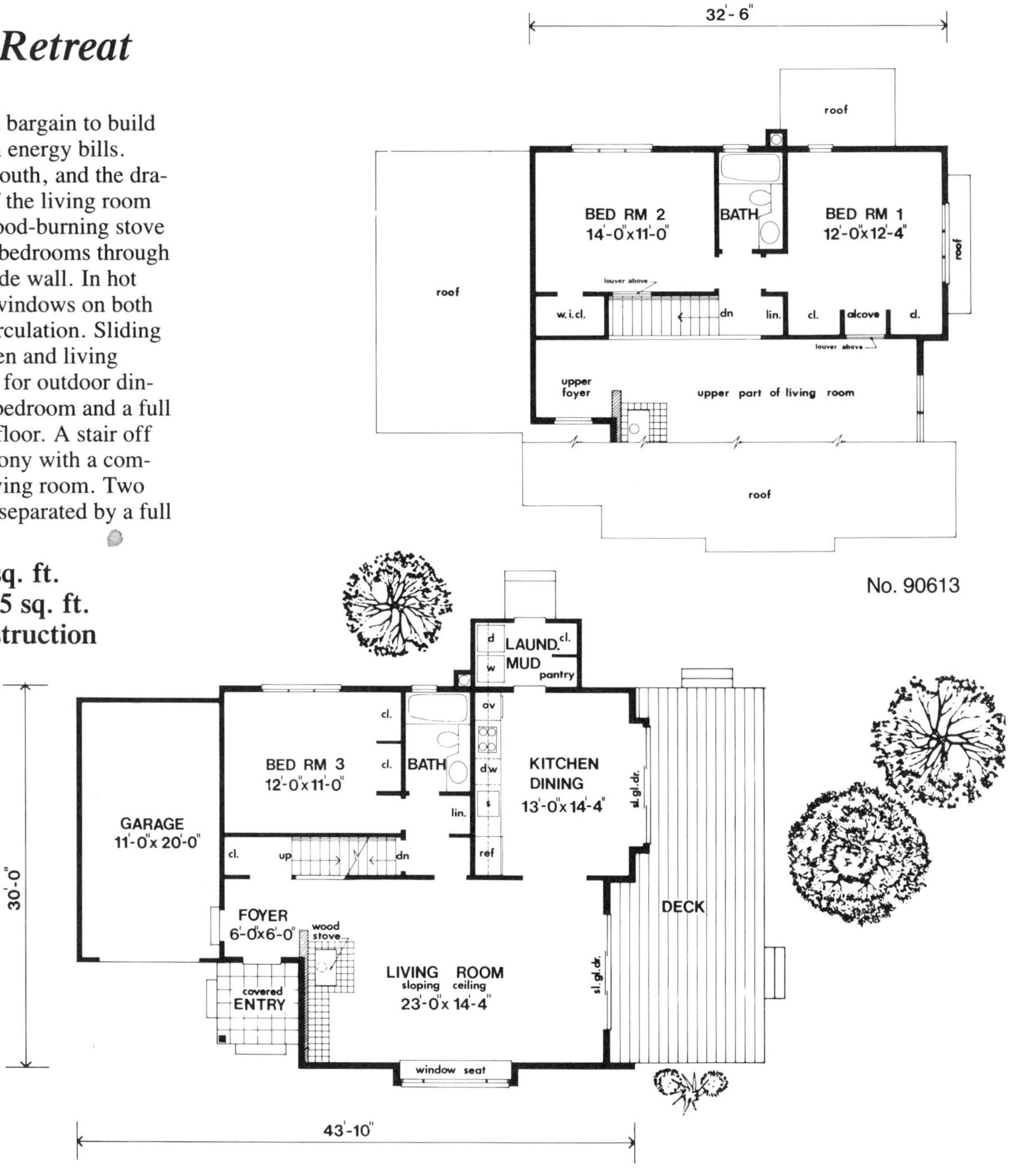

Cathedral Ceiling With Studio

No. 90420

This rustic/contemporary modified A-Frame design combines a high cathedral ceiling over a sunken living room with a large studio over the two rear bedrooms. The isolated master suite features a walk-in closet and compartmentalized bath with double vanity and linen closet. The two rear bedrooms include ample closet space and share a unique bath-and-a-half arrangement. On one side of the U-shaped kitchen and breakfast nook is the formal dining room which is separated from the entry by a planter. On the other side is a utility room which can be entered from either the kitchen or garage. The exterior features a massive stone fireplace, large glass areas and a combination of vertical wood siding and stone.

First floor — 1,860 sq. ft.
Second floor — 343 sq. ft.

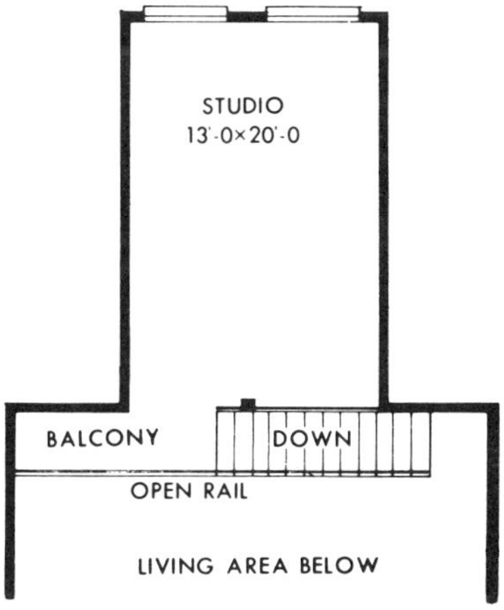

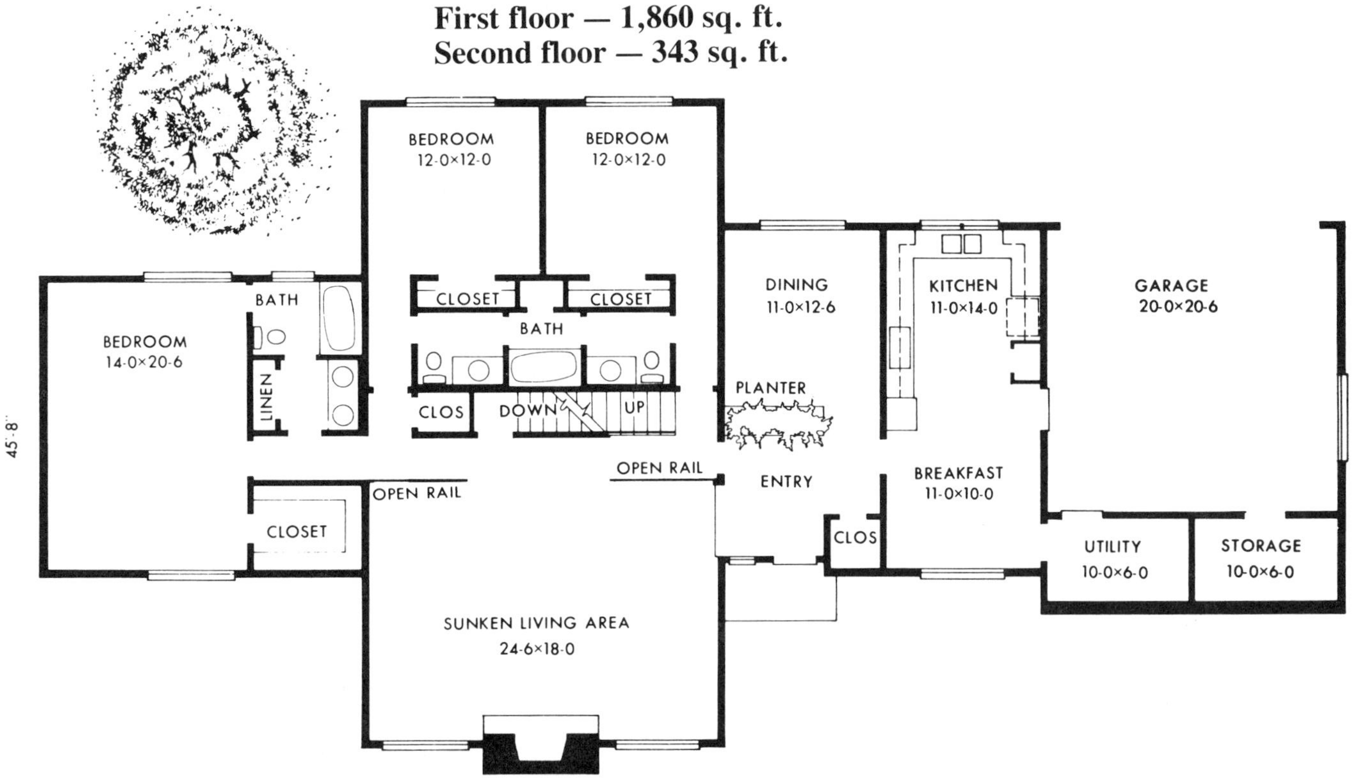

Wood, Stucco, Stone Lend Rustic Warmth

No. 90617

This luxurious split-level home has the charm and beauty of an English country estate. Directly ahead of the large entrance foyer, the living and dining room share a two-way fireplace and a glass wall that runs almost unbroken for 35 feet. The large front kitchen has a separate dinette and adjoining laundry, lavatory and service entry. Four bedrooms occupy the upper level along with two large baths. Off the lower-level recreation room, the study with bath can double as a bedroom. Sliding glass doors lead to rear terraces from both the recreation and living rooms.

Total living area — 2,927 sq. ft.

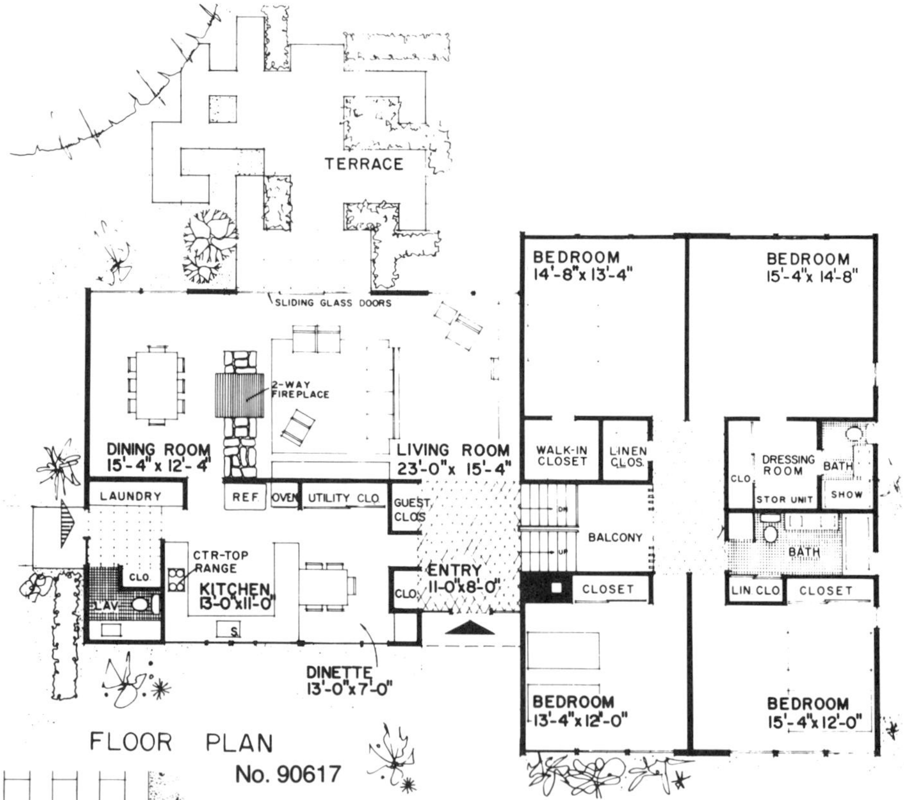

FLOOR PLAN
No. 90617

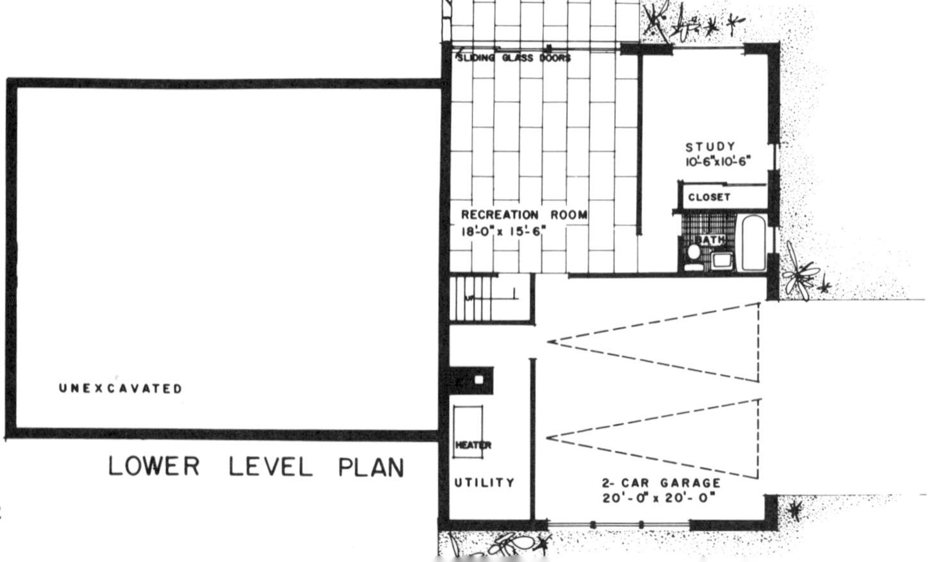

LOWER LEVEL PLAN

True French Provincial Features Four Bedrooms

No. 90408

This French Provincial design features a master suite with a spacious deluxe bath that includes a garden tub, shower, linen closet, double vanity and large walk-in closets share a second compartmentalized bath. Living and dining rooms are lcoated to the side of the formal foyer. Both the family room, with fireplace and double doors opening onto a screened-in back porch, and a U-shaped kitchen, with an island counter open to the breakfast bay, allow more casual living. Fixed stairs in the family room provide access to attic storage above. Also included is a utility room with half bath.

Area — 2,968 sq. ft.

Great Traffic Pattern Highlights Home

No. 90901

Victorian styling and economical construction techniques make this a doubly charming design. This is a compact charmer brimming with features: a sheltered entry leading to the two-story foyer; an island kitchen with convenient pass-through to the formal dining room; a cozy living room brightened by a bay window; an airy central hall upstairs surrounded by large bedrooms with plenty of closet space. And look at that lovely master suite with its sitting area in a bay window.

Main floor — 940 sq. ft.
Second floor — 823 sq. ft.
Basement — 940 sq. ft.
Garage — 440 sq. ft.
Width — 54 ft.
Depth — 33 ft.

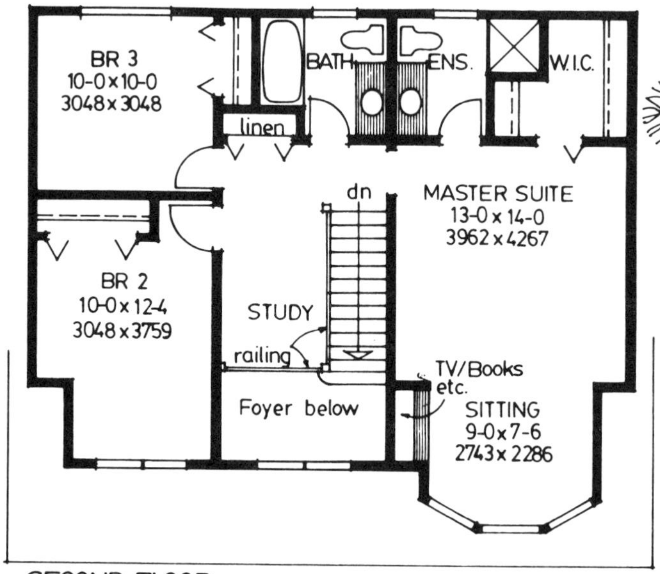

SECOND FLOOR

No. 90901

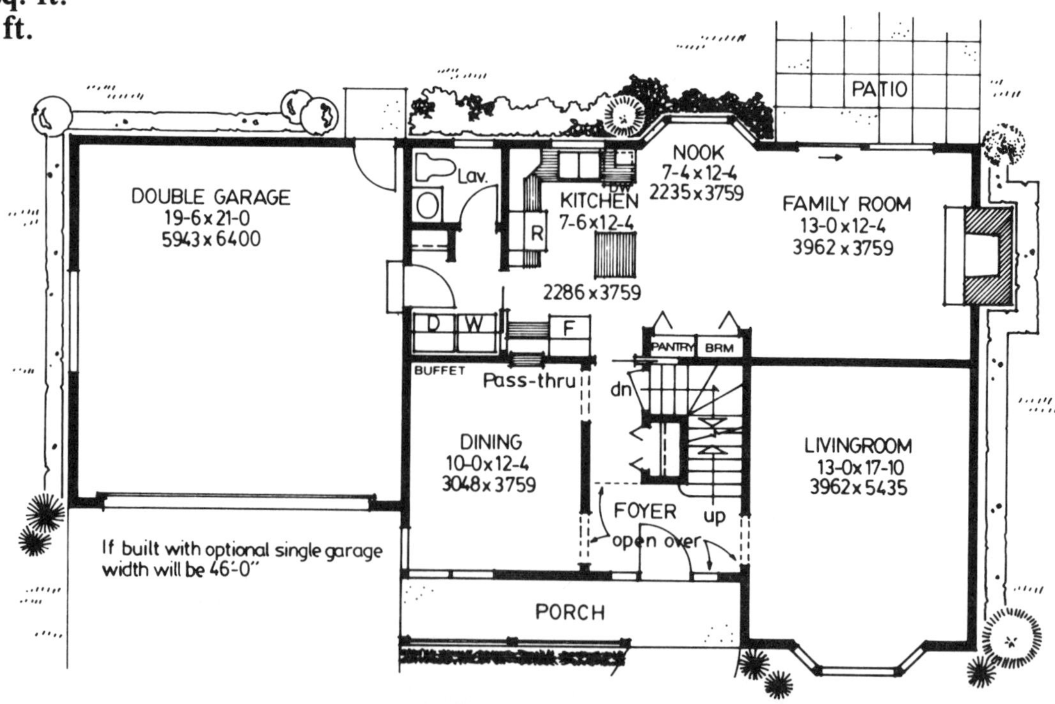

Accent on Luxury

No. 10655

Your houseguests may never want to leave this updated 5 bedroom manor home. Sturdy brick construction and elegant detailing — such as recessed octagonal ceilings, built-in cabinets, shelves and pantry — make this a special place. Extra amenities include the hexagonal sunny breakfast room with access to the deck, two powder rooms, guest bedroom, and full bath all on the first floor. The soaring two story foyer, flanked by the library and dining room, offers a view of the curved staircase and a glimpse of the woodbeamed great room beyond. Walk up the stairs and find a huge master bedroom suite with skylit bath, along with three more bedrooms and two full baths.

First floor — 2,526 sq. ft.
Second floor — 2,062 sq. ft.
Basement — 2,493 sq. ft.
Garage — 976 sq. ft.

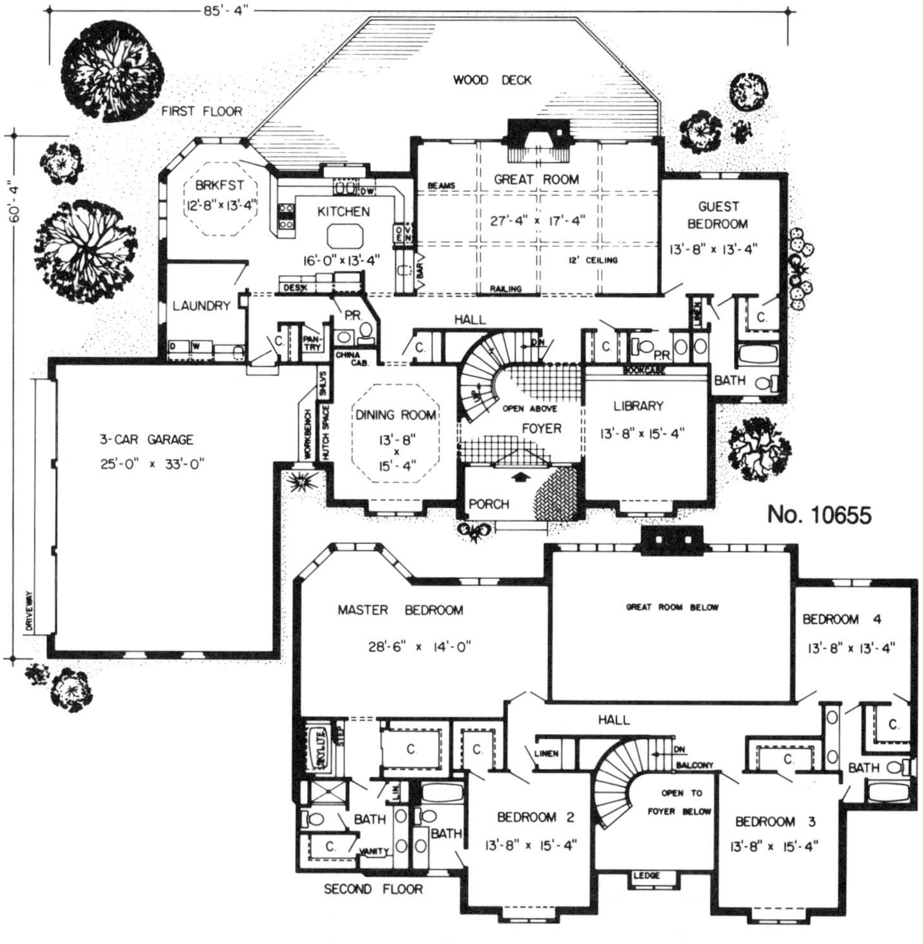

Family Living, Contemporary Style

No. 90628

Convenient living space surrounds the spacious foyer of this compact contemporary. An L-shaped stairway leads to four bedrooms and two baths on the second floor. But on the main level, active family life is the main focus. Gain easy access to both patio and garage from the open kitchen/dinette, which spills into the family room. Rainy weather shouldn't be a problem for the kids; they can play under the covered porch off the living room.

First floor — 988 sq. ft.
Second floor — 936 sq. ft.
(optional slab construction available)

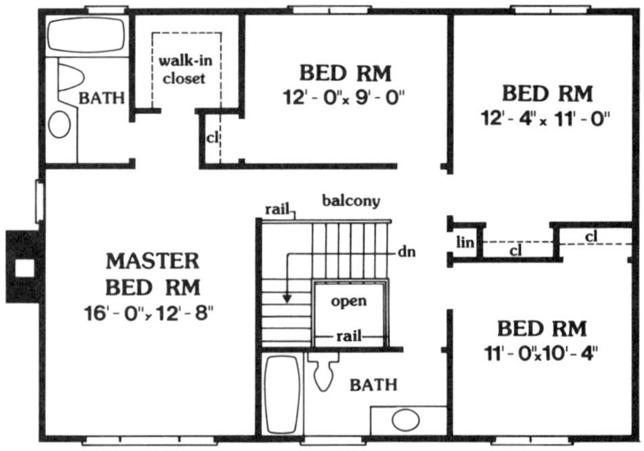

No. 90628

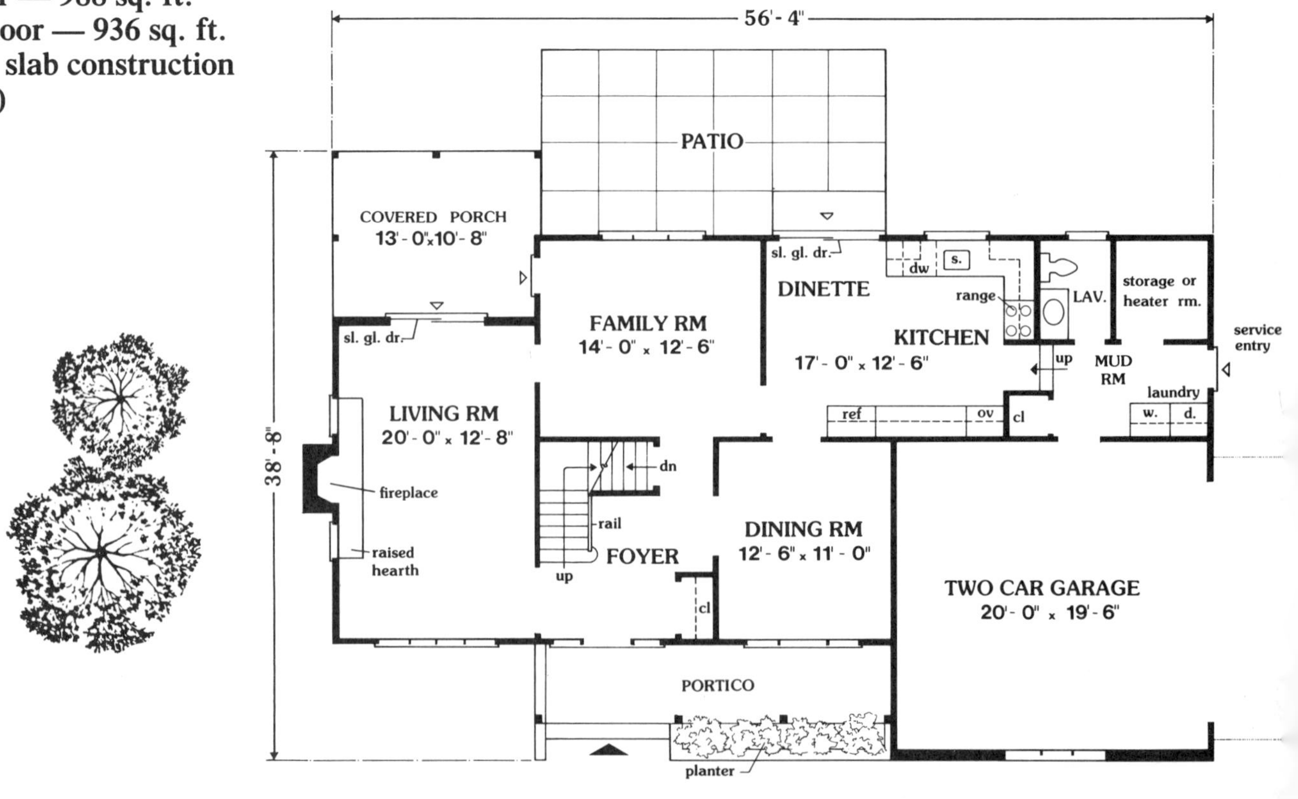

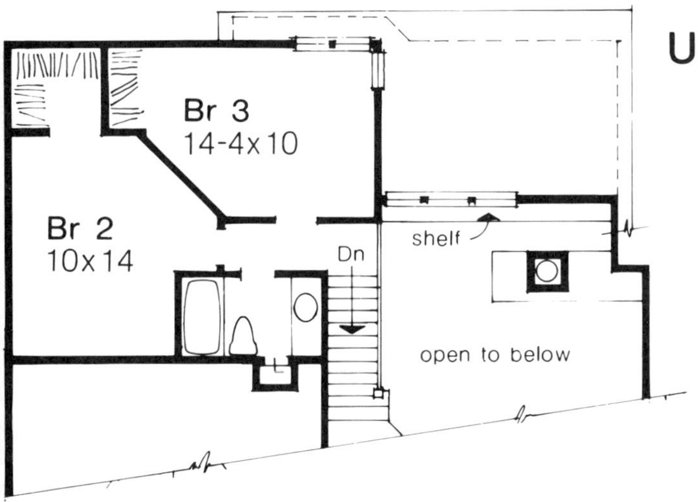

Upper Floor

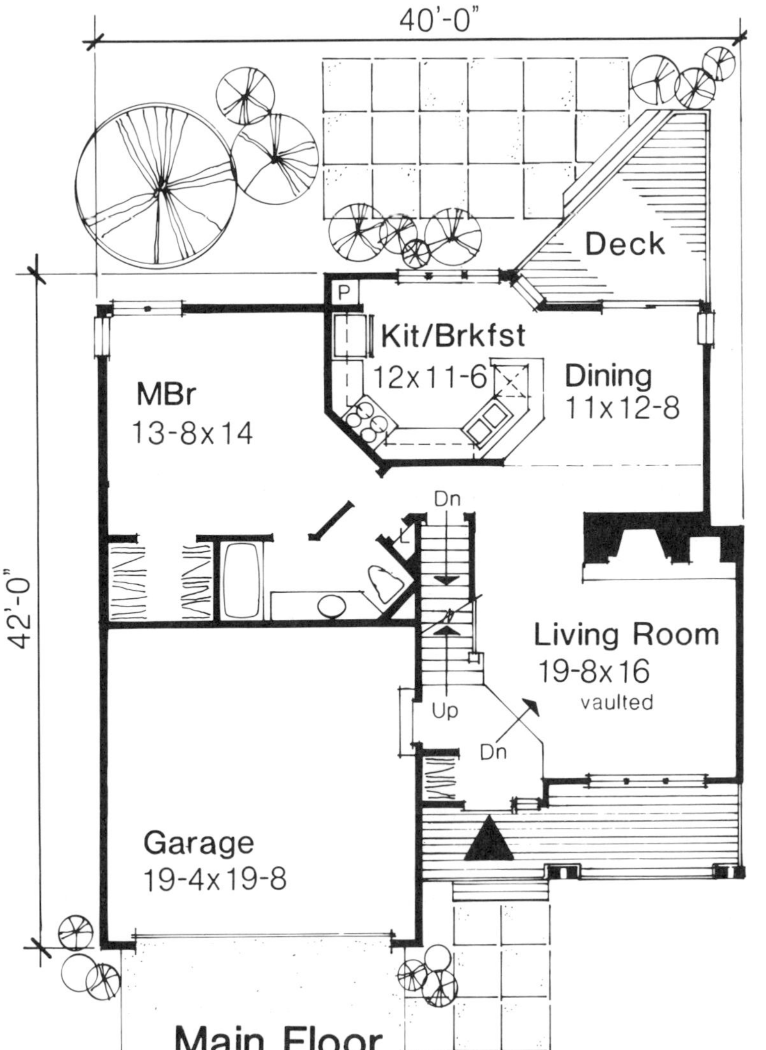

Main Floor

U-Shaped Kitchen Offers Breakfast Bay Window Area

No. 90372

Perceived value, that sales appealing characteristic that justifies the high cost of a new home in your customer's mind, is strongly featured in this home. The exterior has substantial mass and interest. The interior has lots of impact and volume. Combined, the package also features the master bedroom suite on the main floor, the open U-shaped kitchen with breakfast bay, the vaulted living room with tall wall fireplace focus. The style is very "today", quite contemporary in spirit but very reflective of traditional story and a half homes values of the past.

First floor — 1,006 sq. ft.
Second floor — 437 sq. ft.

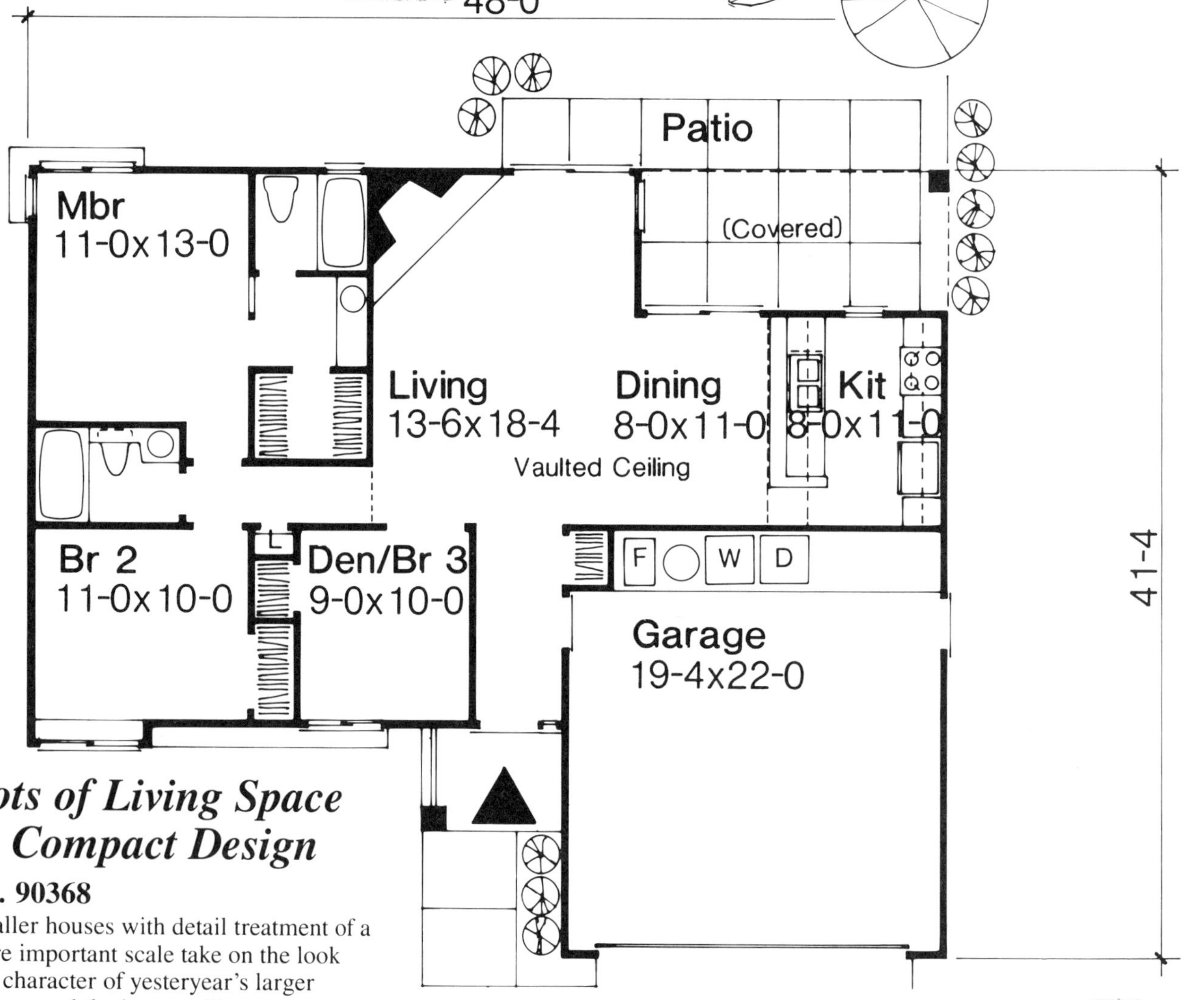

MAIN FLOOR

Lots of Living Space in Compact Design

No. 90368

Smaller houses with detail treatment of a more important scale take on the look and character of yesteryear's larger homes, and the buyer will perceive greater value from this minimum added design expenditure. Then, if your smaller house, like this one, opens to flowing living spaces, rear yard views, and provides a luxurious master bedroom suite, the house will seem to have the essential lifestyle characteristics of a larger home, too.

Area — 1,081 sq. ft.

Built-In Entertainment Center for Family Fun

No. 90615

Up-to-date features bring this center hall colonial into the 20th century. The focus of the Early American living room is a heat-circulating fireplace, framed by decorative pilasters that support dropped beams. Both dining areas open to the rear terrace through sliding glass doors. And, the convenient mud room provides access to the two car garage. Four bedrooms and two baths, including the spacious master suite, occupy the second floor.

Total living area — 1,973 sq. ft.
Garage — 441 sq. ft.
(optional slab construction available)

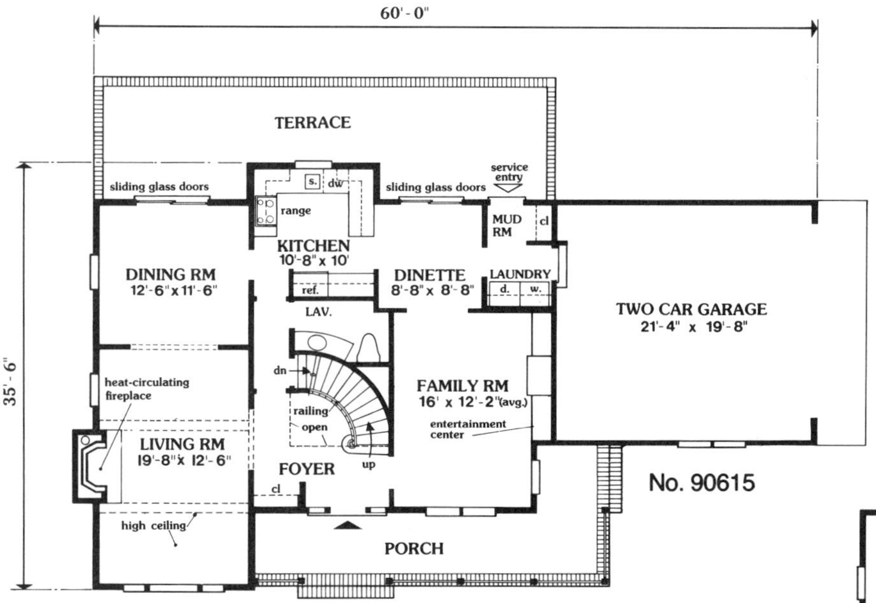

FIRST FLOOR PLAN

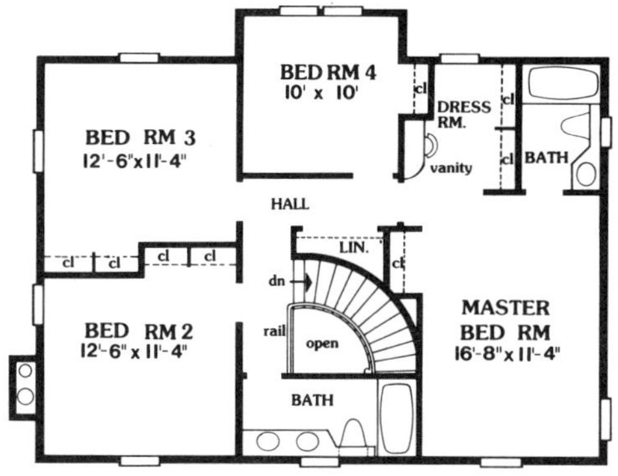

SECOND FLOOR PLAN

Studio Above Garage in Dutch Colonial

No. 90143

This attractive Dutch Colonial design has many outstanding features, but one of the most sought after is the studio loft located above the garage. On the first level, a half bath and laundry facilities are located near the hallway, and an exit is nearby leading out to a porch area. Additionally, the family room connects with the kitchen, while the living room lies just off the kitchen. The second level has two baths. A sewing room is located next to the stairwell. A two-car garage is offered in this plan.

First floor — 1,196 sq. ft.
Second floor — 1,012 sq. ft.
Studio loft — 627 sq. ft.

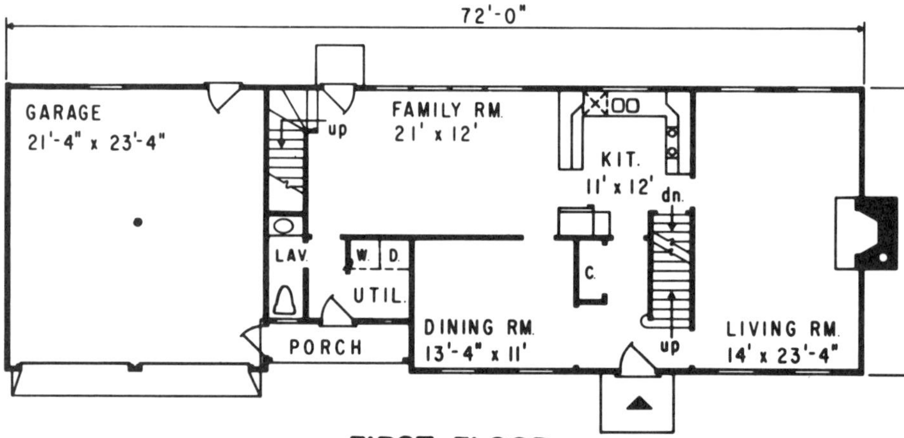

FIRST FLOOR

No. 90143

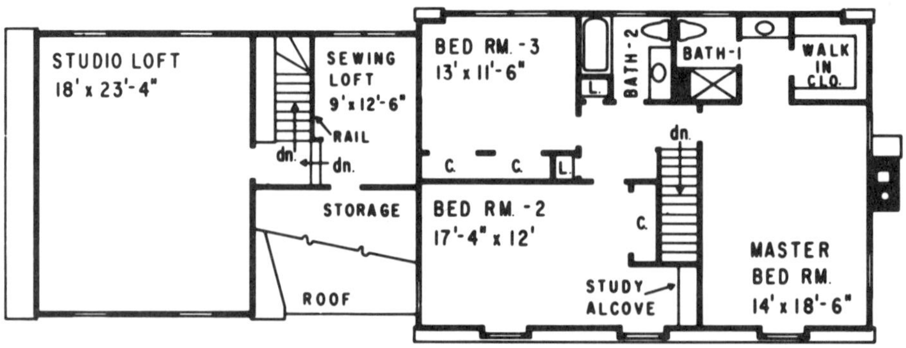

SECOND FLOOR three bedrooms

Bavarian-Style Cottage Plan

No. 90036

Materials are an important design and maintenance aspect of this Bavarian-style vacation cottage. The casual air and easy care associated with the vacation life are assured by hand-split red cedar shingle roof, rough cut horizontal wood siding, and rugged native stone. Inside, vertical, rough sawn board and exposed beams carry out the theme. Other details are made to order for vacation living. A large porch accessible from the dining area is covered for shelter, can be screened for extended use, and enjoys an outdoor barbeque. Indoors, the living-dining area and kitchen are merged spaces; the kitchen is planned for efficiency. One of the attractive stylistic features of this house is the bedroom balcony which gives the living room two ceiling heights. The house is planned to sleep a good sized family or one with frequent guests, as it includes four bedrooms.

First floor — 925 sq. ft.
Second floor — 518 sq. ft.

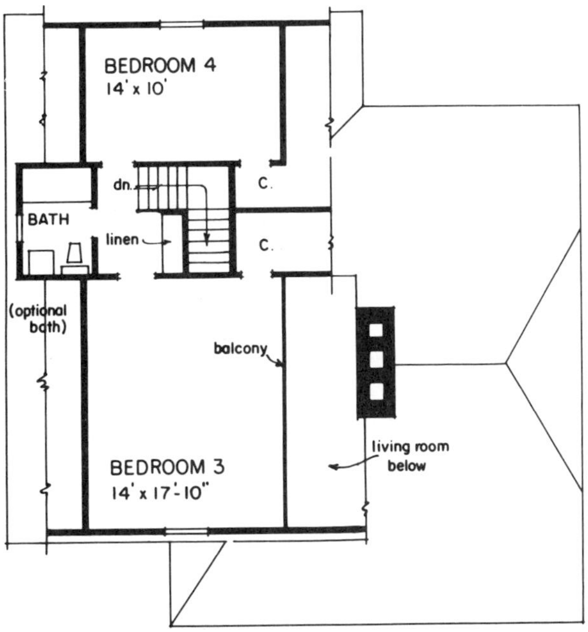

Second floor plan

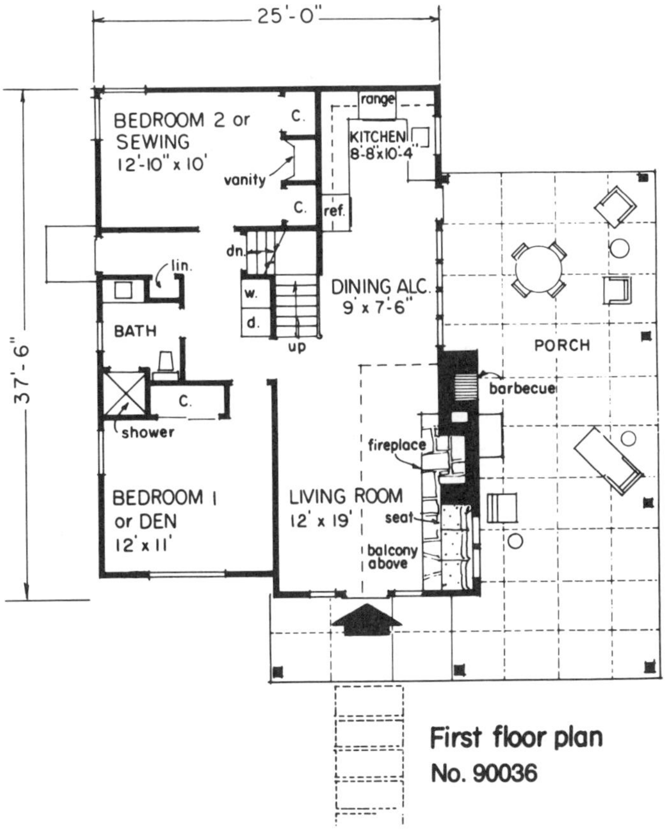

First floor plan
No. 90036

Compact Victorian Ideal For Narrow Lot

No. 90406

This compact Victorian design incorporates four bedrooms and three full baths into a thirty foot wide home. The upstairs master suite features two closets, an oversized tub and a sitting room with vaulted ceiling and bay window. Two additional bedrooms and a second full bath are included in the upper level. A fourth bedroom and third full bath on the main floor can serve as an in-law or guest suite. Between the dining and breakfast rooms is a galley kitchen. The dining room has a bay window and the breakfast room a utility nook. A large parlor with a raised-hearth fireplace completes the main floor. The porches add to the overall exterior appearance and help to protect the front and side entrances.

ELEVATION A

First floor — 954 sq. ft.
Second floor — 783 sq. ft.

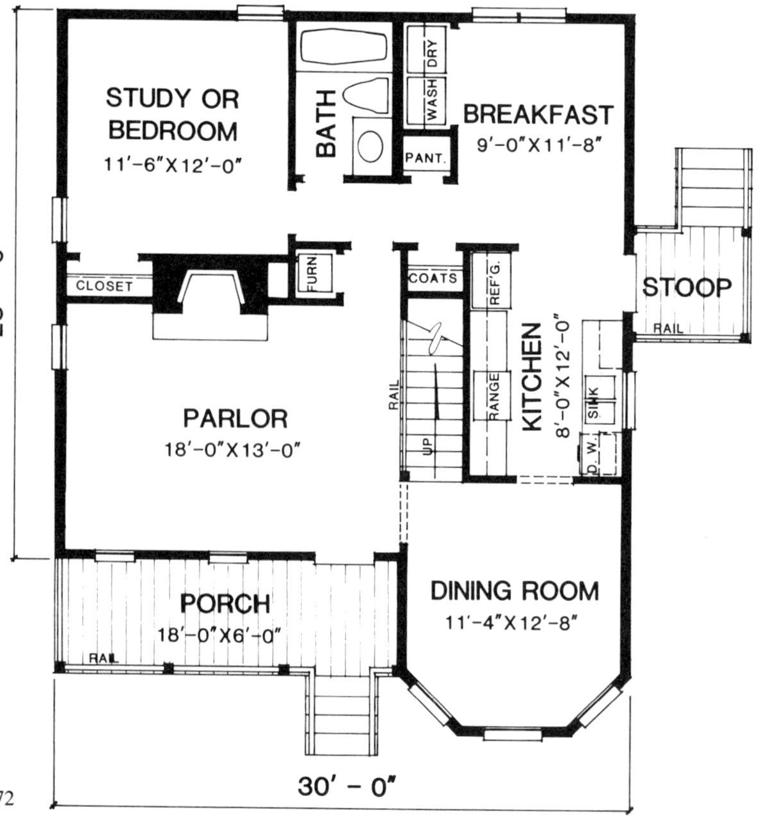

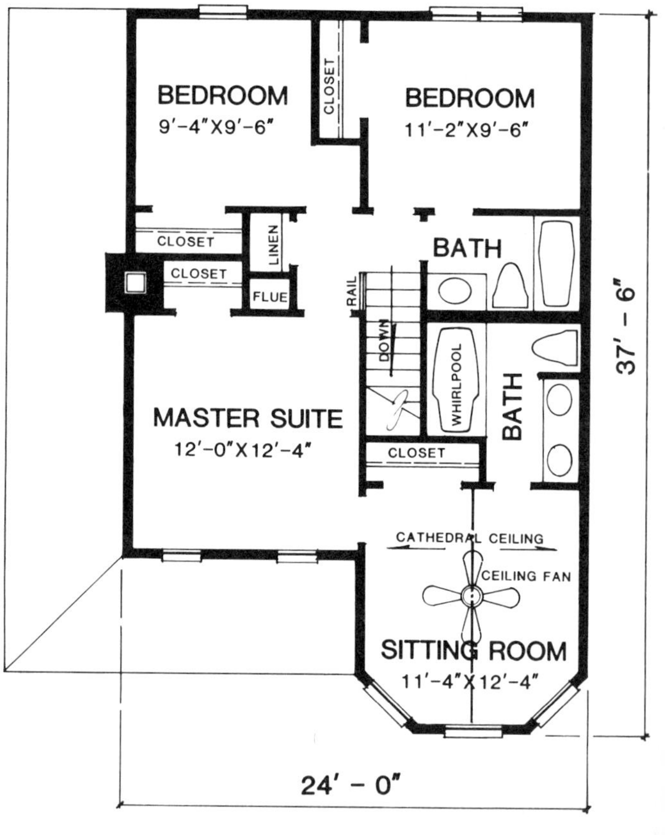

Dramatic Interior Adds Atmosphere

No. 90508

From the moment you enter this home, you sense something special. The oversize entry faces a sweeping stairway and dramatic angled entrances to the living and dining areas. The sense of something special is especially evident in the master suite whose unusual shape, private deck, and walk-in wardrobe add flair and style. The other 3 bedrooms are notable for their roominess and ample closets. Downstairs, the heart of the home is the spacious kitchen with corner sink, cooking island, pantry and desk. From the kitchen, atrium style doors lead to a covered deck. The family room has a remarkable openness thanks to a vaulted ceiling, plenty of glass, and the large passageway to the kitchen.

First floor — 1,525 sq. ft.
Second floor — 1,367 sq. ft.

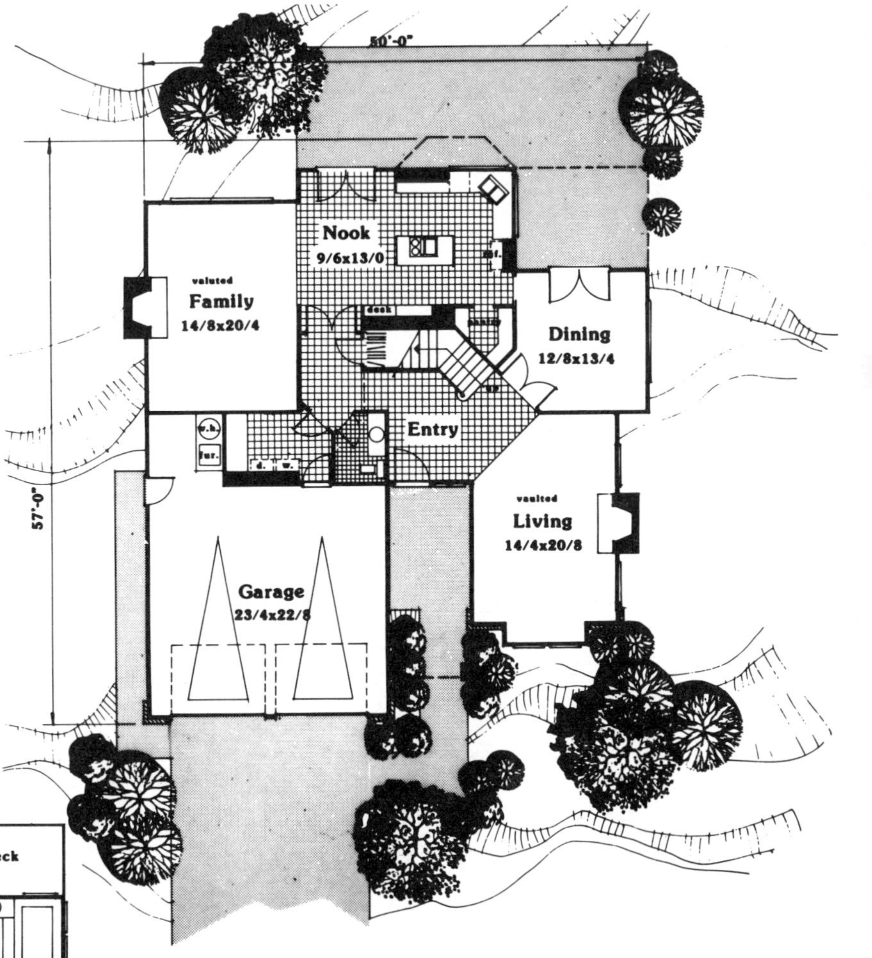

No. 90508

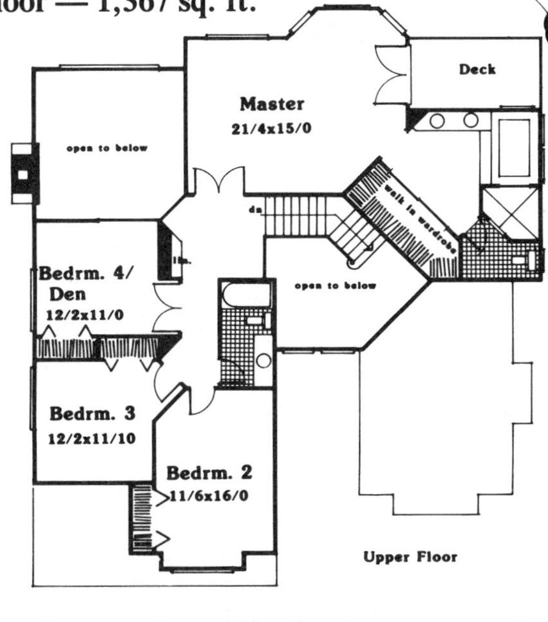

Rocking Chair Living

No. 90409

The open floor plan of this rustic design virtually eliminated wasted hall space. The centrally located great room features a cathedral ceiling with exposed wood beams. Living and dining areas are separated by a massive fireplace. The isolated master suite features a walk-in closet and compartmentalized bath. The galley type kitchen is between the breakfast room, with bay window, and formal dining area. A large utility room and storage room complete the garage area. On the opposite side of the great room are two additional bedrooms and a second full bath.

Area — 1,670 sq. ft.

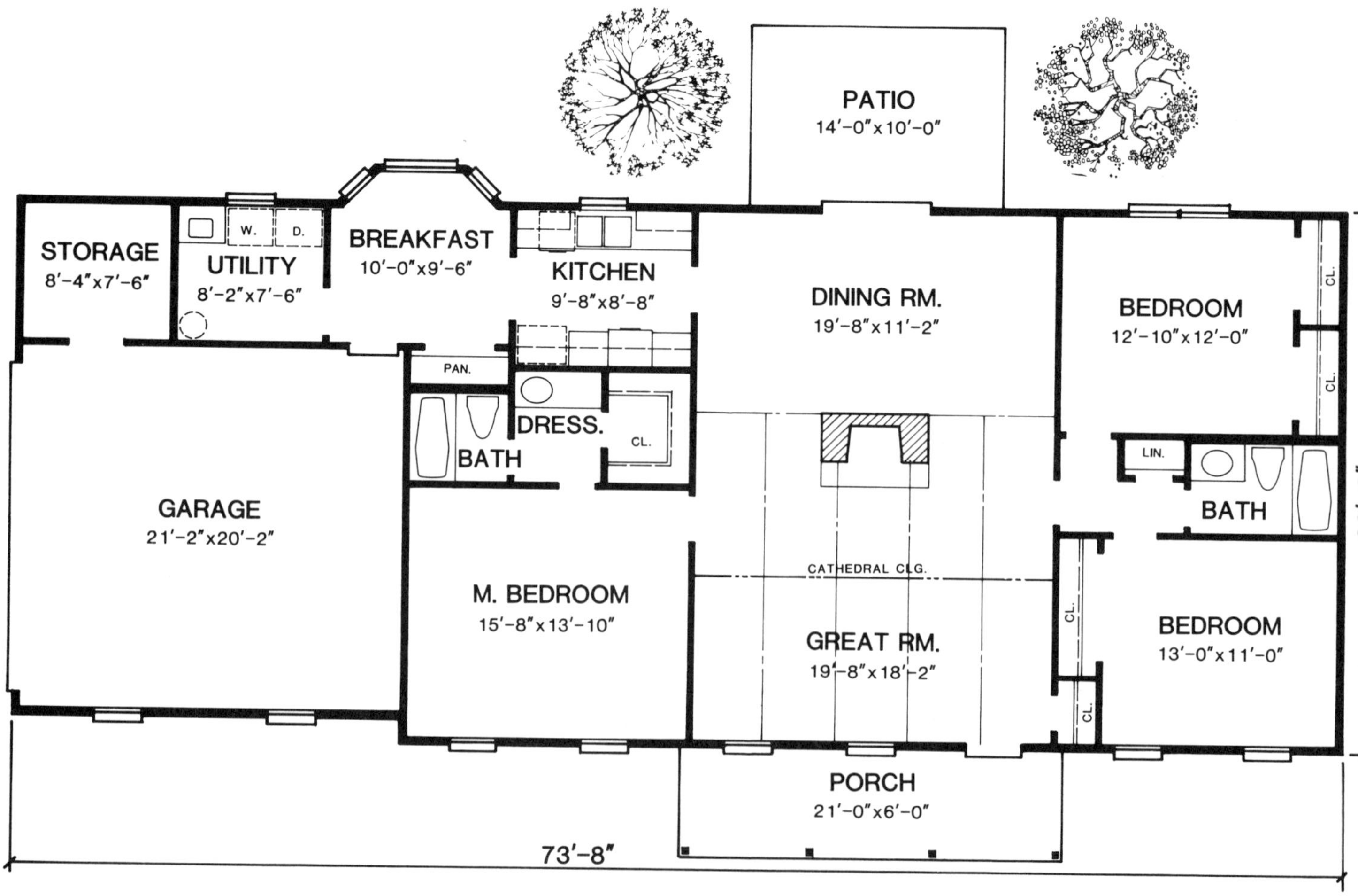

Bay Windows and Skylights Brighten this Tudor Home

No. 10673

Step from the arched fieldstone porch into the two-story foyer, and you can see that this traditional four bedroom home possesses a wealth of modern elements. Behind double doors lie the library and fireplaced living room, bathed in sunlight from two skylights in the sloping roof. Step out to the brick patio from the laundry room or bay windowed breakfast room. For ultimate relaxation, the master bedroom suite contains a whirlpool tub. One bedroom boasts bay windows; another features a huge walk-in closet over the two car garage.

First floor — 1,265 sq. ft.
Second floor — 1,210 sq. ft.
Basement — 1,247 sq. ft.
Garage — 506 sq. ft.

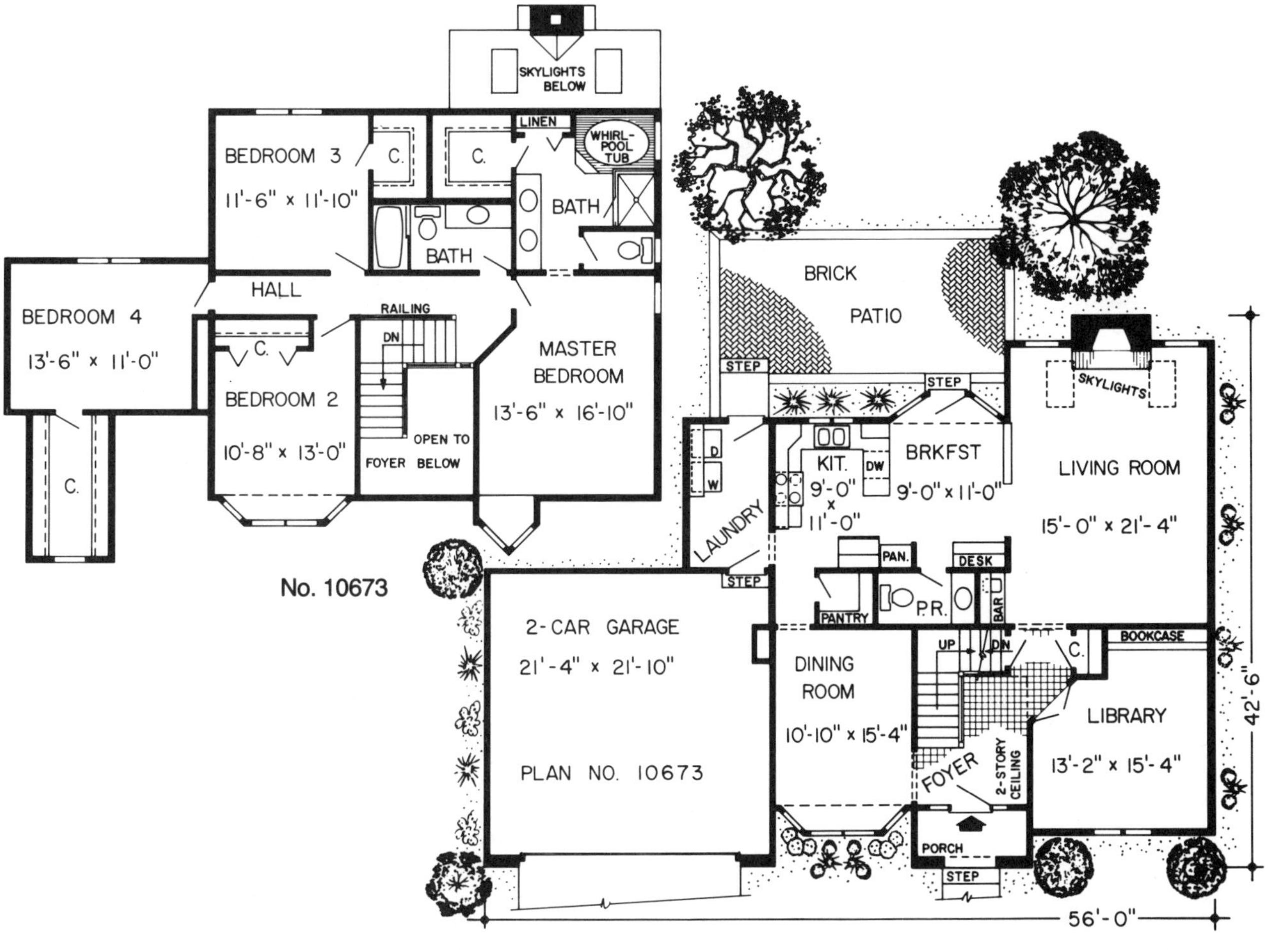

Rustic Exterior; Complete Home

No. 10140

Although rustic in appearance, the interior of this cabin is quiet, modern and comfortable. Small in overall size, it still contains three bedrooms and two baths in addition to a large, two-story living room with exposed beams. As a hunting-fishing lodge or mountain retreat, this compares well.

First floor — 1,008 sq. ft.
Second floor — 281 sq.ft.
Basement — 1,008 sq. ft.

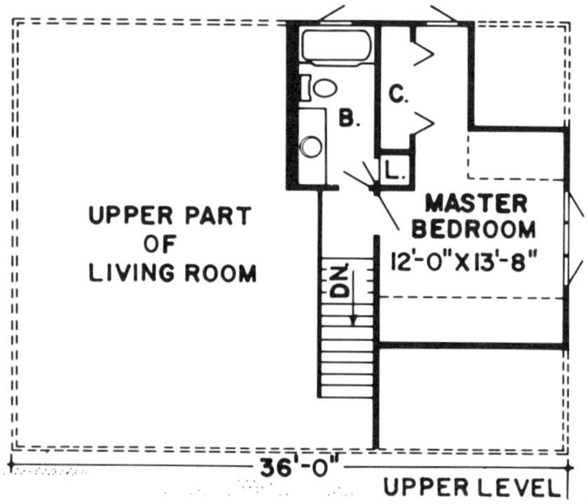

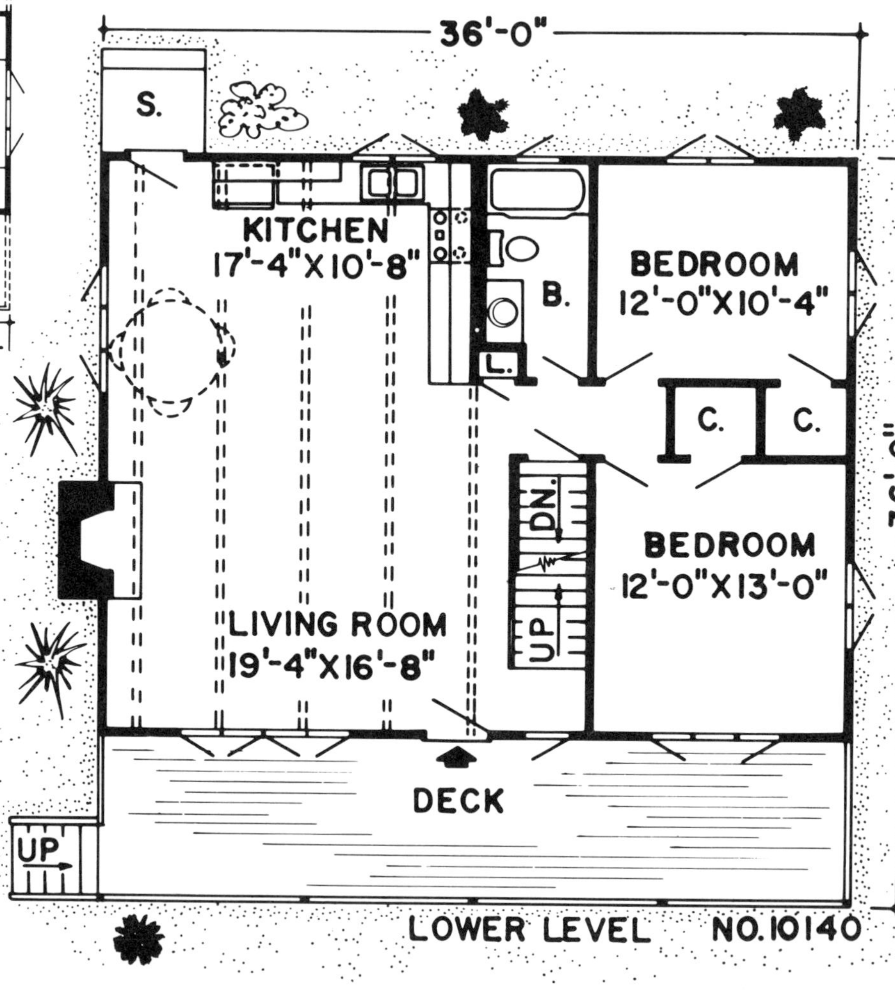

Multiple Levels Make Plan Special

No. 91016

Arched, bump-out windows lend a special elegance to the facade of this four-bedroom beauty. Entering the skylit foyer, you'll discover that those extra-large windows provide a wonderful unity of interior and exterior space. Extra touches combine to make this a special home: a built-in curio shelf, a sunken living room with a cozy fireplace, an eat-in kitchen for family meals, an extra bedroom on the family room level. And, with the bedroom wing a flight of stairs away from main living areas, you're assured of a restful bedtime atmosphere.

Main level — 1,398 sq. ft.
Lower level — 632 sq. ft.

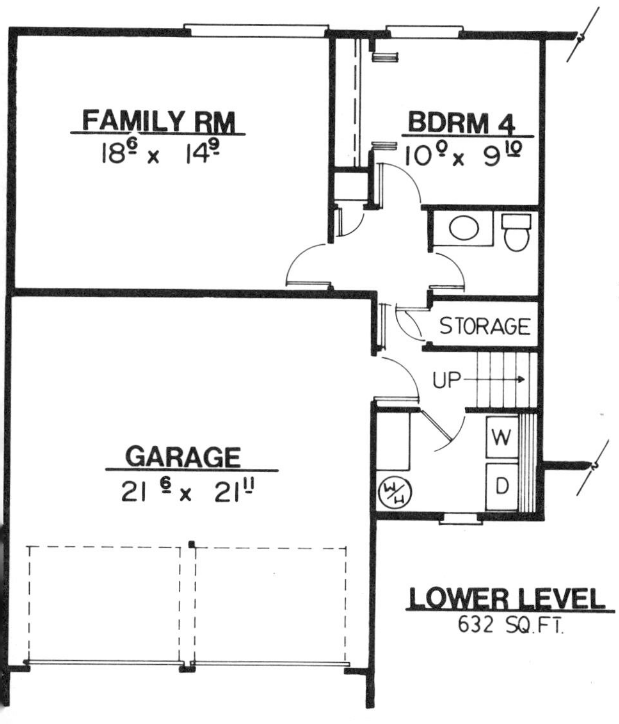

38'-6"

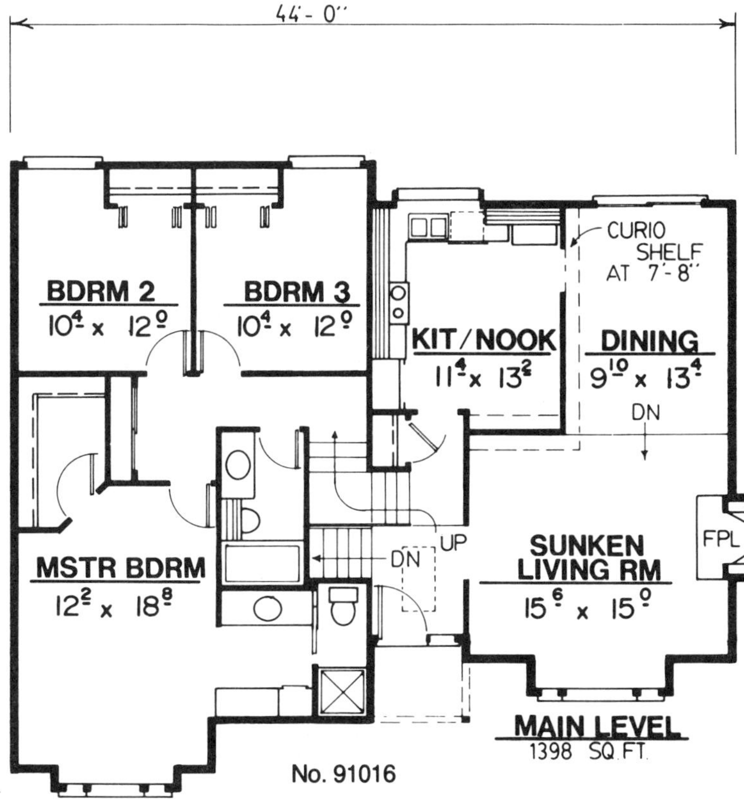

Home Away from Home

No. 90307

The instant you step into this vacation home your spirits will rise. The ceiling of the large living area soars to the loft above. A prefabricated fireplace cheers winter evenings. Built-in banquettes provide seating and sleeping space for guests or children. A full and convenient kitchen, separate laundry-storage room, and full bath makes use of core plumbing as does the upstairs lavatory between the master bedroom and a sitting room or sleeping area. Easy on the upkeep and maintenance, this house deserves to be called a home.

Living Area — 1,152 sq. ft.

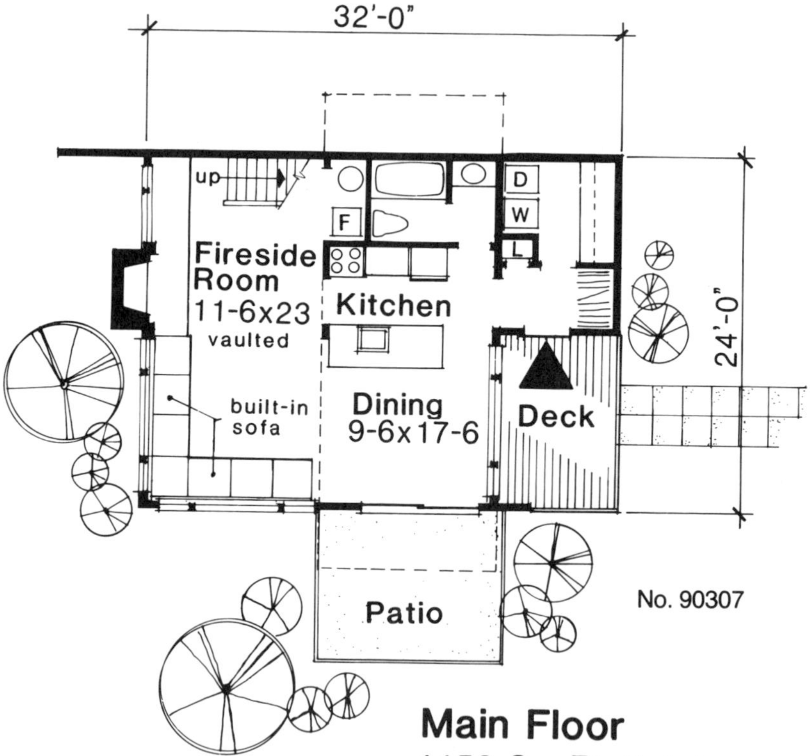

Main Floor
1152 Sq. Ft. Total

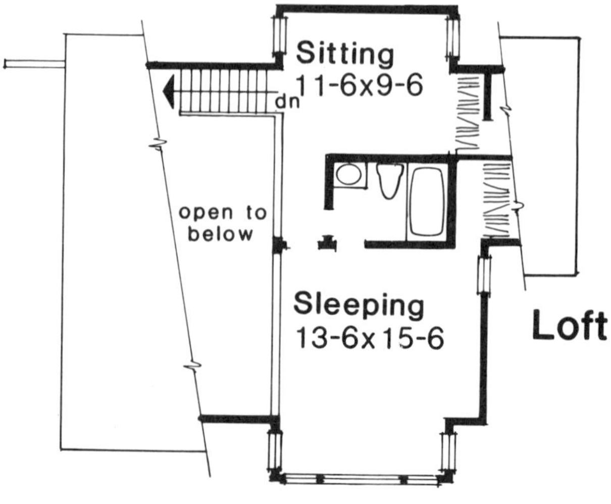

Good Things Come in Small Packages

No. 91028

Do you have a small lot? Here's the solution to your problem. This ingenious design packs lots of living into a compact home. Active areas are open for a spacious feeling. Extra-large windows unite interior spaces with the great outdoors.

Look at the beautiful bay nook in the living room and the handy kitchen that opens to dining and sunken family rooms. An L-shaped stairway at the rear of the house leads to three bedrooms, including the spacious master suite with its own bath and huge walk-in closet.

First floor — 820 sq. ft.
Second floor — 702 sq. ft.

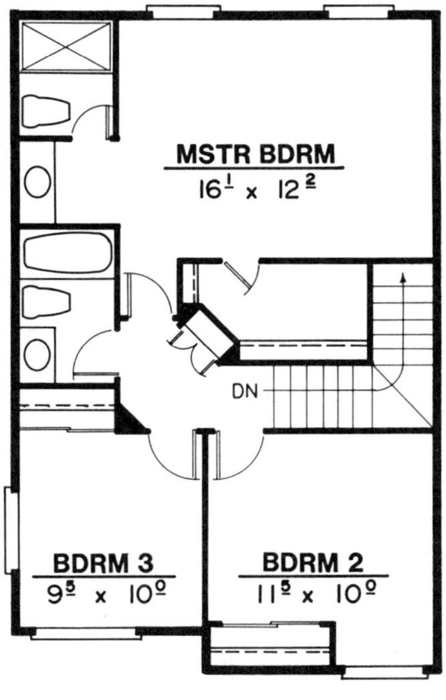

UPPER LEVEL

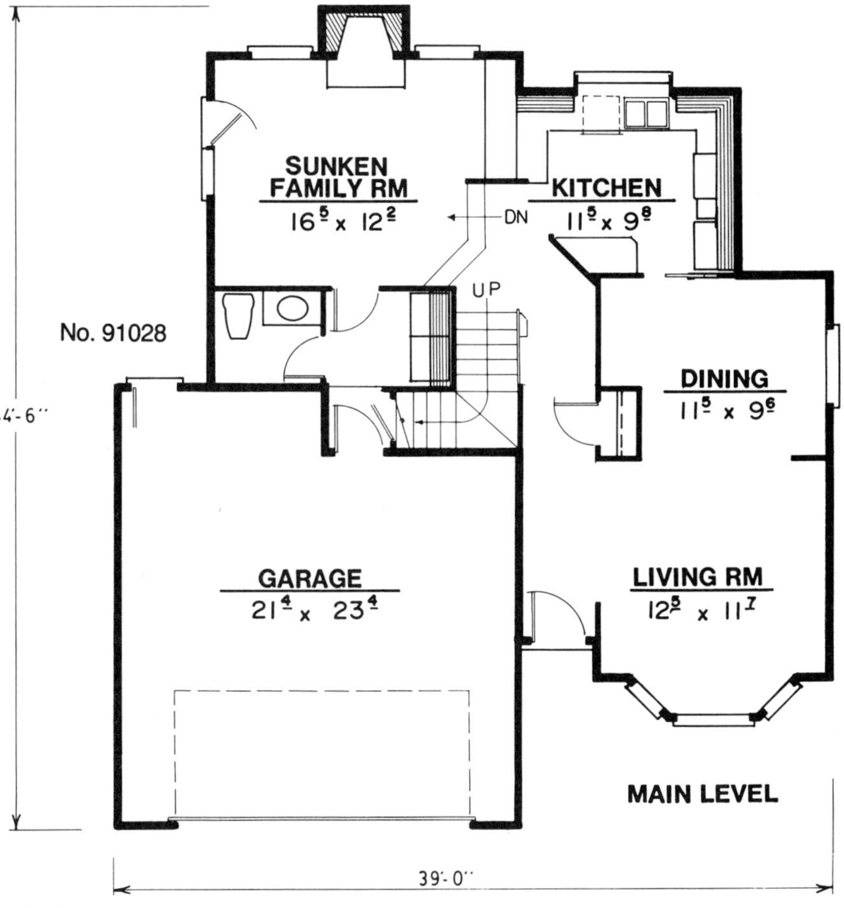

MAIN LEVEL

Two-Level Master Suite Is Luxurious Retreat

No. 90627

Beyond the tasteful exterior of this traditional home is an exciting and imaginative interior. The large entrance foyer sweeps two stories high over an open staircase. In a wing to itself lies the sunken living room with cathedral ceiling, fireplace, and windows on three sides. You'll enjoy the patio off the dining room. The adjacent kitchen with cheerful bay-windowed dinette and pass-through to the comfortable family room makes mealtimes a breeze. Four bedrooms and two baths share the second floor.

First floor — 1,350 sq. ft.
Second floor — 1,001 sq. ft.
Partial basement (optional slab construction available)

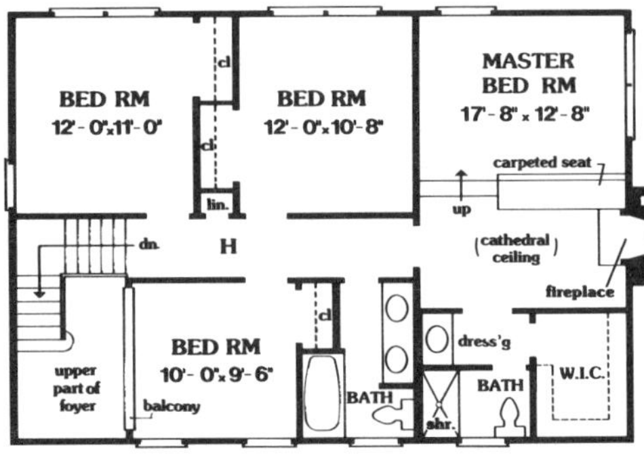

SECOND FLOOR

No. 90627

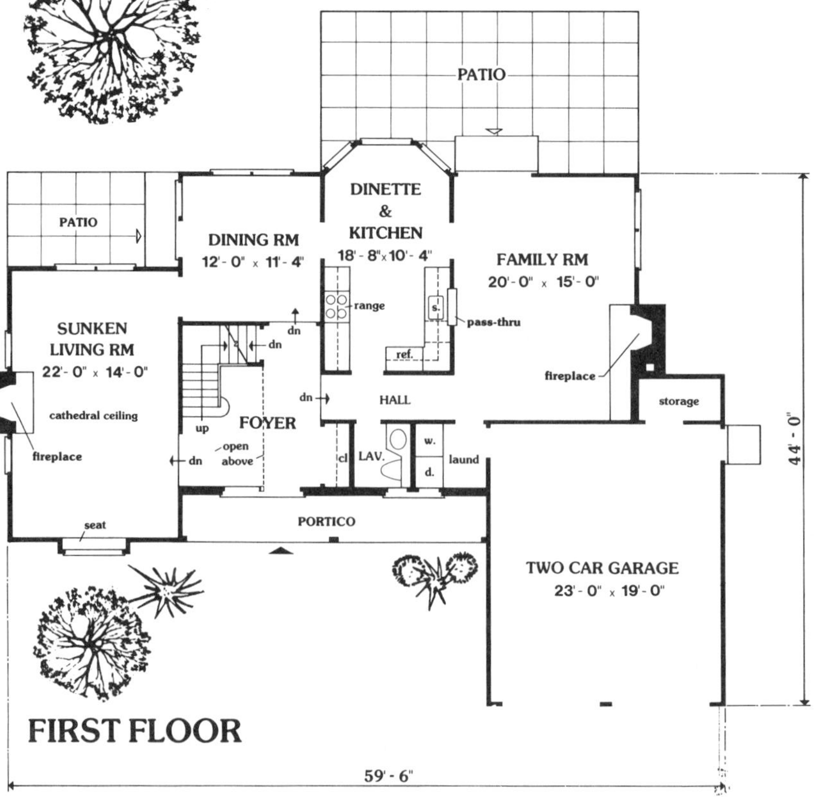

FIRST FLOOR

Cozy Cape Cod

No. 90115

This homey Cape home will blend beautifully in any setting. The formal living and dining rooms are completely separated from the family room, enabling adults and children to enjoy undisturbed everyday living. Notice the location of the first floor bath in relation to the dining room —a plan feature that permits this room to be used as a first floor bedroom, if desired. Back service entrance, mud room and laundry convenient to the kitchen are favorable points of the plan, too. On the second floor, the huge master bedroom has its own dressing area and entrance to the vanity bath.

First floor — 1,068 sq. ft.
Second floor — 804 sq. ft.

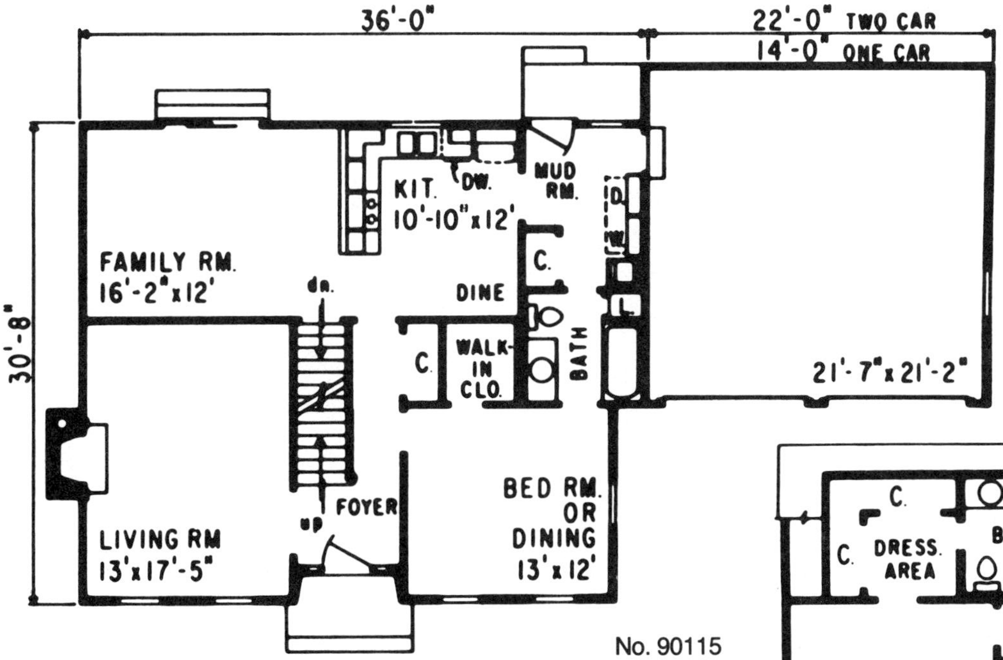

No. 90115

FIRST FLOOR

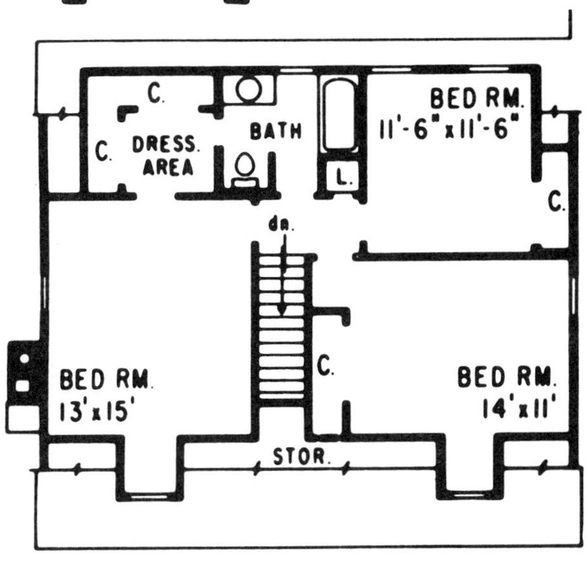

SECOND FLOOR

Charming and Cozy Rooms

No. 90126

Here a home that balances both individual and family needs. The traditional design encloses ample space for a large family, while preserving areas for comfort and quiet. The large family room, with cozy fireplace and sliding doors to the patio, is far away from the living room to simplify entertaining. Complementing the formal dining room is an eat-in nook. The efficiently organized kitchen serves either area well. Upstairs, the master bedroom has a large walk-in closet. Two other berooms are nearby for nighttime security.

first floor — 1,260 sq. ft.
Second floor — 952 sq. ft.

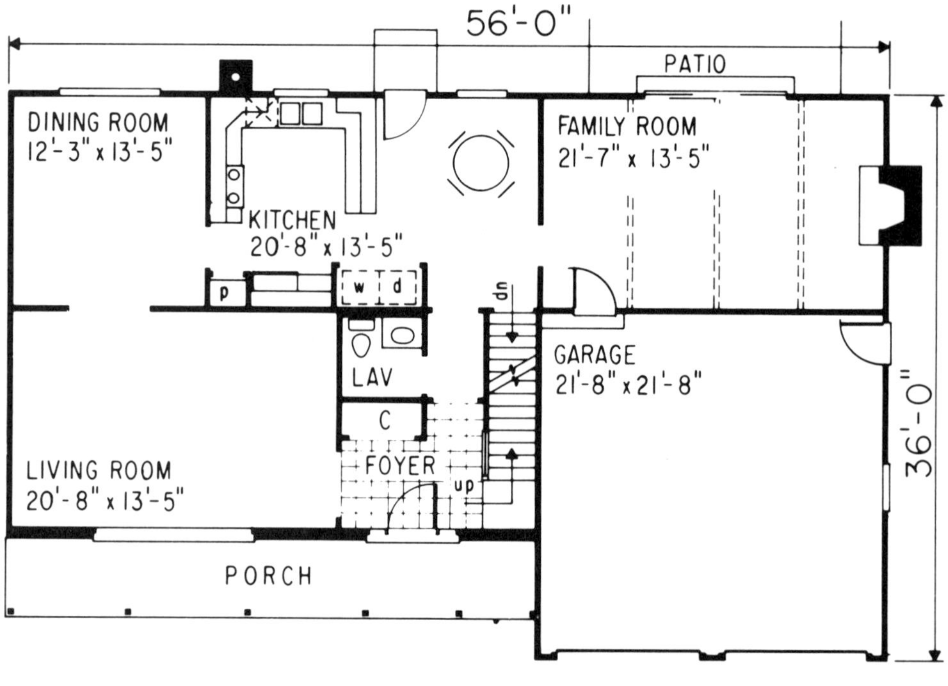

No. 90126

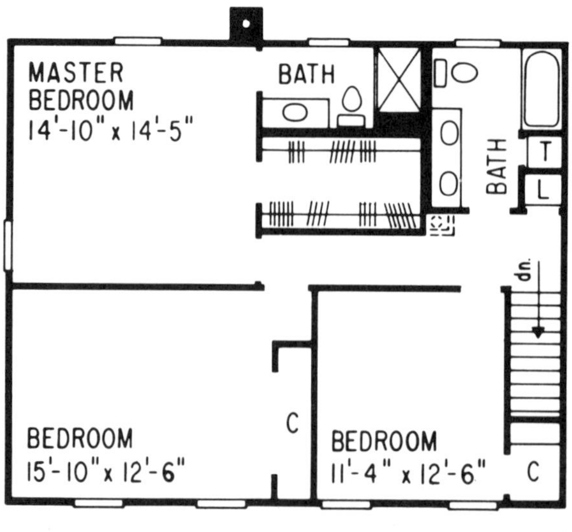

SECOND FLOOR

Romantic Elegance

No. 91014

Even though most living areas are on one level, the addition of a second-story loft make this a one-of-a-kind home with dramatic distinction. Bedrooms are grouped to one side of the stairs for privacy. Walk-in closets and baths keep the sounds from active areas of the house at a minimum. The master suite is flooded with light from its stacked bay window arrangement. Living areas form one magnificent, united space made even larger by the two-story hexagonal dining bay. French doors flanking the fireplace open to a covered patio off the living room. Use the loft upstairs for extra guests, a home office, or just for enjoying the panorama below.

First floor — 1,459 sq. ft.
Upper level — 345 sq. ft.

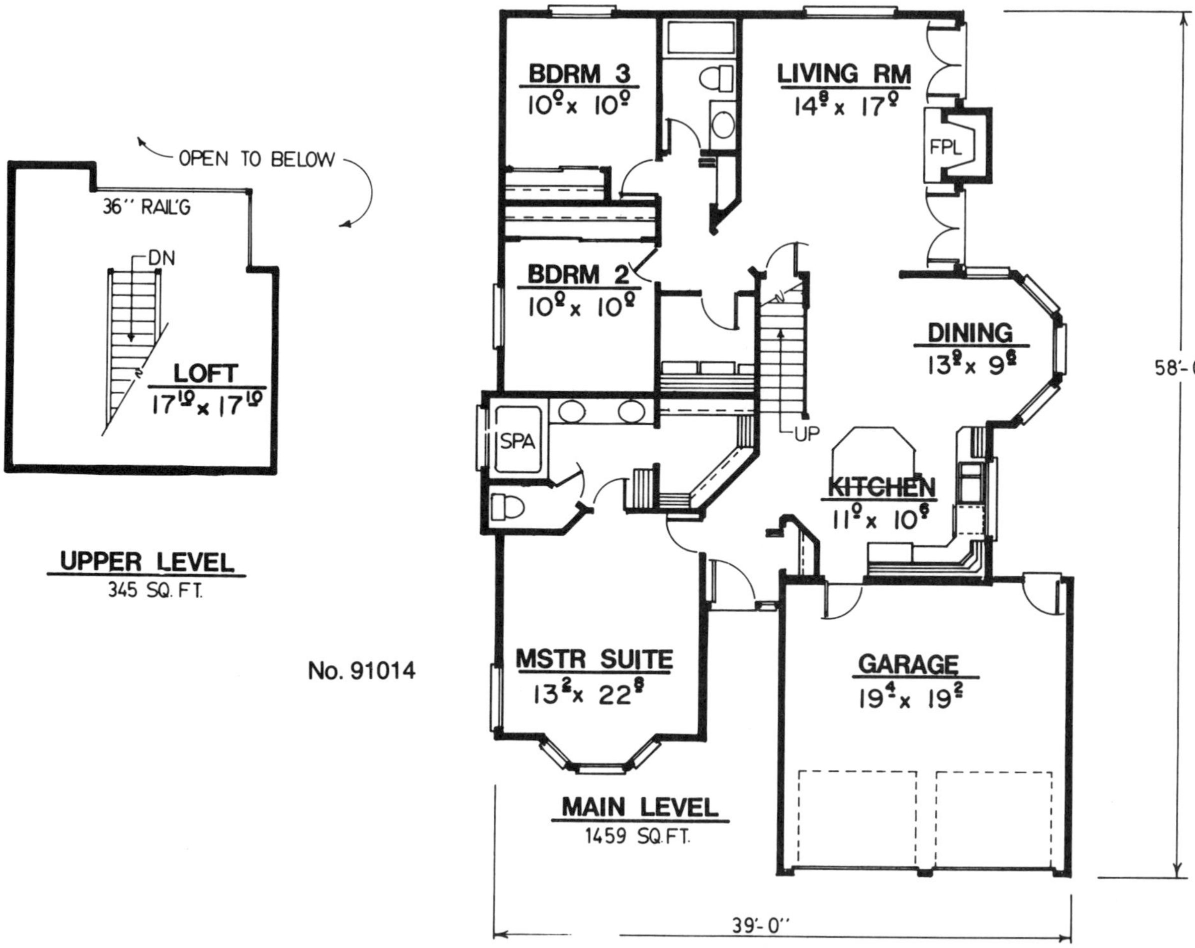

Clean Lines Graced by Window Box

No. 90301

There's no wasted space in this handsome design which slightly elevates the first floor to tuck in a double garage. The first floor contains two bedrooms each with lots of closet space plus a full bath. The living areas on this first floor are open to the loft above. The dining area views the adjacent deck through sliding glass doors while the living room is highlighted by a fireplace. The second story loft features a roof window for access to light and gentle breezes. The master bedroom incorporates a full wall of closet area and a roomy bath with separate vanity area.

Total area — 1,667 sq. ft.

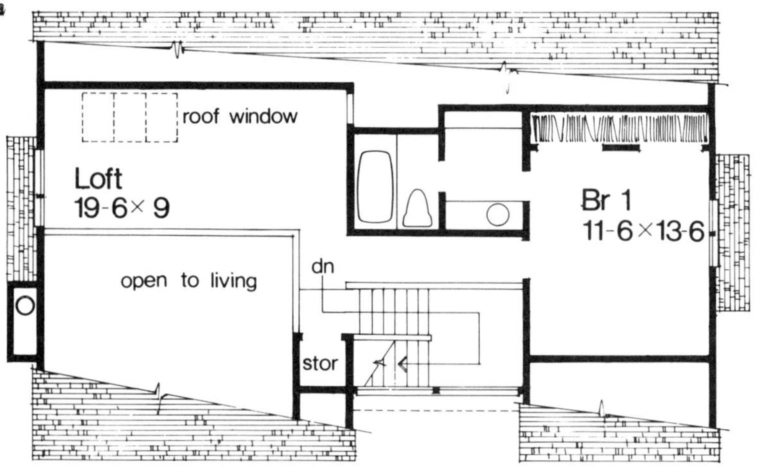

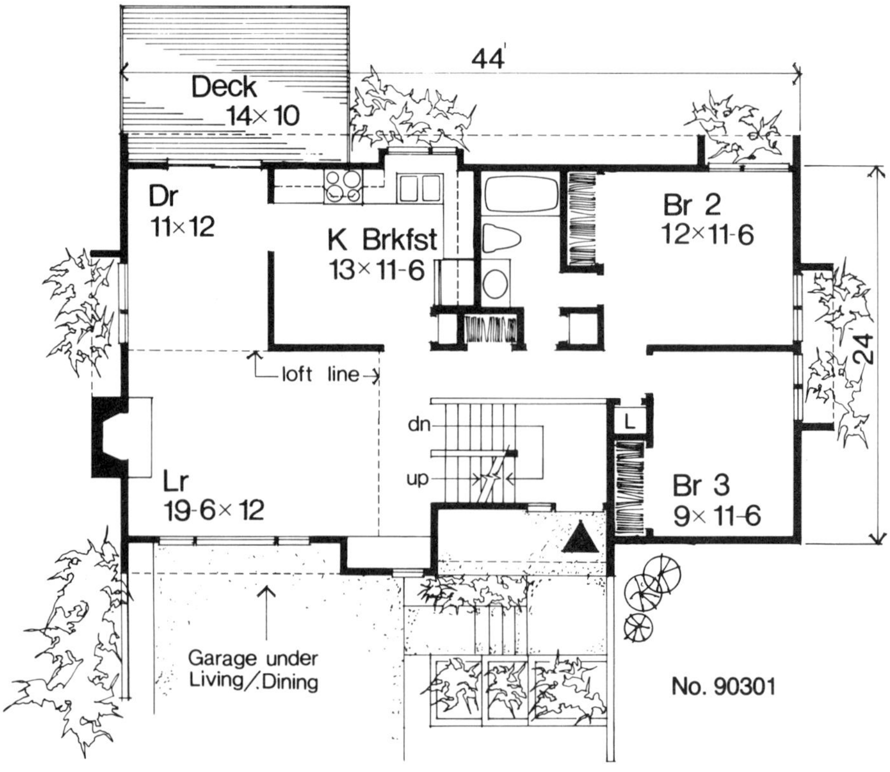

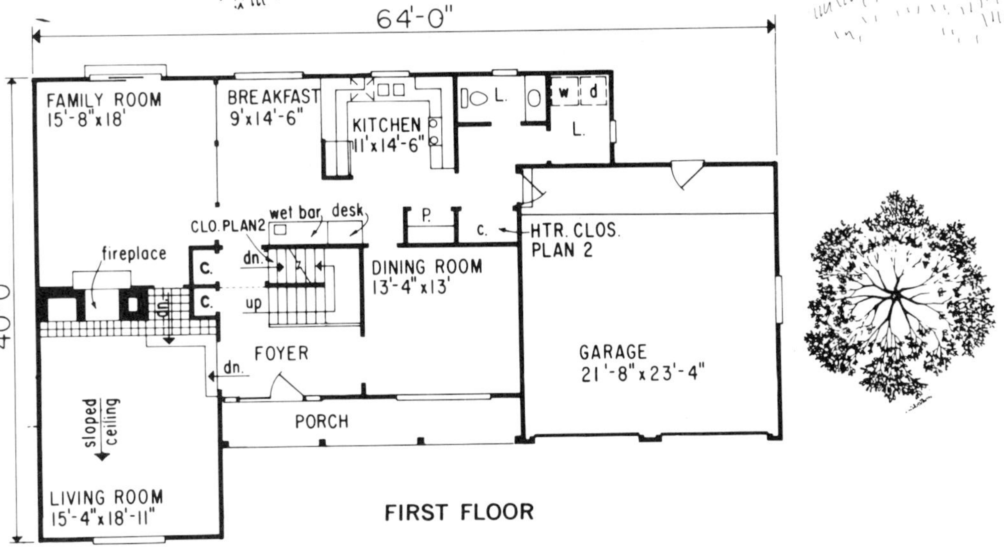

FIRST FLOOR

Varied Roofline Features Modern Amenities

No. 90156

The spacious foyer allows easy traffic flow to all areas of the home. The sunken living room has a sloped roof to the second floor balcony library. A two-way fireplace opens to both the living and family rooms. The kitchen provides abundant counter space, pantry and wet bar. The master suite offers a dressing area, walk-in closet and deluxe bath with the added feature of a balcony library overlooking the living room. Three additional bedrooms and a bath complete the second floor.

First floor—1,432 sq. ft.
Second floor-1,319 sq. ft.

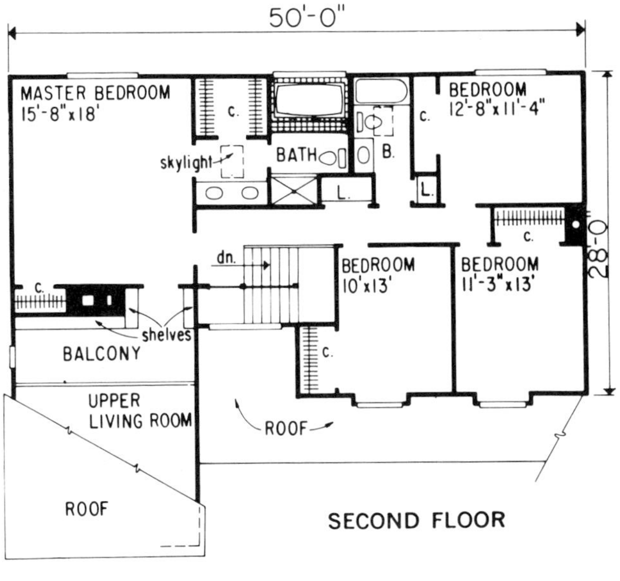

SECOND FLOOR

First Floor Master Suite is Special

No. 90624

American as apple pie, this three-bedroom colonial classic has a welcoming charm that will capture your fancy. Special features abound throughout the house. The two-story foyer is lit from above by a skylight. You can access the terrace or garage through the family room. A convenient kitchen serves both family and formal dining areas with ease, and a heat-circulating fireplace is flanked by shelves in the living room. The spacious master suite, housed in a separate wing, has vaulted ceilings and is illuminated by spectacular windows on three walls. With a whirlpool tub and its own entertainment center, this room is bound to be your favorite retreat.

Total living area — 1,973 sq. ft.
Basement — 1,340 sq. ft.

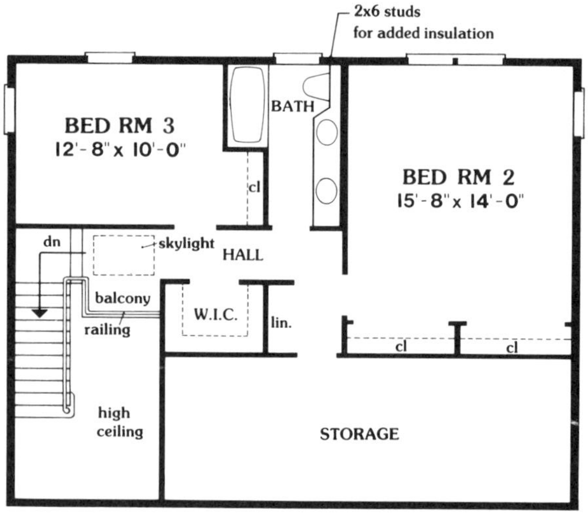

No. 90624

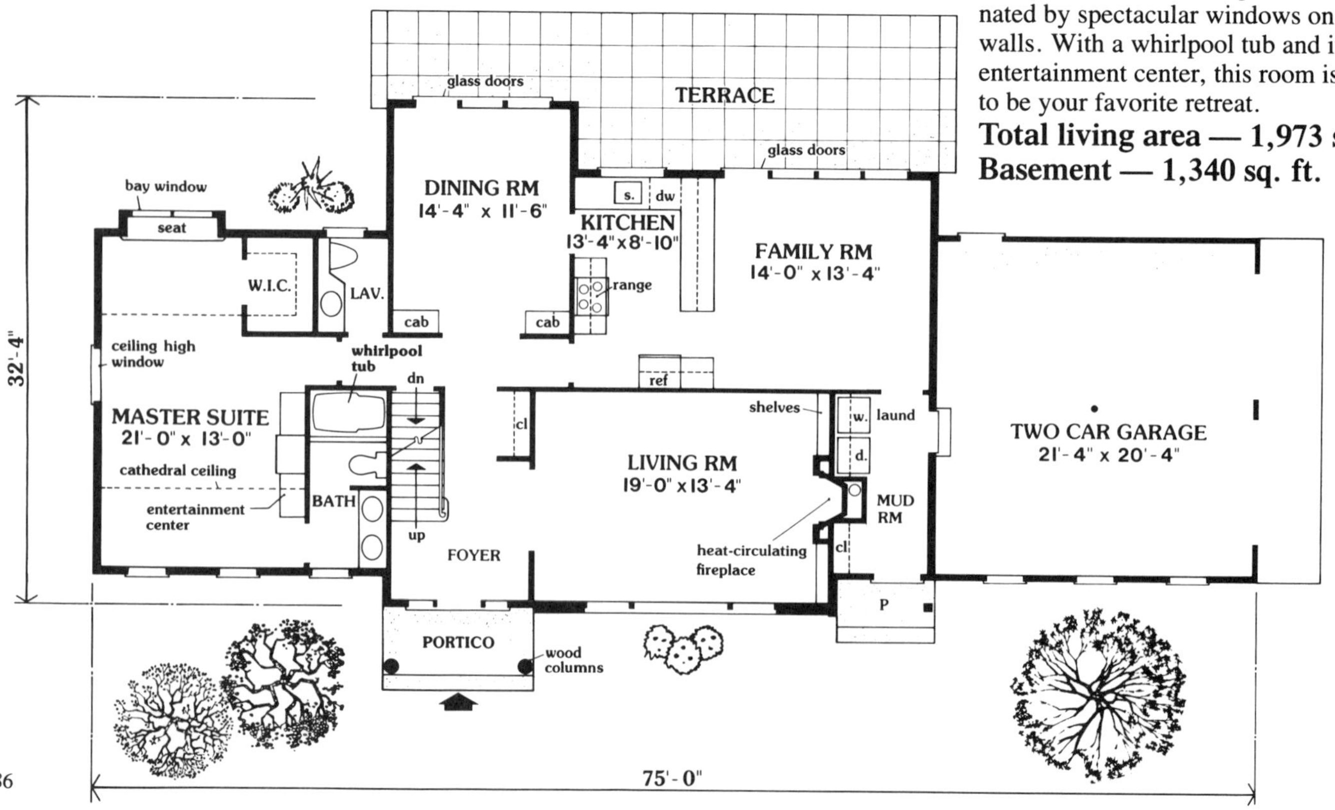

Covered Patio Ideal for Relaxing

No. 90510

Soaring peaks distinguish the facade of this compact country home. View the vaulted entry and living room from the sitting area at the top of the angular staircase. Three bedrooms and two baths, including the spacious master suite, grace the upper level. Arranged for convenient entertaining, the fireplaced family room, breakfast nook, island kitchen, and dining room feature abundant windows that let the sun shine in.

First floor — 1,112 sq. ft.
Second floor — 948 sq. ft.

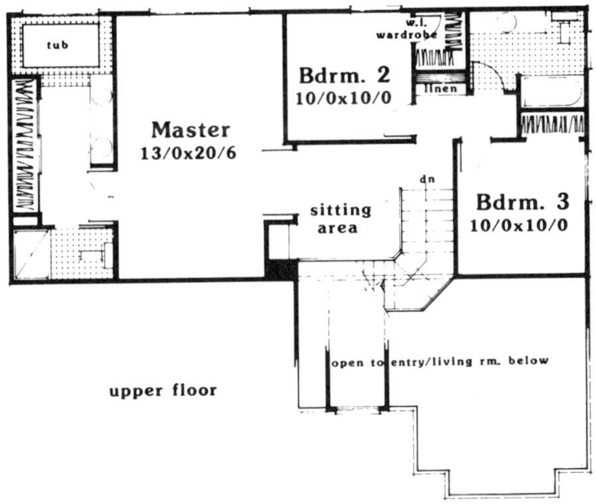

No. 90510

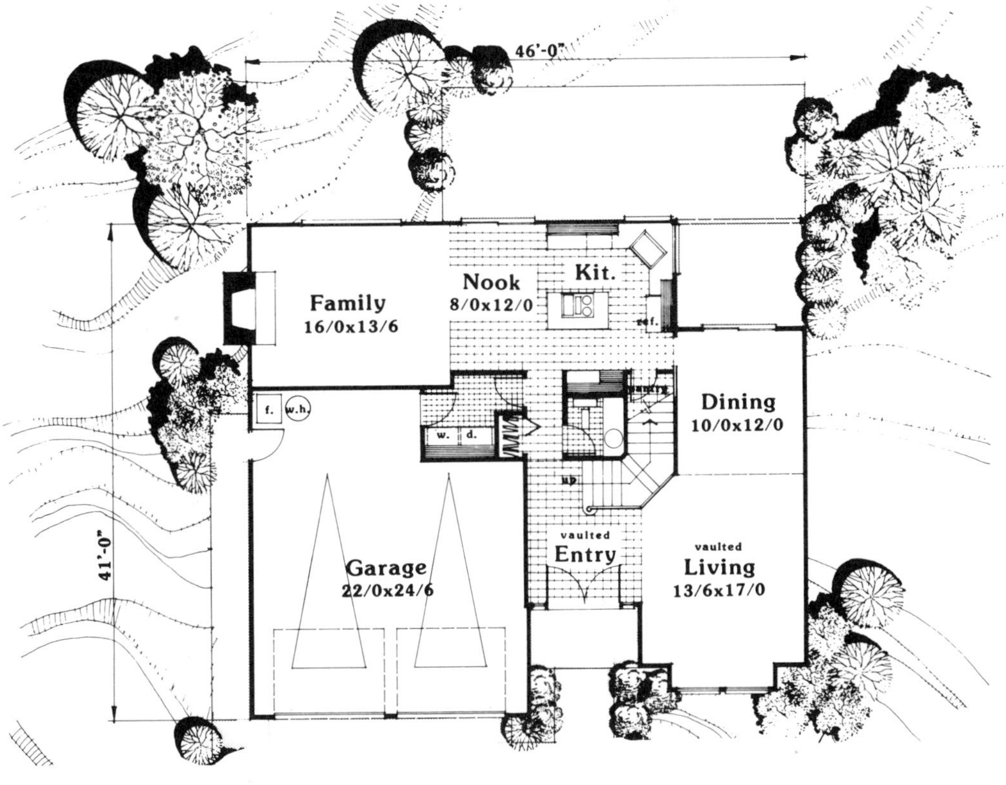

A Touch of Tudor

No. 90518

Here's a terrific little gem for folks that love outdoor activities or just enjoy watching the birds. Windows and sliding glass doors unite the back yard, partially covered deck, and family living areas in this cheery, compact dwelling. Vaulted ceilings and bay windows add expansive open space to the living room, breakfast nook, and master suite. Large windows brighten the soaring foyer and angular bedrooms upstairs.

First floor — 995 sq. ft.
Second floor — 790 sq. ft.

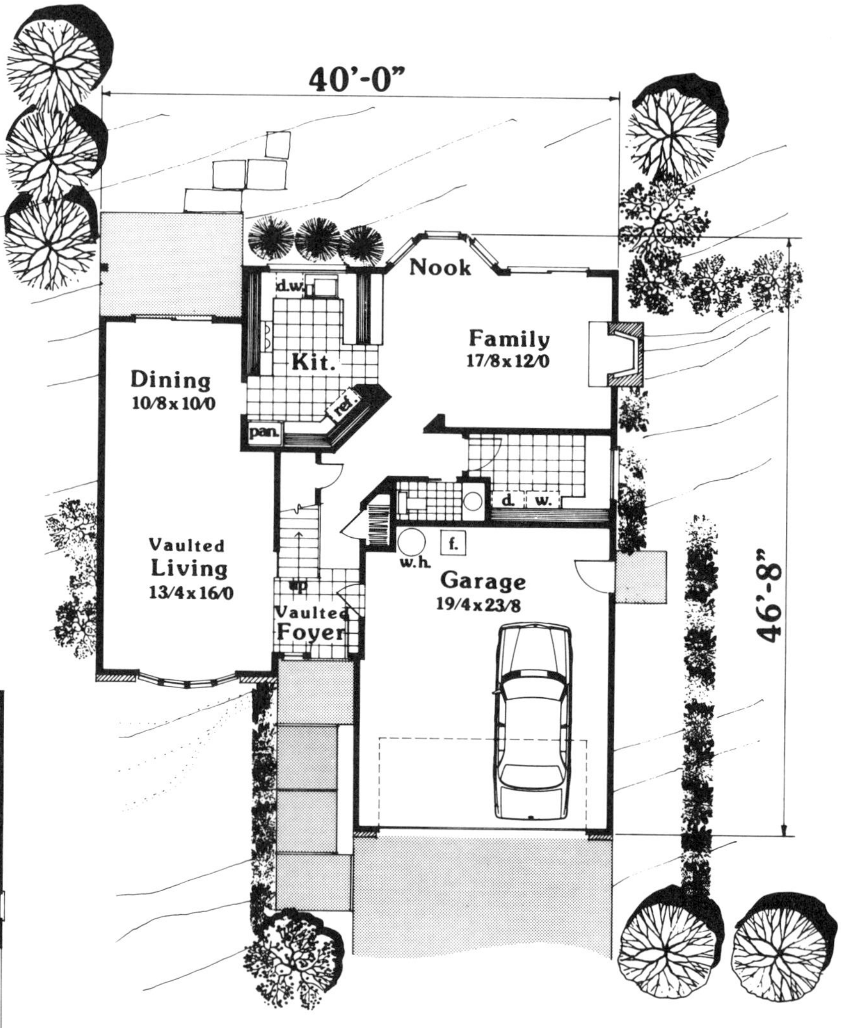

No. 90518

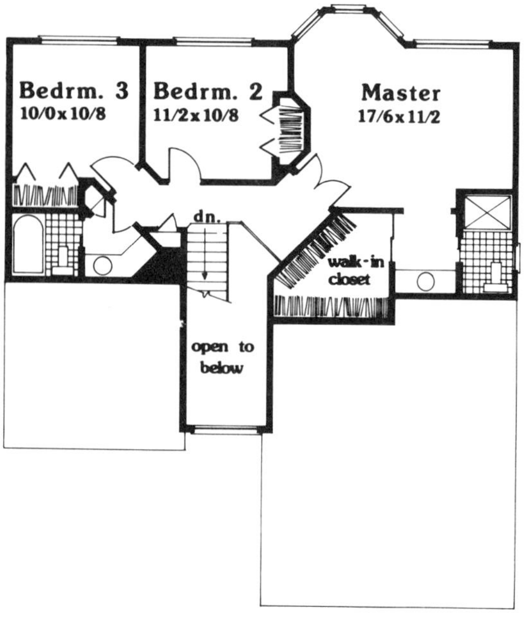

A Home for All Seasons

No. 90629

The natural cedar and stone exterior of this contemporary gem is virtually maintenance free, and its dramatic lines echo the excitement inside. There are so many luxurious touches in this plan: the two-story living room overlooked by an upper-level balcony; a massive stone wall that pierces the roof and holds two fireplaces; both a kitchen oven and an outdoor barbecue. Plus, outdoor dining is a pleasure with the barbecue so handy to the kitchen. All the rooms boast outdoor decks, and each bedroom has its own. The front entrance, garage, a dressing room with bath, and laundry room occupy the lower level.

Main level — 1,001 sq. ft.
Upper level — 712 sq. ft.
Lower level — 463 sq. ft.

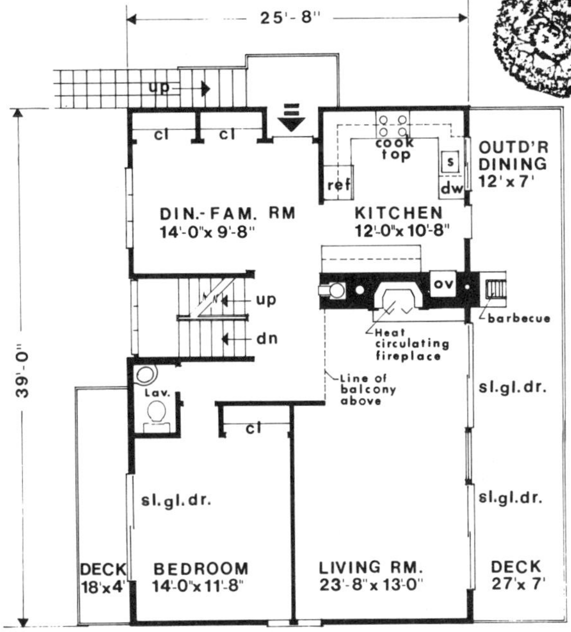

MAIN FLOOR PLAN

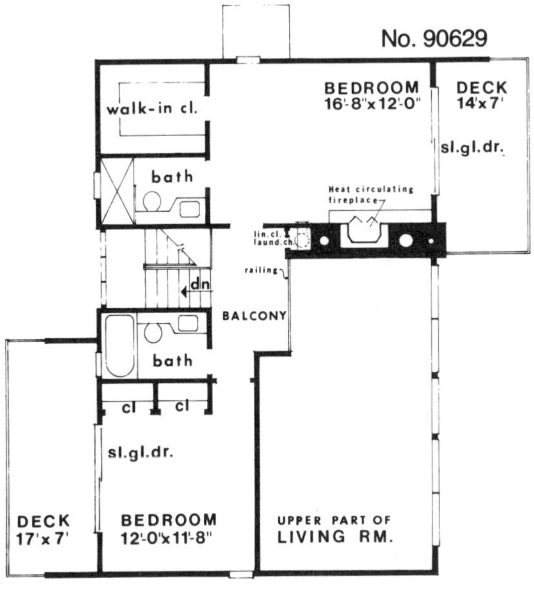

UPPER FLOOR PLAN

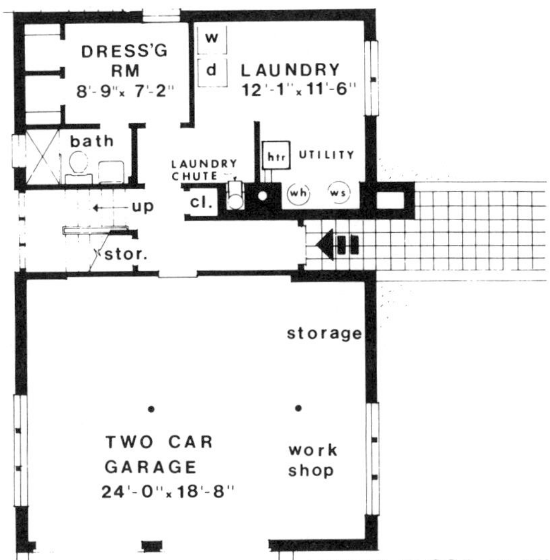

LOWER FLOOR PLAN

Sunlight Streams Into Many Windows

No. 10456

Nine-foot beamed ceilings grace the expansive living room with its patio-facing window wall. The adjoining dining room is defined by a lower ceiling and enhanced by an over-sized bay window of leaded glass. The spacious kitchen features many cabinets, a walk-in pantry, center work island, and a nook overlooking the patio. The master bedroom has a five-piece bath with a skylight, plus an extra large walk-in closet. The two smaller bedrooms share a full bath. A third bedroom located between the kitchen and dining room might find use as a guest bedroom or study.

First floor — 2,511 sq. ft.
Garage — 517 sq. ft.

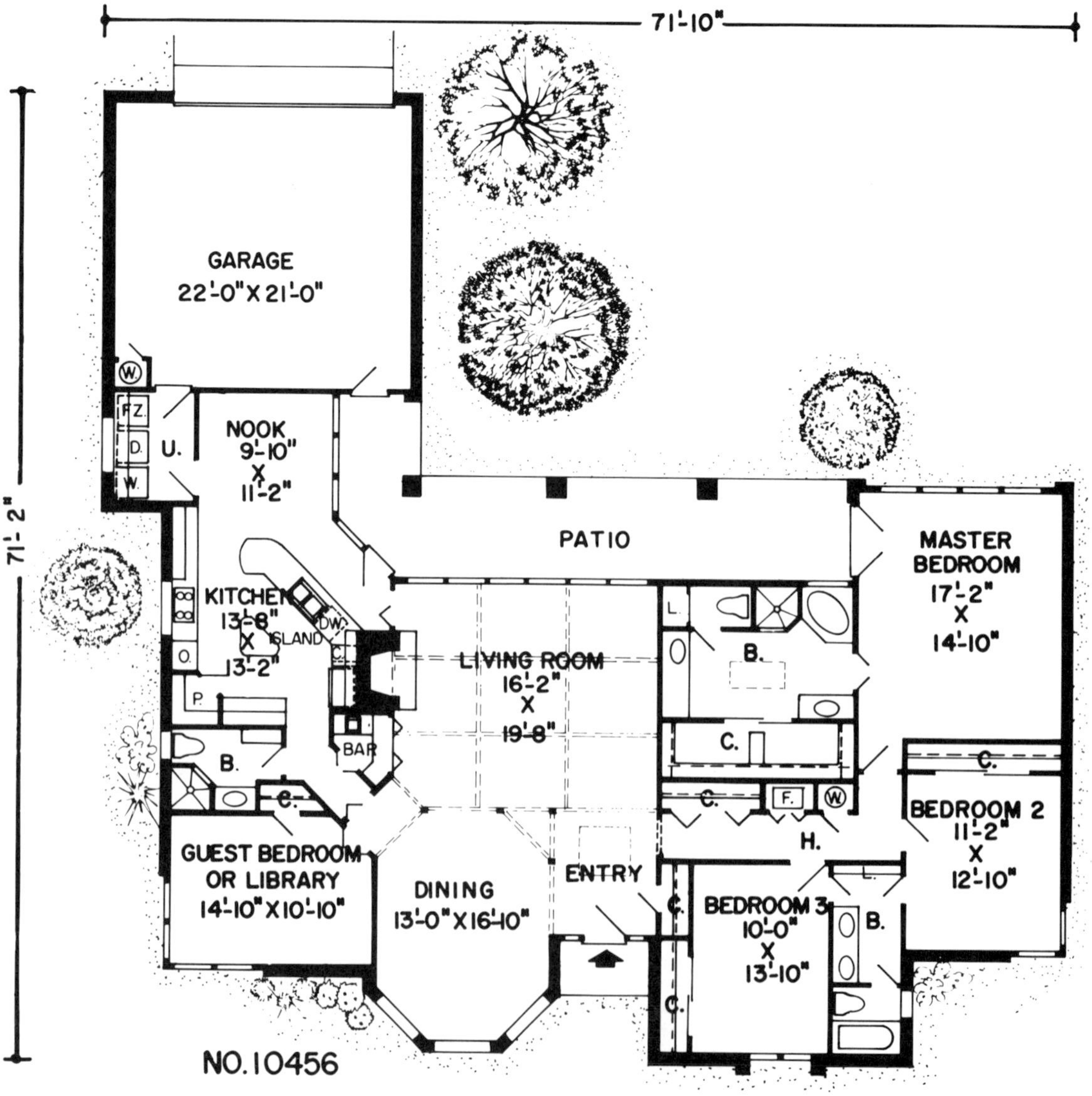

Modified Cape for Family Living

No. 10634

With a graceful porch sheltering three sides of this inviting abode, and a patio off the back, you can enjoy all your summer evenings outside. Walk out for a breath of fresh air after a full meal in the formal dining room or sunny breakfast nook. The adjoining kitchen and cozy family room are located across the central foyer from the spacious living room. Sharing the second floor with three bedrooms and two baths, the master suite features a hexagonal sitting room.

First floor — 1,412 sq. ft.
Second floor — 1,382 sq. ft.

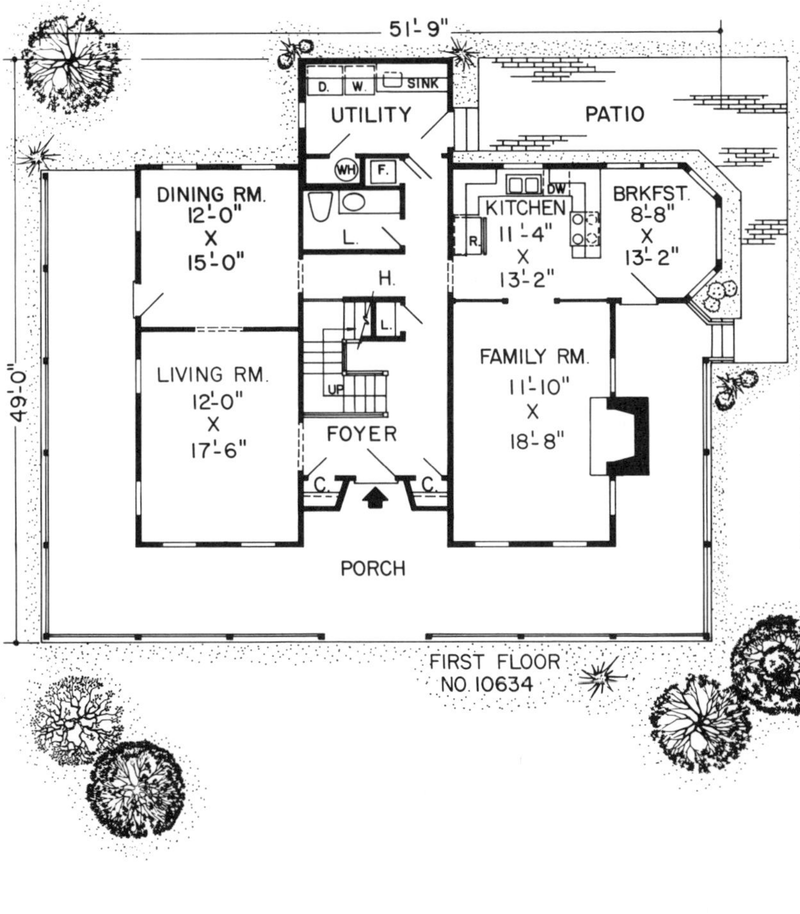

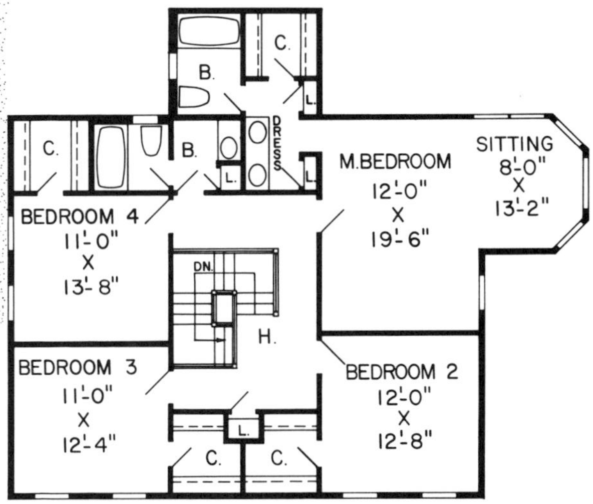

Open Floor Plan Enhanced by Sloped Ceilings

No. 90125

A step down from the tiled entrance area, guests may overlook an expansive living area composed of the great room and the dining room. Warmed by a fireplace and further enhanced by sliding doors opening onto the patio, this welcoming area is easily served by the L-shaped kitchen which shares a snack bar with the dining room. The three bedrooms are separated from the living areas by the careful placement of the bathrooms and the laundry. The master bedroom features two closets, including a walk-in, plus a private bath.

Living area — 1,440 sq. ft.

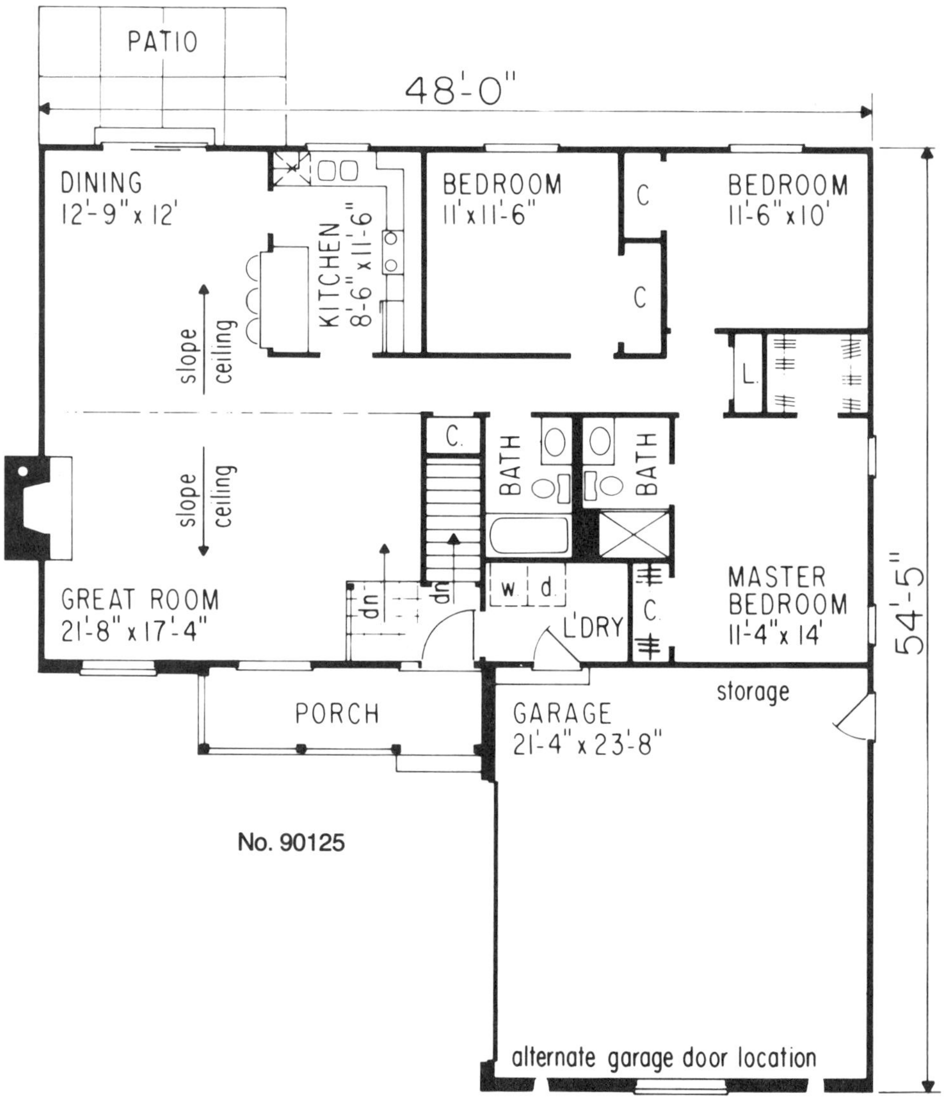

No. 90125

Gracious Design for Family Living

No. 90133

Designed for a family with children, this home contains four sizable bedrooms, a family room and outside terrace. Additional features include the beamed ceiling and optional fireplace in the family room, zoning of active and formal living areas, convenient location of the kitchen, and a mud room with first floor laundry. Unique in this home is the loft over the garage reached by disappearing stairs. This room makes an ideal hobby or game room. The overhanging second floor, clapboard siding and hay loft doors over the garage add up to an exterior that is unusual and definitely attractive.

First floor — 1,149 sq. ft.
Second floor — 988 sq. ft.

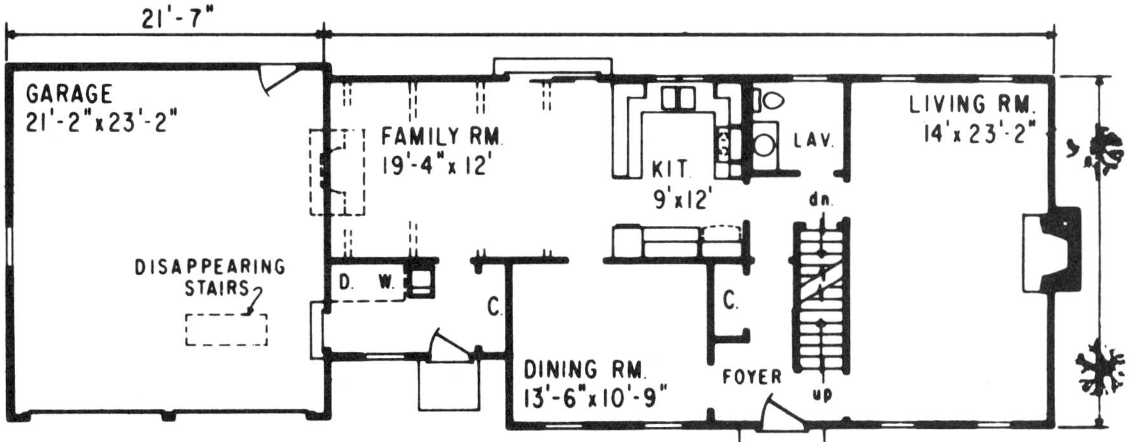

FIRST FLOOR

No. 90133

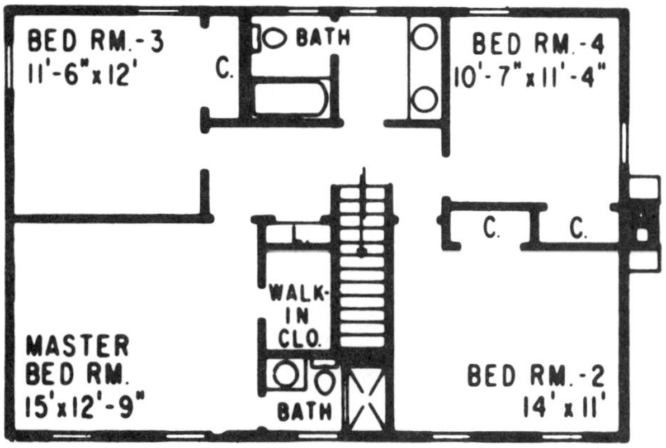

SECOND FLOOR

Glass Captures Views & Sun

No. 90121

Abundant glass floods this plan with light and offers images of the surrounding scenery from three sides, as well as serving as a solar energy feature. Large exterior exposed beams crisscross the glass giving a massive, rugged appearance. The center of family activity begins in the family room and proceeds to the deck which flows into a dining patio on the left side. Your family may relax over meals here or in the dining/kitchen area just inside glass doors. Two bedrooms, a full bath and laundry facilities complete the first level. An open wooden stairway beckons you to the second level which opens into a large fireplaced sitting room and balcony overlooking the family room.

First floor — 1,126 sq. ft.
Second floor — 603 sq. ft.

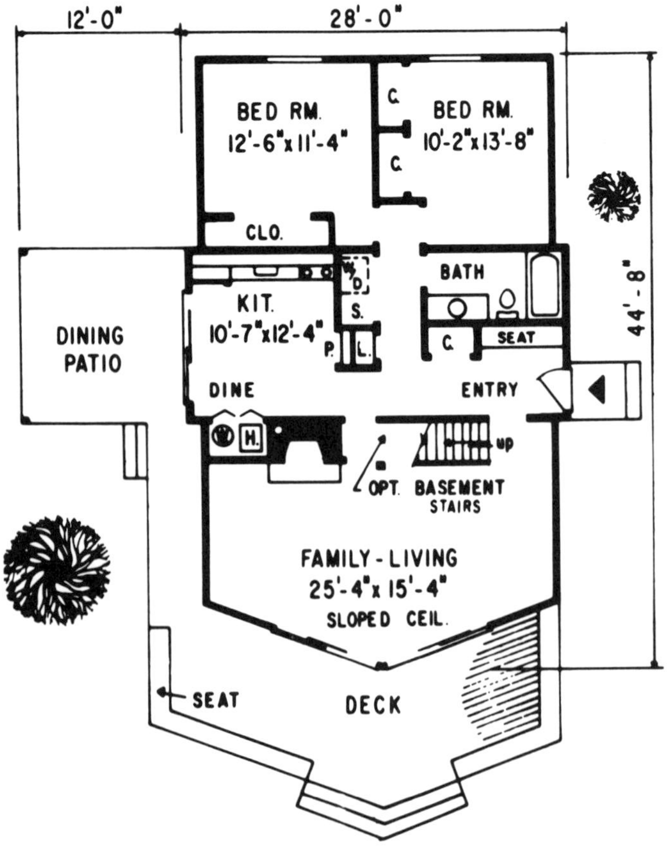

FIRST FLOOR

No. 90121

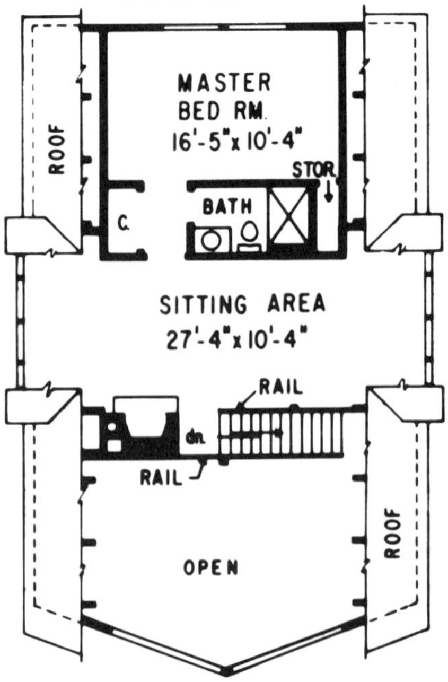

SECOND FLOOR

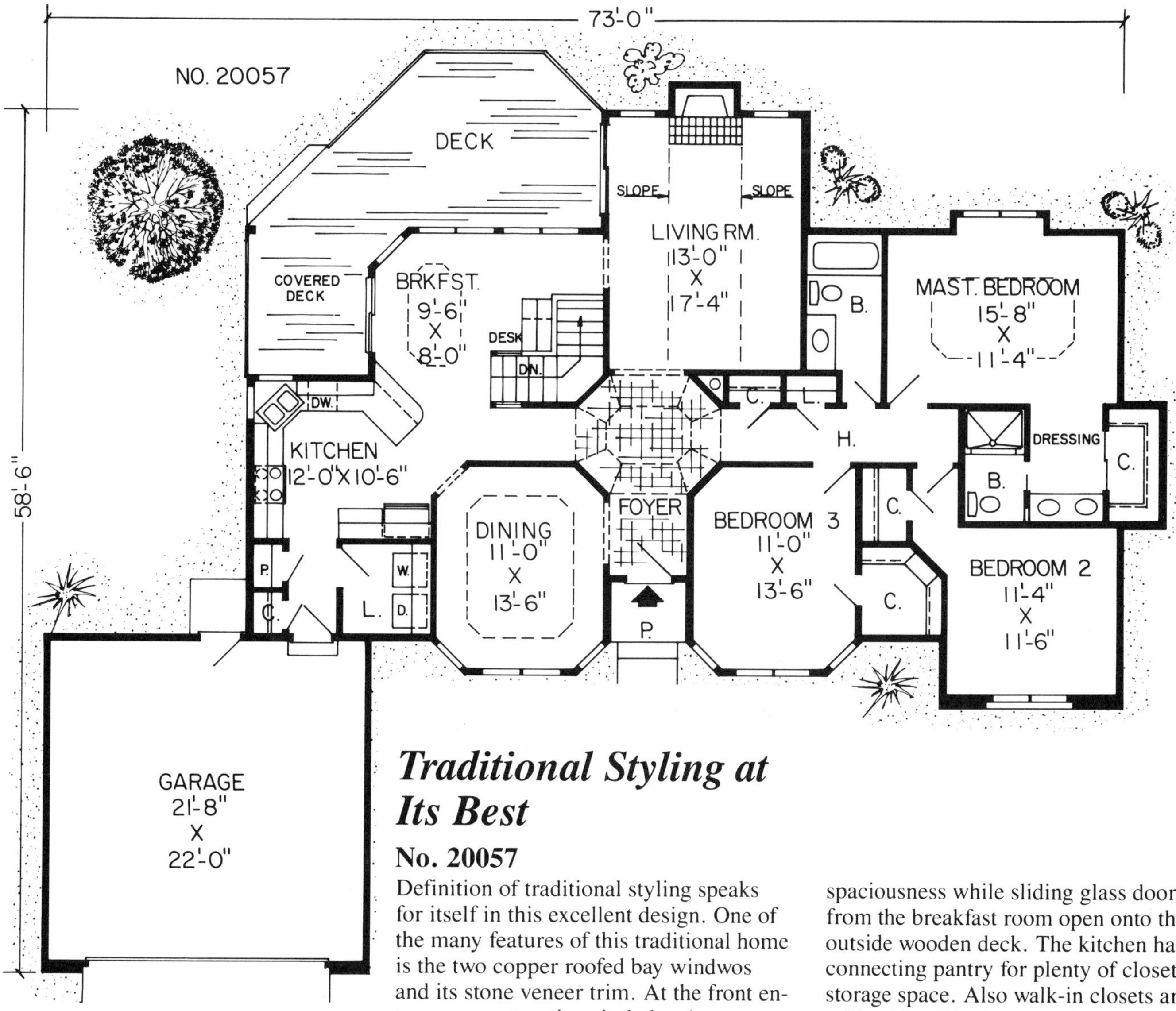

Traditional Styling at Its Best

No. 20057

Definition of traditional styling speaks for itself in this excellent design. One of the many features of this traditional home is the two copper roofed bay windwos and its stone veneer trim. At the front entrance, an attractive circle head transom above the weather protected front door adds refinement to this plan. Vaulted ceilings extend in the foyer, master bedroom, dining room and the breakfast room giving these rooms added spaciousness while sliding glass doors from the breakfast room giving these rooms added spaciousness while sliding glass doors from the breakfast room open onto the outside wooden deck. The kitchen has a connecting pantry for plenty of closet and storage space. Also walk-in closets are utilized in all bedrooms while the master bedroom has a dressing room in its bath area. A full basement is offered in this plan.

First floor — 1,804 sq. ft.
Basement — 1,804 sq. ft.
Garage — 499 sq. ft.

Detailed Ranch Design

No. 90360

Stylish houses to suit the higher design expectations of the sophisticated first time and move up buyer need to present lot of visible value. Starting with the very 1980's exterior look of this home with its arcaded living room sash, thru its interior vaulted spaces and interesting master bedroom suite, this house says "buy me". Foundation offsets are kept to the front where they count for character; simple main roof frames over main house body and master bedroom cantilever. Note, too, the easy option of eliminating the third bedroom closet and opening this room to the kitchen as a family room plus two bedroom home.

Main level — 1,283 sq. ft.

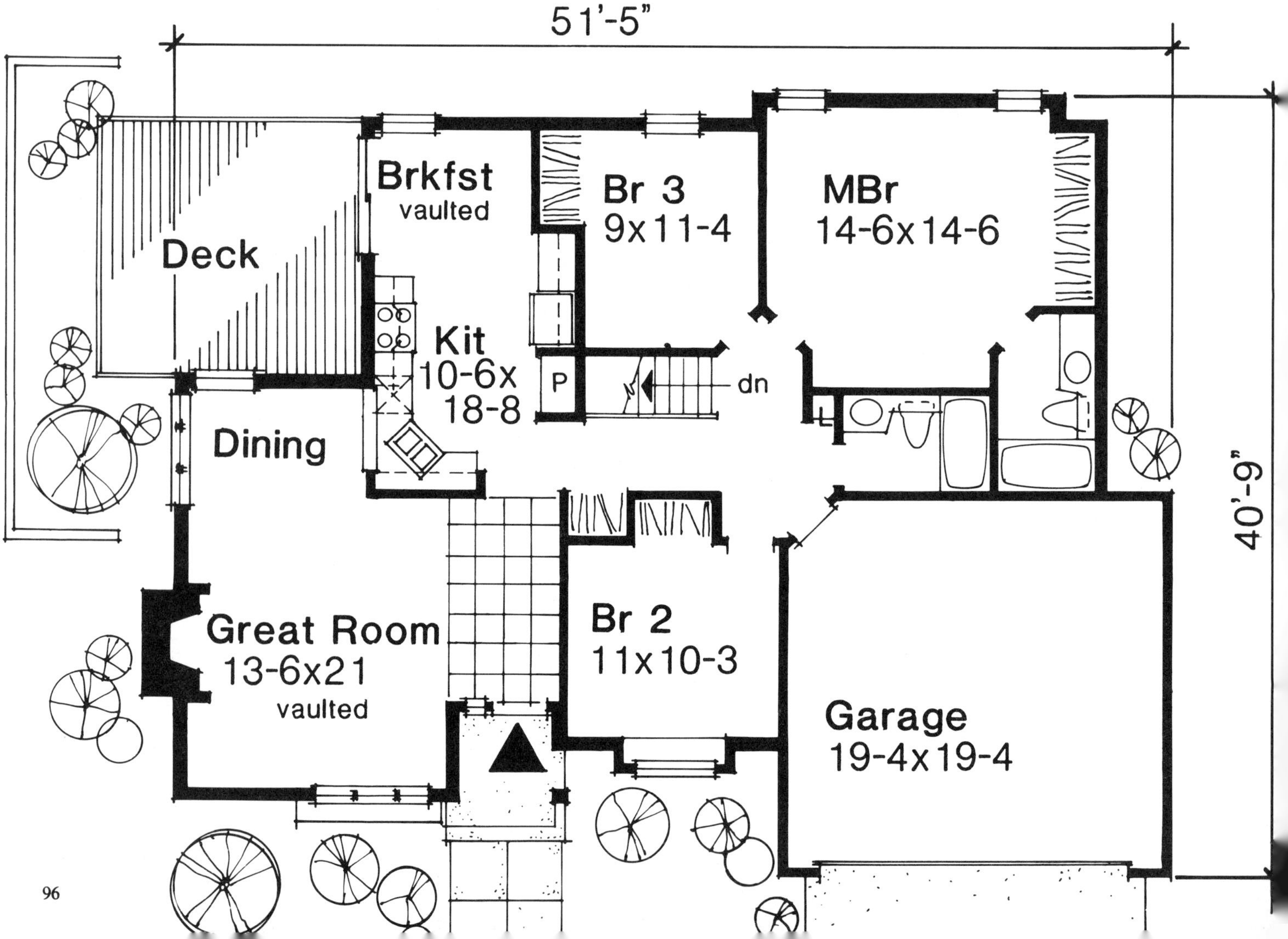

Two-Sink Baths Ease Morning Rush

No. 90622

Save energy and construction costs by building this friendly farmhouse colonial. The inviting covered porch opens to a center hall, enhanced by the stairway leading to the four-bedroom second floor. Flanked by formal living and dining rooms, the foyer leads right into the open, beamed family room, island kitchen, and bay window dinette. The rear porch adjoins both family and living rooms.

First floor — 1,563 sq. ft.
Second floor — 1,013 sq. ft.
(available with or without basement)

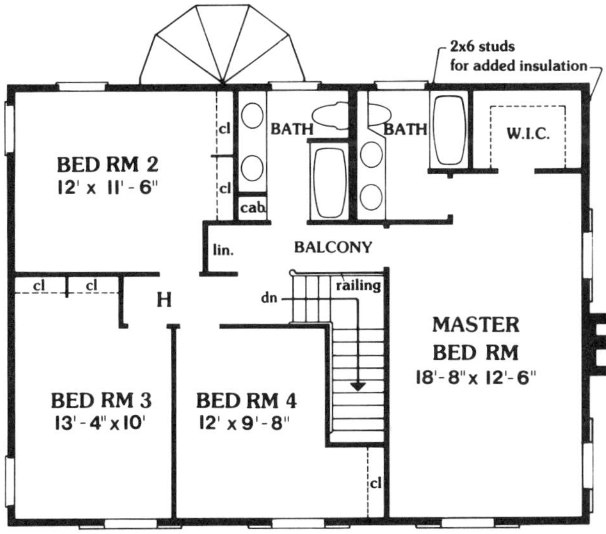

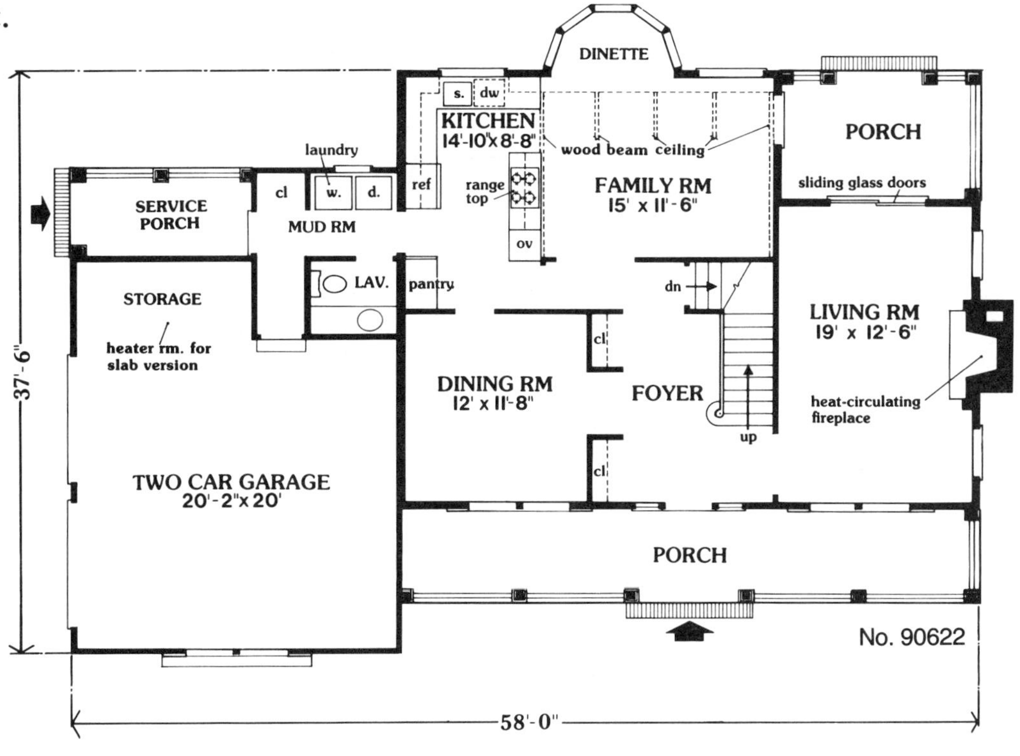

Compact Two-Story Design Ideal For Small Lot

No. 10517

Extra space is provided by the intricate angles incorporated into this design. The living room has a sloped ceiling and tiled hearth. The angular kitchen has direct access to the rear deck. A two-story foyer leads to the second floor which has two bedrooms, a bath, and individual dressing rooms. The master suite has a walk-in closet and complete bath.

First floor — 1,171 sq. ft.
Second floor — 561 sq. ft.
Basement — 1,171 sq. ft.
Garage — 484 sq. ft.

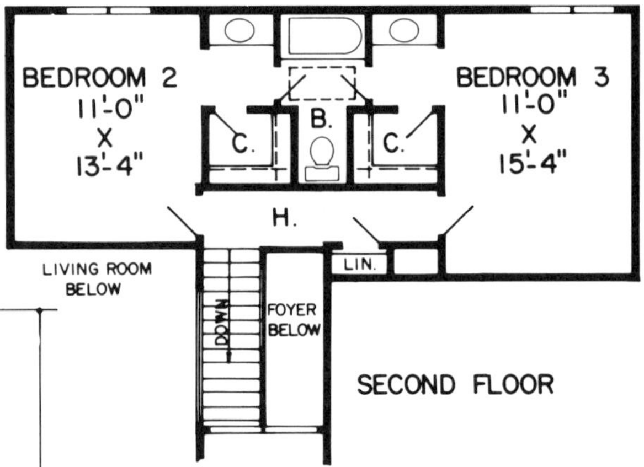

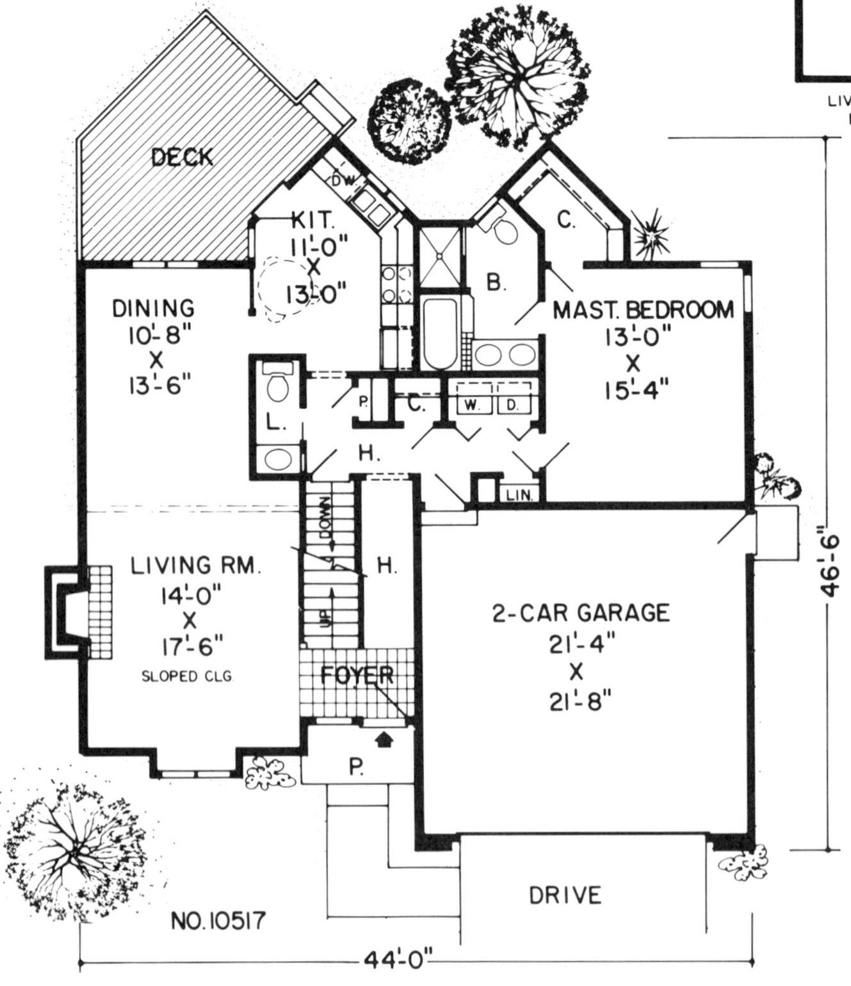

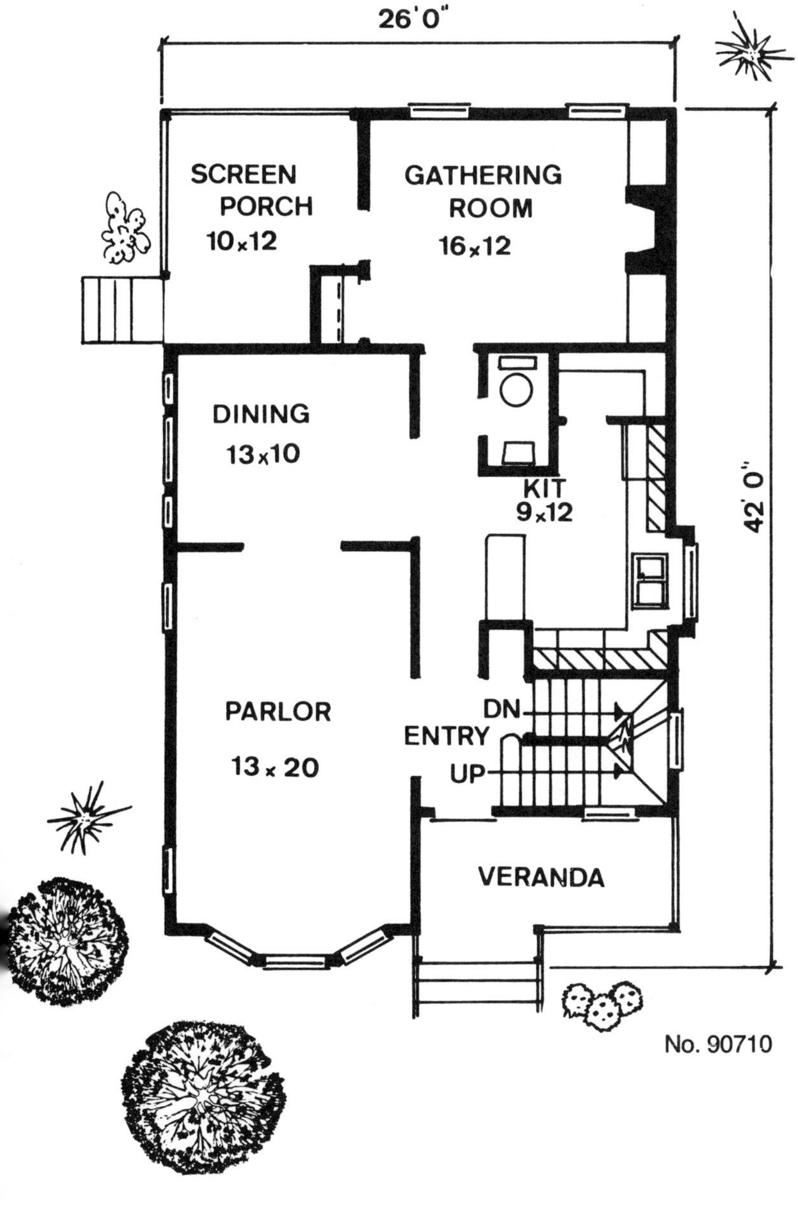

Private Balcony for the Master of the House

No. 90710

With a huge parlor, fireplaced gathering room, and screened porch, this comfortable home provides lots of room for entertaining. Across from the kitchen with walk-in pantry lies the sunny dining room. For a colorful glow, you might want to tuck a bit of stained glass in the window that illuminates the staircase. Two bedrooms share a huge bathroom with separate shower and tub.

First floor — 1,068 sq. ft.
Second floor — 868 sq. ft.

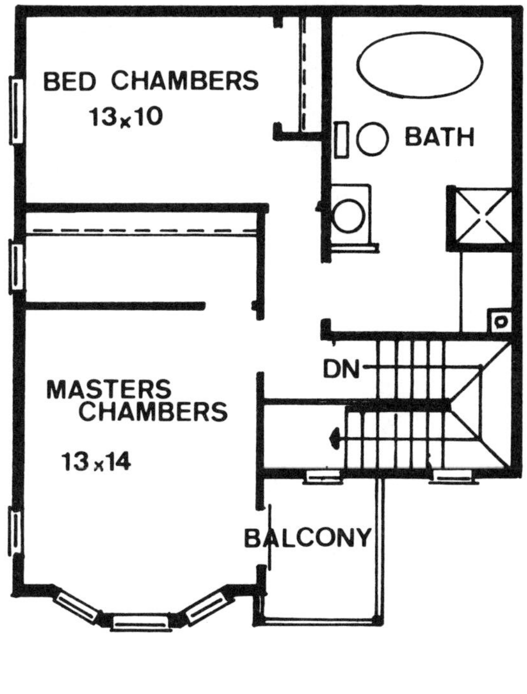

A-Frame Ideal as Vacation Home

No. 90025

It's no wonder that the A-frame has proven to be a popular vacation design, since it is dramatic to look at, practical to live in, and economical to build. The natural earthy feeling of this home would be ideal for a wooded or seaside lot.

Highlights of this design are the fieldstone chimney that soars up through the roof, vertical boards and battens, stained red cedar wood shingles and a redwood sundeck that creates an interesting exterior. For year-round living, provision is made for a supplemental heating unit in the utility room. Although the plan is of basementless design, a full basement is possible if the physical land characteristics permit, with the basement stair located under the main stair where the closet is now shown.

First floor — 884 sq.ft.
Second floor — 441 sq.ft.

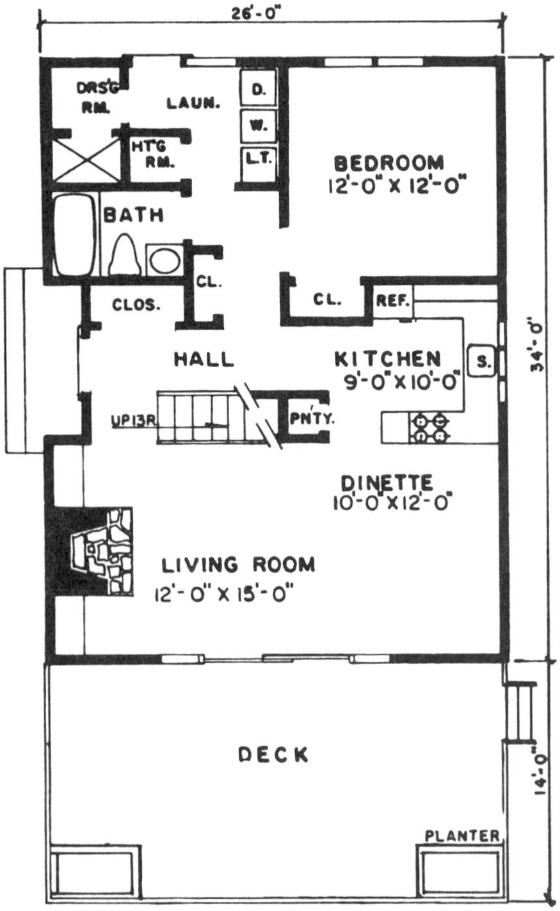

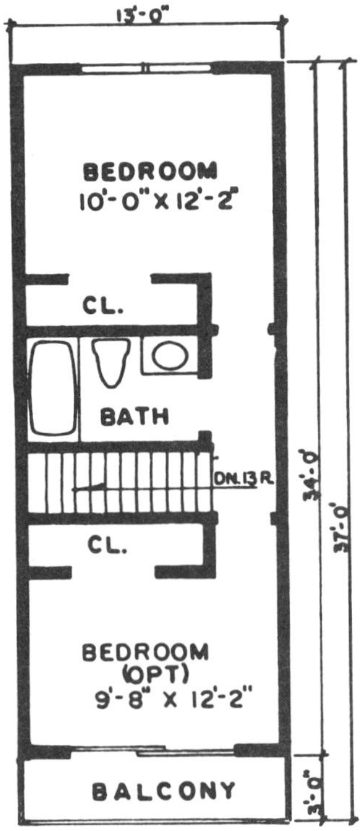

SECOND FLOOR

No. 90025

Tudor Charm and Comfort

No. 90022

The charm of this Tudor adaptation, reminiscent of Old England, could hardly be improved upon. Its fine proportions and exquisite use of exterior materials — half timber, stucco, multi-paned windows, and trimmed circular entrance — result in a most distinctive home. Even the attached garage, with its hipped dormer, diamond shaped leaded window, and extended wall, adds impact to this design. Designed to contribute to your feeling of personal luxury, the master bedroom suite has a dressing area with three closets and a private bath with mirrored vanity and tiled shower stall. Each of the other three bedrooms is served by the main bath, which has a tub and a full-length mirrored vanity.

First floor — 1,082 sq.ft.
Second floor — 916 sq.ft.
Garage — 506 sq.ft.
Patio — 160 sq.ft.

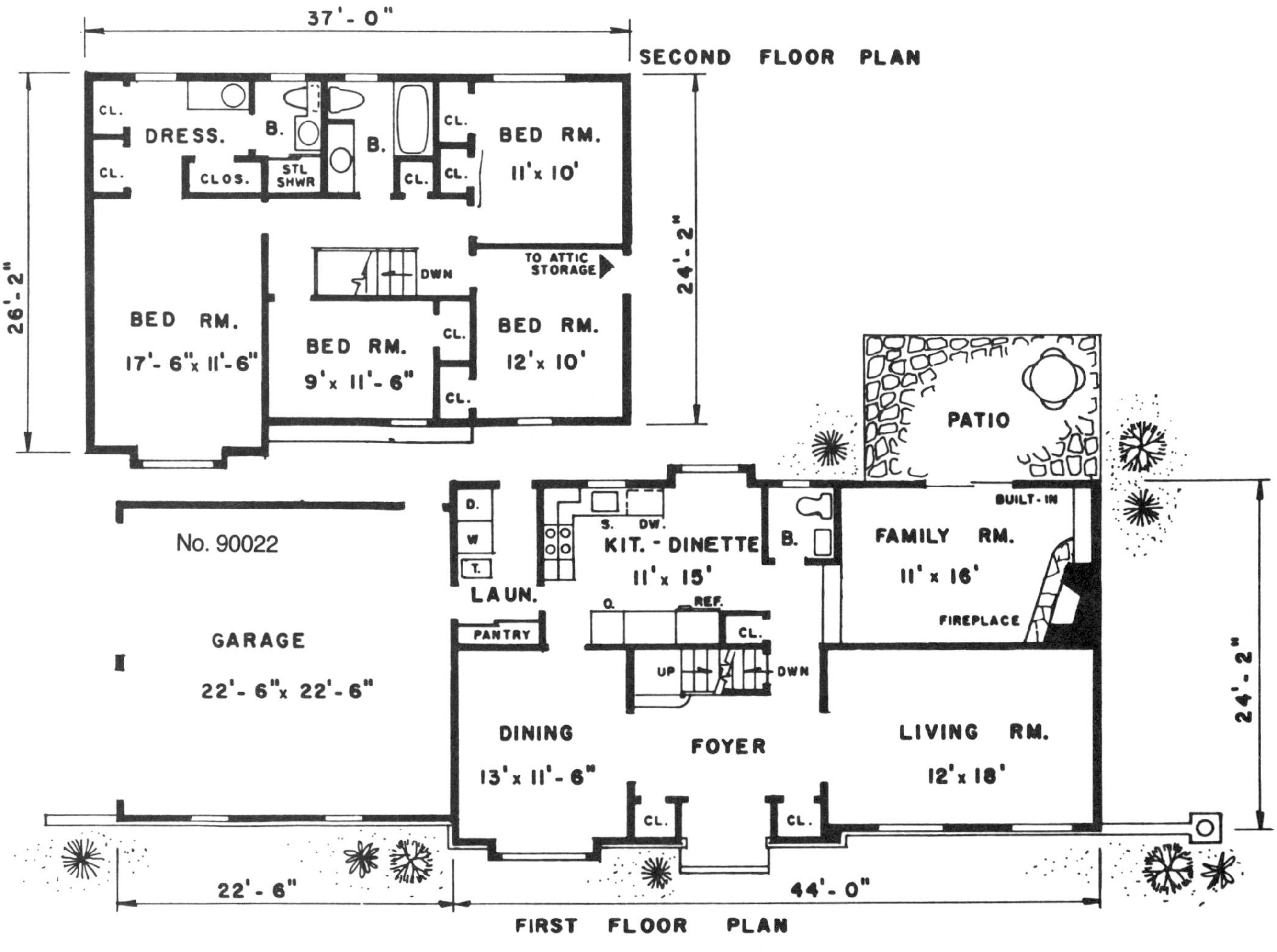

Luxurious Master Suite Lies Behind Double Doors

No. 90513

Two fireplaces warm this three bedroom abode with loads of outdoor living space. One covered porch shelters the entry. Another provides a perfect place to enjoy coffee off the dining room. And, a deck off the hallway upstairs and the breakfast nook below affords a golden opportunity for star gazing. Matching bay windows brighten the fireplaced living room and den. The sunny family room is just a step down from the island kitchen and breakfast nook.

First floor — 1,412 sq. ft.
Second floor — 1,080 sq. ft.

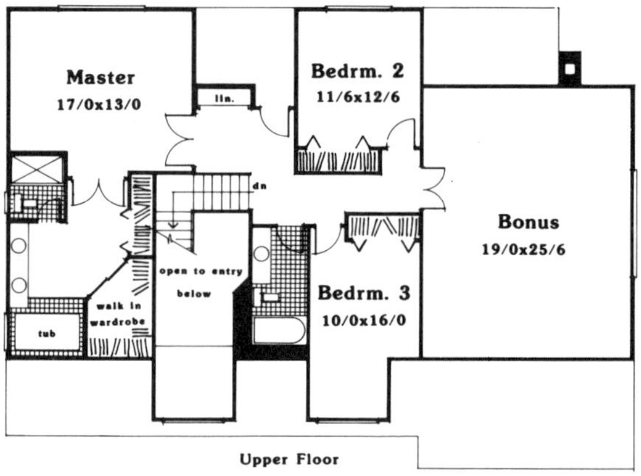

Upper Floor

No. 90513

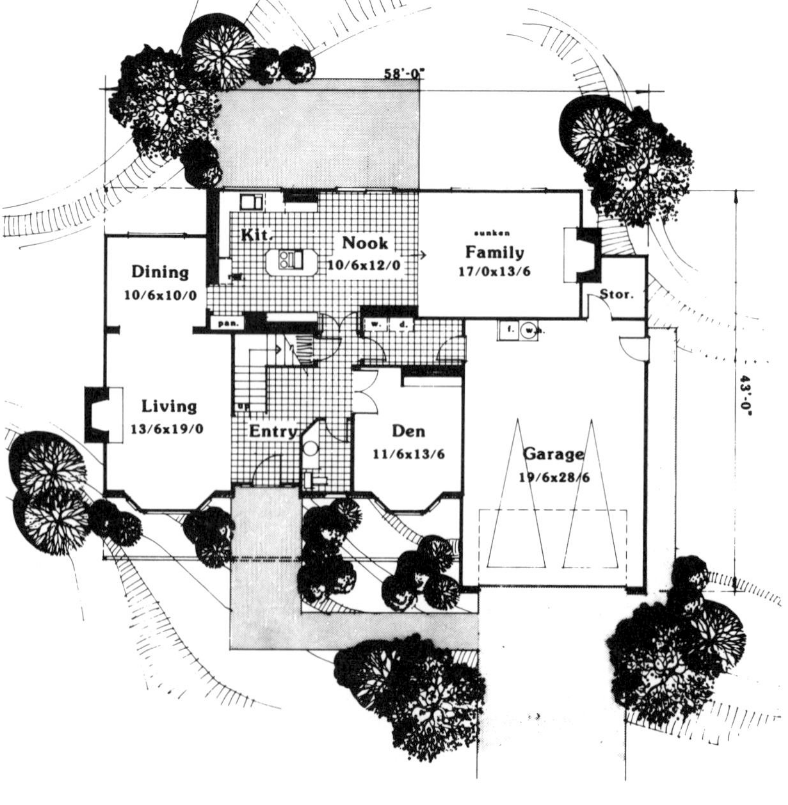

Family Kitchen Highlight

No. 90319

Bring the family together in this large family kitchen. The food preparation area is designed for maximum counter and cabinet space. There's even a coat closet next to the garage entrance and a built-in pantry. The bump out window is an ideal location for the dining table, and the laundry is hidden in a closet. In addition to a living room with window-flanked fireplace, the first floor also includes the large master bedroom suite. The two story entry unifies this design by incorporating two skylights. A third skylight enhances one of the second floor bedrooms.

Main level — 876 sq. ft.
Upper level — 504 sq. ft.
Basement — 859 sq. ft.
Garage — 436 sq. ft.

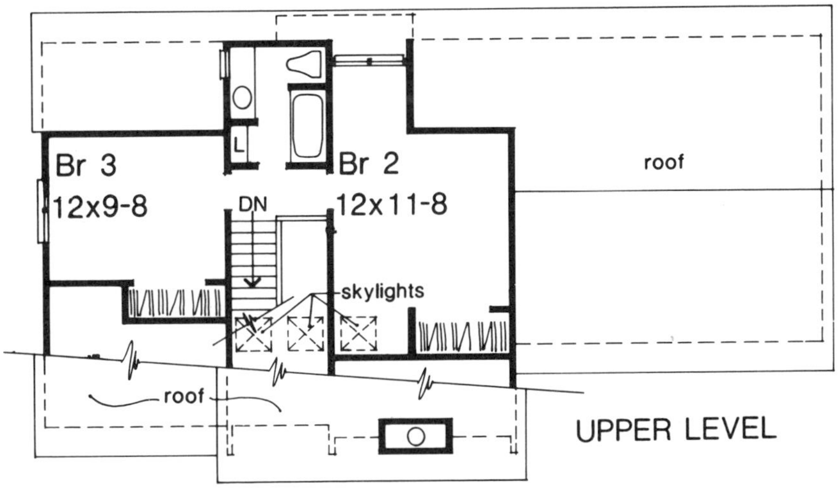

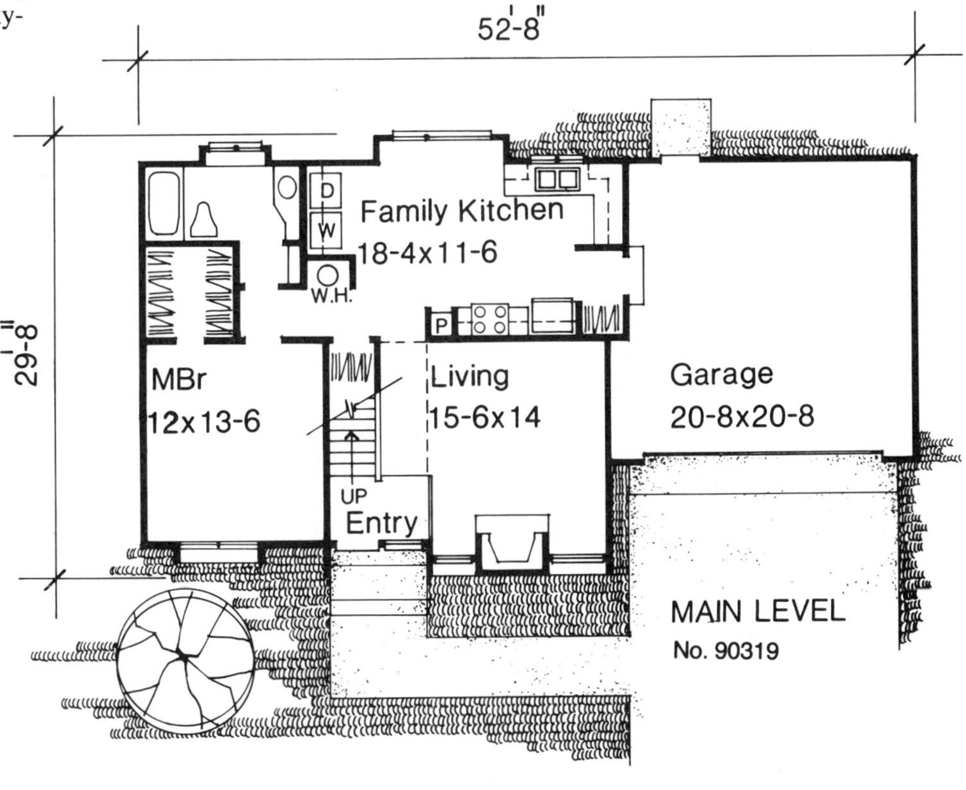

Sunlit Rooms Spread Tranquility

No. 90519

Special window treatments flood the home with light and spaciousness. Cathedral style windows enhance the front bedrooms, and bay windows accent the living room and breakfast nook. The adjoining living and dining areas exemplify roominess. An efficient kitchen has quick access for formal dining or a casual breakfast. The master bedroom features skylights in the dressing room and bath. A laundry area and half bath complete the 1st floor.

First floor — 730 sq. ft.
Second floor — 680 sq. ft.

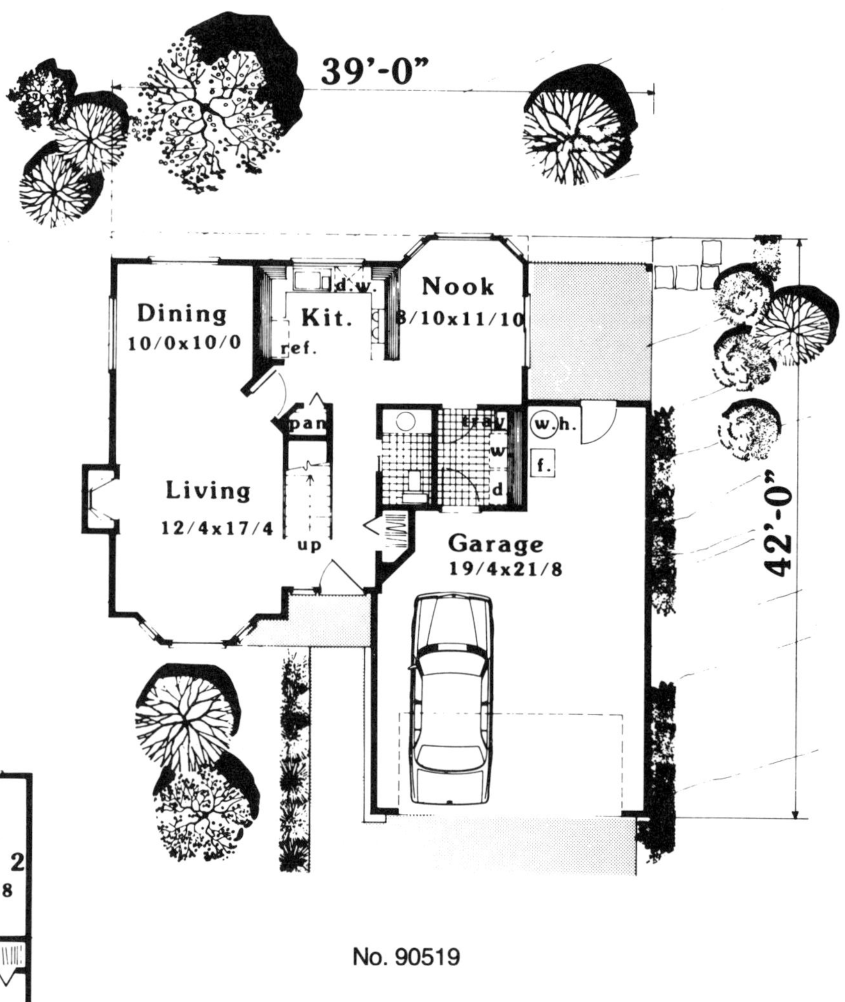

No. 90519

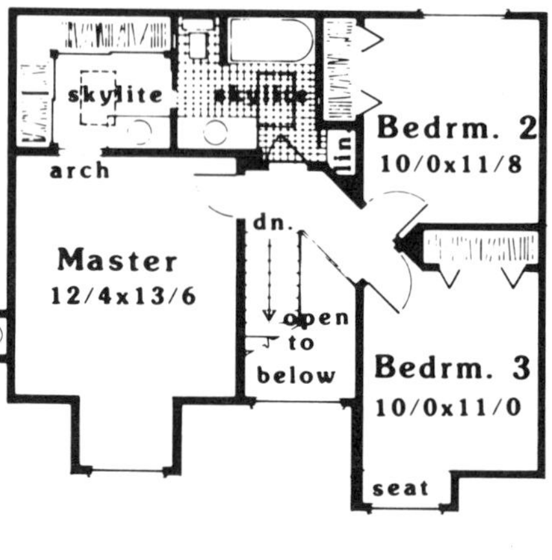

Loft Overlooks Attractive Foyer

No. 10583

This hillside home, characterized by enormous rooms and two garages, is built on two levels. From the foyer, travel down one hall to a cozy bedroom, full bath, island kitchen, laundry and garage. Or, walk straight into the sun-filled great and dining rooms with wrap-around deck. One room features a massive fireplace, built-in bookshelves, and access to the lofty study; the other contains a window greenhouse. For ultimate privacy, the master bedroom suite possesses a lavish skylit tub. On the lower level are two additional bedrooms, a bath, and a rec room with bar that opens onto an outdoor patio.

First floor — 2,367 sq. ft.
Basement (unfinished) — 372 sq. ft.
Basement (finished) — 1,241 sq. ft.
Loft — 295 sq. ft.
Garage (lower level) — 660 sq. ft.
Garage (upper level) — 636 sq. ft.

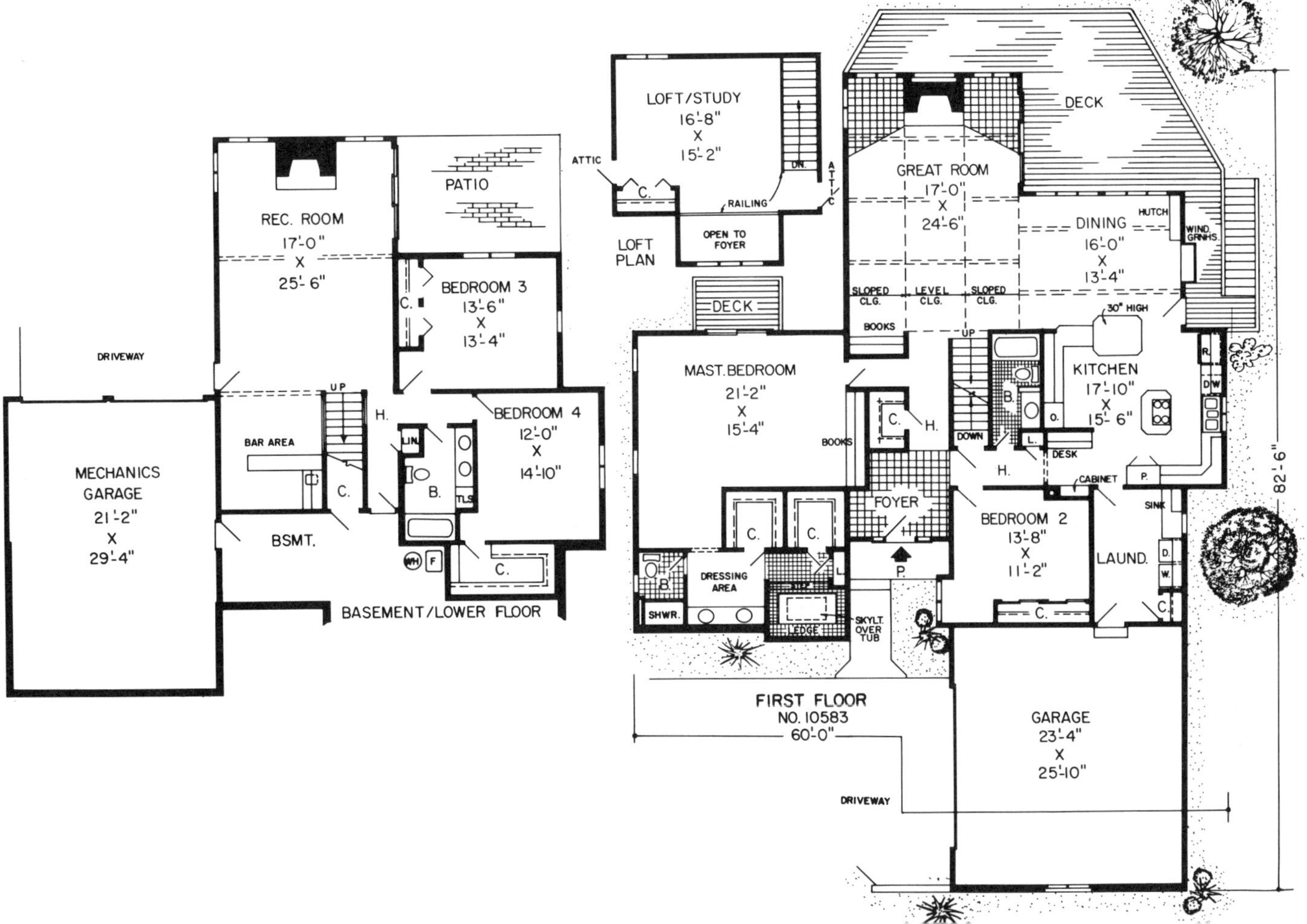

Plan for the Future

No. 90906

There's plenty of space for growth in this attractive basement-entry design. A lovely spacious foyer sets the theme for the main event upstairs. Atop the beautiful open staircase are three large bedrooms, all grouped together to one side of the home for privacy. The master suite has its own private bath and walk-in closet. On the living side, a large family kitchen complete with nook will make family mealtimes a delight. And, beyond the nook through sliding glass doors, a roomy sundeck is available for your leisure hours.

Main floor — 1,184 sq. ft.
Basement — 964 sq. ft.
Garage — 462 sq. ft.
Width — 45 ft.
Depth — 38 ft. (plus 8 ft. sundeck)

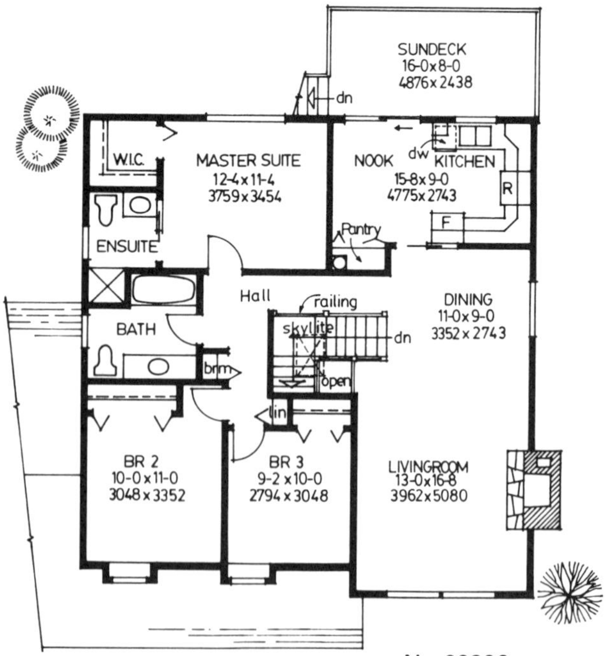

No. 90906

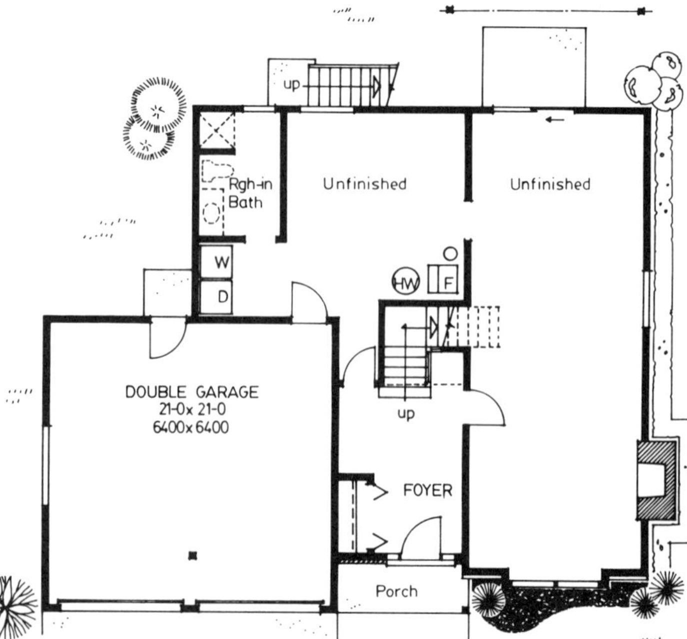

BASEMENT PLAN

If built with optional single garage width will be 34'-0"

Compact Home is Surprisingly Spacious

No. 90905

Searching for a design where the living room takes advantage of both front and rear views? Look no further. And, this cozy ranch has loads of other features. An attractive porch welcomes guests and provides shade for the big living room window on hot summer days. A large covered sundeck adjacent to the living room, dining room and kitchen will make entertaining a delight. The roomy bedrooms, including the master suite with full bath and a walk-in closet, are protected from street noise by the two-car garage.

Main floor — 1,314 sq. ft.
Basement — 1,488 sq. ft.
Garage — 484 sq. ft.
Width — 50 ft.
Depth — 54 ft.

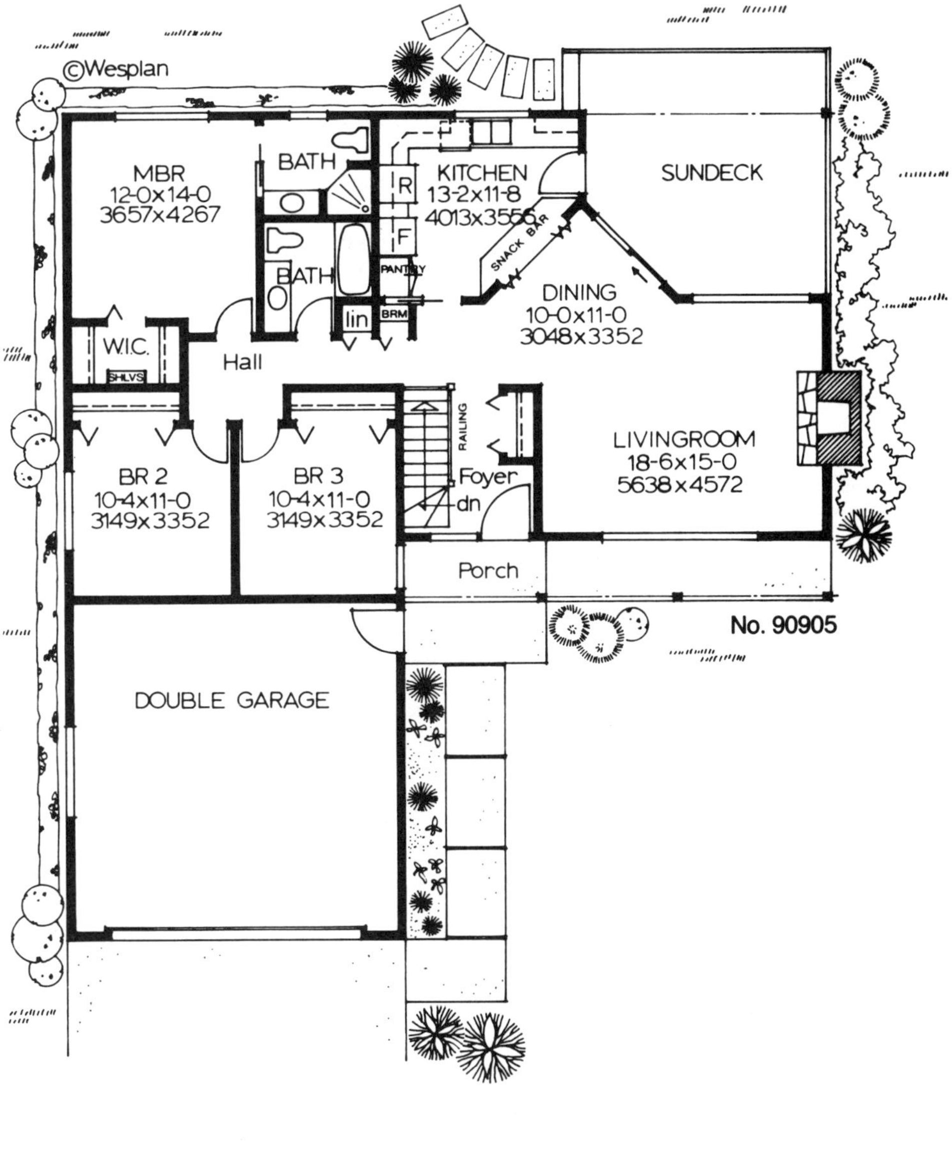

Family Living on a Higher Plane

No. 90913

Loaded with up-to-date features, this distinctive basement-entry design offers a comfortable haven inside a traditional exterior. From the foyer, a beautiful open staircase, illuminated by the skylight in the vaulted ceiling overhead, leads you to the center of the main floor. From this point you may proceed to any room; good zoning of living areas according to their function is a strong point in this plan. On the basement level, there's plenty of room for future expansion. Study this design carefully, it deserves a second look.

Main floor — 1,578 sq. ft.
Basement — 1,304 sq. ft.
Garage — 474 sq. ft.
Width — 41 ft.
Depth — 49 ft. 6 in. (plus 13 ft. for stairs & deck)

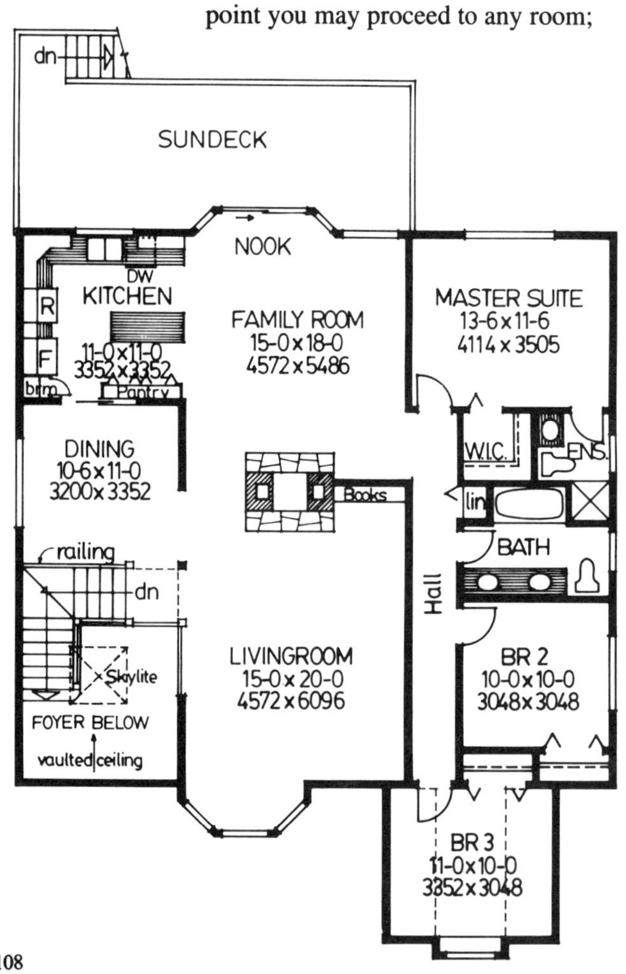

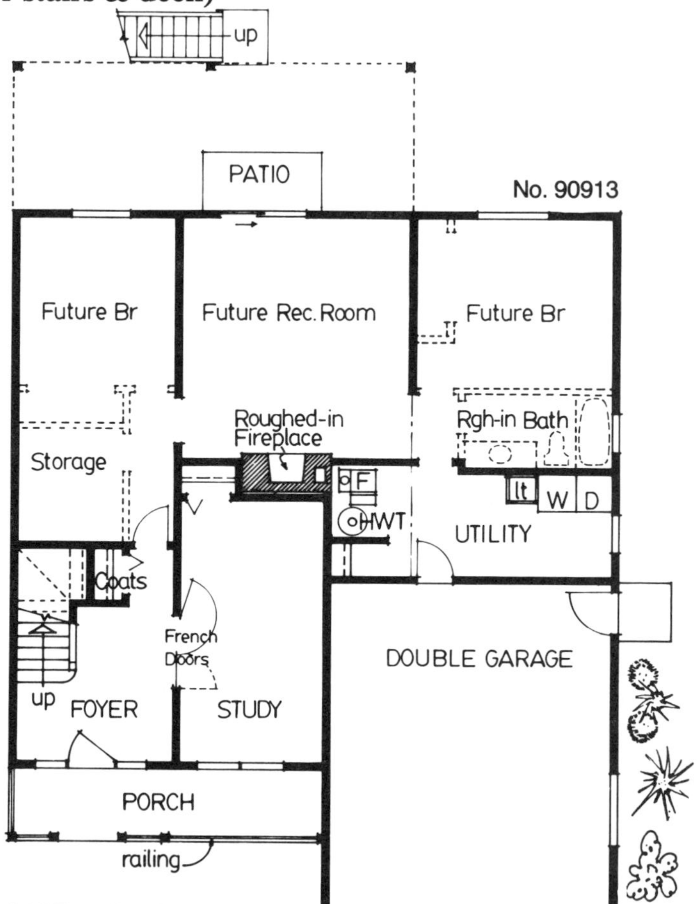

BASEMENT FLOOR PLAN

Built-In Planter Surrounds Split Level

No. 90916

Here's a house on three levels that's brimming with features. The master suite boasts a walk-through dressing area and a 3/4 bath. The family bath is huge, and contains a practical double-basin vanity for hectic mornings. Looking from the breakfast area through a railing into the sunken family room, the visual effect is spectacular. And, the convenient, central kitchen location makes food service to all the living areas a breeze.

Main floor — 1,350 sq. ft.
Second floor — 648 sq. ft.
Basement — 704 sq. ft.
Garage — 418 sq. ft.
Width — 48 ft.
Depth — 52 ft.

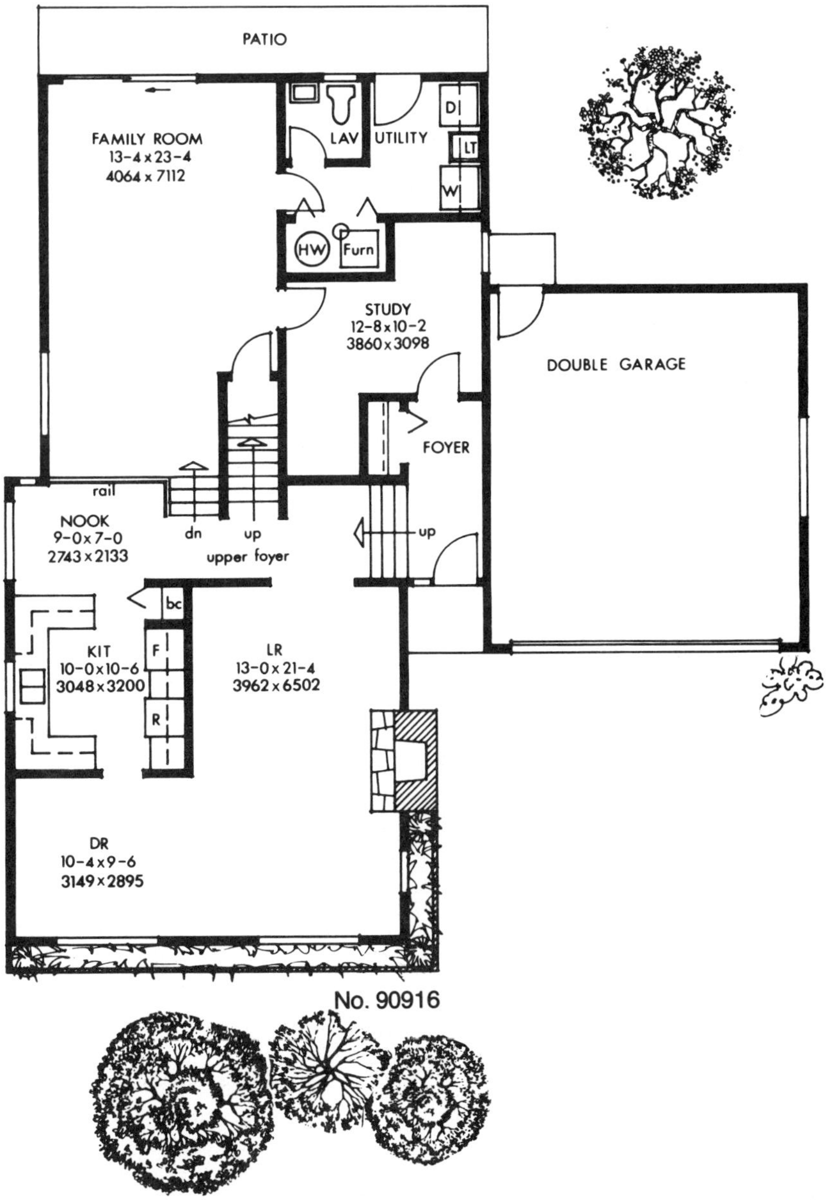

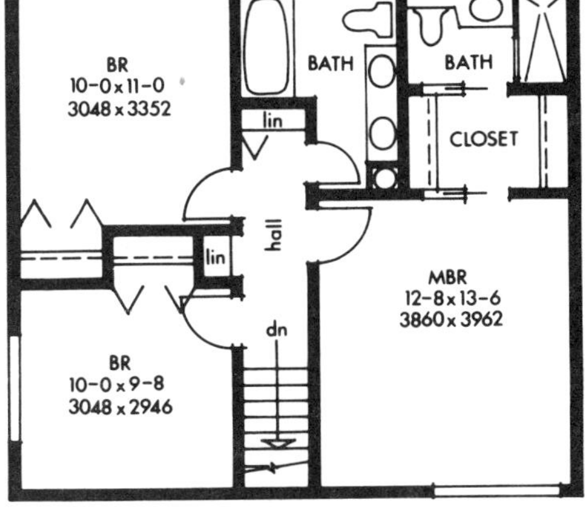

Glass Walls Brighten Second-Story Living

No. 90912

If you can't be outside on the sundecks, you can certainly enjoy your view from anywhere in this three-bedroom beauty. The protected portico enters into an attractive foyer that leads to the family room, extra bedroom, and practical, full-sized utility space. Up the open staircase, the main floor is spacious and comfortable. You'll immediately notice the corner fireplace and soaring, vaulted ceiling of the sunken living room. The ample kitchen, with loads of counter space, is adjacent to family and dining rooms for convenient entertaining.

Main floor — 1,464 sq. ft.
Basement — 1,183 sq. ft.
Garage — 422 sq. ft.

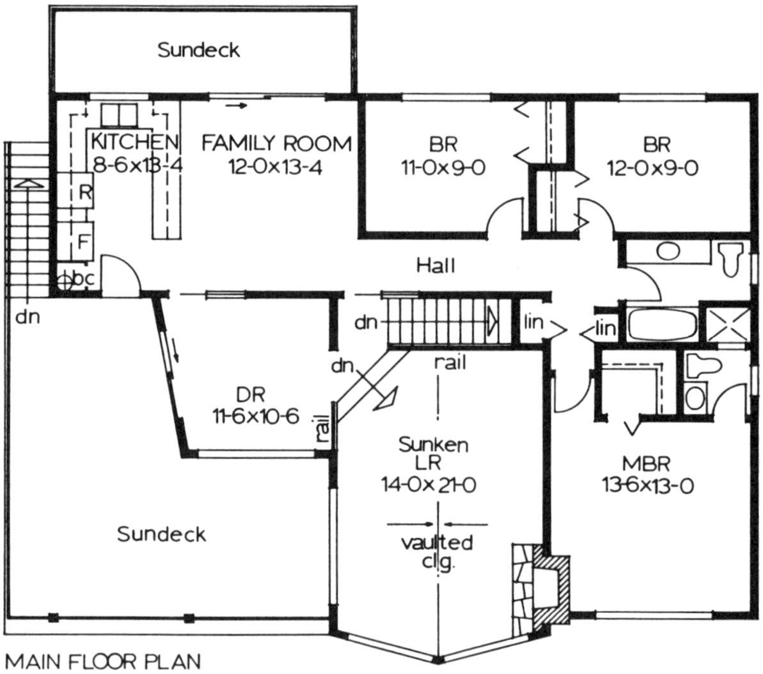

MAIN FLOOR PLAN

No. 90912

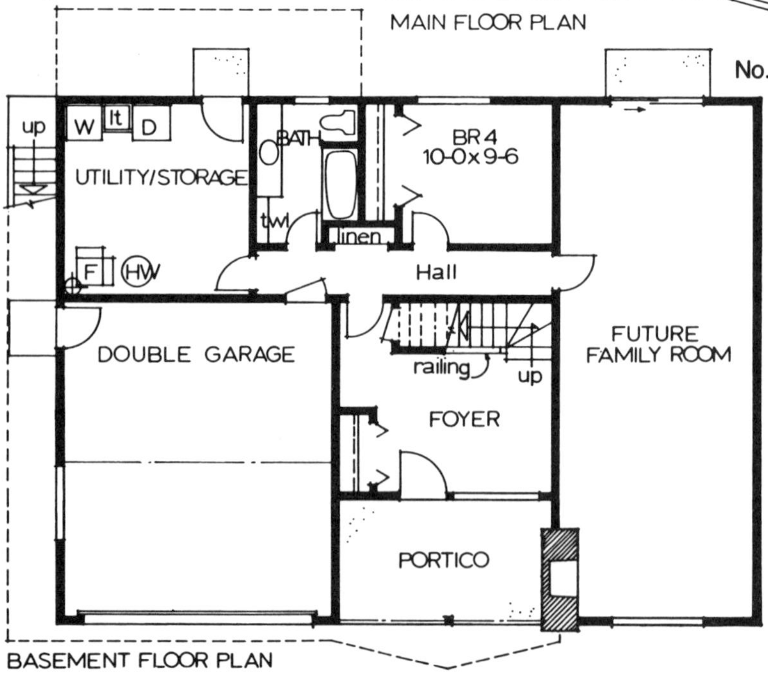

BASEMENT FLOOR PLAN

Width — 48 ft. (plus 3 ft. walkway & stairs)
Depth — 39 ft. (plus 6 ft. deck)

Picket Fence Insures Privacy

No. 90701

Soaring roof lines and an attached greenhouse distinguish this handsome, three-bedroom residence. The master suite with skylit bath is in its own wing off the two-story entry. French doors lead to the huge deck outside, which is also accessible from the dining room. Light pours into the island kitchen from an adjoining two-story sun room. The loft upstairs is like a bridge overlooking the dining room and entry. It connects two bedrooms, a bath, and bookshelf-lined study.

First floor — 1,347 sq. ft.
Second floor — 921 sq. ft.

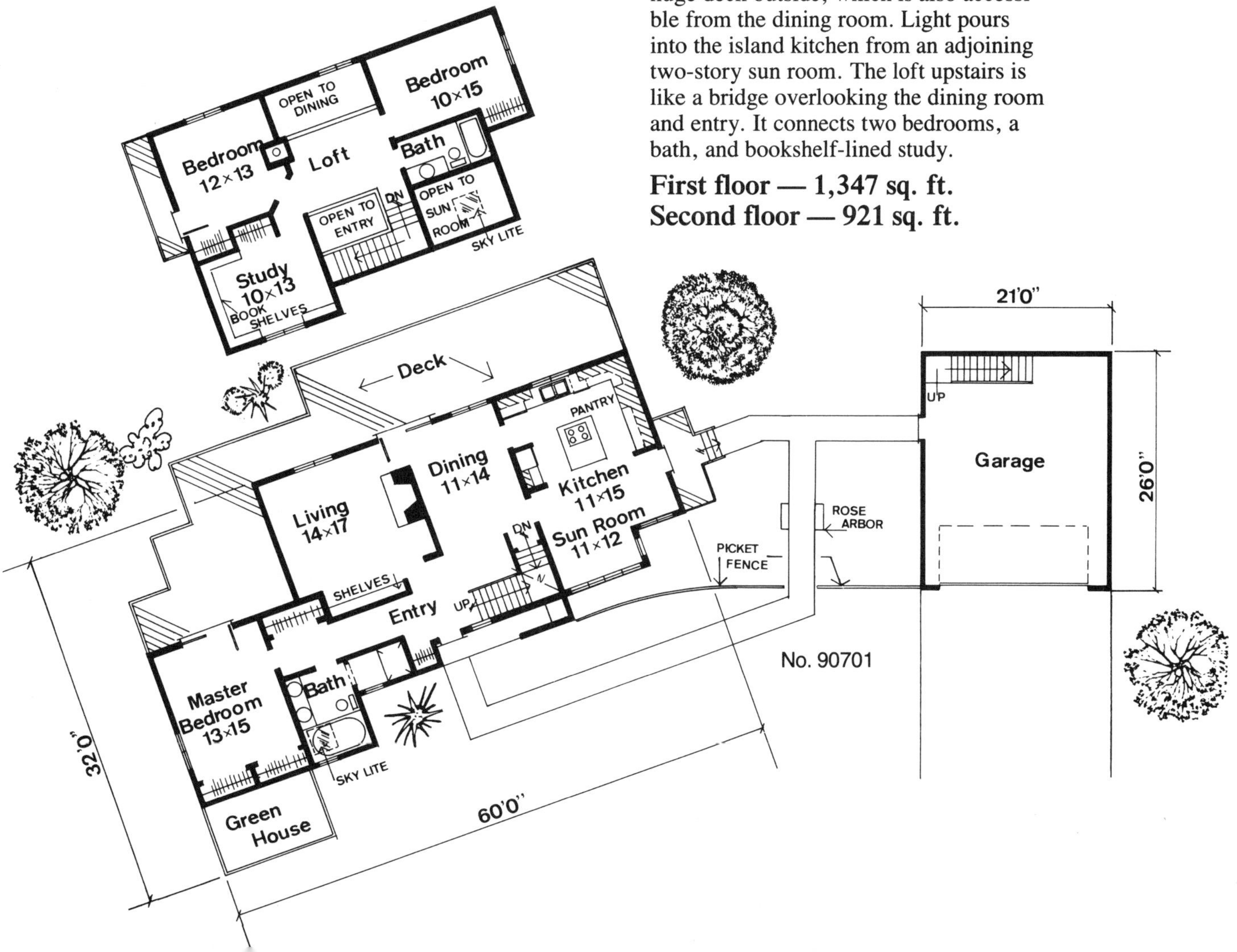

A Hint of Victorian Nostalgia

No. 90909

High roofs, tower bays, and long, railed porches give this efficient plan an old-fashioned charm that's hard to resist. The foyer opens on a classic center stairwell, wrapped in short halls that separate traffic without subtracting from room sizes. The highlight of this home for many homeowners is sure to be the lively kitchen with its full bay window and built-in eating table.

Main floor — 1,206 sq. ft.
Second floor — 969 sq. ft.
Garage — 471 sq. ft.
Basement — 1,206 sq. ft.
Width — 61 ft.
Depth — 44 ft.

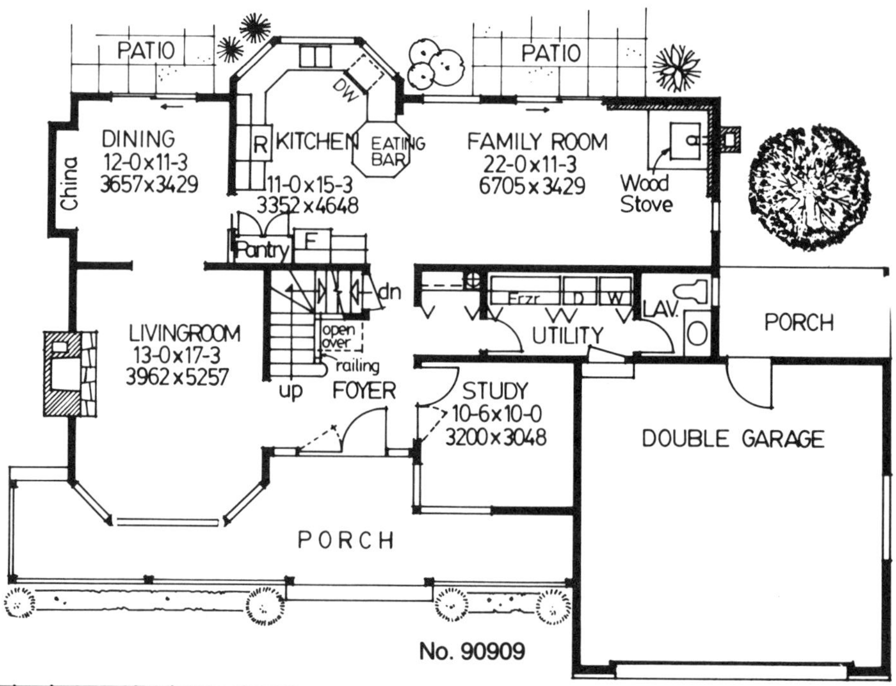

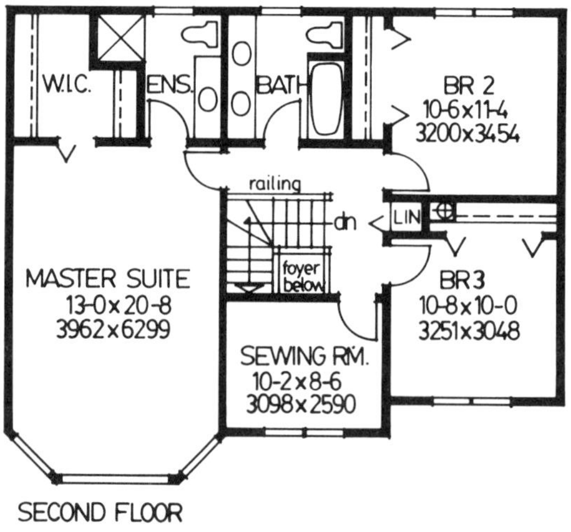

Designed for a Hillside

No. 90807

Wrapped around a skylit central foyer, the open, L-shaped arrangement of common living areas gives this design an airy feeling and a convenient traffic pattern.

Double windows brighten every room. A deck off the sunken living room and adjoining dining room makes outdoor entertaining a breeze. Note the very convenient utility and washroom just off the family room. The master bedroom includes a shower and walk-in closet.

Main Floor — 1,595 sq. ft.
Unfinished daylight basement — 1,595 sq. ft.
Garage — 473 sq. ft.
Width — 54 ft.
Depth — 55 ft.(plus 6 ft. deck)

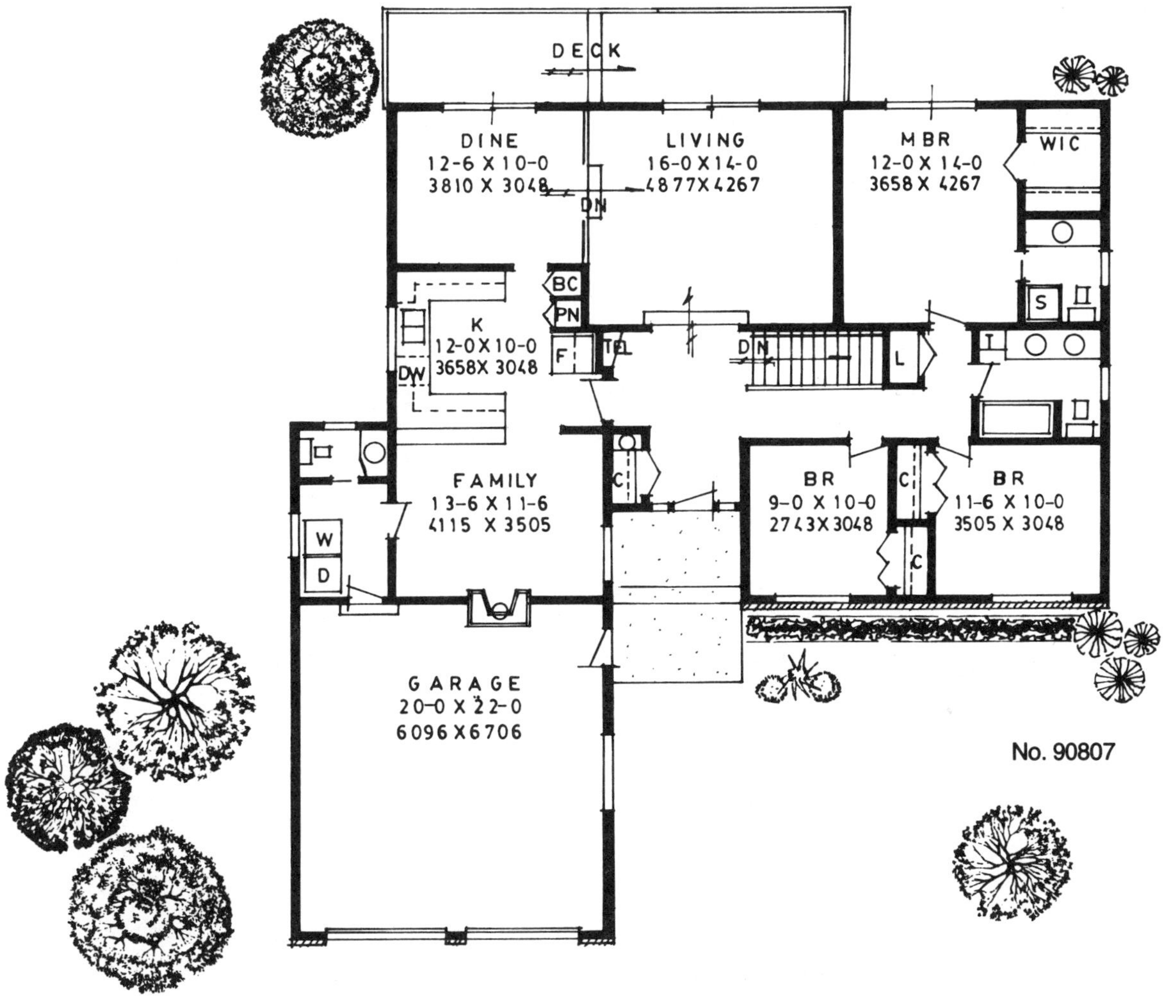

Country Kitchen Accents Design

No. 90119

Joining the U-shaped kitchen to the informal dining area is a serving bar which may also be used as additional counter space for a larger work area. These two areas are adjacent to the family room so there's ample space for family get-togethers. Toward the front of the house is the living room which opens onto the formal dining room whose double windows look out onto the yard or garden. The second floor bedrooms are arranged around a central bath. In addition to the master bedroom's private bath and walk-in closet, one other bedroom also incoporates a roomy walk-in closet.

First floor — 1,104 sq. ft.
Second floor — 1,092 sq. ft.

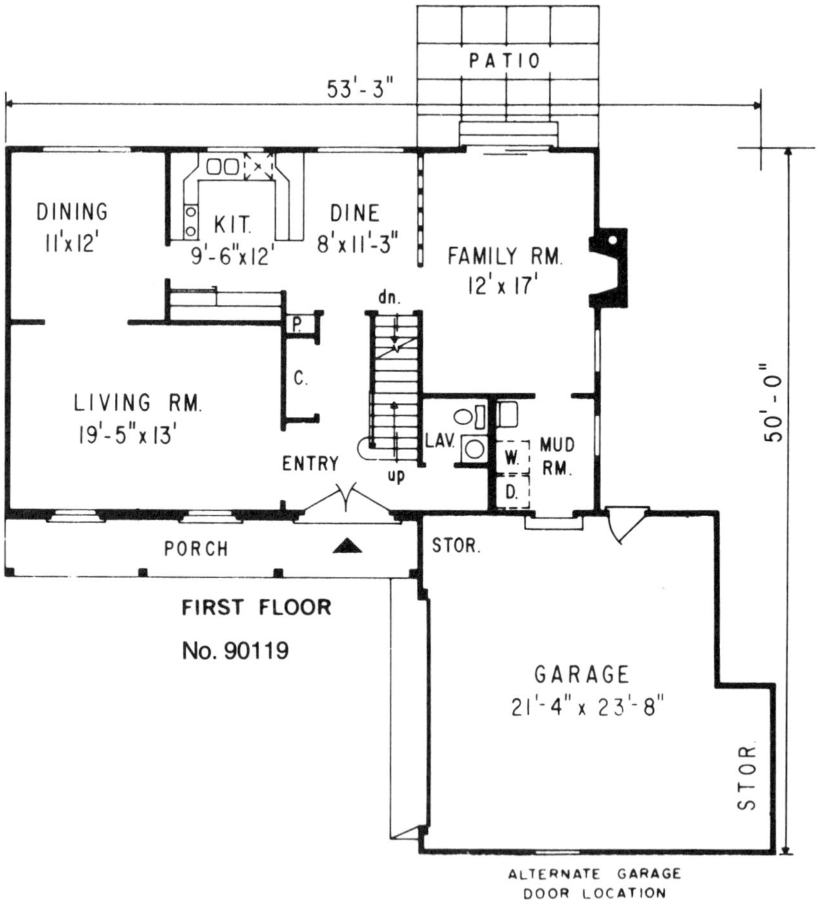

FIRST FLOOR

No. 90119

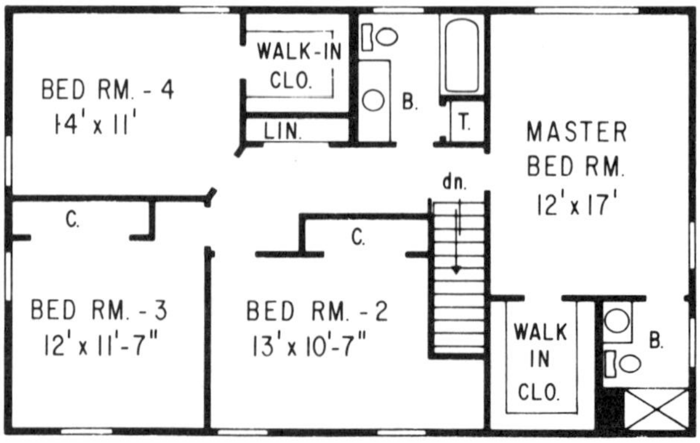

SECOND FLOOR

Olde Tavern-Style Cottage

No. 90003

This evocation of an old English tavern, both inside and out, is a novel approach for vacation or retirement living. Projecting bay windows, dormer windows, half-timber decorative work, and a large chimney are authentic period details. Past the porte-cochere, the trophy foyer helps recall the mood of earlier days with its wooden beams, paneling, and peg flooring. A unique log-storage pass-through stores wood for fireplaces in the taverna (living room) and grog room (dining room). The long service area at the rear, entitled galley and grog room, could be divided into kitchen and dining room by a folding partition.

First floor — 760 sq. ft.
Second floor — 570 sq. ft.

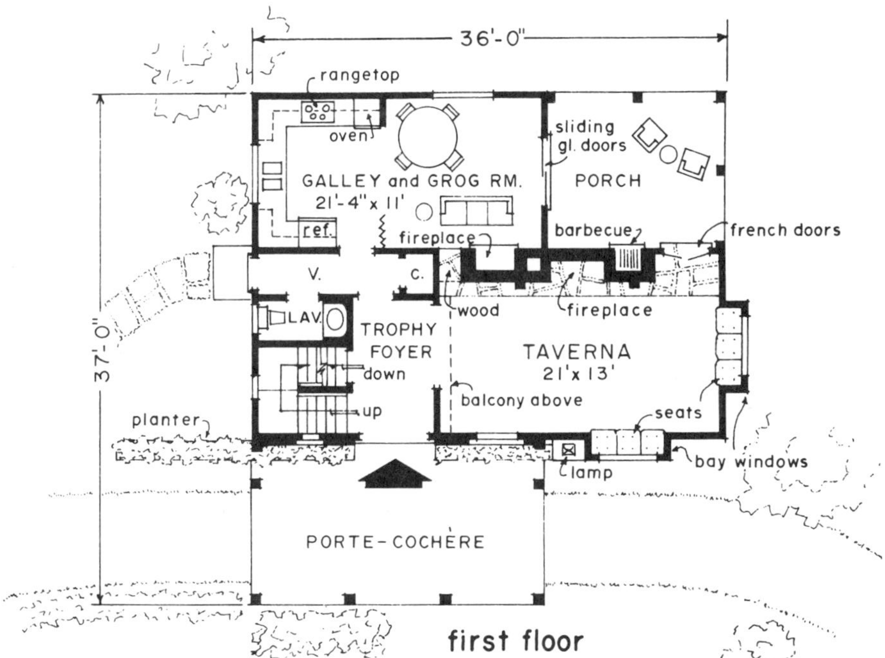

first floor
No. 90003

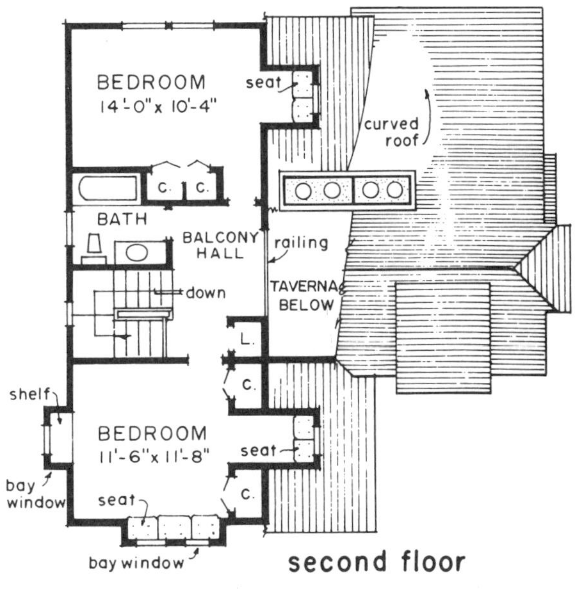

second floor

Enjoy the View

No. 90833

Here's a house that will take advantage of your location to create an irresistible view from the second floor. On the lower level, you'll find a bayed family room complete with a fireplace just off the foyer. But, the main living areas are upstairs. The L-shaped staircase brings you right into the living room. Bay windows, the open railing, and adjacent dining area with sliding glass doors to the sundeck give this area a spacious feeling. The family kitchen is large enough to accommodate a table for informal meals. Past the pantry and full bath, three bedrooms occupy the rear of the house, away from active areas and the noise of the street.

Basement floor — 994 sq. ft.
Main floor — 1,318 sq. ft.
Garage — 378 sq. ft.

FLOOR AREA = 1318 sq.ft.
WIDTH: 40'-0"
DEPTH: 40'-0"

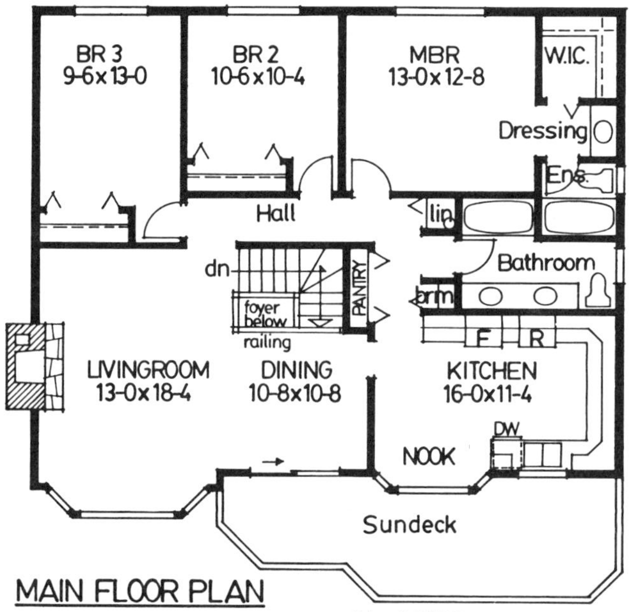

MAIN FLOOR PLAN

No. 90833

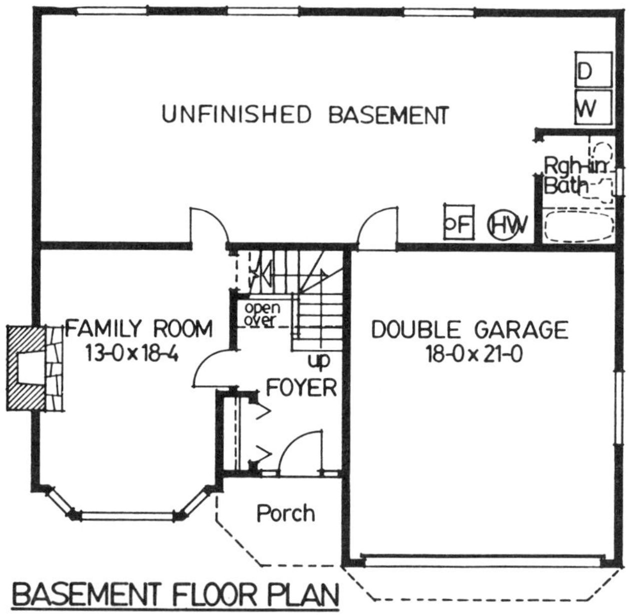

BASEMENT FLOOR PLAN

Den Offers Peaceful Haven

No. 90923

Here is an exquisite victorian adaptation. The exterior, with its interesting roof lines, window treatment, and inviting entrance porch, could hardly be more dramatic. Inside, the delightfully large, two-story foyer has a beautiful curved staircase and controls the flexible traffic patterns. There's loads of room in this house for formal entertaining. For the family's informal activities, family room, covered patio, nook and kitchen areas conveniently interact. Notice the large pantry in the kitchen. Upstairs, via an open balcony hall, you'll find four spacious bedrooms, including the lovely master suite with lavish, sunken tub.

Main floor — 1,264 sq. ft.
Second floor — 1,001 sq. ft.
Basement — 1,279 sq. ft.
Garage — 456 sq. ft.
Width — 42 ft.
Depth — 56 ft.

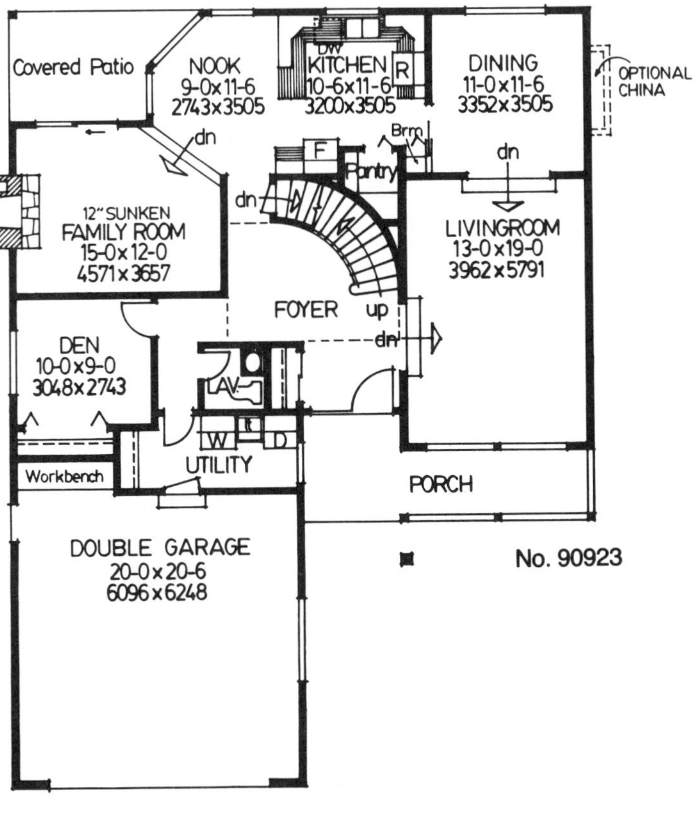

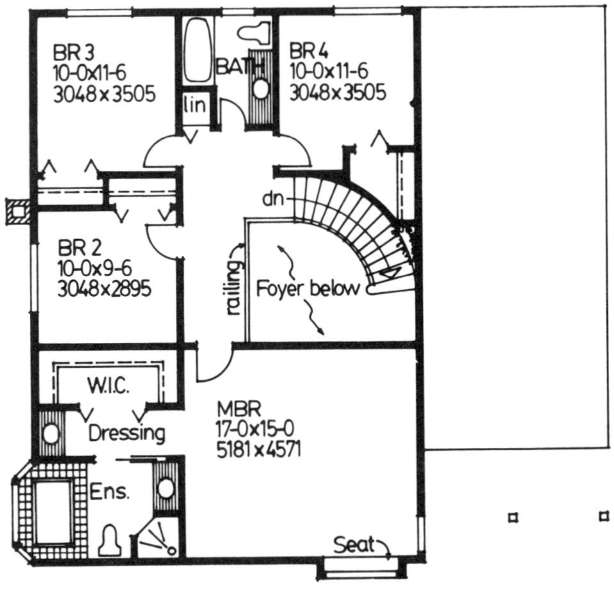

SECOND FLOOR

Compact, But Airy

No. 90509

As you enter this rustic home through the front door, expect to be treated to a panoramic view of the first floor. Living, dining, and family rooms are separated only by the compact kitchen. In nice weather, move outside to the deck off the fireplaced family room. Up the central staircase, you'll find three bedrooms and two baths, including the master suite, which features a bay window that's ideal for bird watching.

First floor — 948 sq. ft.
Second floor — 808 sq. ft.

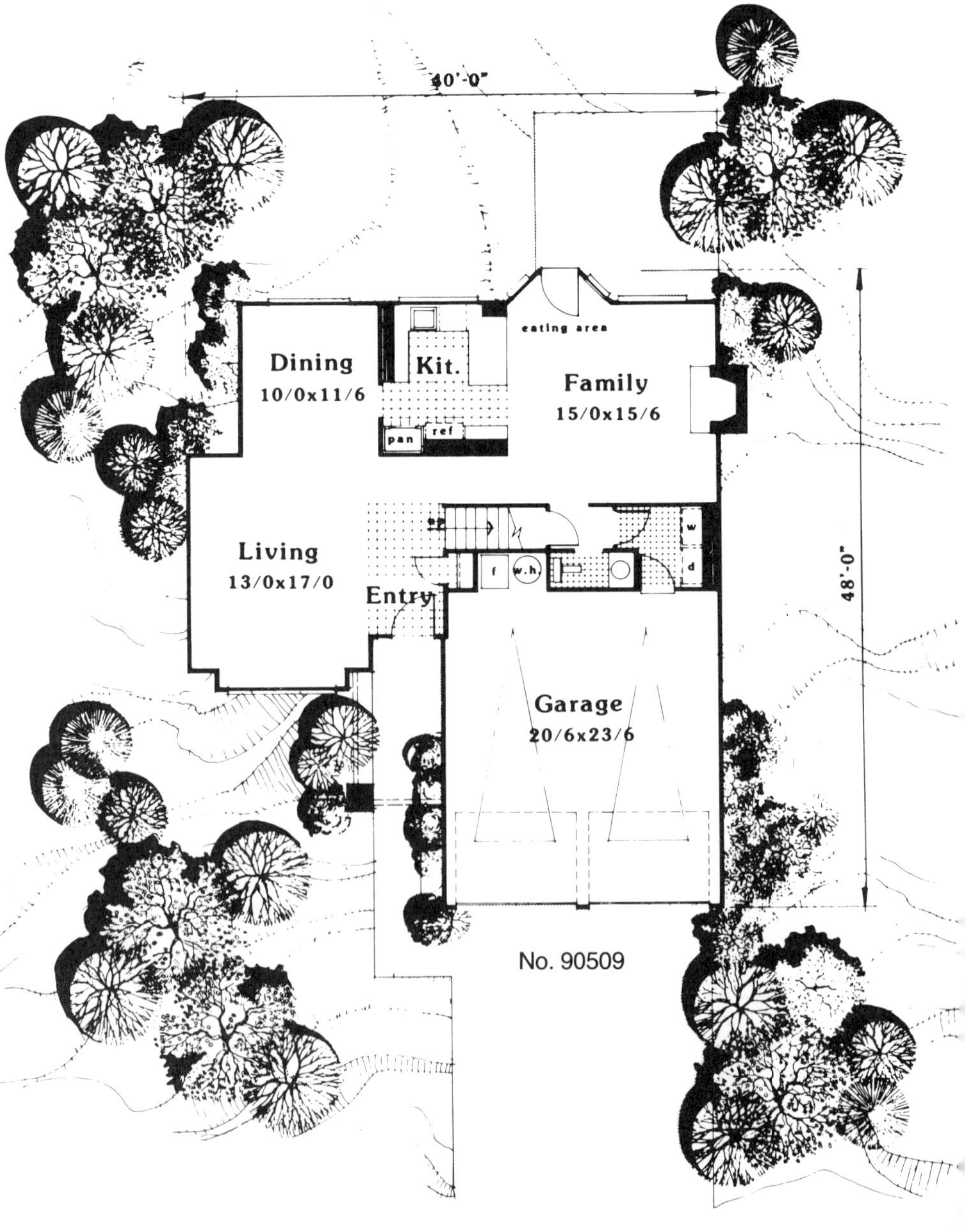

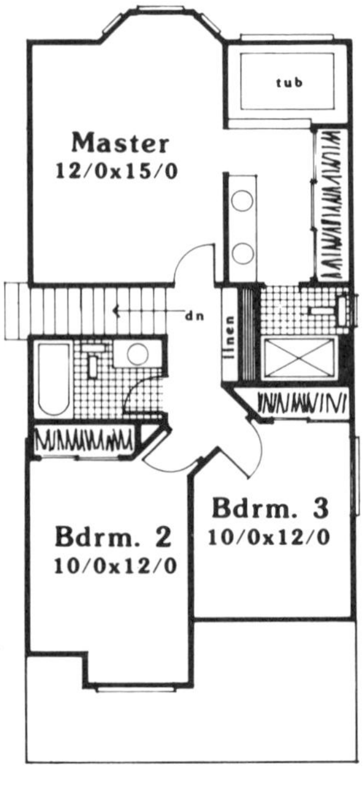

upper floor

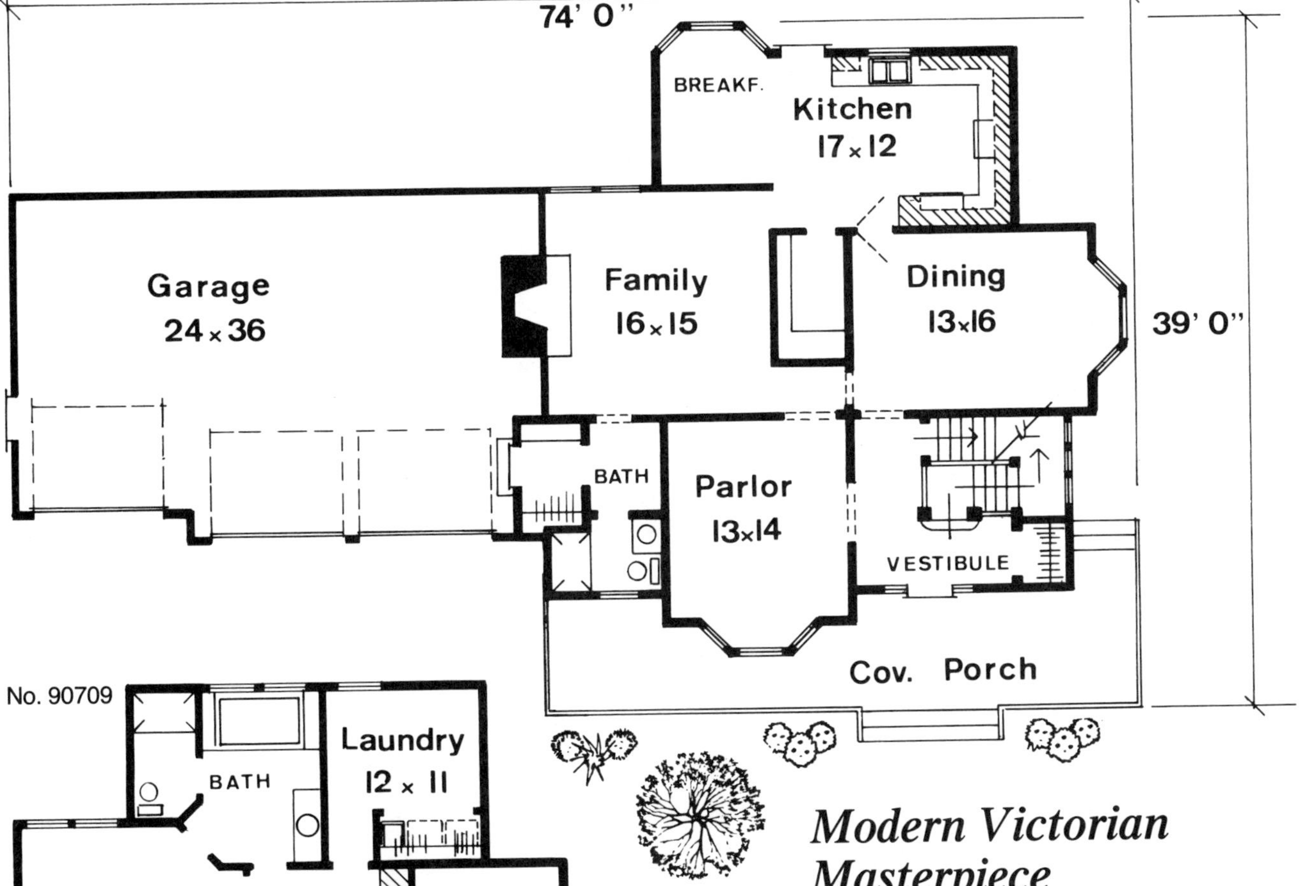

No. 90709

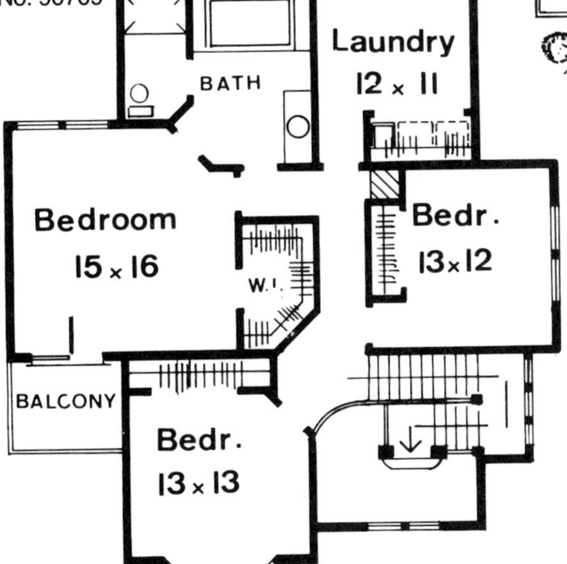

Second Level

Modern Victorian Masterpiece

No. 90709

Whimsical gingerbread trim and bay windows in four rooms adorn this beautiful family home. Enjoy the night air on the covered porch or the balcony off the master suite. The laundry is conveniently located upstairs near the bedrooms. Other amenities include an extra large kitchen, fireplaced family room, and three car garage.

First floor — 1,264 sq. ft.
Second floor — 1,152 sq. ft.

English Tudor Utilizes Distinctive Materials

No. 90032

English Tudor homes are among the most favored in America today. The varied roof lines, distinctive materials such as brick and half-timber, and the unique architectural treatment of diamond paned windows, massive chimney, double-entrance oak doors, and half-dormers contribute to the popularity. To the left of the foyer is the one-half story beamed ceiling living room that features a balcony library at the end of the room with its dramatic, spiral wrought iron stair. The main circular stairs lead to the four bedrooms on the second floor. The master bedroom suite is on the right, and includes a dressing area with two room-size closets, a private dressing lounge, and a luxury bath with Roman whirlpool tub.

First floor — 2,120 sq. ft.
Second floor — 1,815 sq. ft.
Basement — 1,855 sq. ft.
Garage — 644 sq. ft.

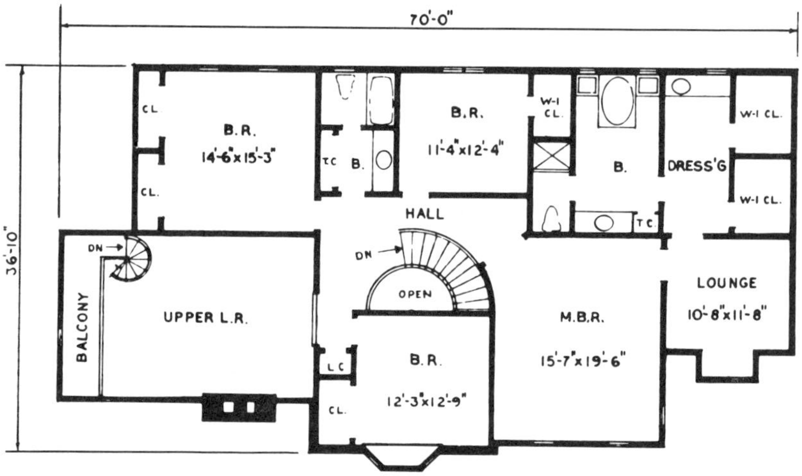

SECOND FLOOR PLAN

No. 90032

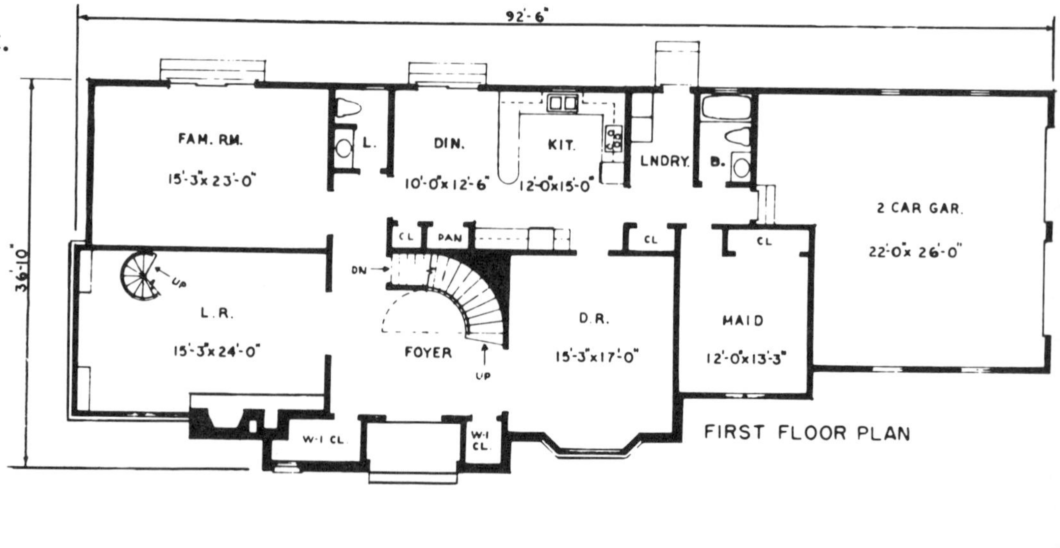

FIRST FLOOR PLAN

Breezeway Connects To Angled Garage

No. 90011

A pleasing treatment of home design is presented by this large, farmtype residence. The garage is turned about 20 degrees, which allows the house to be located at various angles on the property or take advantage of an irregular lot shape. The driveway may sweep across the lawn past the front entrance with this arrangement. The interior is full of pleasant surprises including a sunken living room, private master bath with dressing area and access to porch, glazed hot house for the plant enthusiast, and private den off breezeway.

Living Area — 1,876 sq. ft.

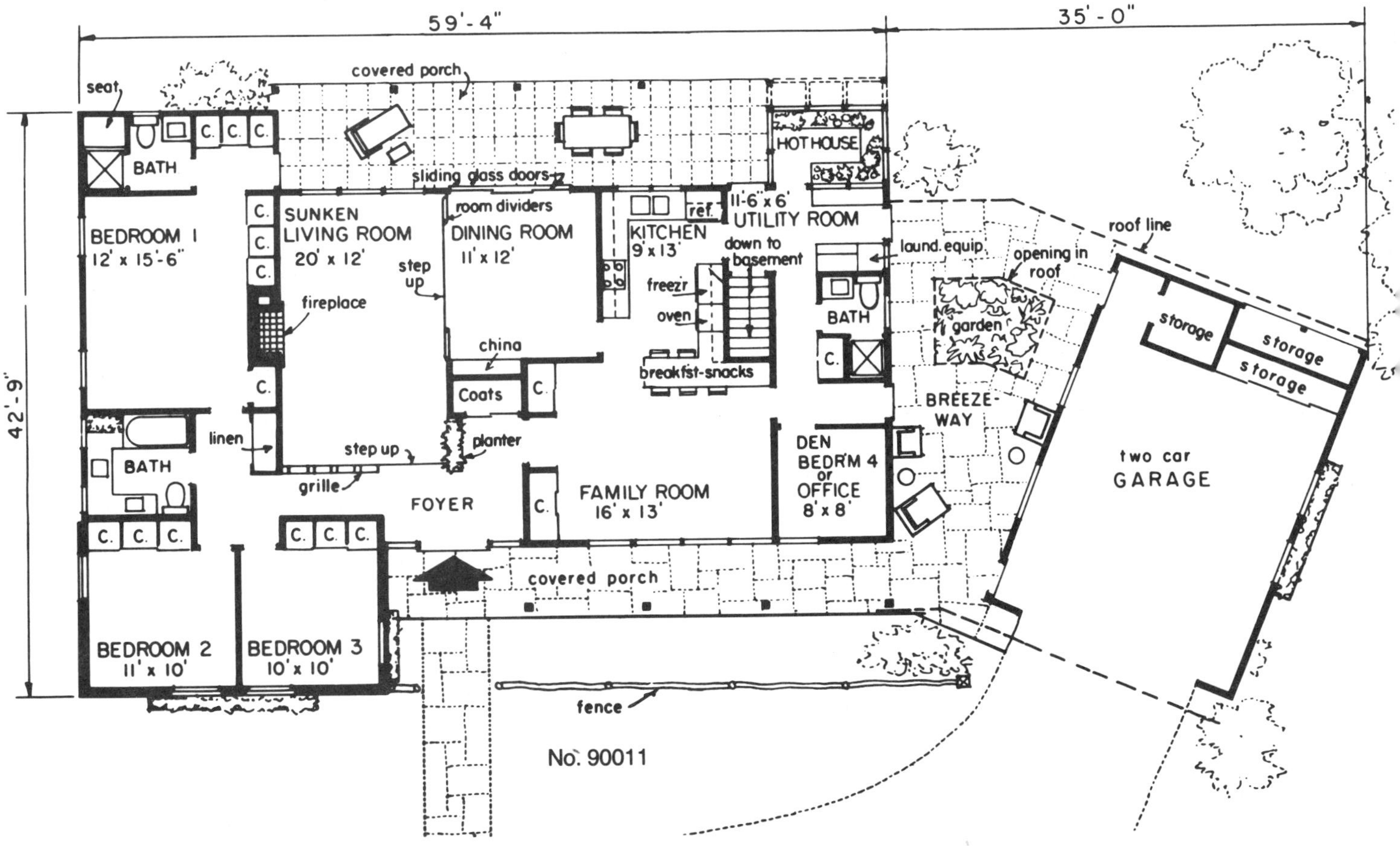

Ideal Plan For Narrow Lot

No. 90342

Close at hand in this plan is a large kitchen area with laundry facilities. You'll find it ideal for a growing family. The first level has an open floor plan that provides needed space. The living-dining room has both flexibility and charm and enjoys a wood-burning fireplace. Through the hallway, a half-bath lies near the stairwell that leads to the second level. On the second floor, three bedrooms share two full baths. Other features include two wooden decks and a two-car garage.

Living Area — 1,418 sq. ft.

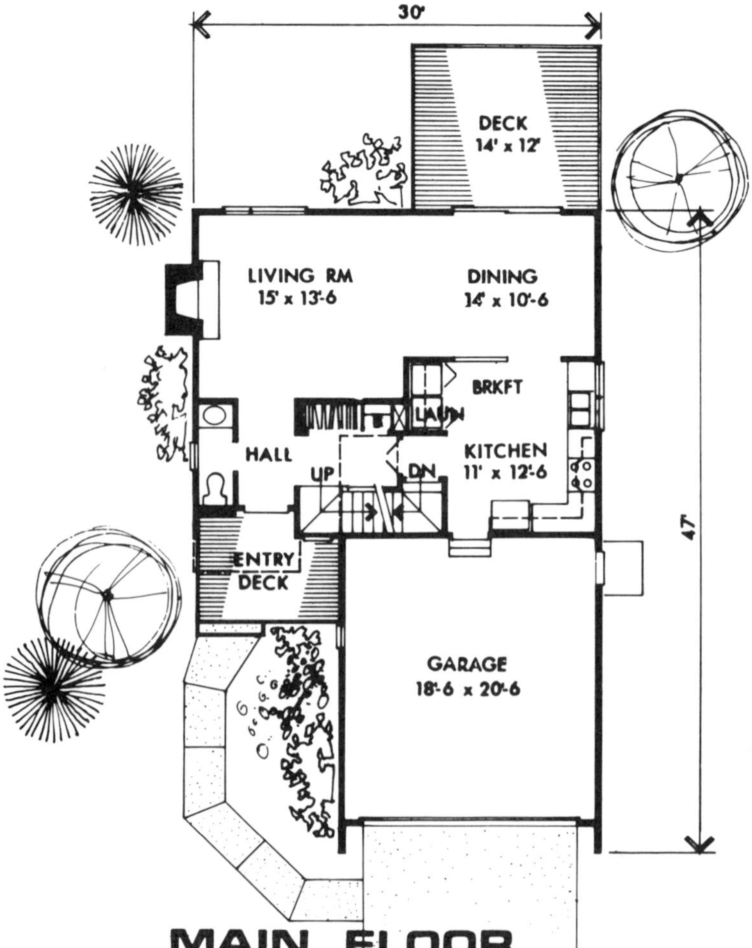

MAIN FLOOR

UPPER FLOOR

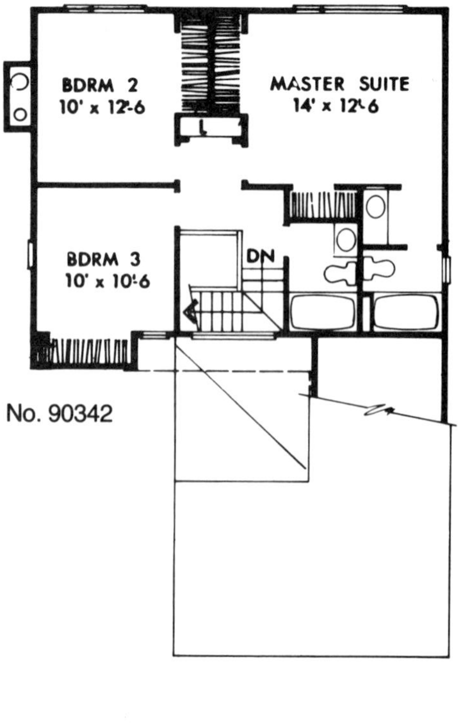

No. 90342

Private Spa Surrounded by Sunlight

No. 91045

Who said one-level homes had to be boring? Just look at this elegant wood and brick classic. A sweeping view from the spacious entry commands a grand entry to the soaring family, living, and dining rooms. But, the excitement doesn't end there. Notice the efficient island kitchen, centrally located for easy meal service and the sunny eating nook and adjacent family room, warmed by a roaring fire. Walk down the hall to the bedroom wing, where the third bedroom can double as a den if you prefer. Then, take in the luxurious atmosphere of the vaulted master suite, tucked away behind double doors at the rear of the house.

First floor — 1,919 sq. ft.

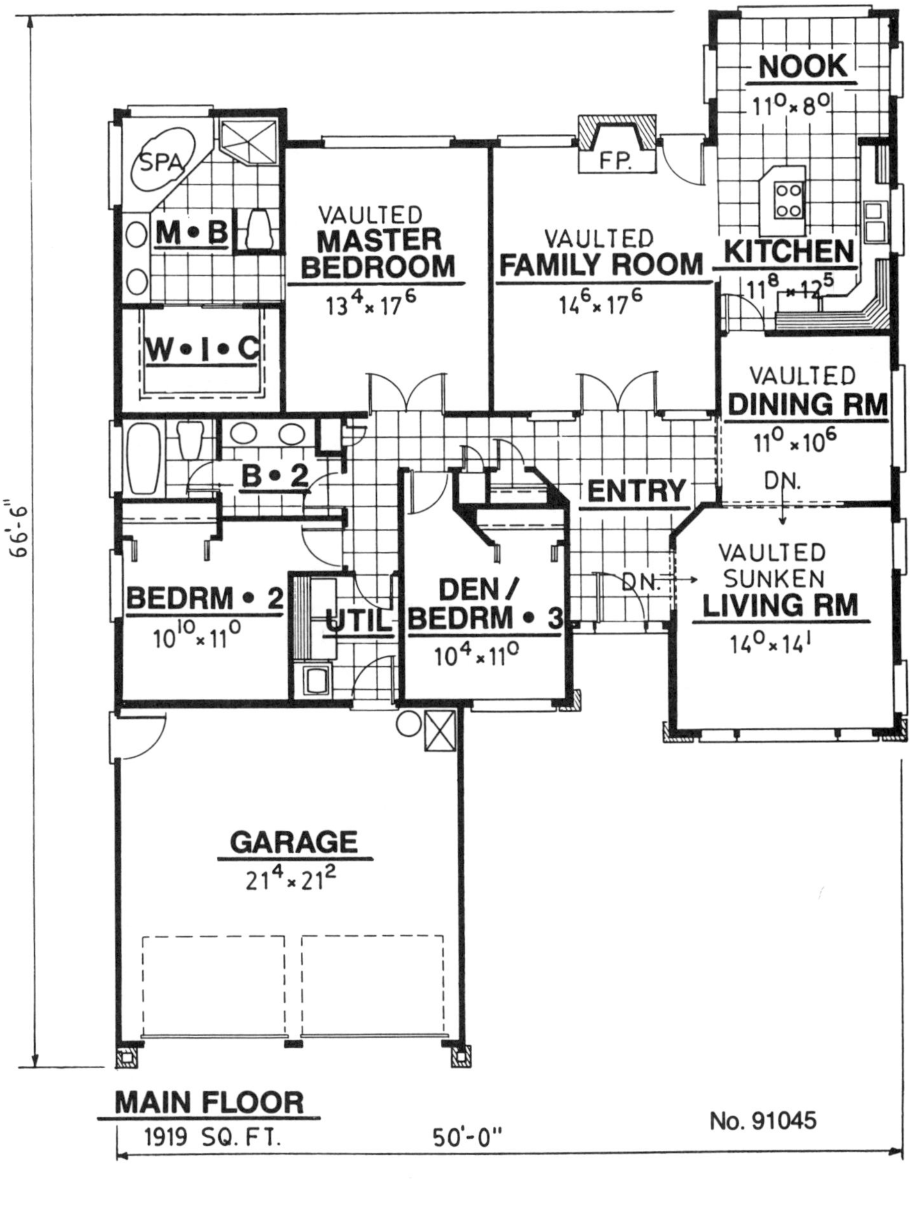

Country Living in a Doll House

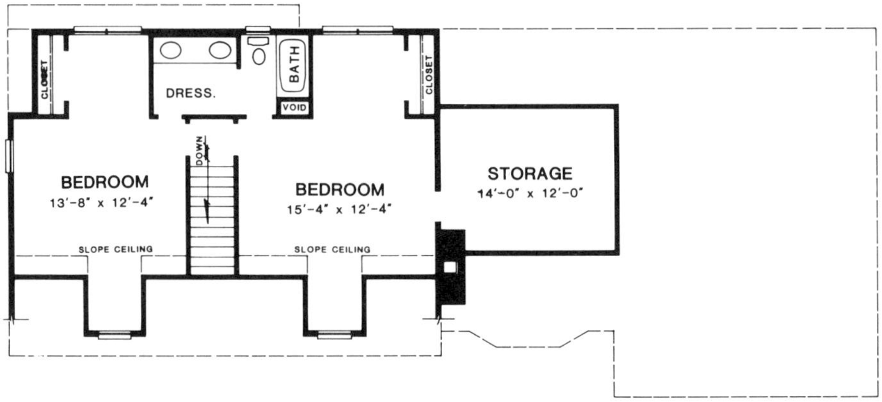

No. 90410

Front porch, dormers, shutters and a bay window on the exterior of this rustic design are complemented by an informal interior. The main floor is divided into three sections. The eat- in country kitchen with island counter and bay window and a large utility room which can be entered from either the kitchen or garage. The second section is the great room with fireplace, an informal dining nook and double doors opening on to the rear deck or screened-in porch. The master suite features a walk-in closet and compartmentalized bath. The second floor consists of full bath and two bedrooms and a large storage room.

First floor — 1,277 sq. ft.
Second floor — 720 sq. ft.

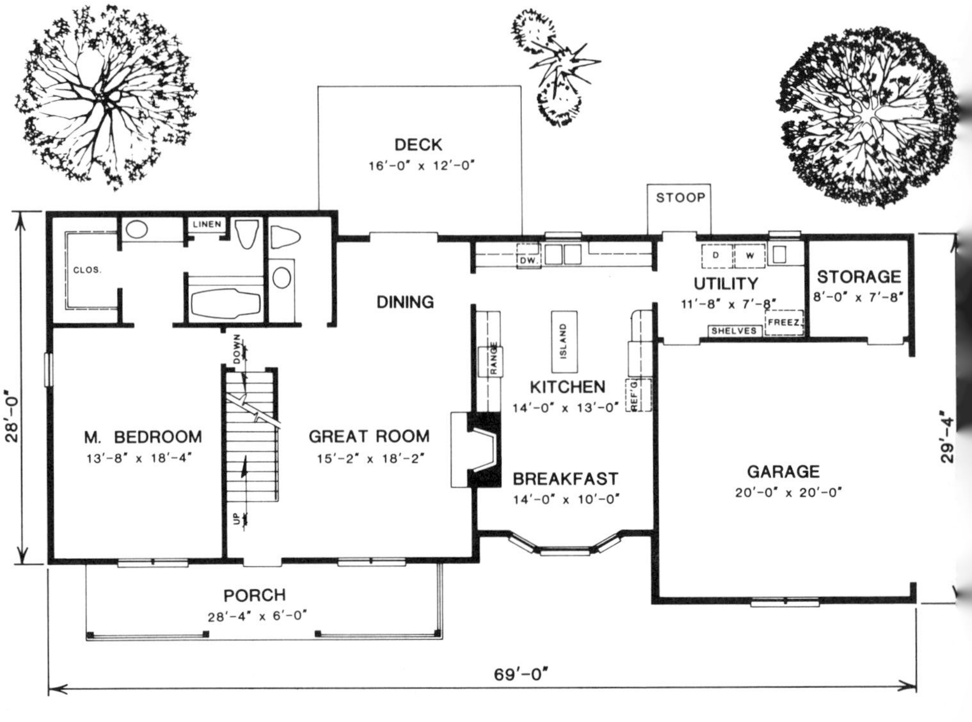

Take Advantage of a Spectacular View

No. 90903

This three-bedroom, contemporary Victorian home is geared towards comfortable family living. A spacious central foyer on the ground floor leads conveniently to any area of the home. The main floor plan incorporates a number of bay windowed areas, offering an exciting challenge to the interior decorator. And, the possibilities for future development on the ground floor are endless.

Main floor — 1,132 sq. ft.
Basement — 992 sq. ft.
Garage — 410 sq. ft.
Width — 42 ft.
Depth — 40 ft.(plus 8 ft. sundeck)

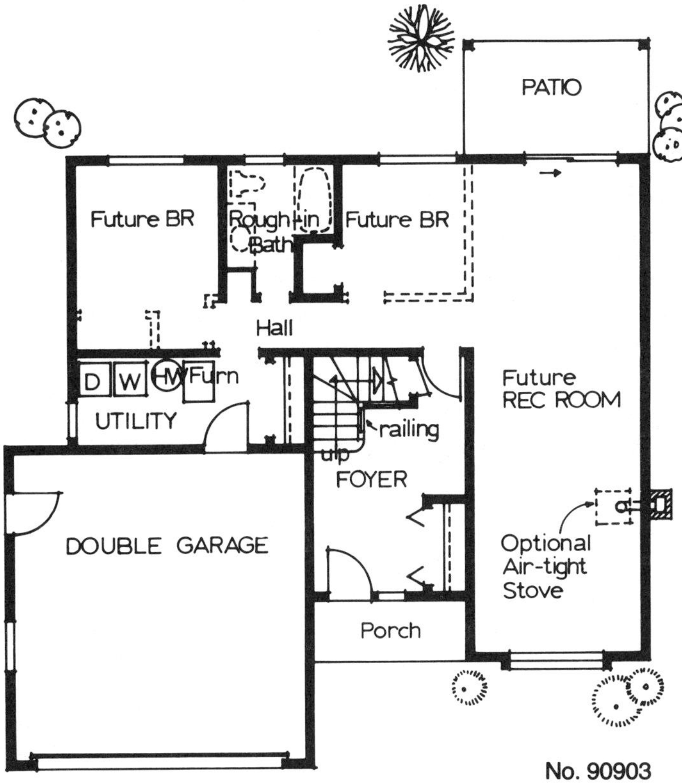

No. 90903

LOWER FLOOR

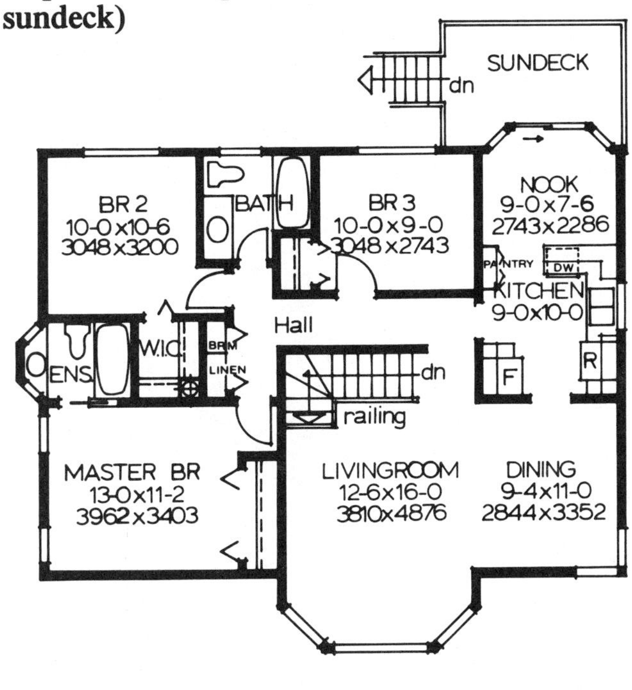

Southern Colonial with Modern Interior

No. 90411

Four columns, large windows, front widow's walk and a formal entry enhance this Southern Colonial Home. The first floor master bedroom suite features a large bath with garden tub, separate shower, twin vanities and walk-in closet. Also, the first level consists of separate living and dining rooms, family room, breakfast area, kitchen and utility room. The second floor, has four bedrooms each connected to a full bath.

First floor — 1,775 sq. ft.
Second floor — 1,148 sq. ft.

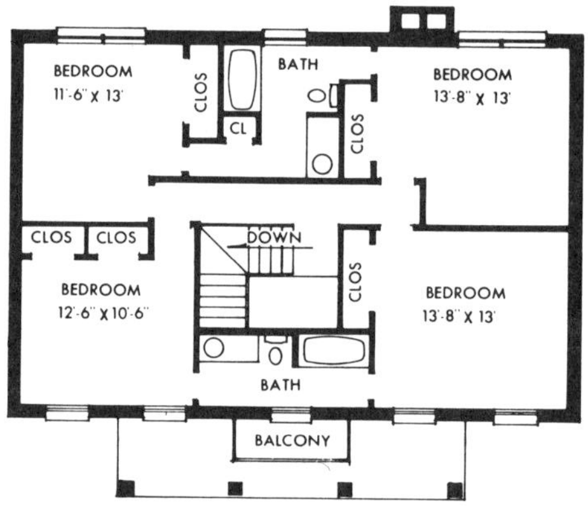

SECOND FLOOR

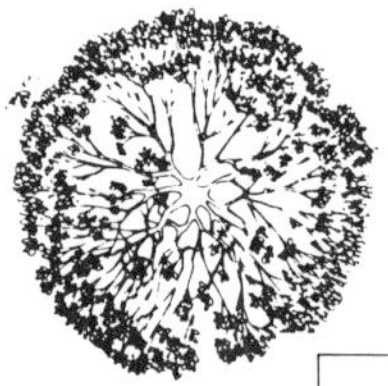

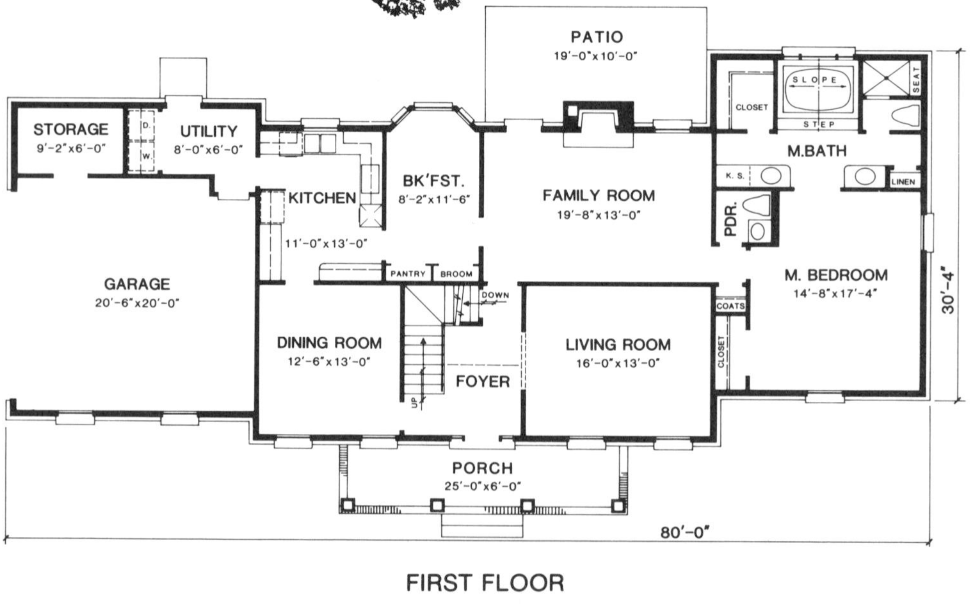

FIRST FLOOR

Bay Windows Adorn Four Bedroom Home

No. 90707

The two porches on this updated Victorian will double the breezes you'll enjoy on a hot summer night. Entering the foyer, you'll find the family room with wet bar, bay window, and fireplace. A matching bay window brightens the kitchen/breakfast room. The adjoining formal dining room, which opens to a cozy living room, has sliding glass doors to a covered deck. Three bedrooms upstairs are bathed in sunshine. And, in the master suite, a third bay window provides a comfortable sitting nook.

First floor — 1,188 sq. ft.
Second floor — 1,120 sq. ft.

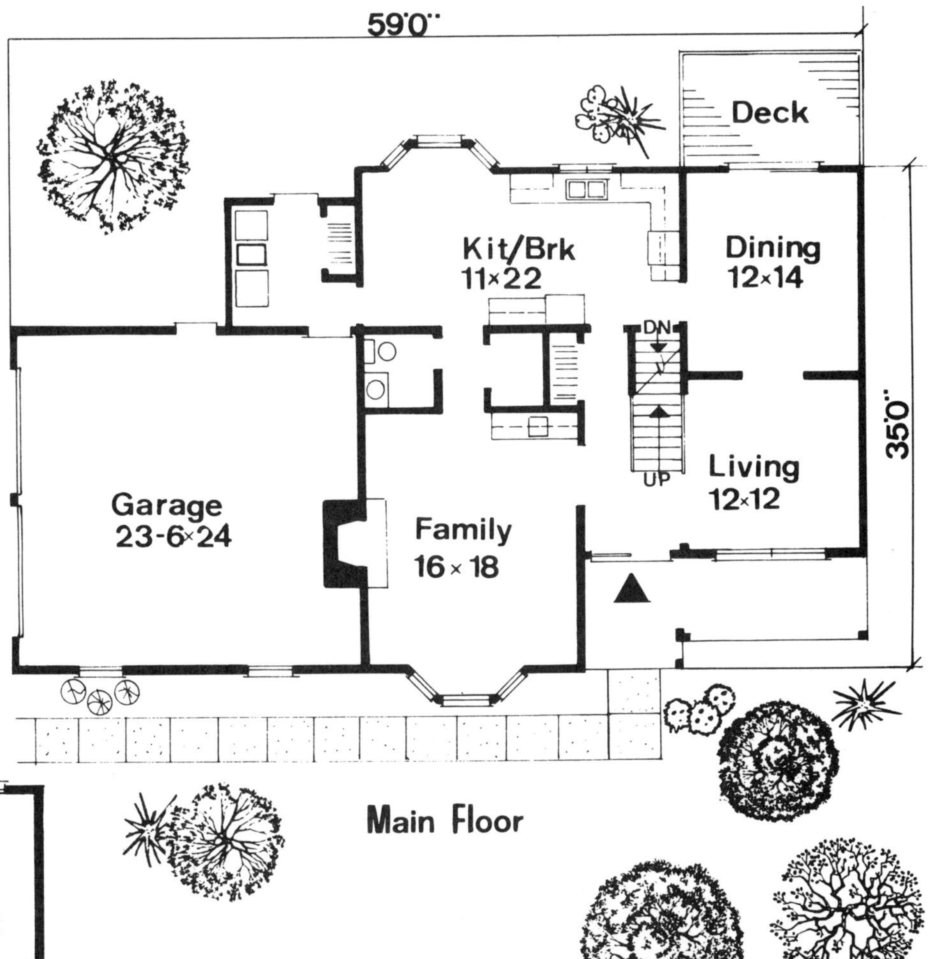

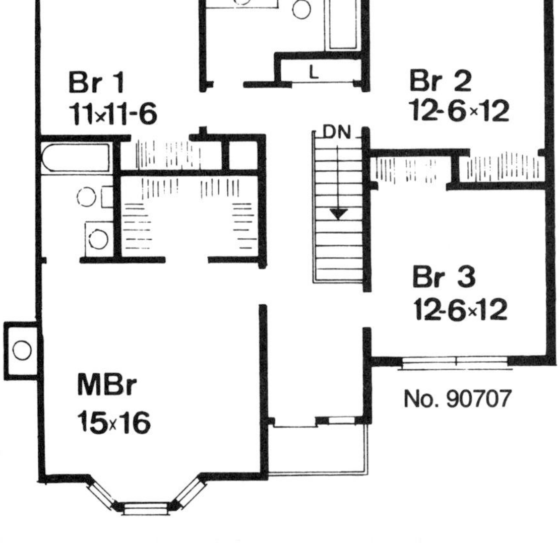

No Wasted Space

No. 90412

The open foor plan of this modified A-Frame design virtually eliminated wasted hall space. The centrally located great room features a cathedral ceiling with exposed wood beams and large areas of fixed glass on both front and rear. Living and dining areas are visually separated by a massive stone fireplace. The isolated master suite features a walk-in closet and sliding glass doors opening onto the front deck. A walk-thru utility room provides easy access from the carport and outside storage areas to the compact kitchen. On the opposite side of the great room are two additional bedrooms and a second full bath. A full length deck and vertical wood siding with stone accents on the corners provide a rustic yet contemporary exterior. Specify crawlspace, basement or slab foundation when ordering.

Area — 1,454 sq. ft.

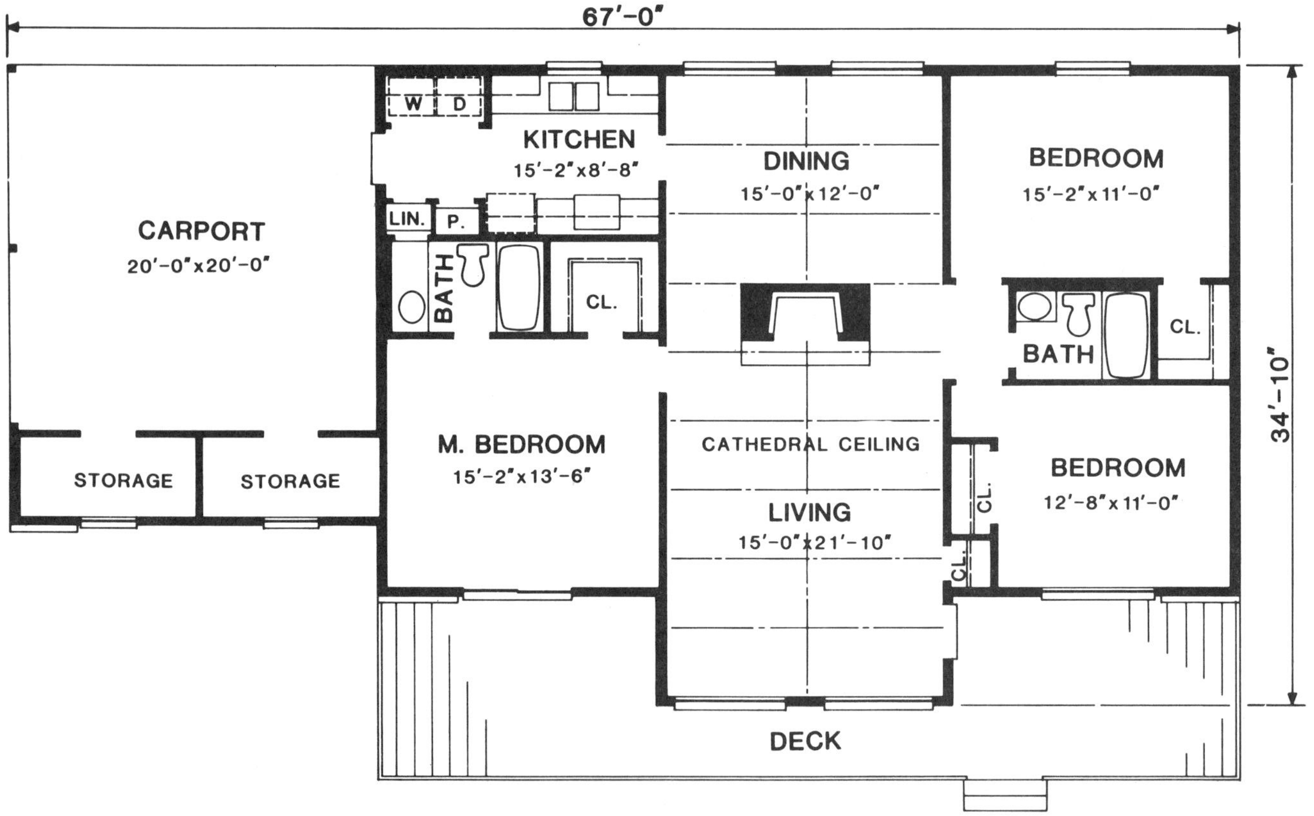

Graceful Arches Distinguish Facade

No. 90832

Hang the family portraits in the second floor gallery of this beautiful traditional home. And, while you're upstairs, look at the three roomy bedrooms and two full baths. You'll love the sunny sunken living room just off the main entry downstairs. Combined with the formal dining room, this is a great spot for entertaining. There's a wonderful bayed dining nook right off the island kitchen for family meals. Steps away, the cozy family room features a fieldstone fireplace and sliding glass doors that lead to the back yard.

First floor — 1,223 sq. ft.
Second floor — 899 sq. ft.
Basement — 1,160 sq. ft.

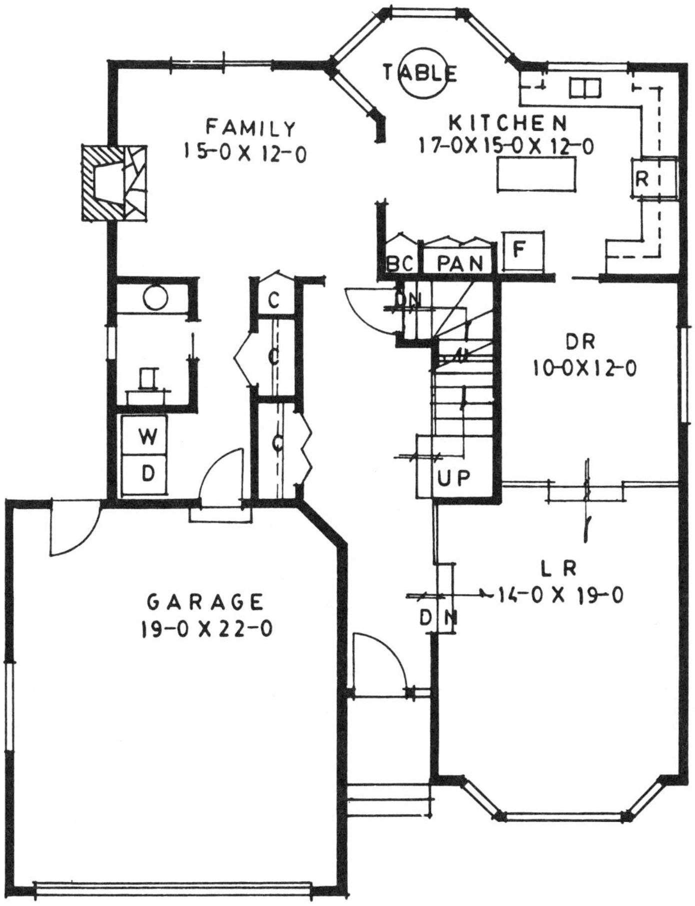

GROUND FLOOR

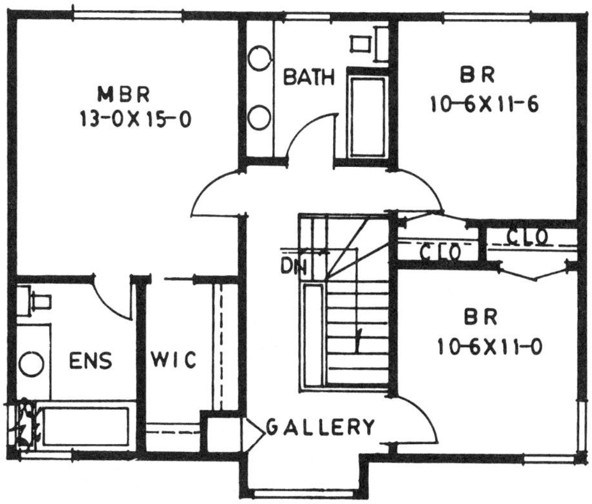

SECOND FLOOR

No. 90832

FRONT ELEVATION

Passive Solar With Sun Room

No. 90417

This ranch design features large areas of glass in the master suite and kitchen, and a sun room accessible from both the family room and breakfast room. A recessed entry and a limited amount of glass on the north wall help keep the warm air in during the winter, and over-heating during the summer months is prevented by eliminating glass from the east and west walls. The master suite features a walk-in closet and a compartmentalized bath with linen closet, a second walk-in closet and a dressing area with double vanity. One of the two front bedrooms has a double closet and direct access to a second full bath and the other has a walk-in-closet. A centrally located utility closet and two hall closets complete the left wing. Separating the sunken living room and the foyer area is a massive stone fireplace. A formal dining room can be entered from either the living room or the kitchen. The U-shaped kitchen has a bar counter open to the breakfast area and a mud room with coat closet and access to the garage, which acts as a buffer from northwestern winter winds.

Area — 1,859 sq. ft.

FLOOR PLAN

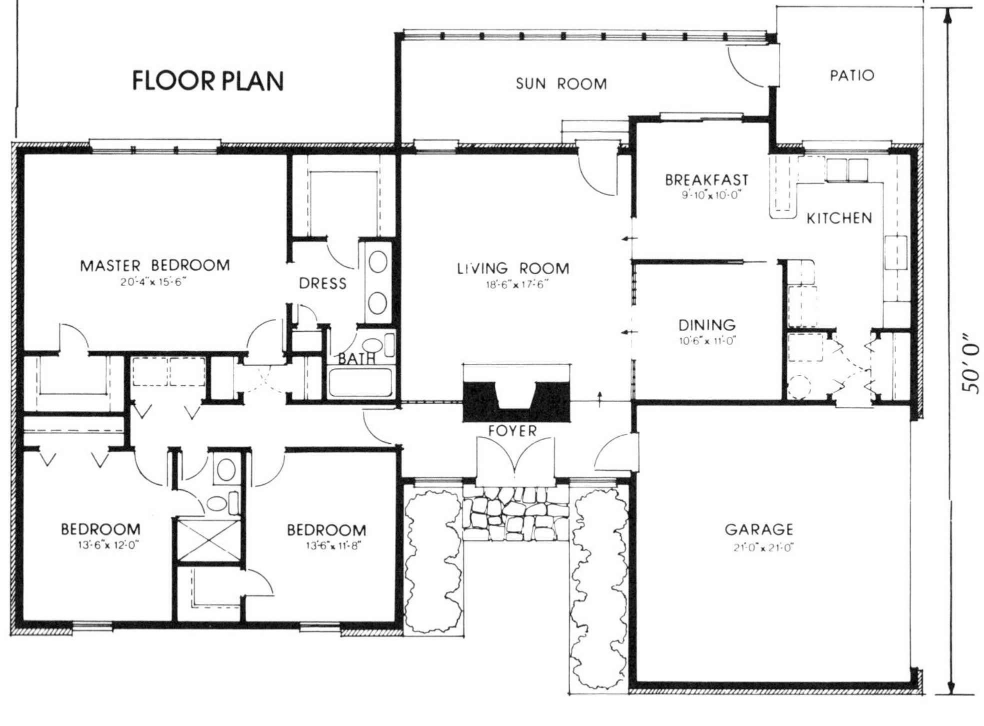

SOUTH ELEVATION

Traditional Design Enhanced by Open Loft

No. 90305

The sunken living room with its vaulted ceiling and fireplace provides a focal point for this lovely home. The master bedroom is on the main level, while two other bedrooms are situated on the upper level. The master bedroom has a separate vanity area just off the full-sized bath. The U-shaped kitchen is arranged for efficiency and convenience with direct access to the dining room, the patio and the garage. The upper level bedrooms with their large closets share a full bath and are separated by a loft, which serves to lend a feeling of openness and provide an additional area for relaxation.

Total area — 1,680 sq. ft.

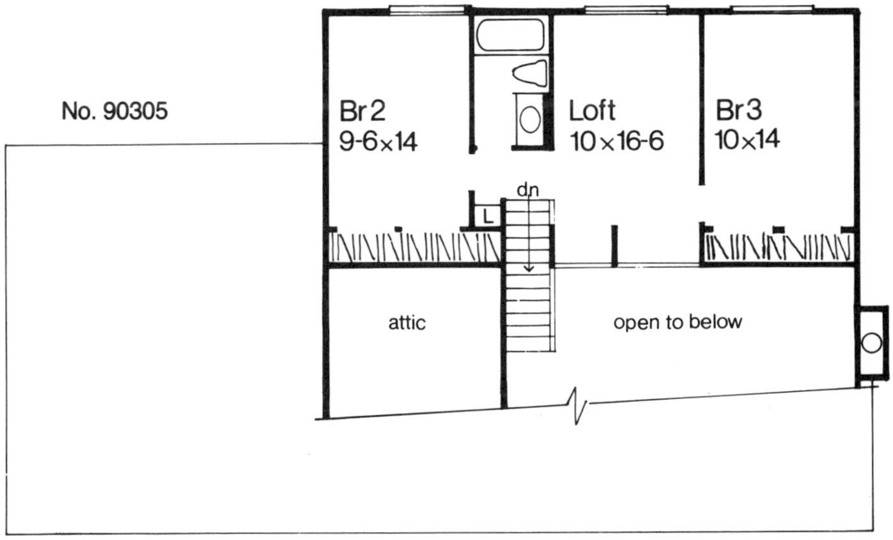

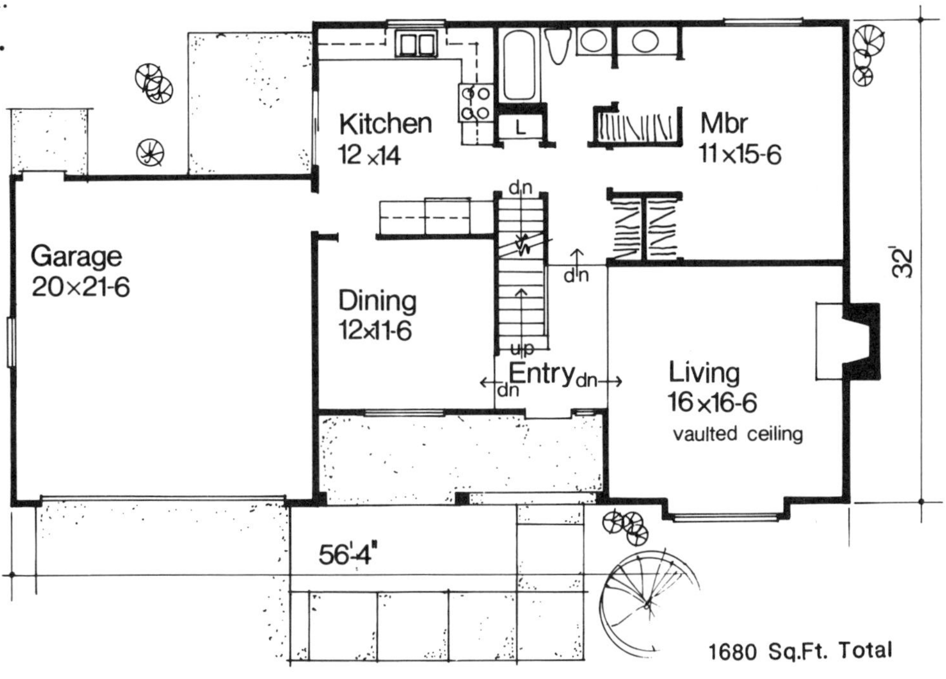

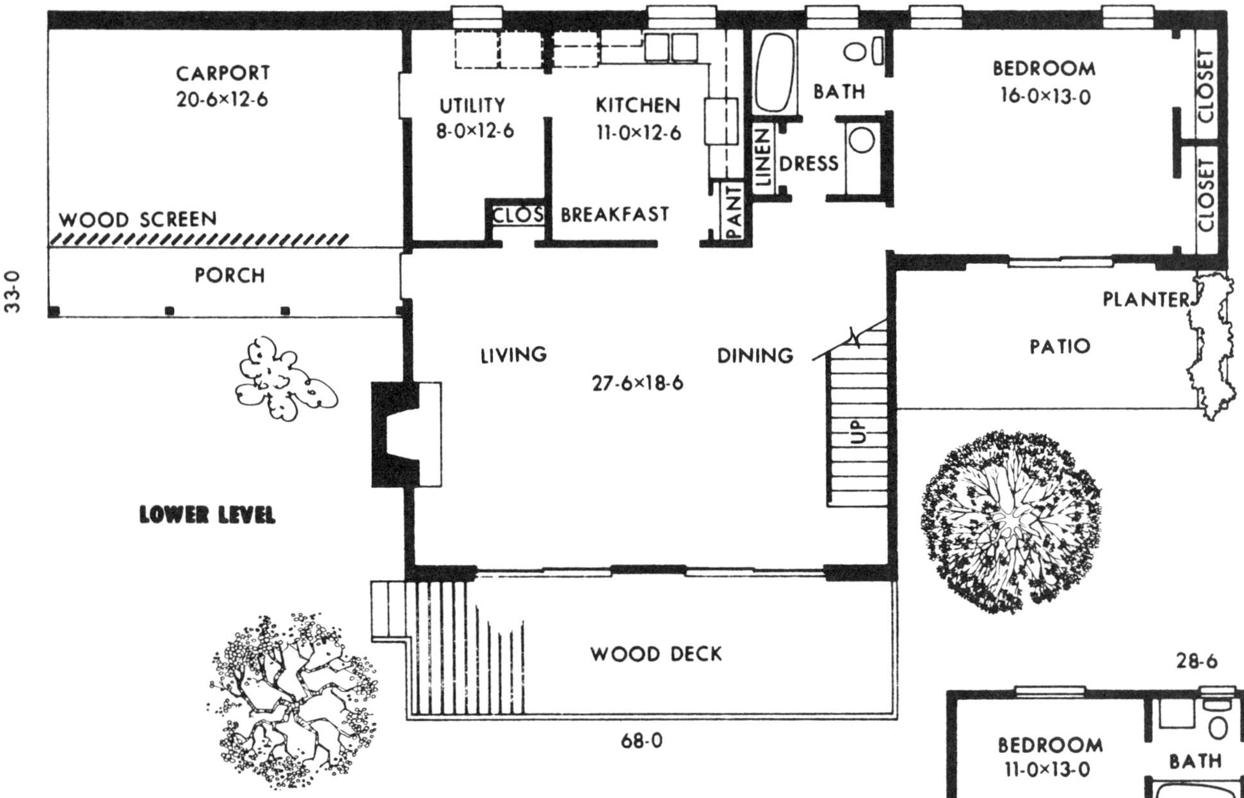

House with a View

No. 90418

Modest in appearance this vacation home offers open living area. The two-level home has two bedrooms and a bath located on the upper level and another bedroom and bath on the lower level. A kitchen and utility room are located off the living-dining area.

First floor — 1,304 sq. ft.
Second floor — 303 sq. ft.

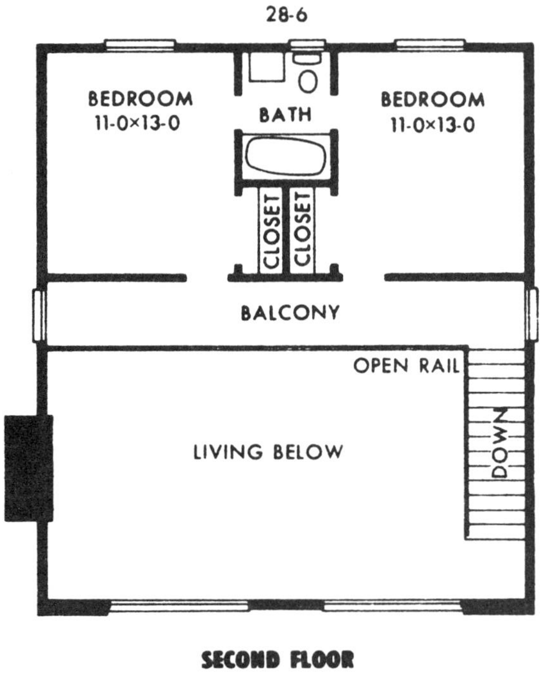

SECOND FLOOR

Expandable French Provincial Features Three to Five Bedrooms

No. 90402

This lovely home features a master suite with a deluxe compartmentalized bath which includes a vaulted ceiling with skylights, garden tub, shower, linen closet and a separate dressing room with double vanity and large walk-in closet. Two additional bedrooms with ample closet space share a second compartmentalized bath. Living and dining are lcoated to the side of the formal foyer. A family room with a formal fireplace and double doors on to a screened-in back porch and a U-shaped kitchen with an island counter open to the breakfast bay allow more casual living. Open rail stairs in the family room provide access to the second floor. The second floor can be either unfinished or finished with one or two bedrooms and a large bath.

First floor — 2,400 sq. ft.
Second floor — 751 sq. ft.

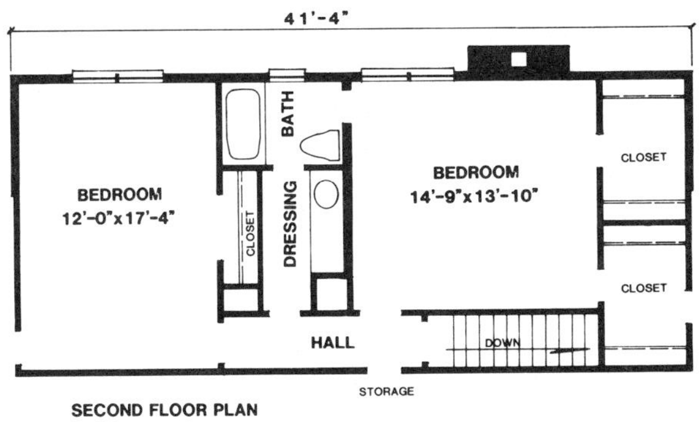

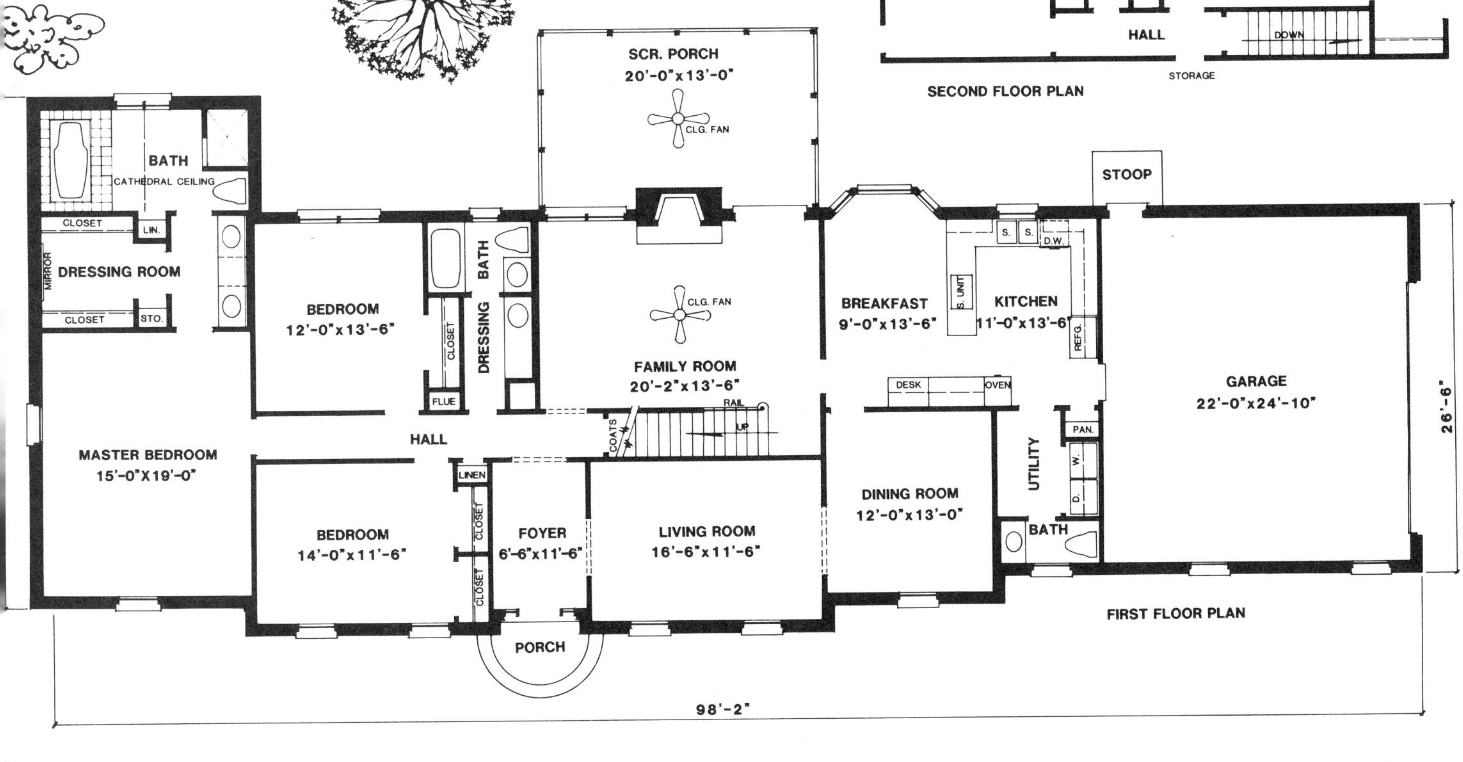

Country Kitchen and Great Room

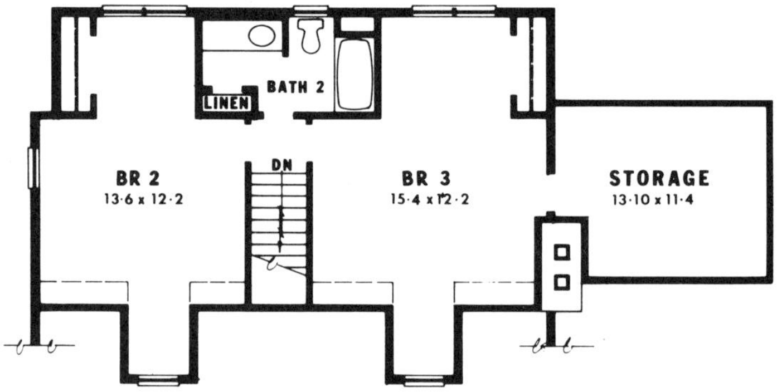

No. 90419

Front porch, dormers, shutters and multi-paned windows on the exterior of this Cape Cod design are complimented by an informal interior. The main floor is divided into three sections. In the first section is an eat-in country kitchen with island counter and bay window and a large utility room which can be entered from either the kitchen or garage. The second section is the great room with inside fireplace, an informal dining nook and double doors opening onto the rear deck. The master suite features a walk-in closet and compartmentalized bath with linen closet. The upper floor consists of a second full bath and two bedrooms with ample closet space and window seats. A large storage area is provided over the garage.

First floor — 1,318 sq. ft.
Second floor — 718 sq. ft.
Basement — 1,221 sq. ft.
Garage — 436 sq. ft.

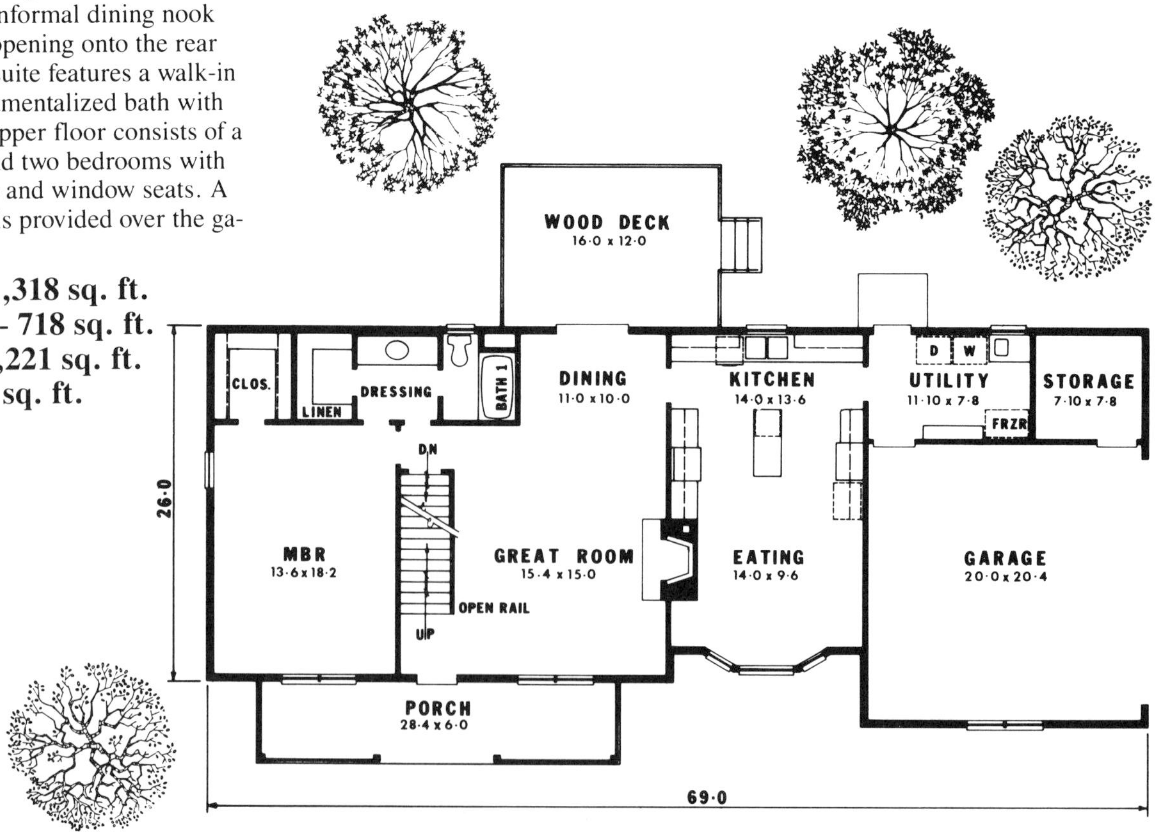

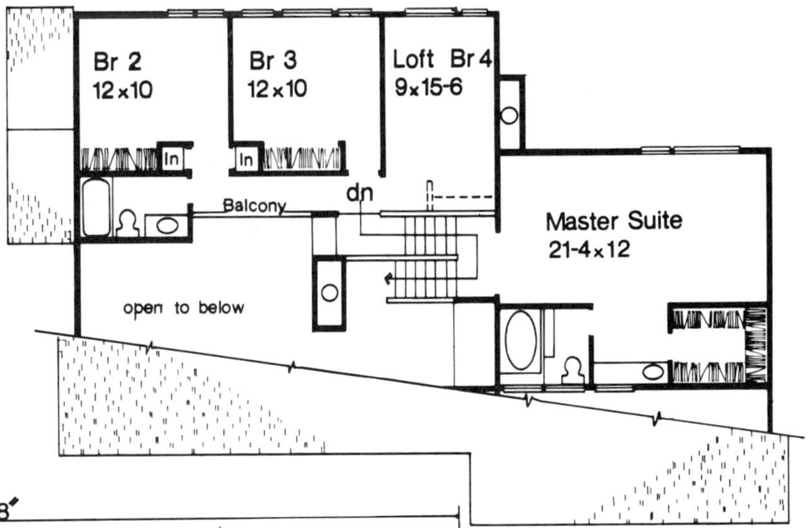

Wet Bar Located in Family Room

No. 90364

A suburban home exudes a friendly warmth with neither stuffiness nor the avant-garde. Massive roof provides a welcoming envelopment for the high-ceilinged living room with bedrooms off a balcony. The master suite over the garage has a level of its own; the kitchen blends with the family room.

Area — 2,110 sq. ft.

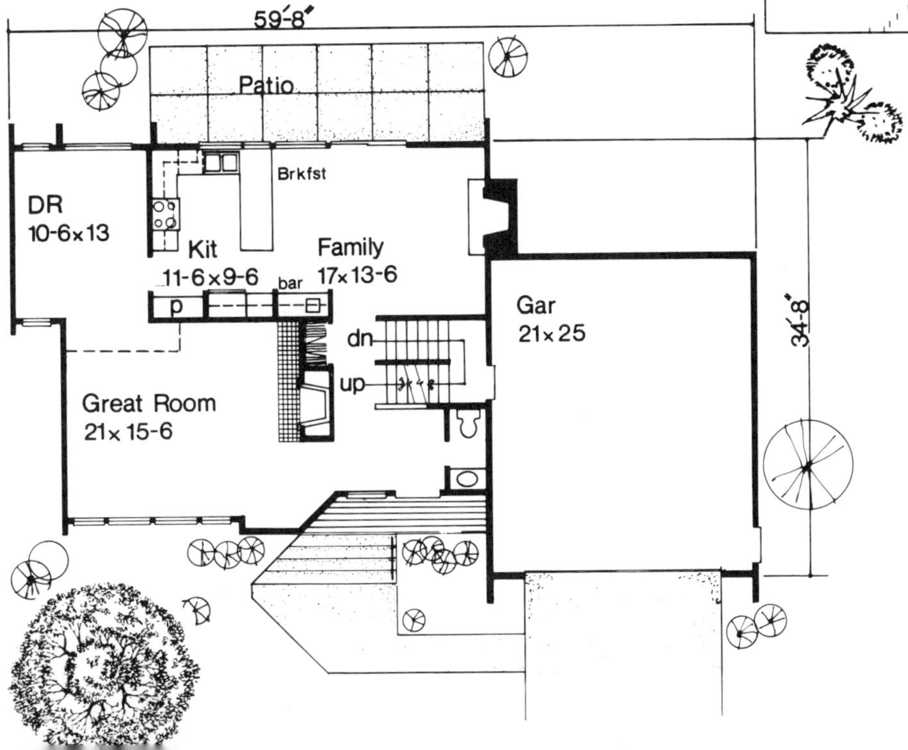

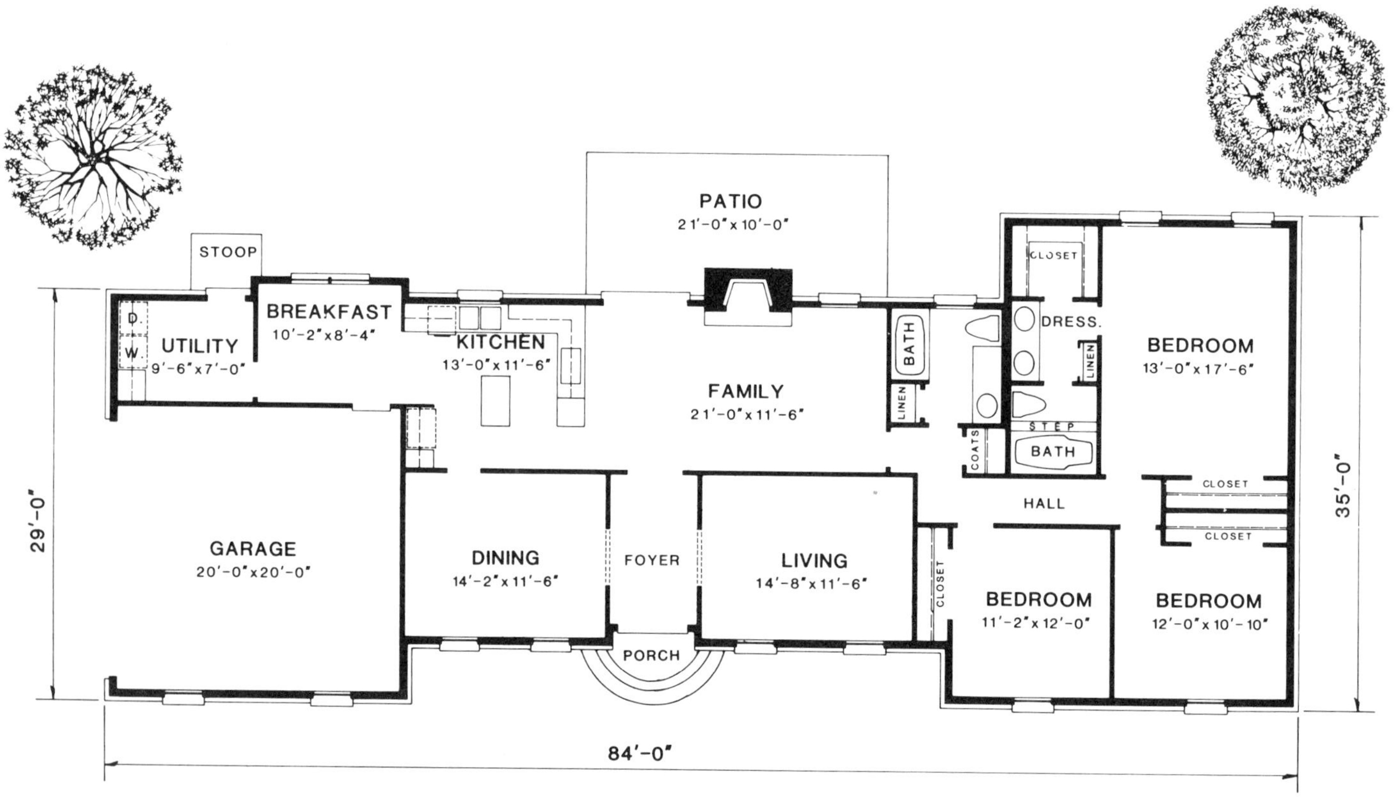

Ideal for Formal Entertaining

No. 90421

This lovely French Provincial design features a formal foyer flanked by the living room on one side and the dining room on the other. A family room with a raised-hearth fireplace and double doors to the patio, and the L-shaped island kitchen with breakfast bay and open counter to the family room allow for more casual living. Adjacent to the breakfast bay is a utility room with outside entrance. The master suite includes one double closet and a compartmentalized bath with walk in closet, step-up garden tub, double vanity and linen closet. Two front bedrooms and a second full bath with linen closet complete the design. A recessed entry and circular porch add to the formal exterior.

Area — 1,940 sq. ft.

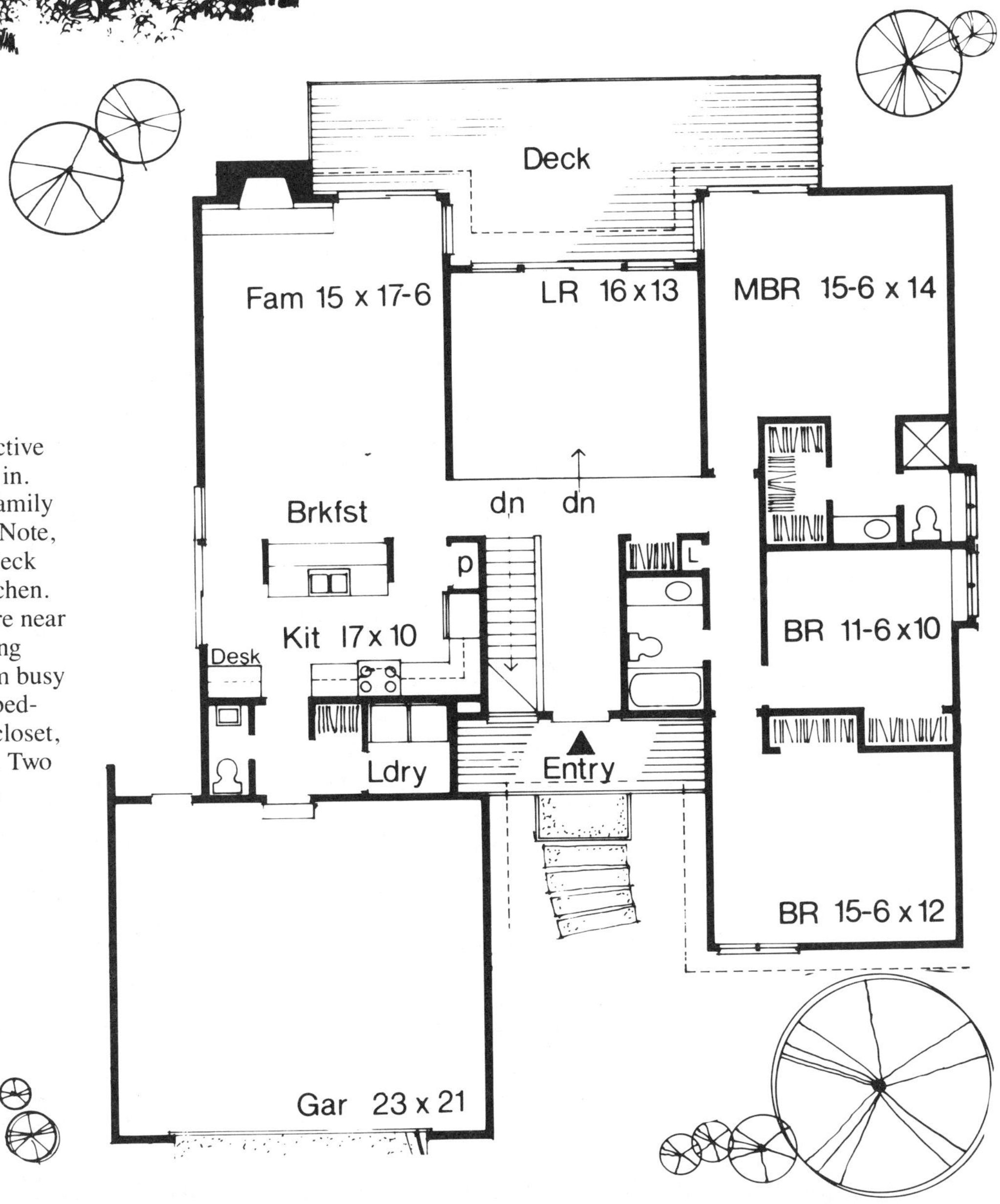

Attractive Ranch Design

No. 90347

Appealing inside and out, this attractive all-on-one-floor home is fun to live in. The vaulted ceiling in the paneled family room lends a lot of spatial volume. Note, too, the well-placed fireplace, the deck view, the pass-through from the kitchen. Lavatory, laundry and coat closet are near the entry to the garage. Sunken living room is an island of quiet away from busy family room hustle bustle. Master bedroom suite has a generous walk-in closet, a divided lavatory and shower bath. Two other bedrooms share the hall bath. Home has a basement.

First floor — 1,826 sq. ft.

Deluxe Master Suite

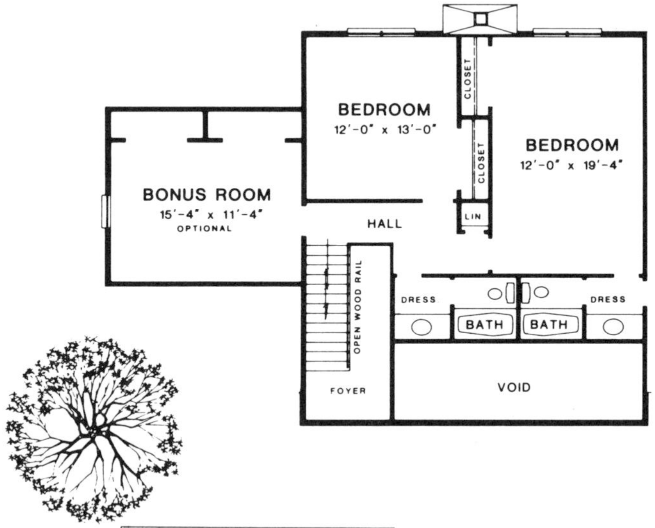

No. 90422

Covered porch, stone and painted siding enhance a very livable floor plan. Main level consist of a separate living room, dining room, family room, kitchen, breakfast nook, utility room and master bedroom suite. Upper level consist of three bedrooms and two full baths. Bonus features are three and one-half baths, open stairs in foyer wet bar and attic storage.

First floor — 1,947 sq. ft.
Second floor — 705 sq. ft.
Bonus room — 203 sq. ft.

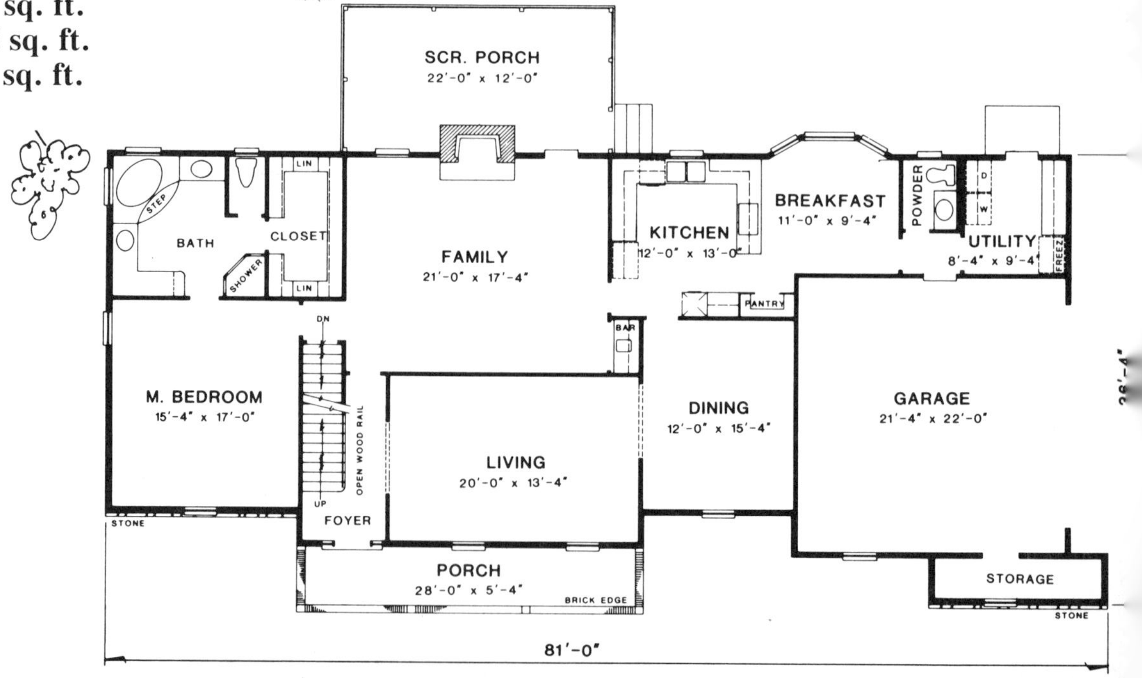

Compact Contemporary With Clerestory

No. 90403

This contemporary design features a large family room with a stone fireplace, double doors to the rear patio, dining area, open stairwell to the full basement and a vaulted ceiling with exposed wood beams and triple clerestory windows. The master suite includes two walk-in closets and a private bath. Both front bedrooms have a walk-in closet and share a second full bath. The eat-in kitchen includes access from the dining area as well as the front opening garage. Additional features include a coat closet off the foyer, vertical wood siding with stone, and a recessed entry with a front porch. Specify basement or crawlspace foundation when ordering.

Area — 1,457 sq. ft.

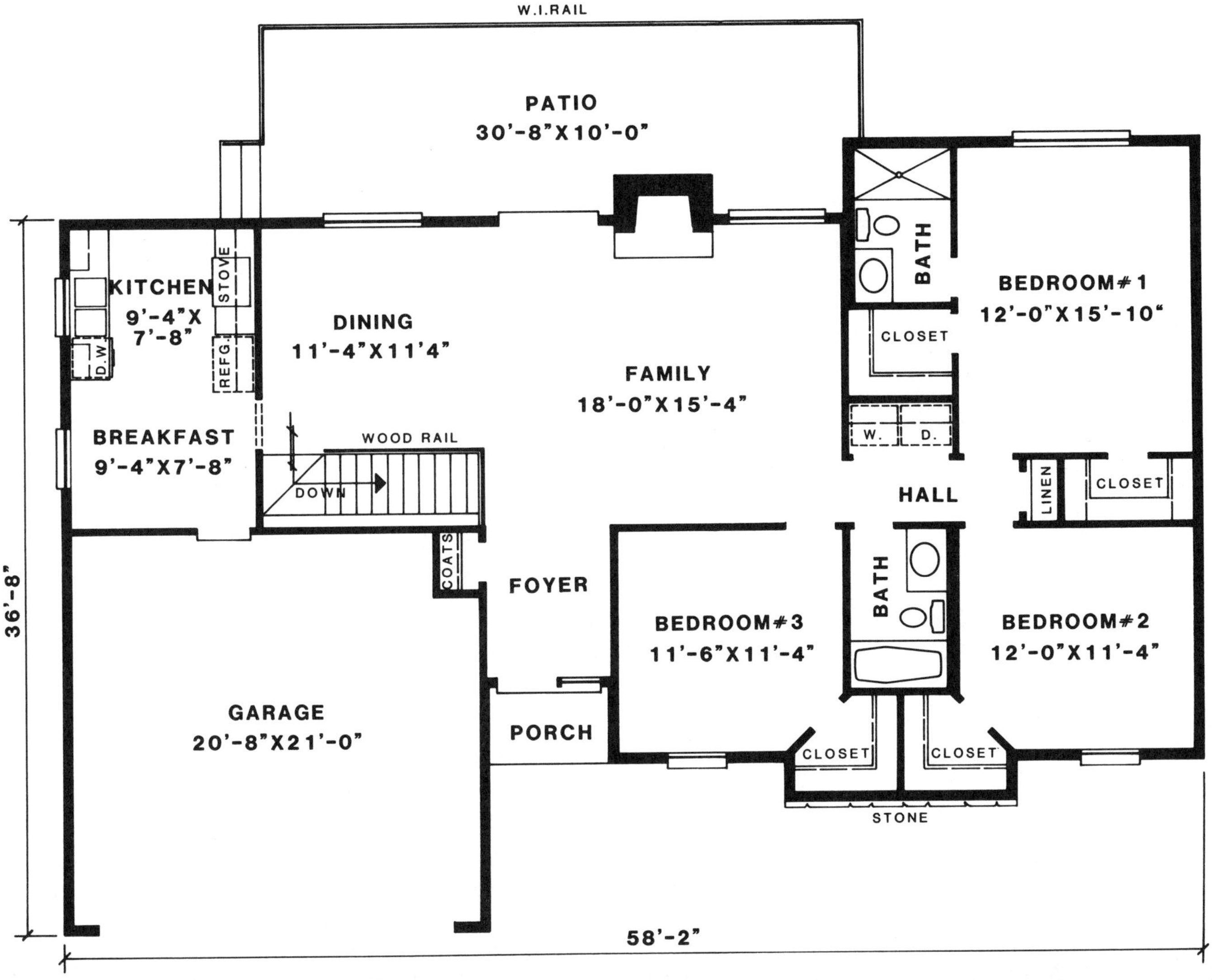

Rustic Home for Relaxed Living

No. 90423

A screened-in breezeway provides a cool place to dine out on warm summer days and nights and the rustic front porch is ideal for relaxed rocking or a swing. A great room to the left of the entry has a fireplace and connects the dining area to the country kitchen. The large master suite contains separate shower, garden tub, vanities and walk-in closets.

Area — 1,773 sq. ft.

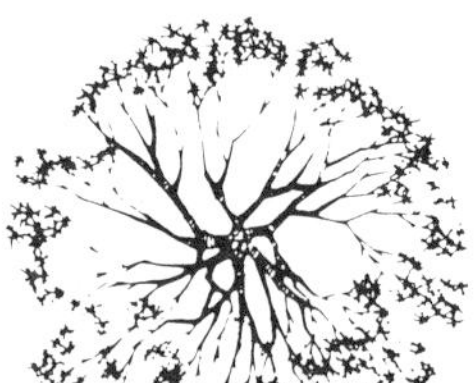

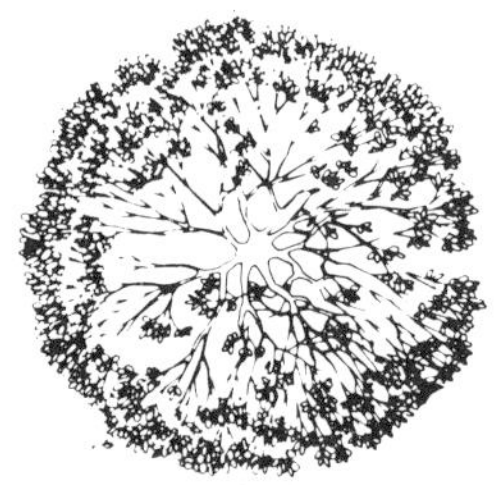

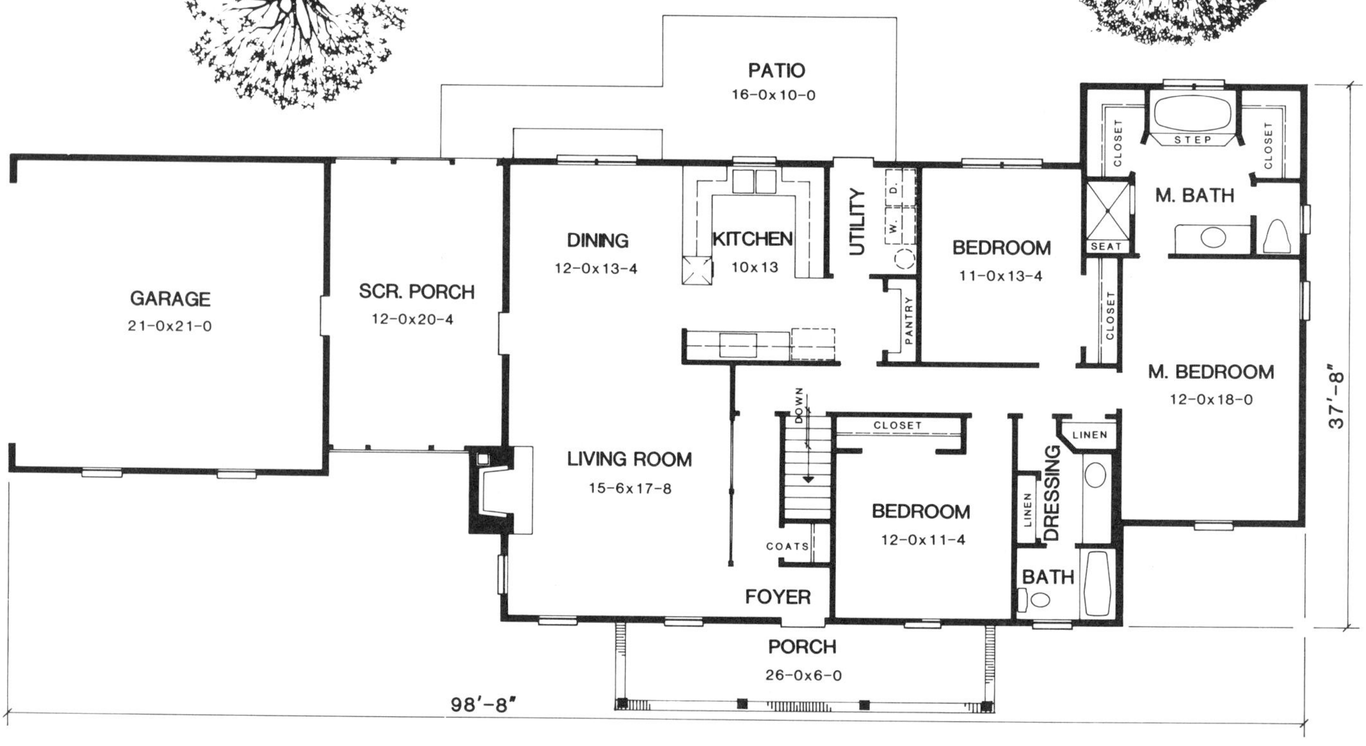

Place This House For Solar Gain

No. 90620

This modest ranch with generous rooms and passive solar features provides comfortable living for the family on a budget. The soaring, skylit central foyer provides access to every room. Straight ahead, the living room, dining room, and greenhouse form a bright, airy arrangement of glass and open space. The adjacent kitchen conveniently opens to a spacious, bay-windowed dinette. A separate wing contains three bedrooms and two baths, including an ample master suite.

Total living area — 1,405 sq. ft.
Basement — 1,415 sq. ft.

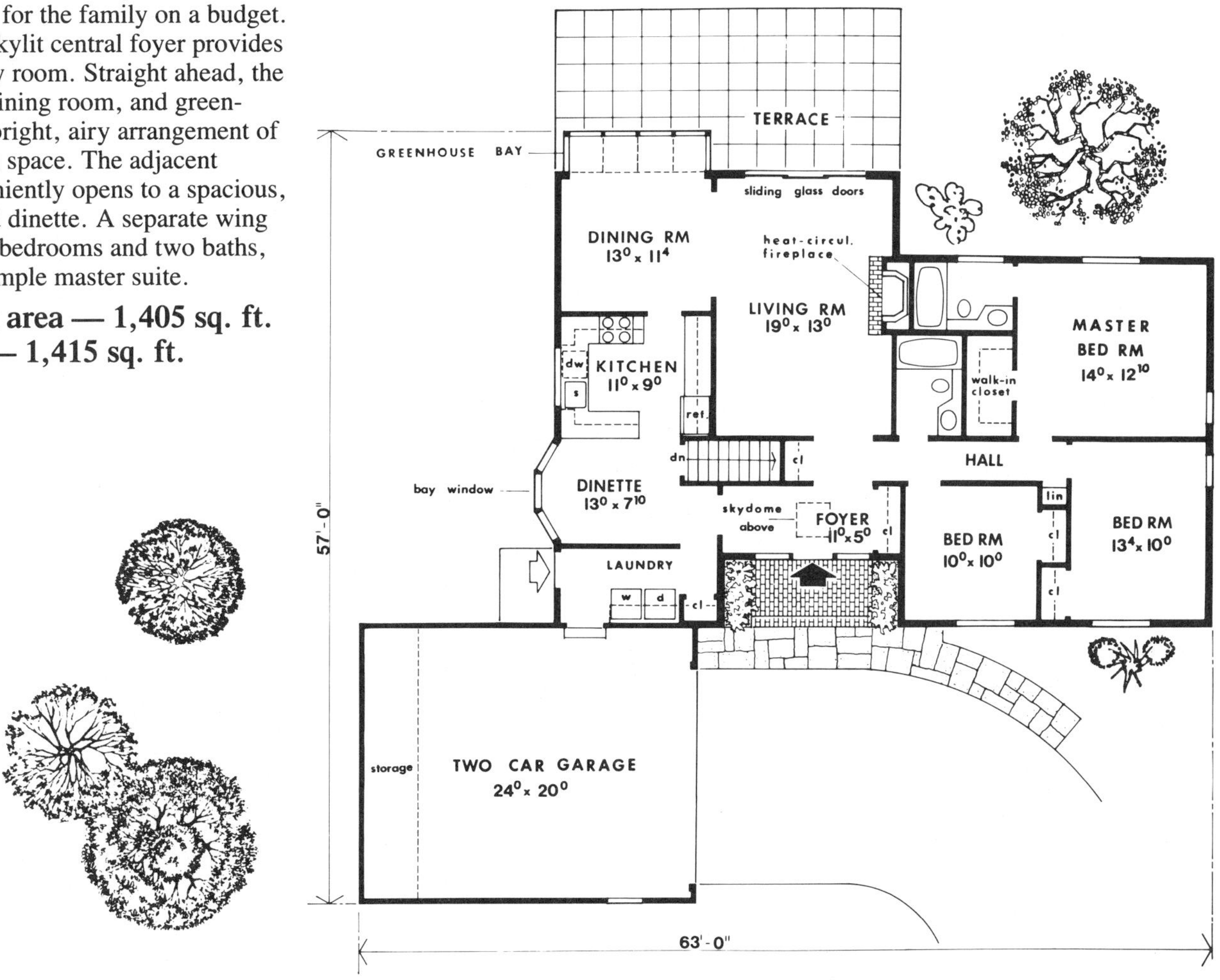

No. 90620

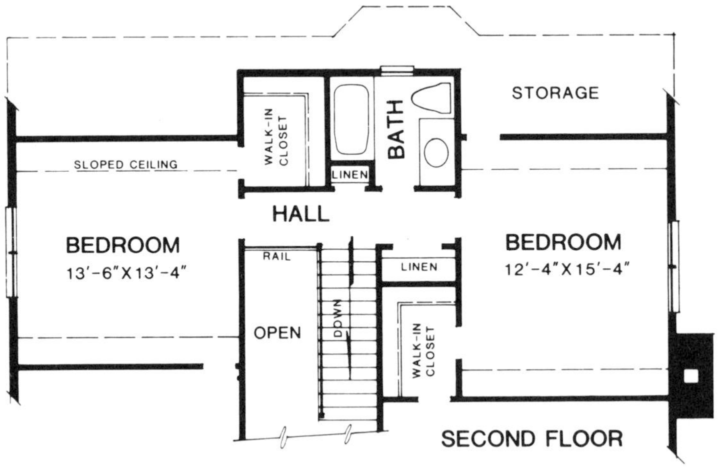

Basement with Drive-Under Garage

No. 90401

This rustic design includes a two-car garage as part of its full basement. All or part of the basement can be used to supplement the main living area. The master suite features a large walk-in closet and a double vanity in the master bath. An L-shaped kitchen with dining bay, a living room with raised-hearth fireplace and a centrally located utility room complete the main floor. The open two-story foyer leads to the upper floor consisting of two bedrooms with walk-in closets and a second full bath with two linen closets. Front porch, multi-paned windows, shutters and horizontal wood siding combine for a rustic exterior. Basement foundation only.

First floor — 1,100 sq. ft.
Second floor — 660 sq. ft.

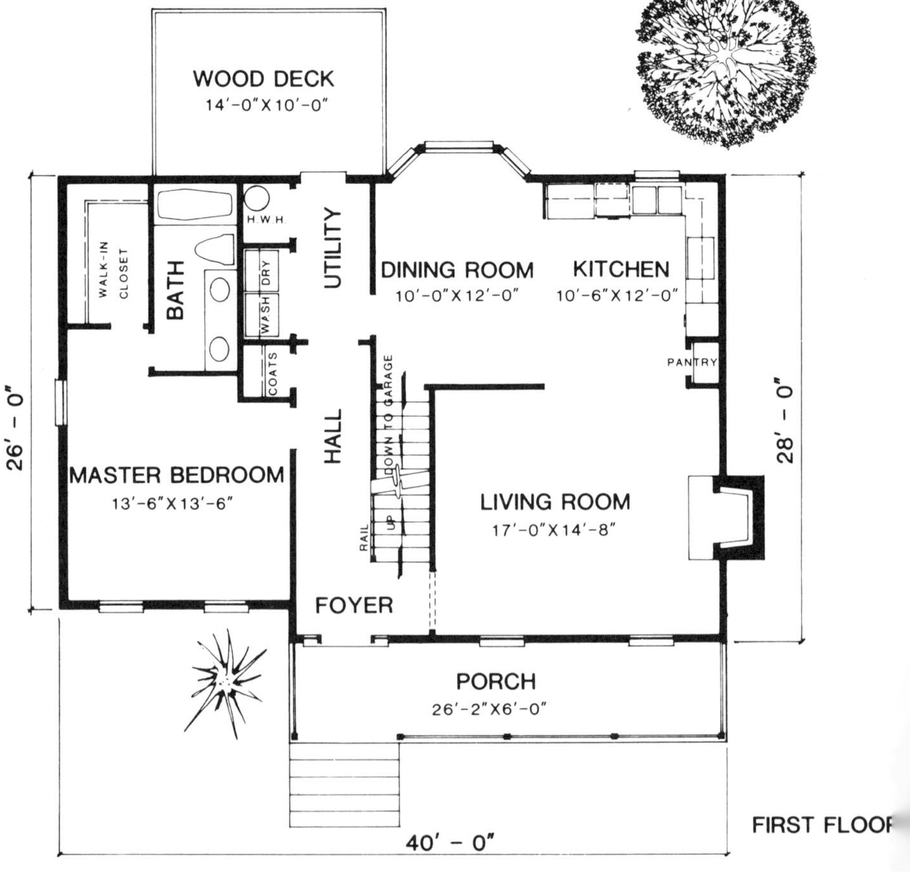

Deluxe Master Bath Includes Vaulted Ceiling and Garden Tub

No. 90404

This lovely French Provincial design features a master suite with a deluxe compartmentalized bath which includes a vaulted ceiling with sky lights, garden tub, shower, linen closet and a separate dressing room with double vanity and large walk-in closet. Two additional bedrooms with ample closet space share a second compartmentalized bath. Living and dining rooms are located to the side of the formal foyer. A family room with a raised hearth fireplace and double doors onto a screened-in back porch and a U-shaped kitchen with an island counter open to the breakfast bay allow more casual living. Fixed stairs in the family room provide access to attic storage above. Also included is a utility room with a half bath.

Area — 2,400 sq. ft.

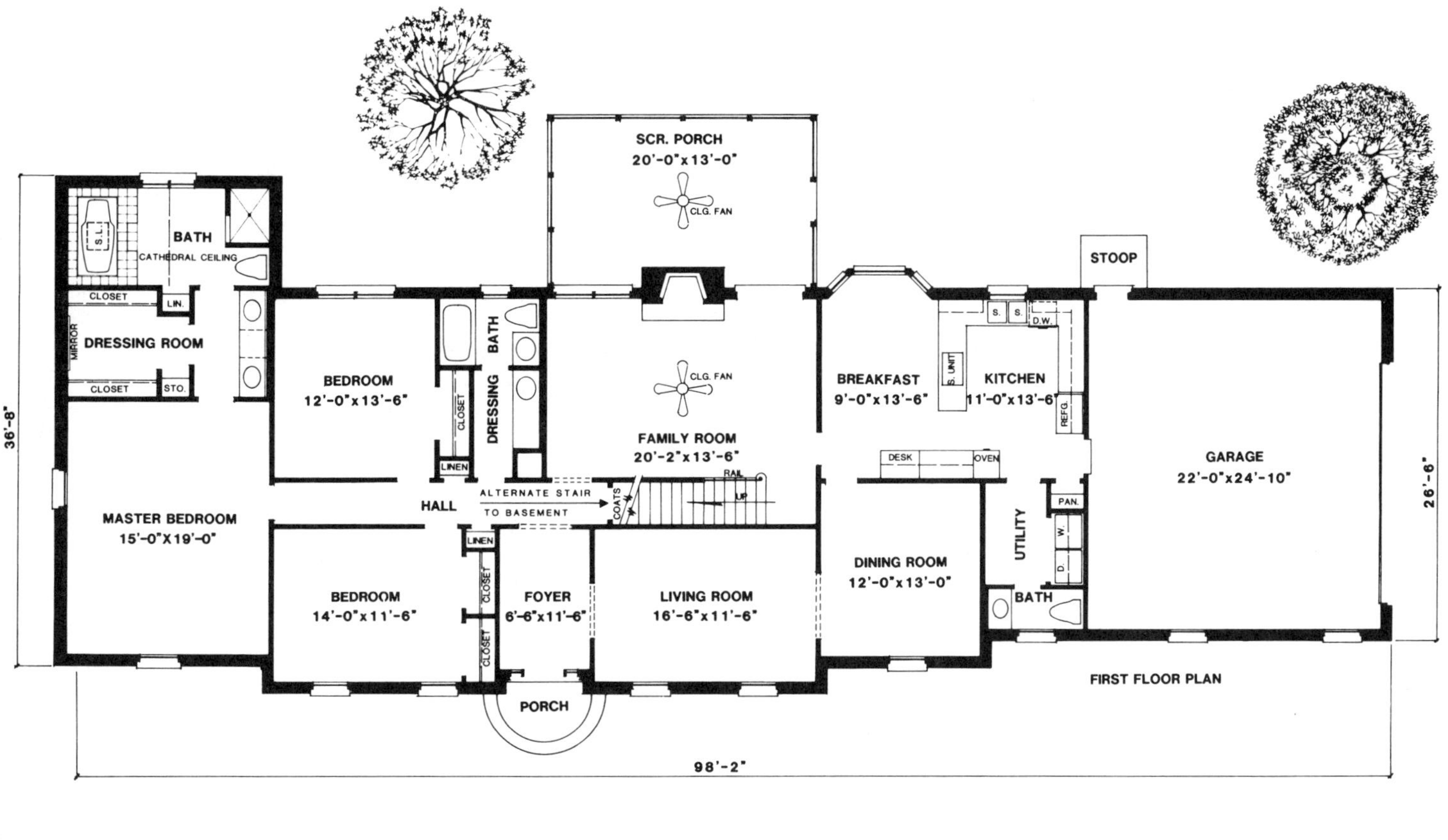

Early American Home for Today

No. 90605

This house reflects the charm and warmth that was prevalent in the early American home 200 years ago. The shuttered, double-hung windows, the moldings at the eaves, the large chimney, and the clapboard siding are elements that capture a colonial flavor. This is reflected in the interior, especially in the "Keeping Room", the early American family gathering place. Located to the rear of the living room, it's used for dining, cooking, and family fun. A counter-height fireplace, pegged plank flooring, beamed ceiling, and colonial-style kitchen cabinets continue the early American motif.

Total living area — 1,260 sq. ft. (optional slab construction available)

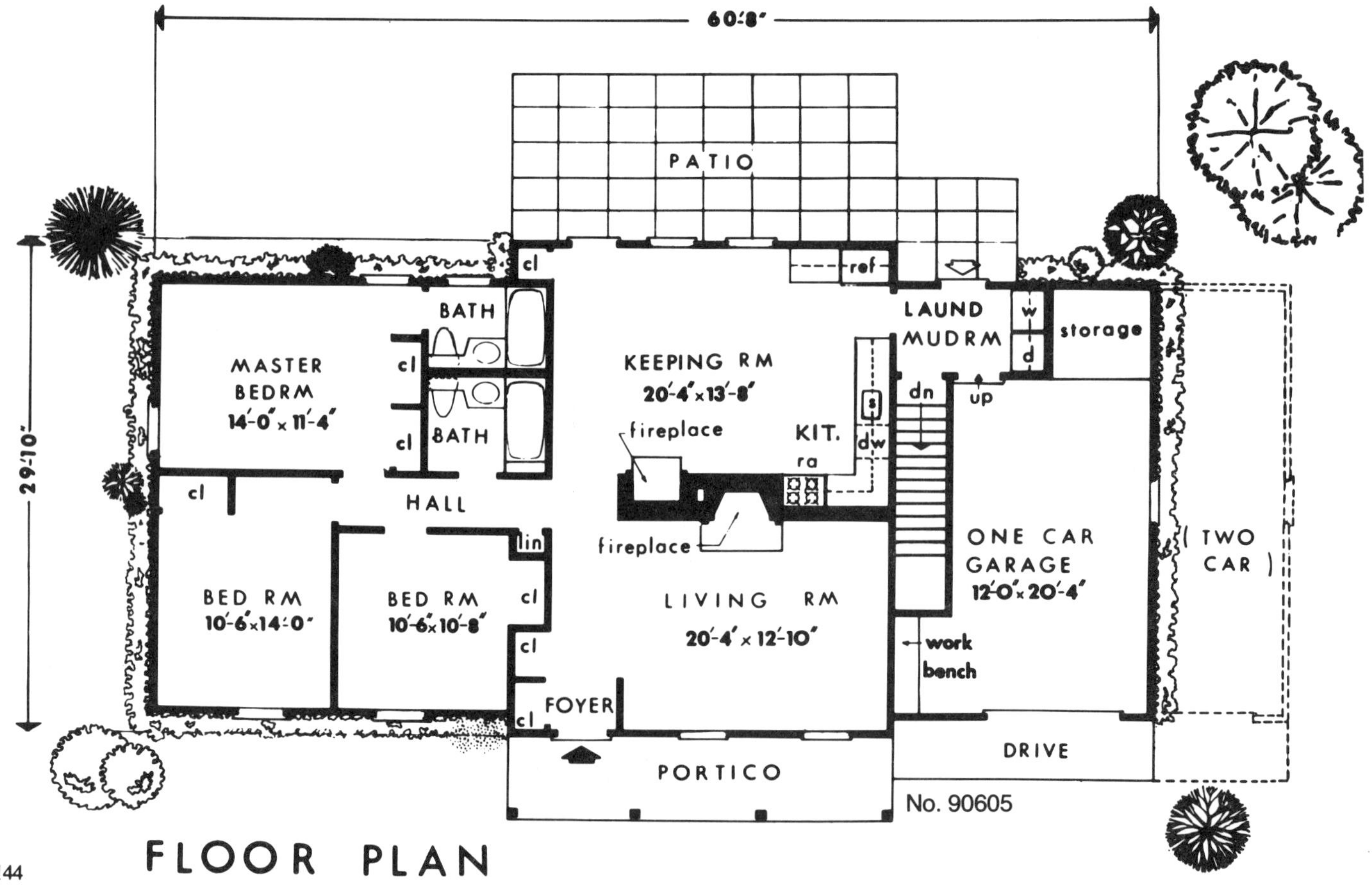

FLOOR PLAN

Contemporary Design Has Style

No. 90333

With an exterior of vertical wood siding, this contemporary design provides homeowners with ease of maintenance and upkeep. The interior floor plan uses openness to give growing families more living space. On the first level the living and family rooms are together, and both have exits to the outdoor patio at the rear of the house. The L-shaped kitchen contains a breakfast room that provides ample eating space. A more formal dining room is located by the kitchen also. The second level has two bedrooms plus the master bedroom which has its private bath area and a walk-in closet. The other two bedrooms share a full bath. A basement plus a two car garage are offered in this plan.

Living area — 1,800 sq. ft.

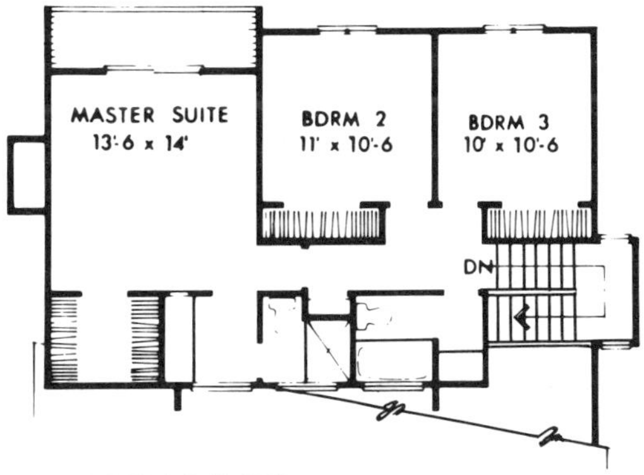

UPPER LEVEL

No. 90333

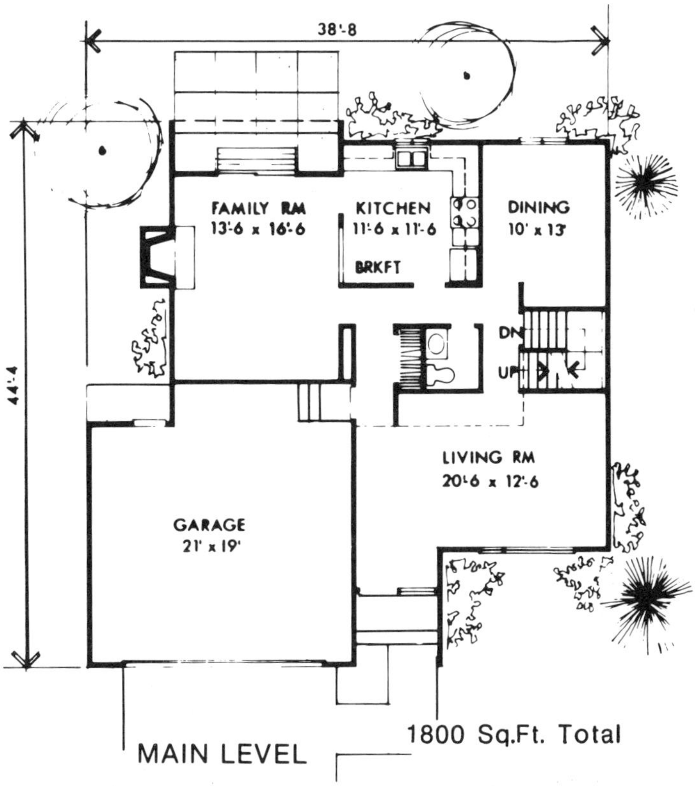

MAIN LEVEL

1800 Sq.Ft. Total

Stucco and Stone Reveal Outstanding Tudor Design

No. 10555

This beautiful stucco and stone masonry Tudor design opens to a formal air-lock foyer that leads through double doors into a well-designed library which is also conveniently accessible from the master bedroom. The master bedroom offers a vaulted ceiling and a huge bath area. Other features are an oversized living room with a fireplace, an open kitchen and a connecting dining room. A utility room and a half-bath are located next to a two-car garage. One other select option in this design is the separate cedar closet to use for off-season clothes storage.

First floor — 1,671 sq. ft.
Second floor — 505 sq. ft.
Basement — 1,661 sq. ft.
Garage — 604 sq. ft.
Screened porch — 114 sq. ft.

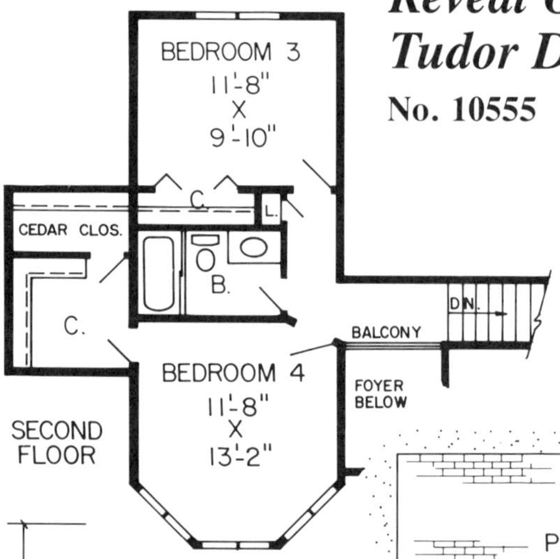

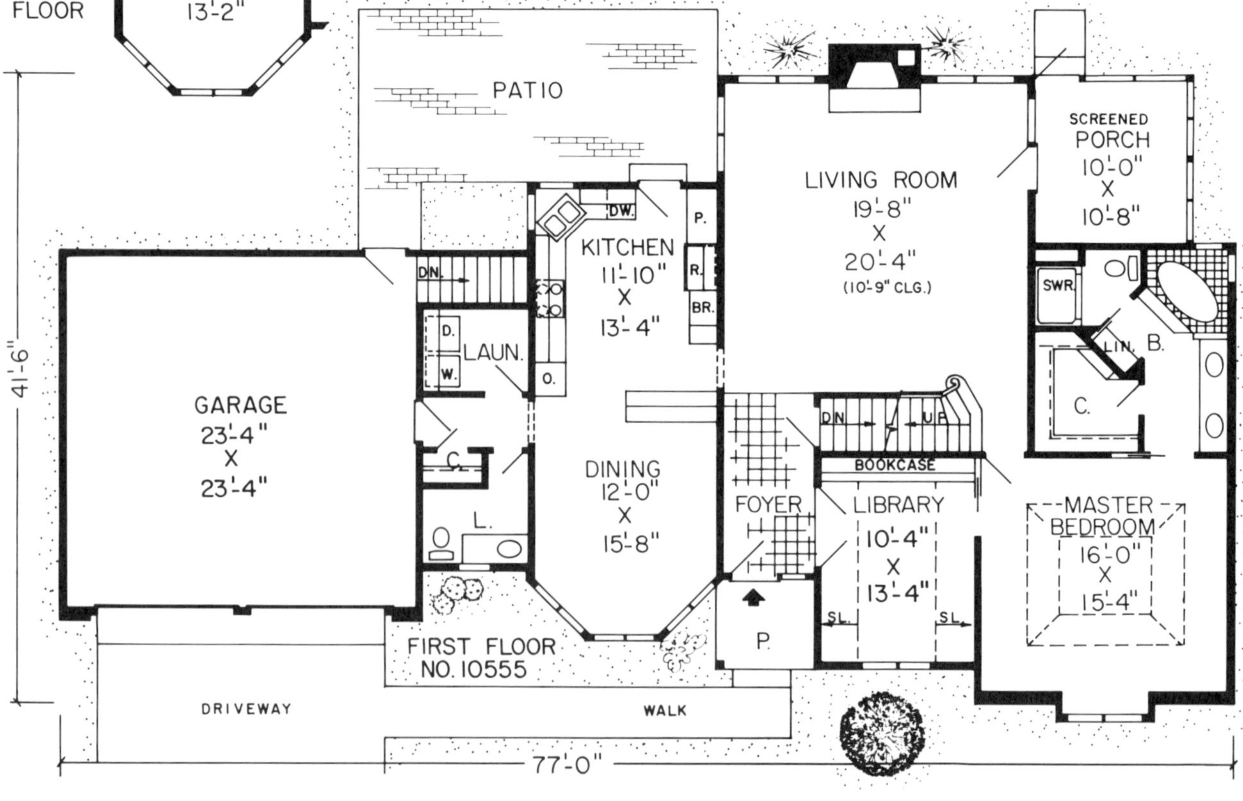

Massive Fireplace Adds Warmth & Charm

No. 90831

Whether you're thinking about retirement or just starting out, this versatile one-level home is an economical and practical design you're sure to appreciate. With three bedrooms, there's plenty of room for the kids, or your guests. And, with no stairs to climb, household chores are simplified. Active areas enjoy a spacious feeling thanks to an open plan and lots of oversized windows. The utility room is spacious and convenient and serves as a mudroom entrance from the garage. If you're an outdoor lover, the rear deck off the eat-in kitchen will provide extra living space when the weather's nice.

First floor — 1,389 sq. ft.
Basement — 1,335 sq. ft.

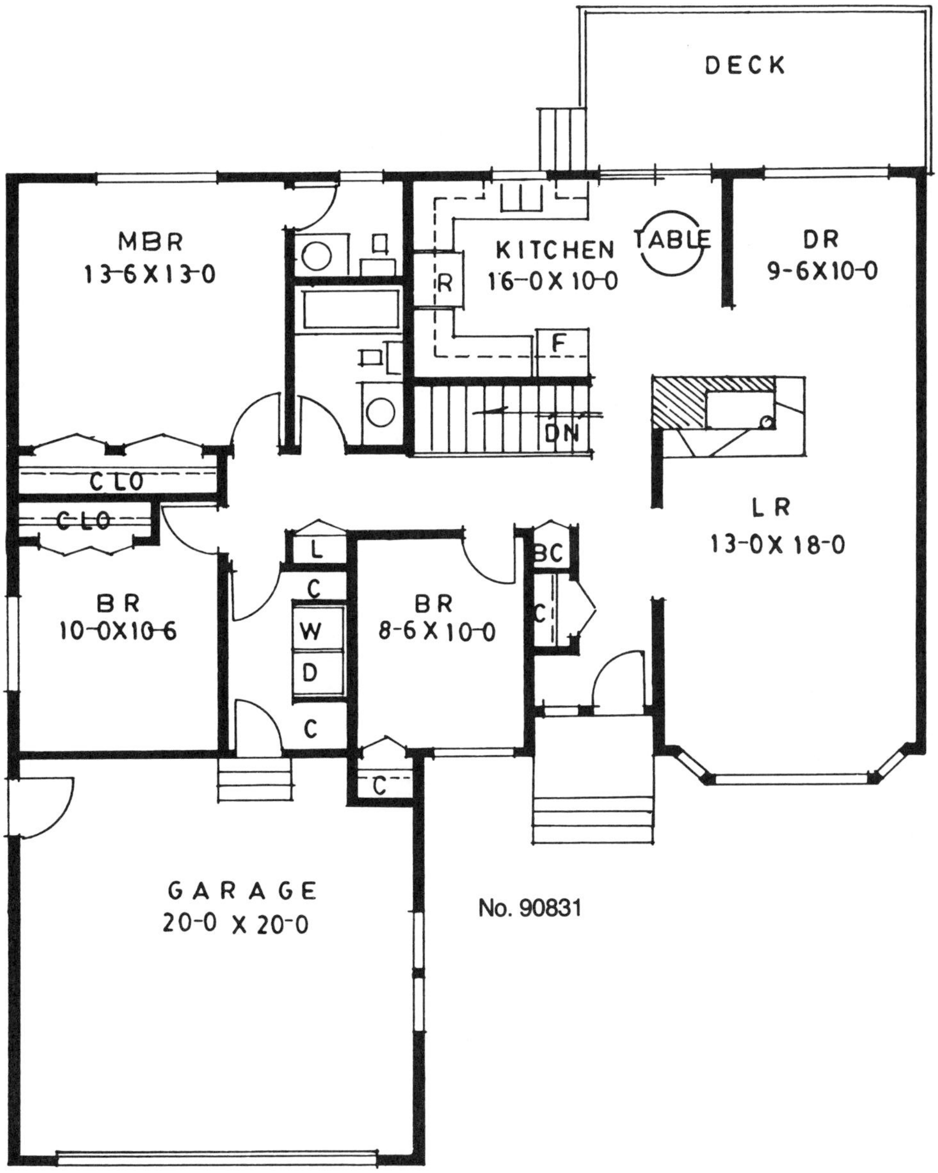

Fireplaces Warm Roomy Ranch

No. 90908

Here's a delightful one-level home you can build for a bargain. Save foundation costs with this no-basement design. Also, note that careful planning has placed laundry across from the family bath to eliminate extra plumbing. A wide covered porch shelters the front entry. You'll fall in love with the skylit foyer which provides easy access to all points of this plan. The formal areas are well separated from the family areas. The kitchen, nook, and family rooms form plenty of casual living space. Beyond the nook through sliding glass doors is an ideal location for future deck or grade level patio.

Total living area — 1,499 sq. ft.
Garage — 452 sq. ft.
Width — 42 ft.
Depth — 51 ft.

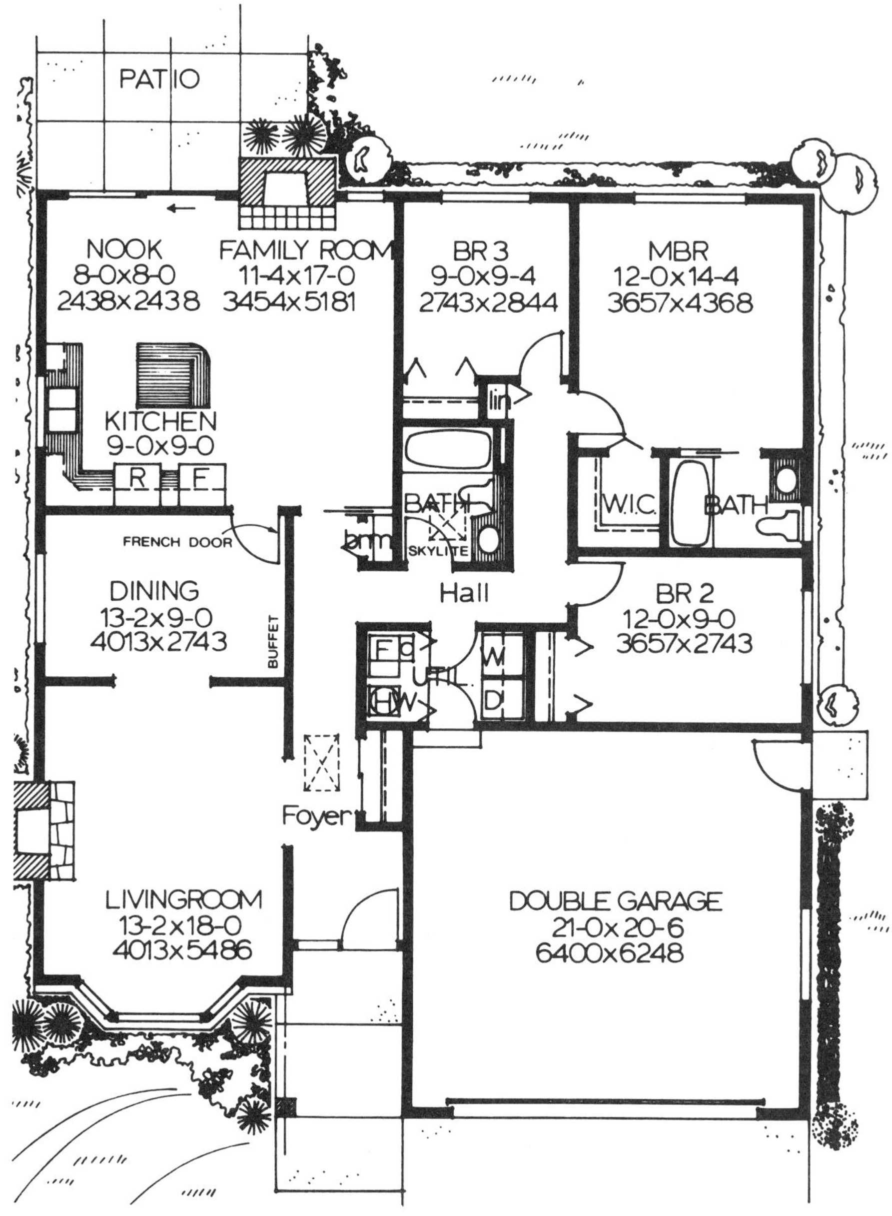

No. 90908

Cathedral Window Graced by Massive Arch

No. 20066

A tiled threshold provides a distinctive entrance into this spacious home. There's room for gracious living everywhere, from the comfortable living room with woodburning fireplace and tiled hearth to the elegant dining room with vaulted ceiling to the outside deck. Plan your meals in a kitchen that has all the right ingredients: a central work island, pantry, planning desk, and breakfast area. A decorative ceiling will delight your eye in the master suite, which includes a full bath and bow window.

First floor — 1,664 sq. ft.
Basement — 1,656 sq. ft.
Garage — 503 sq. ft.

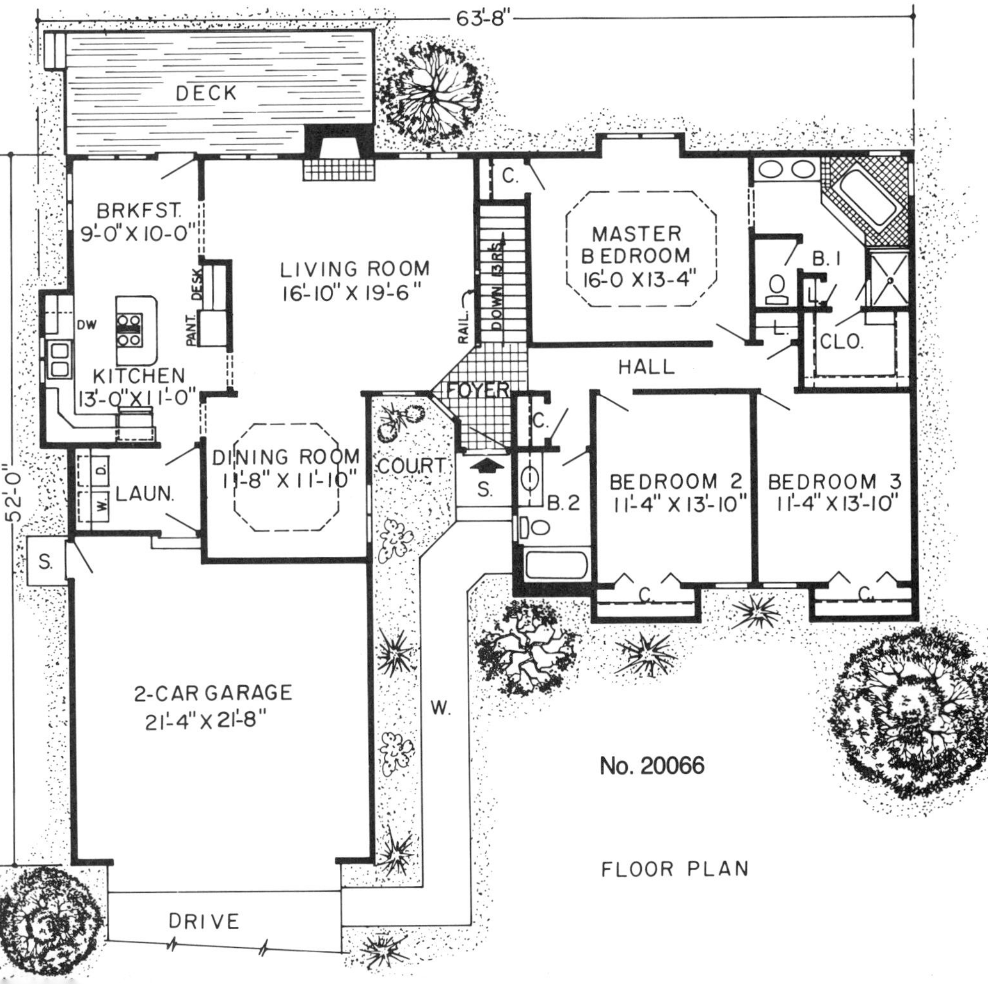

Designed for Family Living

No. 90604

The grand, circular staircase will charm your guests as they enter this traditional three-bedroom loaded with family features. Flanked by formal dining and living rooms, the foyer leads straight into the family living area of the house, with utility room entry for muddy kids and grocery-laden parents. The cozy family room with raised hearth is a comfortable center for group activities. Four bedrooms, two baths, and closets galore make this a house you can enjoy for many, happy years.

First floor — 952 sq. ft.
Second floor — 892 sq. ft.
(excluding garage, laundry, storage)

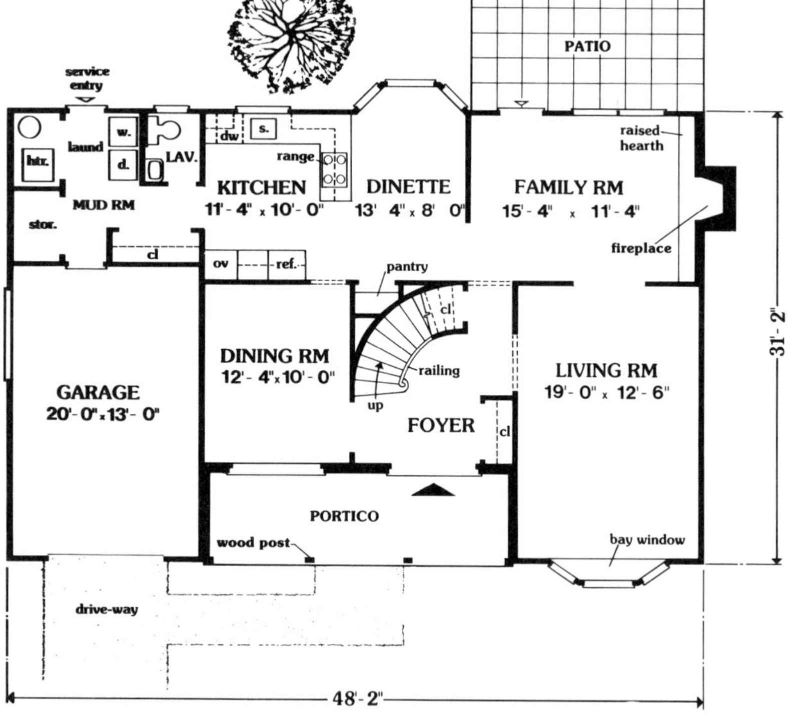

No. 90604

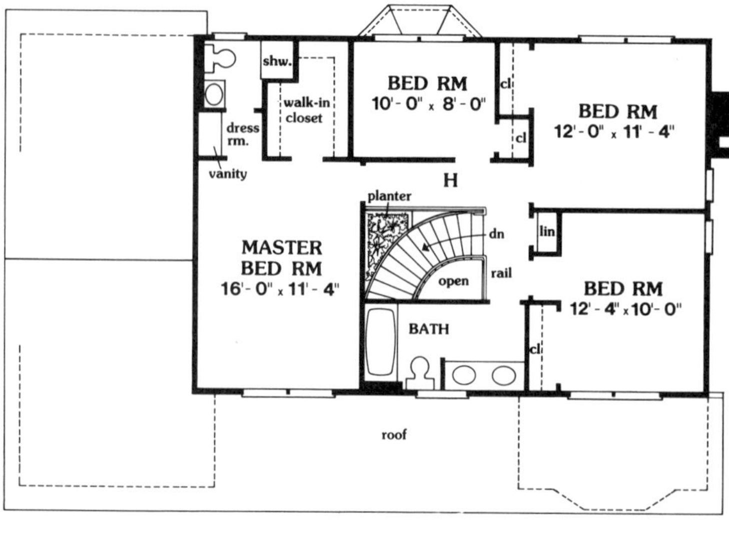

SECOND FLOOR

Expansive, Not Expensive

No. 90623

Despite its compact area, this home looks and lives like a luxurious ranch. A decorative screen divides the entrance foyer from the spacious, comfortable living room, which flows into the pleasant dining room overlooking a rear garden. The roomy, eat-in kitchen features a planning corner. And, the adjacent laundry-mudroom provides access to the two-car garage and to the outdoors. Here also lie the stairs to the full basement, a valuable, functional part of the house which adds many possibilities for informal family living. The private bedroom wing includes three bedrooms and two baths.

Total living area — 1,370 sq. ft.

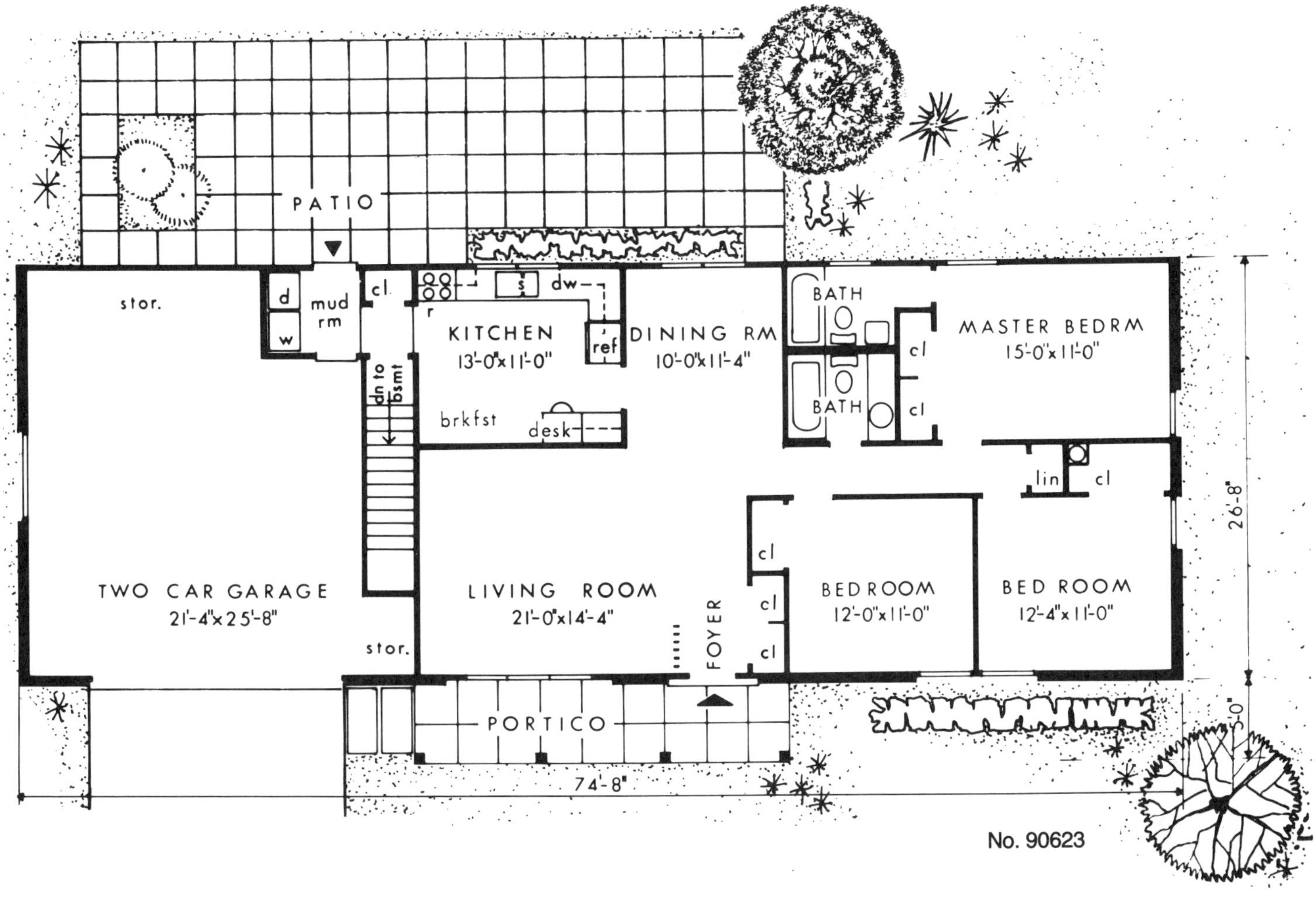

No. 90623

Separate Sleeping Wing Insures Restful Atmosphere

No. 90505

Massive columns guard the central entry of this one-level, three bedroom home. Adorned by rustic timbers, enormous windows lend an airy atmosphere to every room. Double doors give the dining room a quiet formality. Adjoining the family room, the breakfast nook features sliding glass access to an outdoor deck.

Floor area — 1,739 sq. ft.

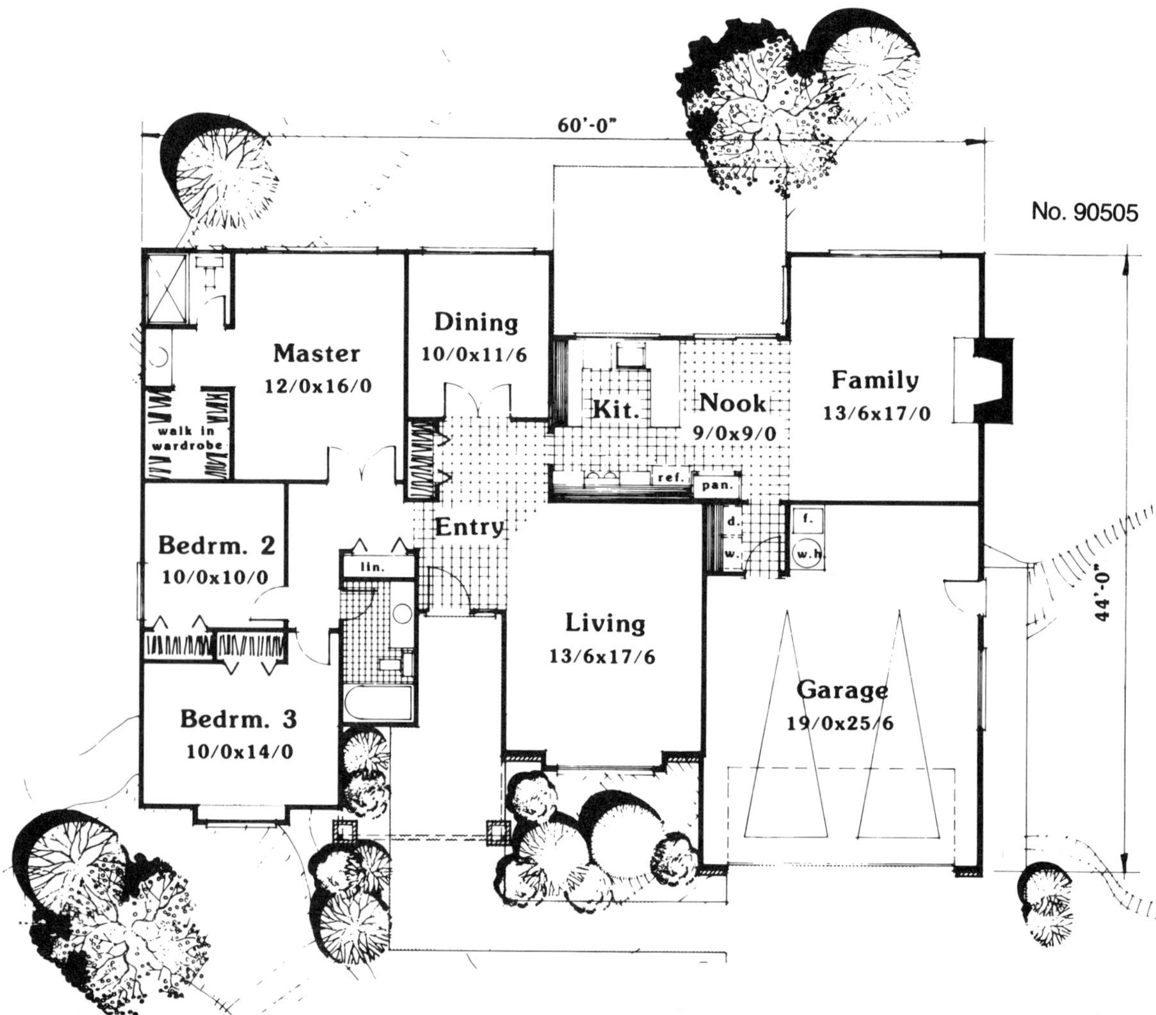

Vaulted Ceiling Enhances Central Living Area

No. 90306

The entry deck accented by windows and attractive plantings leads into the spacious living room of this home. This room also separates the activity area from the sleeping quarters. The master bedroom has a separate bath and double closets plus access to the patio. Two other bedrooms share a bath. The activity area of the house incorporates the family room, dining room, and the kitchen, with its convenient laundry room. All three of these areas flow into each other so that there is the illusion of more space. The family room is enhanced by its fireplace and access to the patio.

Living Area — 1,440 sq. ft.

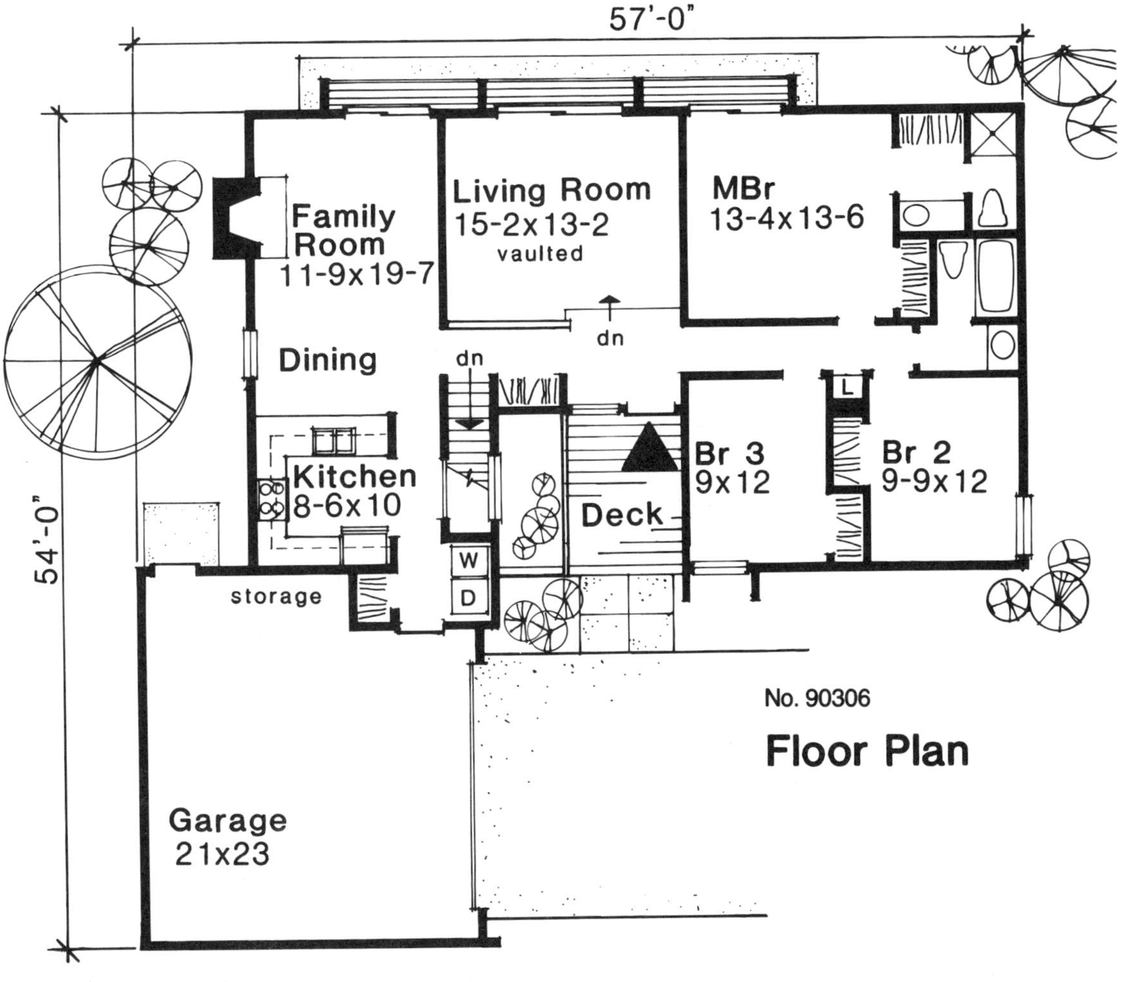

No. 90306

Floor Plan

Surround Yourself with Luxury

No. 10615

A magnificent home in every detail, this stately 5 bedroom residence surrounds you with thoughtful luxury. Enter the oversized, tiled foyer and view the grand staircase whose landing splits the ascent into separate wings and creates an aura of privacy for a guest or live-in relative in bedroom 4. Serenity reigns throughout the home thanks to the courtyard plan that insulates the master bedroom complex and bedroom 2 from the main living areas. The kitchen is designed to serve the eating areas and family room and reserve the vast living room for more formal entertaining. Most of the home shares access to, and wonderful views of, the patio, covered by the 2nd floor deck, and pool area.

First floor — 4,075 sq. ft.
Second floor — 1,179 sq. ft.
Garage — 633 sq. ft.

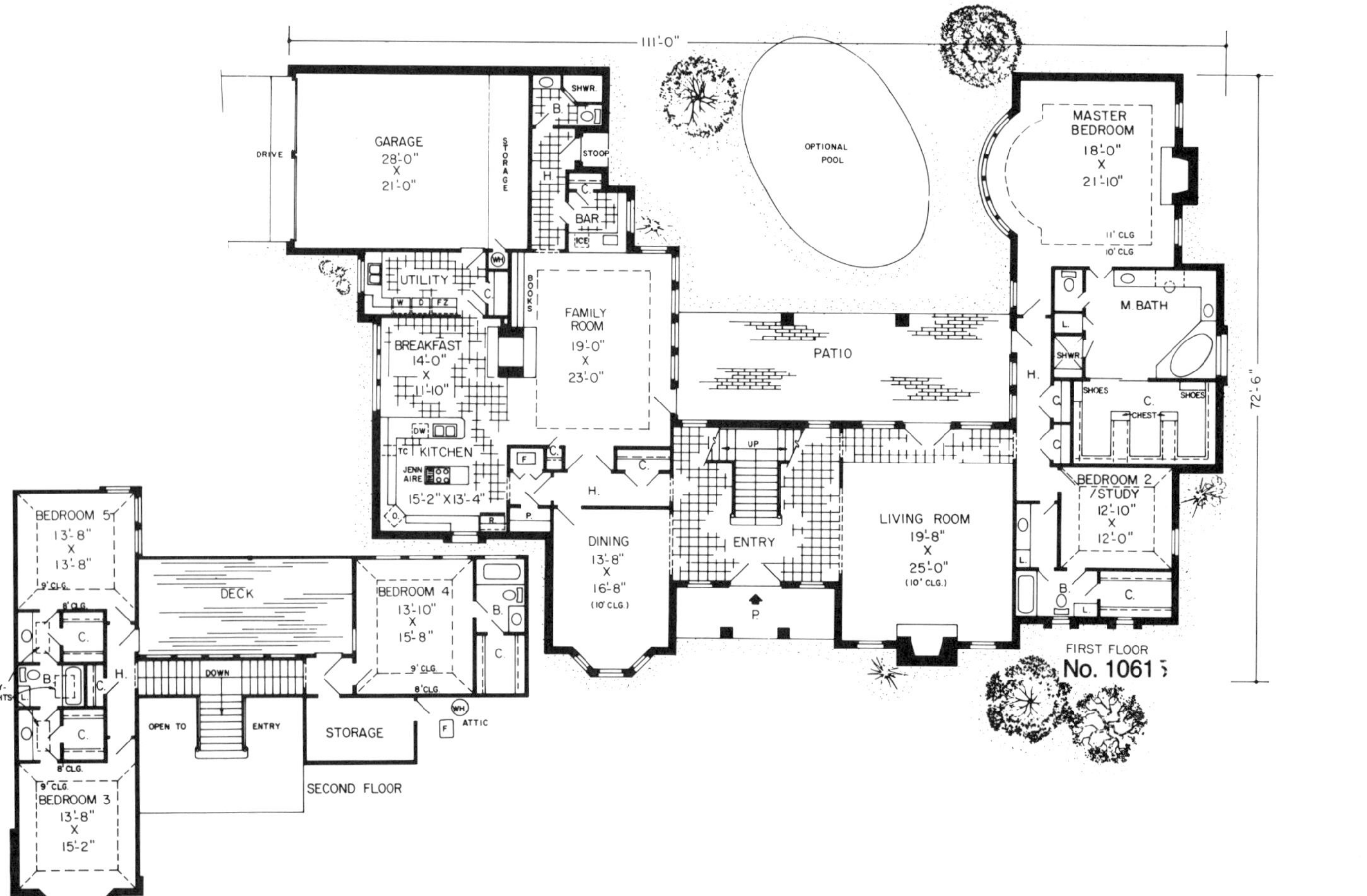

Single-Floor Family Living

No. 90829

With three spots to choose from, you'll have a hard time deciding where to dine in this one-level charmer. On nice days, the back porch is a delightful place for morning coffee. Enjoy family meals in the breakfast nook off the kitchen, or entertain guests in the formal dining room that adjoins the bayed living room. Whatever your choice, meal service is sure to be convenient with the centrally-located kitchen. And note the pantry storage. The bedrooms, located at the rear of the house and buffered from noise by the garage, feature ample closets and easy access to the washer and dryer.

First floor — 1,325 sq. ft.
Basement — 1,168 sq. ft.

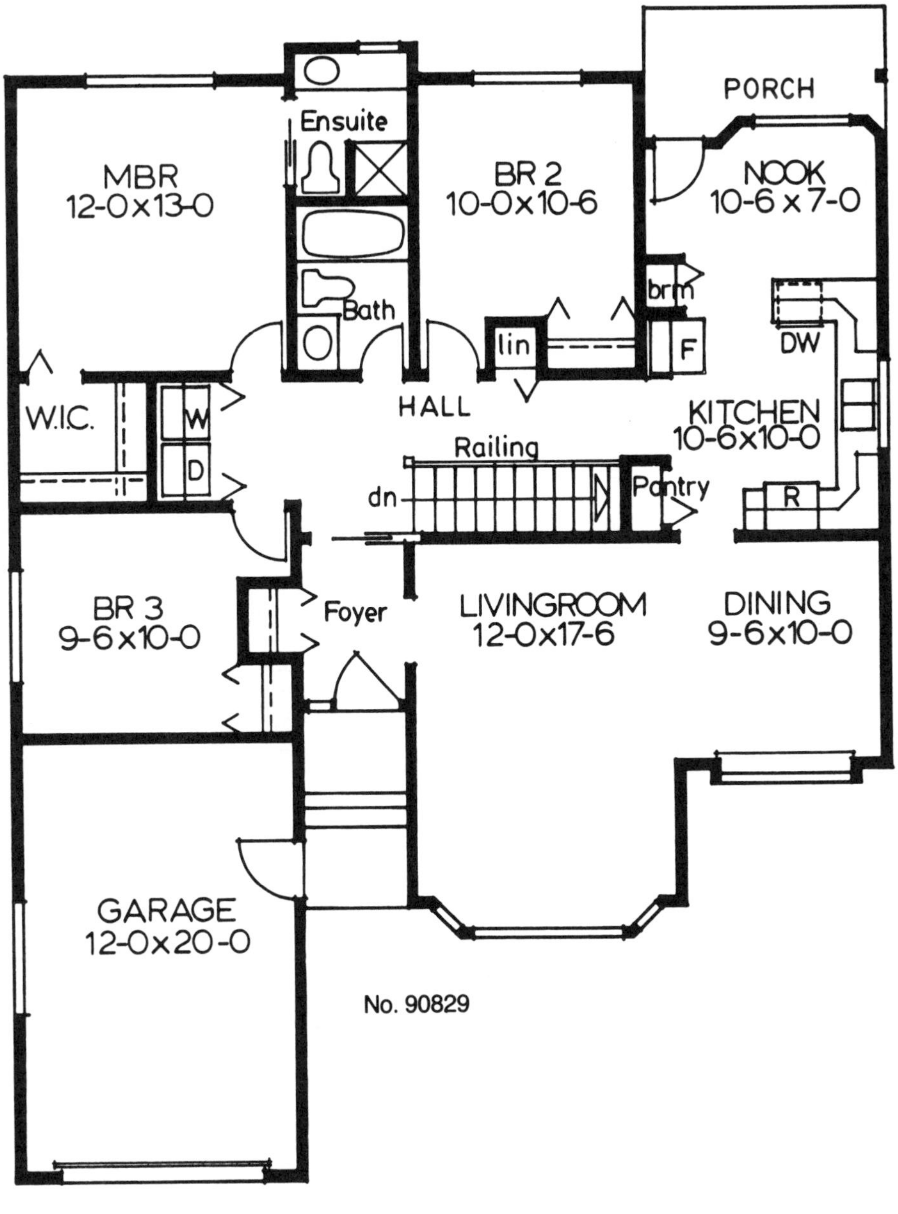

Elegant Yet Energy Efficient

No. 90110

From the central foyer, the staircase rises to the elegantly arranged bedrooms. The master bedroom features a dressing room, master bath and walk-in closet. The other bedrooms are convenient to the other upstairs bath with its double lavatory. The first floor encompasses several distinct living areas, including a family room with fireplace, a formal dining room, and a kitchen with its own dining area.

First floor — 1,398 sq. ft.
Second floor — 1,266 sq. ft.

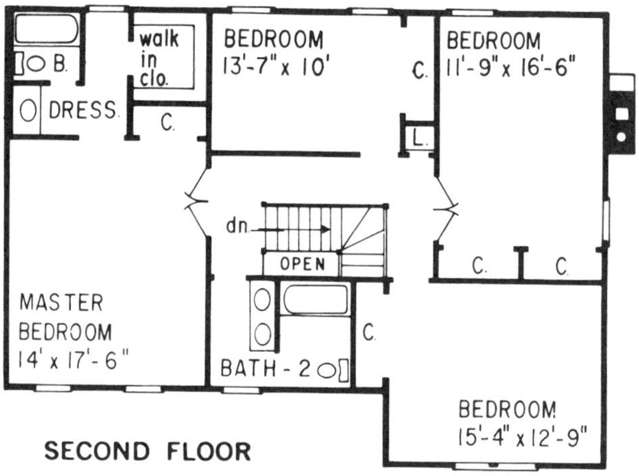

SECOND FLOOR

No. 90110

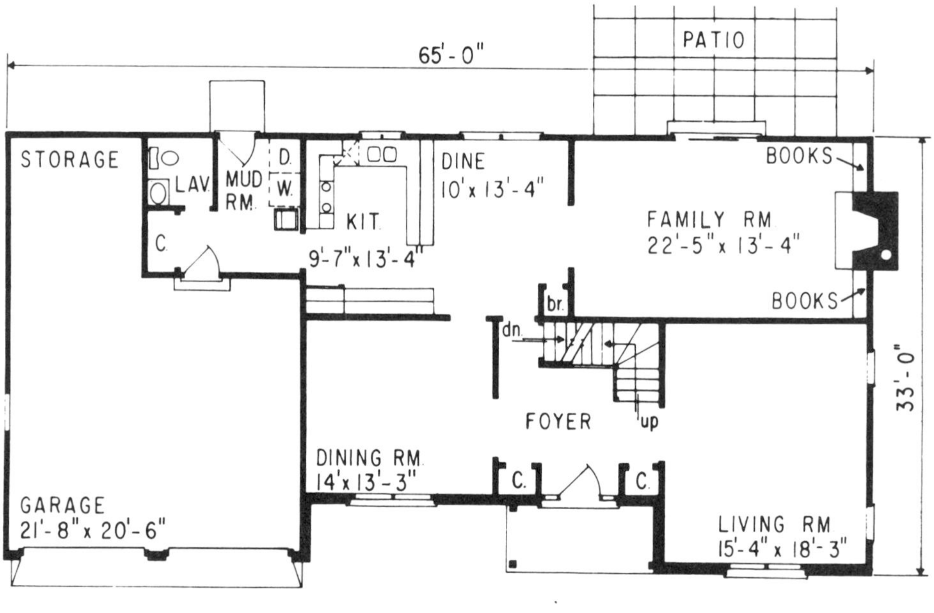

FIRST FLOOR

Charming Kitchen and Family Room

No. 90102

Enjoy family time together in the efficient kitchen that opens onto the family room. The centrally located laundry facilities streamline those mundane chores, and the built-in storage along the back of the carport keeps everything organized. The full bath is convenient to all three bedrooms which each contain a spacious closet.

Living Area — 1,120 sq. ft.

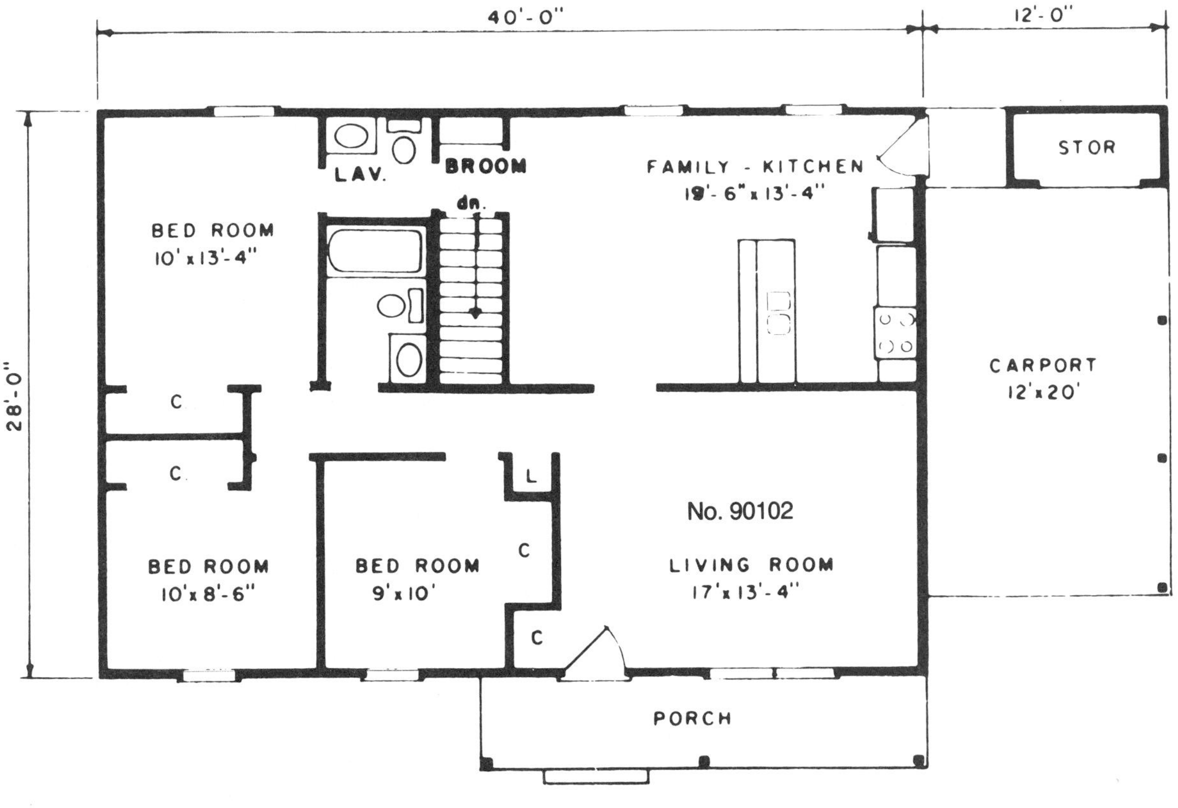

Classic Styling, Exceptional Plan

No. 90155

An appealing exterior is accented by the second floor overhang and gabled windows. A snack counter divides the U-shaped kitchen and breakfast area. Steps lead down from the kitchen into the sunken living room, which features a brick fireplace. A powder room and mudroom with entry from the garage allow for clean up before entering the main living areas. The master suite is enhanced by a large walk-in closet and deluxe bath with corner deck tub and double vanity. Three additional bedrooms, two with walk-in closets, complete this exceptional layout.

First floor — 1,212 sq. ft.
Second floor — 1,160 sq. ft.

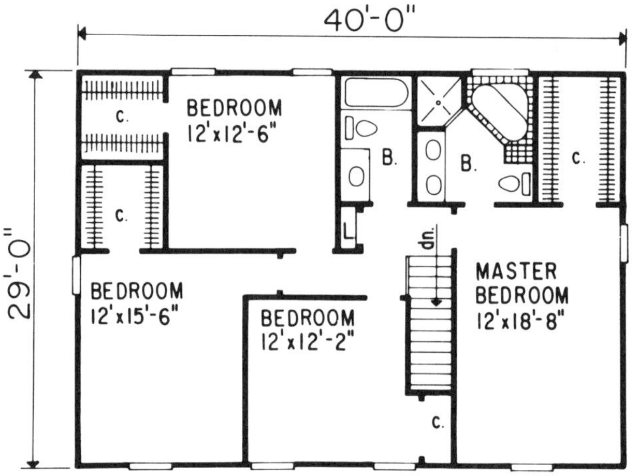

SECOND FLOOR

No. 90155

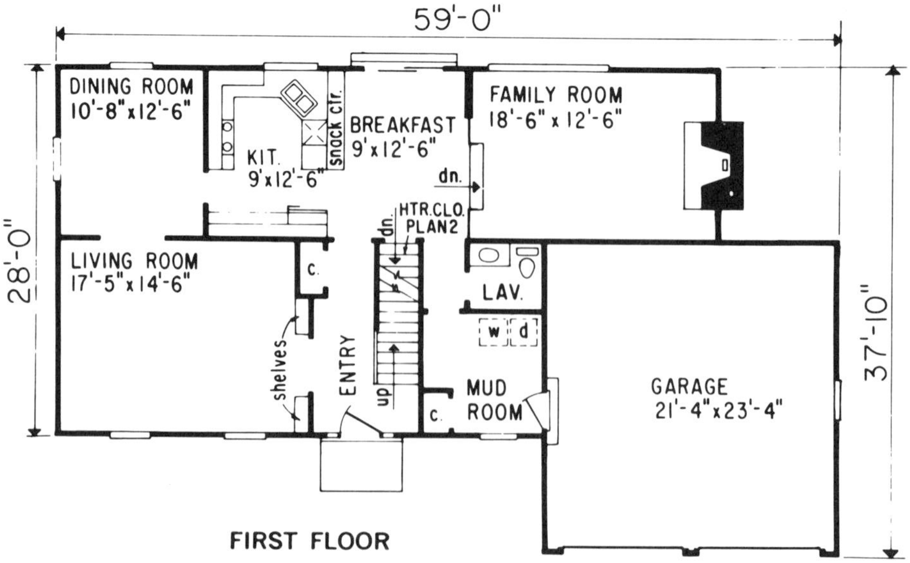

FIRST FLOOR

Design Incorporates Informal and Formal

No. 90317

The main level of this two-story home is divided into formal and informal living areas by the central placement of the staircase and the kitchen. The two-story living room and the dining room with its unique bump-out window are located to one side of the home. On the other side are the family room with its inviting fireplace and the breakfast room which has sliding glass doors onto the deck. Four bedrooms comprise the second floor. The expansive master bedroom features a five-piece bath and two walk-in closets.

Main level — 1,413 sq. ft.
Upper level — 1,245 sq. ft.
Basement — 1,413 sq. ft.
Garage — 689 sq. ft.

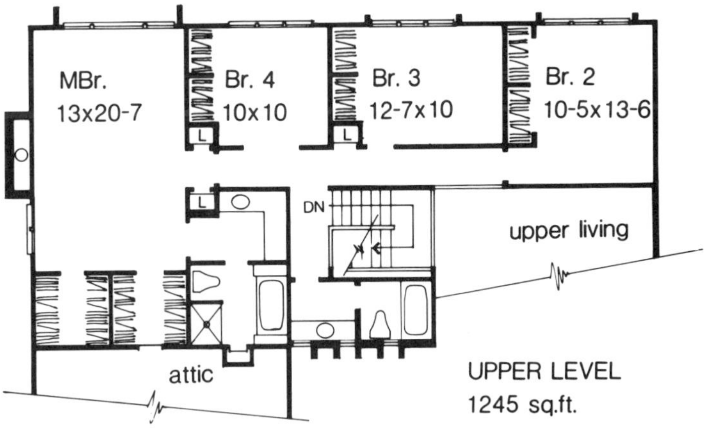

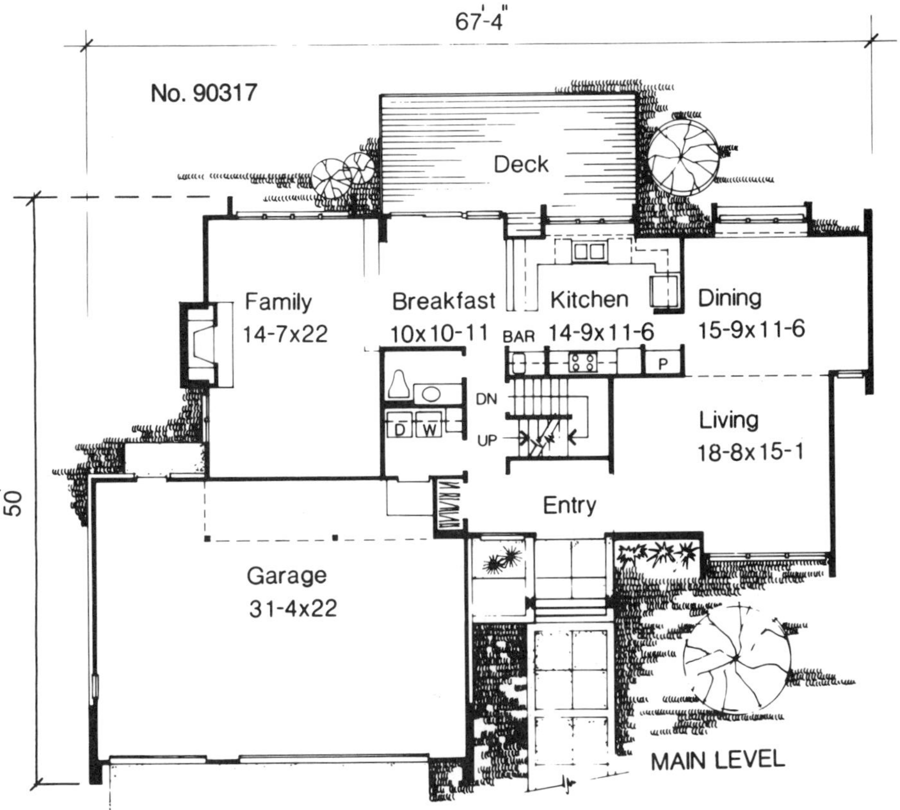

Compact Home for a Small Space

No. 90500

A massive bay window is the dominant feature in the facade of this cozy home with attached two-car garage. From the entry, there are three ways to walk. Turn left into the fireplaced living room and adjoining dining room. Or walk straight into the kitchen and breakfast nook, which extends to a covered porch. Step down the hall on the right to the master suite, full bath, and a second bedroom. The TV room, which can double as a third bedroom, completes the circular floor plan in this convenient, one-level abode.

Floor area — 1,299 sq. ft.

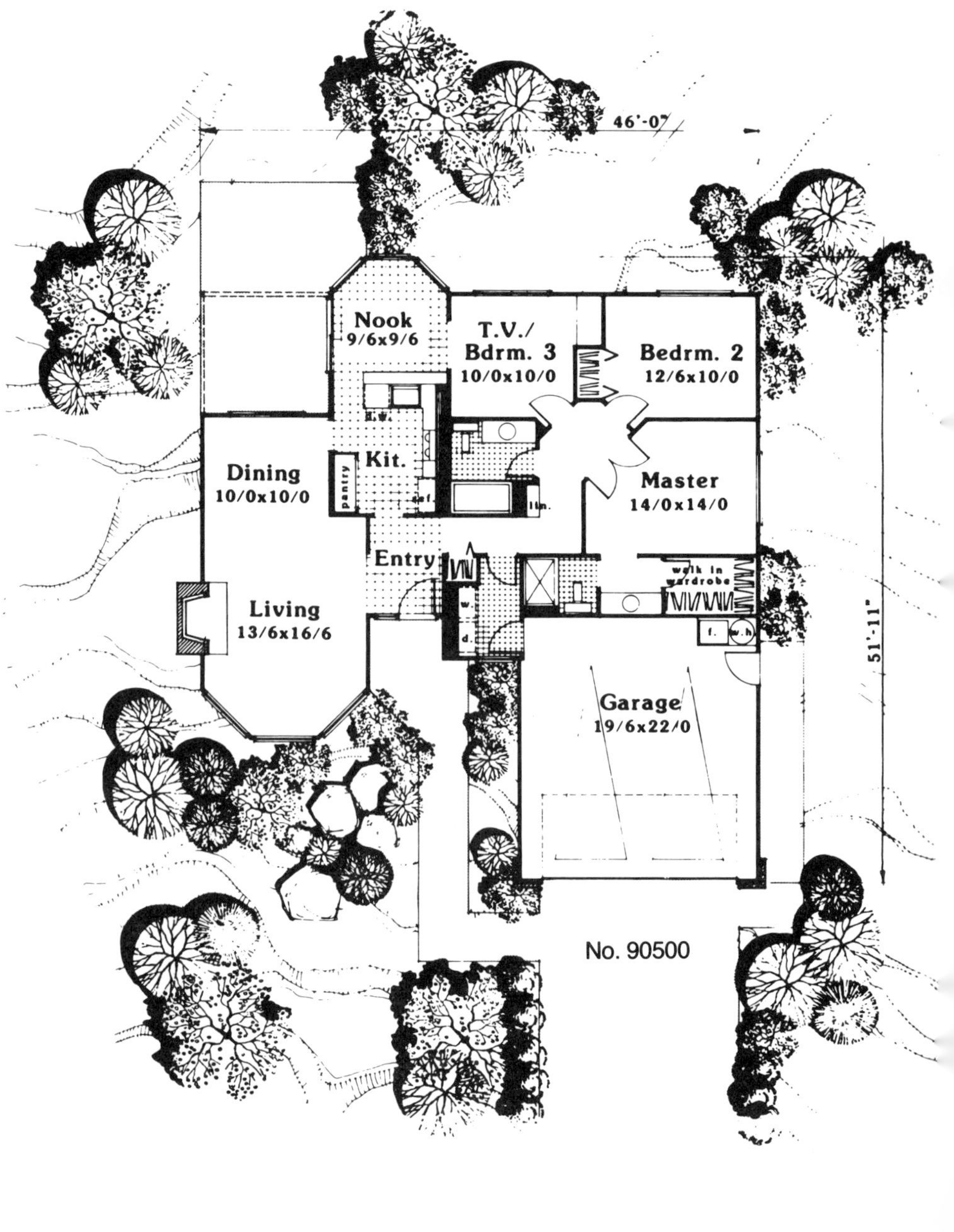

Multiple Levels Make Life Interesting

No. 90828

From the sheltered porch to the cozy, sunken family room, this house is a warm, inviting place. The skylit entry rises to the second floor, where you'll find three spacious bedrooms and two full baths. Up a half level, a studio and a third full bath occupy a quiet spot away from the rest of the house. Back on the ground floor, the spacious, sunken living room just off the foyer is a step away from the formal dining room with built-in china cabinet and adjoining deck. The centrally located kitchen will make meal service simple, whether you're feeding the family or a huge gathering.

First floor — 1,307 sq. ft.
Second floor — 1,462 sq. ft.
Basement — 701 sq. ft.

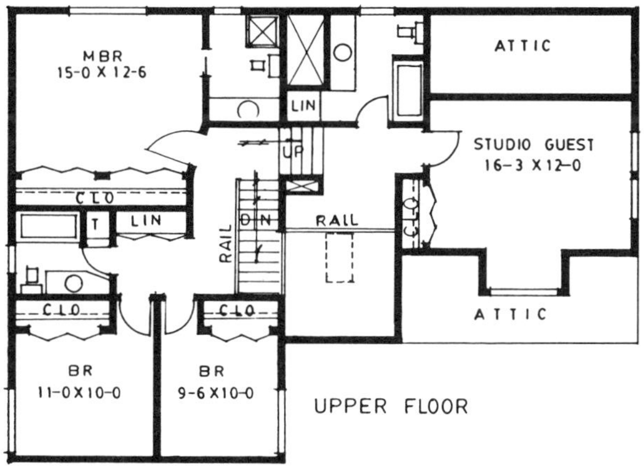

No. 90828

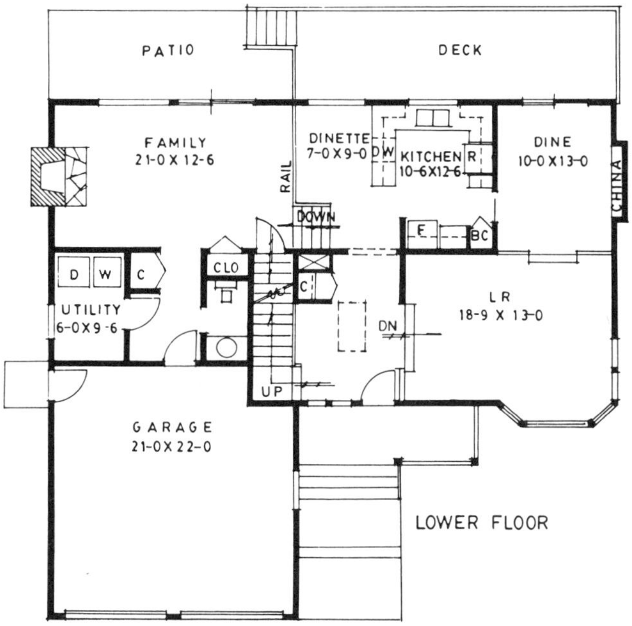

Designed for the TV Buff

No. 90621

No matter where you decide to build, you'll be sure to get perfect TV reception in the living room of this passive solar home. A satellite dish shares south-facing roof space with skylights and hot water solar collectors. And, the entertainment center is visible from all the living areas, grouped together in one, open space. The entrance foyer leads to the main rooms and the master bedroom off the bathroom hall. The upstairs hall, two bedrooms, and bath are brightened by clerestory windows. With energy-saving construction features, this home will give you years of enjoyment with minimal energy costs.

First floor (exluding deck) — 967 sq. ft.
Second floor — 389 sq. ft.

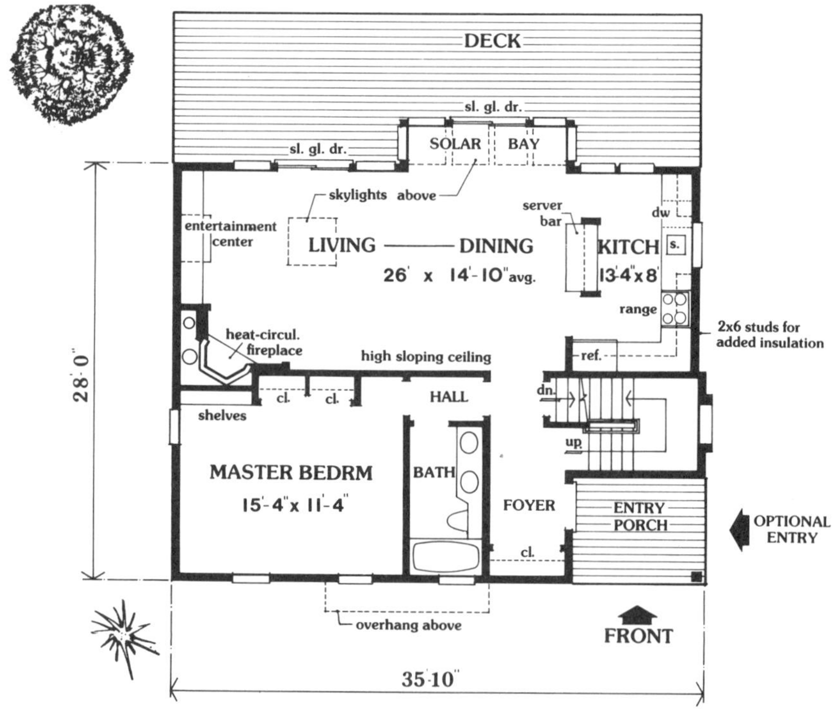

FIRST FLOOR PLAN

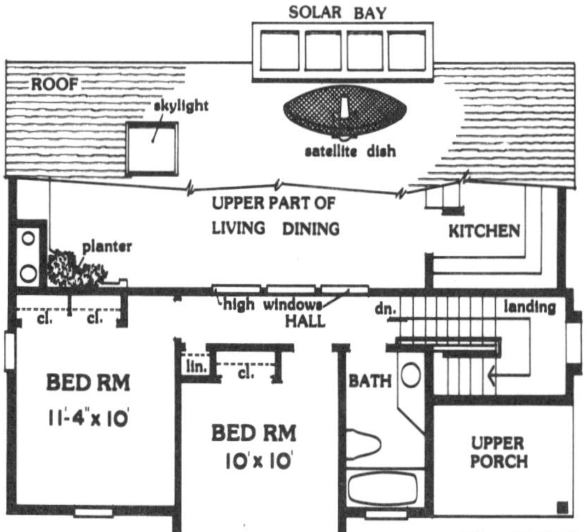

No. 90621

Three Different Designs from One Plan

No. 90600

Here's a home that's as small or as large as your changing needs. The basic house is an economical, cozy five-room cottage. The bedroom wing off the foyer houses one spacious master bedroom suite with a fireplace, full bath, and porch access, or two separate bedrooms. Need more family space? Expand off the kitchen by adding a family room and trellised patio. Not enough bedrooms? You can add three bedrooms and a bath upstairs. A large family may want to build the entire home at once, but a growing one can expand this versatile home as the need arises.

Total living area — 1,409 sq. ft.
Second floor expansion — 825 sq. ft.

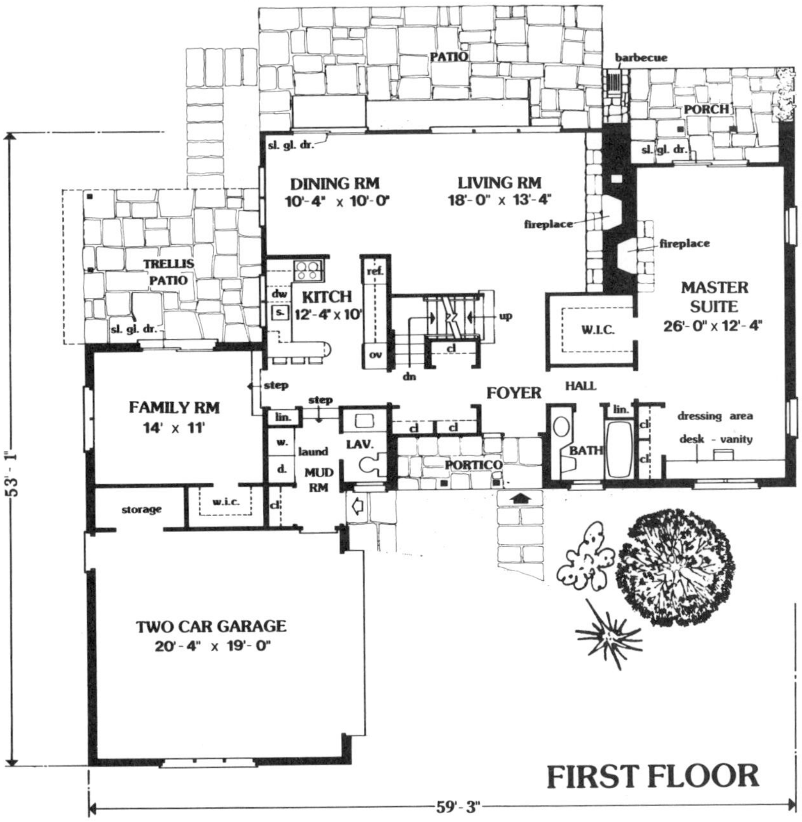

FIRST FLOOR

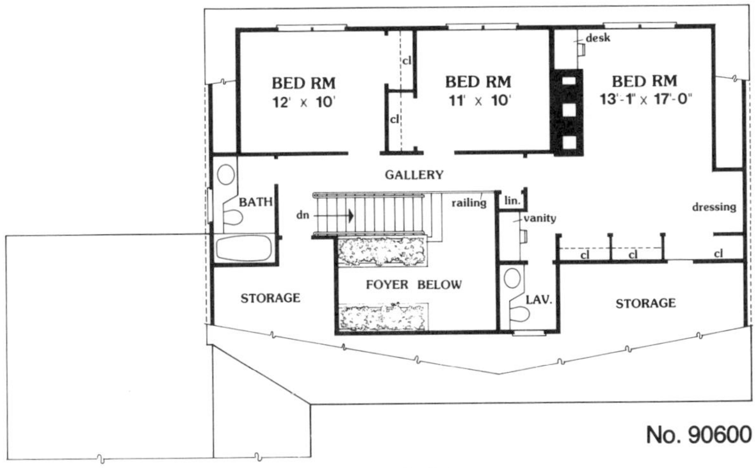

No. 90600

SECOND FLOOR

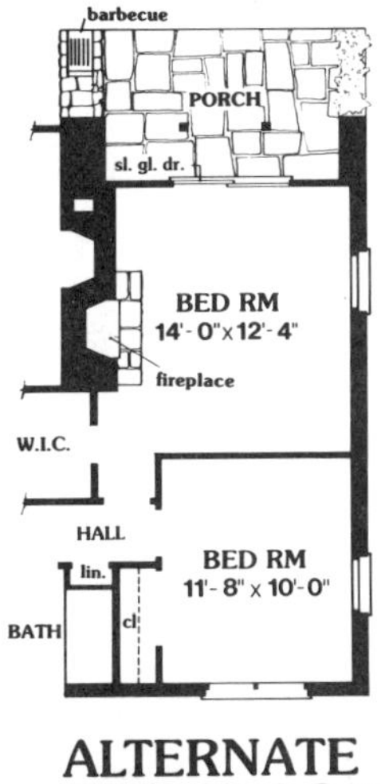

ALTERNATE 2-BEDROOM

Distinctive Styling with Vaulted Ceiling

No. 90516

Elegant lines are accented by french windows and brick facade on this stylish home. A sunken family room with fireplace and vaulted ceiling is overlooked by the 2nd floor balcony. The master bedroom has luxury touches like a sunken tub and large walk-in closet. Tile floors extend from the foyer into the oversized kitchen. Note the excellent traffic patterns to the dining area, family room, and deck.

First floor — 1,516 sq. ft.
Second floor — 1,153 sq. ft.

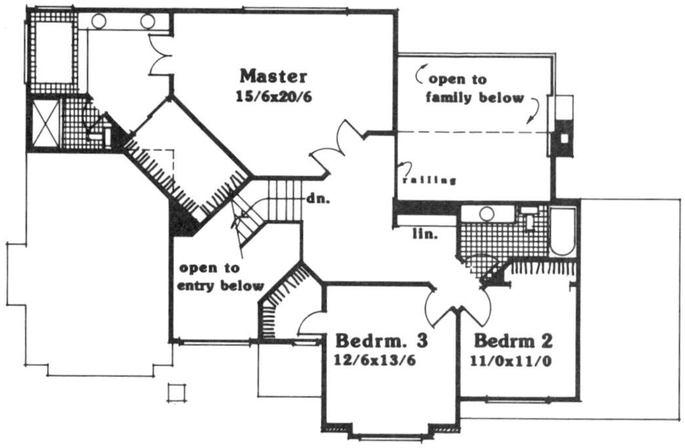

No. 90516

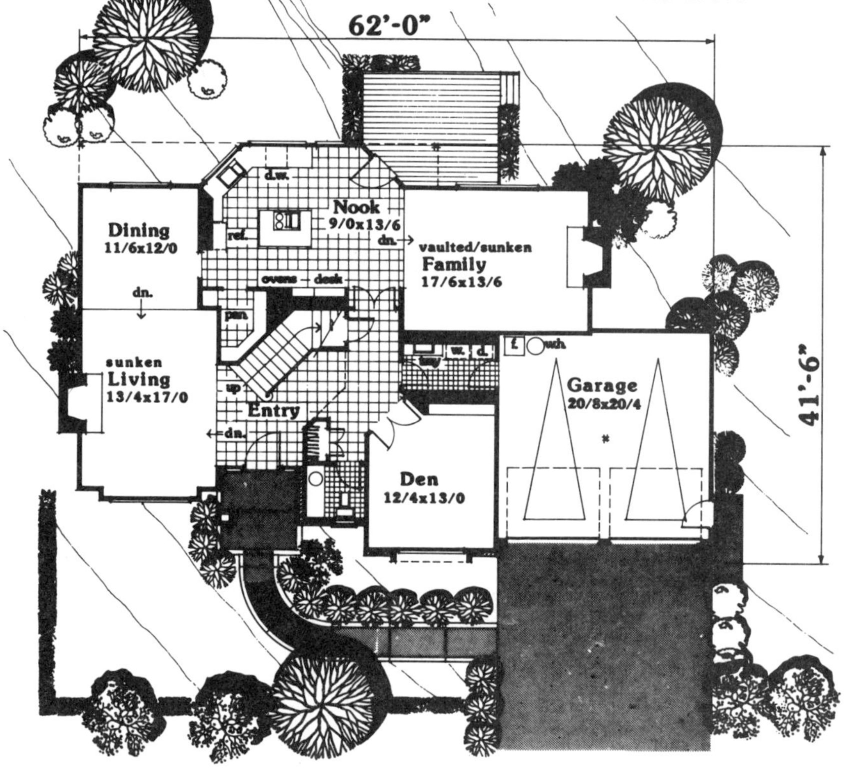

Luxurious Master Bedroom Suite

No. 90310

The main floor of this contemporary design welcomes guests into the sunken great room whose vaulted ceiling extends beyond the second floor. In addition to two large windows, it also includes a fireplace with an extended hearth. Just a step up from the great room is the dining room. A wet bar serves both rooms and is convenient to the efficient U-shaped kitchen. The adjacent breakfast room opens onto the deck and is separated from the kitchen by a serving bar. The master bedroom has an additional, private suite with a fireplace and sliding doors onto the deck. The upper floor is comprised of three more bedrooms; one of which has a private bath, four roof-windows and a walk-in closet.

Main floor — 2,082 sq. ft.
Upper floor — 1,279 sq. ft.
Basement — 2,082 sq. ft.
Garage — 684 sq. ft.

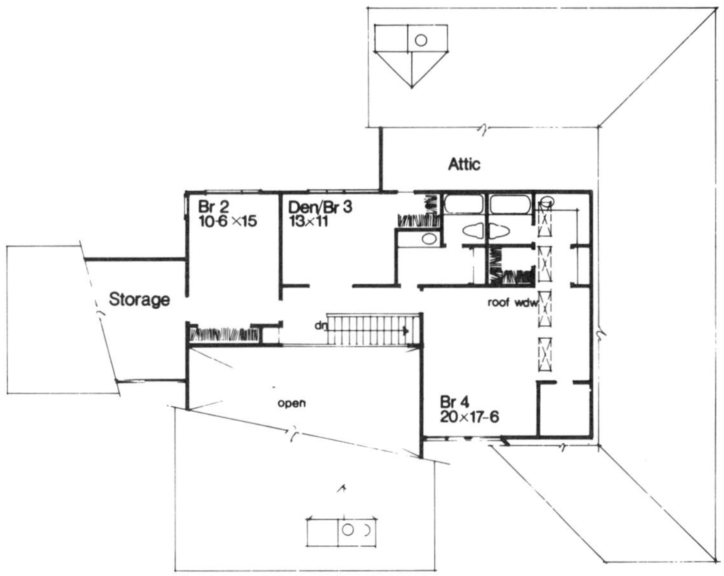

UPPER FLOOR 1085 sq.ft.

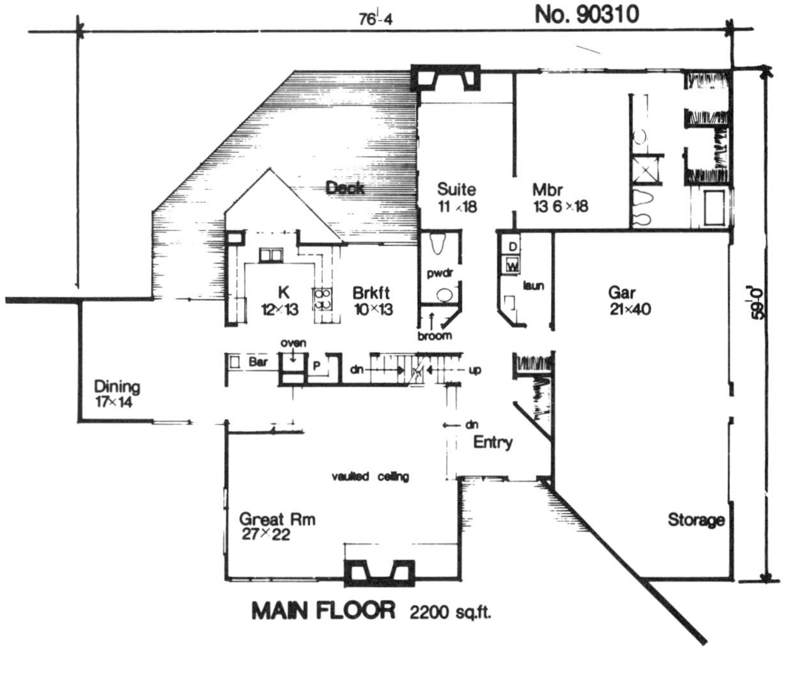

MAIN FLOOR 2200 sq.ft.

Bedrooms Zoned for Privacy

No. 90614

As you pass through the welcoming atrium into the foyer, you can sense the fine spatial organization that sets this home apart from the ordinary. Just ahead, the large sunken living room boasts a bold stone fireplace, and a rear wall of windows with a sliding glass door to the patio. A cathedral ceiling unites living and dining space, separated by a railing. The comfortable master suite features a dressing alcove, walk-in closet, and full bath. This home clearly demonstrates the effectiveness of contemporary design: integrated outdoor areas, privacy where needed, open and flowing spaces for a light, cheerful atmosphere.

Total living area — 1,540 sq. ft.

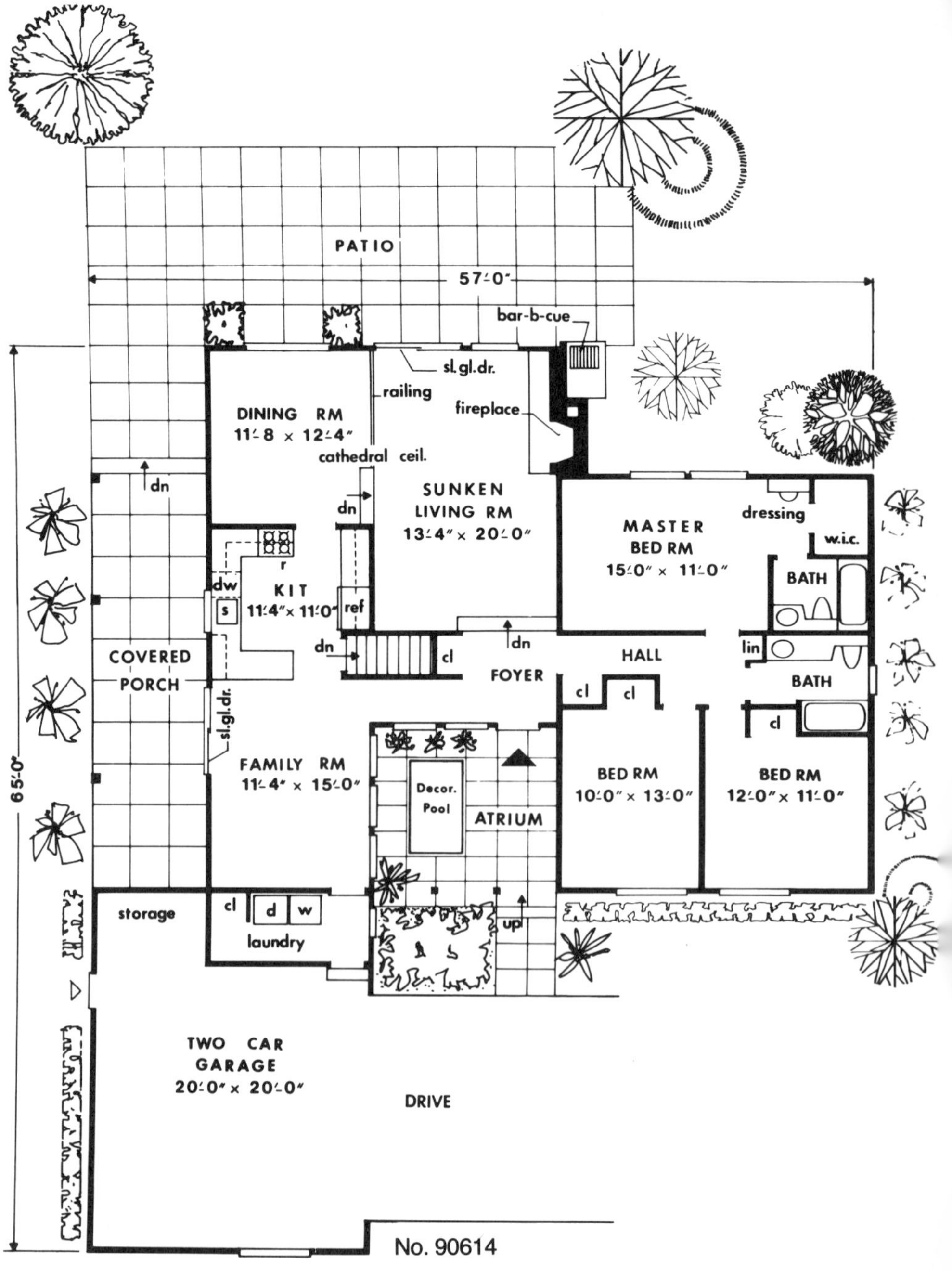

No. 90614

Entire Glass Front Distinguishes A-Frame

No. 90026

In this distinctive variation of the popular A-frame, the structure is built in the conventional manner of wood studs, rafters and joists. The entire front facade is glass, making it a wonderful house for any scenic property. Sunshine streams into the living area to create a cheerful, outdoor atmosphere. Although the plan now shows no basement, a full basement can be built by locating the stairs where the utility room is now.

First level — 962 sq. ft.
Second level — 578 sq. ft.

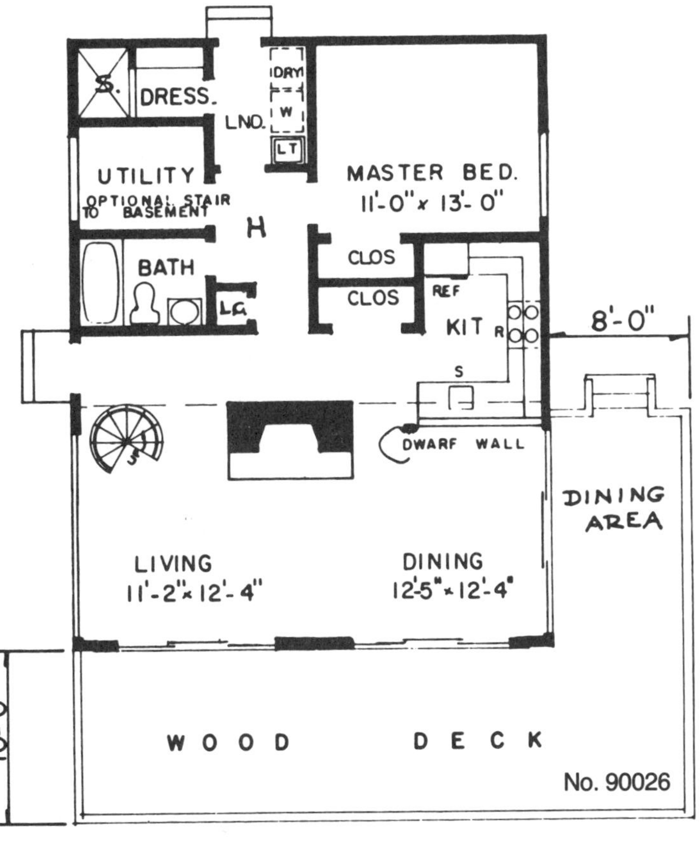

FIRST FLOOR

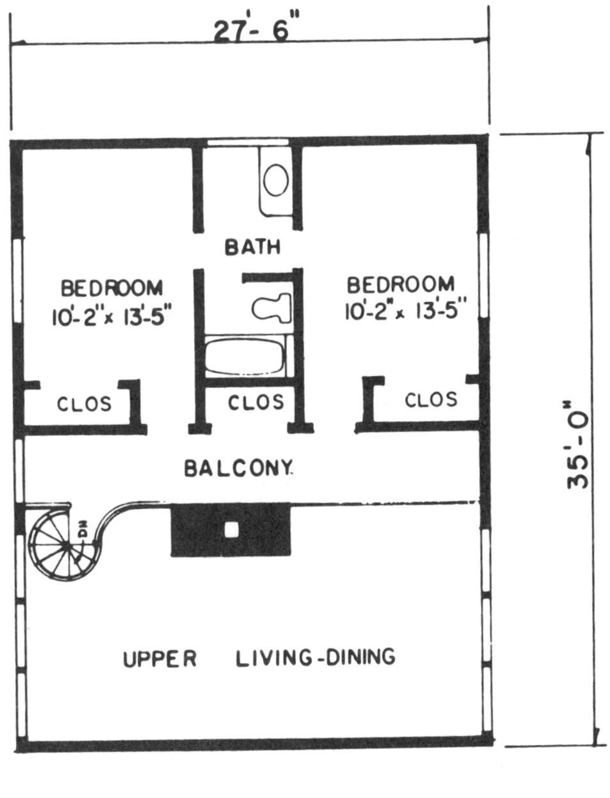

SECOND FLOOR

Ideal for Smaller Lot

No. 90322

All three bedrooms, including the master bedroom, plus a two entry bath, are located on the upper floor of this family home. The main floor is dominated by the family kitchen and the great room. The spacious great room features a vaulted ceiling and hearthed fireplace. The family kitchen runs the width of the house and opens onto both the backyard and the partially enclosed patio. The main entrance to the home incorporates a double door entry for increased energy efficiency all year. The laundry area and main floor powder room are centrally located.

Main floor — 834 sq. ft.
Upper floor — 715 sq. ft.
Basement — 823 sq. ft.
Garage — 440 sq. ft.

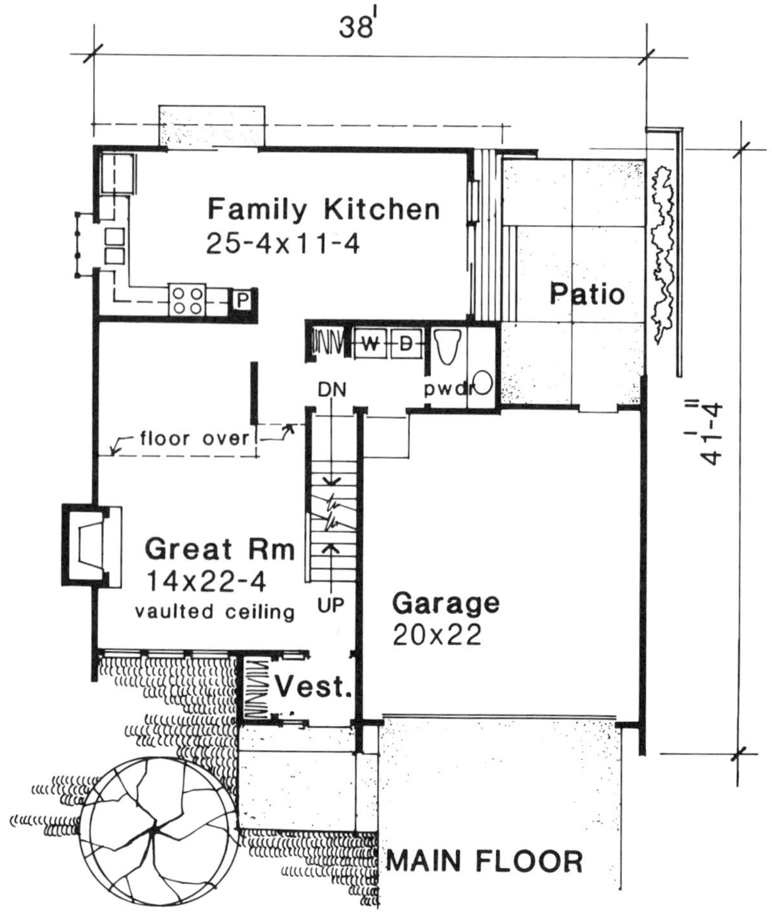

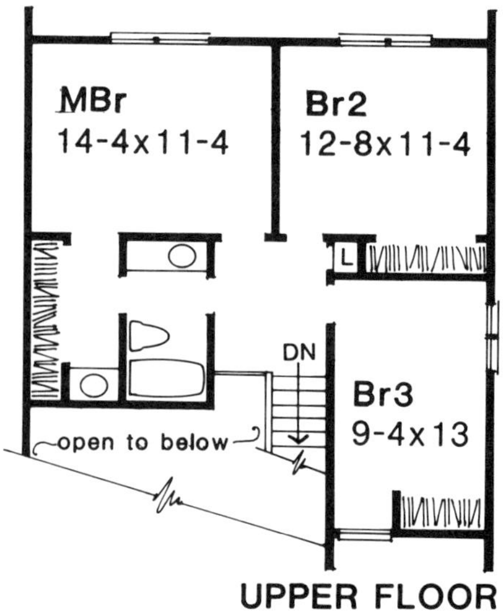

No. 90322

Arched Master Bedroom Window

No. 20055

The arched master bedroom window above the garage gives this three-bedroom, two and a half bath home a special appearance. The spacious kitchen opens onto a deck and adjoins a breakfast room with pantry. The entrance foyer lends access to the living room, formal dining room or stairs. The sloped ceiling in the master bedroom, a large bath with linen closet, dressing area and walk-in closet provide a sense of drama and complete privacy.

First floor — 928 sq. ft.
Second floor — 773 sq. ft.
Garage — 484 sq. ft.

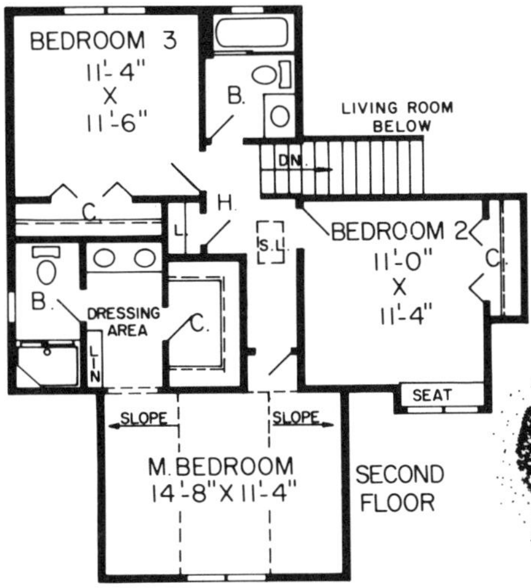

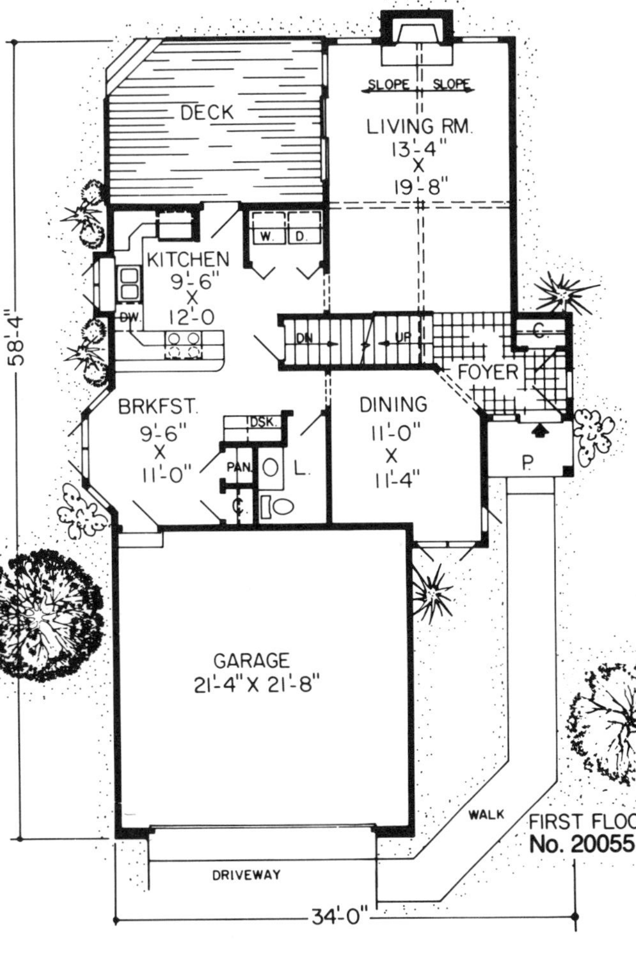

Distinctive Tudor Design

No. 90047

This Tudor adaptation stands out as a home of distinction. Its elegant exterior appearance is matched only by the quality of the interior design. Inside, the unusually large foyer makes a fine reception area with its two coat closets and is the key to efficient circulation, distributing traffic effectively throughout the first floor and by an attractive staircase to the two bedrooms on the second floor. To the left is the formal dining room. The oak-paneled family room directly behind the living room features a stone fireplace with a raised flagstone hearth flanked with casement windows on either side. There is no doubt that the romance and rustic charm of the English half-timber style of this three bedroom two-story design should delight families with a taste for Continental design.

First floor — 1,458 sq. ft.
Second floor — 539 sq. ft.
Basement — 1,552 sq. ft.
Garage & Laundry — 639 sq. ft.

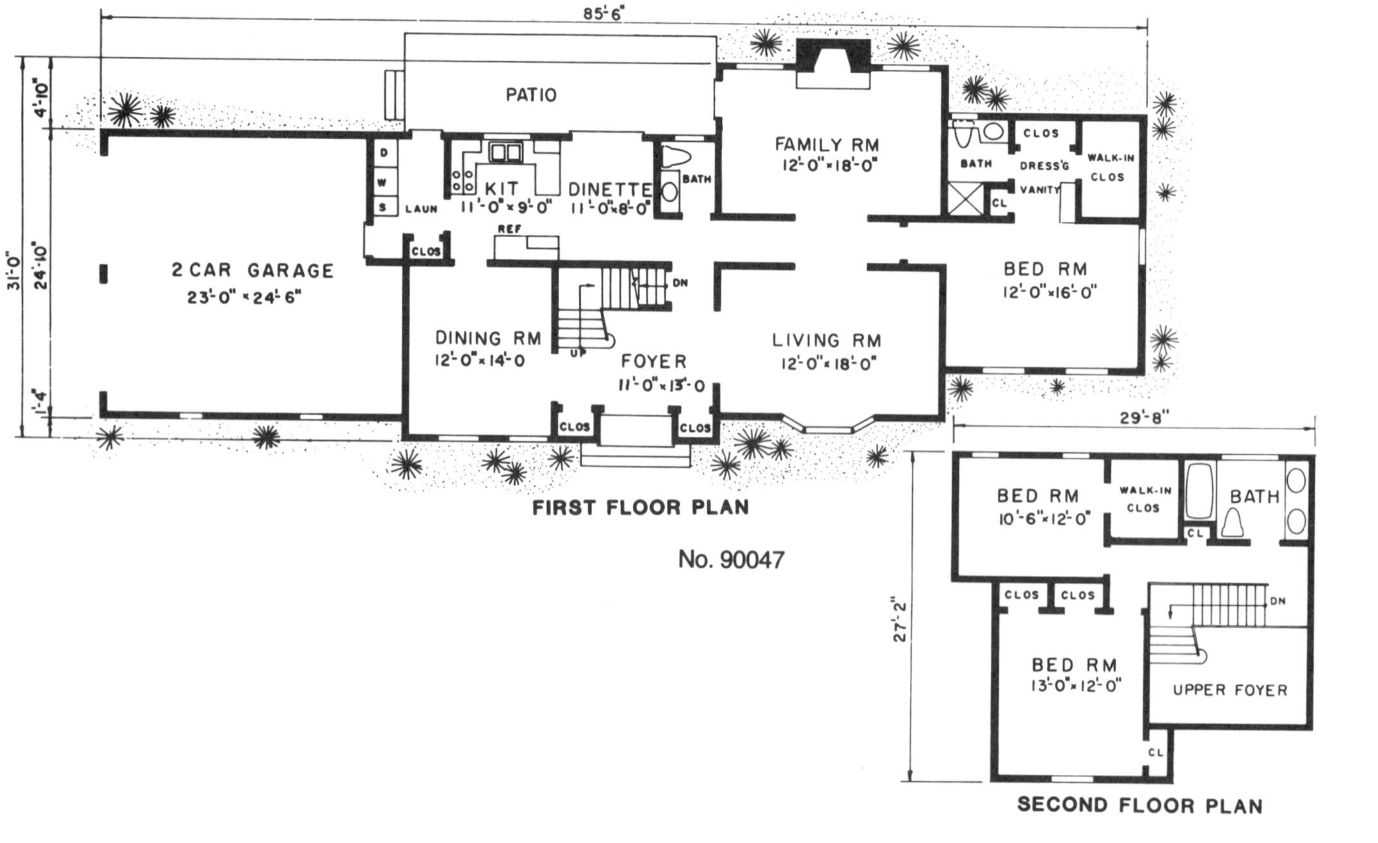

Delightful Colonial Design

No. 90138

A quick study of this traditional colonial design will highlight many features desired by homemakers. The exterior of this plan exhibits traditional double-hung windows and horizontal siding all around the house. The first floor living room is completely separated from all other rooms for formal entertaining. The informal family room is at the rear of the house and features a wood-burning fireplace. Sliding glass doors in the breakfast area lead to an outdoor patio which shares its view with the kitchen. A large pantry is located within the kitchen while the laundry facilities are close by. The second floor features four bedrooms and two full baths.

First floor — 1,152 sq. ft.
Second floor — 1,152 sq. ft.

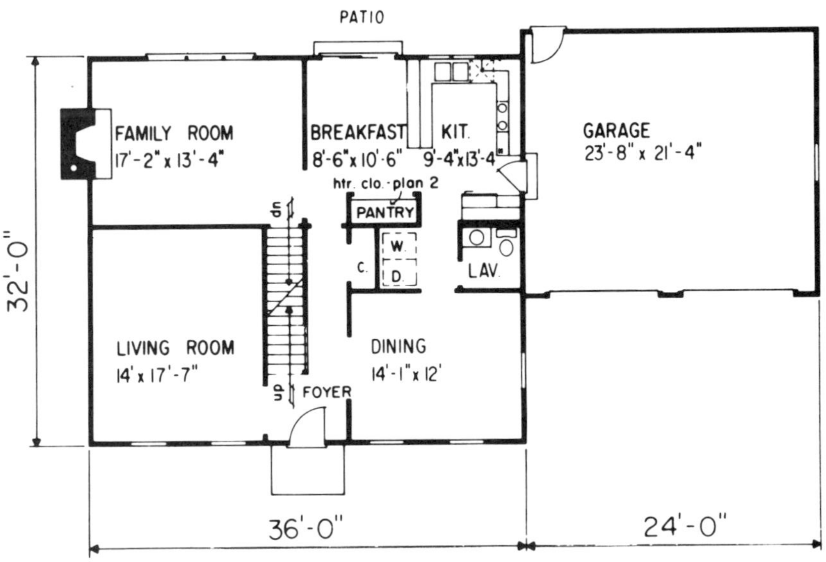

FIRST FLOOR
PLAN 1 WITH BASEMENT
PLAN 2 WITHOUT BASEMENT

No. 90138

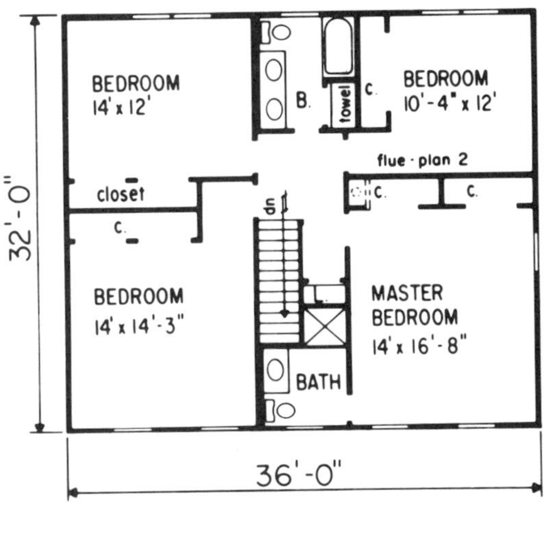

SECOND FLOOR

An Octagon For Open Holiday Living

No. 90009

An octagon living area ringed by an outdoor, sheltered porch gives this house a vacation air. Leisurely living is provided by a swimming pool that reaches almost into the living room and an outdoor dining- and living porch curving away at either side of the pool. The living-dining room is dominated by a central, circular chimney with a fireplace facing the living area and a grille facing the kitchen. An open counter between kitchen and dining area facilitates formal and informal service while keeping diners out of the kitchen. The octagonal section of the house is completed by a bath with double lavatory and a laundry area. In contrast to the wide-open living octagon, the bedroom wing is enclosed for privacy, particularly on the facade.

Living Area — 1,183 sq. ft.

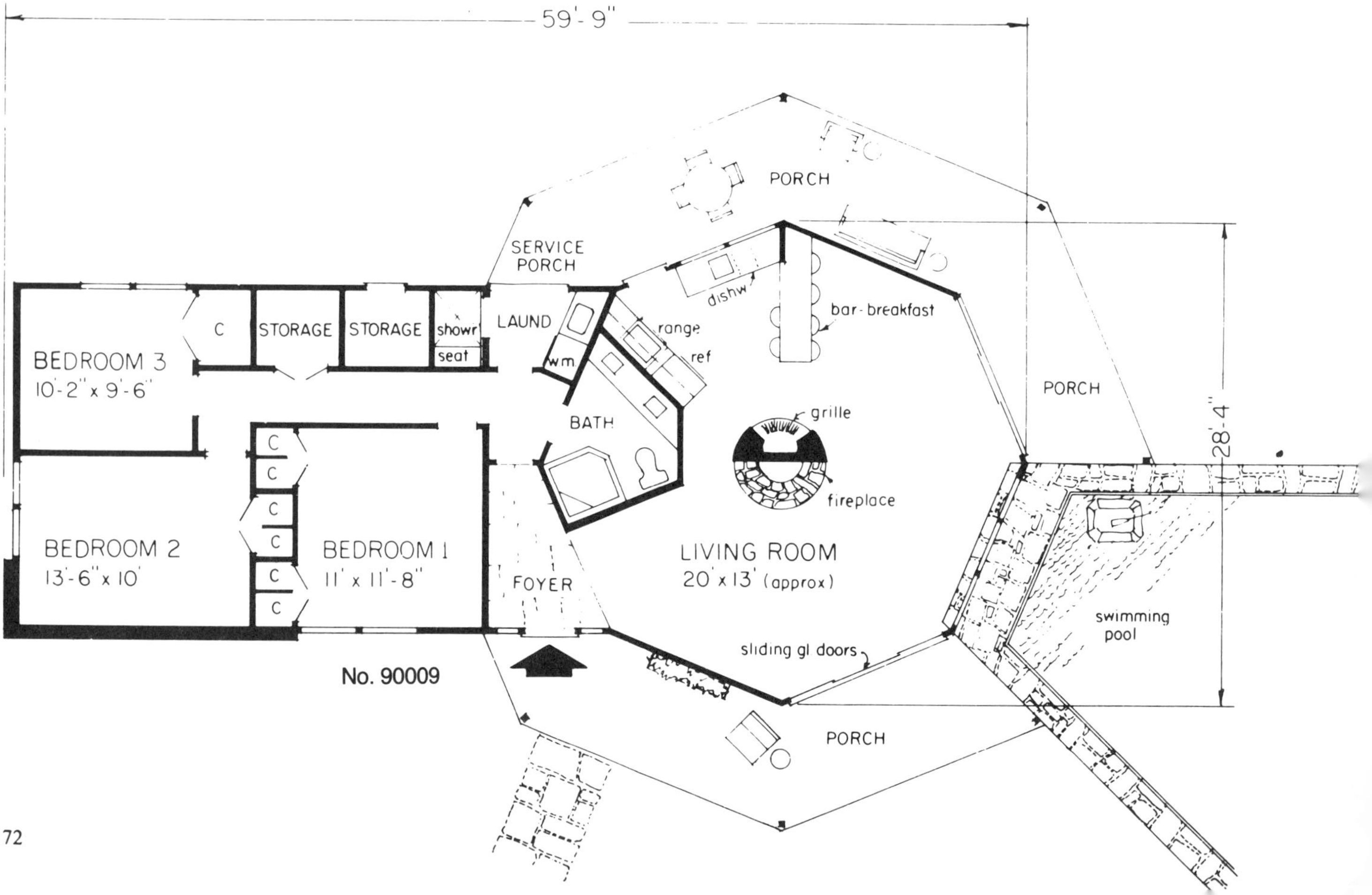

No. 90009

Classic ranch Features French Styling

No. 90019

Formal homes, although always popular, are now enjoying a marked revival in many parts of the country. In this ever popular ranch design, the corner quoins, long entrance porch, shuttered windows, circular brick arches and steep roofs capture the traditional look of classic French styling. A centrally located entrance foyer assures good circulation by channelling traffic in three directions: to the dining room straight ahead, to the three bedrooms on the left, and to the interior focal point to the home, a sunken living room separated from the foyer by a decorative wrought iron railing. The cathedral ceiling kitchen-family room is especially desirable because of the massive brick fireplace where the family is likely to spend most of its leisure time and because of its access to the rear pool terrace through the sliding glass doors.

Living area — 1,645 sq.ft.
Garage — 522 sq.ft.

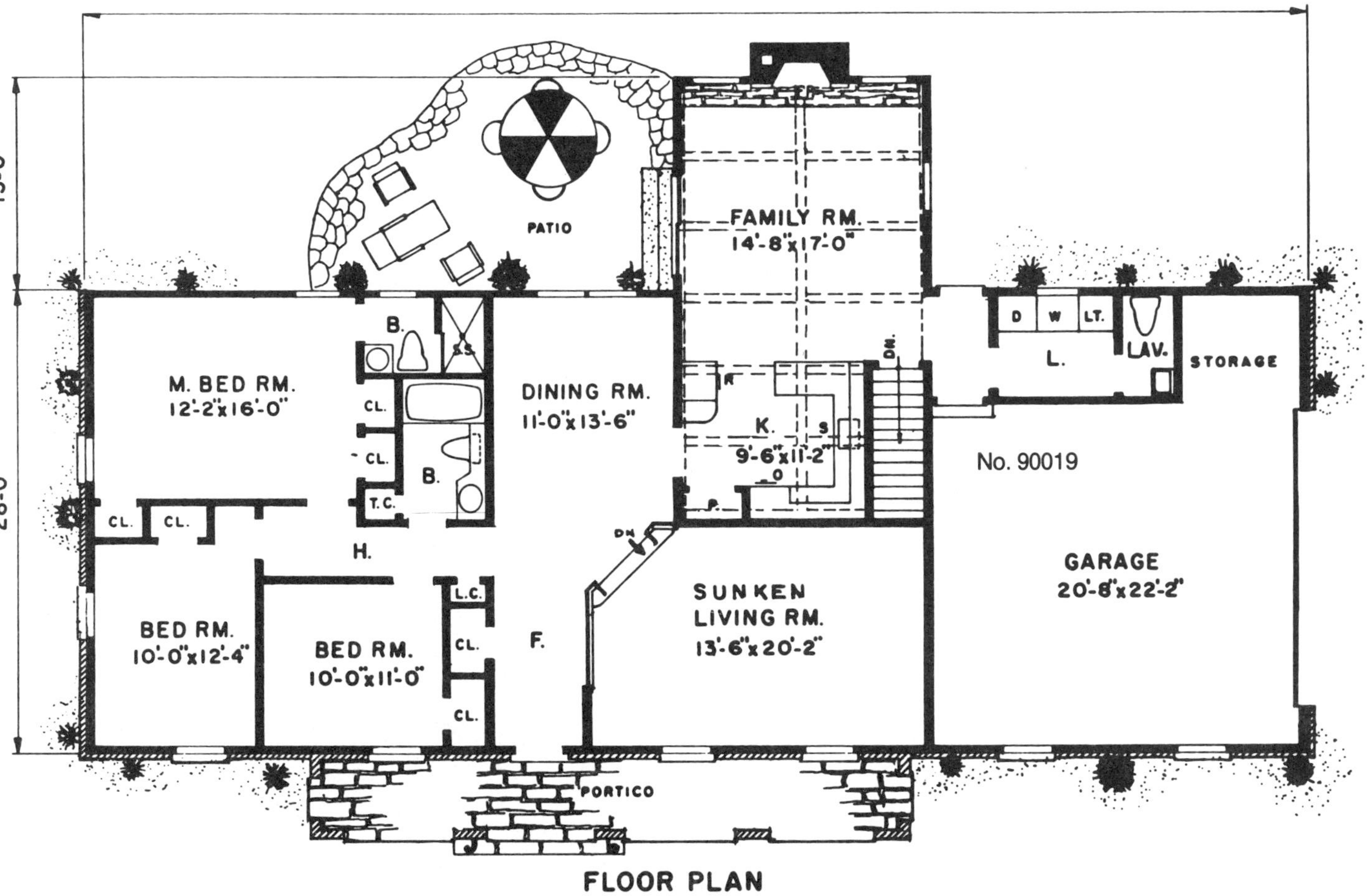

FLOOR PLAN

Lots of Closets and Storage Space

No. 90318

This compact three-bedroom design is ideal for placement on a narrow lot. The living room features a cathedral ceiling which reaches up to the second floor loft and a bump-out window that would be perfect for a window seat. The family room includes a fireplace and sliding glass doors giving access to the patio. The garage entrance to the family room incorporates closet space for the family's coats. The U-shaped kitchen is separated from the family room by a convenient food preparation center. The first floor bedroom has built-in storage plus a double closet. Two additional bedrooms are located on the upper level.

Main level — 929 sq. ft.
Upper level — 491 sq. ft.
Basement — 929 sq. ft.
Garage — 436 sq. ft.

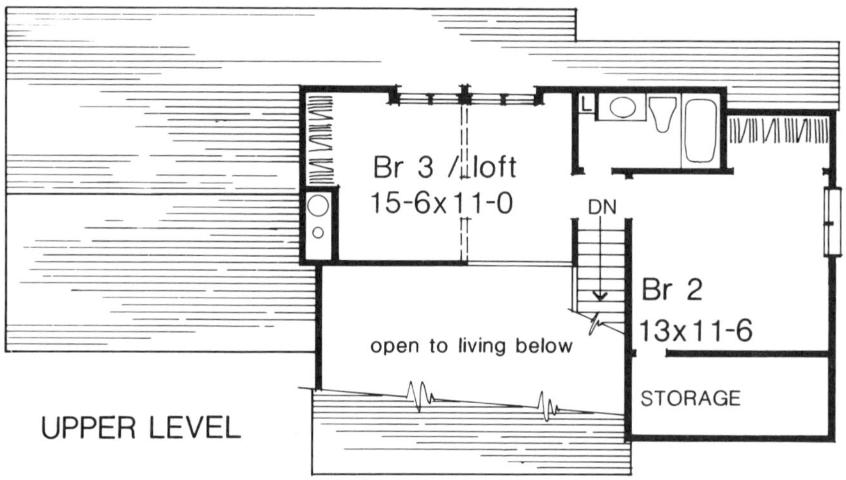

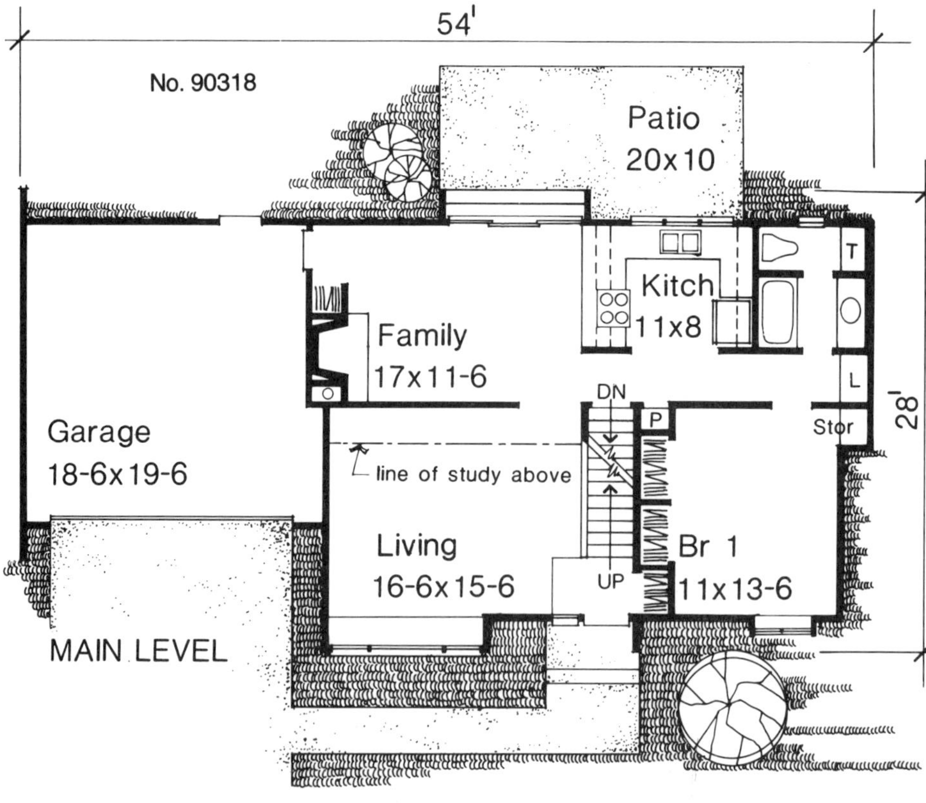

Outdoor Lovers' Dream Home

No. 90640

Enjoy the best of old and new in one sparkling design. Even your plants will love this Tudor-styled contemporary with solar bays and energy-saving 2 X 6 stud construction. Sun-filled family areas at the rear of the house are flanked by porches and surrounded by a huge terrace. At mealtime, choose breakfast bar service to the family room, or eat in the formal dining room. Both are adjacent to the kitchen. And, the fireplaced living room off the foyer allows entertaining on a grand scale. Sequestered upstairs for a quiet atmosphere, four bedrooms include the spacious master suite.

First floor — 1,020 sq. ft.
Second floor — 876 sq. ft.
Basement — 796 sq. ft.
Garage and storage — 481 sq. ft.

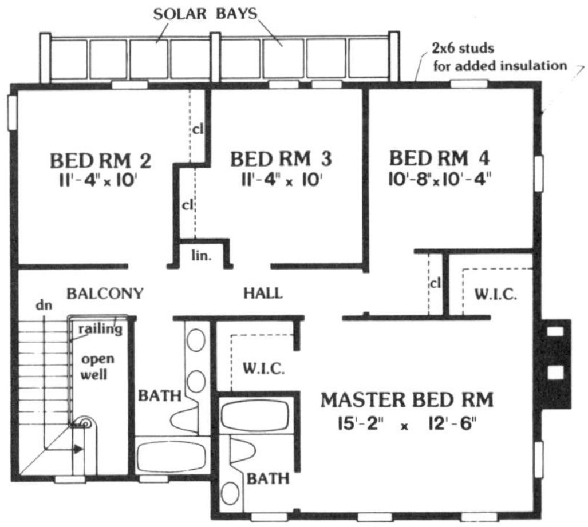

SECOND FLOOR PLAN

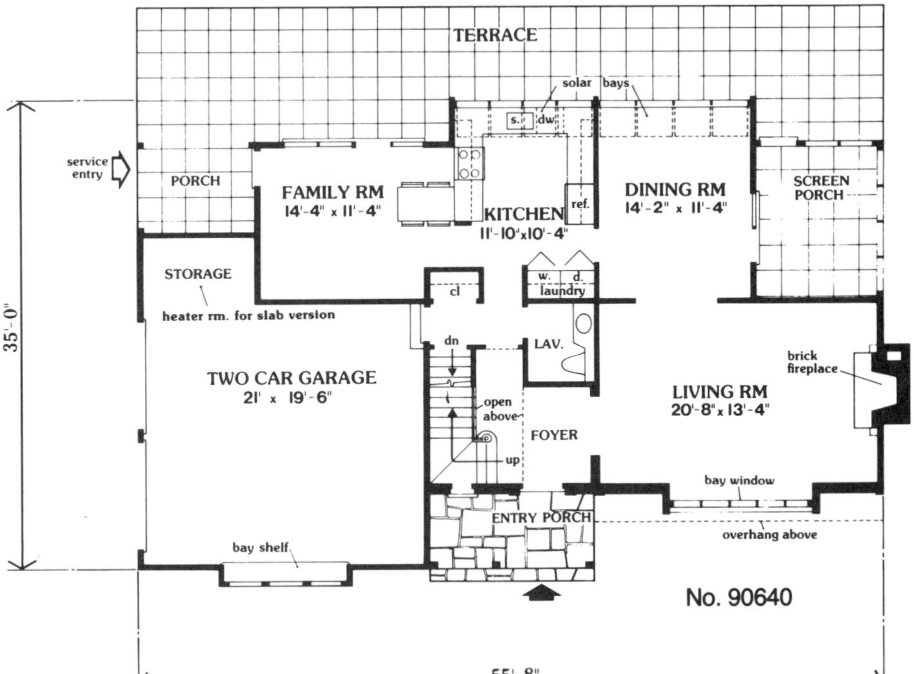

FIRST FLOOR PLAN

Flexible Plan Create Many Options

No. 90324

Add a third bedroom, include a cozy den, or expand the dining area according to the family's needs. This flexible plan is designed to let you decide. The inviting great room views blooming plants in season through the multiple windows and features a vaulted ceiling plus a fireplace and built-in bookcase. The roomy eat-in kitchen opens onto the partially enclosed deck through sliding glass doors. Its L-shaped design provides for convenient meal preparation and easy access to storage. The comfortable master bedroom has a private bath, large walk-in closet and charming window seat. The second full bath is convenient to the second bedroom as well as the living areas of the house.

Living area — 1,016 sq. ft.

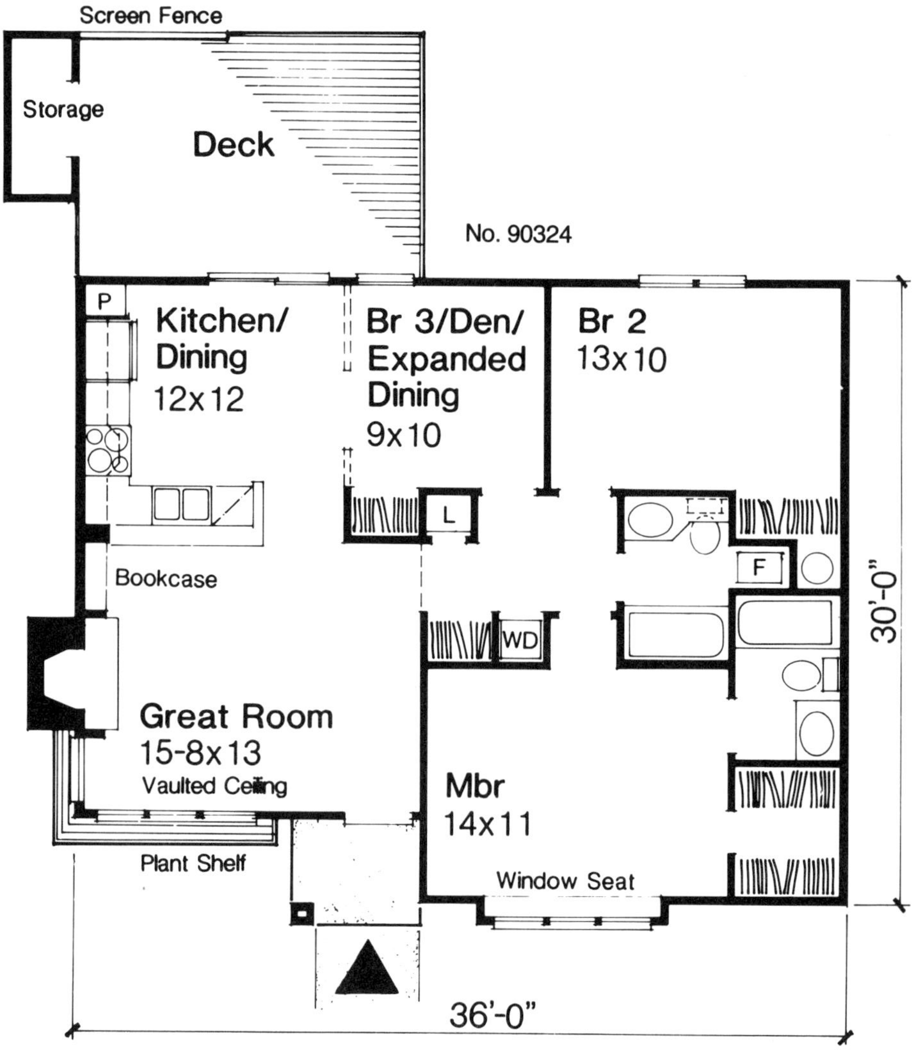

Soaring Ceilings and Multiple Levels Enlarge Living Areas

No. 91047

Behind double doors, just off the two-story foyer, the den in this exciting home will give you a quiet place to work or greet clients. And, the charming living room with adjoining dining room is a great place to entertain. The huge island kitchen can handle a crowd of any size. Watch your guests arrive from the window seat in the sitting room of your master suite, a cozy spot with a fireplace and built-in bookcase. Skylights brighten the bedroom, walk-in closet, and both upstairs baths without compromising your privacy. And, on busy mornings when everyone's in a hurry, you're sure to appreciate the double vanities.

Main floor — 1,831 sq. ft.
Upper floor — 1,269 sq. ft.

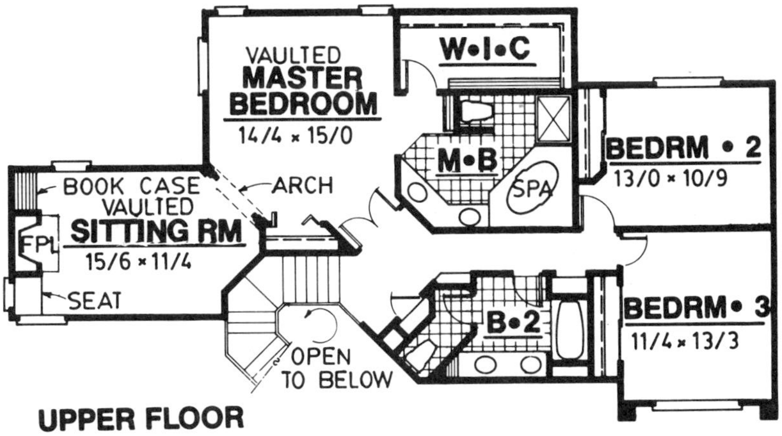

UPPER FLOOR
1269 SQ. FT.

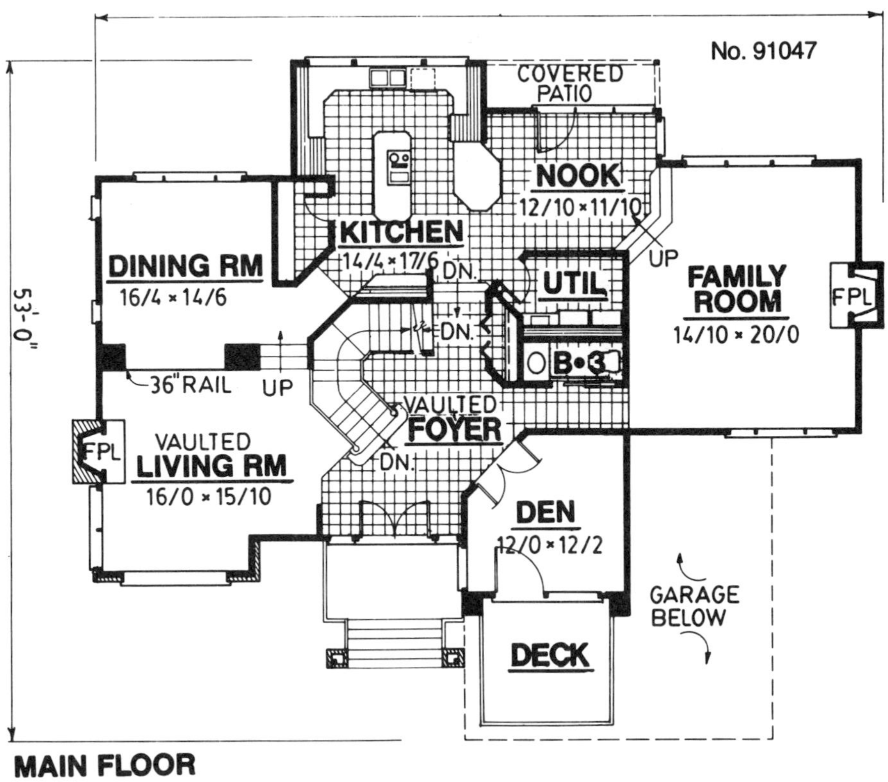

MAIN FLOOR
1831 SQ. FT.

Compact, Contemporary Design

No. 90101

This compact home is designed so that you can finish each section as needed or all at the beginning. This type of plan is perfect for a flexible budget or a growing family. Ideal for a narrow lot, this home features a vaulted ceiling above the open living room which blends into the dining area adjacent to the efficiently designed kitchen. The first floor also includes two bedrooms and a roomy bath. Second floor bedrooms and bath may be completed at a future date, as may the optional garage.

First floor — 988 sq. ft.
Second floor — 520 sq. ft.

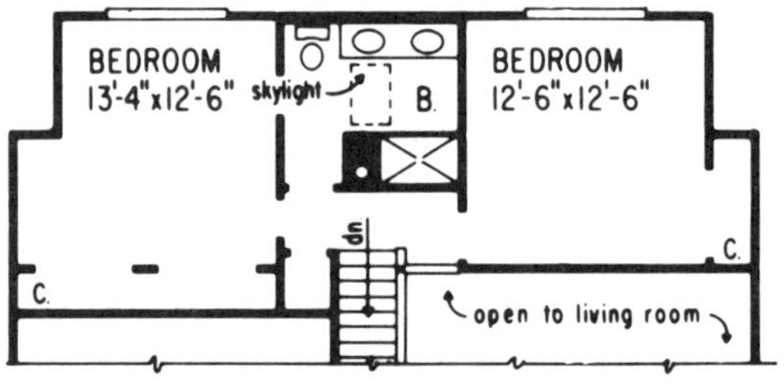

SECOND FLOOR

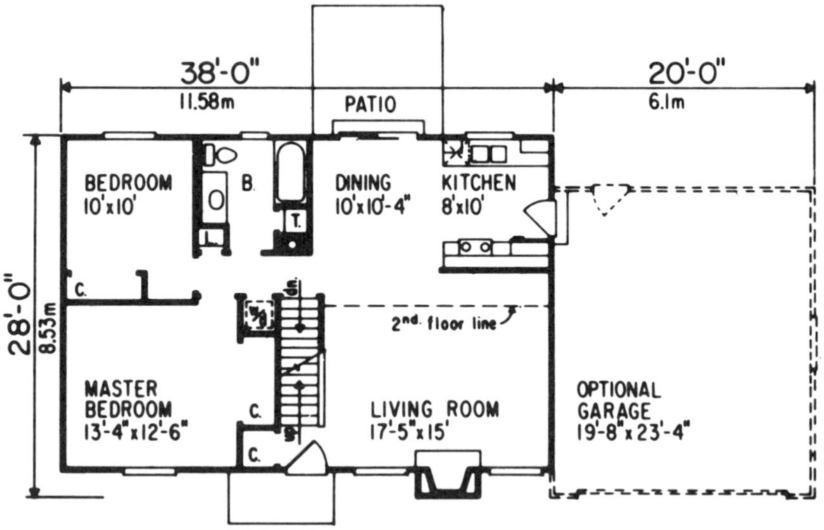

FIRST FLOOR PLAN 1 WITH BASEMENT
No. 90101

Distinctive Split-Level

No. 90010

From its dramatically handsome entrance to the master bedroom's spacious walk-in closet, this home is distinctive in every detail. Exterior appearance is luxurious, with stone, brick and wood shingles excellently combined. The large foyer serves as a traffic hub. A sunken garden outside the large family room is reached through sliding glass doors. The efficient kitchen includes a breakfast balcony overlooking the family room. The bedroom area is served by two complete baths. Another half bath serves the family room area.

Living Area — 1,727 sq. ft.

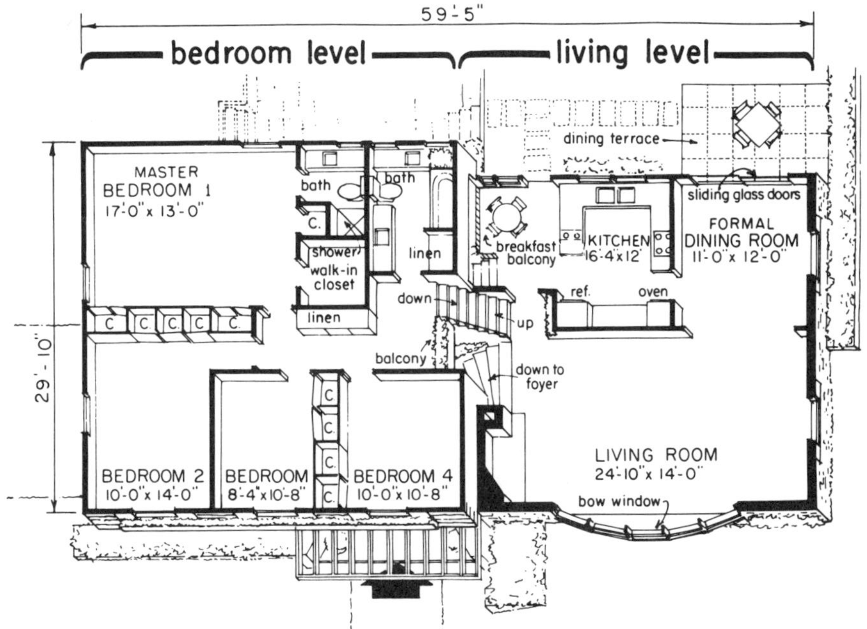

No. 90010

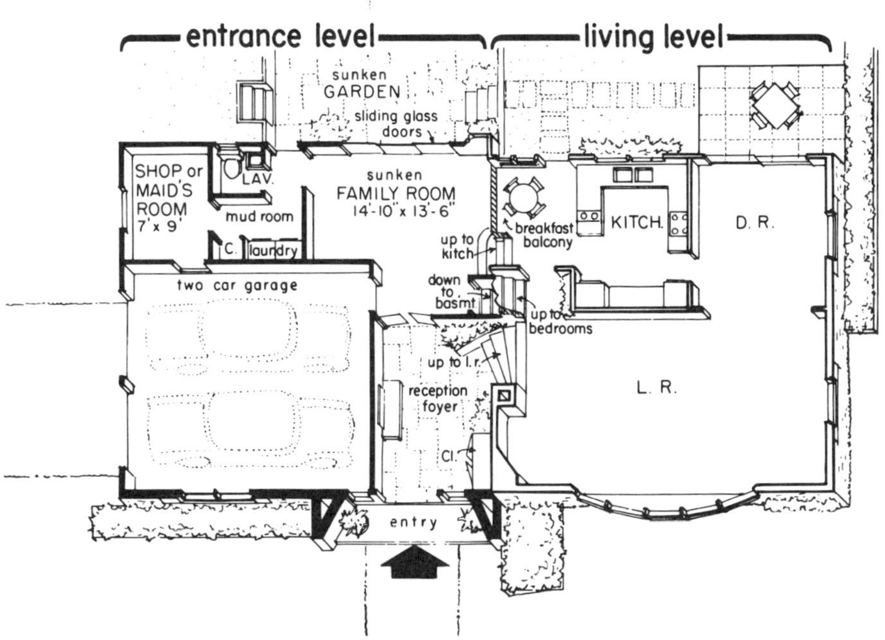

Designed for Entertaining

No. 10587

The double doors of the vaulted entry are just a hint of the graceful touches in this three-bedroom home. Curves soften the stairway, deck, and the huge bar that runs between the formal and informal dining areas. Skylights, bay-, and bump-out windows flood every room with light. And when the sun goes down, you can keep things cozy with fireplaces in the family and sunken living rooms. For a quiet retreat, sneak upstairs to deck off the master bedroom suite.

First floor — 2,036 sq. ft.
Second floor — 1,554 sq. ft.
Garage — 533 sq. ft.

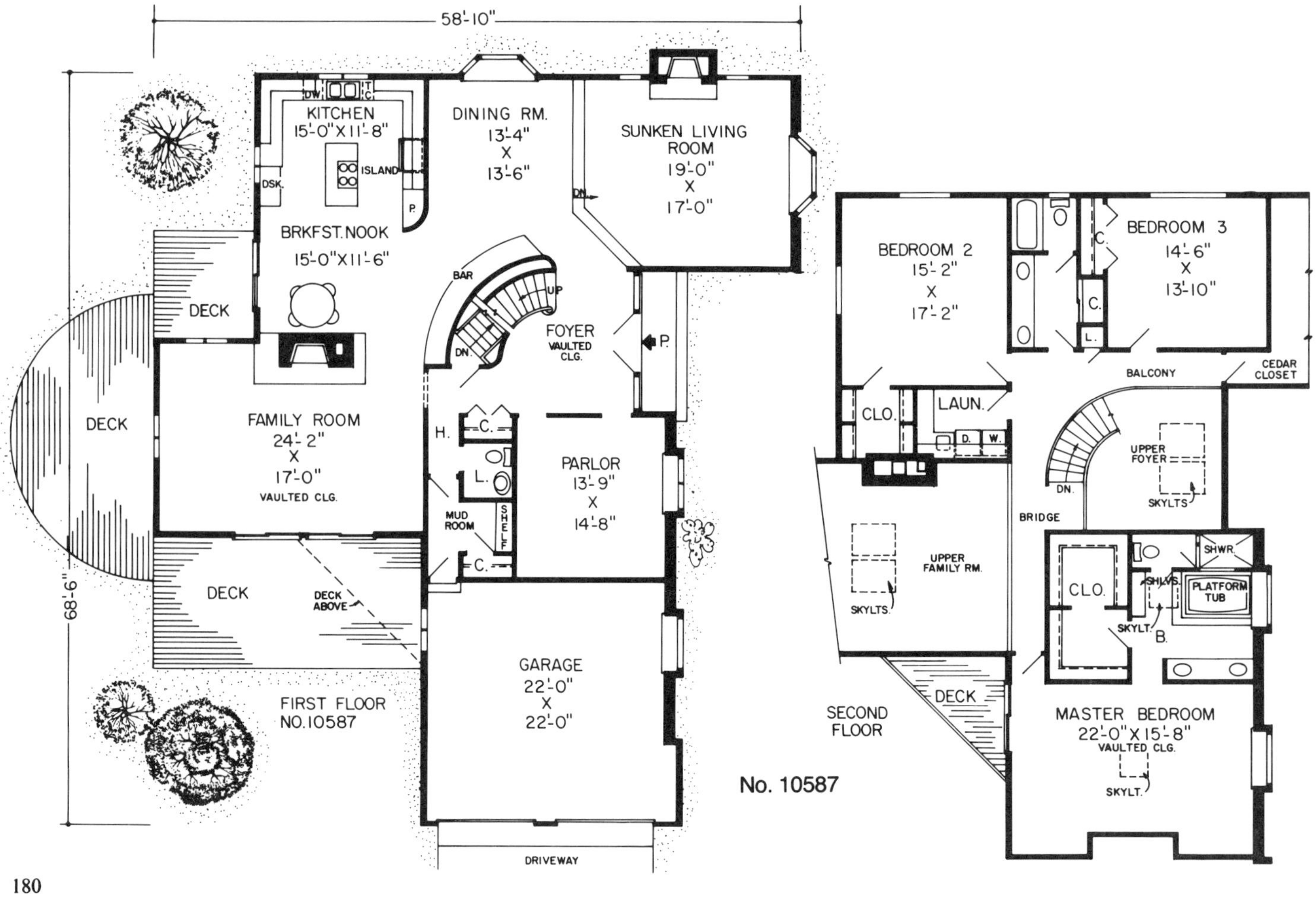

Visual Excitement

No. 90665

Here's an exciting home built for beautiful views inside and out. Standing on the bridge that connects the two upstairs bedrooms and full bath, you can survey your two-story foyer, the sunken living room, and even the rear patio that lies beyond the double sliding glass doors. The view from the dining room is just as exciting. The bow window brings the outdoors inside. And, the brick wall surrounding the fireplace in the adjoining sunken living room rises two stories to a dizzying height. Beauty isn't the only asset possessed by this magnificent home. The convenience of the kitchen to both dining areas, the handy lavatory for your guests, and the quiet repose of a separate bedroom wing are all the result of an ingenious plan with the homeowner in mind.

First floor — 1,458 sq. ft.
Second floor — 470 sq. ft.

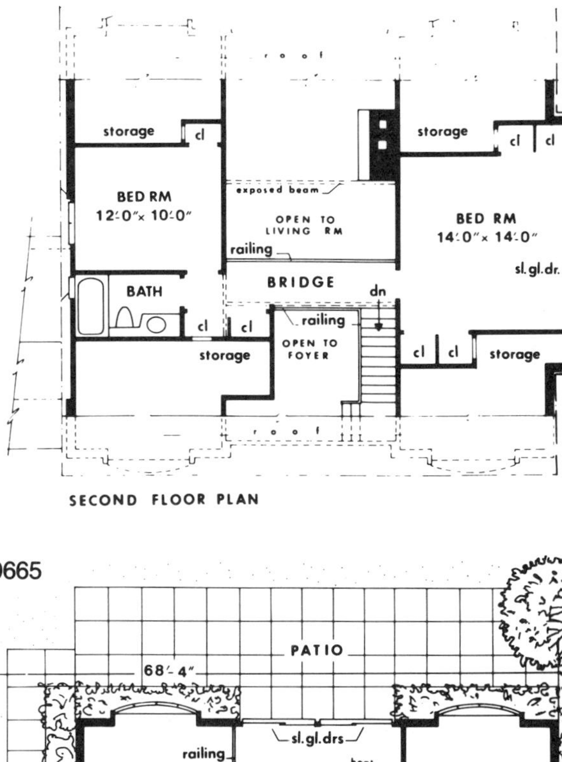

SECOND FLOOR PLAN

No. 90665

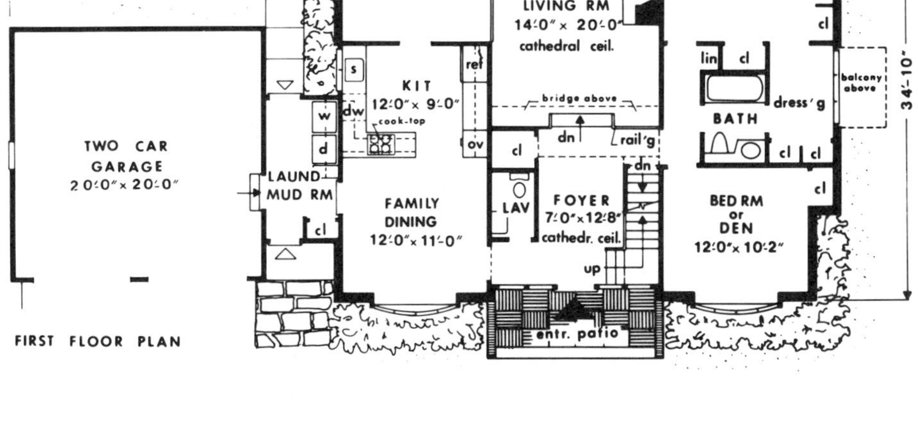

FIRST FLOOR PLAN

Deluxe Master Suite

No. 90507

The master bedroom commands this contemporary 4 bedroom design. With oversized, walk-in closet and dressing room, this king sized bedroom is irresistable. The vaulted, tiled foyer extends to the kitchen and channels traffic for privacy. The formal atmosphere of the living and dining room combination is a delightful contrast to the casual, firelit charm of the family room.

First floor — 1,359 sq. ft.
Second floor — 1,318 sq. ft.

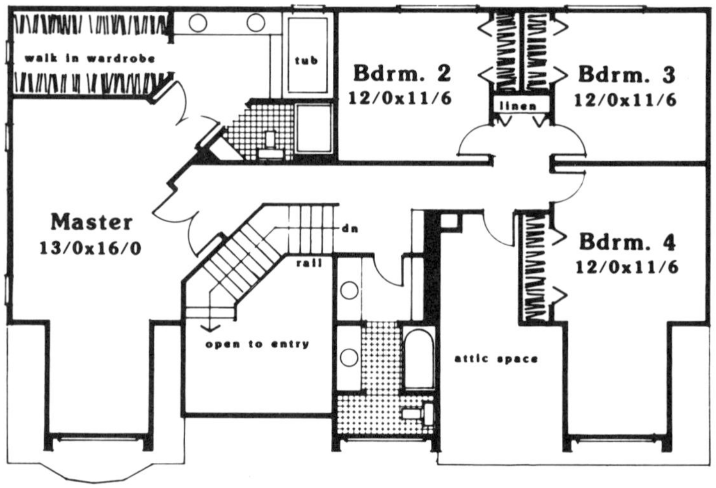

Upper Floor

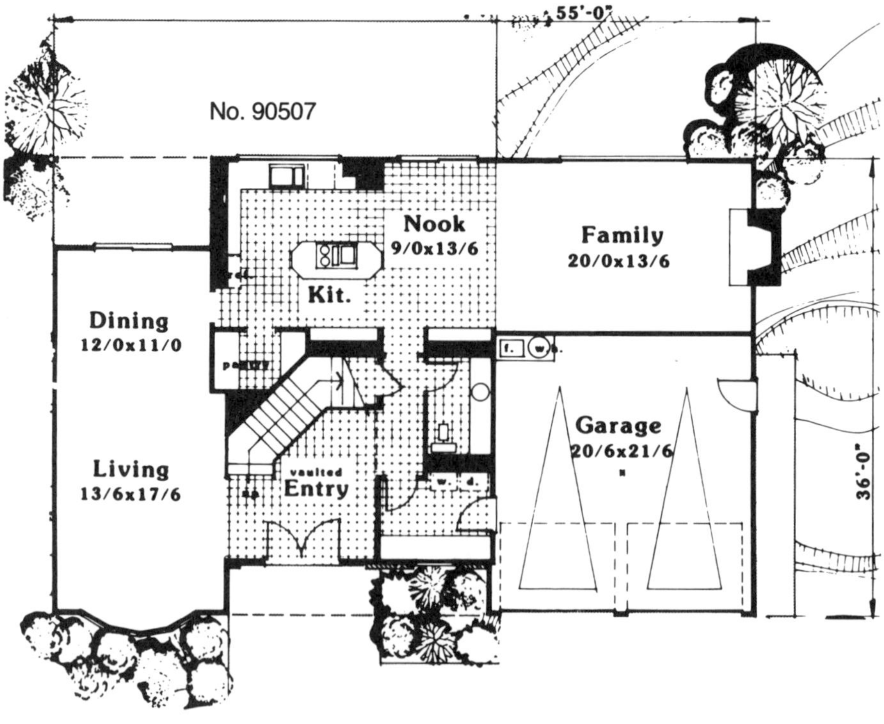

Bridge Above Great Room

No. 90316

The living area of this home is dominated by the large, open plan of the great room and the dining room. Each opens onto the rear deck through sliding glass doors and is further lighted by two stories of windows. The kitchen features a corner sink and adjacent breakfast room which opens onto a private dining patio. The laundry is conveniently located and includes a large closet which serves the garage entrance. Additional features on the first floor include a powder room and a library. The second floor bridge links the master bedroom to the other two bedrooms on this floor and incorporates a linen cabinet as one of the railings.

Main floor — 1,213 sq. ft.
Upper floor — 916 sq. ft.
Basement — 1,164 sq. ft.
Garage — 459 sq. ft.

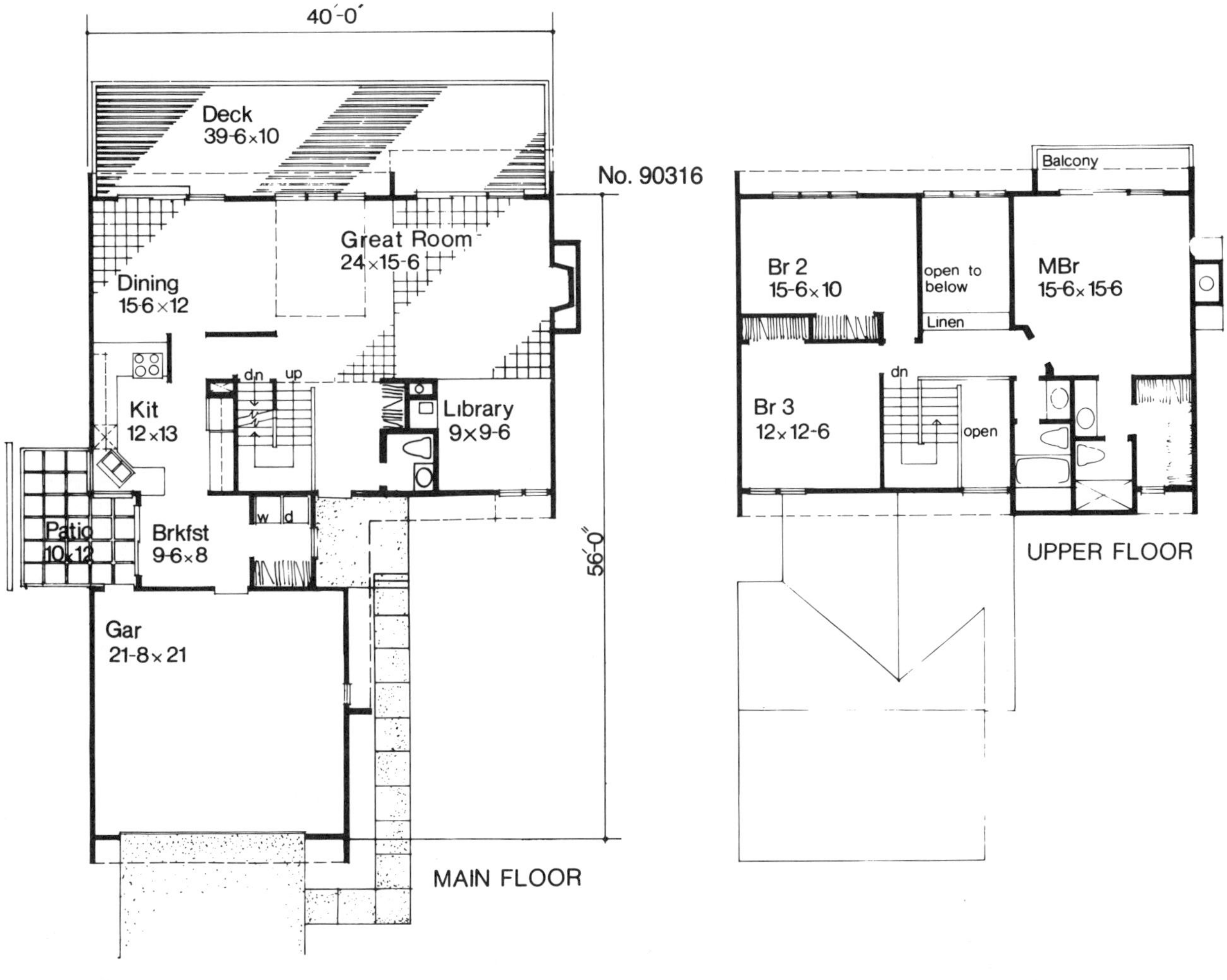

Family Activities Plus Elegant Style

No. 90100

Two garden patios, one off the kitchen and one off the great room, increase the elegant living available in this spacious home. The great room's cathedral ceiling opens onto the loft above and creates an expansive atmosphere which is complemented by the stone fireplace. Two bedrooms across the front of the house might also be used as a den or library or turned to other functional use. The master bedroom's bath is designed for privacy but may also be shared with one of the front bedrooms.

First floor — 1,898 sq. ft.
Second floor — 400 sq. ft.

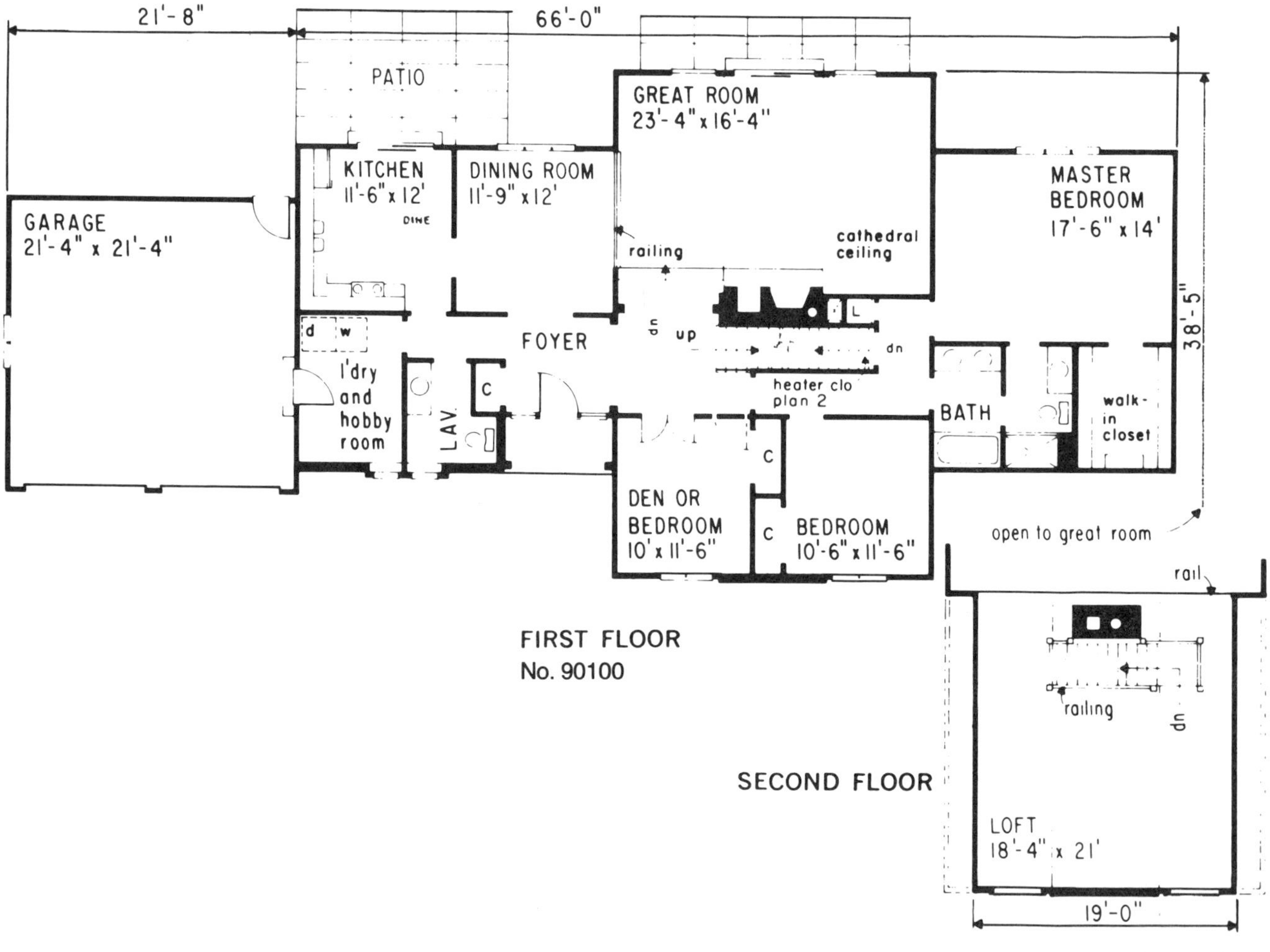

Traditional Warmth and Charm

No. 90664

There's no cozier house than a New England Cape, with its high-pitched roof, shuttered windows, and compact Colonial economy. And many think there's none prettier. This four-bedroom charmer is no exception. A fireplace in the spacious living room adds to the friendly atmosphere and helps keep the heating bills down. Enjoy your meals across the foyer in the formal dining room or use the dinette off off the kitchen. Here's a plus for a retired couple: two first-floor bedrooms adjoin a full bath at the rear of the house. Save the second floor for guests and grandchildren. The two bedrooms upstairs share a full bath.

First floor — 1,102 sq. ft.
Second floor — 465 sq. ft.

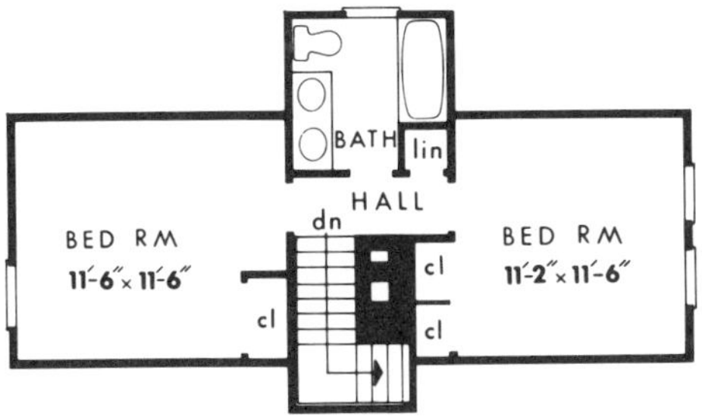

SECOND FLOOR PLAN

No. 90664

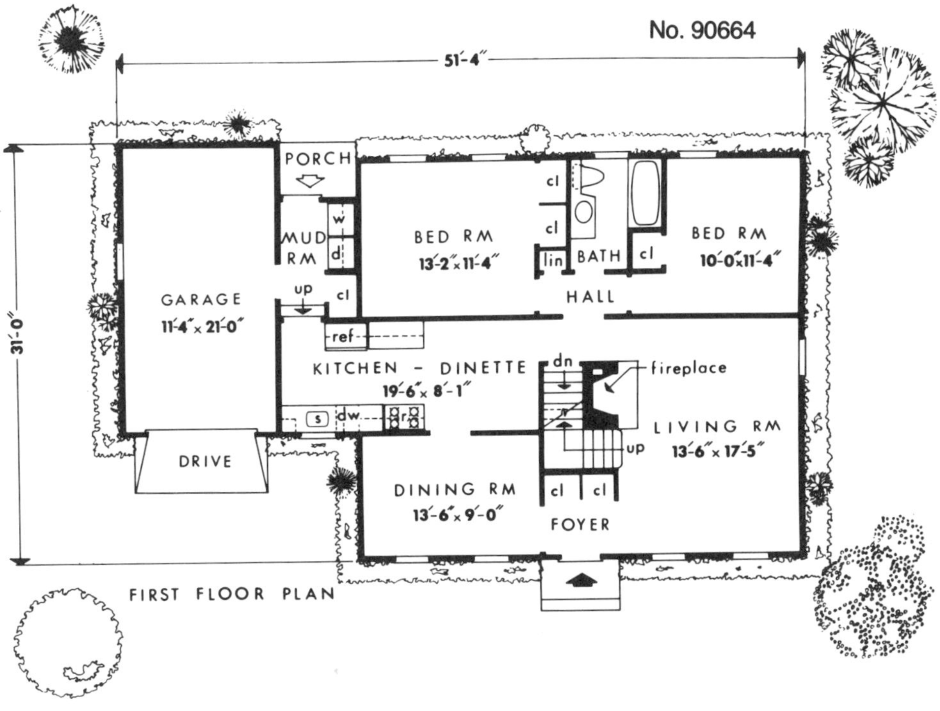

FIRST FLOOR PLAN

Two-story Foyer Marks Fabulous Design

No. 90514

Enter a stunning 2-story foyer with tiled floor. Excellent traffic patterns provide discrete access to kitchen, linen and laundry facilities. The kitchen and breakfast nook boast easy dining and quick access to the deck through sliding doors. The sunken family and living rooms each have a cozy fireplace. The bedrooms are grouped on the 2nd floor, with a walk-in closet and dressing area for the master. Another prominent feature is the 3-car garage.

First floor — 1,599 sq. ft.
Second floor — 1,236 sq. ft.
Bonus room — 429 sq. ft.

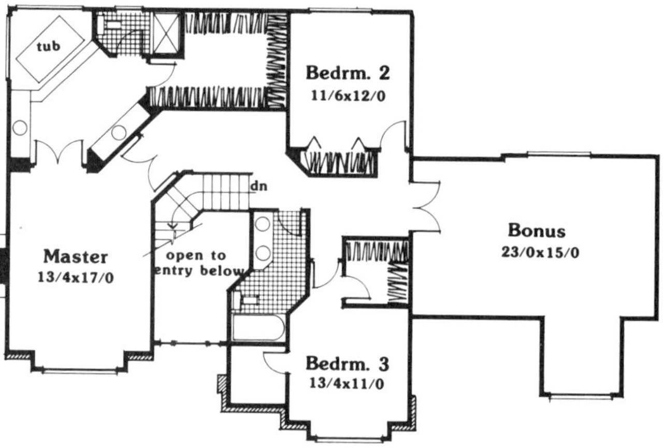

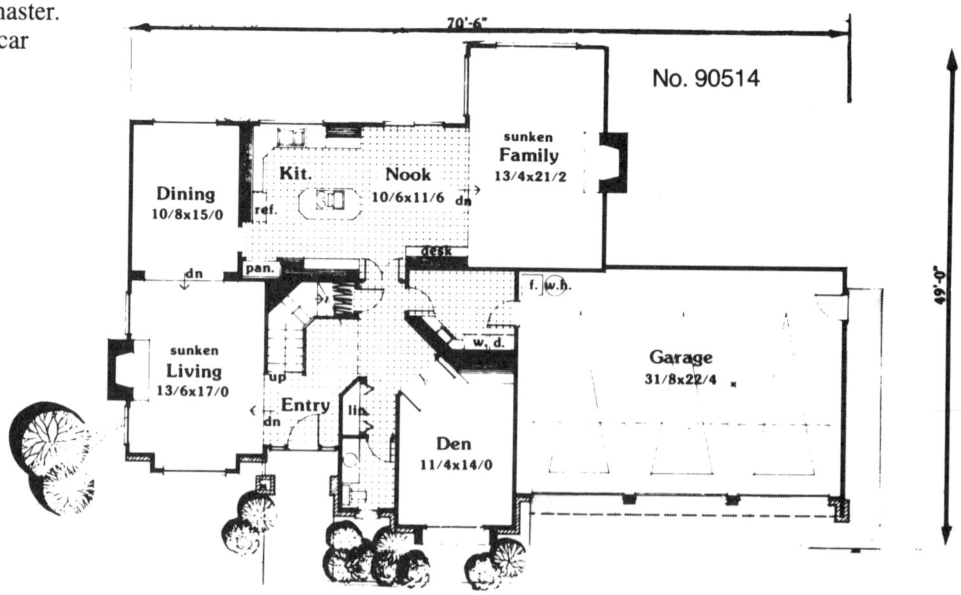

Open Plan Features Great Room and Exterior Options

No. 90328

With a skylight and a vaulted ceiling, the great room will welcome family and guests alike. This inviting room also includes a fireplace, sliding door access to the deck and a wet bar. The roomy eat-in kitchen features an efficient U-shaped work area and lots of windows in the dining area. The three bedrooms and two full baths incorporate unusual angled entries so as the make the most of every foot of floor space. The master bedroom combines its bath and dressing area. The third bedroom would make a cozy den or a handy room for guests.

Main floor — 1,400 sq. ft.
Basement — 1,350 sq. ft.
Garage — 374 sq. ft.

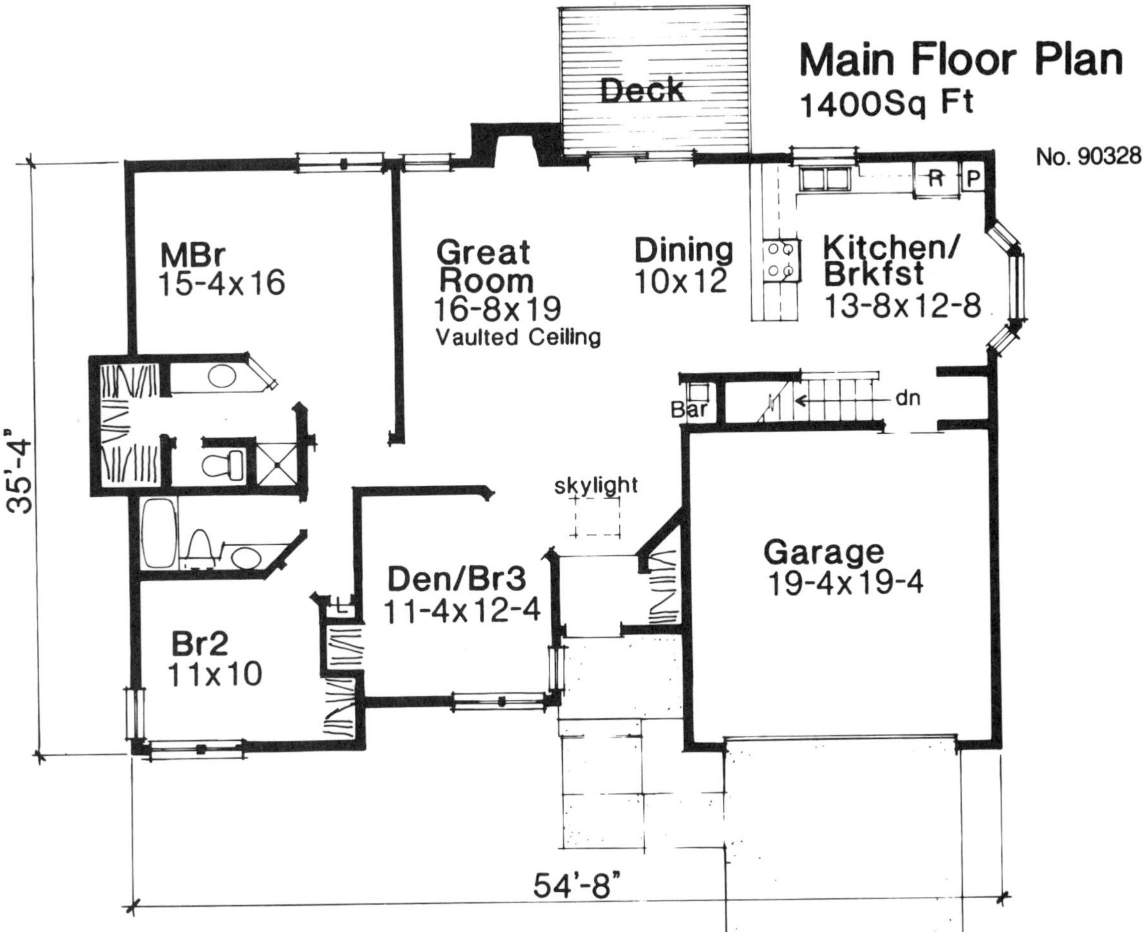

Contemporary Exterior

No. 90327

A spacious feeling is created by the ingenious arrangement of the living areas of this comfortable home. The inviting living room offers a cozy fireplace, a front corner full of windows, a vaulted ceiling and an open staircase. The clerestory windows further accent the open design of the dining room and kitchen. The U-shaped kithen welcomes cook and tasters alike with its open preparation areas. Secluded from the rest of the main floor and the other two bedrooms, the master bedroom features a walk-in closet and a large, compartmented bath which may also serve as a guest bathroom. Two additional bedrooms and a full bath comprise the upper floor.

Main floor — 846 sq. ft.
Upper floor — 400 sq. ft.
Basement — 846 sq. ft.
Garage — 400 sq. ft.

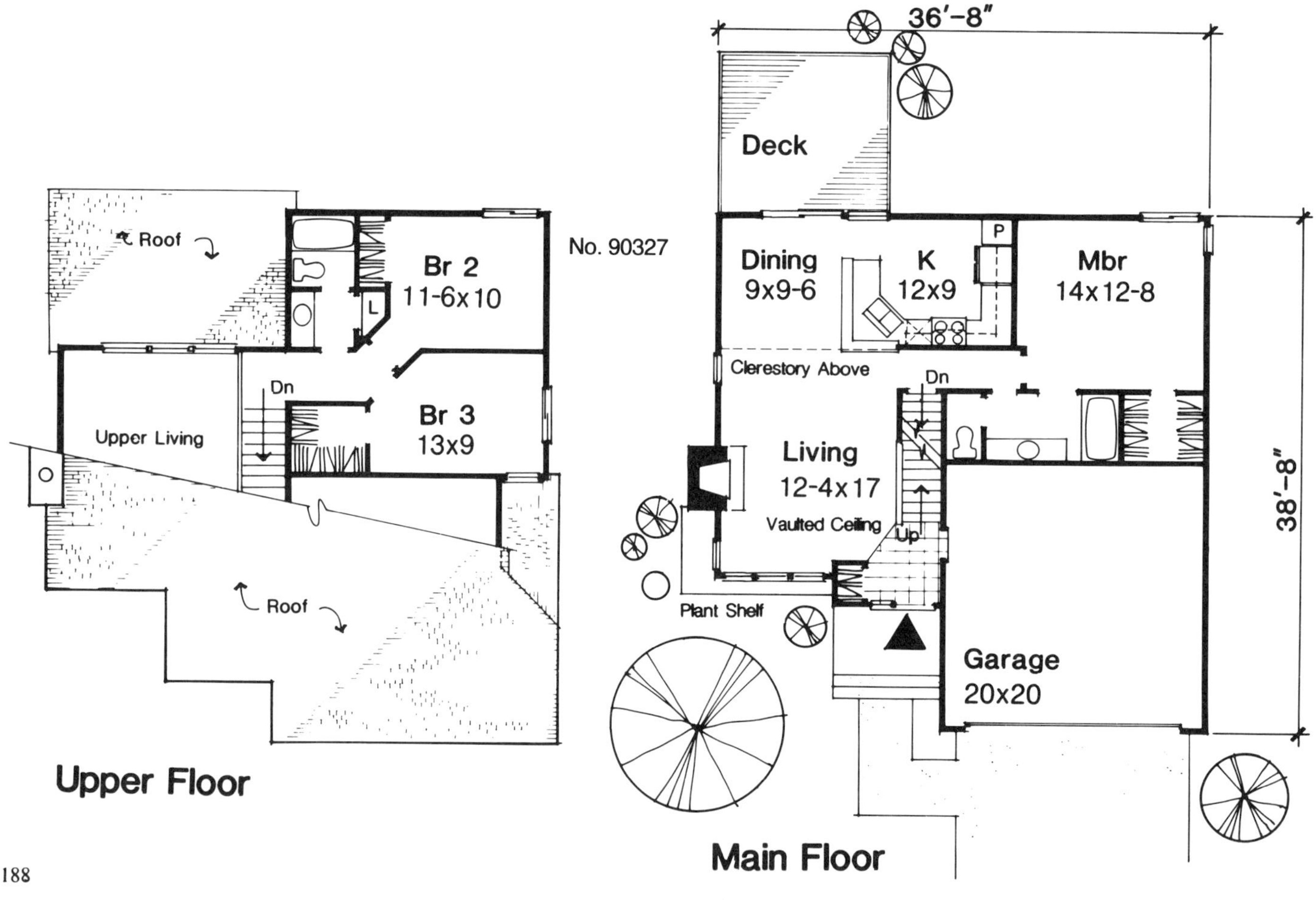

Fireplace Serves Dual Purpose

No. 90657

Vertical columns and a brick facade lend an air of solidity and strength to the exterior of this compact, one-level home. But upon entering the soaring living room, you'll be amazed at the airy atmosphere that envelopes you. Cathedral ceilings, skylights, sliding glass doors and an absence of unneccesary walls combine to create a sun-filled space you'll love coming home to. Look at the kitchen, just steps away from both dining rooms. And, that fireplace in the living room doesn't just look pretty. It circulates warm air throughout the house when the temperature plummets. You can be sure of a quiet rest in the bedrooms, tucked away from active areas and served by two full baths.

First floor — 1,340 sq. ft.

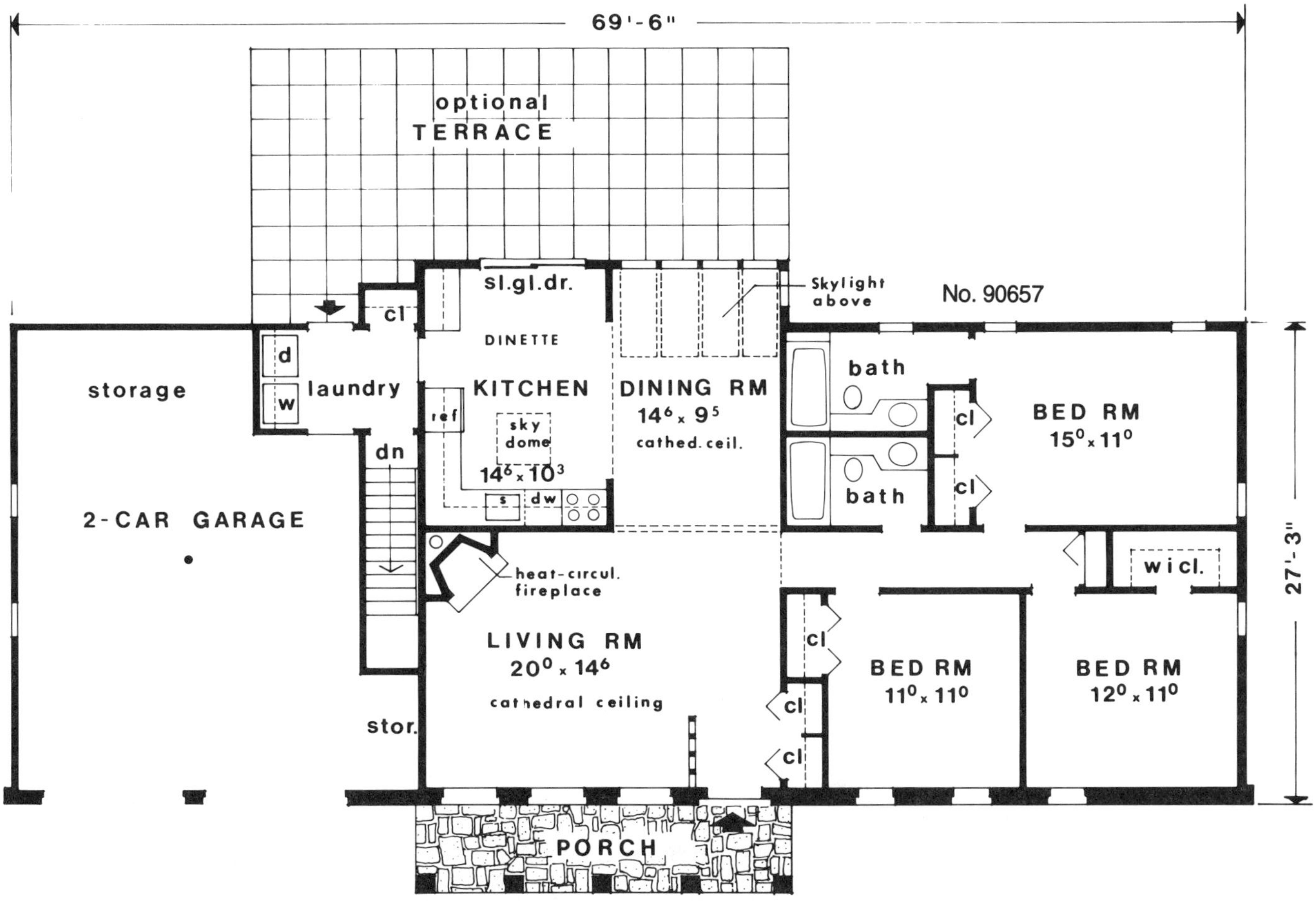

Appealing Multi-level Home

No. 90112

Special activity areas within this multi-level home make family living more congenial. The main level is composed of the garage, the living room, and the unified kitchen and dining areas. The upper level offers a segmented bath with a double lavatory, a large master bedroom in the rear, and two smaller, yet spacious bedrooms along the front of the house. The family room is just a few steps down from the entry way, and there is even room for an additional bedroom or a private den. Laundry facilities and an extra bath are also located next to the family room. Just a few steps from the family room is a large basement with room for a workshop or any of your household projects.

Main level and Upper level — 1,356 sq. ft.
Lower level — 720 sq. ft.

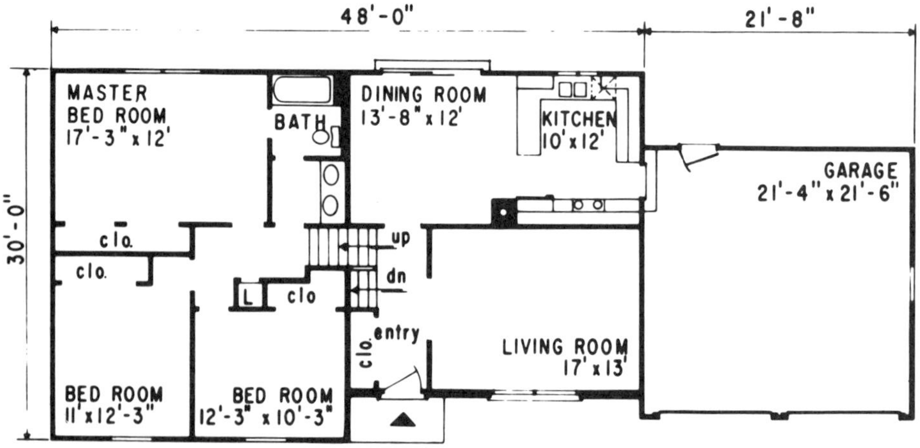

MAIN AND UPPER LEVEL

No. 90112

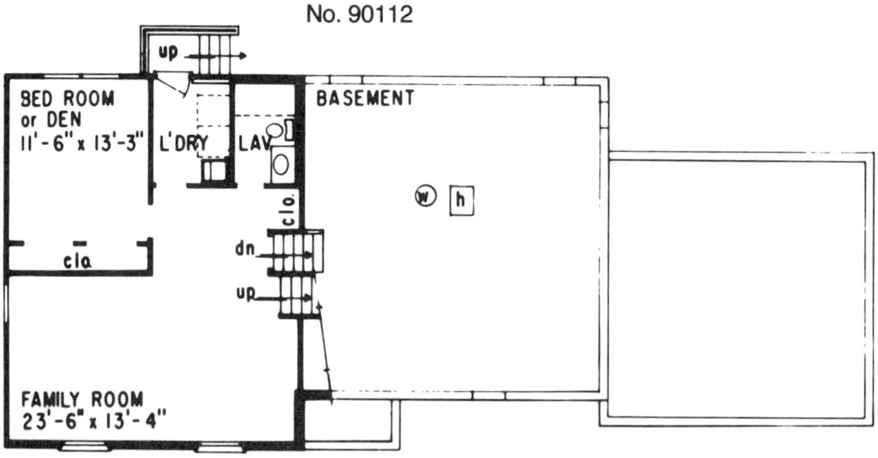

LOWER LEVEL

Stately Tudor

No. 90002

This imposing and impressive facade was designed to satisfy the scrutiny of those who love English details. The eye-catching tower soars above the main roof, housing a dramatic interior stair foyer. The tower is further enhanced by a bay window, shed roofs, dormers, open timber work, and truncated, gabled, and hip roofs. The carved double-entrance doors are flanked by iron grilled side lights. A dual closet vestibule greets guests and flows into a 11 x 13 ft. curved-stair foyer. The living room is large and impressive with its 9 foot high window, 7 foot wide window seat, log burning fireplace with 13 foot hearth, and double French doors leading to the rear porch.

First floor — 1,679 sq. ft.
Second floor — 1,040 sq. ft.

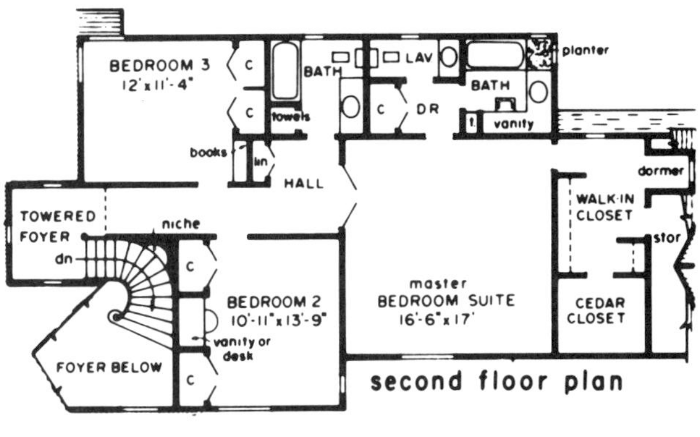

second floor plan

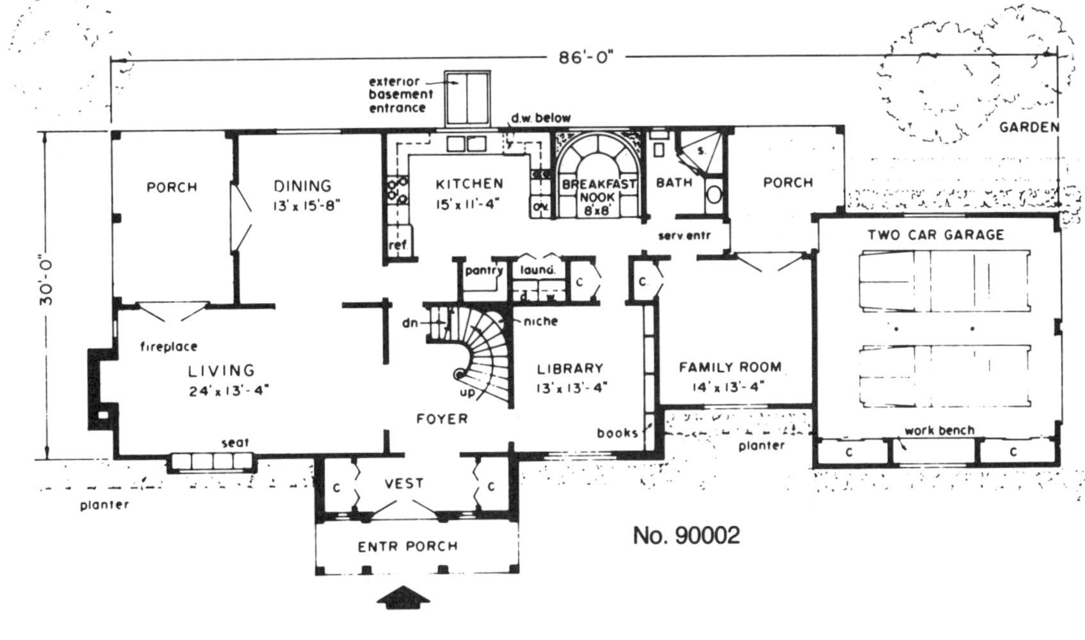

No. 90002

first floor plan

Dormers Provide Cozy Window Seats

No. 91050

Designed with efficiency in mind, this one-and-a-half story home boasts cost-saving features that will help keep your construction budget down. Notice the stacked baths and back-to-back plumbing in the kitchen and utility rooms. A minimum of hallways eliminates wasted space. But, you'll still enjoy a convenient kitchen and adjoining bayed dining nook with a built-in work desk and china cabinet. And, you don't need to do without two spacious first-floor bedrooms with huge closets, or an attached garage with a built-in shop area. You can even have a roomy second-floor bedroom with a walk-in closet and adjoining studio/rec room.

First floor — 1,008 sq. ft.
Second floor — 308 sq. ft.

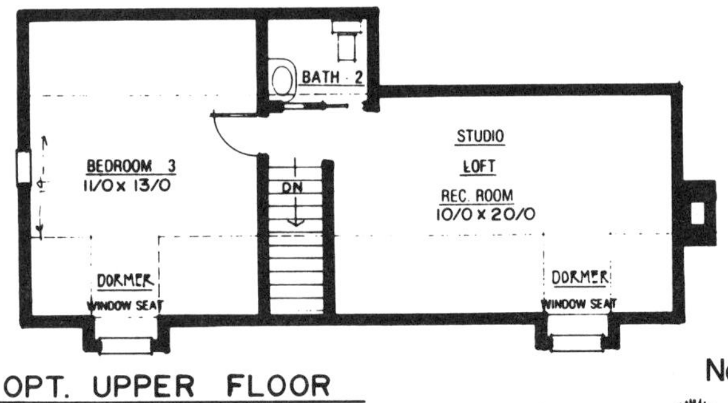

OPT. UPPER FLOOR
308 SQ. FT.

No. 91050

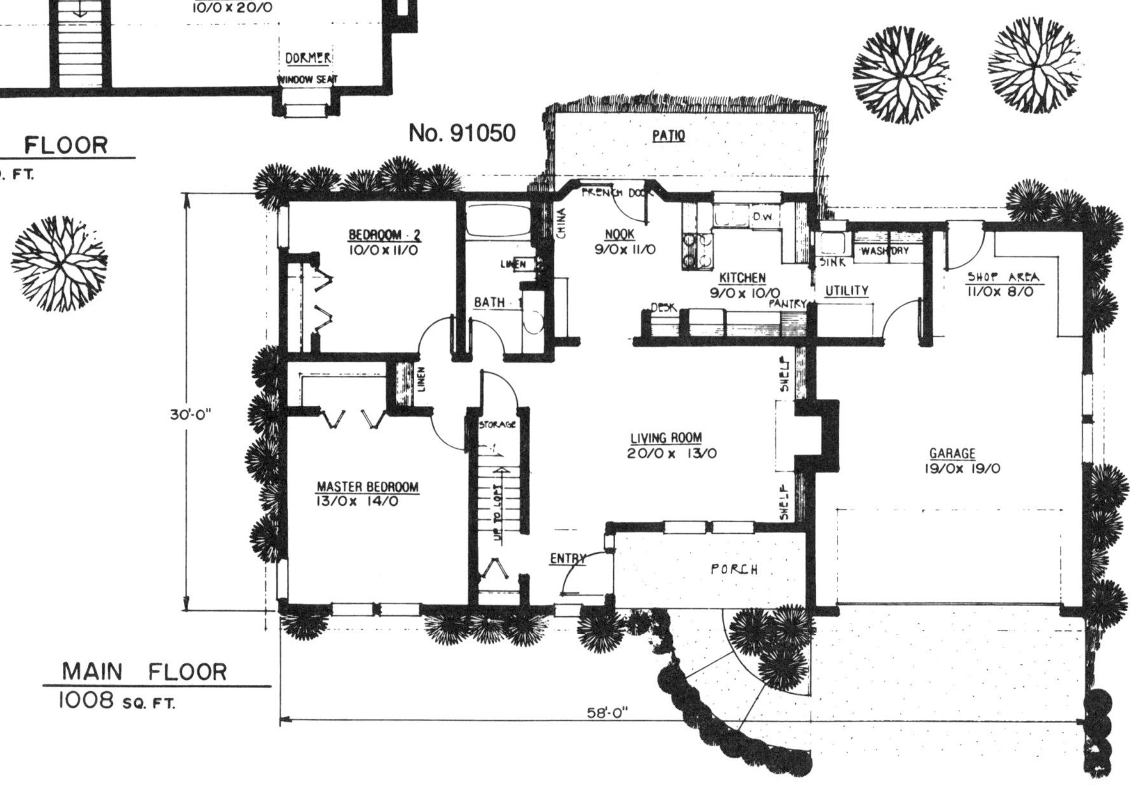

MAIN FLOOR
1008 SQ. FT.

Sunlight Floods Every Room

No. 90511

Walk into the two-story foyer from the garage or sheltered front entry and you'll be struck by the wide-open spaciousness of this compact home. The kitchen is flanked by vaulted living and dining rooms on one side and a fireplaced family room and breakfast nook on the other. Atop the open stairs, the plush master bedroom suite lies behind double doors. Two additional bedrooms share an adjoining full bath.

First floor — 1,078 sq. ft.
Second floor — 974 sq. ft.

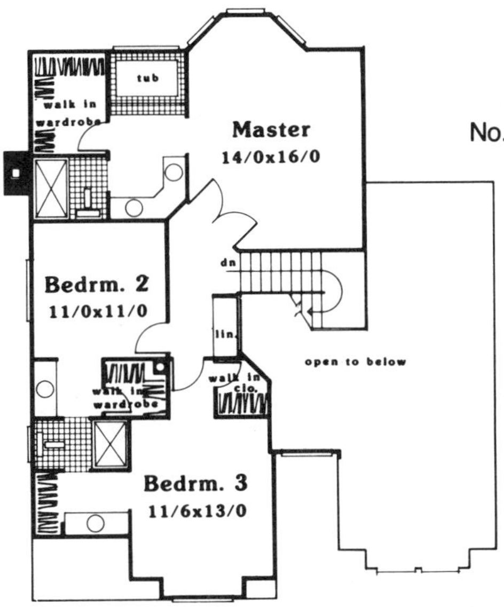

Upper Floor

No. 90511

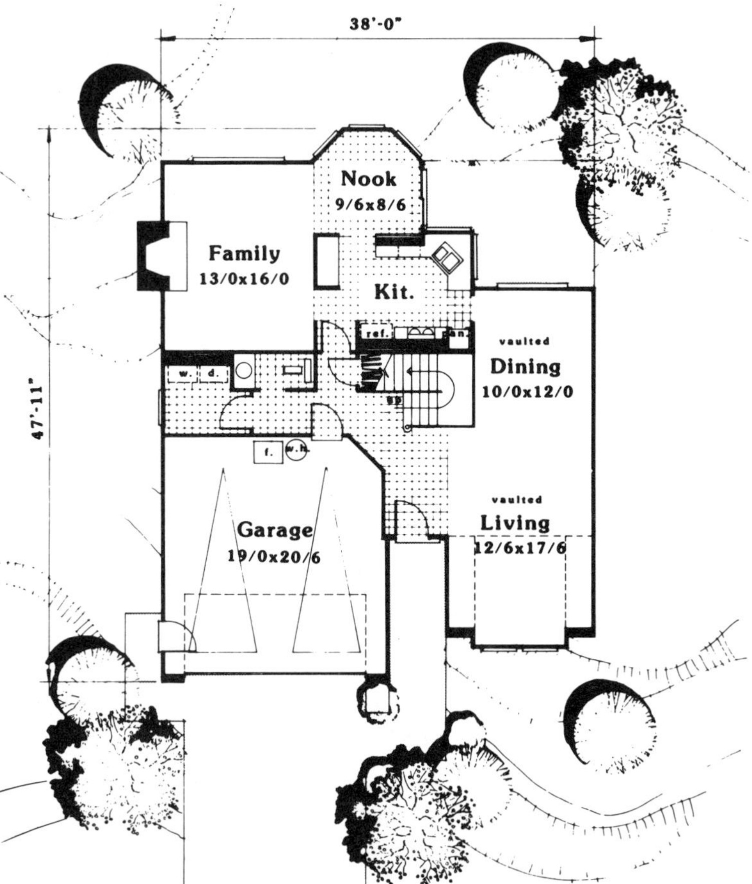

Covered Porch Offered in Farm-type Traditional

No. 20064

This pleasant traditional design has a farmhouse flavor exterior that incorporates a covered porch and features a circle wood louver on its garage, giving this design a feeling of sturdiness. Inside on the first level from the foyer and to the right is a formal dining room complete with a bay window and an elevated ceiling and a corner china cabinet. To the left of the foyer is the living room with a woodburning fireplace. The kitchen is connected to the breakfast room and there is a room for the laundry facilities. A half bath is also featured on the first floor. The second floor has three bedrooms. The master bedroom is on the second floor and has its own private bath and walk-in closet. The other two bedrooms share a full bath. A two-car garage is also added into this design.

First floor — 892 sq. ft.
Second floor — 836 sq. ft.
Basement — 892 sq. ft.
Garage — 491 sq. ft.

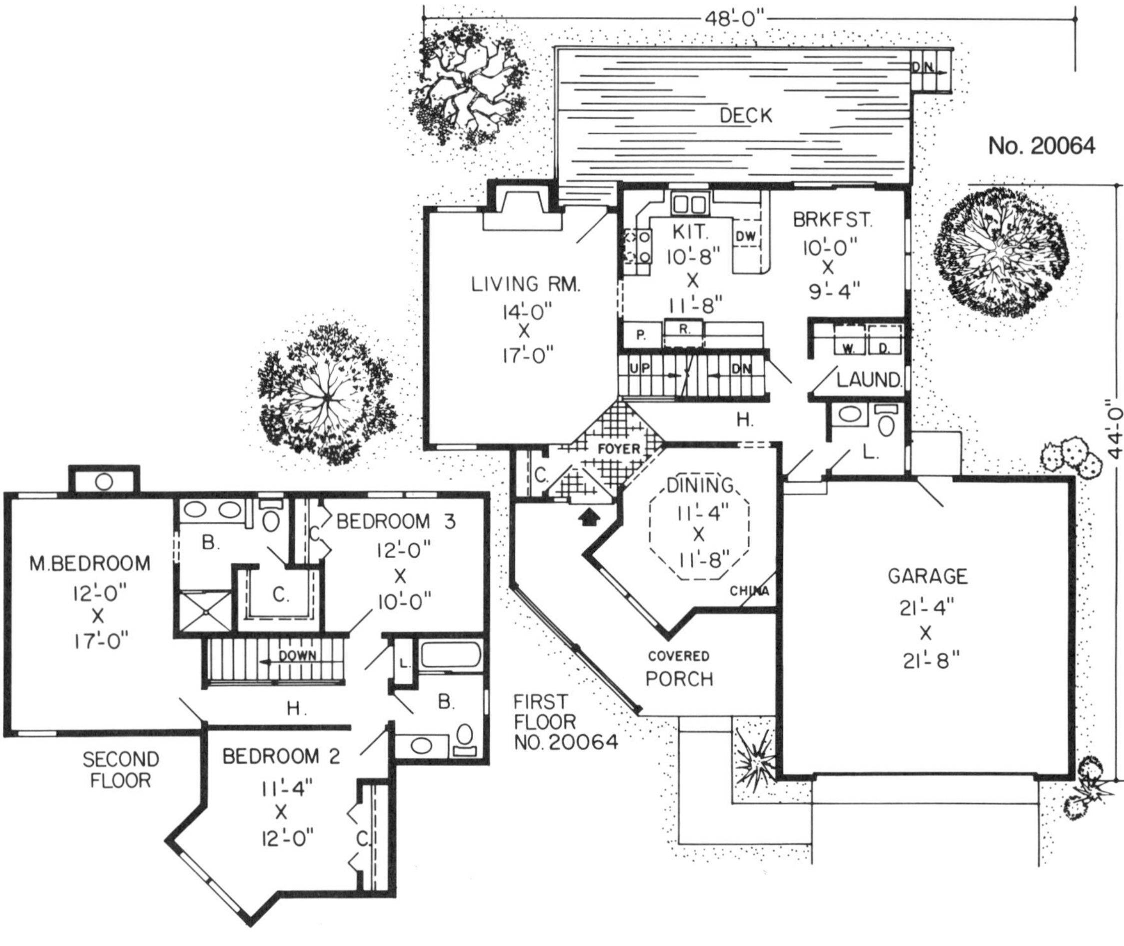

A Unity of Interior and Exterior Space

No. 90650

Energy-efficient construction, a heat-circulating fireplace, and oversized sun-catching windows are just a few of the amenities that make this compact contemporary special. The U-shaped kitchen features pass-through convenience to the family room. And, with sliders to the patio, both the family and dining rooms enjoy a pleasing unity with the back yard. The master suite upstairs features its own full bath and huge, walk-in closet. Sliders lead to a private balcony off the front bedroom, which shares another full bath with the bedroom overlooking the back yard.

First floor — 1,067 sq. ft.
Second floor — 845 sq. ft.

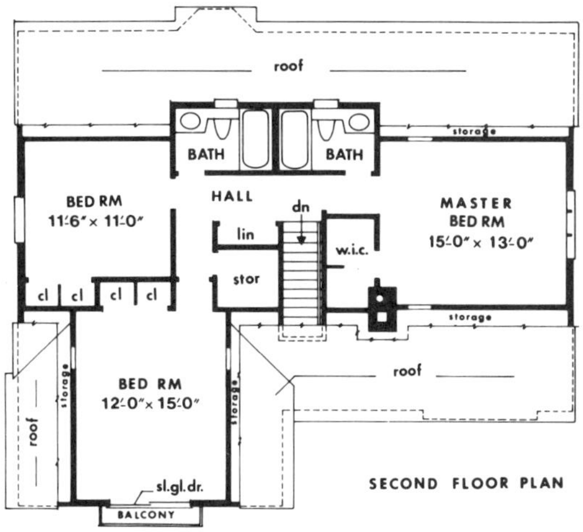

No. 90650

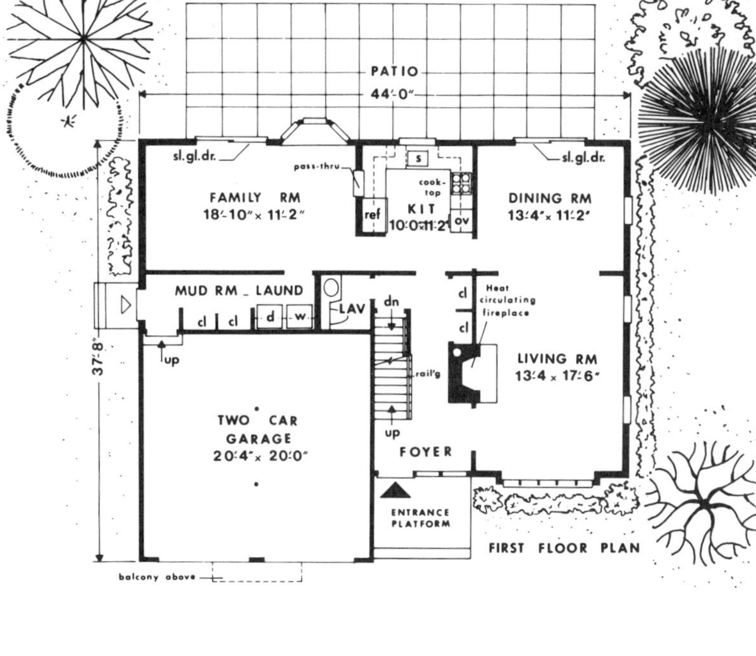

Provincial Charmer Features Energy-Saving Solar Porch

No. 90643

This elegant, brick classic may look traditional, but the modern touches inside make it easy to love. The spacious foyer is dominated by a curving staircase to the four corner bedrooms and two full baths with double sinks. The master bath even features a whirlpool bath. Flanking the foyer, the formal living and dining rooms are designed for gracious entertaining. Guest will appreciate the handy powder room tucked under the stairs. For family meals, the kitchen adjoins a cozy dinette. Sliding glass doors in the family room lead to a full-length terrace at the rear of the house.

First floor — 1,020 sq. ft.
Second floor — 953 sq. ft.

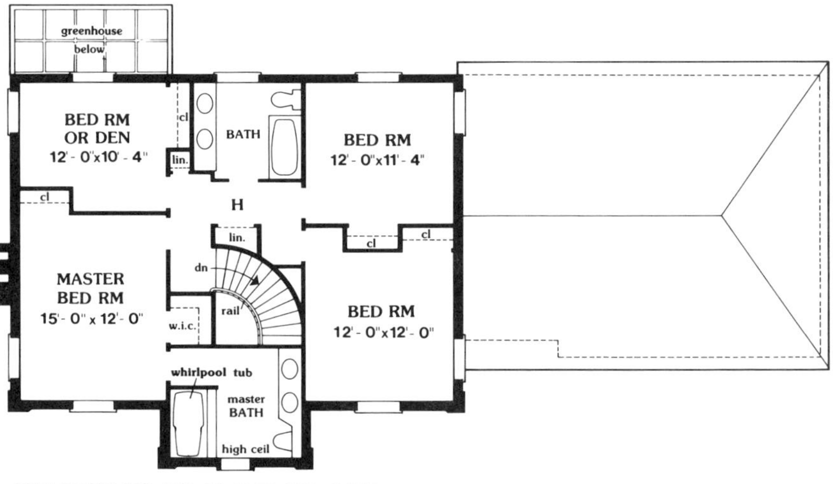

SECOND FLOOR PLAN

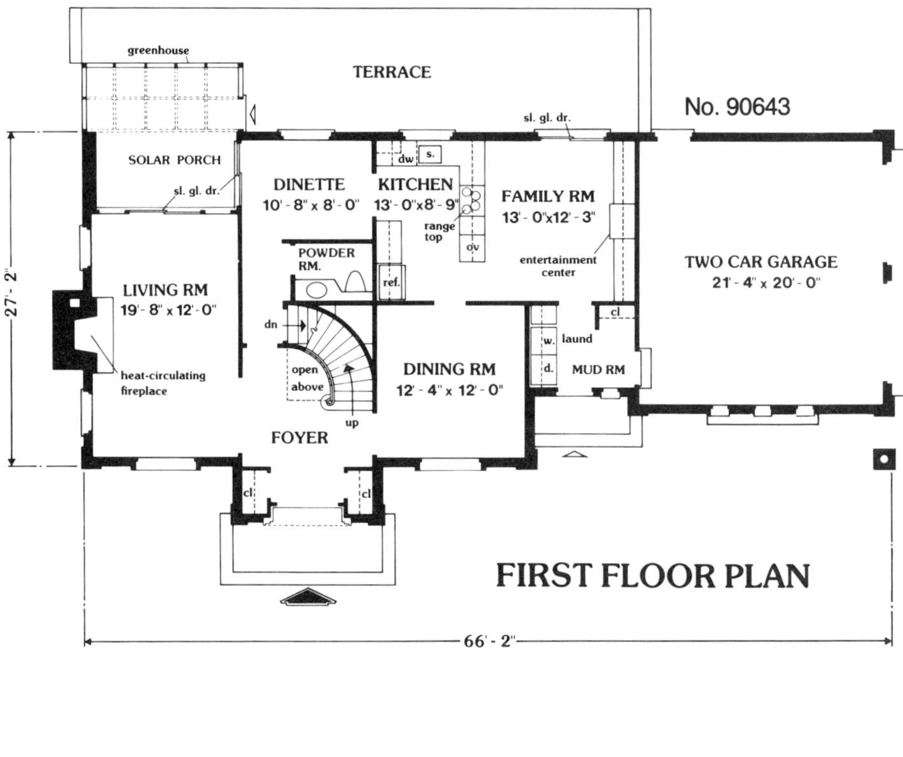

FIRST FLOOR PLAN

Soaring Roof Lines Hint at Exciting Interior

No. 90538

Here's a dramatic contemporary with a versatile floor plan. A clerestory window, an open staircase, and the adjoining vaulted living room give the expansive entry a wonderful atmosphere. Family areas, at the rear of the home past the den, feature window walls that flood every corner with sunlight. You'll appreciate the convenient kitchen with its central cooktop island, just steps away from formal and informal dining rooms. Upstairs, the sunny feeling continues in the bedrooms. A bayed sitting room in the master suite and cozy bump-out window seat in the front bedroom provide wonderful spots for relaxing with a good book.

First floor — 1,286 sq. ft.
Second floor — 920 sq. ft.

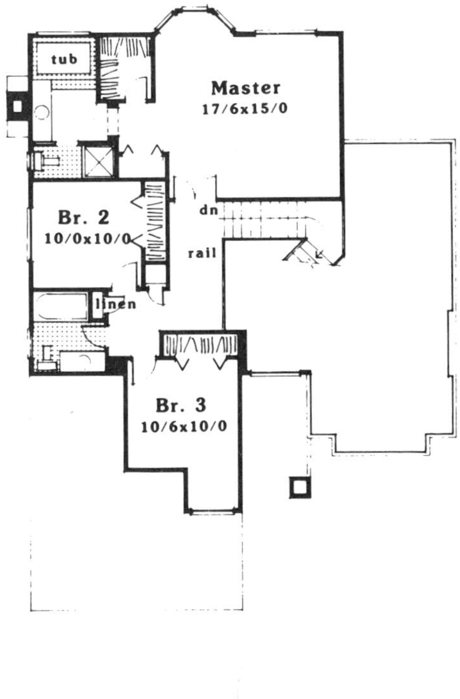

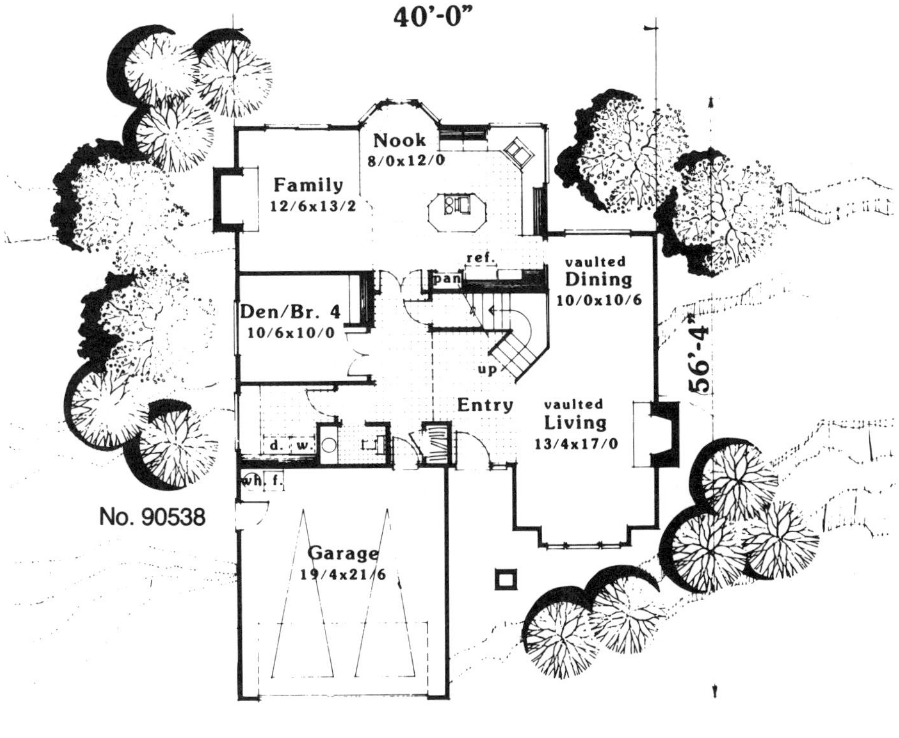

Western Approach To The Ranch House

No. 90007

Here is a house in authentic ranch style with long loggia, posts and braces, hand split shake roof, and cross-buck doors. Two wings sprawl at an angle on either side of a Texas-sized hexagonal living room. Directly across from the double-door entrance, a sunken living room is two steps lower and enhanced by two solid walls (one pierced by a fireplace), two 10' walls of almost solid glass (with sliding doors), and two walls opened wide as entrances from foyer and to dining room. For outdoor living and dining, a porch surrounds the room on three sides.

Living Area — 1,830 sq. ft.

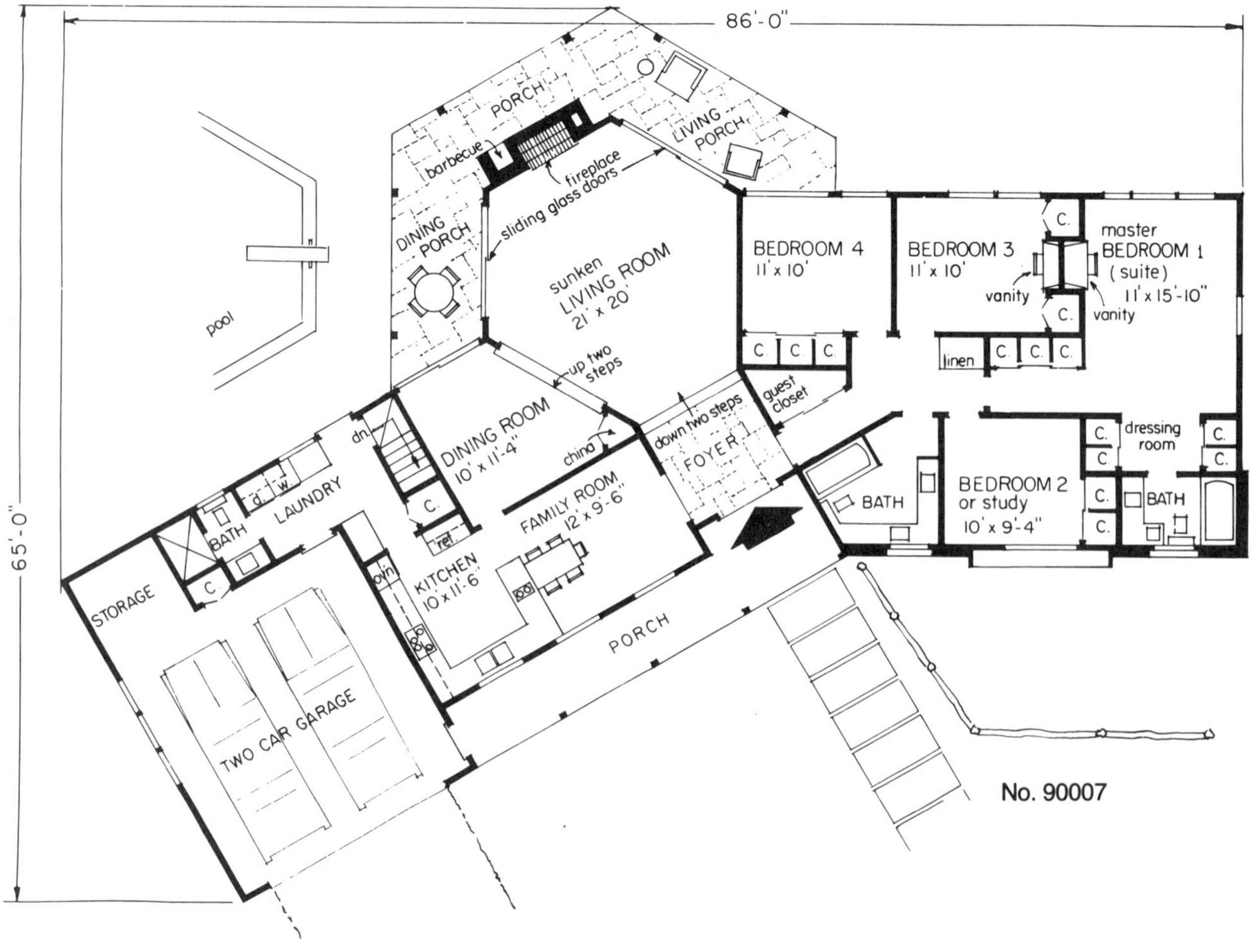

No. 90007

Outdoor Living Space Adds Appeal

No. 90656

Enjoy the elegance of Country Tudor in a compact and affordable home. Can't you imagine a cozy evening with good friends, gathered around the fire in the two-story conversation area off the living room? That's just one of the joys you'll experience in this striking masterpiece loaded with unusual features. You'll love the balcony off the master suite that overlooks the conversation area, and the double sinks in the bath that serves the other upstairs bedrooms. You'll spend lots of happy hours in the sun-washed family room with its bayed breakfast room, just across the counter from the roomy kitchen. And, you'll be glad to have the lavatory by the rear entrance so the kids can clean up after an afternoon of play.

First floor — 890 sq. ft.
Second floor — 922 sq. ft.

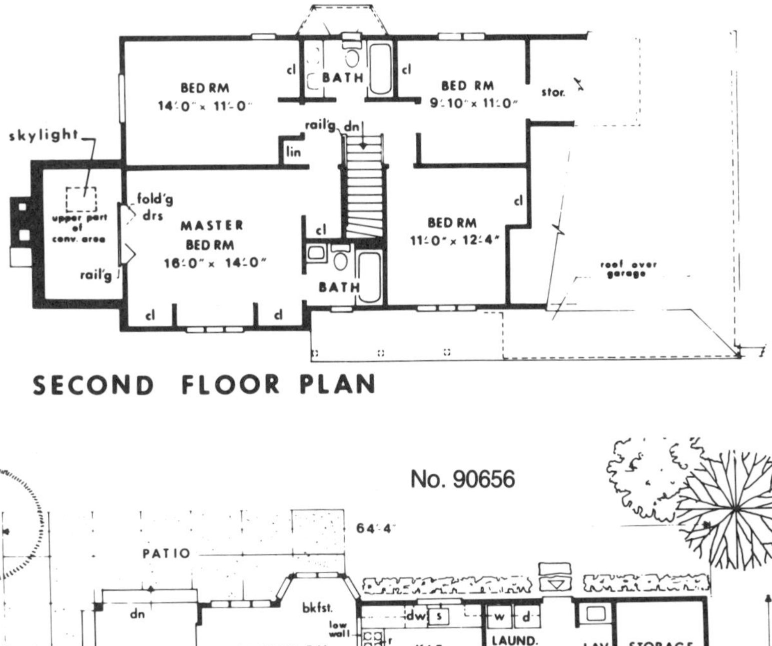

SECOND FLOOR PLAN

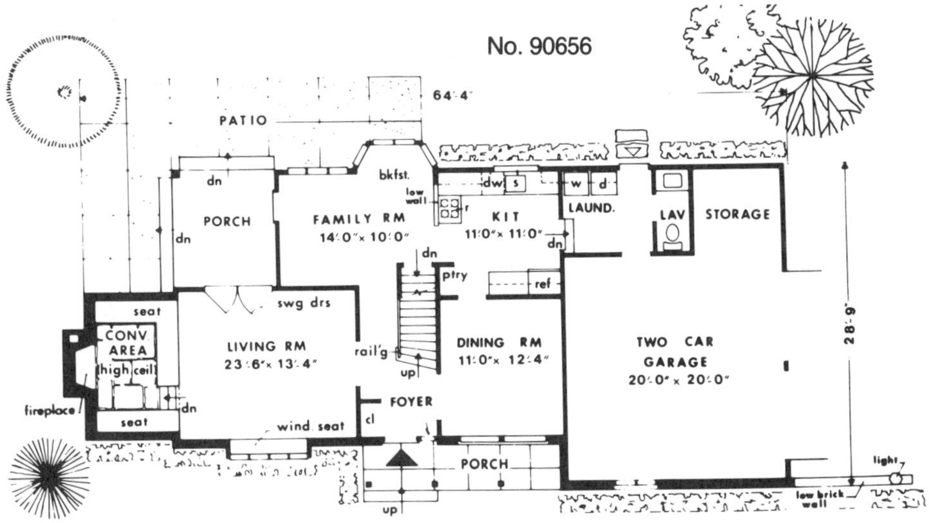

FIRST FLOOR PLAN

Consider the Possibilities

No. 90835

Here's a distinctive ranch with a future. With an unfinished daylight basement, you can expand your dreams later: build an in-law apartment, additional bedrooms, or whatever you need. Built-in planters bring a welcome touch of greenery to the windows in the island kitchen and front bedrooms. Walking through the double doors to the foyer, you'll find a matching planter in the living room along the open staircase. Sliding glass doors in every room at the rear of the house open to a full length balcony and deck, a spot you're sure to appreciate in fine weather. And, when there's a chill in the air, you'll love the massive fireplace that separates the living and dining rooms.

First floor — 1,503 sq. ft.
Daylight basement — 1,392 sq. ft.

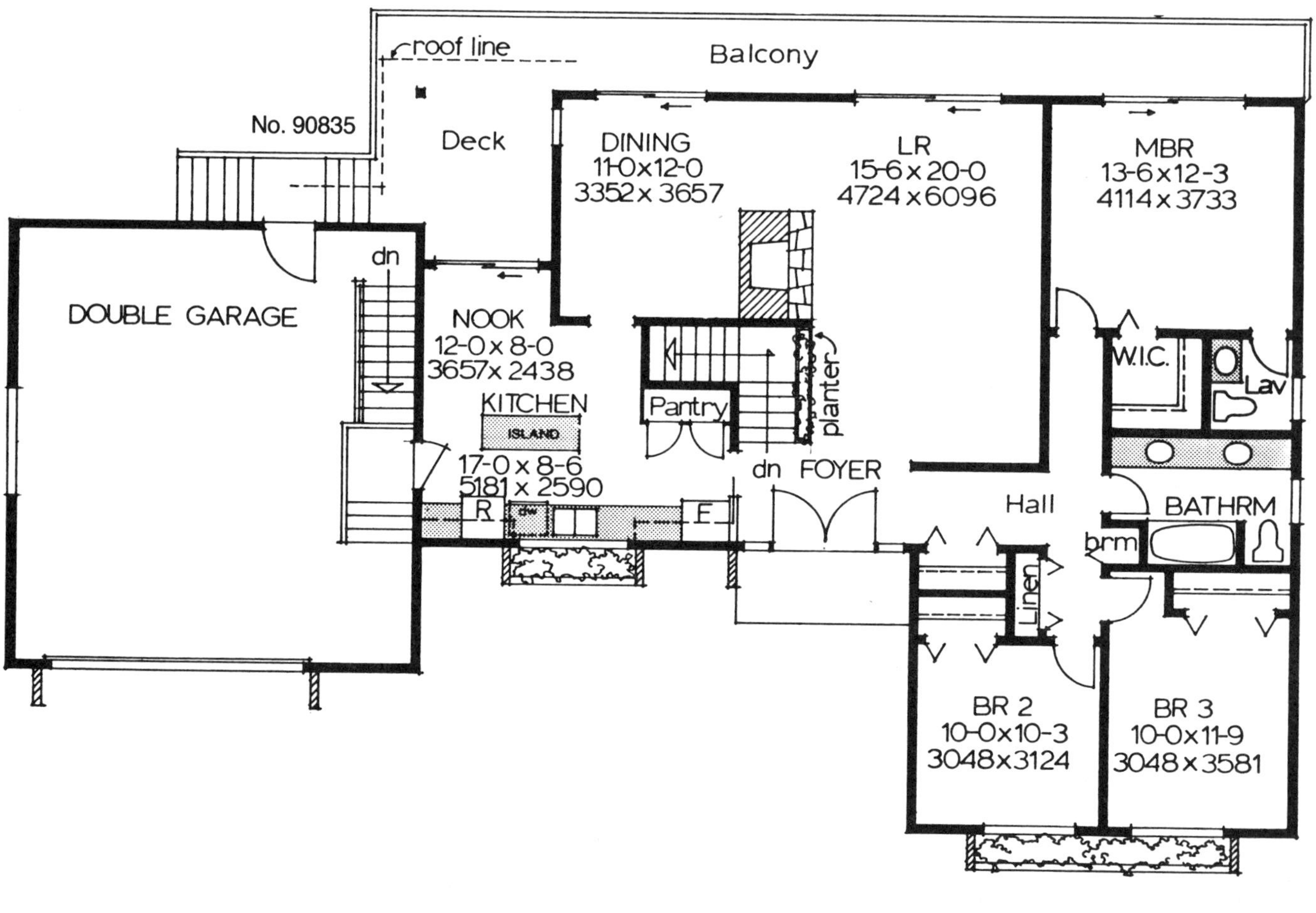

Circular Staircase Makes Stunning Impression

No. 90663

Gather the family around you while you prepare supper in your sunny, well-equipped kitchen. The adjoining glass-walled dinette makes this a cheerful, expansive area for happy family hours. The brick wall surrounding the fireplace in the adjacent family room adds atmosphere and helps store the heat of the crackling fire. Formal areas are just off the foyer. The bow window makes the living room seem even larger than its generous size. Up that sweeping stairway, there are enough bedrooms to give everyone a room. And, double sinks in the front bath will make mornings so convenient, you'll wonder how you ever lived without them.

First floor — 963 sq. ft.
Second floor — 892 sq. ft.

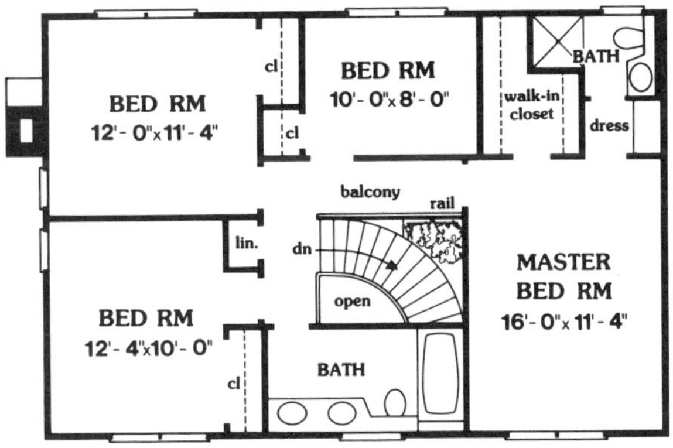

SECOND FLOOR PLAN

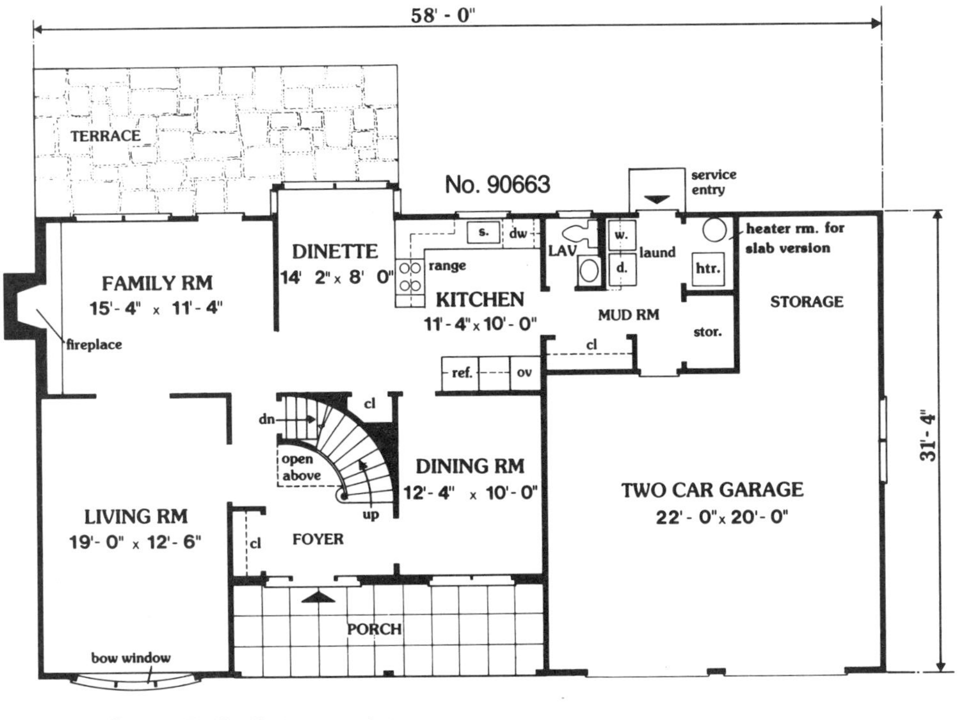

FIRST FLOOR PLAN

Flower Boxes Add Romantic Touch

No. 90658

Walk through the imposing arched entry of this elegant, one-story home, and you'll know you've arrived. The massive great room, and the back yard beyond its four window walls, spreads before you in a splendid panorama. To the left, sliding glass doors unite the dining room with an outdoor terrace. Conveniently located next to the kitchen, it's a lovely spot for a formal meal. Boasting exceptionally large closets and adjacent to two full baths, the bedrooms occupy their own wing, so you can enjoy your privacy.

First floor — 1,542 sq. ft.
Basement — 805 sq. ft.

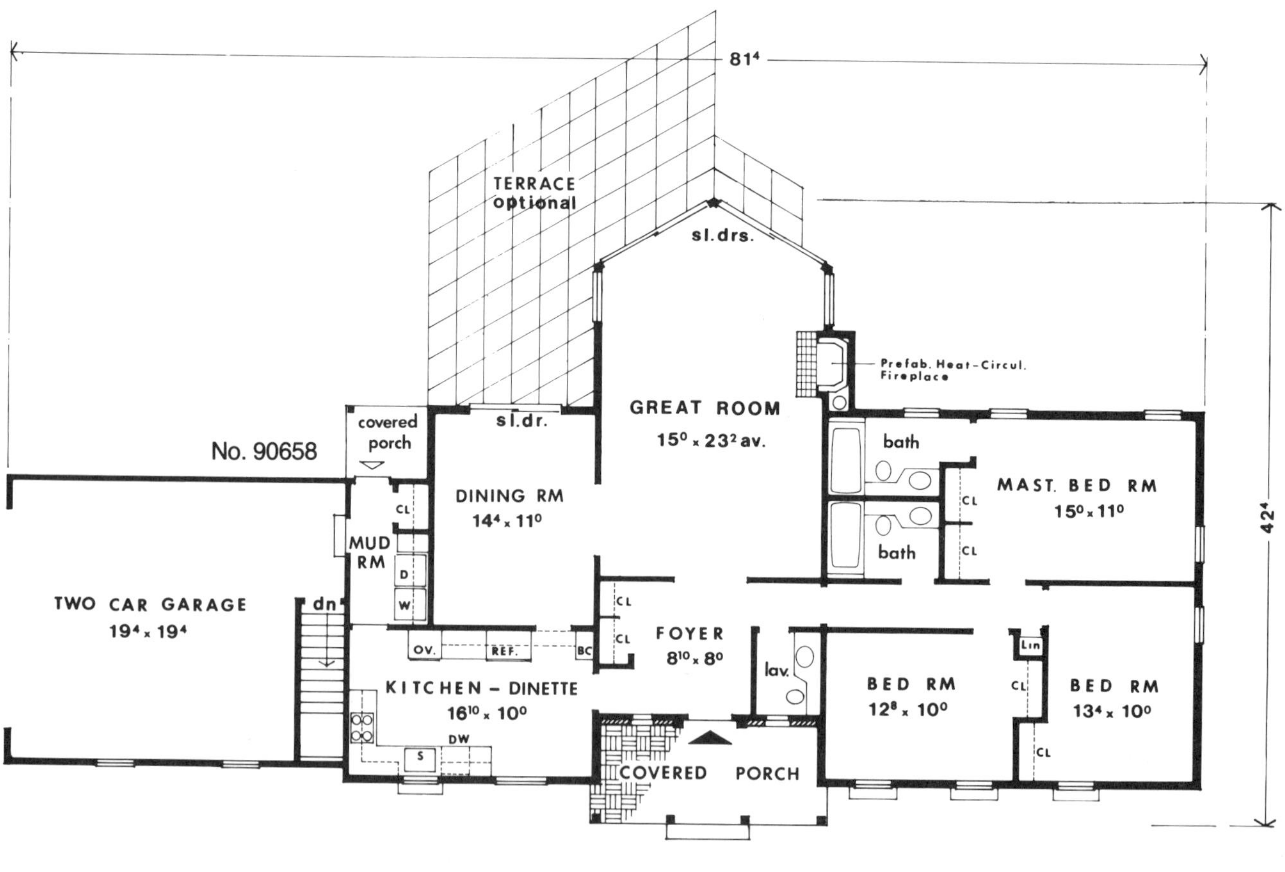

Traditional Energy-Saver

No. 90940

Viewed from the road, this country classic has all the charming elements of a traditional design: a fieldstone facade, an inviting porch, and double hung windows. But, this house also is loaded with modern energy-saving features, from the airlock vestibule to the open plan that allows warm air from the heat-storing solarium to circulate throughout the house. When the sun goes down, the fireplaces in the family and living rooms take over. And in warm weather, venting skylights in the upper gallery release unwanted heat. There's room for the whole family in the three upstairs bedrooms. But, if you need to expand, the unfinished room over the garage will accommodate you.

First floor — 1,603 sq. ft.
Second floor (finished) — 864 sq. ft.
Basement — 699 sq. ft.
Garage — 408 sq. ft.

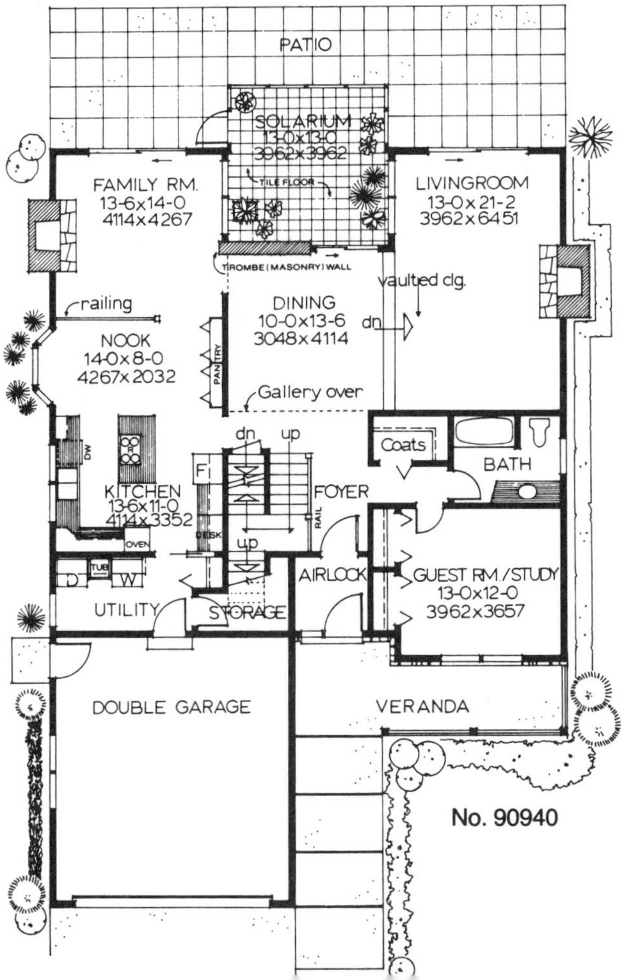

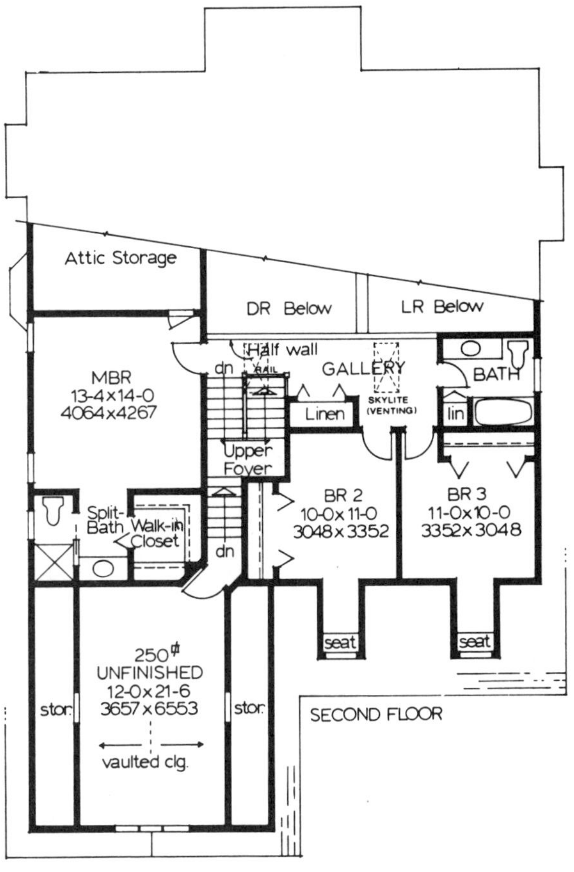

Spanish Two-Story Includes Distinctive Features

No. 90008

An air of exoticism has always recommended Spanish styling, while the practicality of its traditional materials, and the privacy afforded by its characteristic walled facade, make it suitable for contemporary living. This house is distinguished by an intriguing, asymmetrical street front view: four arches conceal the entry, and only two windows can be seen on the facade. The typical Spanish house was usually built around an inner court. Here, however, outdoor living is enjoyed on a roof garden.

First floor — 1,249 sq. ft.
Second floor — 1,134 sq. ft.

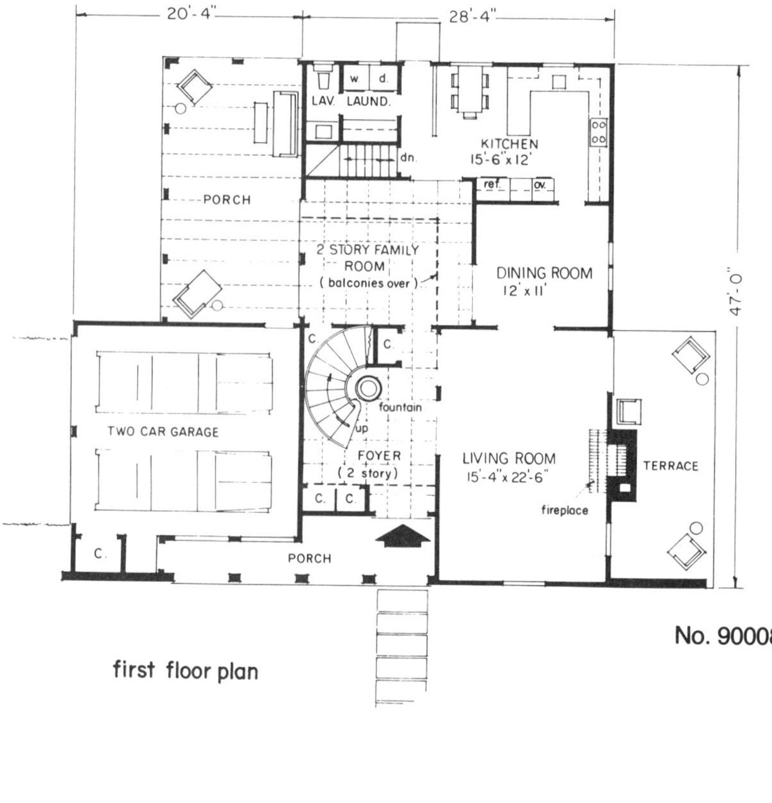

first floor plan

No. 90008

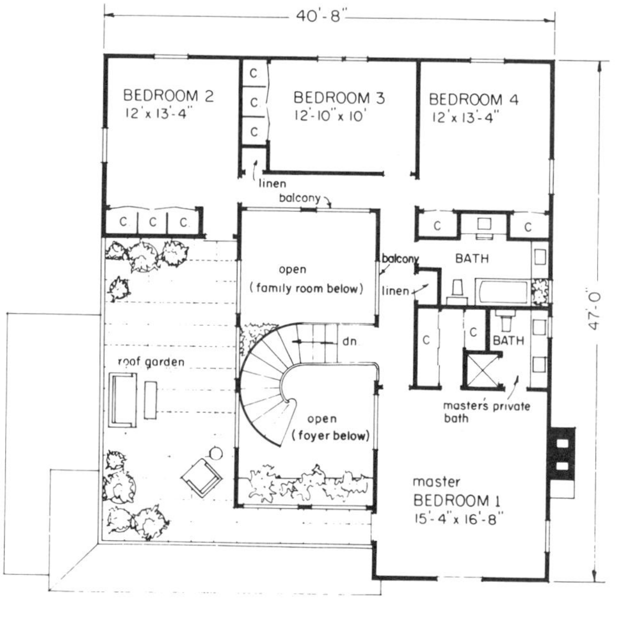

second floor plan

Energy Efficient

No. 90130

Choose either a single or double garage to complement this compact, three bedroom home plan. Lots of living is packed into this space conscious design which is organized around the multipurpose great room. This extra large living area accommodates all of the family's activities by making the galley style kitchen an integral part of the living space. Another advantage of the room arrangement is seen in the separation of the living area from the three bedrooms. This separation is achieved through the placement of the two full baths and of the closets.

Living area — 1,118 sq. ft.

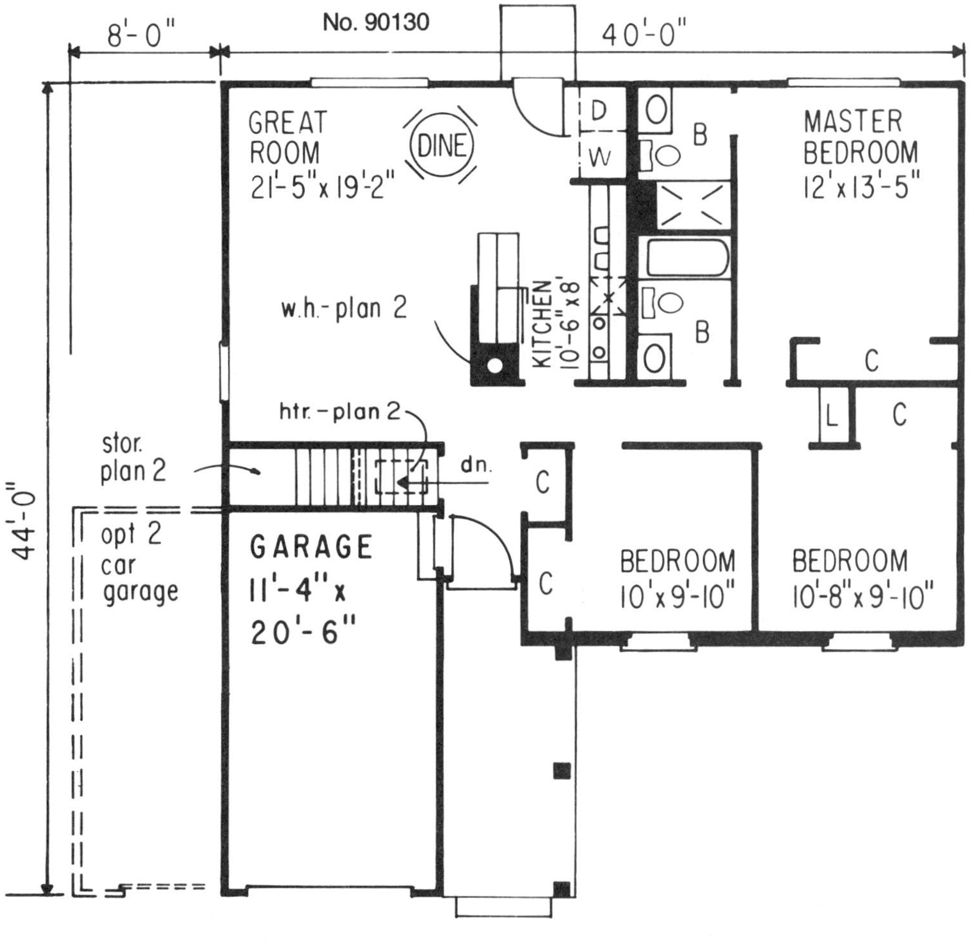

Compact, but Roomy

No. 90529

Consider this one-level, charming home designed for a corner lot or narrow building site. A host of beautiful windows makes it very special. The front entry brings you right into the living room. Need more space? Expand your entertaining area by opening the double doors to the den. Family areas at the rear of the house feature window walls, and an open plan that unites the U-shaped kitchen with dining and fireplaced family rooms. Two bedrooms, tucked away in their own wing, include the spacious master suite with private bath and double closet.

First floor — 1,215 sq. ft.

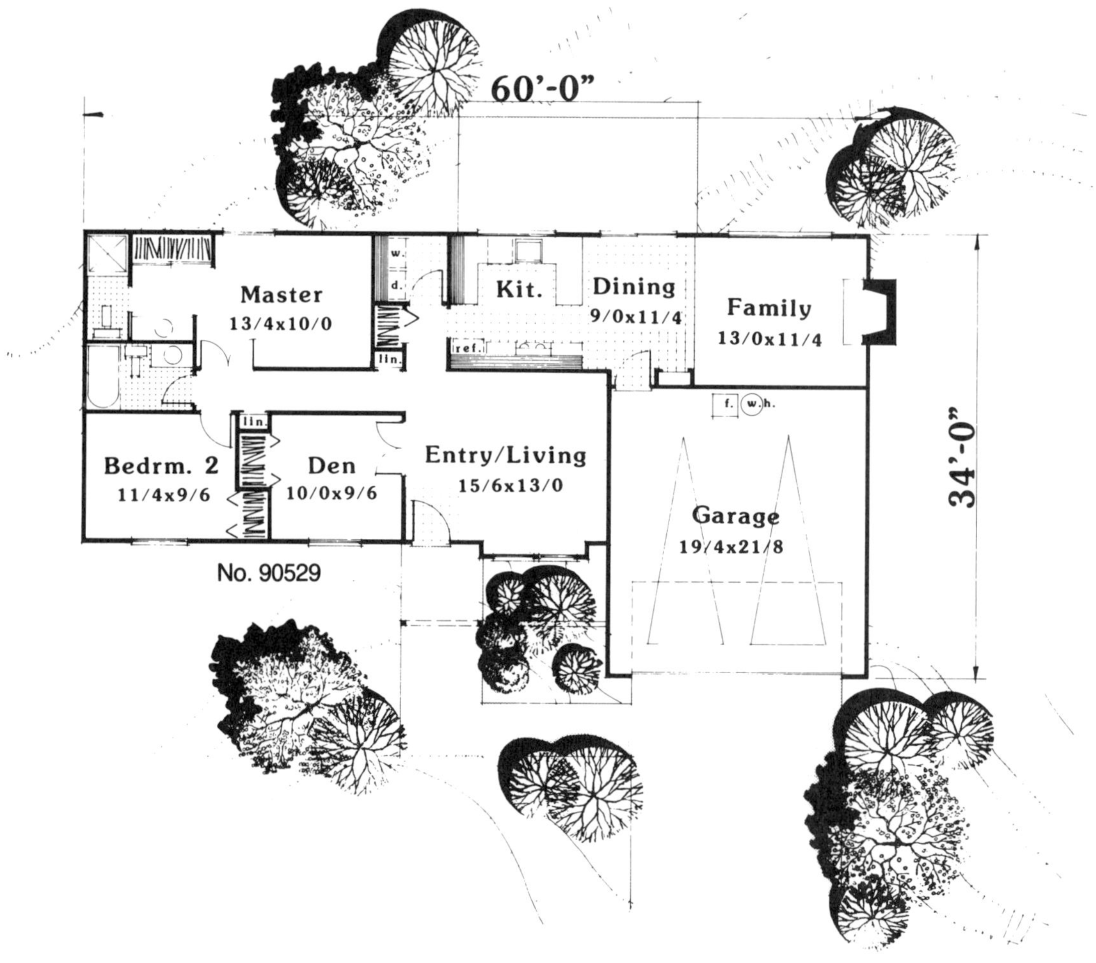

No. 90529

Take Advantage of a Spectacular View

No. 91041

This gracious contemporary deserves a beautiful hilltop location. Look at the non-traditional reversal of active and sleeping areas and the extensive windows in all the rear rooms. Flanked by the vaulted dining room and open staircase, the impressive entry leads to a fireplaced living room and private den with soaring ceilings. Stargazing is a treat on the deck off the family area. But, if you prefer a secluded spot, retreat downstairs to the deck off the master suite, which features a walk-in closet, shower and luxurious spa. Two additional bedrooms share a full bath with double vanities. And, with the utility room right next door, laundry day is convenient.

Main floor — 1,651 sq. ft.
Lower floor — 1,573 sq. ft.

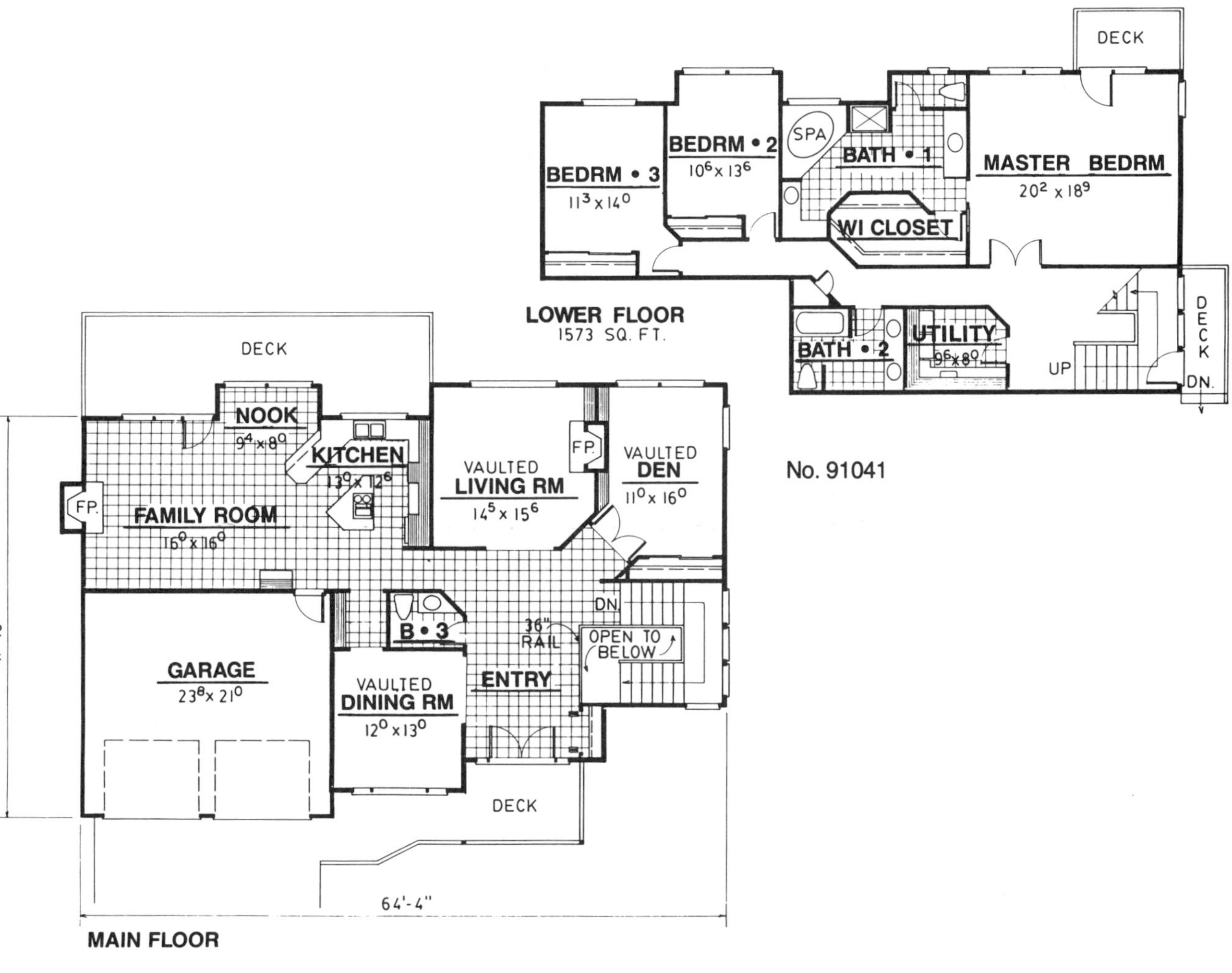

Outstanding Luxury Design is Always Popular

No. 10531

Here's a stately home that's a treasure chest of popular features, including a sunken great room, a spectacular breakfast nook, and a bridge-like balcony on the 2nd floor. The luxurious, 1st floor master suite is a marvel, with two huge walk-in closets, a 5-piece bath, and a sitting room with bay window. The 2nd and 3rd bedrooms each have a walk-in closet and private bath. The great room features a bar, fireplace, and built-in cabinets for TV and stereo, all crowned by a sloping, beamed ceiling. Both the dining room and the foyer have cathedral ceilings and are overlooked by the 2nd floor balcony. A fully equipped kitchen enjoys a sweeping view of the patio and opens to the stunning nook. All in all, this is a fabulous and impressive home.

First floor — 2,579 sq. ft.
Second floor — 997 sq. ft.
Basement — 2,579 sq. ft.
Garage & Storage — 1,001 sq. ft.

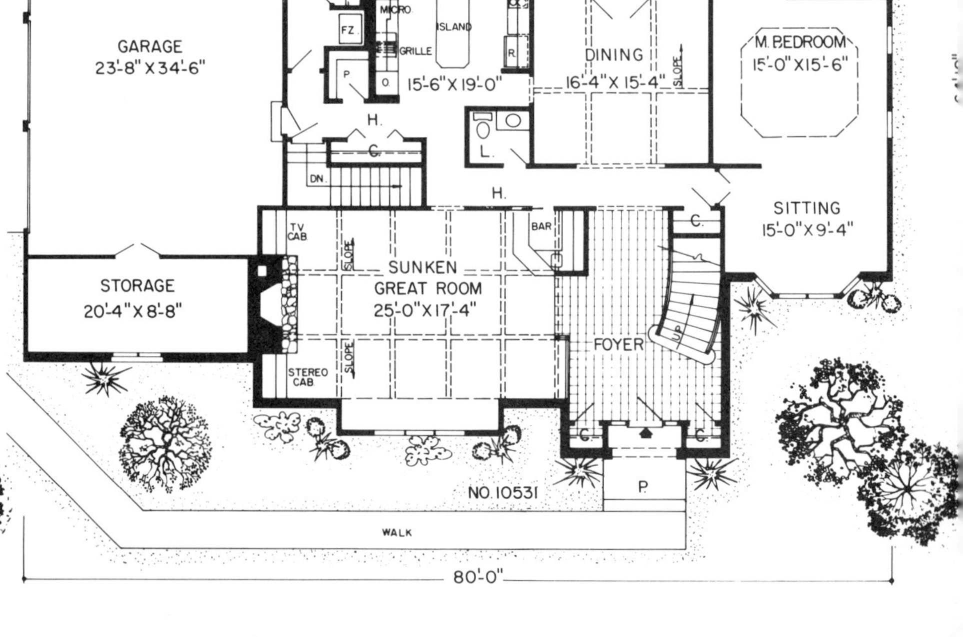

Traditional Warmth

No. 90817

Here is a country charmer with a cozy feeling. A wrap-around front porch shelters the front door, which opens to a central foyer and a view of the living room and patio. Both living and family rooms feature back to back fieldstone fireplaces. The pantried kitchen and dining area are conveniently connected. With three large bedrooms and two full baths upstairs, this home has plenty of room for a growing family.

First floor — 1,161 sq. ft.
Second floor — 972 sq. ft.
Basement — 1,131 sq. ft.
Width — 63 ft.
Depth — 41 ft.

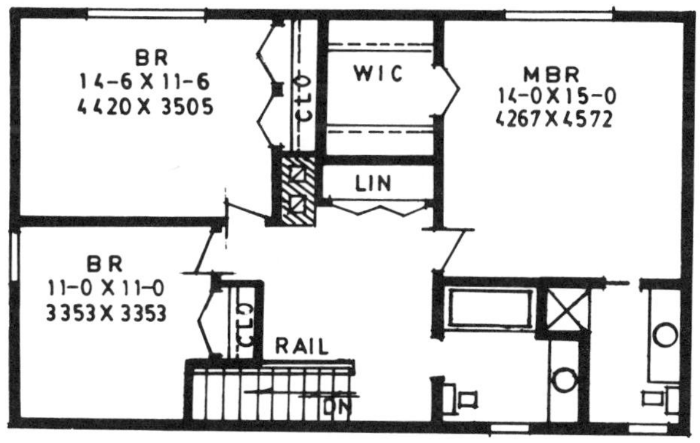

SECOND FLOOR

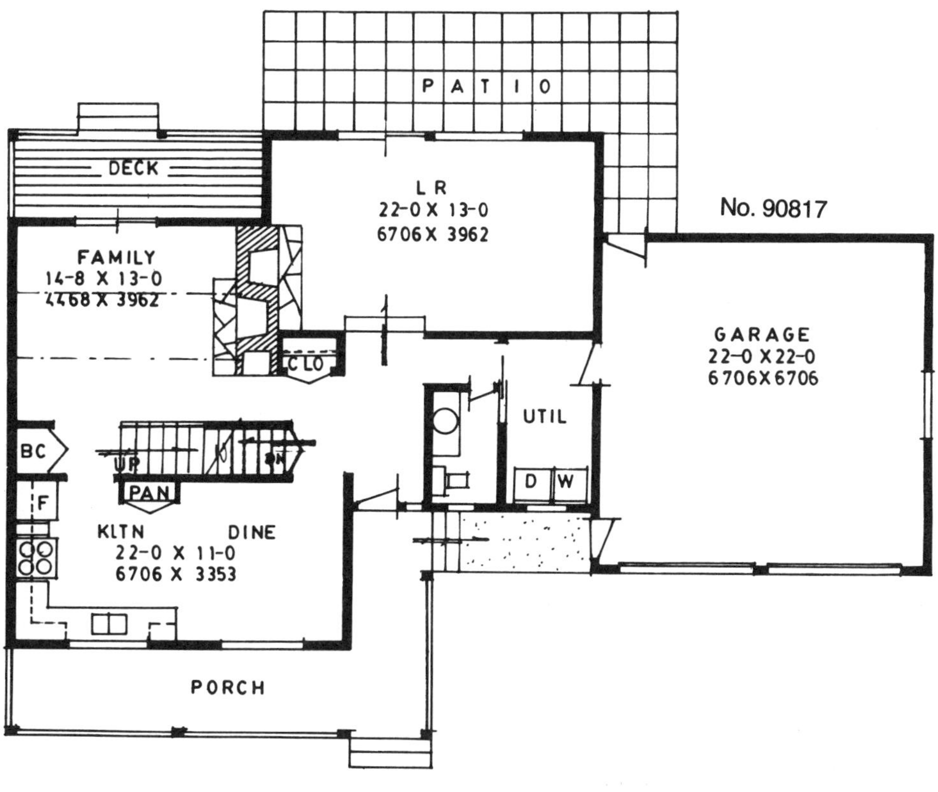

No. 90817

Formal Tiled Entry Leads Guests Into Gracious Living Room

No. 90109

Double doors highlight the exterior of this lovely ranch home which boasts space and elegance. The central living room is accented by its sloped ceiling. The family room opens onto the rear patio and adjoins the breakfast room just off the kitchen. This arrangement makes it easy to serve both informal family meals and large numbers of party guests. The efficiently organized kitchen is also just a few steps from the formal dining room located along the front of the house. The master bedroom has a private bath and a spacious walk-in closet. The other three bedrooms share a five-piece bath.

Living area — 2,305 sq. ft.

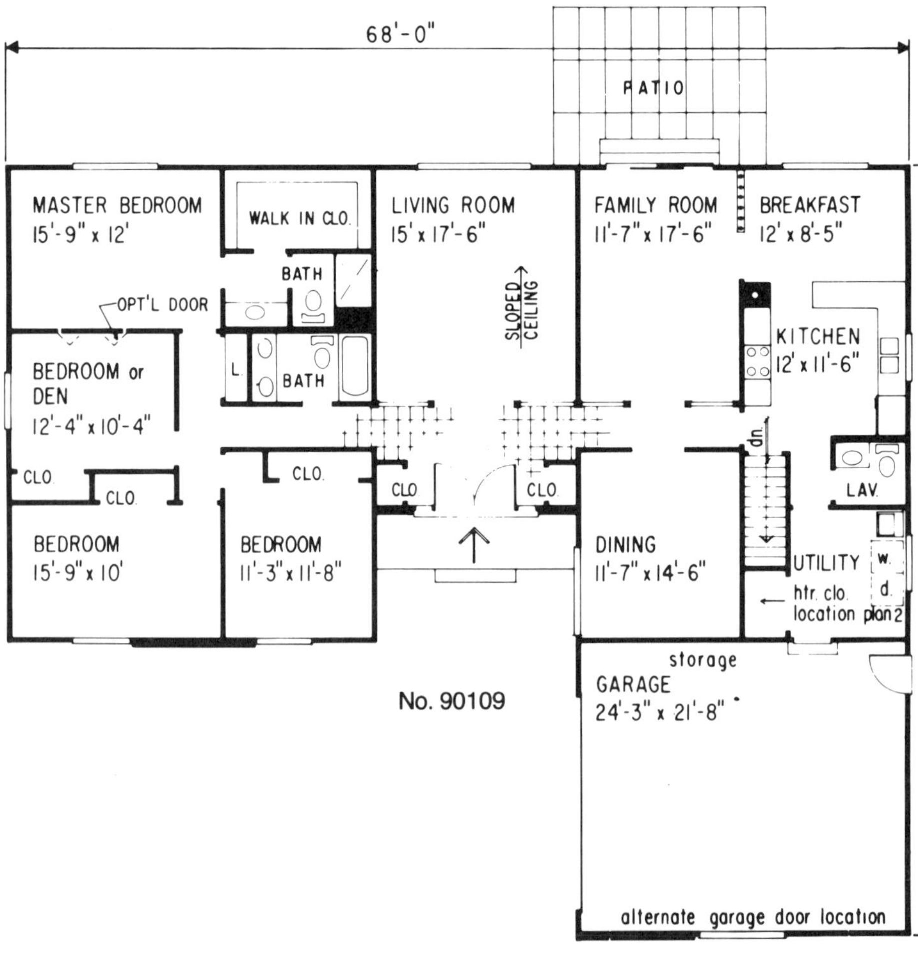

Plenty Of Space For Family Living

No. 90104

This well-designed home features plenty of living space on the first floor, especially in the adjacent living and dining areas. The living room is enhanced by the large, front picture window. Functional traffic patterns are created by the placement of the kitchen between the formal dining room and the family room. The kitchen is of two wall design with plenty of storage and direct access to the family room which opens onto the patio through sliding glass doors. Upstairs are the four bedrooms and two baths.

First floor — 732 sq. ft.
Second floor — 800 sq. ft.

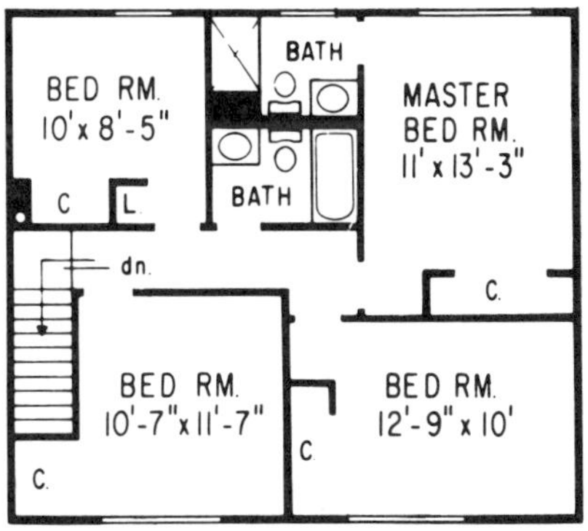

SECOND FLOOR

No. 90104

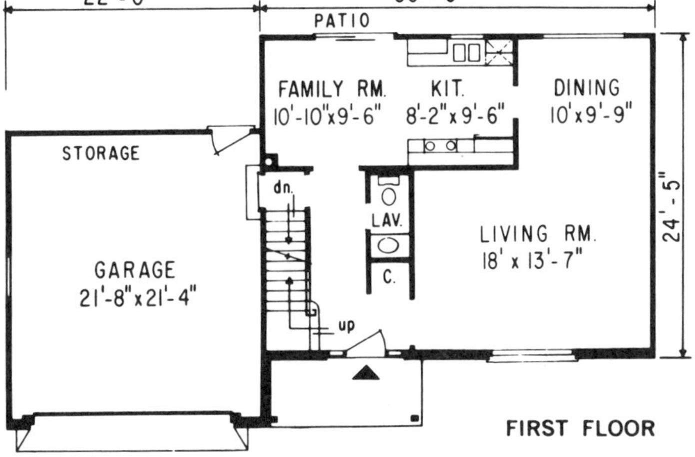

FIRST FLOOR

Angled Wing Houses Bedrooms

No. 90662

A fieldstone facade, flower boxes, and a distinctive, angular shape set this attractive three-bedroom design apart from the typical ranch. The foyer entry provides convenient access to every area of the house, but when your arms are loaded with groceries, you'll want to save steps by using the handy door off the garage. The nearby kitchen serves the dinette, dining room, and sunken family room with ease. Sliding glass doors in the family and living rooms flood each room with natural light, as well as providing access to a lovely rear patio. You'll appreciate the privacy of your corner master suite, with its own bath and double closets.

First floor — 1476 sq. ft.

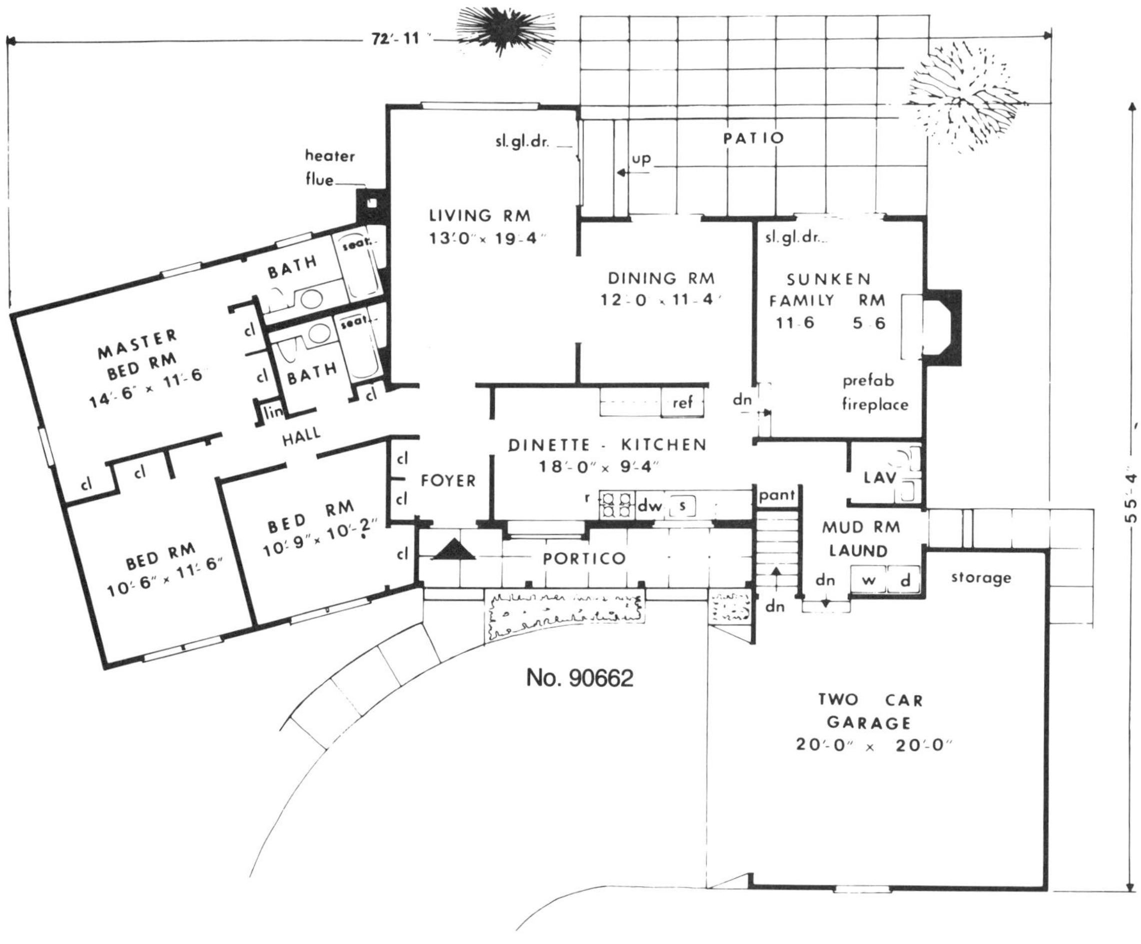

At Home on a Hillside

No. 10644

You'll just love the excitement of living in this 4 bedroom, 3 1/2 bath beauty; every room has an interesting shape! From the foyer, view the recessed ceilings of the dining room, the bump-out windows of the parlor, and the fireplaced family room with patio. Beyond the central stairwell lies the angular kitchen with skylit breakfast nook. The master bedroom suite is right down a short hall. Each of the upstairs bedrooms has direct access to a full bath. And, don't worry about carrying a heavy laundry basket down the stairs. A centrally located chute delivers dirty clothes to the laundry room.

First floor — 1,593 sq. ft.
Second floor — 818 sq. ft.
Basement — 863 sq. ft.
Garage — 720 sq. ft.

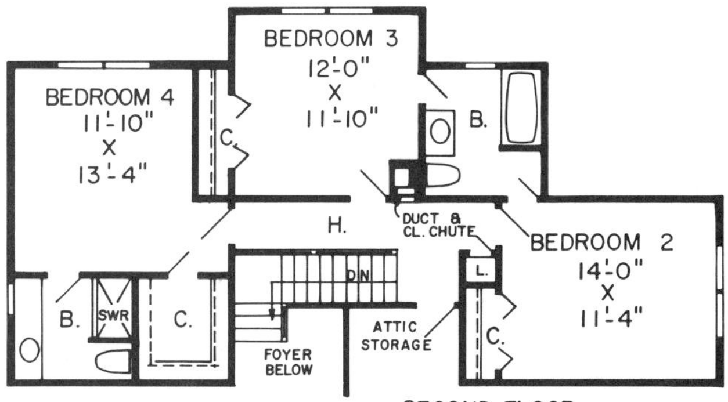

SECOND FLOOR

No. 10644

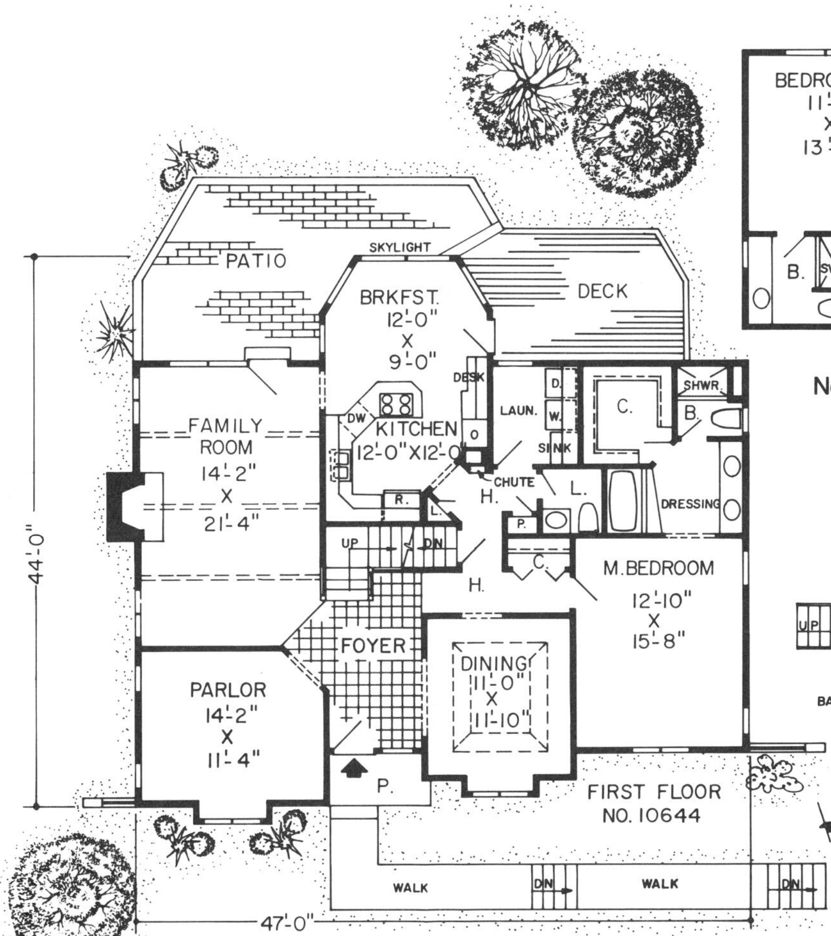

FIRST FLOOR
NO. 10644

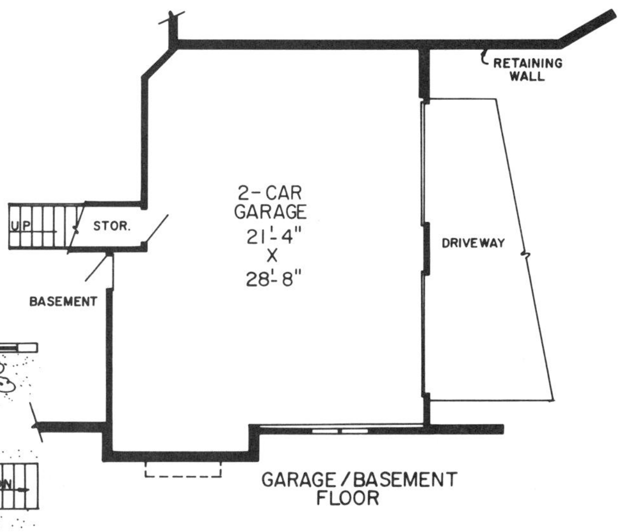

GARAGE / BASEMENT FLOOR

Relax and Enjoy the Terrace

No. 90649

Clapboard siding, shuttered, double-hung windows, and a welcoming porch lend traditional grace to this adaptable family home. With bedrooms and a full bath downstairs, you can lower your building budget now, and finish the second floor when you need it. Save on energy bills by using the heat-circulating fireplace in the living room, building the optional greenhouse off the dining room, and siting the rear of the house to the south to expose the window walls in the formal dining room and informal dinette to the sun's warming rays.

First floor — 1,127 sq. ft.
Second floor — 578 sq. ft.

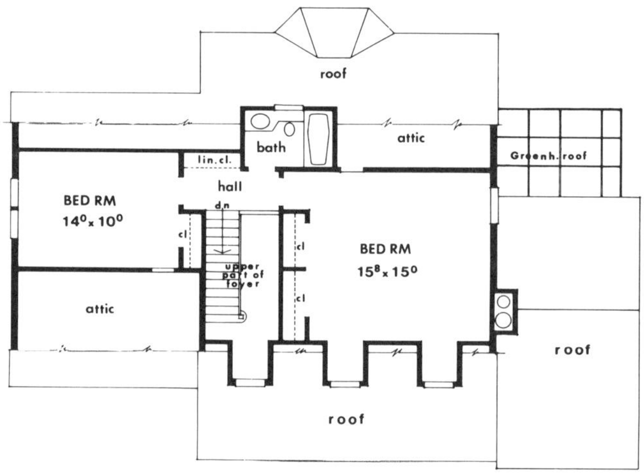

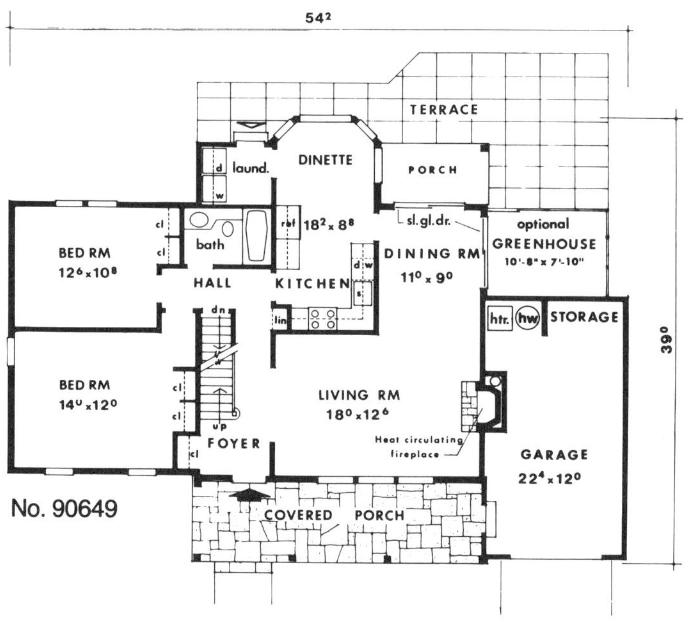

No. 90649

Indulge Yourself in a Master Suite Retreat

No. 90530

Walk through the sheltered entry of this compact home, and you'll know you're in a special place. To your left, past the utility area, an efficient kitchen with adjoining breakfast nook makes family meal service a pleasant task. Through the angled passage, the open living and dining rooms are warmed by a massive fireplace, fixed windows, and sliding glass doors to the rear patio. And around the corner, you'll find the bedroom wing. Two bedrooms share a full bath. And, off behind gracious double doors, you'll find a special treat: the master suite boasts its own skylit bath, a huge, built-in vanity, a walk-in wardrobe, and a sunny, bayed sitting area.

First floor — 1,298 sq. ft.

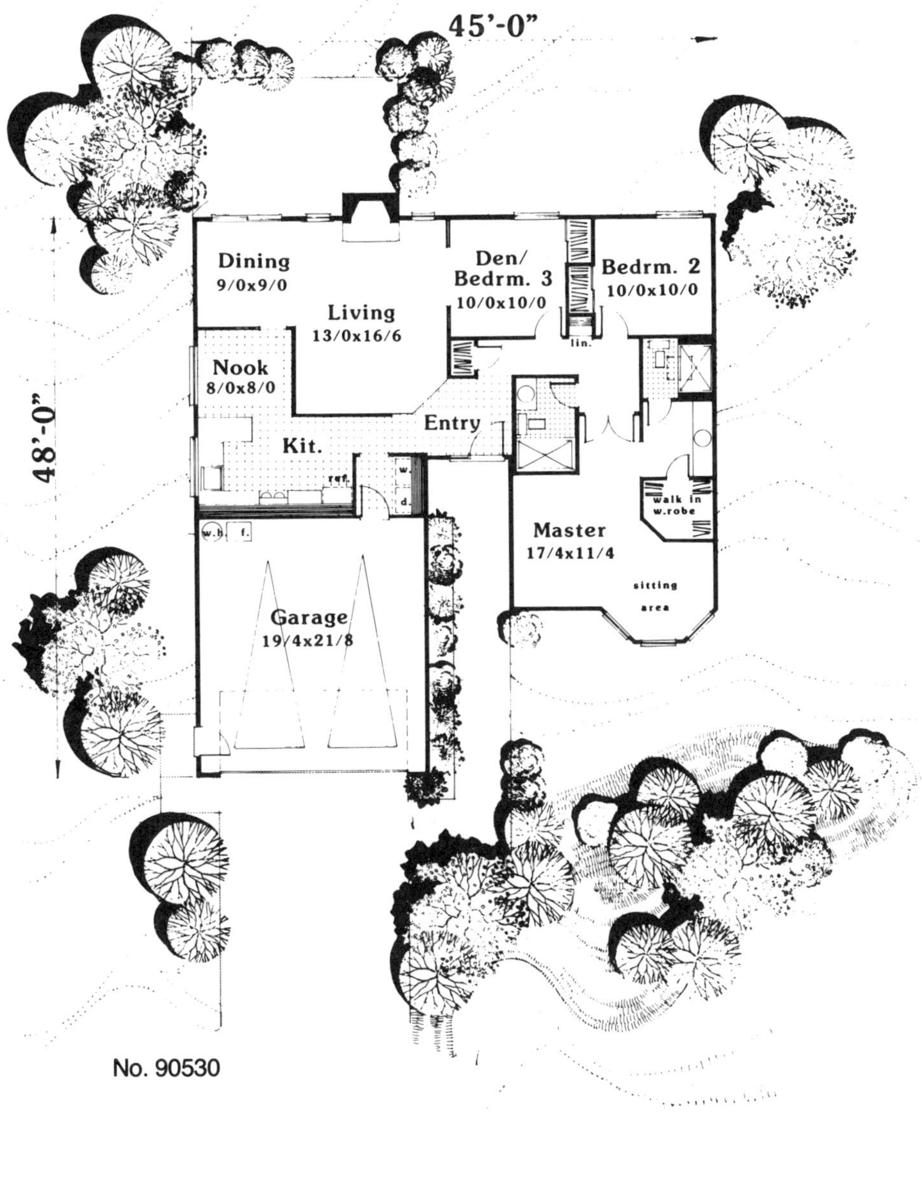

No. 90530

Windows are Highlights

No. 90118

Double windows in the living room and formal dining room, plus a bay window off the kitchen's dining area, enhance the livability of this spacious home. With your choice of four or five bedrooms, all located upstairs for privacy, individuality flourishes. There's even a mud room conveniently located to the rear of the garage and adjacent to the kitchen for cleaning up after yard work.

First floor — 1,392 sq. ft.
Second floor — 1,282 sq. ft.

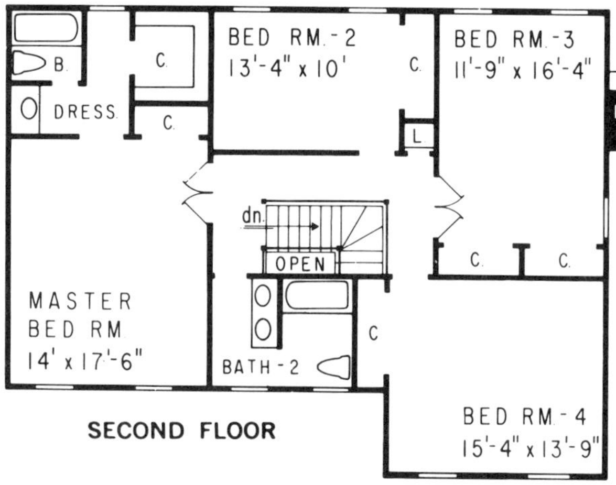

No. 90118

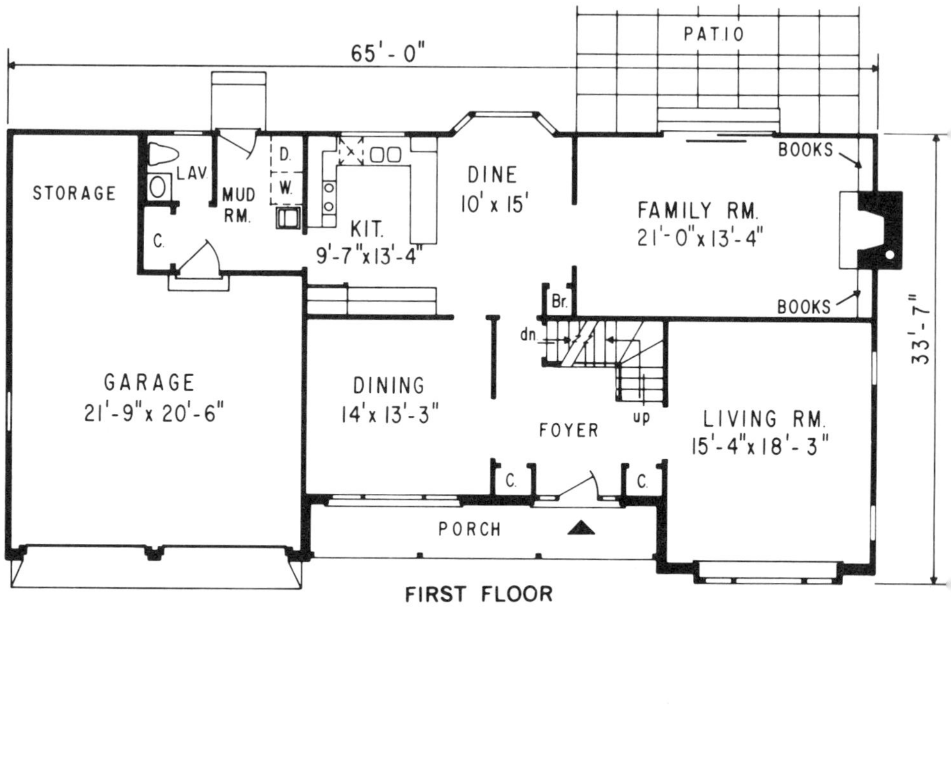

FIRST FLOOR

Three Porches Offer Outdoor Charm

No. 90048

Summer fun can be enhanced by the atmosphere this beautiful home provides. It has been designed so it can be used in winter and summer. A basement is provided which could be easily eliminated if not required. Three porches offer maximum outdoor living space. The one on the left is for clean up for the sportsman returning from his activities. A laundry with utility sink and a stall shower are provided, plus a closet for gear. The interior is as dramatic as the exterior. Note the oversized log burning fireplace on the right wall. Three bedrooms and two baths can be built by finishing the second floor. Note the U-shaped kitchen with adjoining dining porch.

First floor — 972 sq. ft.
Second floor w/ balcony — 321 sq. ft.

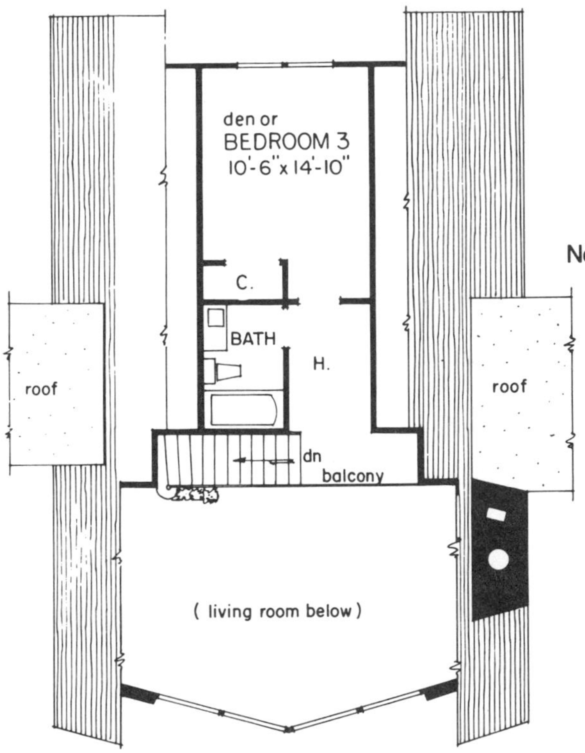

second floor plan

No. 90048

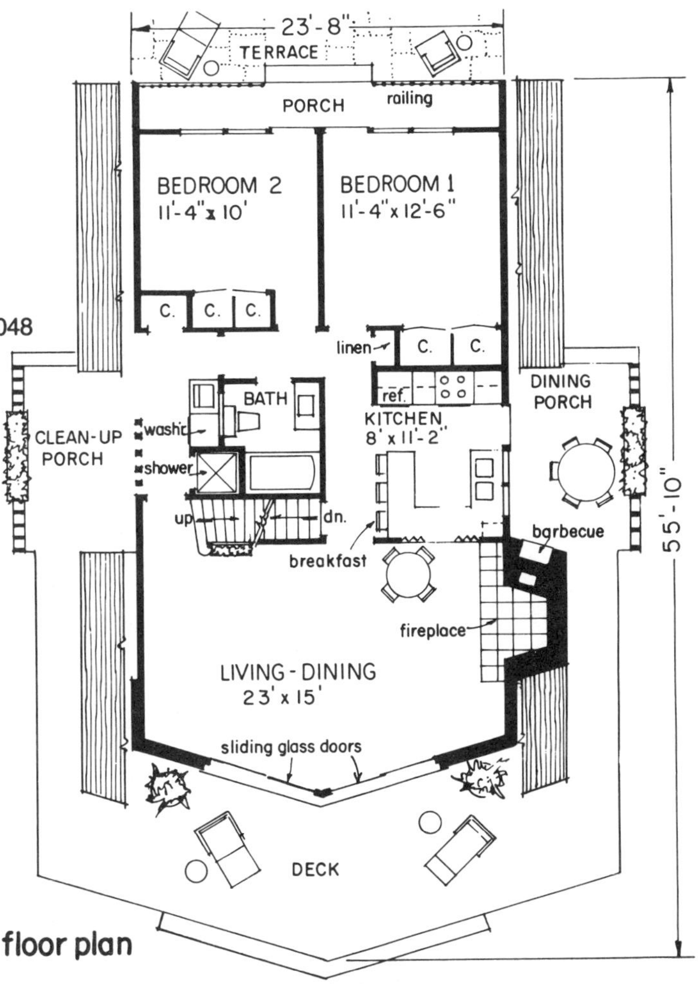

first floor plan

Compact and Cost Effective

No. 91049

Did you find a great buy on an unusually shaped or narrow lot? With a width of just 32 feet, this three-bedroom home is compact enough to fit any space, yet the clever plan is roomy enough to house your family in comfort. The entry opens to a huge great room adjoining a cozy dining room. The convenient, U-shaped kitchen is just steps away from the first floor bath and utility area. Look at the interesting angles in the bedrooms upstairs, including the ample master suite with private bath and two large closets. There's even a bonus room over the garage. Use it for storage now, and finish it when you need more living space.

Main level — 798 sq. ft.
Upper level — 780 sq. ft.

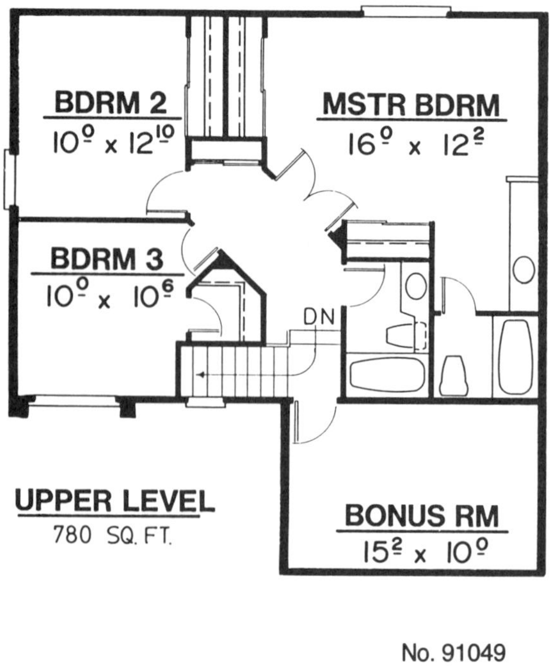

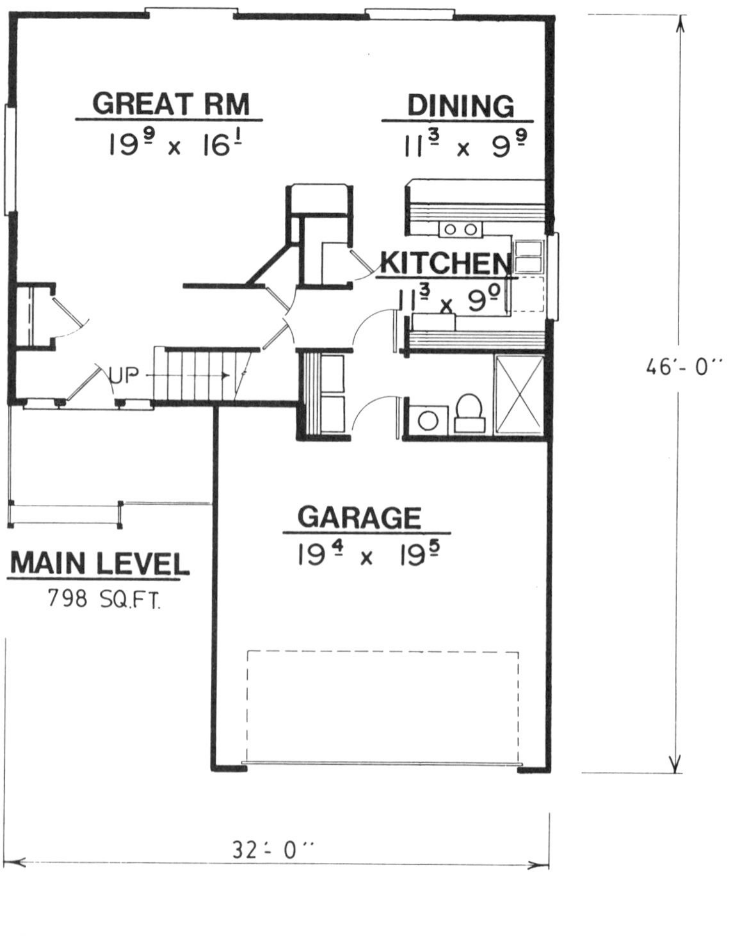

No. 91049

Designed for Sun Lovers

No. 90539

Are you looking for one-level living with a sunny atmosphere and a clever design? Here's your home. A central hallway off the entry separates living and sleeping areas for maximum quiet at bedtime. Sheltered from street sounds by the two-car garage, every bedroom features lots of closet space. The master suite boasts a private bath with double vanities. On the active side of the house, an island sink divides the kitchen, fireplaced family room, and skylit nook, providing a wonderful, open feeling to the entire area. For formal entertaining, use the barrel-vaulted living room just off the entry.

First floor — 1,685 sq. ft.

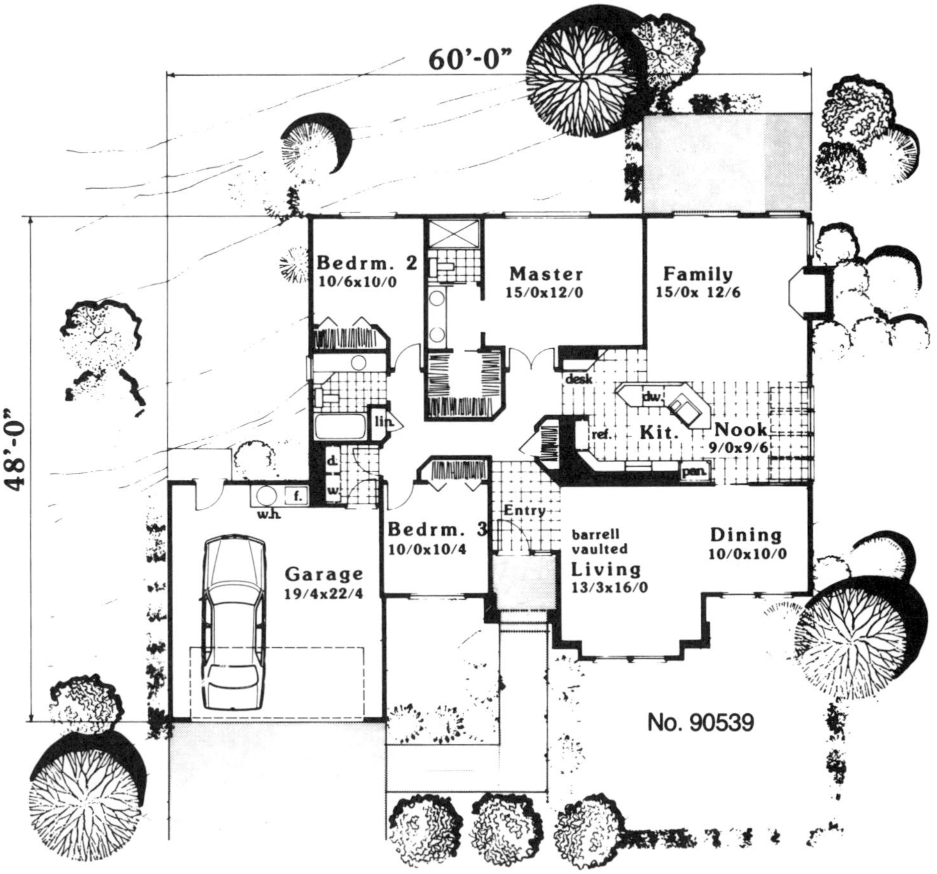

Angled for Excitement

No. 90653

You can be sure that this distinctive ranch will make a lasting impression on passers-by. But, the facade only hints at the dynamic plan that unfolds as you enter the foyer. A glance to the left reveals the conveniently arranged kitchen, flanked by the sunny dining room and breakfast nook. A corner window over the sink will let you keep a watchful eye on the kids playing outside. Look straight ahead into the soaring, hexagonal family room, featuring a spectacular three-way view of the yard, sliders to the patio, and a two-way fireplace that services the adjacent living room. And, away from it all in their own private wing, three ample bedrooms include the master suite with full bath and walk-in closet.

First floor— 2,495 sq. ft.

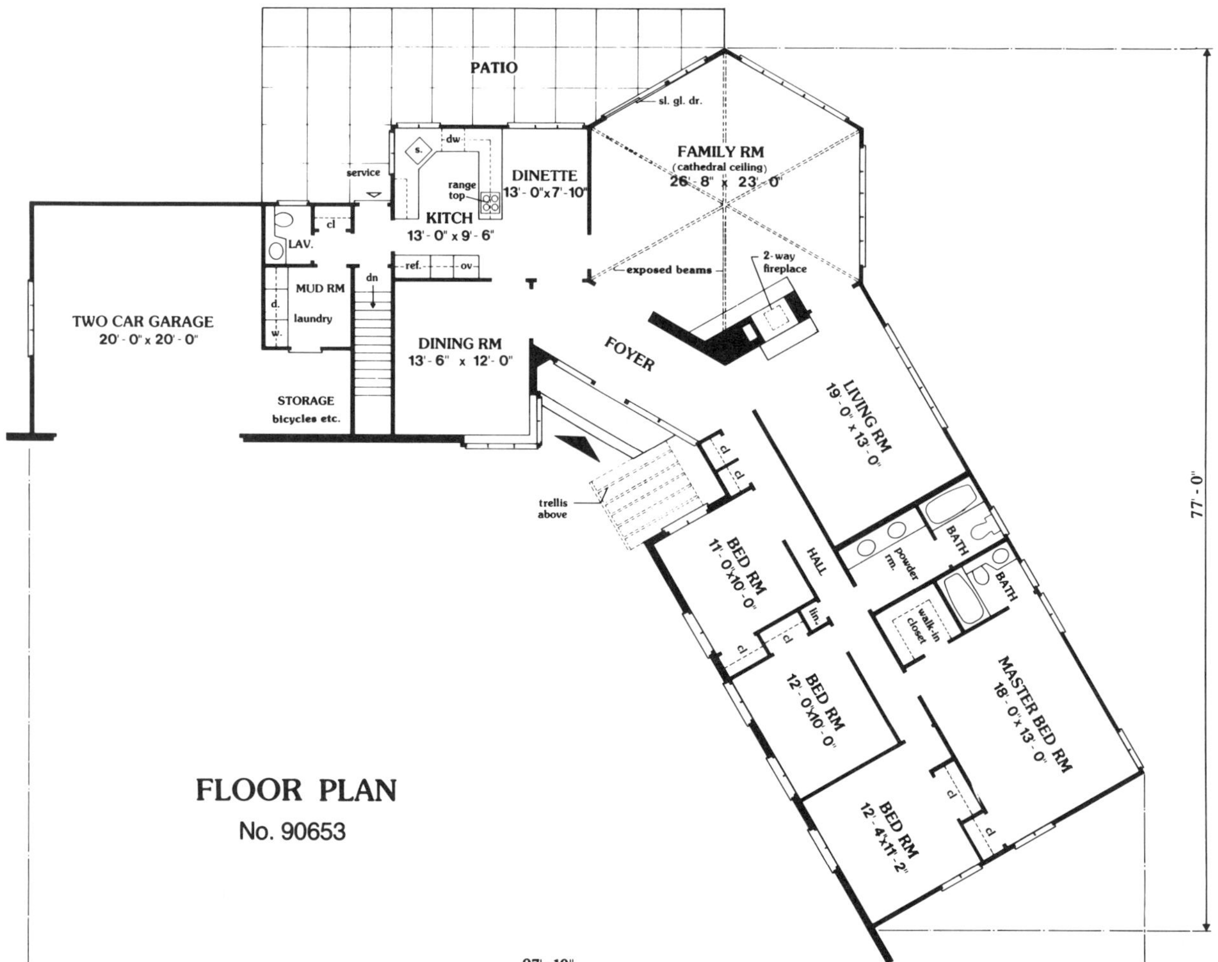

Family Plan Boasts Hidden Features

No. 90939

An inviting country porch, shutter-trimmed windows, and a big brick chimney are among the traditional elements that give this four-bedroom house a welcoming atmosphere. The elimination of wasted space, the sun-flooded central foyer, the secret sundeck off the expansive master suite, and a wide-open plan for the family living areas make this a special home for your family. Look at the U-shaped kitchen, designed to make mealtime easy… whether you serve supper in the dining room, the breakfast nook, or on the patio just outside. And, notice the door into the garage, a perfect entrance for the kids, who can leave their muddy boots in the utility room.

First floor — 1,104 sq. ft.
Second floor — 845 sq. ft.
Basement — 991 sq. ft.
Garage — 494 sq. ft.

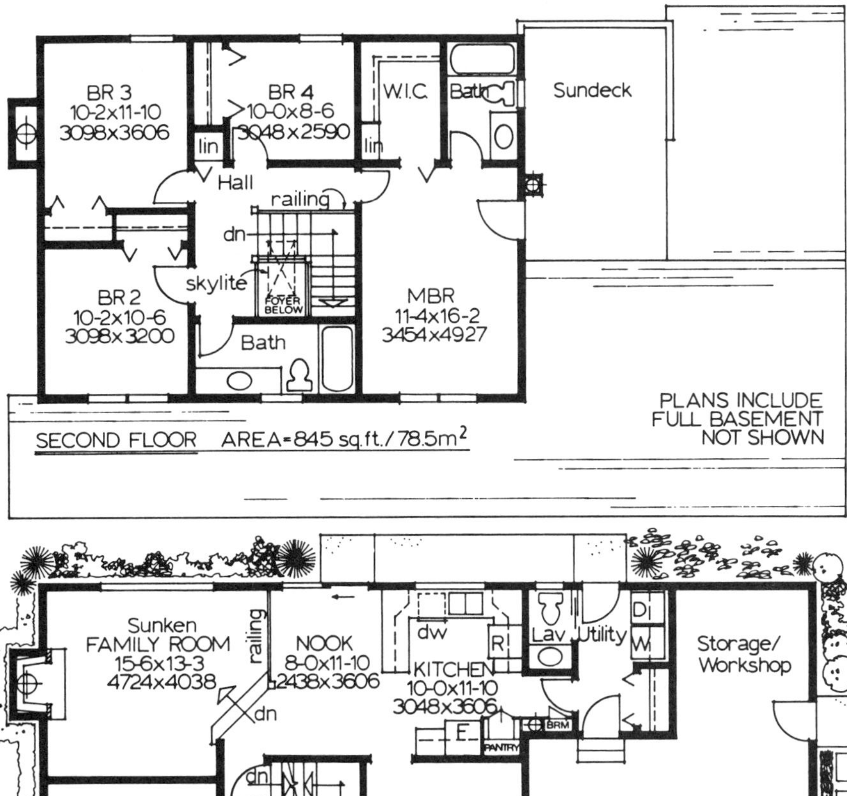

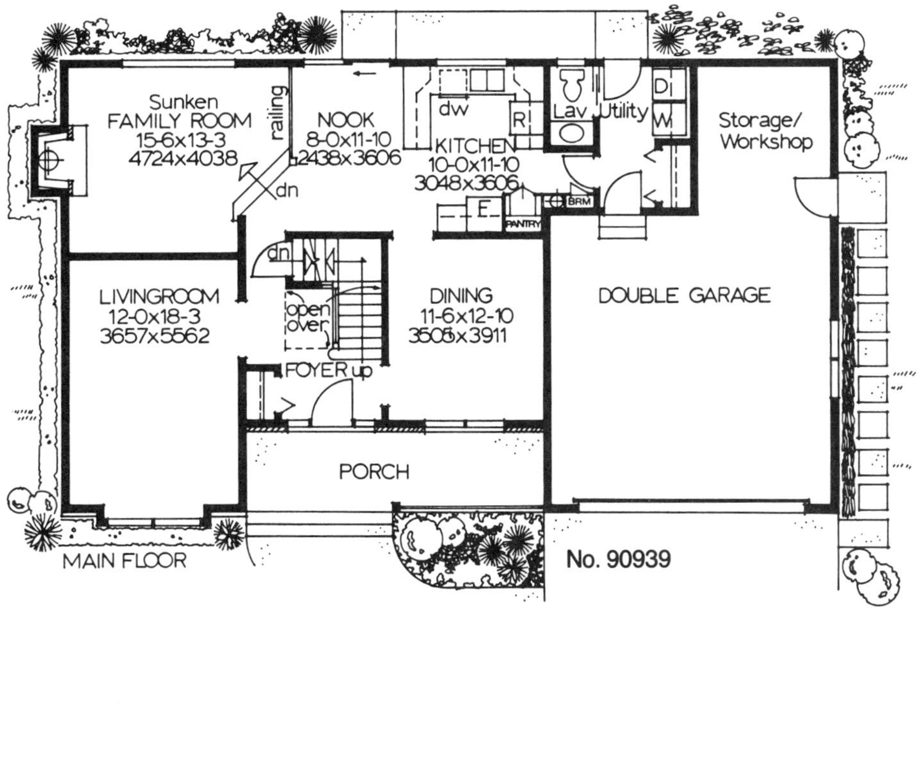

No. 90939

Enjoy A Lofty Retreat

No. 91039

This contemporary beauty on three levels will house your family in style and give you a private escape at the end of the day. From the main entry, walk down to a roomy fourth bedroom and utility room, or, step up to the to the living room on the main level. There, you'll be treated to a full view of active family areas, flooded with sunlight from oversized windows. Two bedrooms, one with its own private deck, flank a convenient full bath. Climb the stairs to the lofty master suite overlooking the living room. With a double vanity, walk-in shower and spa tub all to yourself, you'll be glad you chose this comfortable home.

Main level — 1,021 sq. ft.
Upper level — 418 sq. ft.
Lower level — 330 sq. ft.

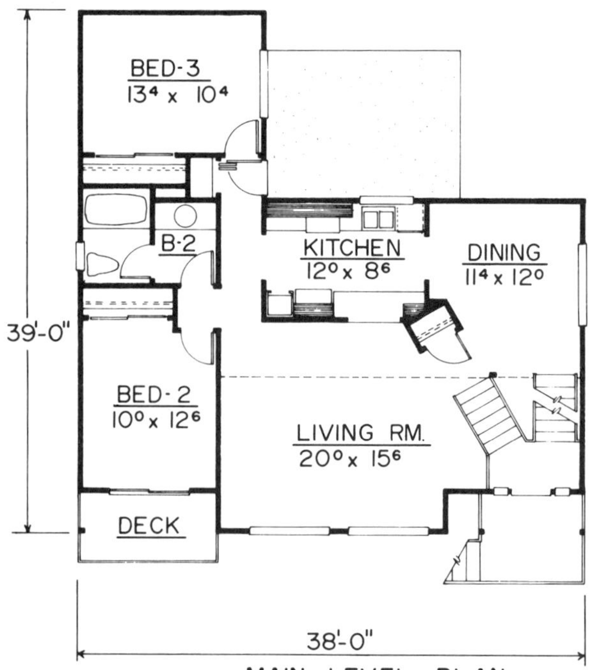

MAIN LEVEL PLAN

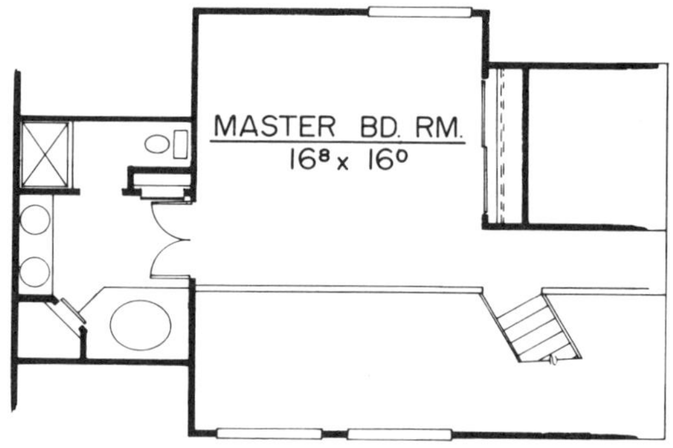

UPPER LEVEL PLAN

No. 91039

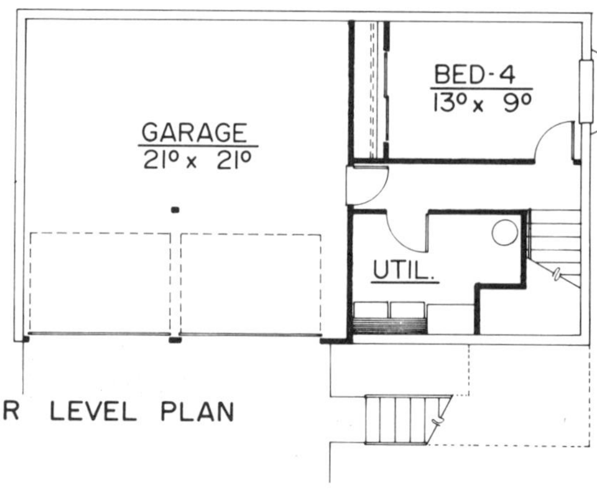

LOWER LEVEL PLAN

Elegant Half-Round Window Crowns Peak

No. 90659

Two bedrooms and a full bath enjoy a cozy retreat at the top of this charming home sheathed in cedar shingles. The huge entry foyer is flanked by the bedroom wing on the right, and by an efficient, skylit kitchen with adjoining dinette on the left. Straight back and a step down, the elegant, sunken living room is warmed during the day by three walls of windows, and at night by a heat-circulating fireplace. Sliding glass doors in the dining room make the terrace an attractive possibility for your after-dinner coffee.

First floor — 1,480 sq. ft.
Second floor - 560 sq. ft.
Basement — 1,085 sq. ft.
Garage — 268 sq. ft.

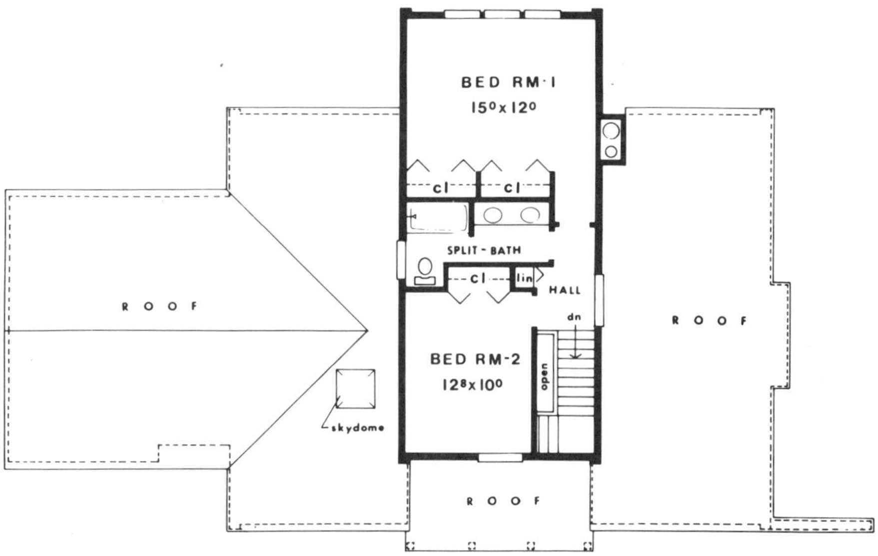

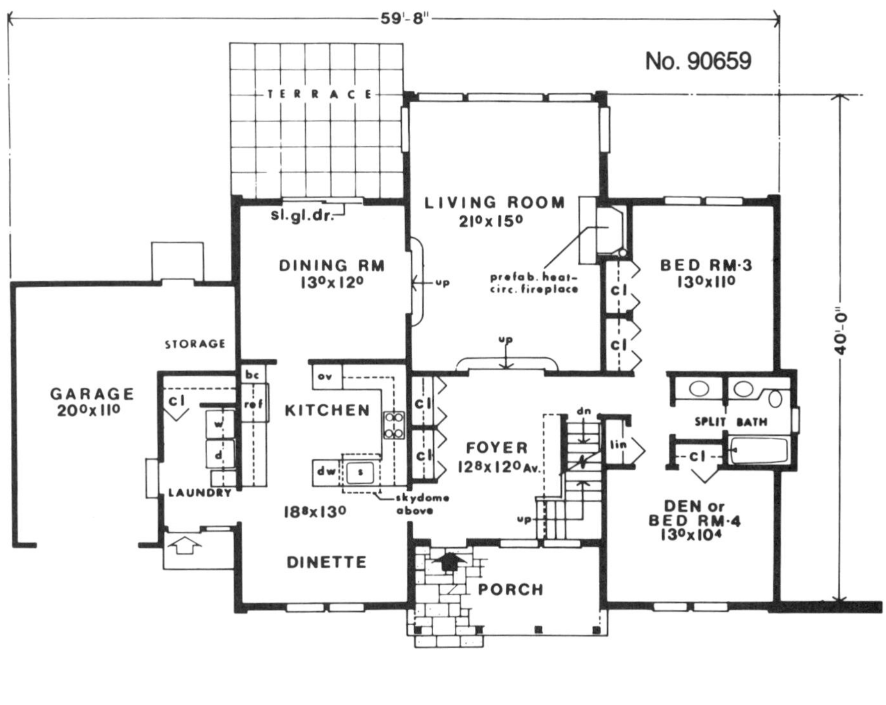

One-Level Budget Booster

No. 90937

Relax and enjoy the cost-saving advantages, and all the wonderful features, of this cozy ranch. From the central foyer, turn right to the sleeping wing. Tucked behind the garage away from active areas, the three bedrooms boast easy access to the utility room and two full baths. Or, walk straight past the general storage areas into the family eating nook and kitchen with sliders to the rear patio. Step down from the entry into the fireplaced, sunken living room. Bay windows and a wide-open view of the dining room give this formal area a delightful, sunny atmosphere.

Main living area — 1,238 sq. ft.
Garage — 399 sq. ft.

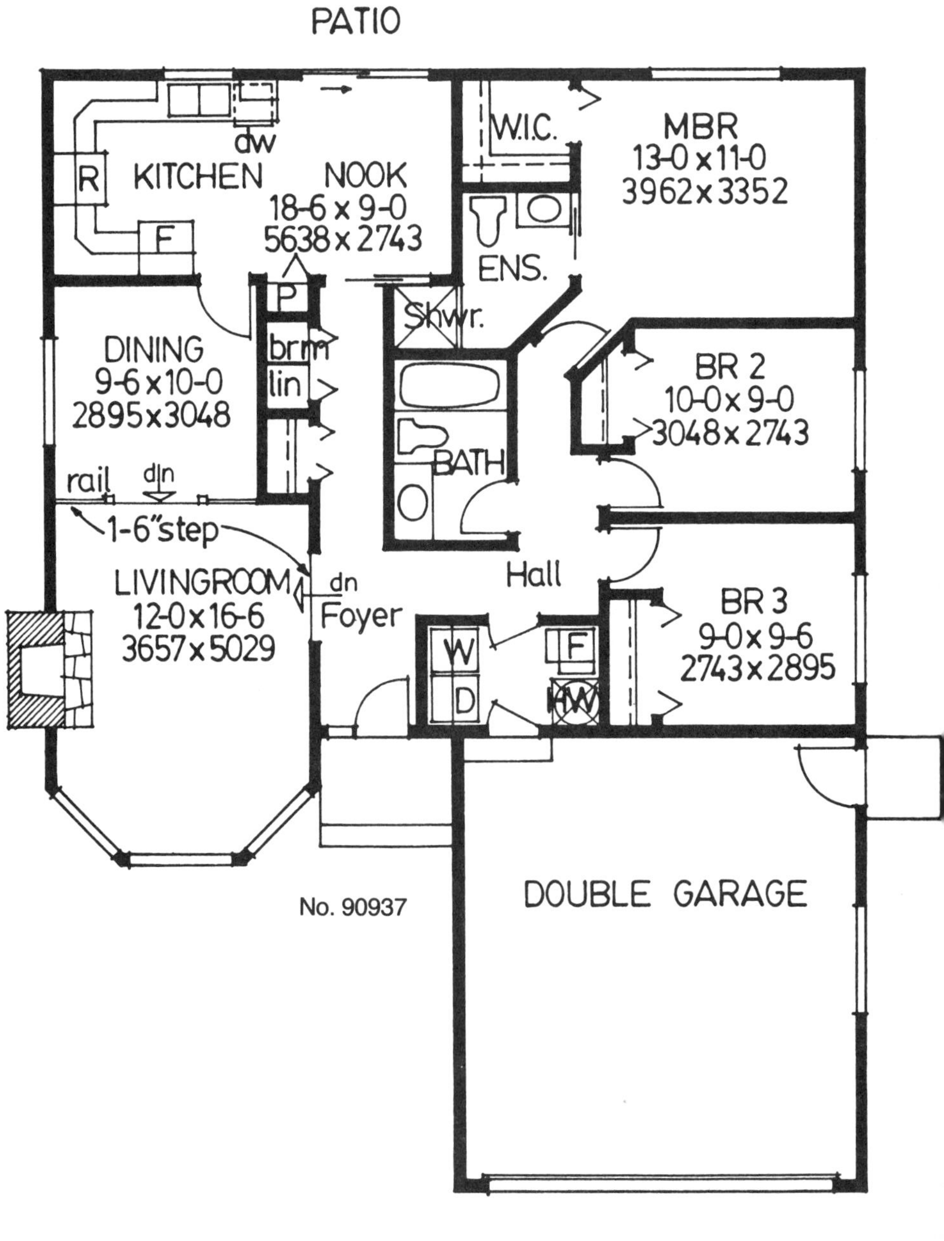

Country Farmhouse with Modern Touches

No. 90639

Enjoy this updated treatment of the classic salt box design. Don't worry about the kids tracking mud all over the house. The old-fashioned porch that surrounds this inviting home shelters two convenient entrances: one for guests and one for the kids with muddy shoes! The central foyer is flanked by the family room and a lovely sunken living room with an efficient heat-circulating fireplace. At the rear of the house, the kitchen serves formal and family dining rooms with ease. Walking up the circular stairs, you'll find three roomy bedrooms, including the master suite with skylit bath and dressing area.

Total living area — 1,950 sq. ft.
Basement — 1,159 sq. ft.
Garage — 439 sq. ft.

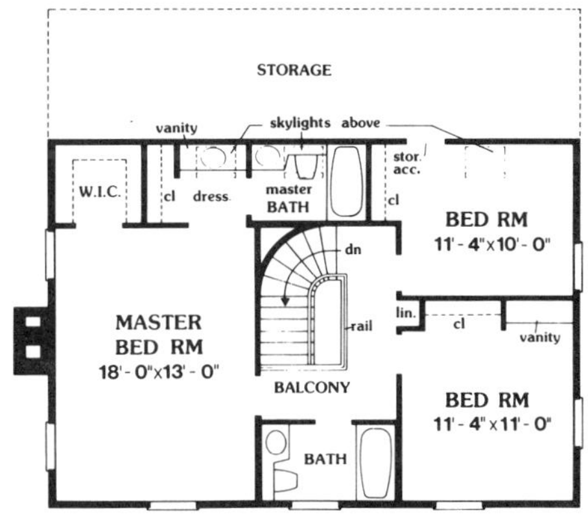

SECOND FLOOR

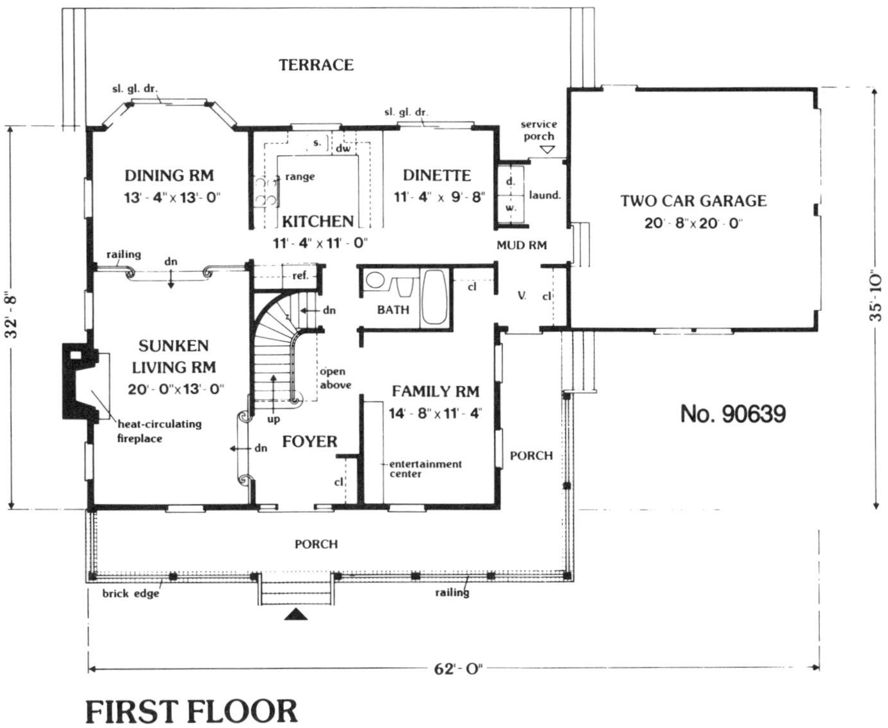

FIRST FLOOR

Delightful Cottage Plan

No. 90041

Square footage is held to a minimum in this delightful cottage to keep the cost attractively low, yet the use of the space allows maximum livability. A 20-foot-long, family-dining kitchen promotes spaciousness and efficiency. The master bedroom is quite large and sports two closets totalling 11 feet. The expansion attic, or second floor, has a good space in which two bedrooms and a bath can be finished, and a smaller room has two balconies to add to its stature. One is outdoors and frames against the stone chimney. The other is 11 feet long and overlooks the living room below. Exterior materials used are stylish: hand split wood roof shakes, horizontal wood siding, stone and wood hung windows.

First floor — 1,018 sq. ft.
Attic — 556 sq. ft.

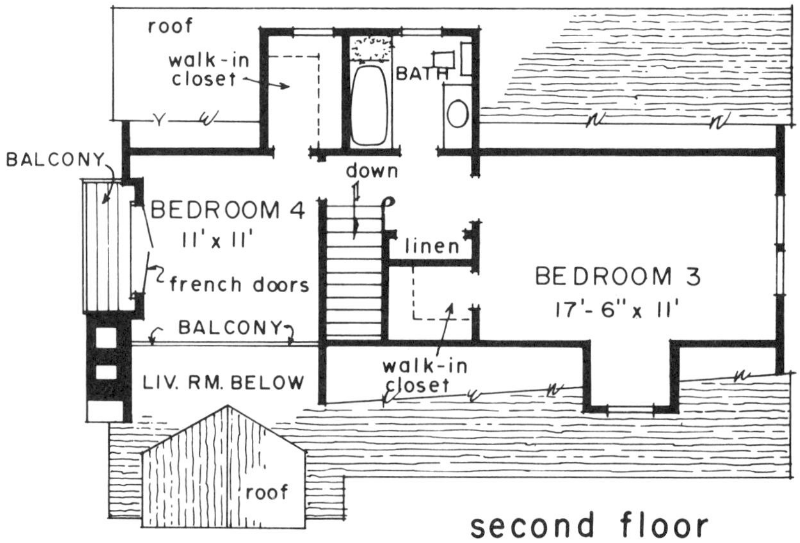

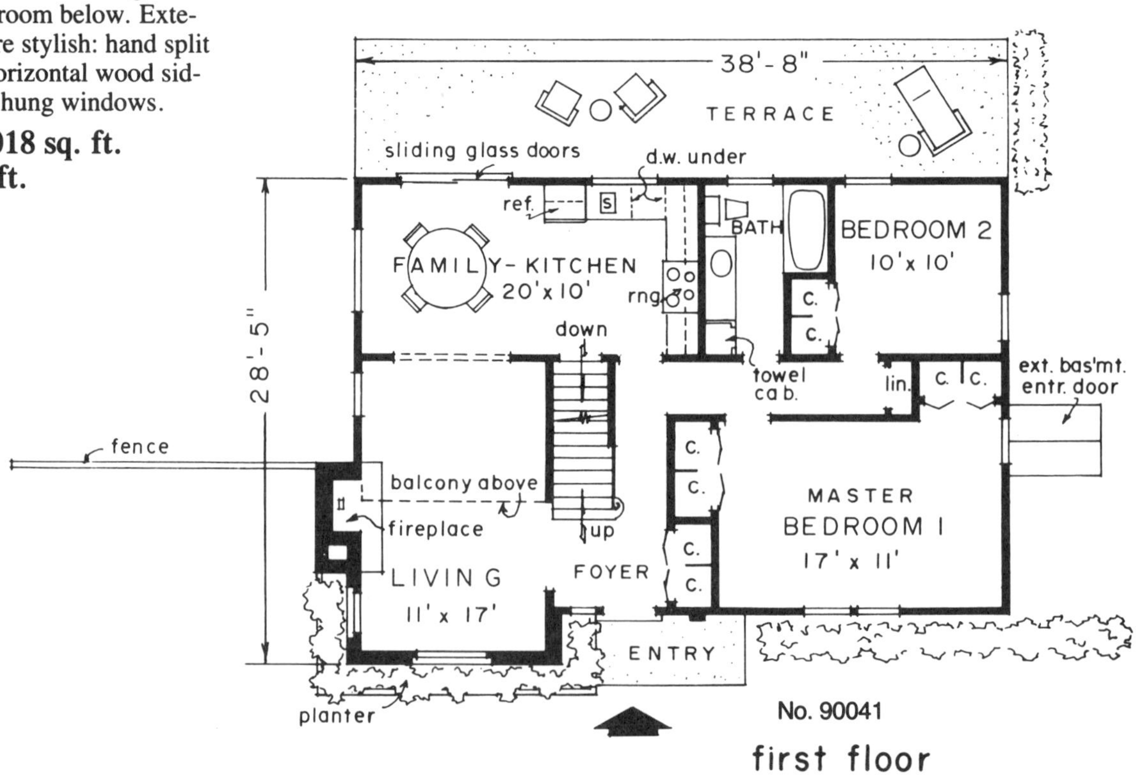

Solar Room More Than Just a Greenhouse

No. 90611

Thanks to the year-round solar room, this passive home will save you a bundle on your heating bills. Open the sliding glass doors on sunny days and close them at night to hold the heat inside the two-story living/dining room. A wraparound deck adds warm weather living space. Two roomy bedrooms and a full bath complete the first floor. The master suite enjoys lofty views of the living area below. With a balcony, bath, and private sitting room, it's a pleasant retreat at the end of the day.

First floor — 1,242 sq. ft.
Second floor — 490 sq. ft.
(excluding solar room and deck)

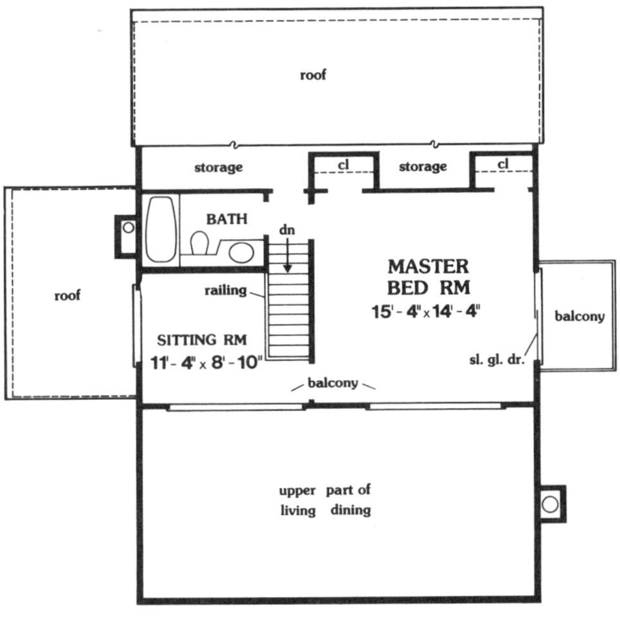

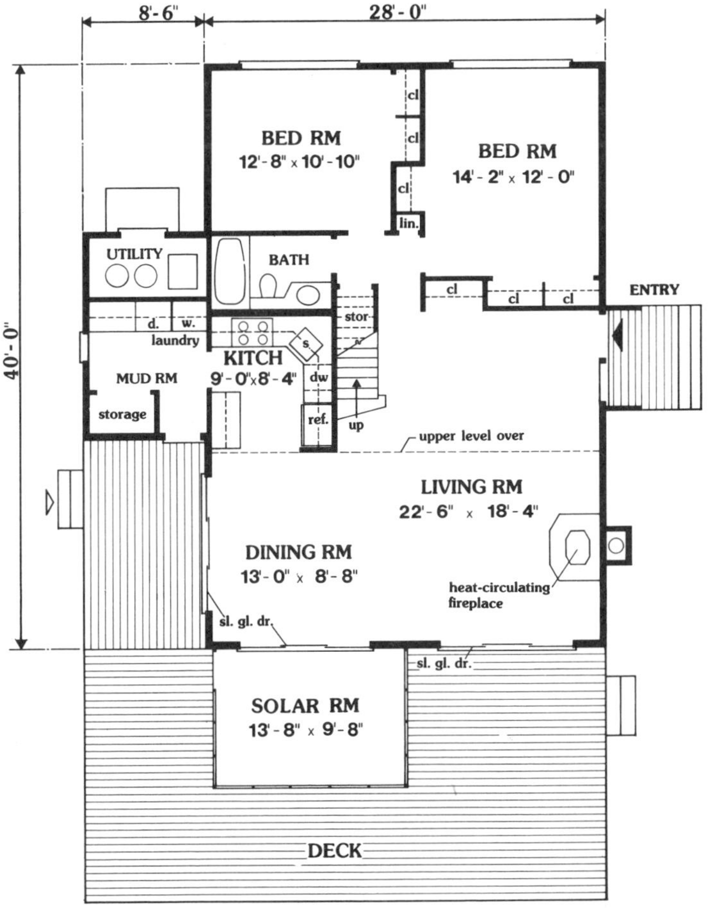

FIRST FLOOR

No. 90611

Perfect Union of Inside and Out

No. 90534

There's lots of living space packed into this compact two-story gem. Downstairs, active areas surround the soaring entry. A handy den is a well suited for privacy. The living- and dining rooms connect to form an attractive, airy space. You'll be amazed at the effect that comes from a combination of expansive windows, sliding glass doors, and an open plan. The roomy, adjacent kitchen features a pantry for storing all those extra groceries. Upstairs, you'll find loads of closet space in every bedroom, as well as bump out windows in the front rooms. The 2nd and 3rd bedrooms benefit from a quiet placement over the garage. You're sure to enjoy your private sunbathing deck off the master suite.

First floor — 768 sq. ft.
Second floor — 698 sq. ft.

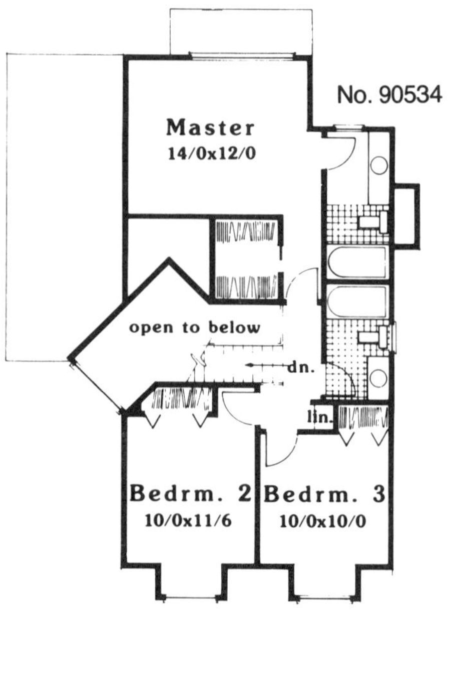

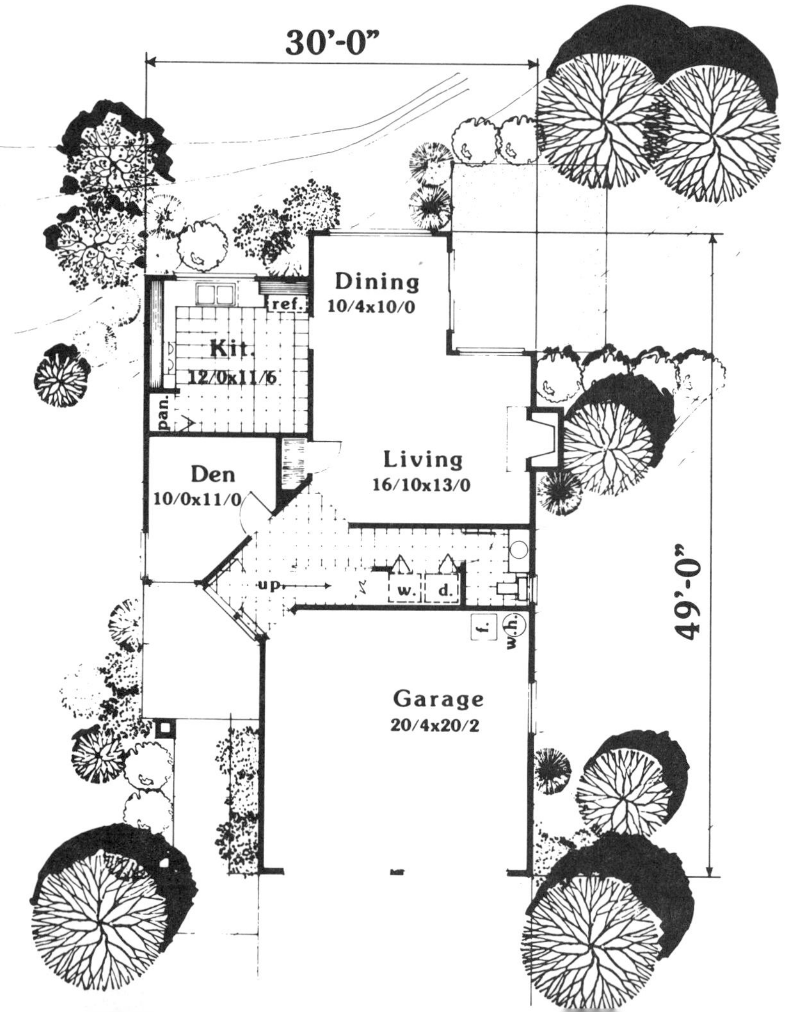

Choose Two Bedrooms or Four

No. 90651

Here's a house you can build now, and finish later. Fieldstone siding gives this one-an-a-half story gem a rustic charm that's easy to love. But, flexibility is an advantage that's hard to resist. The two first-floor bedrooms, full bath and lavatory are right off the foyer, but far enough from active areas to keep bedtime quiet. Straight ahead and two steps down, the sunken living and dining rooms combine a spectacular view of the back yard with a cozy fireplace to create an atmosphere you'll want to come home to. And, with a kitchen this efficient, mealtimes should be a breeze.

First floor — 1,300 sq. ft.
Second floor — 548 sq. ft.

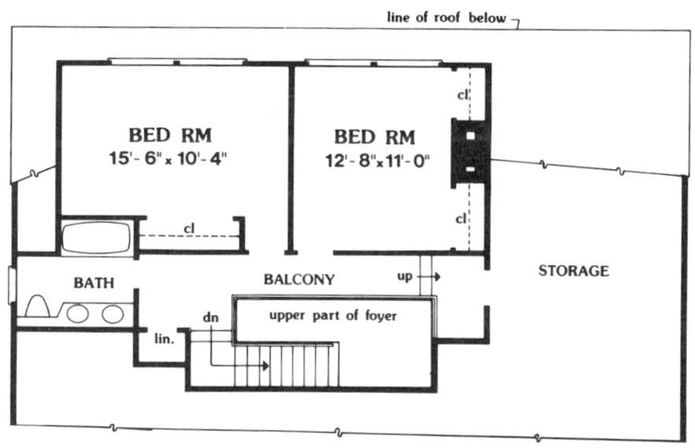

SECOND FLOOR

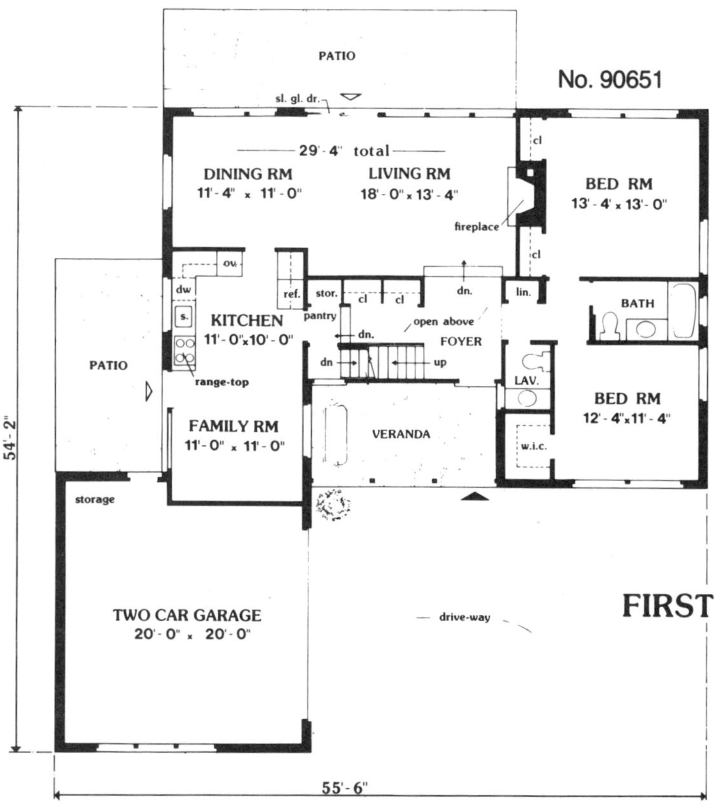

FIRST FLOOR

Abundance of Cabinets in Ranch Design

No. 90147

This modest ranch is very appealing to the first-time homeowner. Traditional vertical siding with lots of windows displays an attractive exterior. Inside, two bedrooms exist with a third possibly coming from the study, and they share two full baths. The kitchen is connected with the dining-family room combination which provides a very relaxed atmosphere for family activities. The laundry facilities are centrally located with the bedrooms for convenience.

Living area — 1,288 sq. ft.

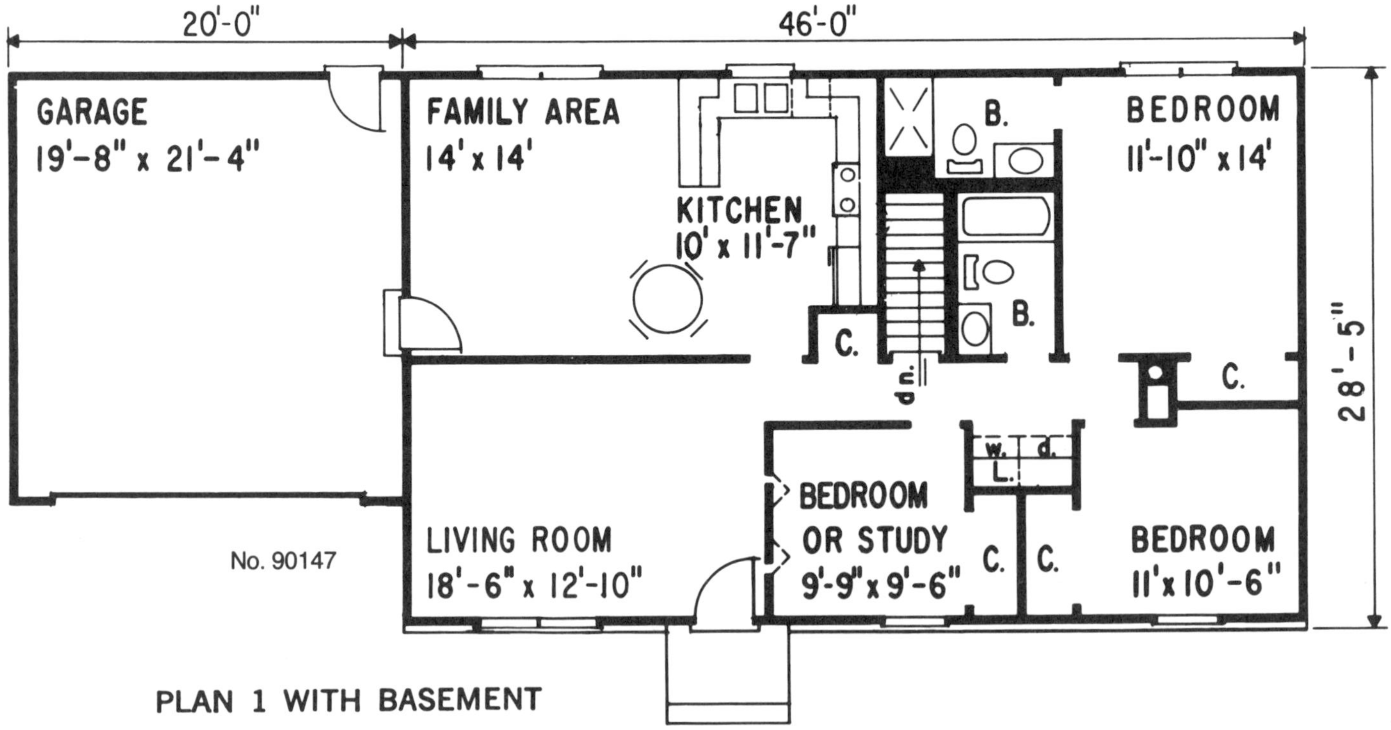

PLAN 1 WITH BASEMENT

Four-Bedroom English Tudor

No. 90031

The fine proportions of this impressive exterior —with its stone and brick veneer, half-timber, stucco, half-dormers, diamond and multi-paned windows— identifies the Tudor heritage of this two-story, four-bedroom design. Added to the impact is the stone trimmed arched entrance, massive brick chimney, and the extended decorative wall. Visual variety, so pleasing outside, is continued indoors with a breathtaking array of highlights that will cater to the whims of a large family. Designed to contribute to a feeling of personal luxury, the lavish secluded master bedroom suite has a dressing area with three closets and a private bath with mirrored vanity and a glass-enclosed, tiled shower stall.

First floor — 1,094 sq. ft.
Second floor — 934 sq. ft.
Garage — 506 sq. ft.
Patio — 160 sq. ft.

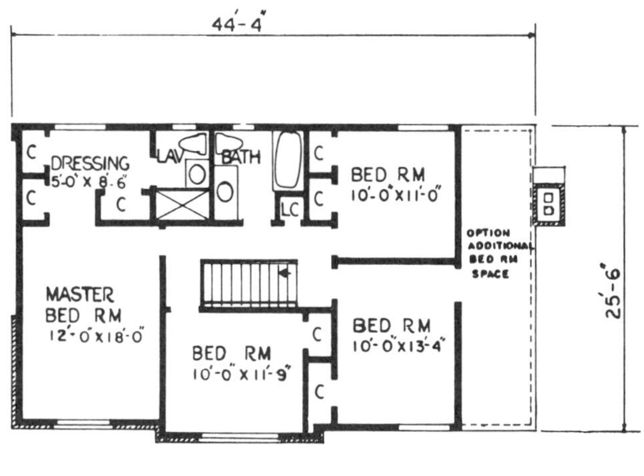

SECOND FLOOR PLAN

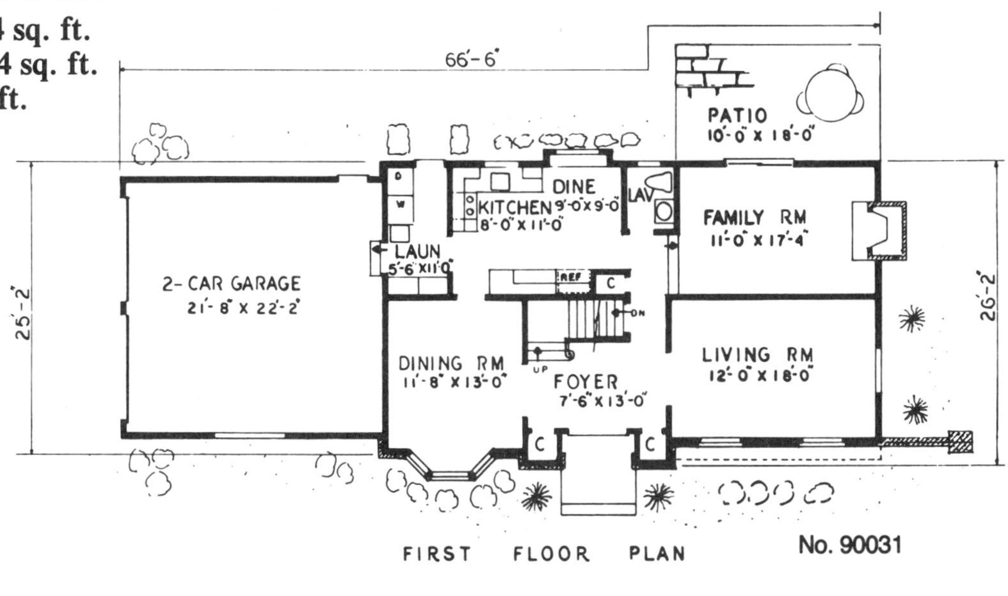

FIRST FLOOR PLAN

No. 90031

Huge Closets Keep Clutter Down

No. 90531

Imagine how easy it would be to live in this bright and airy gem. From the charming covered porch to the rear patio, you'll find special touches everywhere. An open plan and plenty of oversized windows give active areas a roomy and light feeling. You'll enjoy the convenience of the adjacent kitchen and dining room. You may even want to serve lunch on the patio just beyond the sliding glass doors. Thanks to lots of windows, the secluded bedrooms boast the same, bright atmosphere found in family areas. And, the proximity of the utility area to the bedrooms will make laundry day easy.

First floor — 1,157 sq. ft.

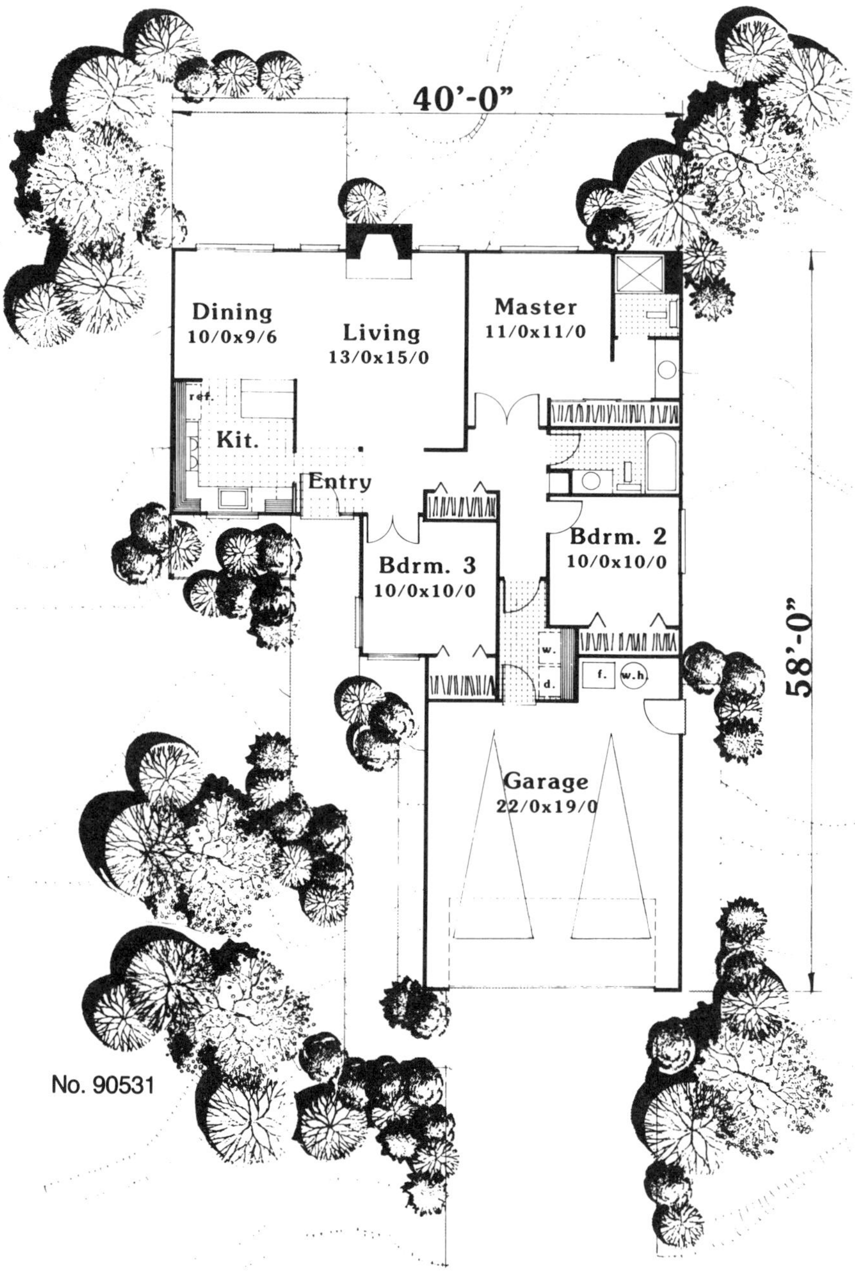

No. 90531

Master Suite Commands Private Wing

No. 90655

From its clapboard and fieldstone facade to its distinctive roof-line, this four-bedroom home has loads of curbside appeal. But best of all, the prospect of a luxurious, first-floor master suite will appeal to you. Right off the soaring, central foyer, you'll find an expansive formal living room brightened by a huge, five-panel window. Past the handy powder room, you'll discover the dining room, conveniently placed adjacent to the kitchen. Sliders lead to the rear patio, a nice place to enjoy a barbecue on a warm summer day. And, when there's a chill in the air, stoke up the fireplace heater in the massive multi-purpose room. Just look at the closet space in the upstairs bedrooms. And, notice the double sinks in the nearby bath that will keep morning traffic moving.

First floor — 1,396 sq. ft.
Second floor — 615 sq. ft.

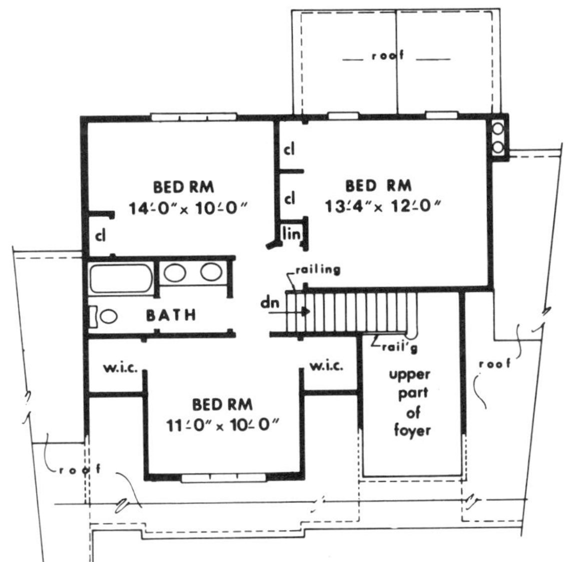

SECOND FLOOR PLAN

No. 90655

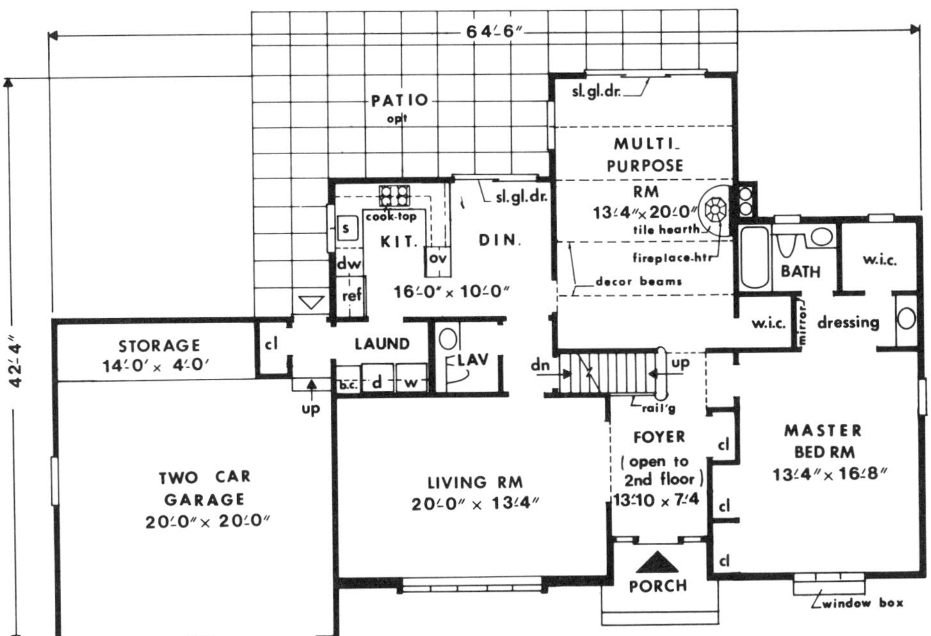

FIRST FLOOR PLAN

Hand-hewn Timbers In English Tudor

No. 90030

Once again, English architecture is enjoying wide popularity. There is something special about the dark hand-hewn timber and stone exterior, the paned and diamond-shaped windows, and the overall look that gives an impression of enduring comfort and security. Typical of this style is the open staircase which leads directly from the entrance foyer to the four bedrooms and open balcony on the second floor. A decorative metal circular staircase provides ready access to the upper balcony library that is located at the end of the living room, while directly behind is the beamed ceiling family room which connects with the outdoor terrace.

First floor — 1,565 sq. ft.
Second floor — 1,455 sq. ft.
Basement — 1,200 sq. ft.
Garage — 560 sq. ft.

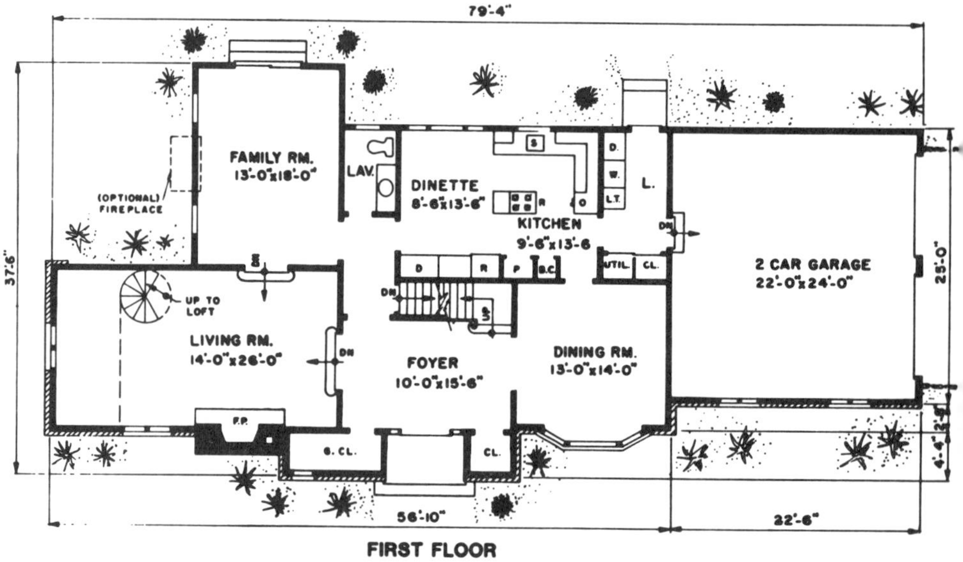

FIRST FLOOR PLAN

No. 90030

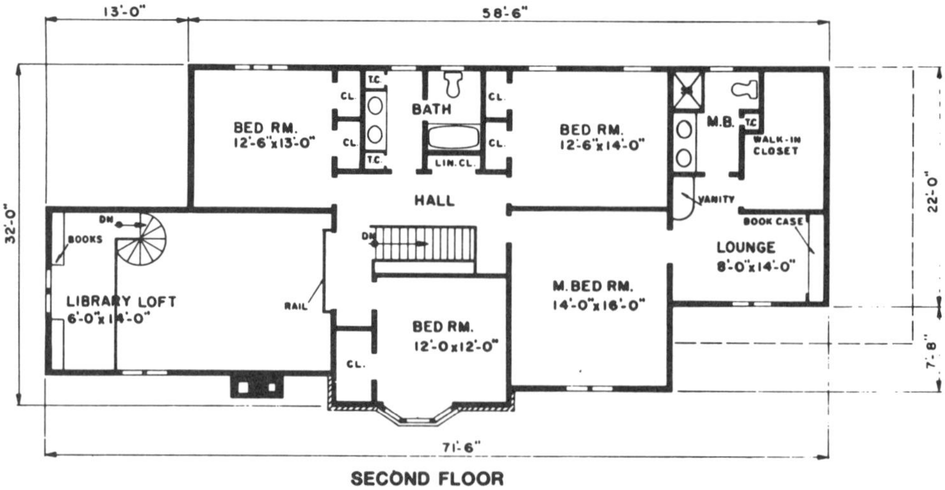

SECOND FLOOR PLAN

Two Story Foyer for a Grand Entrance

No. 90625

An interesting play of one and two-story wings gives the exterior of this four-bedroom Colonial a visual suggestion of large size. The materials used are traditional: wood shingles, brick veneer, and board and batten siding. A recessed front portico provides a sheltered entry. Just off the foyer, the living room features exposed beams, a cathedral ceiling, and glass doors to a covered porch. A built-in cabinet and large front windows enhance the dining room. For family meals, the U-shaped kitchen adjoins a lovely bay-windowed dinette. The family room, with a large window overlooking the garden, is warmed by a brick fireplace.

First floor — 1,147 sq. ft.
Second floor — 850 sq. ft.

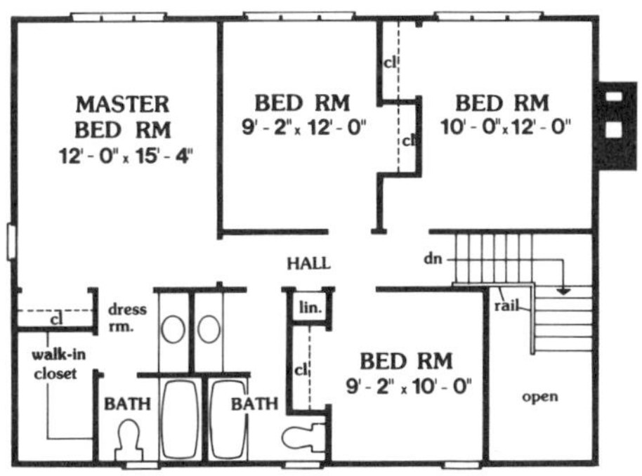

SECOND FLOOR PLAN

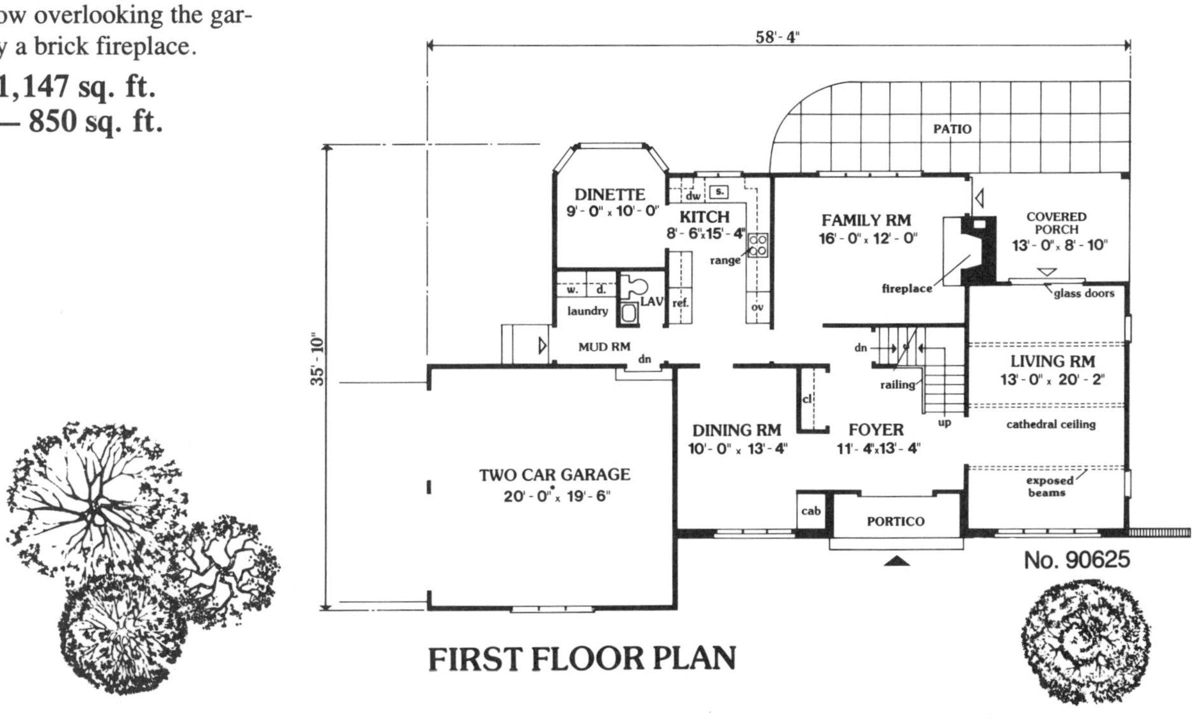

FIRST FLOOR PLAN

Stacked Bays Create Dramatic Impression

No. 90537

High ceilings and graceful arches give this stately brick home a elegant character that won't go out of style. Formal entertaining is a pleasure in the adjoining living and dining rooms just off the entry. Close the double doors to the efficient island kitchen and your guests will never guess how hard you or your helpers have worked. Informal eating and living areas at the rear of the house are wide open for lots of family interaction. Past the study and up the stairs, you'll find three roomy bedrooms and two full baths. Designed for maximum comfort and convenience, the master suite features double walk-in closets, double vanities, a walk-in shower and a tub.

First floor — 1,447 sq. ft.
Second floor — 926 sq. ft.
Storage — 138 sq. ft.

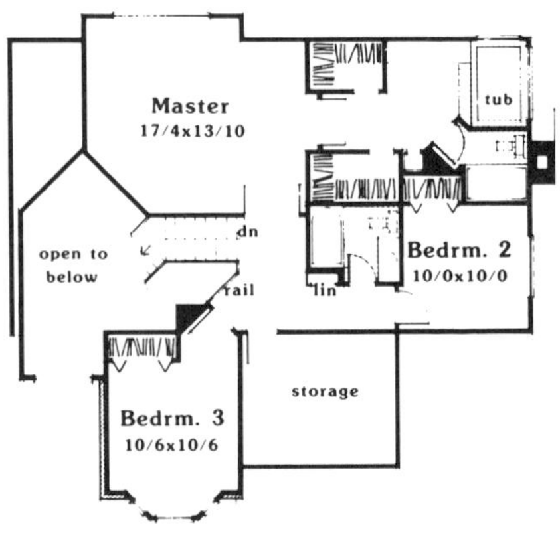

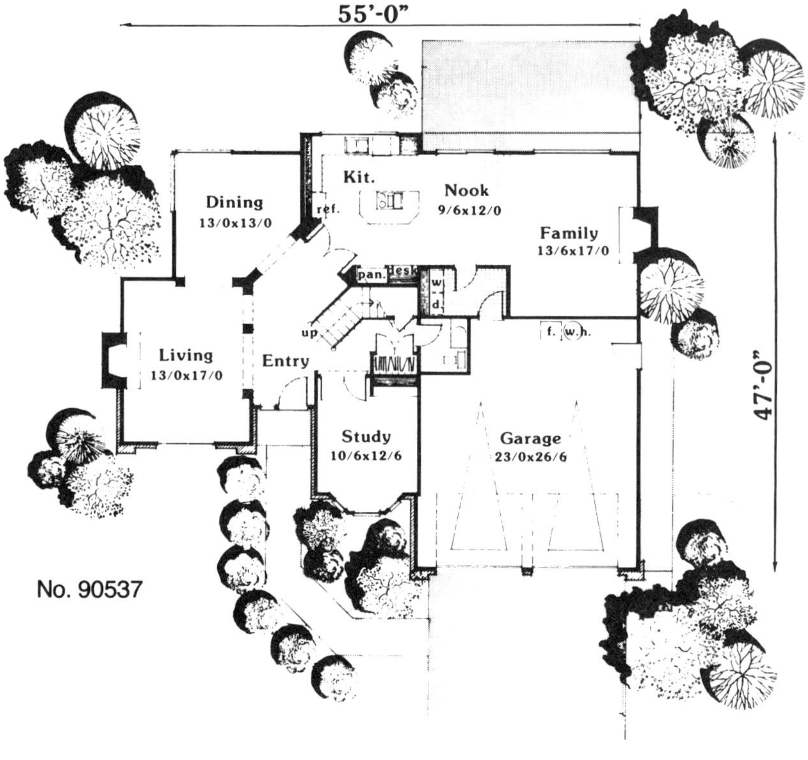

Tudor Accents for a Modern Plan

No. 90652

Take classic Tudor styling, add an ingenious one-level plan zoned for privacy, and you've got the house of your dreams. Thanks to placement in their own wing off the foyer, the three bedrooms and two full baths are amazingly quiet. Active areas surround the galley kitchen, strategically located for maximum efficiency. A heat-circulating fireplace adds a warm glow, and separates the living and dining rooms without compromising their open atmosphere. Sliders to the rear patio accentuate the airy feeling.

First floor — 1,588 sq. ft.

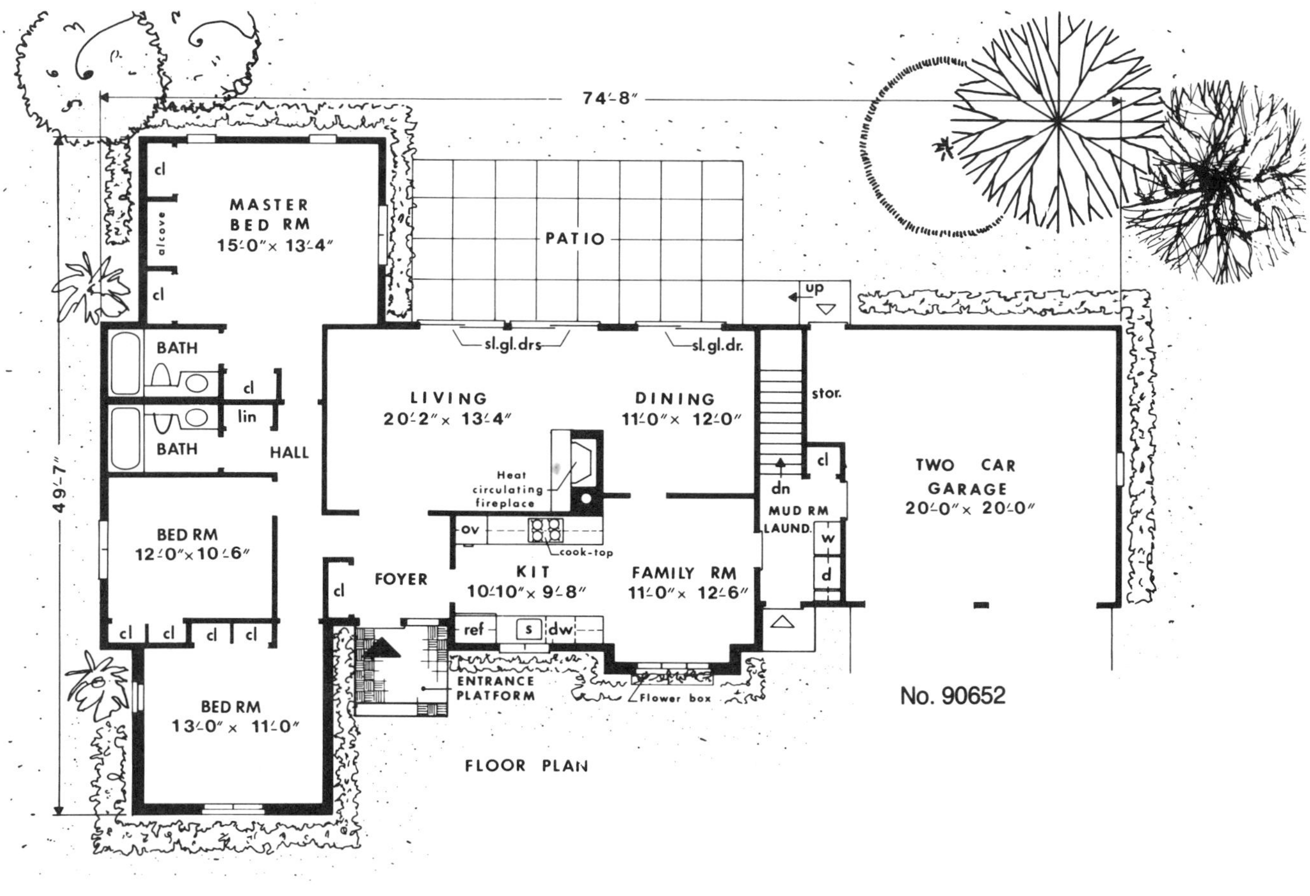

Sunworshippers' Dream House

No. 90660

Here's a beautiful passive solar design that hides a wonderful surprise inside. The traditional facade, complete with a nostalgic flower box, doesn't even hint at the modern interior of this one-level home. Energy-saving features include the airlock vestibule, the glass-walled solar room, and the rustic, beamed living room with its brick thermal wall and heat-circulating fireplace. Sliding glass doors in both the living and dining rooms open to the rear patio. In the master suite, which features a full bath and walk-in closet, a built-in window seat occupies most of the south wall. Two bedrooms at the front of the house adjoin another full bath.

First floor — 1,886 sq. ft.

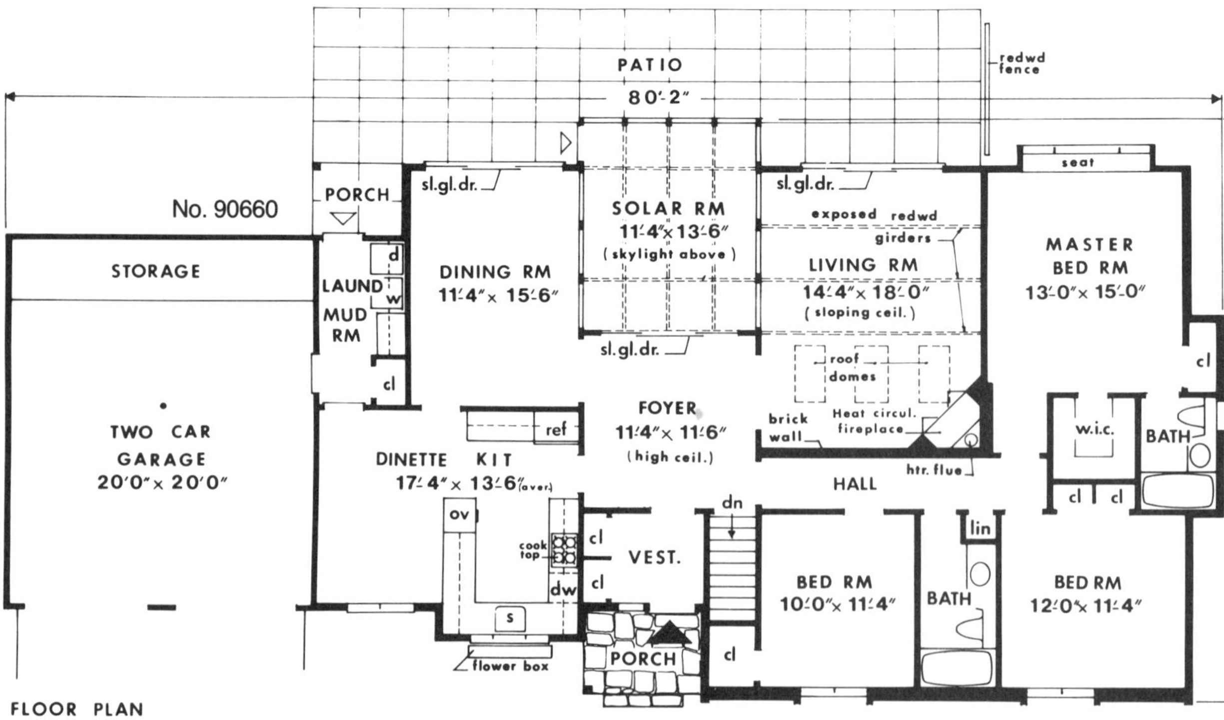

Enjoy Outdoor Dining on the Patio

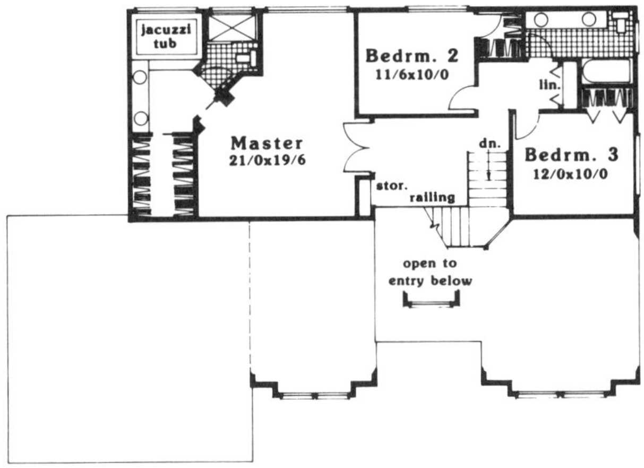

No. 90535

It would hard to find a grander home in the same square footage. Soaring ceilings and two-story windows provide dramatic interior and exterior views in this contemporary brick and wood classic. And, with huge glass expanses in every room, you're guaranteed a cheerful atmosphere year-round. The convenient floor plan will make you cheerful, too. The island kitchen, flanked by the formal dining room and bayed breakfast nook and handy to the family room, eases meal preparation and creates a convivial atmosphere. The three bedrooms upstairs open to a central hallway with a view of the entry. You'll find double vanities in both full baths. And, the master suite even boasts a jacuzzi!

First floor — 1,510 sq. ft.
Second floor — 1,000 sq. ft.

No. 90535

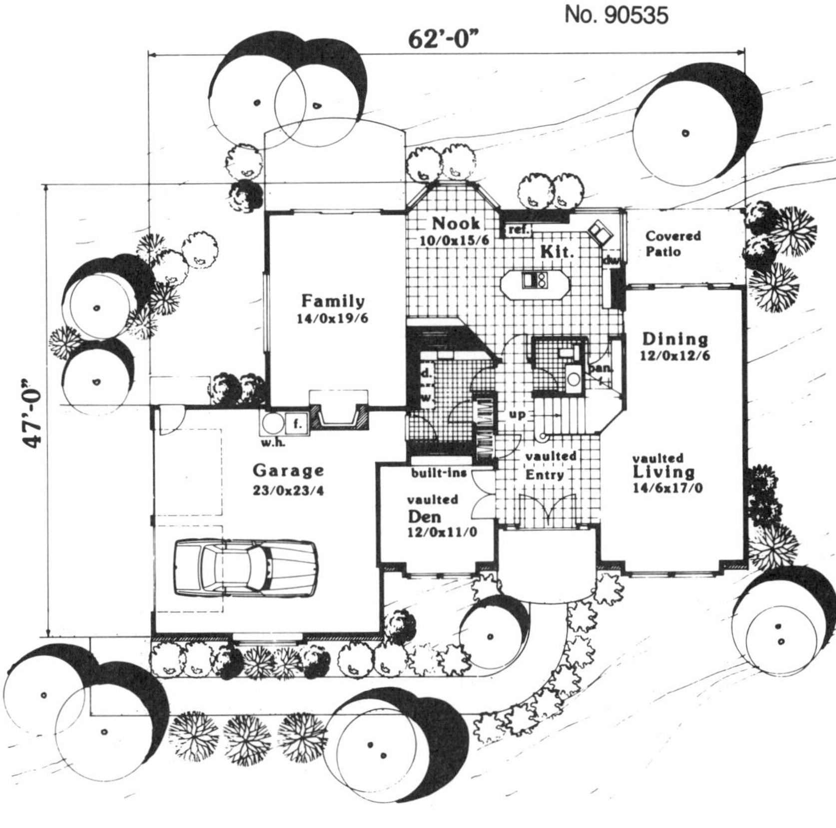

Modest Tudor With A Massive Look

No. 90012

Specifically designed to make its presence felt in any neighborhood, this stately Tudor home contains fewer square feet, and is more affordable, than one would imagine. Broken and steeply sloping roof lines, dormers, a large cantilevered bay, and a Gothic shaped, unique entrance way —as well as the charming stone, brick, and half-timber materials—all add keen interest to the exterior. The living/dining space is an open 34 ft. area designed to be an impressive focal point; a large log burning fireplace is centrally located on the far wall. The triple windows in the front allow for a grand view.

First floor — 1,078 sq. ft.
Second floor — 1,131 sq. ft.

No. 90012

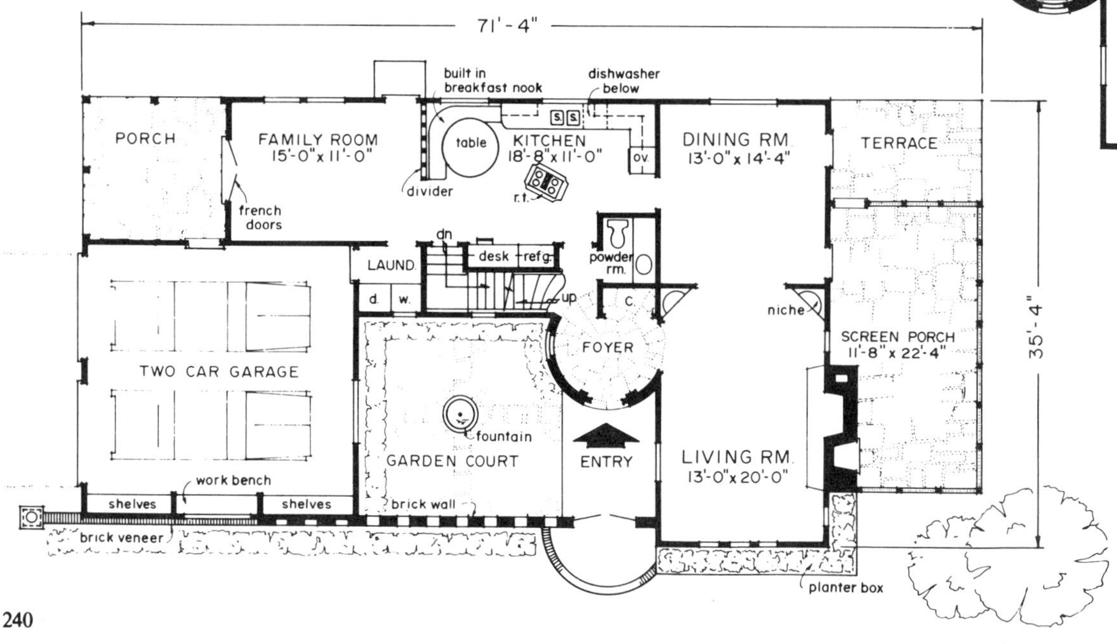

Book-lined Family Room

NO. 90117

Relax in this comfortable family room among the books and curl up in front of the fire. Or, on warmer days move through the glass doors and onto the patio which augments your living area. The formal living room and dining room are adjacent to the central foyer which incorporates a coat closet and a half bath for the convenience of guests. Family dining is accommodated by an area between the family room and the well planned kitchen. The second floor contains four bedrooms with the master bedroom having a double walk-in closet and a private bath. Linked to these rooms is an optional studio above the double garage.

First floor — 1,452 sq. ft.
Second floor — 1,158 sq. ft.
Optional studio — 264 sq. ft.

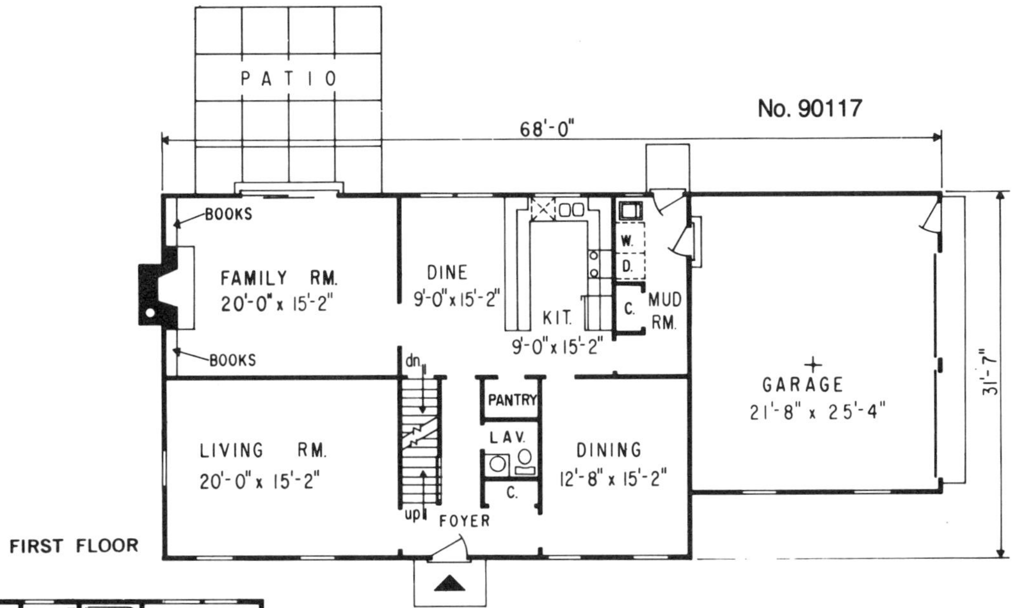

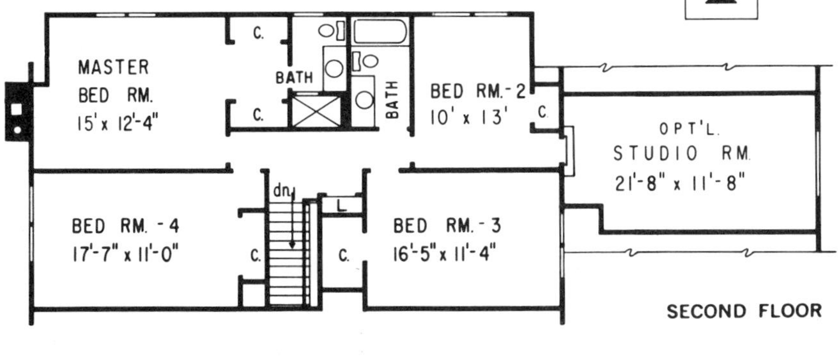

Versatile Hillside Home

No. 90830

Do you have big plans for the future and a limited budget today? This charming two-bedroom is perfect for an economical hillside lot, and practical to build, too! Start with one level. The master suite off the entry foyer features a private bath and walk-in closet. A second bedroom is steps away from the washer and dryer and another full bath. Expansive windows and sliding glass doors afford living areas at the rear of the house that great hillside view. And, when the weather's nice, move out to the sundeck. The daylight basement remains cheery and is the perfect place for economical expansion.

First floor — 1,172 sq. ft.
Daylight basement — 1,068 sq.ft.

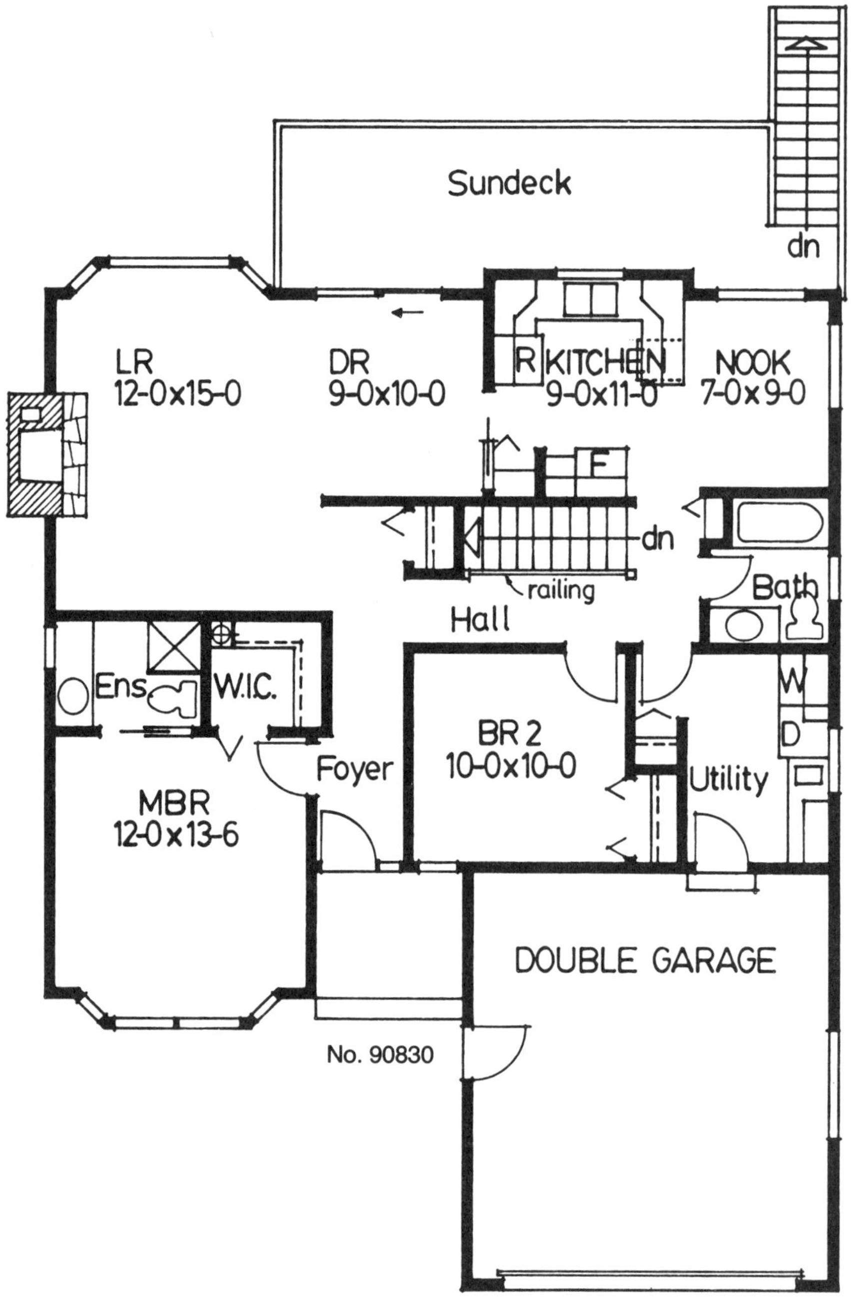

Multiple Peaks Hint at Exciting Interior

No. 91044

Stand at the top of the open, U-shaped staircase and enjoy a full view of the soaring living room, two-story entry, and the yard outside this magnificent, contemporary castle. And, while you're upstairs, notice the interesting angles and extra-large closets in every bedroom, the double vanities and spa in the master suite, and the corner window treatments that create a special glow. Downstairs, the wide-open feeling of the vaulted living room continues throughout the sun-washed family areas. Eat in the cozy nook or the formal dining room. The efficient island kitchen, loaded with counter space, is handy to both.

Main floor — 1,158 sq. ft.
Upper floor — 952 sq. ft.

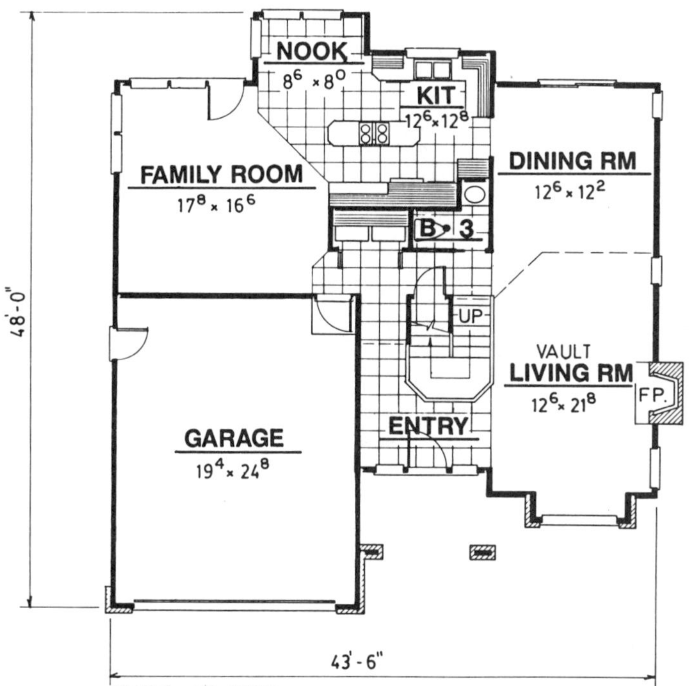

MAIN FLOOR
1158 SQ. FT.

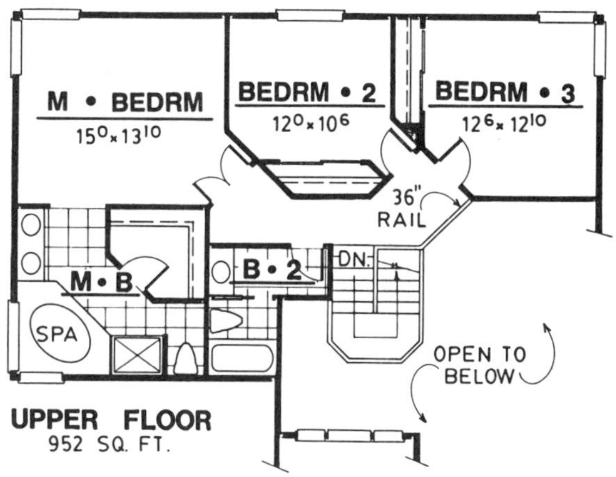

UPPER FLOOR
952 SQ. FT.

No. 91044

Family Home Boasts Sunny Atmosphere

No. 90938

The moment you enter the skylit, two-story foyer of this three-bedroom charmer, you'll fall in love with its sunny, open plan. French doors provide separation of formal and family areas without cutting off the sunlight that streams through the window walls at the rear of the house. The island in the U-shaped kitchen works the same way, maintaining the airy atmosphere of the expansive family room and informal nook. Entertain in the formal dining and living rooms, which feature a built-in china cabinet and cozy fieldstone fireplace. Upstairs, three roomy bedrooms include the master suite with its own private bath and bump-out sitting area.

First floor — 1,028 sq. ft.
Second floor — 734 sq. ft
Basement — 883 sq. ft.
Garage — 400 sq. ft.

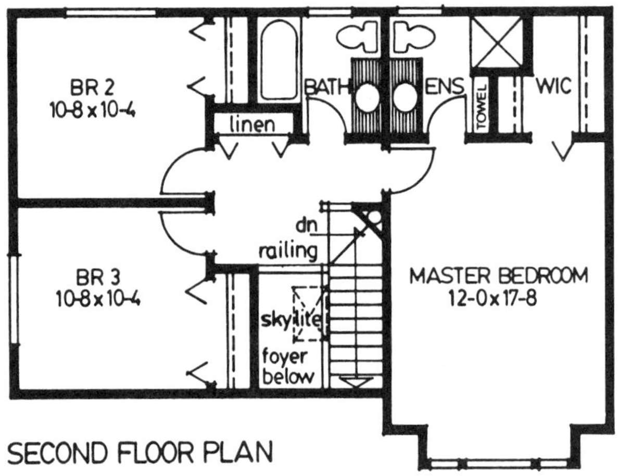

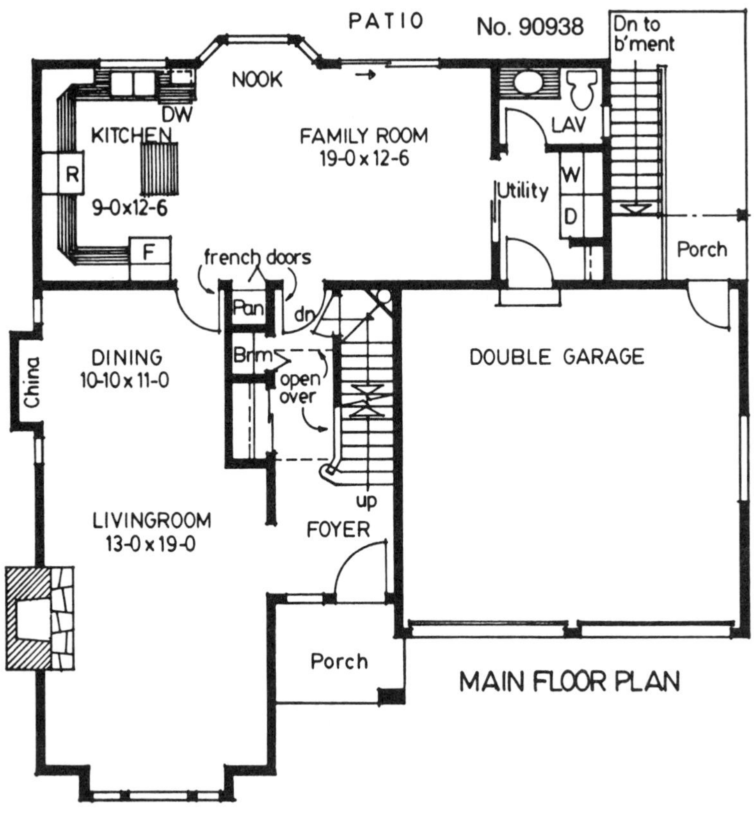

Octagonal Window Adds Interest

No. 90528

Prepare supper as you watch the world go by from the U-shaped kitchen of this easy-living home. And, with a pass-through to the vaulted dining room, meal service couldn't be easier! You'll love the airy feeling in the fireplaced, sunken living room. Expansive windows at the rear of the house unite the open living and dining rooms with the back yard. Upstairs, three bedrooms feature loads of storage space, sport interesting angles, and share a view of the entry below. And you'll especially enjoy the attractive private bath in the roomy master suite.

Total living area — 1,342 sq. ft.

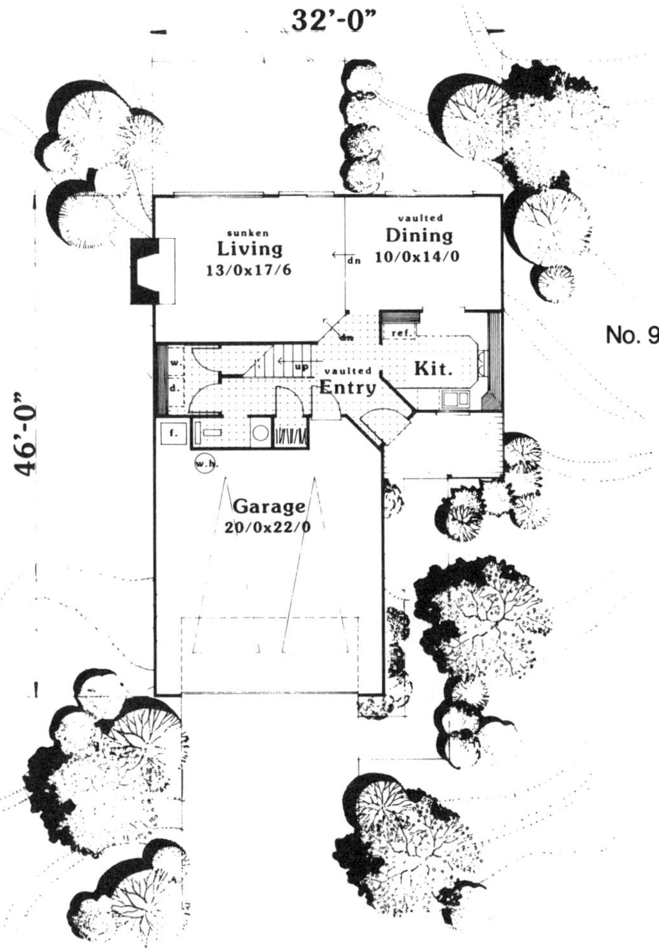

No. 90528

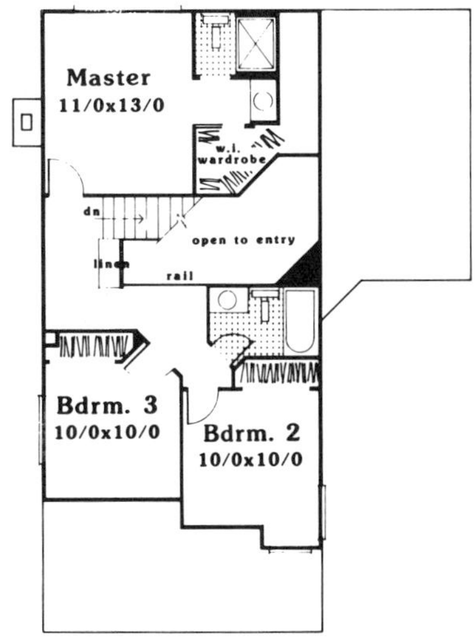

Upper Floor

Three Bedroom Contemporary Design

No. 90042

Flowers and shrubs in a permanent L-shaped brick planter grace the entrance to this one story, three bedroom contemporary ranch design. The entrance foyer does more than serve as the starting point for good traffic circulation; it creates an excellent first impression with decorative wrought iron railings separating it from the living room at the left. Excellent decorating possibilities abound in the sunken living room, which has a corner, brick-faced fireplace, corner windows and wall space. The spartan simplicity of this contemporary design meets the demands for convenience and ease of maintenance required by many families, yet it will suit almost any surrounding in any part of the country.

First floor — 1,490 sq. ft.
Basement — 1,490 sq. ft.
Garage — 300 sq. ft.

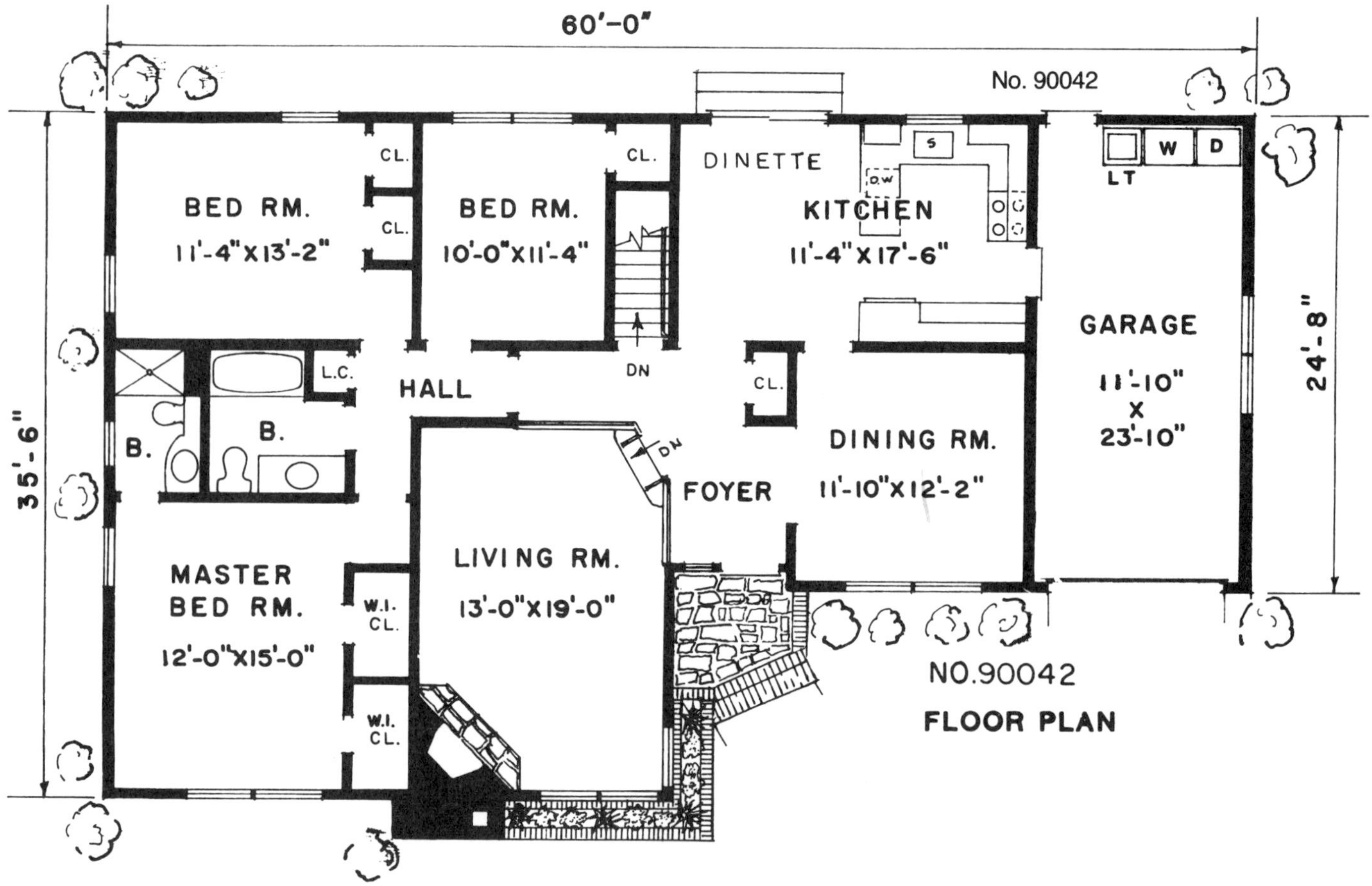

NO.90042
FLOOR PLAN

Three Private Dressing Rooms

No. 90039

The front and rear exposed living room with its log burning fireplace and covered rear porch, the double access family room, the curved walled dining room with porch entry, and kitchen providing a circular breakfast nook, planning desk and concealed laundry make up the impressive balance of the first floor. The second floor, comfortably housing three large bedrooms offers unique features: a balconied hall, three private dressing rooms, large four-fixture bath with two windows, luxurious closet space and a master bedroom suite with private bath, three rear sky windows, four front windows and a 15 x 20 foot storage room.

First floor — 1,064 sq. ft.
Second floor — 947 sq. ft.

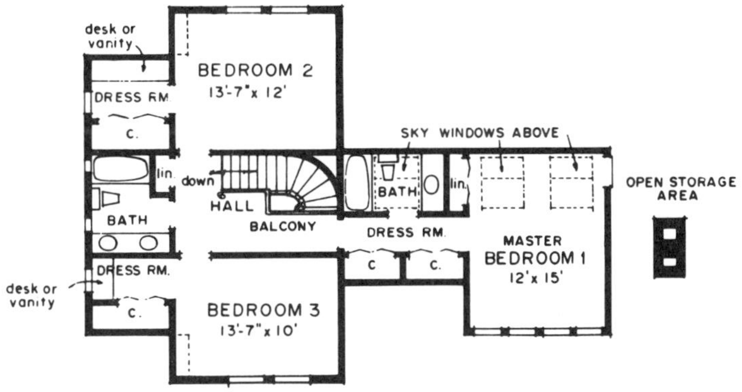

second floor plan

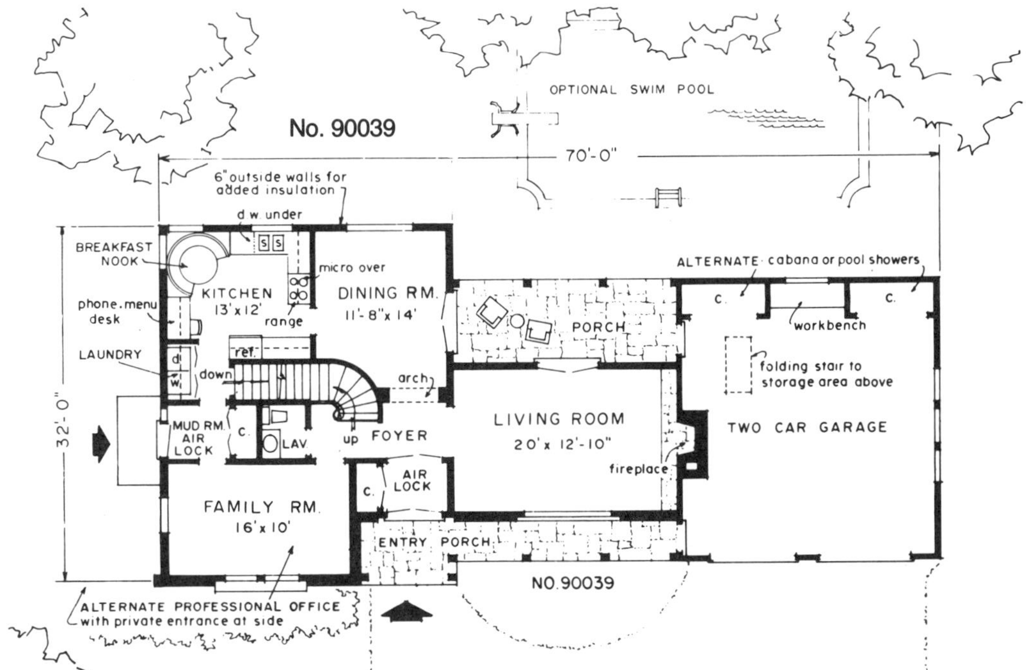

first floor plan

Enjoy a Hint of Victorian Charm

No. 91001

Stepping through the curved brick archway of this contemporary gem, you'll encounter a spacious, two-story entry flooded with light. The open feeling continues throughout the main floor. Glass walls unite the formal and informal dining and fireplaced family rooms with your back yard. The convenient kitchen mirrors the angles in the bay-windowed breakfast nook, creating interesting angles in every room. Upstairs, enjoy quiet hours behind the double doors of the study, or in the luxurious master suite.

Total area — 2,176 sq. ft.

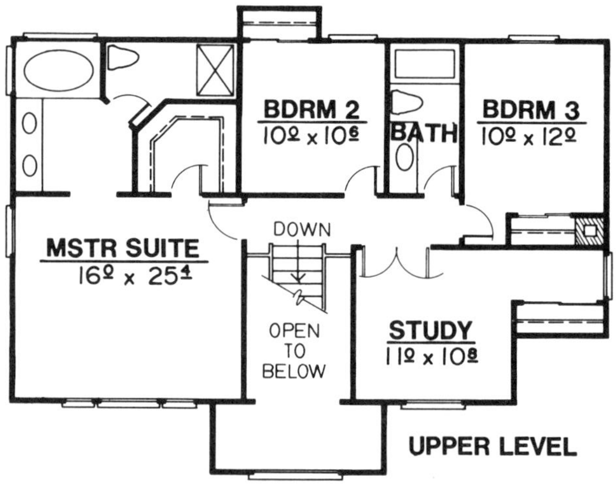

UPPER LEVEL

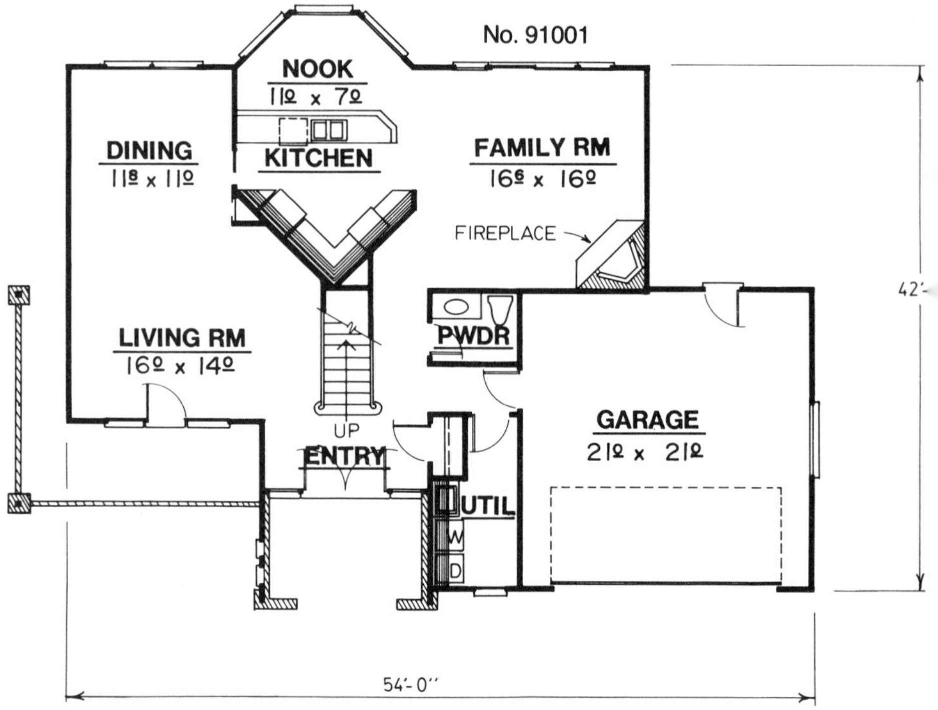

MAIN LEVEL

Designed for an Informal Life Style

No. 90325

You'll find daily living relaxed and comfortable in this stylish plan. Both the great room and the kitchen/dining room of this home are accented by vaulted ceilings. In addition to having a conveniently arranged L-shaped food preparation center, the dining area overlooks the deck through sliding glass doors. The great room incorporates all adjacent floor space and is highlighted by the corner placement of the fireplace. Two bedrooms are secluded from the living areas and feature individual access to the full bath. The master bedroom also includes a separate vanity in the dressing area.

First floor — 988 sq. ft.
Basement — 988 sq. ft.
Garage — 400 sq. ft.

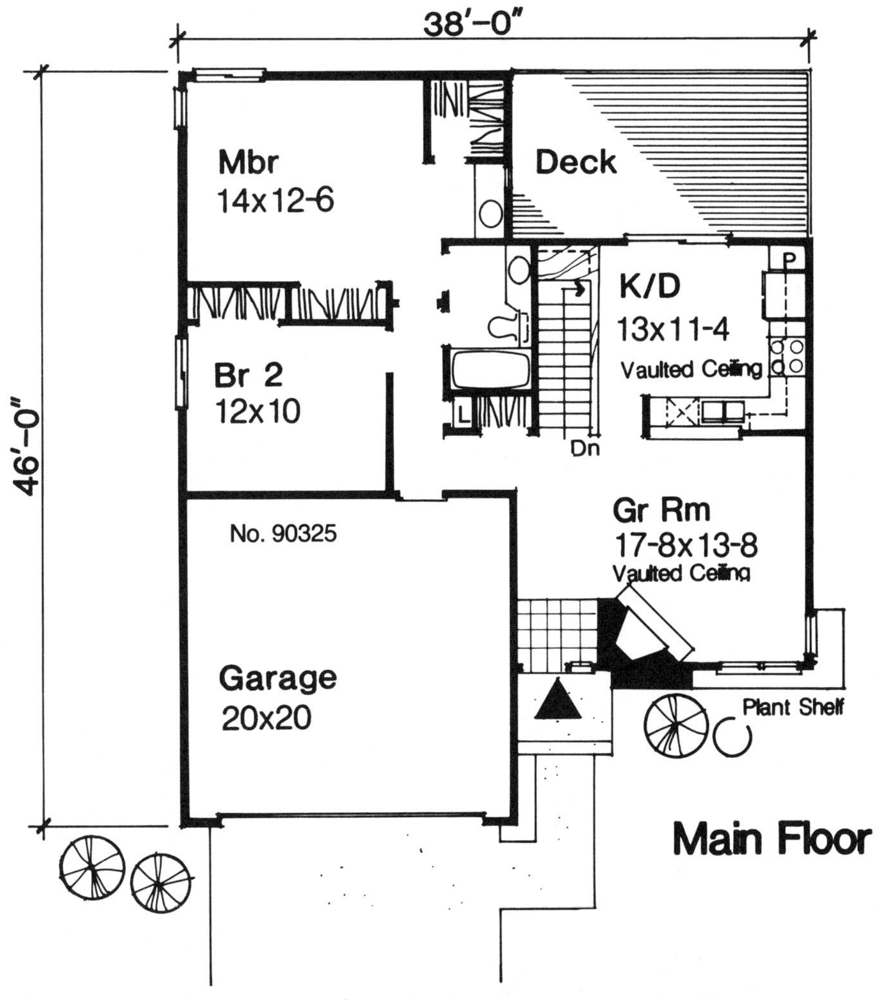

Moat And Bridge Greet Guests

No. 90001

Impressive in length and form, this rustic, sprawling western ranch in not as huge as it looks, thanks to the clever design that makes the most out of its modest size. Its angled walls, exposed beams, planters, timber posts, split rail fence, two chimnies, and cupola all blend together to make this a charming residence. Inside the double front entrance doors, the angled plan creates the striking, octagonal shape of the large living room. The entrance to the room is dramatically designed with a moat and bridge. A large log burning, stone fireplace centers in the entrance on the opposite wall.

Living Area — 2,177 sq. ft.

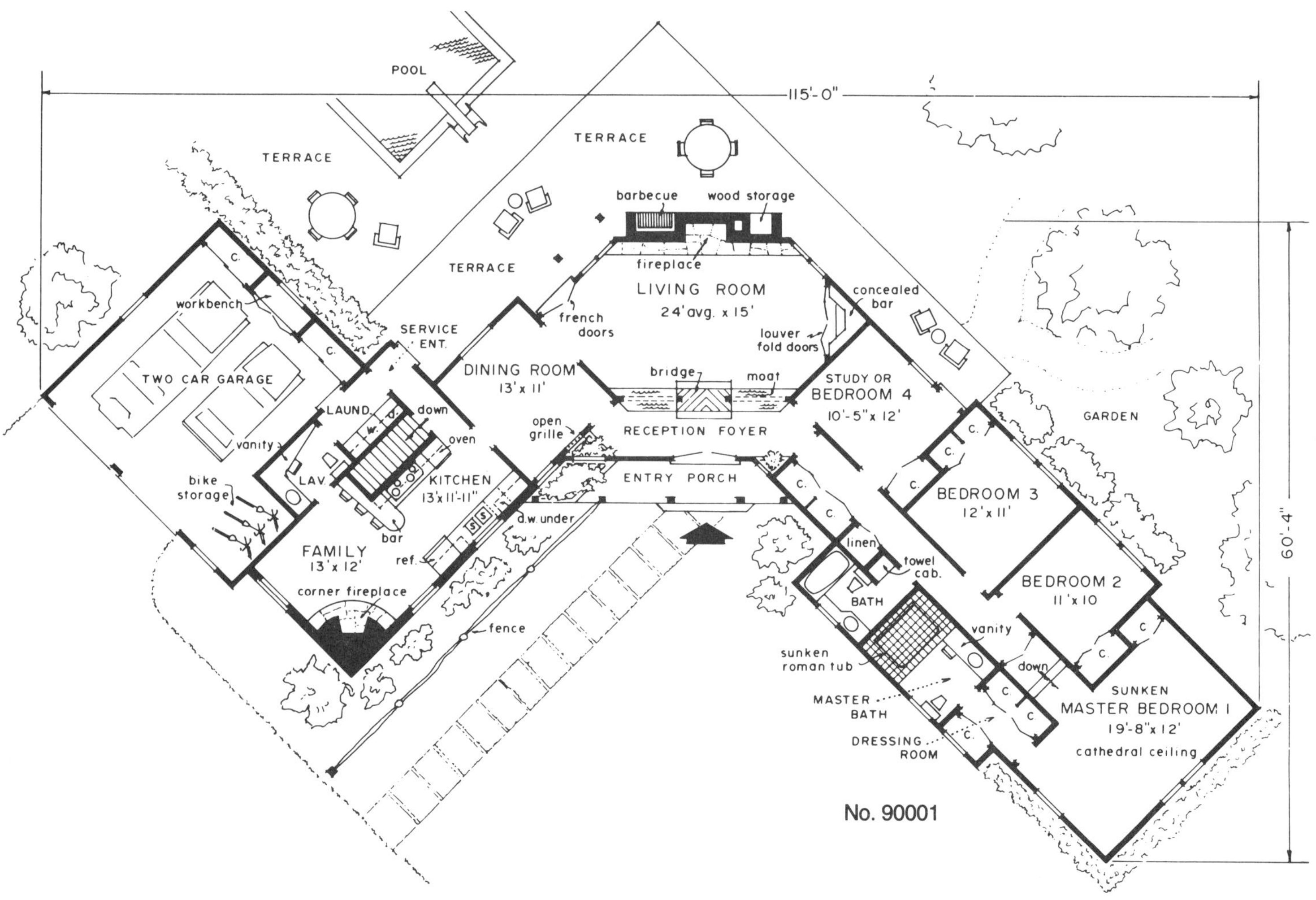

New England Tradition

No. 90608

This salt box classic appeals to almost everyone. It copies the best from the Colonial residential tradition and adds modern conveniences and efficiencies. A spacious foyer channels traffic to all parts of the house. The large, U-shaped kitchen serves the dinette, dining room, and patio. The ground floor bedroom can be easily adapted as a den; note the two entrances to the bath. Three bedrooms on the 2nd floor have plenty of closet space. The master bedroom has a walk-in closet and plush bath.

First floor — 1,132 sq.ft.
Second floor — 840 sq.ft.

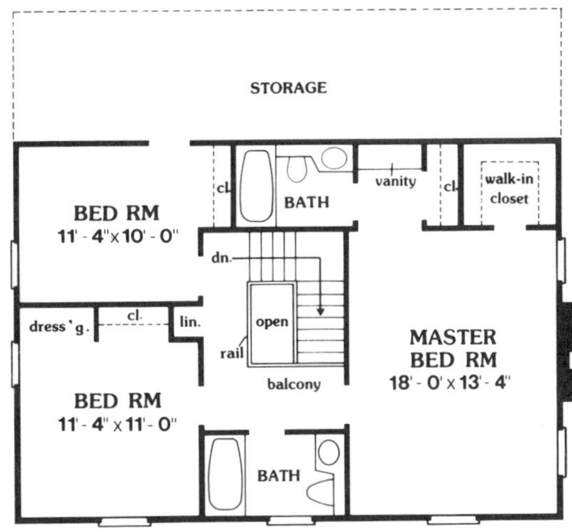

SECOND FLOOR PLAN

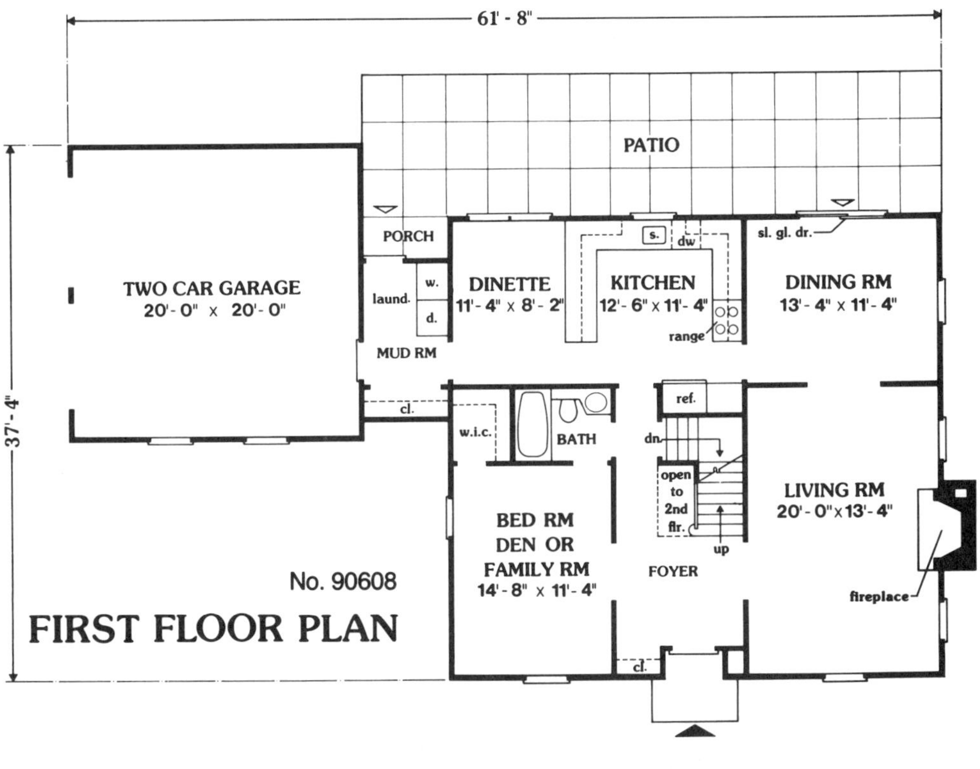

No. 90608

FIRST FLOOR PLAN

Expansive, Elegant Living

No. 90006

This impressive house contains over 4,000 square feet on two floors plus a third floor for storage or future expansion as a studio, with the addition of a rear dormer. The handsome exterior with its stone, brick, half-timber, stucco, turrets, bays, overhang, and massive chimney is distinctively English Tudor. Visual variety, so pleasing outside, is continued indoors as well. A vestibule forms the primary entrance. Flanked by a turret-shaped powder room and walk-in guest closet, it opens to an octagonal foyer which directs traffic to all parts of the house.

First floor — 1,843 sq. ft.
Second floor — 2,309 sq. ft.

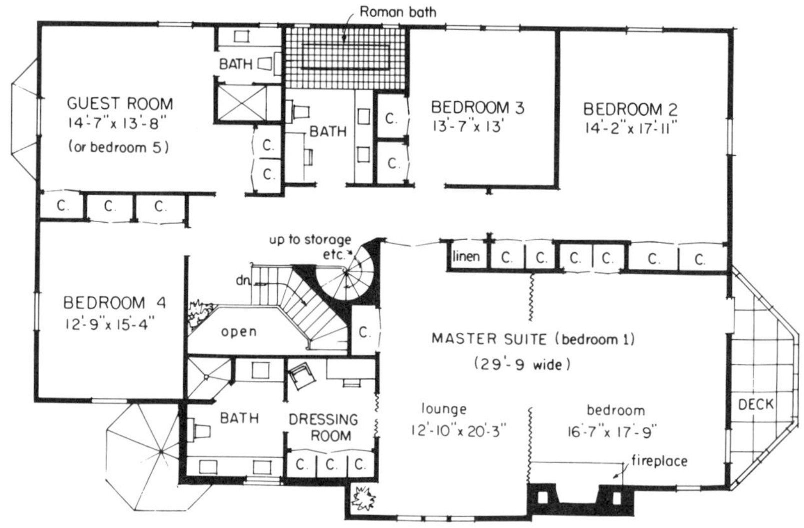

second floor plan

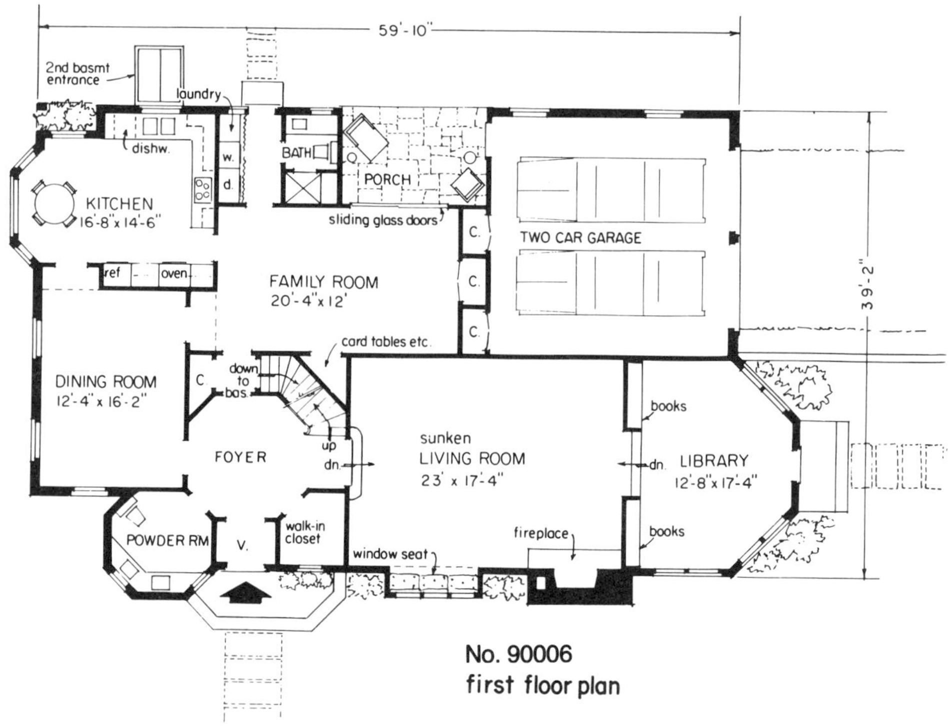

No. 90006
first floor plan

Sloping Ceilings Accent Interior

No. 90108

The sloped ceilings over the foyer and the living room give a feeling of spaciousness to this two level contemporary design. The sunken living room is accented by a fireplace which also warms the adjacent family room. Joining the family room to the U-shaped kitchen is a comfortable breakfast room. On the second level are four bedrooms and two baths. The master bath features a large lavatory just inside the dressing room which incorporates a built-in vanity.

First floor — 1,368 sq. ft.
Second floor — 1,160 sq. ft.

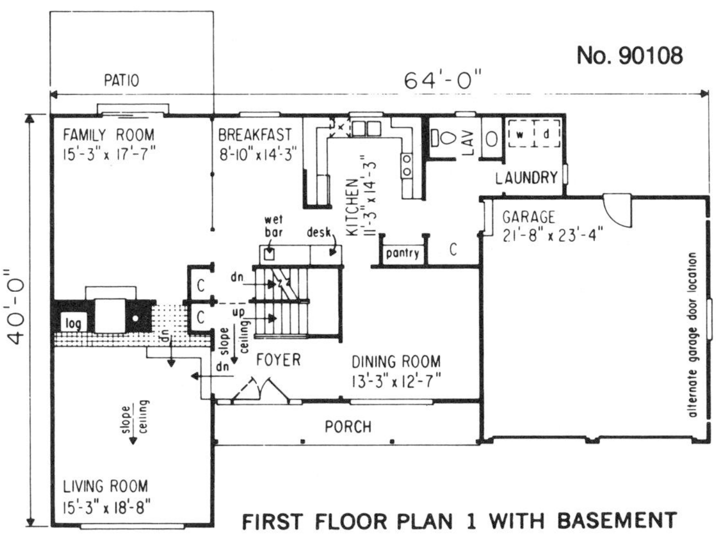

FIRST FLOOR PLAN 1 WITH BASEMENT

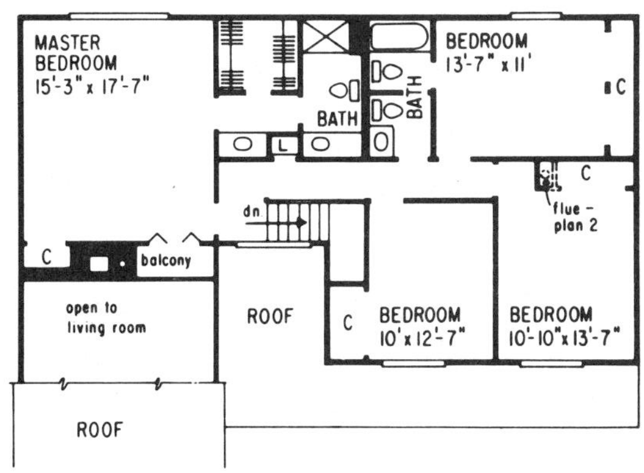

SECOND FLOOR

Twin Fireplaces for a Warm Feeling

No. 91006

Tudor styling and multiple roof angles give the exterior of this home a gracious distinction that will be welcome in any neighborhood. A brick archway shelters entering guests. In the vaulted entry, the open staircase is a dramatic focal point that leads to three spacious bedrooms. A fireplace warms the master suite, which features a huge walk-in closet and double vanities for early morning convenience. Mealtimes will be easy in the galley kitchen flanked by formal and informal dining rooms. Need a home office? A front location right off the entry makes the den the perfect place.

First floor — 1,528 sq. ft.
Second floor — 1,013 sq. ft.
Bonus room — 556 sq. ft.

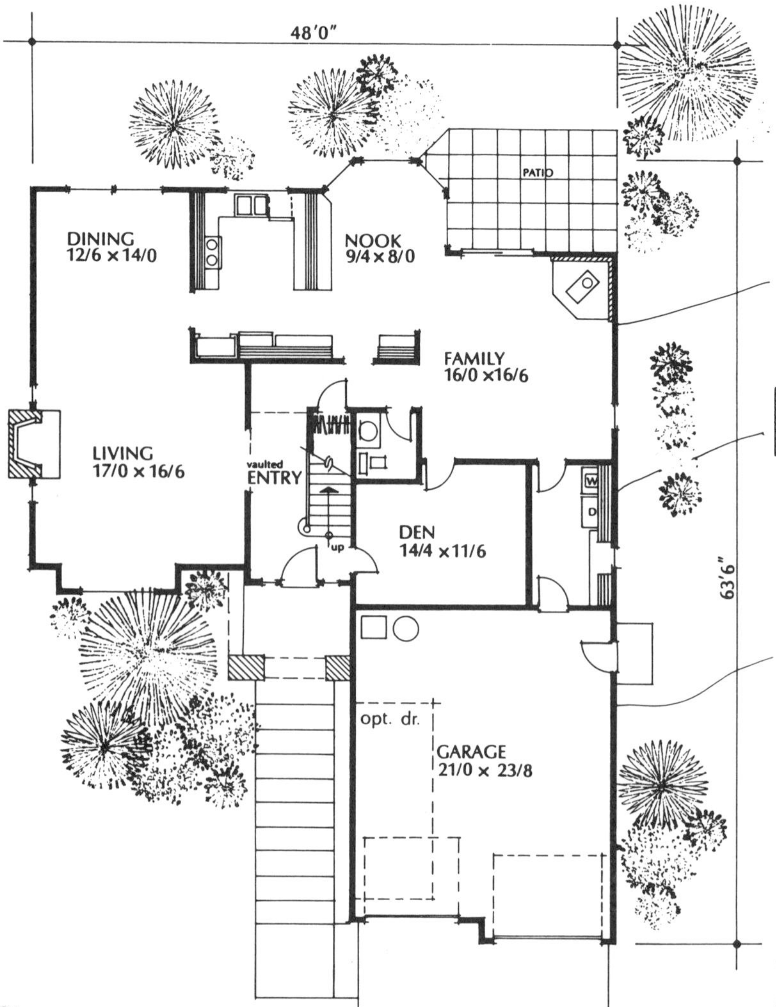

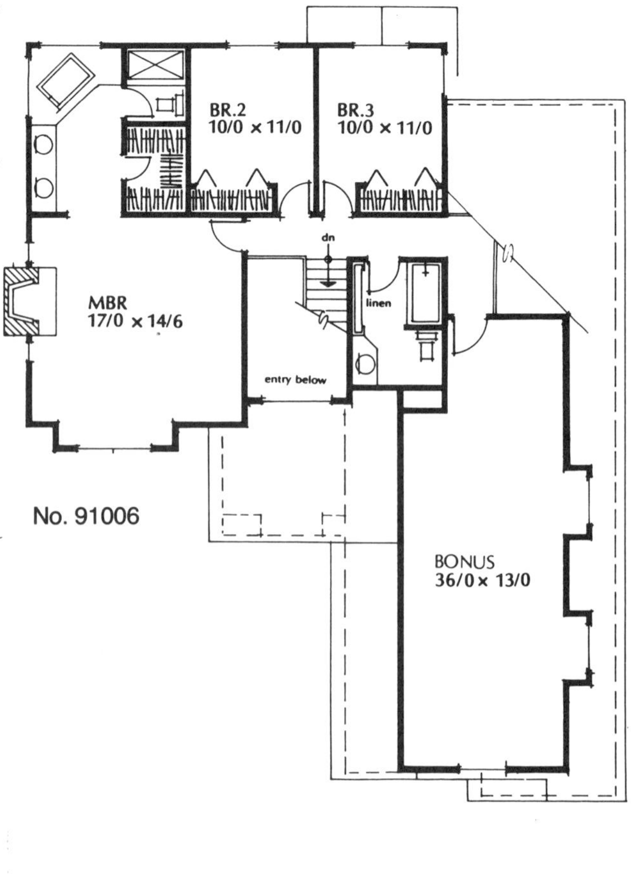

No. 91006

Two-Story Bay Adds Drama

No. 91003

Stand in the entry of this gracious four-bedroom home and feast your eyes on a wide-open view. In one sweeping glance, look at the open staircase, soaring ceiling, cozy study, sunken living room and family areas. And, this house is loaded with convenient features. The baywindowed nook and formal dining room flank the kitchen for easy meals. Past the main floor bedroom, a full bath and mud room make washing up a breeze. Upstairs, double doors lead to the master suite, featuring a toasty fireplace and angular bath with double vanities.

First floor — 1,524 sq. ft.
Second floor — 984 sq. ft.

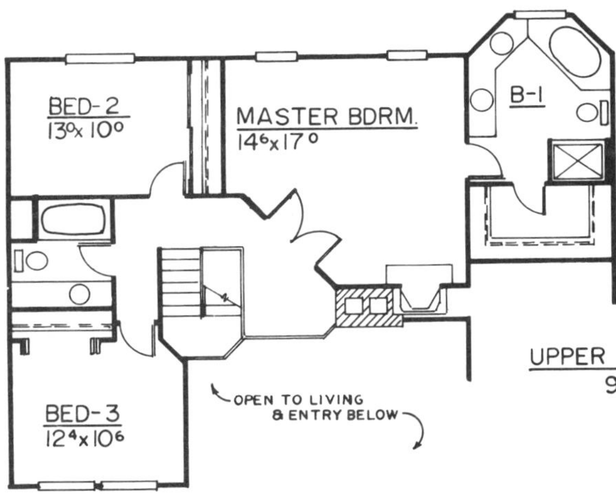

UPPER LEVEL FLOOR PLAN
984 SQ. FT.

No. 91003

MAIN LEVEL FLOOR PLAN

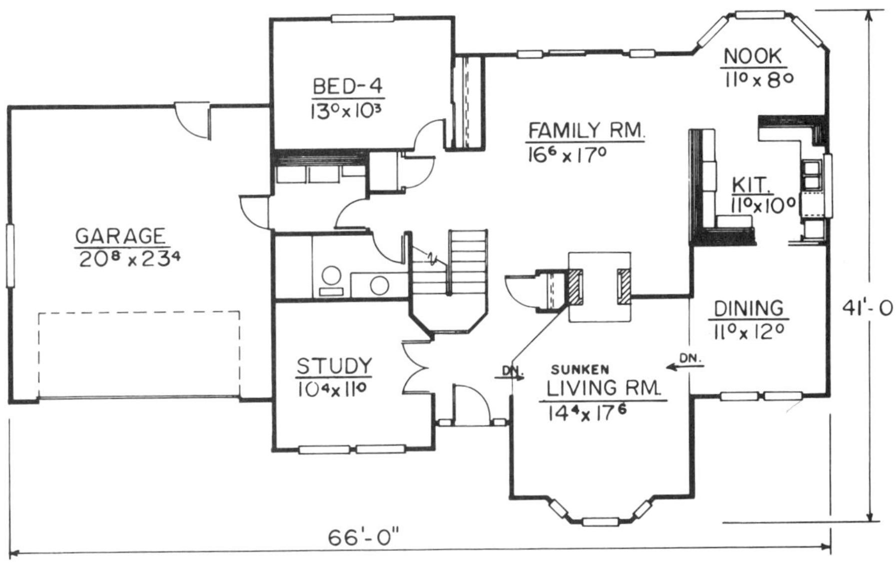

Varied Roof Heights Create Interesting Lines

No. 90601

This rambling one-story Colonial farmhouse packs a lot of living space into its compact plan. The covered porch, enriched by arches, columns and Colonial details, is the focal point of the facade. Inside, the house is zoned for convenience. Formal living and dining rooms occupy the front of the house. To the rear are the family room, island kitchen, and dinette. The family room features a heat-circulating fireplace, visible from the entrance foyer, and sliding glass doors to the large rear patio. Three bedrooms and two baths are away from the action in a private wing.

Total living area — 1,536 sq. ft. (Optional slab construction available)

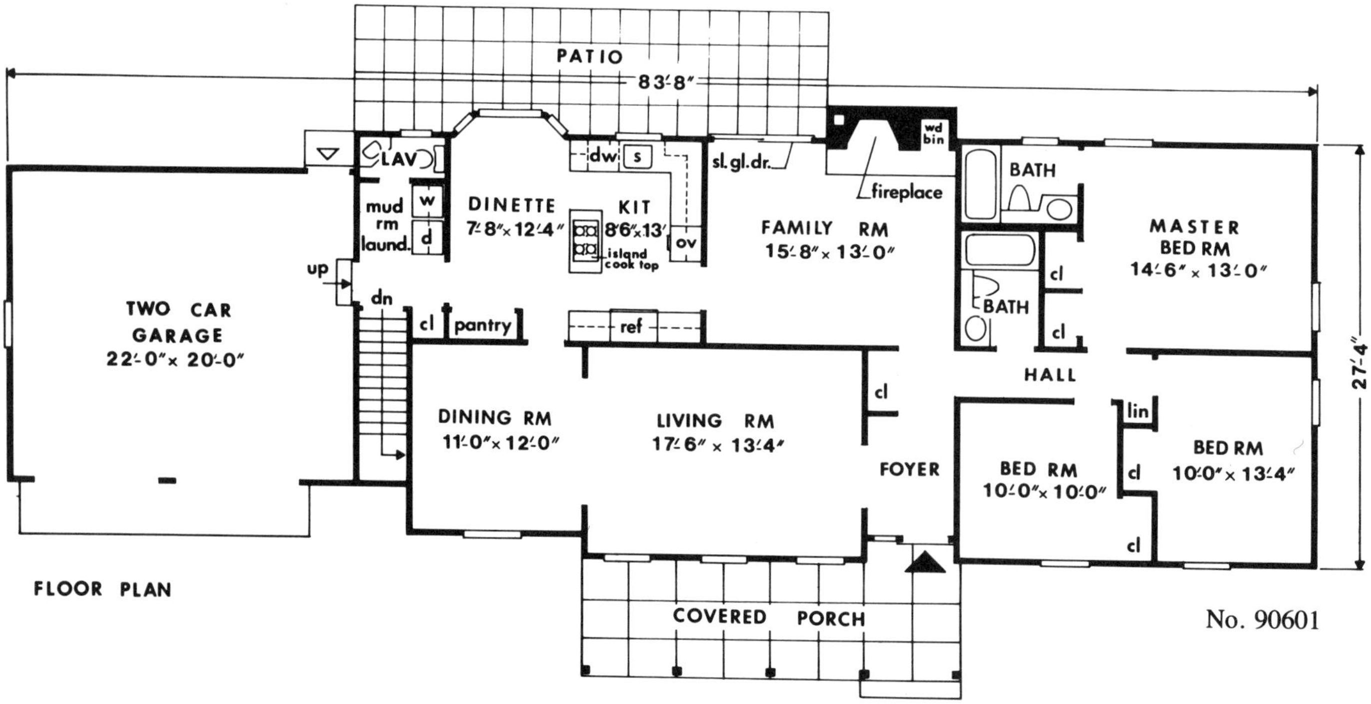

FLOOR PLAN

No. 90601

Modified A-frame At Home Anywhere

No. 90309

The comfortable style of this compact plan is equally at home in surburbia or at a resort. The main floor includes a combined living room/dining room whose ceiling reaches to the second floor loft. This living area is further enhanced by its view of the angled deck through corner windows and two sliding glass doors, plus the fireplace with its large hearth. Located at one end of the rear deck is a roomy outdoor storage cabinet. The galley-style kitchen is conveniently arranged and is located near both the front entrance and the laundry area for convenience. Completing the main floor are a bedroom and a full bath. In addition to the loft on the second floor, there are an optional bedroom and a half bath.

Main Floor — 735 sq. ft.
Upper Floor — 304 sq. ft.

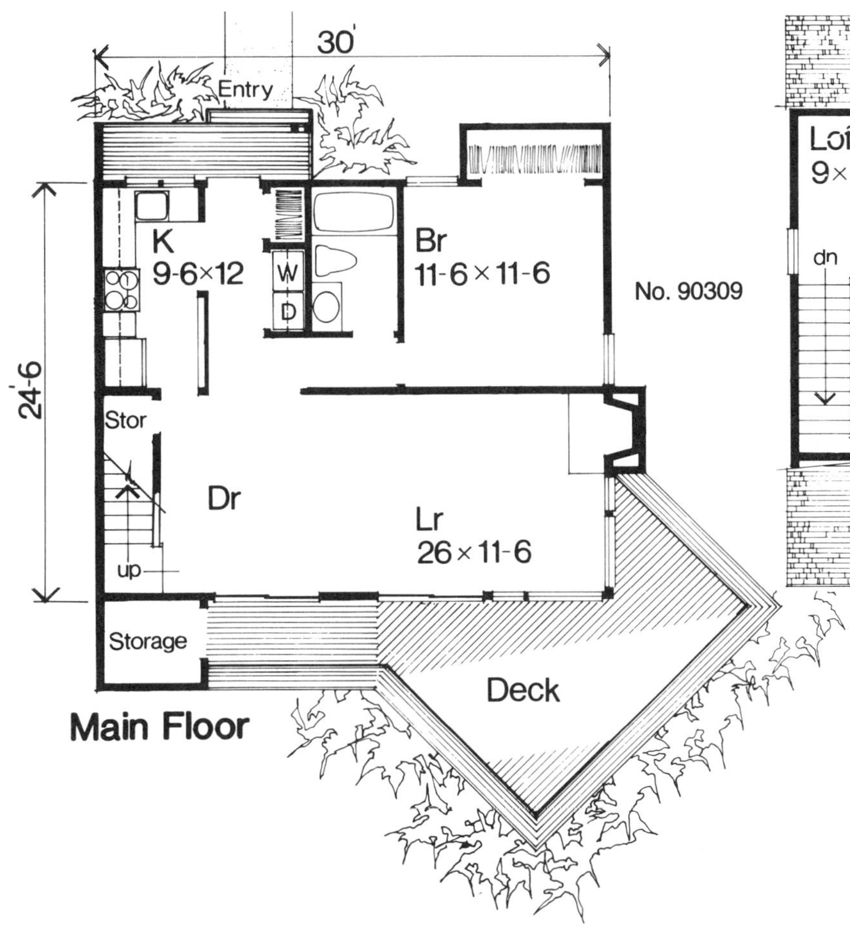

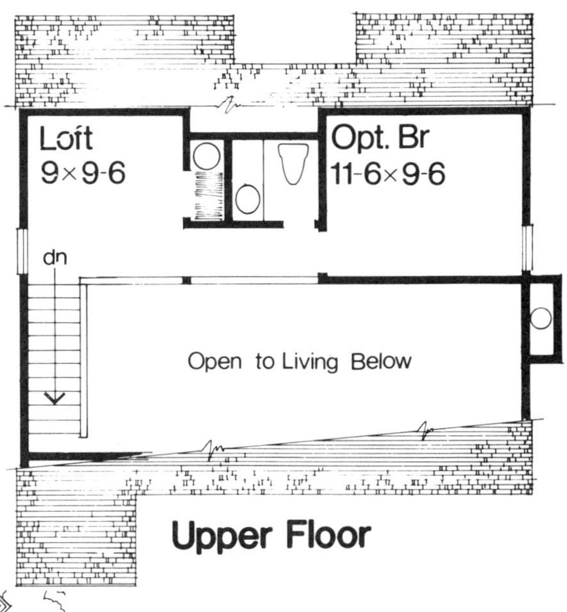

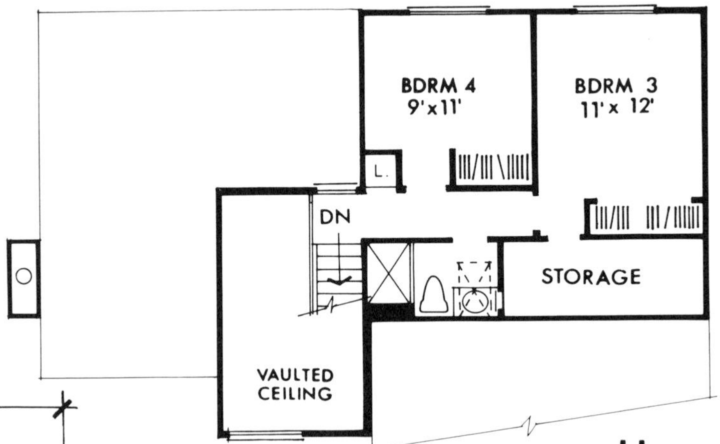

Upper Flo

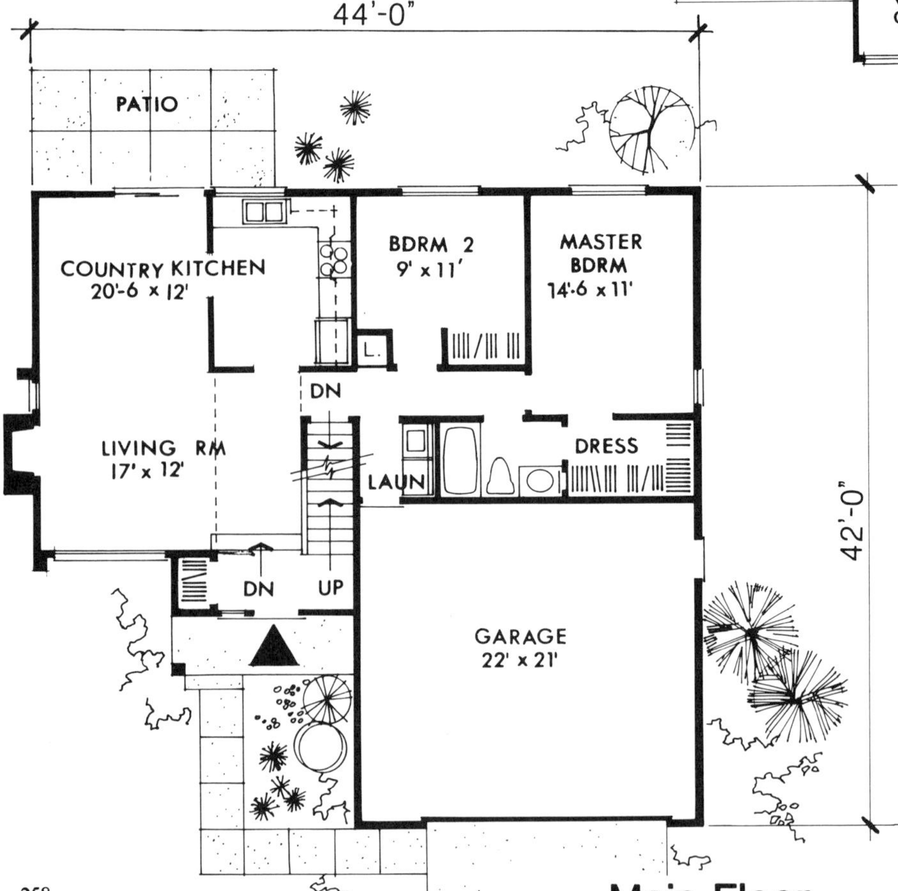

Main Floor

Appealing Contemporary Design

No. 90366

The story-and-a-half house provides an opportunity to combine old fashioned value with contemporary design appeal. This house looks and lives 1970s with its dramatic entrance and vaulted ceiling space, its garden kitchen, its flexible, open living/dining/kitchen area and its generous master bedroom dressing closet. Note, also, the modern convenience of the mud room/laundry entrance. Yet with a door to block hallway access, the upstairs can be left unfinished to reduce initial cash requirements. The two bedrooms and bath with an optional operable skylight can be a do-it-yourself project to be finished later. If built without a basement, mechanical equipment can be placed under the stairs.

Area — 1,460 sq. ft.

Attractive Floor Plan Enhances Traditional Design

No. 20056

This three-bedroom, two-bath home offers comfort and style. The master bedroom is complete with its own bath with a skylight. A beamed ceiling and fireplace in the living area add charm to the more traditional family room. A spacious laundry room adjoins the kitchen and breakfast area. The country-style front porch and large front windows in the breakfast and dining rooms lend a cozy atmosphere to this eye-catching design.

First floor — 1,669 sq. ft.
Basement — 1,669 sq. ft.
Garage — 482 sq. ft.

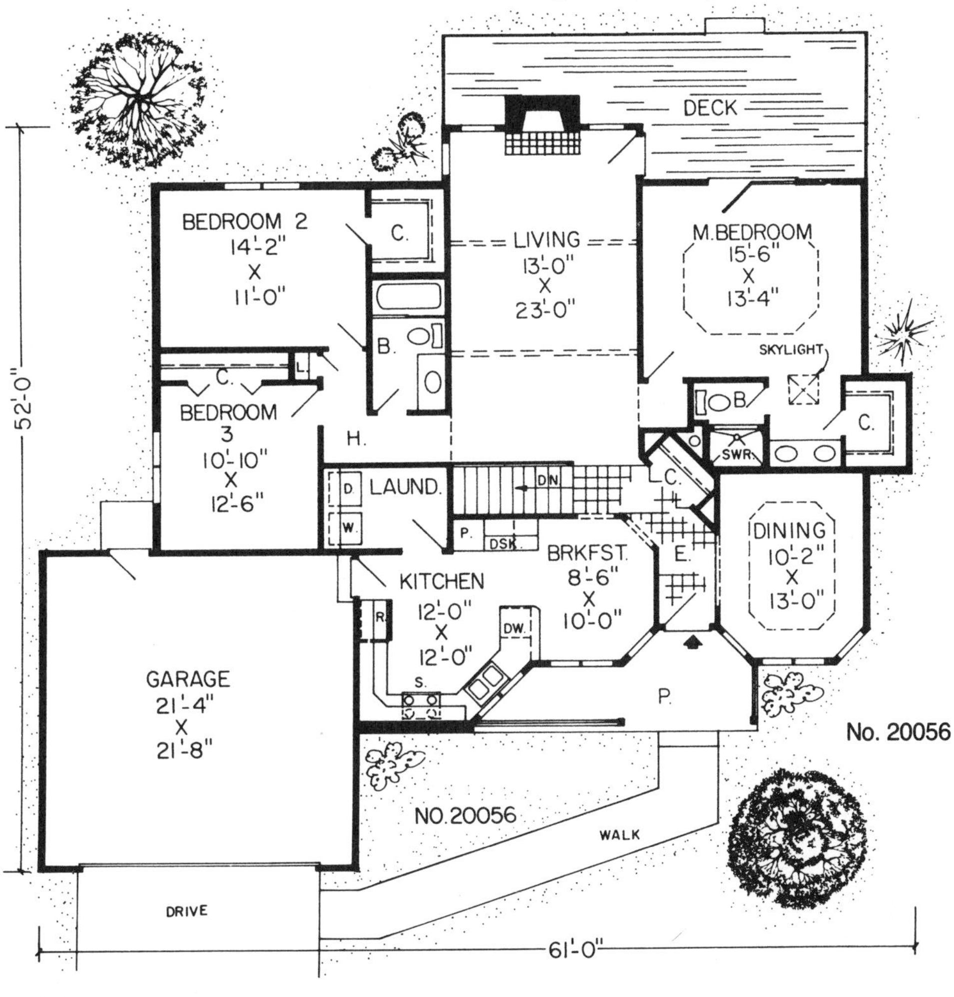

No. 20056

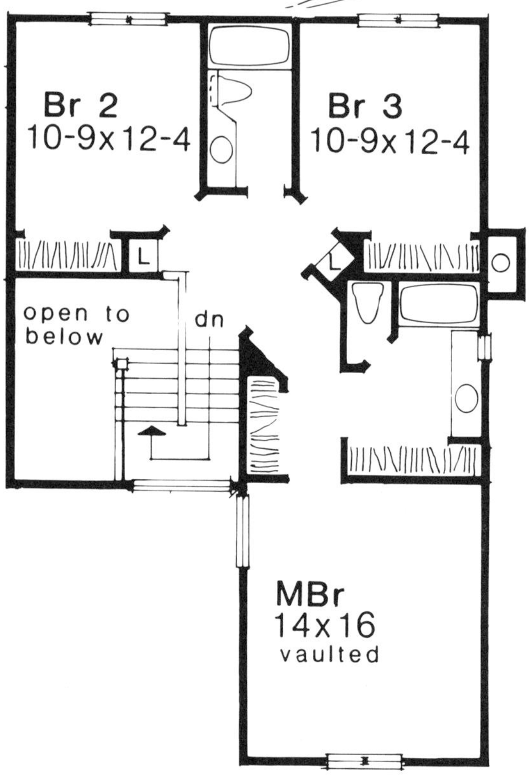

Upper Floor

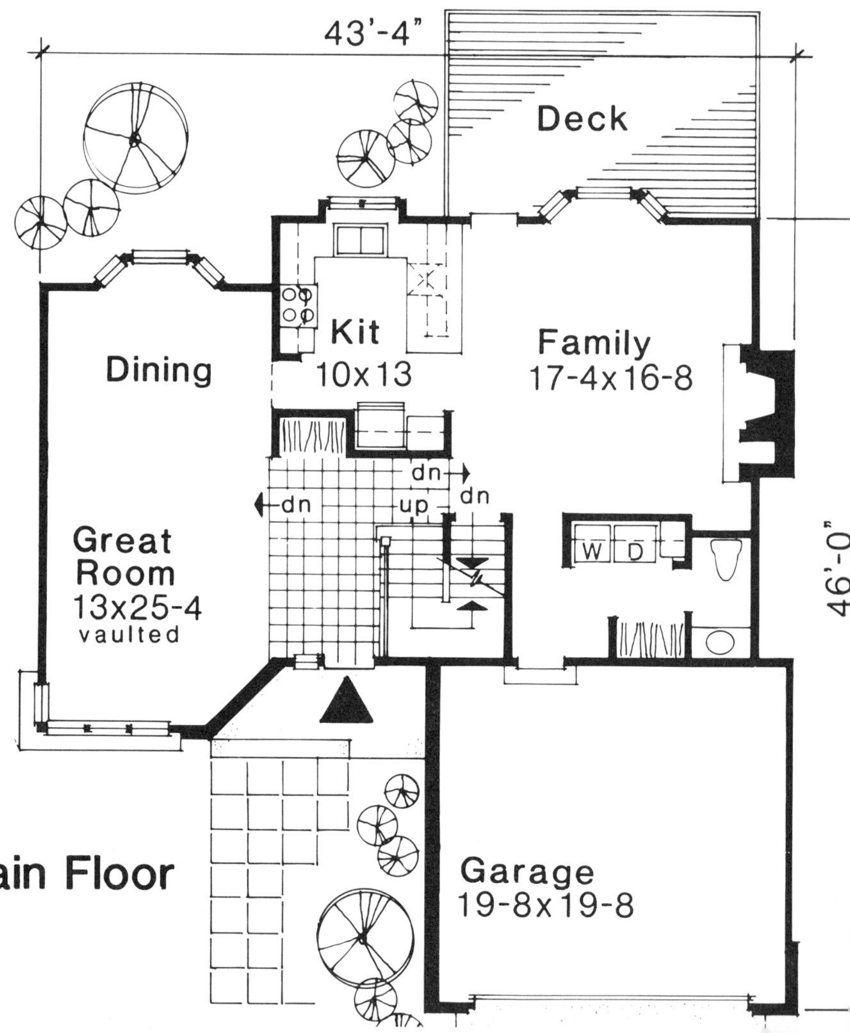

Main Floor

Streetscape Statement

No. 90359

The big family two story is downsized for the '80's but still has the move-up family characteristics of separated formal and informal areas plus a luxurious master bedroom suite. We have added the impact plusses of a vaulted ceilinged entry and great room, a well working U-shaped kitchen, and a moderate overall width to allow construction on smaller lots.

First floor — 1,075 sq. ft.
Second floor — 816 sq. ft.

Comfortable Family Room in Congenial Setting

No. 90520

A secluded porch provides an intimate entrance to this 3 bedroom home. You'll appreciate the large family room with fireplace as the center for many activities. The breakfast nook will be popular with its nearby bow window and will be practible near the pantry and kitchen. The dining area also is easy to serve. The living room will have a wonderful view through the bow window. The master bedroom is complete, including dressing area and walk-in wardrobe.

First floor — 1,048 sq. ft.
Second floor — 726 sq. ft.

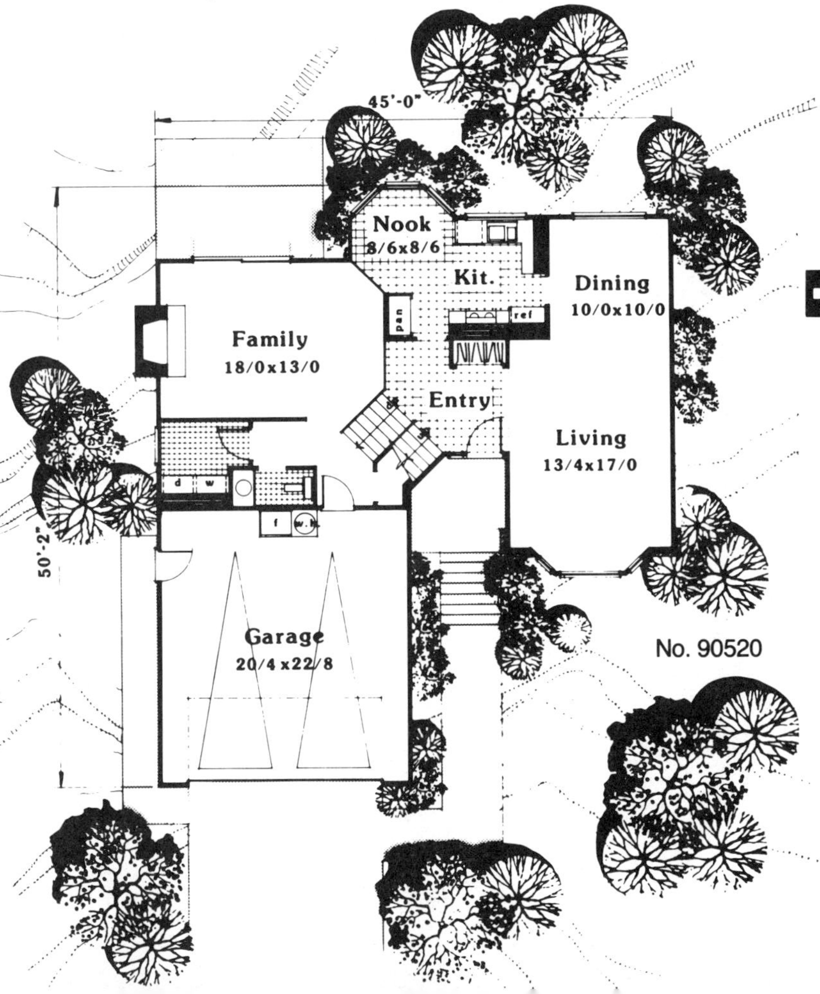

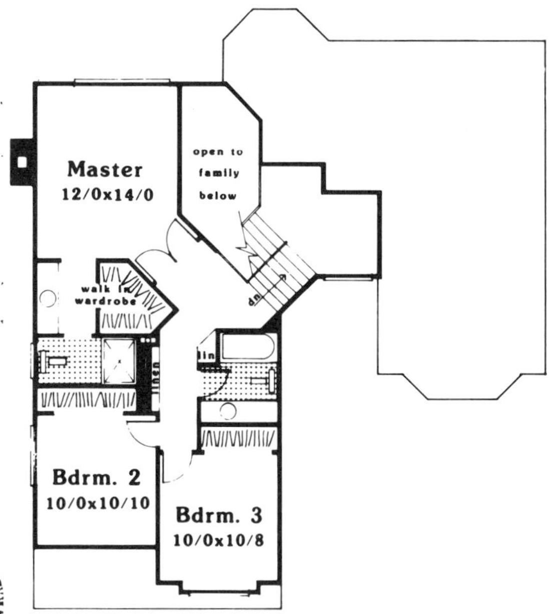

Solar Wall Merges Inner and Outer Space

No. 90609

In addition to offering expansive views of the landscape, the solar wall at the rear of this one-level contemporary provides welcome relief from your winter heating bills. Two roof skylights over the front entrance and the dinette-kitchen area give an added glow to these cheerful spaces. The central foyer leads to all the rooms in the house. Expanded by a cathedral ceiling and the solar bays, the living room and dining room flow together. Three bedrooms and two baths occupy a wing off the foyer.

Total living area — 1,435 sq. ft.
Basement — 1,254 sq. ft.
(optional slab construction available)

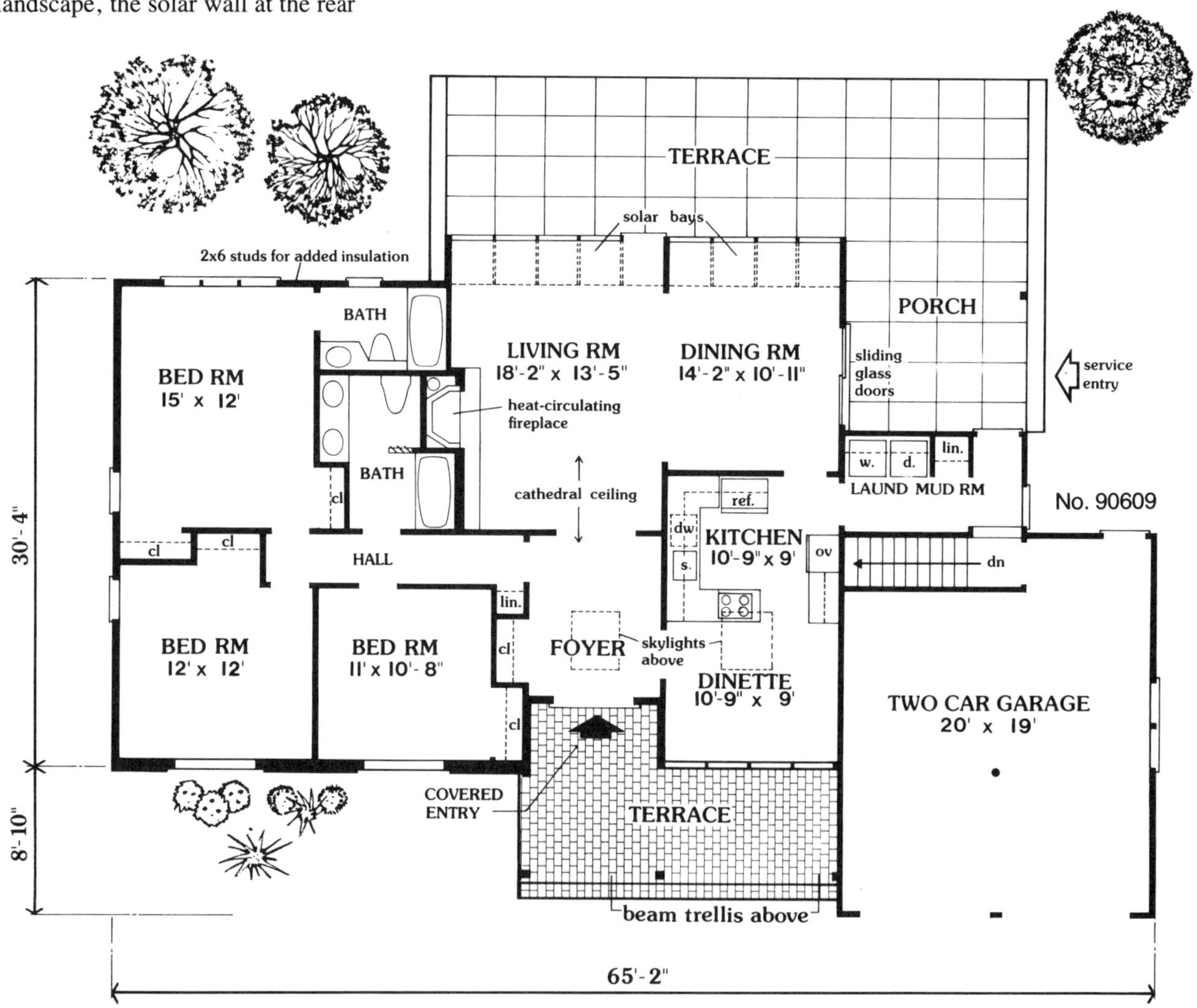

Luxurious Master Suite

No. 90329

On the second floor, the roomy master bedroom with its luxurious master bath and dressing area will be a constant delight. Just a step down from the bedroom itself, the bath incorporates an oversized corner tub, a shower, a walk-in closet, and a skylight. The third bedroom could serve as a loft or sitting room. The open staircase spirals down to the first floor great room with its vaulted ceiling, fireplace, and corner of windows. The adjacent dining room has a wet bar and direct access to the large, eat-in kitchen. Additional living space is provided by the family room which opens onto the deck through sliding glass doors.

Main floor — 904 sq. ft.
Upper floor — 797 sq. ft.
Basement — 904 sq. ft.
Garage — 405 sq. ft.

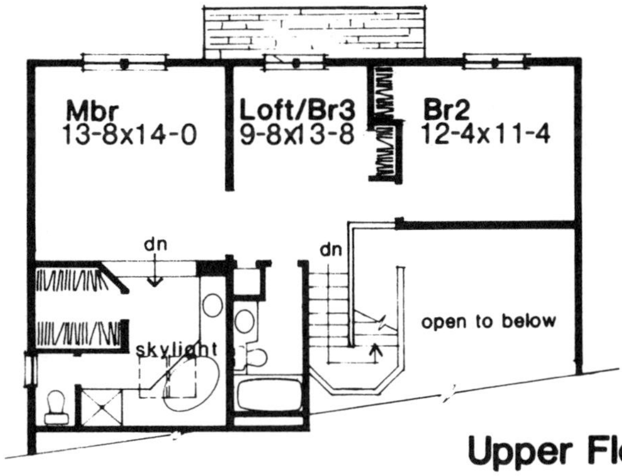

Upper Floor

No. 90329

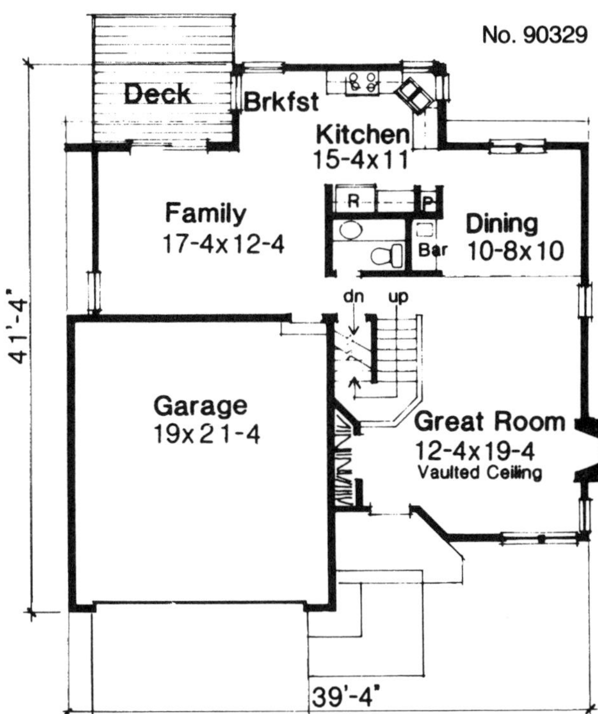

Main Floor

Unique Spanish With A Tower Balcony

No. 90000

This uniquely housed Spanish plan borrows its form from the one story, one and one half story and two story types to create a different and interesting look. A straight front wall about 70 feet long forms the bulk of the facade but the wall does not touch the house proper. A portion of the wall is the front of the garage and more than half of it is used as a roof support. This way it becomes an integral part of the house while performing other duties. It creates a covered court, an open courtyard and gives privacy to both.

First floor—969 sq. ft.
(Excluding garage and court)
Second floor—905 sq. ft.

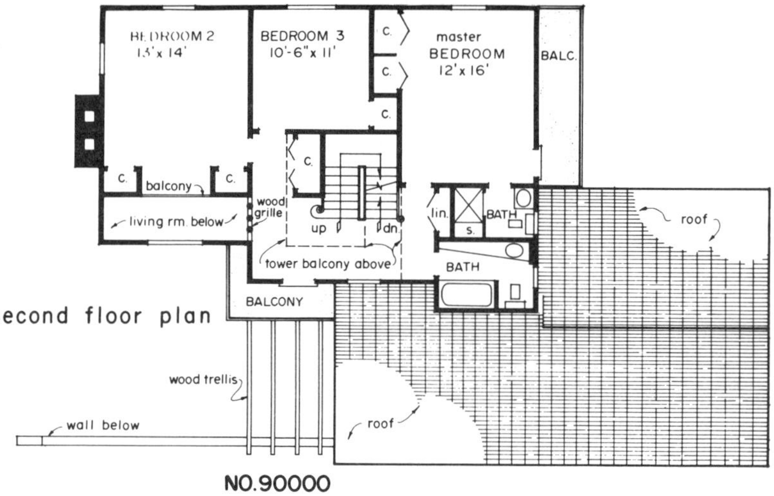

second floor plan

NO.90000

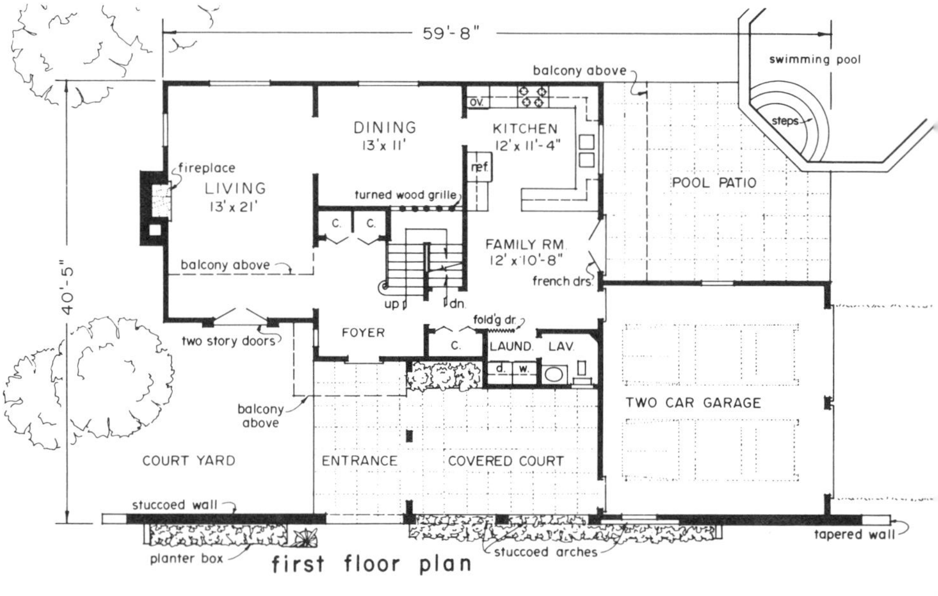

first floor plan

Master Bedroom on First Level

No. 90142

This excellent traditional design has the master bedroom located on the first level and equipped with a walk-in closet and a large bath area that incorporates a skylight over the tub. Also on the first level is a living room with large bay windows allowing natural lighting to fill the room. The kitchen has an abundance of cabinet space and includes a pantry that has plenty of storage space. The laundry room is located just between the kitchen and garage. The second level has three bedrooms and one full bath.

First floor — 1,663 sq. ft.
Second floor — 727 sq. ft.

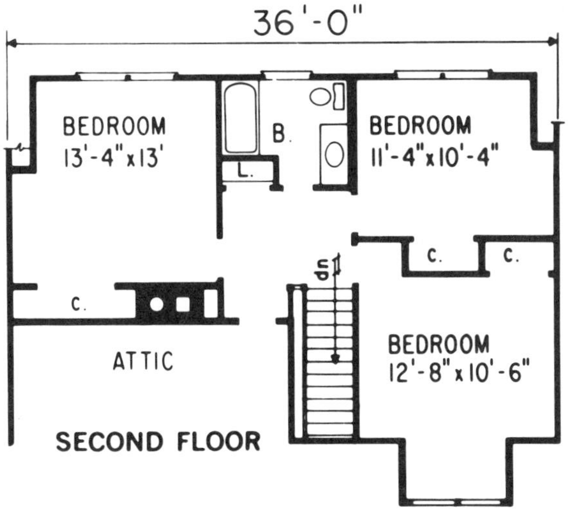

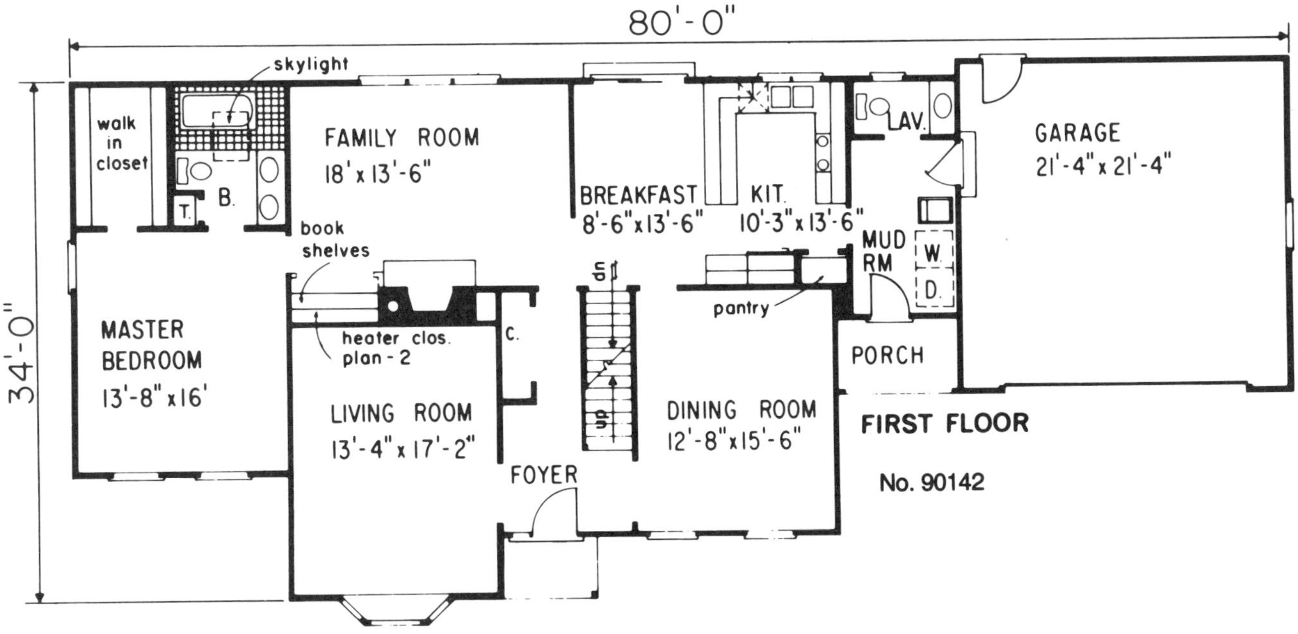

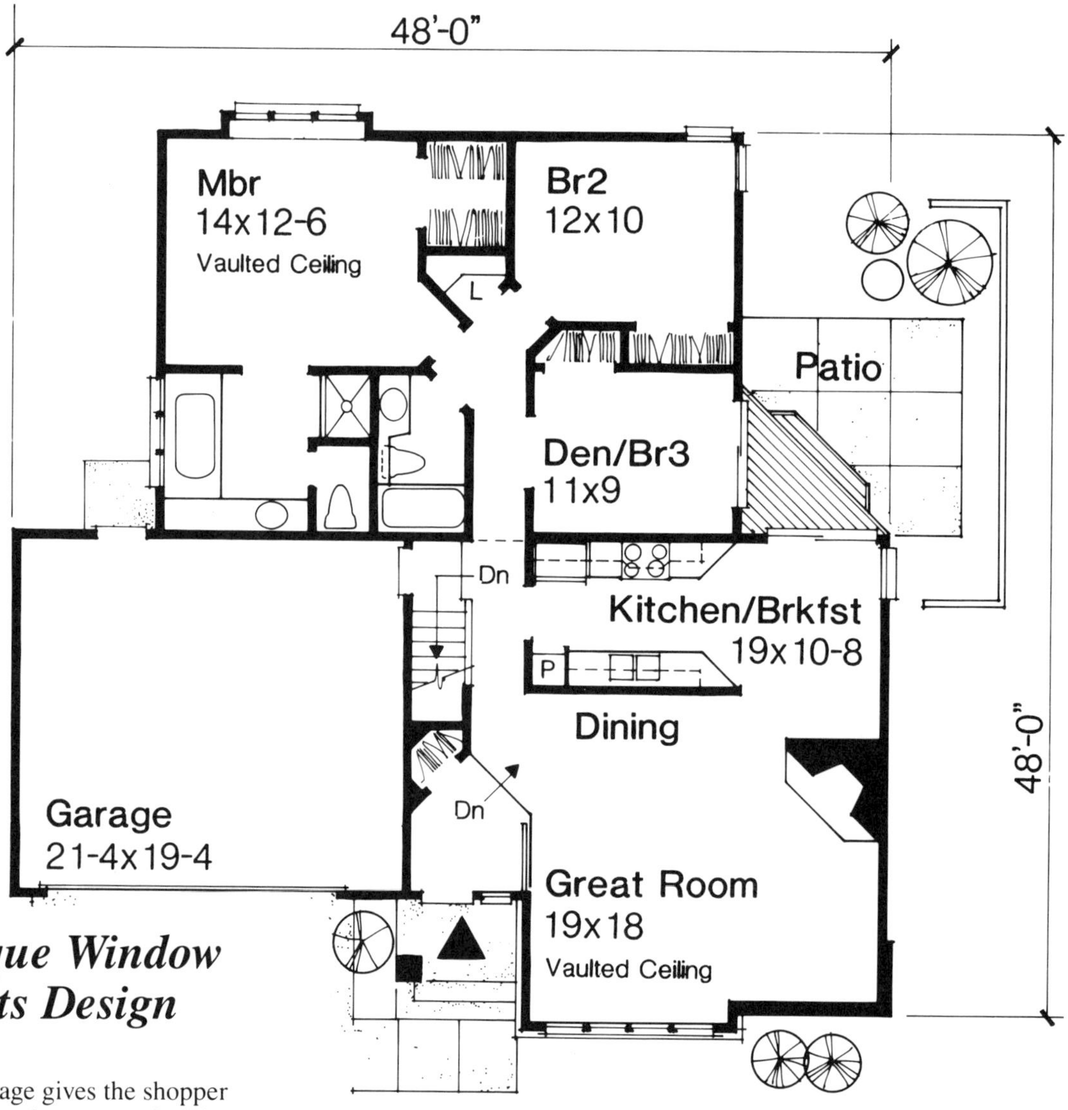

Main Floor Plan

Picturesque Window Highlights Design

No. 90357

This design package gives the shopper the perceived value he expects for his move-up dollar, and gives the buyer the style that makes his investment a daily pleasure.

Area — 1,368 sq. ft.

Two Fireplaces Warm Rustic Retreat

No. 90504

Open space is abundant in this one-level house with attached two-car garage. Spilling into the living and dining rooms, the sheltered entry leads to the open kitchen, family room, and breakfast nook. Separated only by a convenient work island, this sun-filled, three-room suite accesses the deck outside through a door in the breakfast nook. Away from active living spaces lie three bedrooms, including the master suite, which features its own deck for private outdoor lounging.

First floor — 1,735 sq. ft.

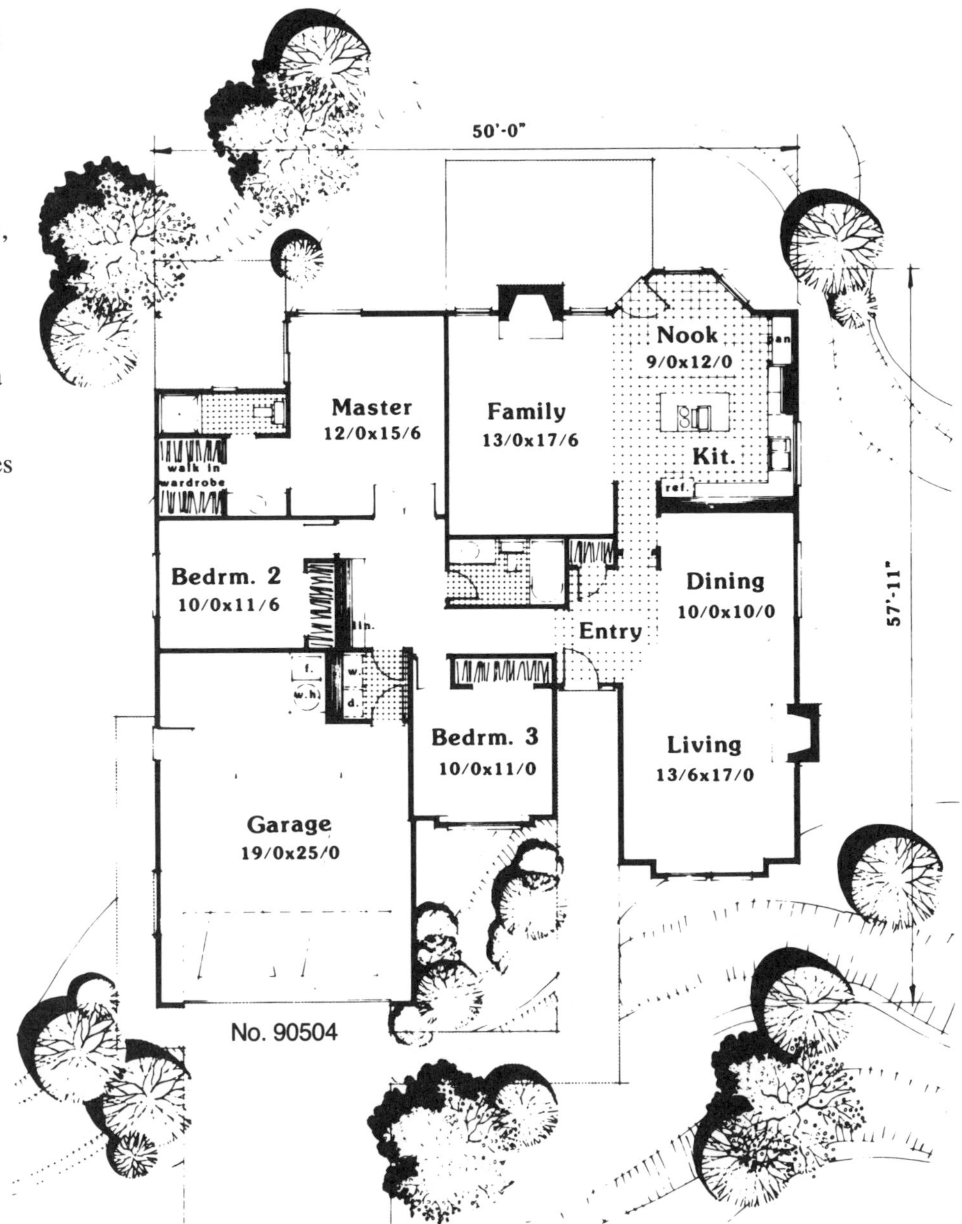

Den Can Double As a Home Office

No. 90816

Traditional styling marks this elegant, four-bedroom home with lots of outdoor living space. Flooded with light from a picture window, the sunken living room lies just off the central foyer. At the rear of the home, the kitchen is flanked by the formal dining room and a breakfast nook. Sliding glass doors open to the sundeck. A single step leads down to the fire-placed family room. Window gables at the top of the gently curving staircase provide pleasing study nooks. The master suite features a luxurious whirlpool bath.

First floor — 1,252 sq. ft.
Second floor — 1,117 sq. ft.
Basement — 1,245 sq. ft.
Garage — 564 sq. ft.
Depth — 35 ft.(plus 8 ft. sundeck)
Width — 71 ft.

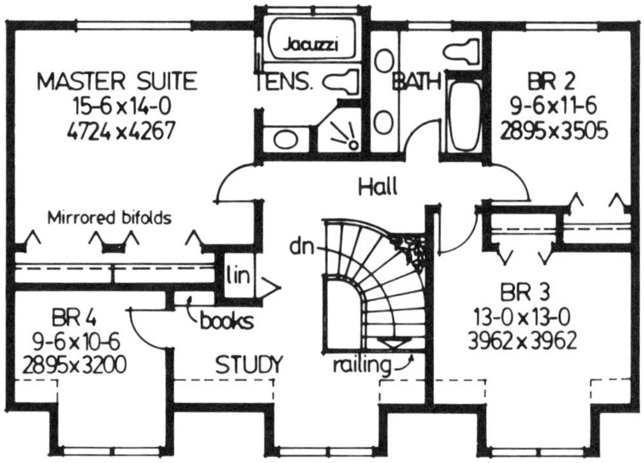

SECOND FLOOR PLAN

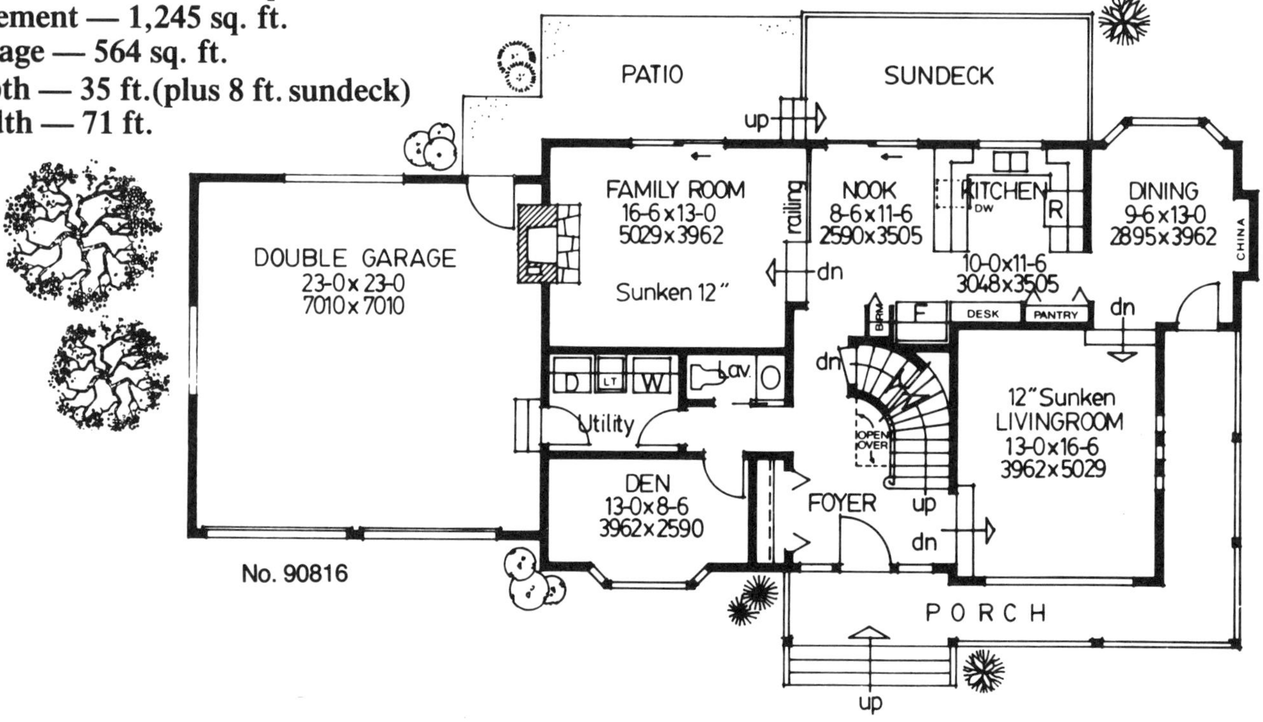

Floor Plan Accents Open Design

No. 90304

A second floor study opens onto the living room below to give the feeling of extra spaciousness. Behind the living room, the family room opens onto the patio and the adjacent kitchen to further the design concept. The U-shaped kitchen offers plenty of storage and a high degree of efficiency plus lots of light provided by its own set of windows onto the patio. The main floor incorporates one bedroom with double closets and a full bath plus linen closet. The second floor makes storage and also allows for the other bedroom and its full-sized bath.

Total area — 1,410 sq. ft.

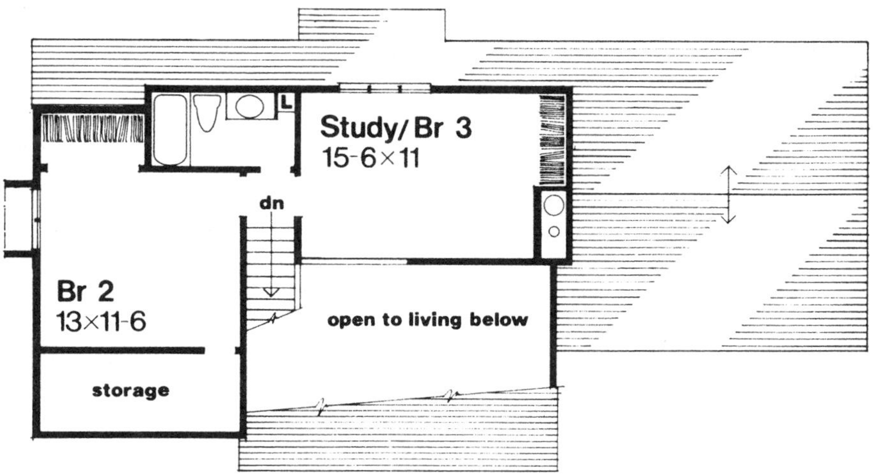

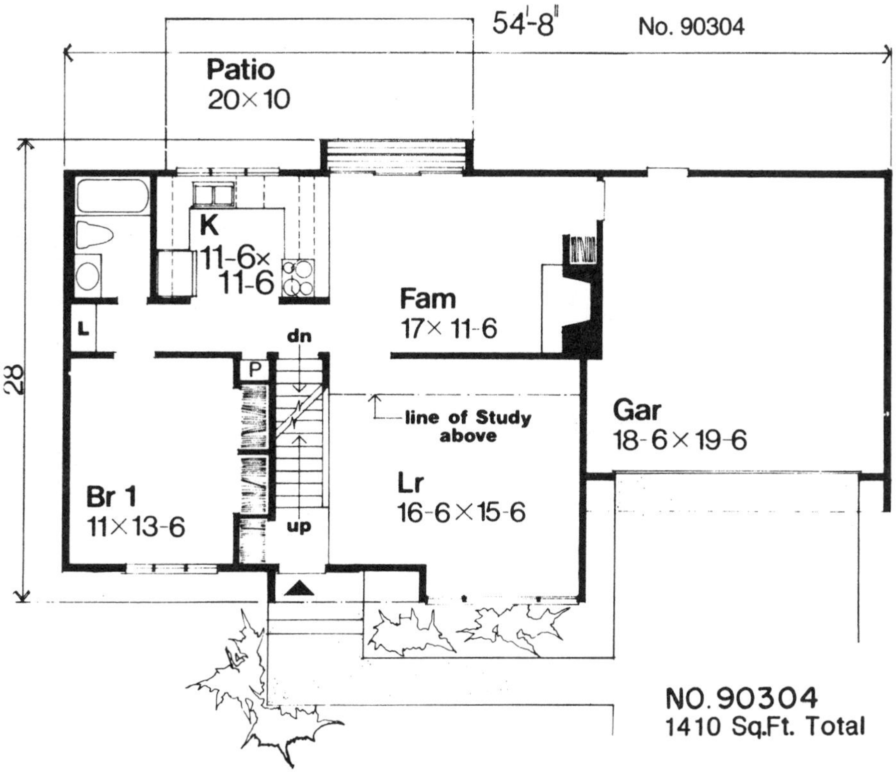

Dormers Provide Cozy Window Seats

No. 90932

You'll find all the conveniences of modern living in this traditional New England Saltbox design. The attractive facade is authentic to the last detail, while inside the large foyer directs traffic with modern efficiency. The master suite on the main floor features his and hers closets. Close at hand is a large split-bath, which doubles as a powder room or guest bath. Mom will appreciate the lavatory next to the mud room at the rear door for youngsters returning from outdoor play. The stairs off the foyer lead up to two airy bedrooms featuring dramatic dormer window seats.

Main floor — 1,228 sq. ft.
Upper floor — 584 sq. ft.
Width — 52 ft.
Depth — 30 ft.

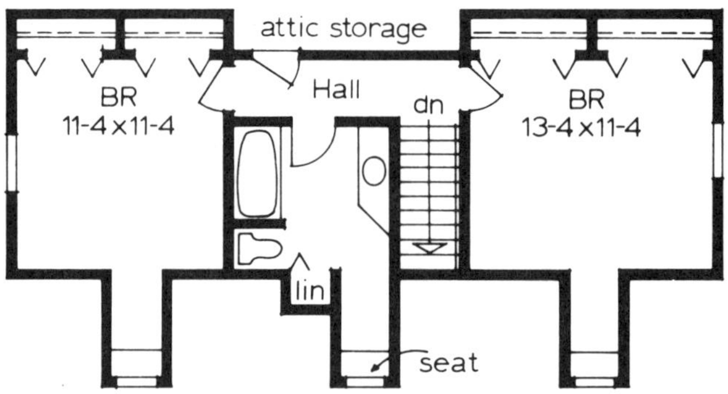

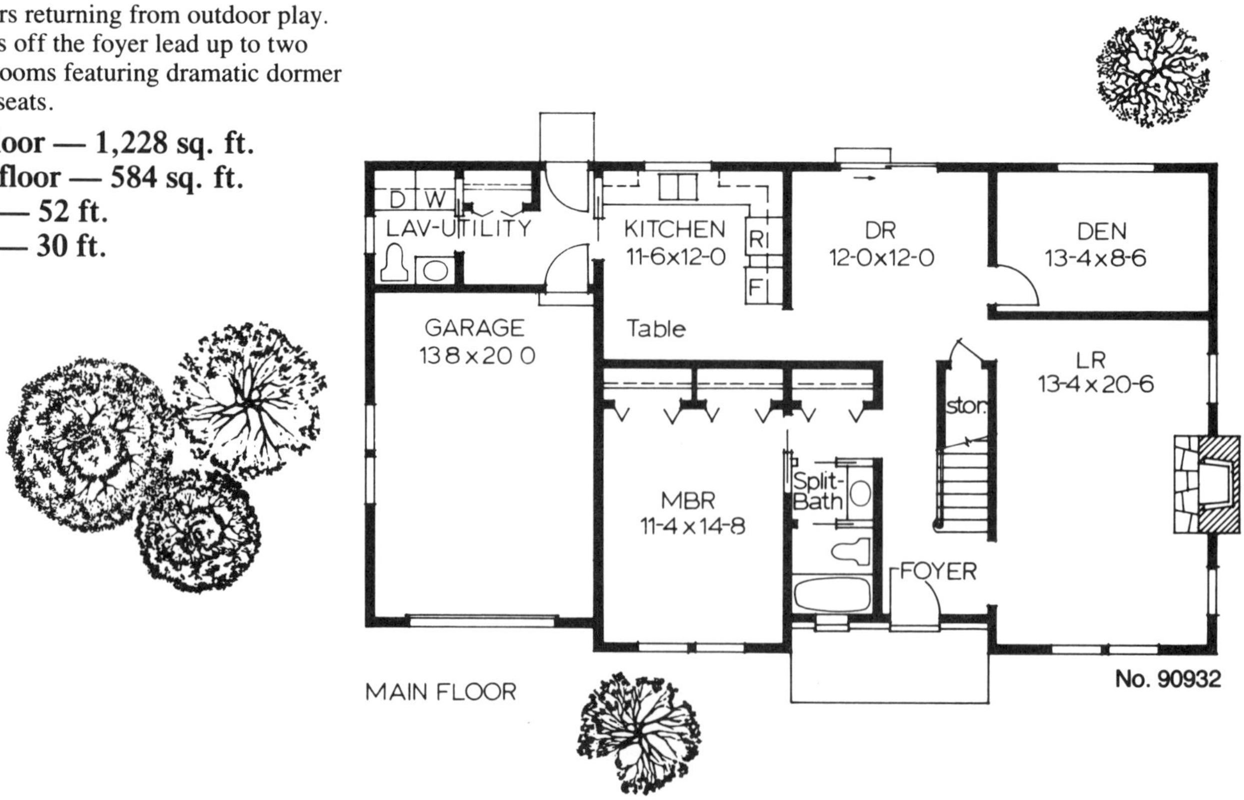

Efficient Single Level Design

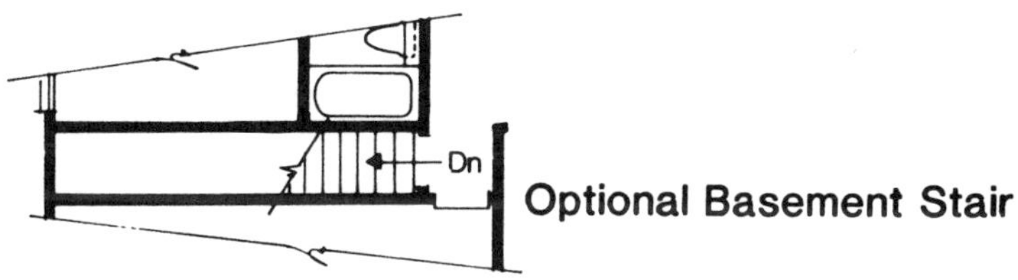

No. 90335

All the conveniences one enjoys and expects are present in this step-saving single level plan. A very large kitchen offers a popular center island with built-in range to speed food preparation. The breakfast room is charming and well lighted by two-level windows. The dining room sports a wetbar, while the great room is distinguished by a vaulted ceiling and corner fireplace. The master bedroom is set off by a very large bath area with skylight and an exit to the deck.

First floor — 1,700 sq. ft.

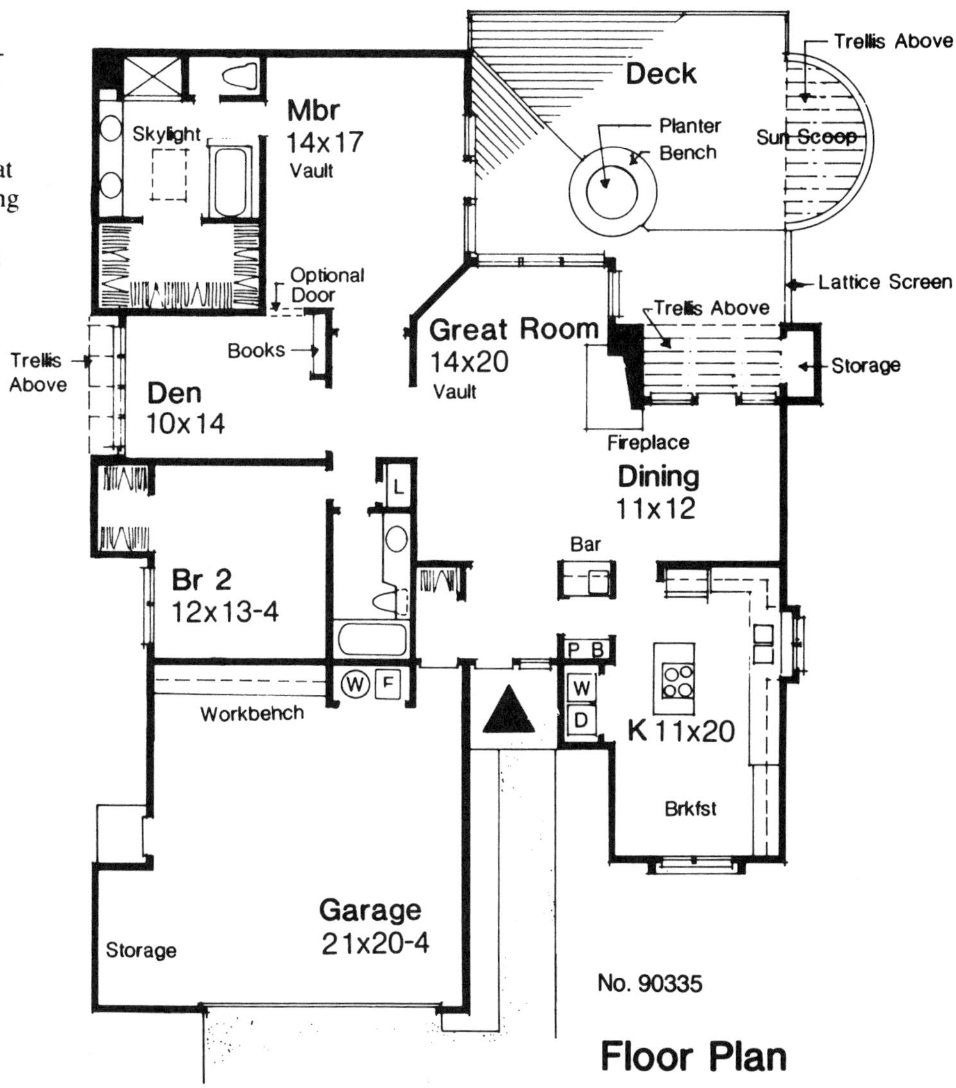

Spiral Stairs Lead to Loft

No. 90127

The central A-frame of this unusual design comprises the core of this home's living areas. The large eat-in kitchen easily serves the formal dining room or the great room which is accented by a cathedral ceiling, fireplace and sliding doors leading to the patio. Three bedrooms and a four-piece bath are gathered on one wing of the home while the master bedroom is further separated from the living areas by the placement of the laundry and the foyer. The master bath features individual dressing areas with a central bathing area. This arrangement is ideal for a working couple with teenagers.

First floor — 2,093 sq. ft.
Loft area — 326 sq. ft.

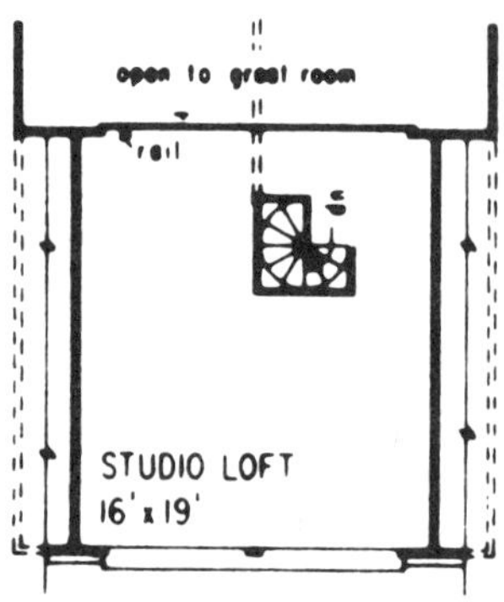

Loft Area

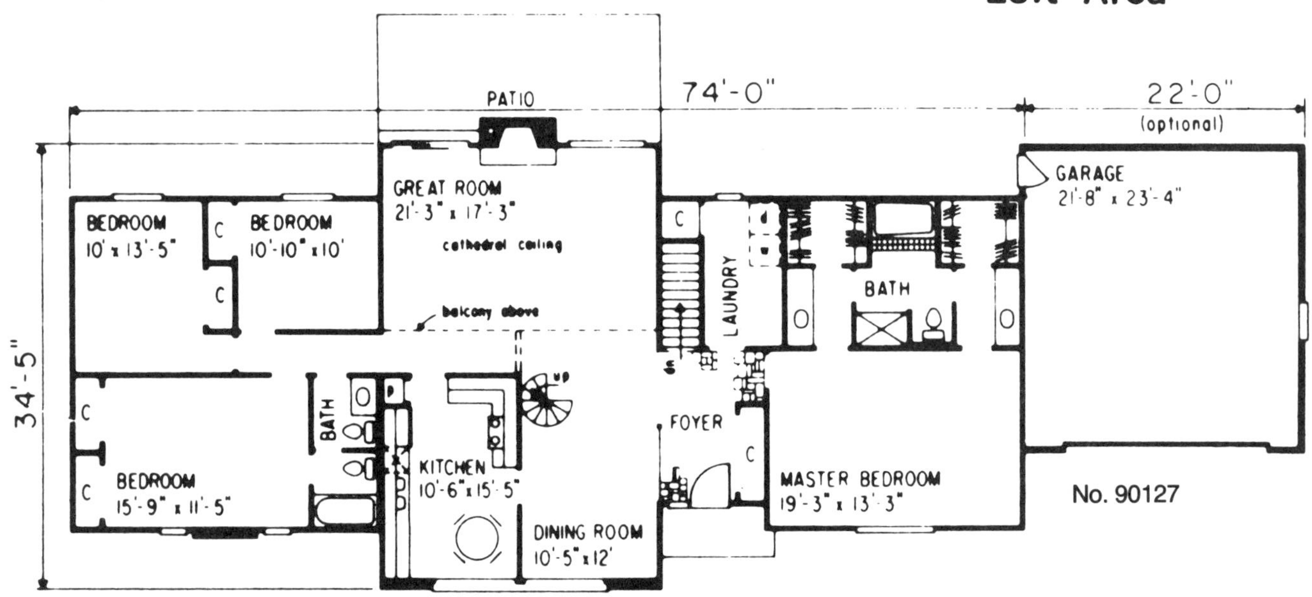

FIRST FLOOR WITH BASEMENT

Impressive Use of Space

No. 90131

The great room is the focal point of this uniquely organized plan; its sloped ceiling rises two stories to the cozy second floor balcony. Also on the second floor is the master bedroom with its own balcony, double closets and roomy bath. The two first floor bedrooms are separated from the living areas by the stairway, a large bath and extra closets. The L-shaped kitchen is conveniently located between the dining area and the garage entrance. Additional kitchen features are the built-in grill and the sliding door to the patio. The laundry room is placed so that it can also serve as a mud room just inside the garage door.

First floor — 1,320 sq. ft.
Second floor — 444 sq. ft.

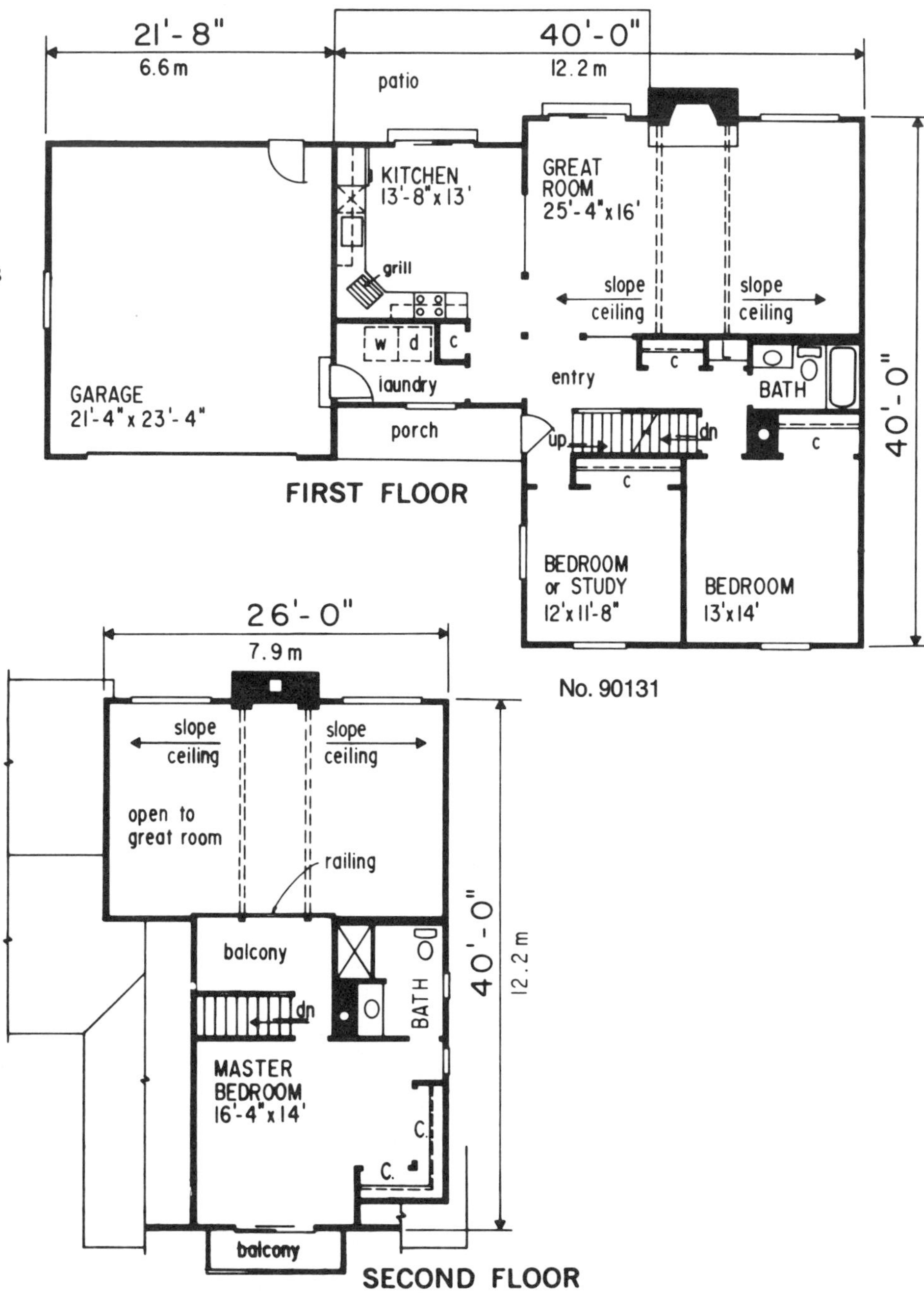

FIRST FLOOR

SECOND FLOOR

Railings Unify Open Design

No. 90900

Vaulted ceilings and open spaces highlight the interior of this delightful contemporary design, finished in horizontal cedar with a shake roof. From the moment you step into the foyer with its 2-story ceiling and skylight, you'll be impressed with the spaciousness of this plan. Every room on the main floor is zoned according to function in a step-saving arrangement. A versatile loft upstairs overlooks the living room and foyer below and provides access to three bedrooms and two baths.

Main floor — 1,156 sq. ft.
Second floor — 808 sq. ft.
Basement — 1,160 sq. ft.
Garage — 473 sq. ft.
Width — 48 ft.
Depth — 47 ft. 6 in.

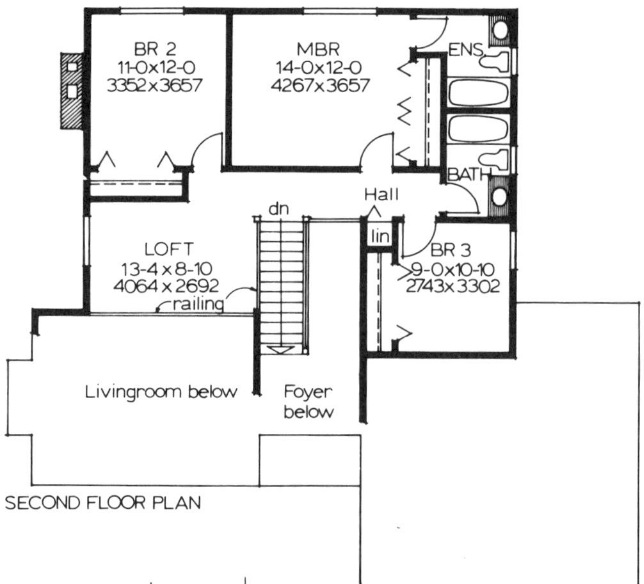

SECOND FLOOR PLAN

No. 90900

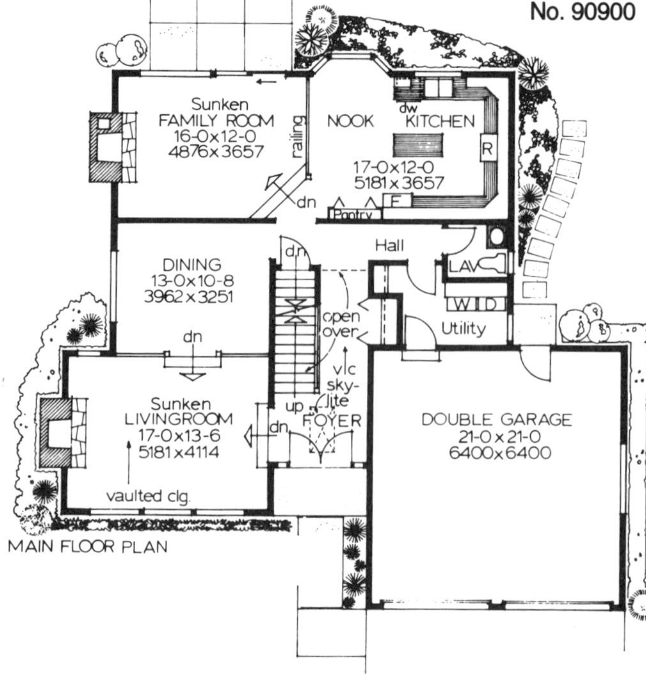

MAIN FLOOR PLAN

Bright and Beautiful

No. 91008

Imagine the attention the brightly-lit stair tower of this smart contemporary will attract after dark. From the bay-windowed kitchen and bedroom to the fireplaced living room, the angles of the tower are mirrored in the shapes of every room. Watch your guests arrive from the convenient kitchen at the front of the house or the balcony upstairs. You'll enjoy the privacy of entertaining in the formal dining room at the rear of the house, or the covered patio just outside. At day's end, the master suite is a roomy and welcoming retreat.

First floor — 1,153 sq. ft.
Second floor — 493 sq. ft.

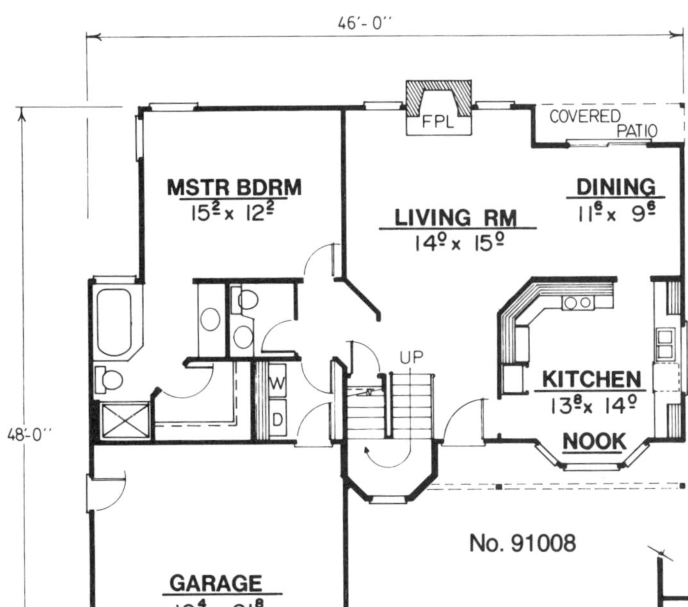

MAIN LEVEL

No. 91008

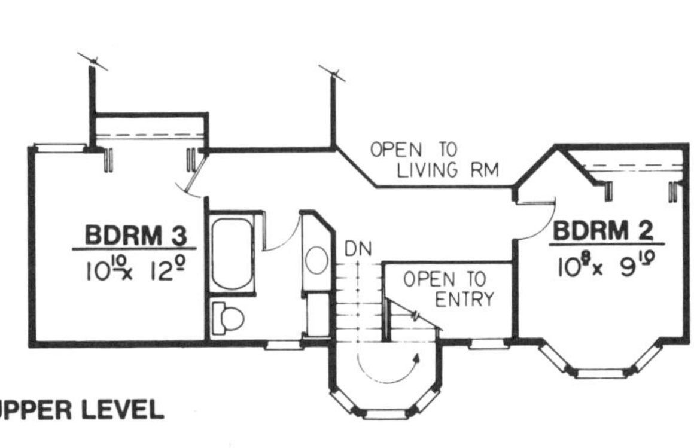

UPPER LEVEL

Great Room Has Vaulted Ceiling

No. 90361

The triple appeal of stylish impact, a great kitchen with charming breakfast area, and a luxurious master bedroom suite give this house high perceived value in today's very competitive mid-priced marketplace. Note how these features are emphasized with balconied stair overlooking living and dining rooms, greenhouse plus bay windowed kitchen, and master bath with platform tub, stall shower, and oversized walk-in closet. Combined with the highly detailed, custom-look exterior, this total design package gives you a lot to like.

First floor — 1,105 sq. ft.
Second floor — 460 sq. ft.

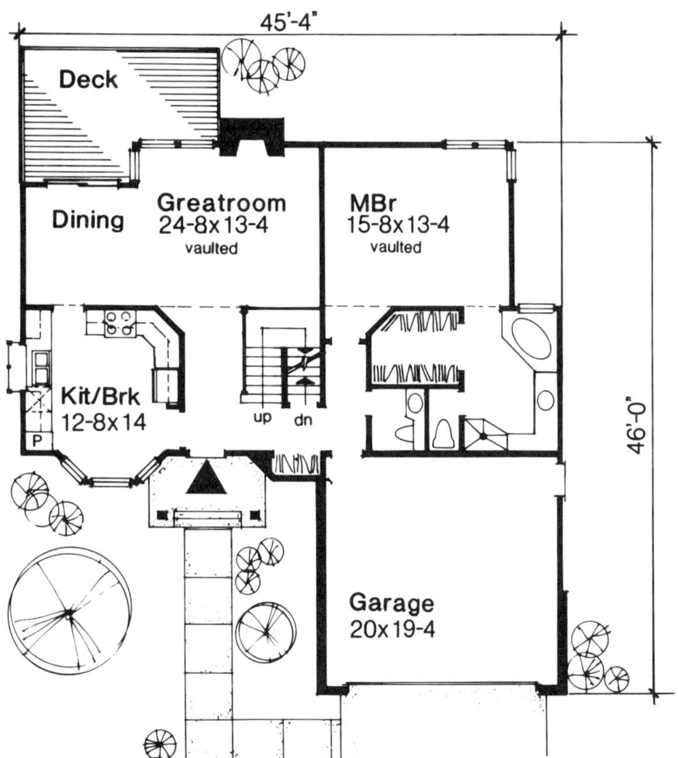

Main Floor

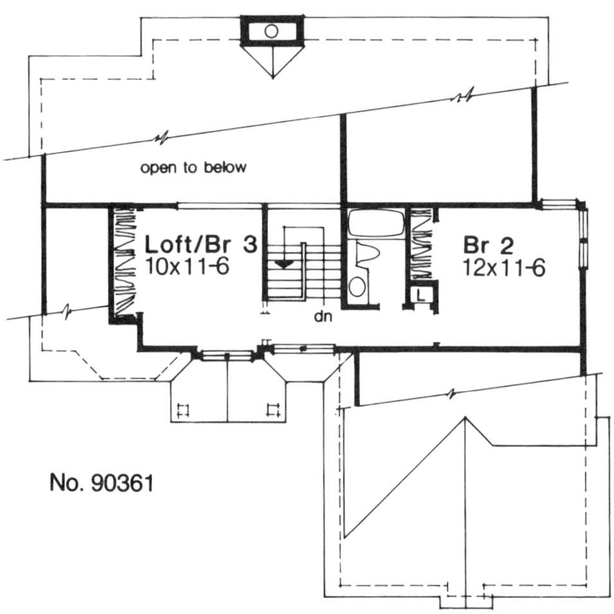

Upper Floor

Contemporary Offers Sunken Living Room

No. 90334

This contemporary design is inviting because of the built-in greenhouse that is located just left of the entry into the house. Inside, a sunken living room is accessible from the hallway. Once in the living room, you're greeted by a vaulted ceiling and a masonry fireplace. A formal dining room is located next to the living room. An efficient kitchen has a connecting breakfast room which appears larger because of its vaulted ceiling. An outside wooden deck is accessible from the kitchen/breakfast rooms. The family room has its own wood-burning fireplace and a wet bar. Laundry facilities are located near the family room. The second floor includes four bedrooms. The master bedroom has a his/hers walk-in closet, a whirlpool bath surrounded by tile and a cathedral ceiling with circle top windows.

First floor — 1,382 sq. ft.
Second floor — 1,328 sq. ft.

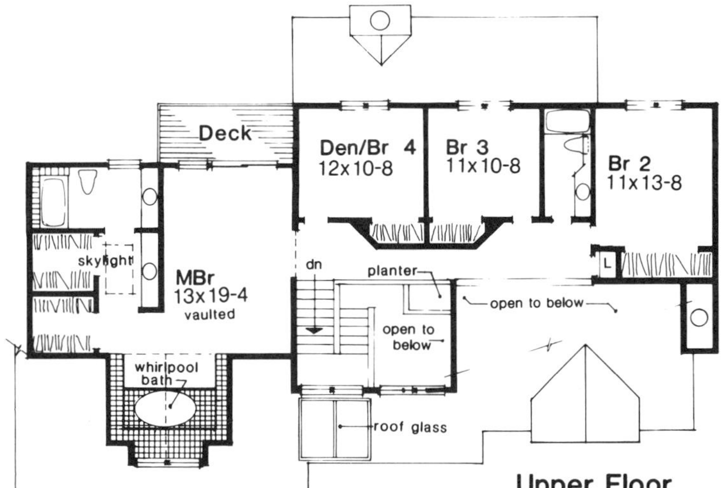

Upper Floor
1328 sq.ft.

No. 90334

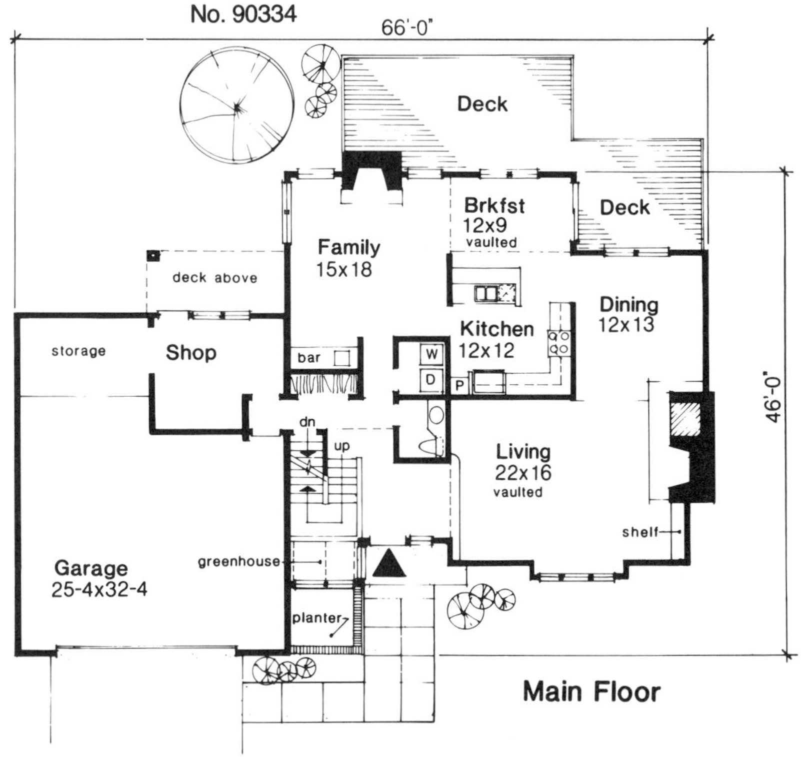

Main Floor

Do-It-Yourself Dream House

No. 90642

Looking for a dramatic, yet simple, vacation home? Here's a compact one-level home that's easy to build and even easier to maintain. And, if you're lucky enough to build in a beautiful setting, the window wall treatment in the active areas will allow you to take full advantage of a spectacular view. Enter the living room and kitchen through sliding glass doors via the deck, or use the back door and come in past the convenient utility room that separates the three bedrooms and two full baths from the rest of the house. The large, fireplaced living room and kitchen with dining area seem even more spacious, thanks to cathedral ceilings that soar to a dizzying height.

Living area — 1,134 sq. ft.

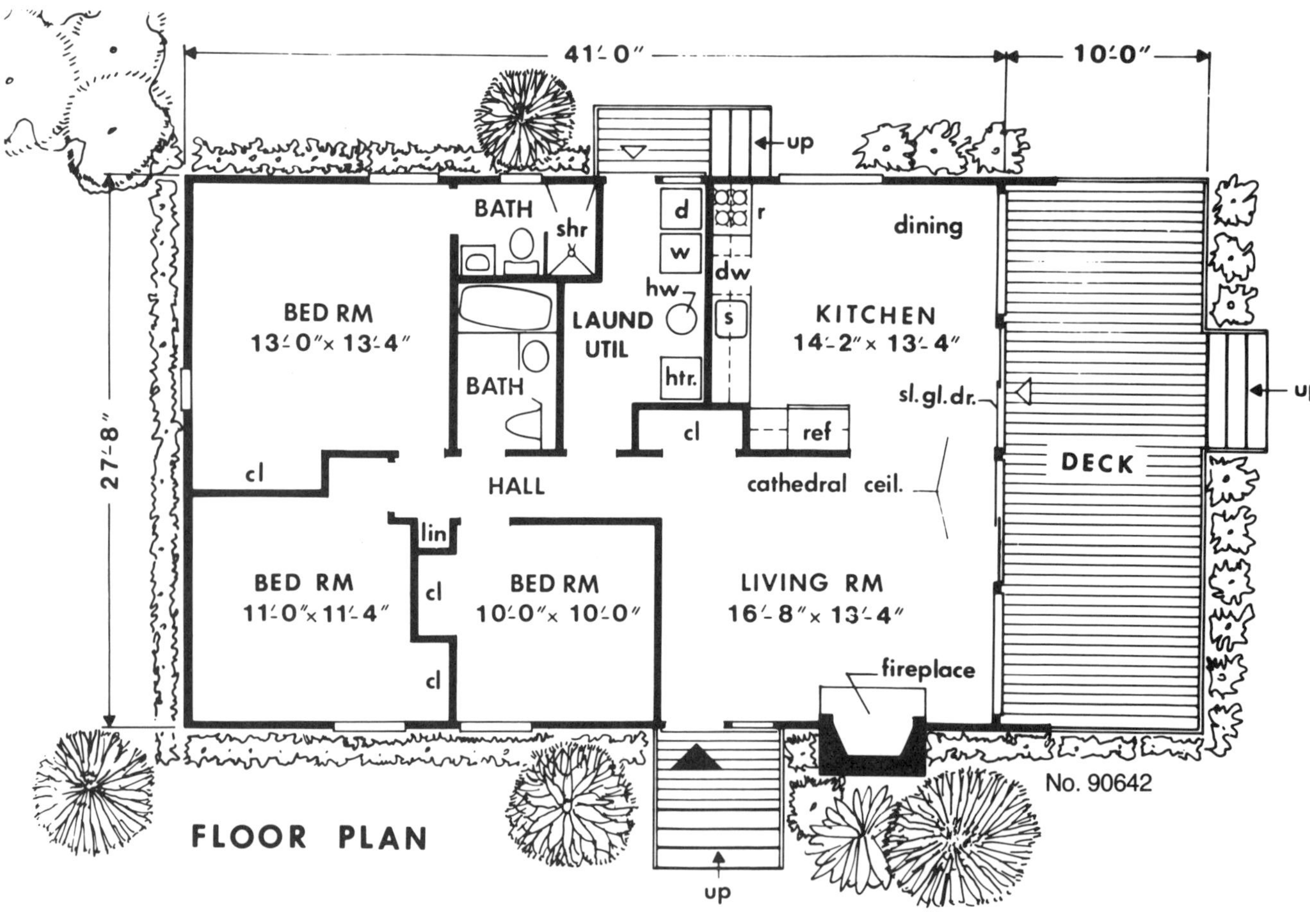

Compact Three Bedroom Zoned for Family Activities

No. 90136

This family home is almost equally divided into the private, bedroom area and the living area. The living area is further divided into formal and informal spaces. The three bedrooms and two full baths are well placed along one side of the home and buffered from street noise by the placement of the garage. The formal living and dining areas are located along the front of the home to welcome guests while the more informal family room and the large, eat-in kitchen overlook the back yard. Because these living spaces flow into one another or are separated by dividers instead of walls, this home gives the feeling of being much larger than it is.

Living Area — 1,380 sq. ft.

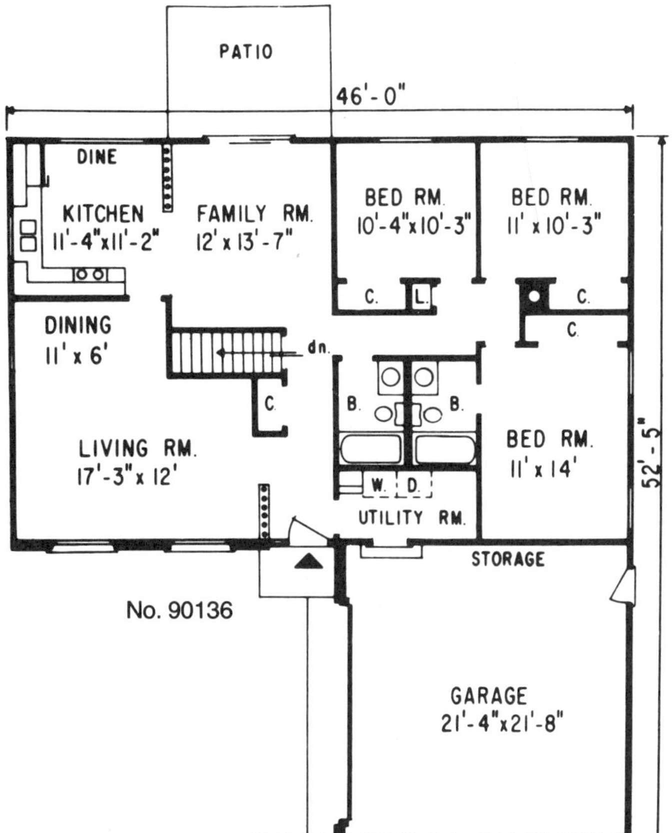

No. 90136

PLAN 1 WITH BASEMENT

Luxury Master Suite, Room to Expand

No. 10525

In addition to three bedrooms, the second floor of this traditional design features a large unfinished area. The luxury master suite has two walk-in closets in the dressing area plus a five-piece bath which features a circular window above the tiled tub enclosure. The first floor is composed of formal dining and living rooms on either side of the tiled foyer, with the family areas organized along the back overlooking the patio. The cozy family room has a fireplace, built-in bookcase and opens onto the patio. The kitchen features a bump-out window over the sink and shares a snack bar with the bright and cheery breakfast nook.

First floor — 1,219 sq. ft.
Second floor — 1,010 sq. ft.
Basement — 1,219 sq. ft.
Garage — 514 sq. ft.

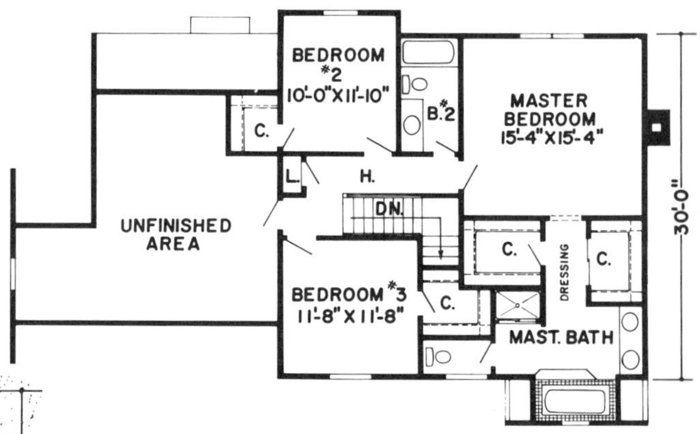

SECOND FLOOR PLAN

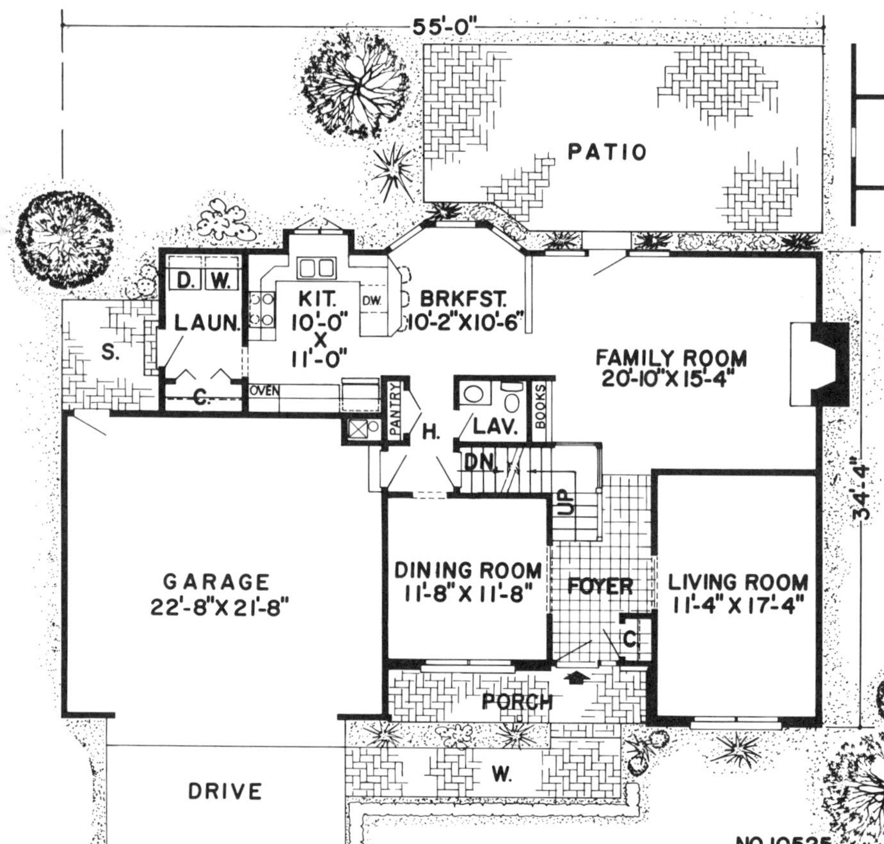

FIRST FLOOR PLAN

Stucco Charm and Durability

No. 91005

There's a hint of things Mediterranean in this four-bedroom tri-level contemporary. Entering through the two-car garage, you'll find a spacious family room, bedroom, and convenient powder room. On the main floor, the living room is just a step down from the eat-in kitchen and formal dining room. And, for restful nights, three bedrooms occupy a separate, upper level. You'll love retreating to the master suite, a luxurious sanctuary with its own deck for private relaxing.

Lower level — 632 sq. ft.
Main floor — 1316 sq. ft.

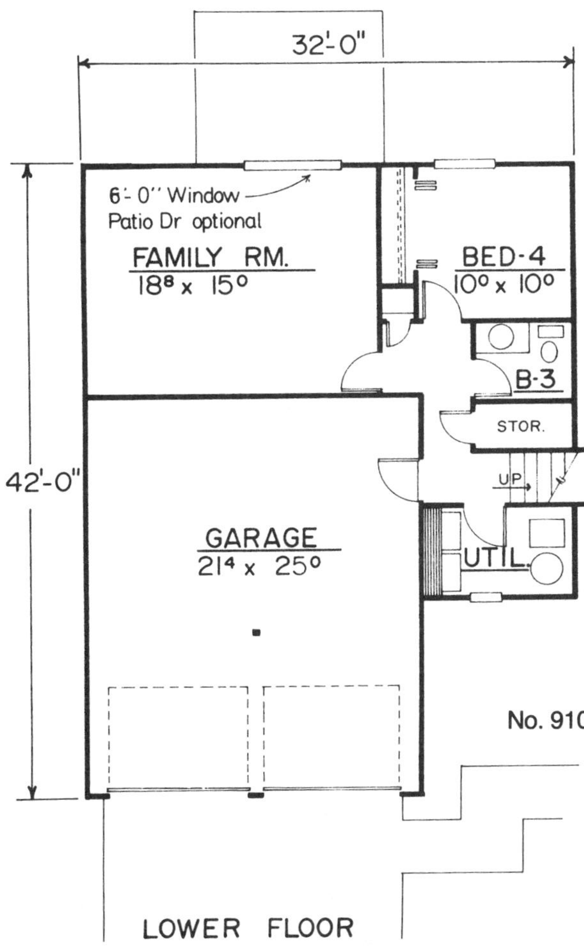

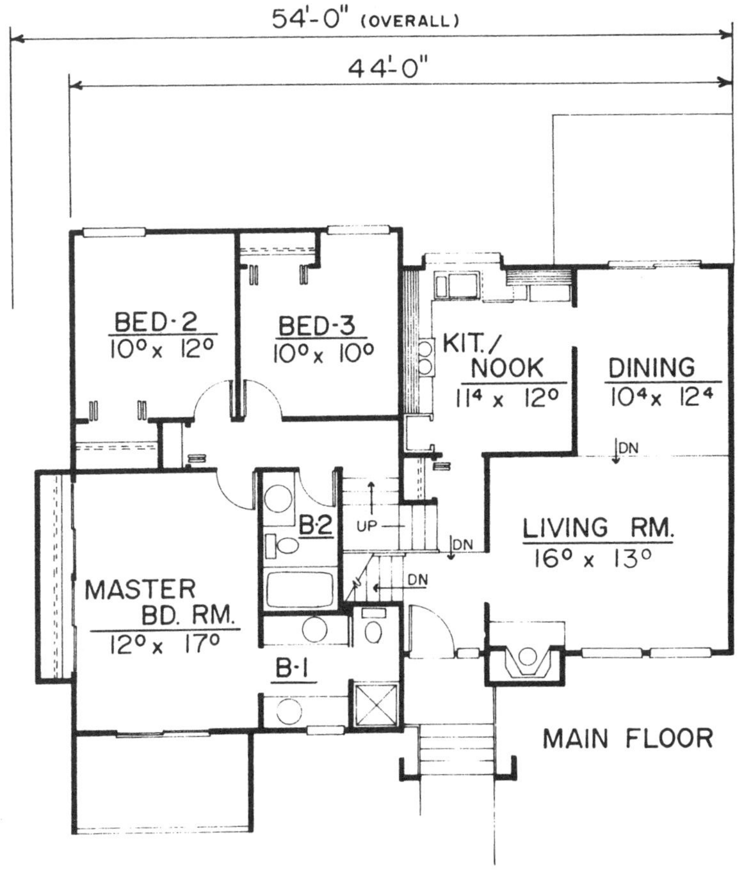

Inviting Victorian Veranda

No. 91007

Traditional style with all the features of a modern floor plan makes this a place you'll love coming home to. Extra large windows brighten every room. You'll appreciate the interesting angles bay windows give to living, dining, and master bedrooms. The central staircase separates formal entertaining from family areas, warmed by a fireplace and wide-open for convenient mealtimes.

First floor — 1,228 sq. ft.
Second floor — 880 sq. ft.

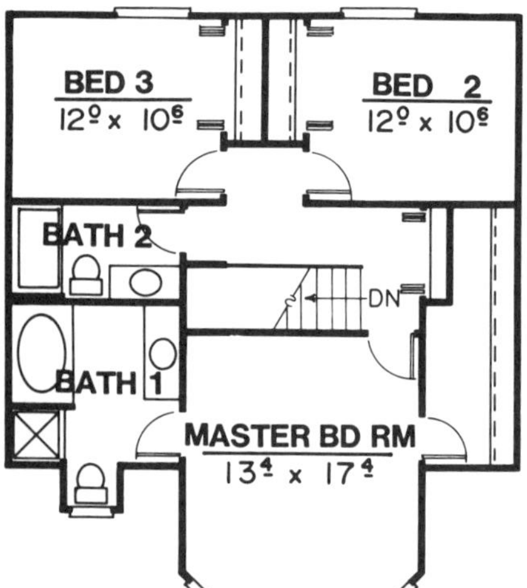

UPPER LEVEL

No. 91007

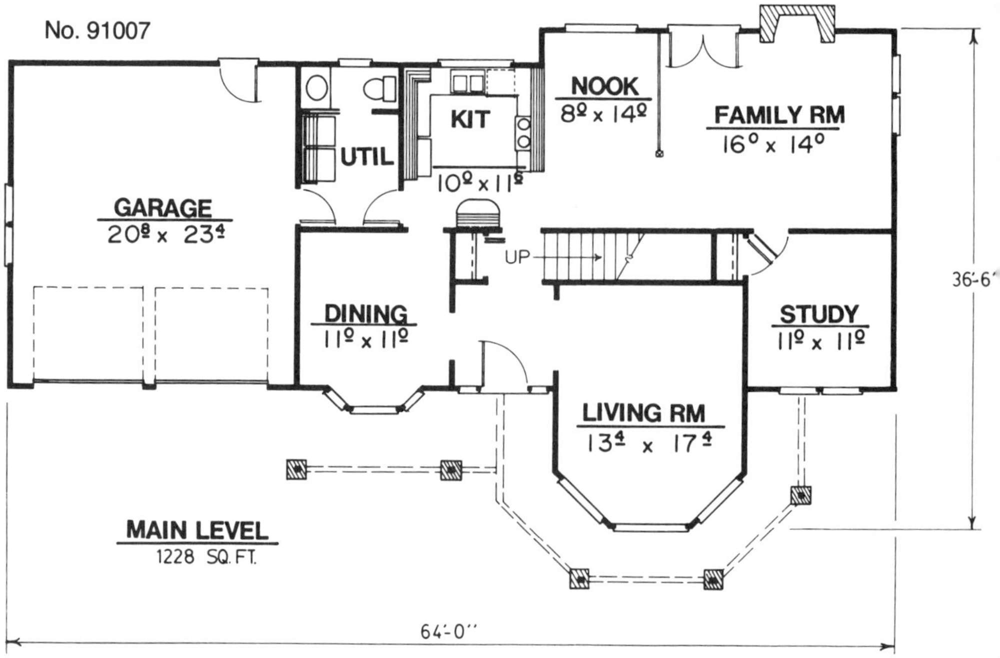

One-Level Convenience

No. 91004

Here's a delightful home designed for a busy family. Enjoy a quiet night's sleep in bedrooms tucked behind the garage and away from main living spaces.

You'll enjoy easy meal service, too, in an angular kitchen that opens to fireplaced family room and breakfast nook. For entertaining, choose the formal dining room graced by a glass wall and a view of the sunken living room.

Living Area — 1,792 sq. ft.

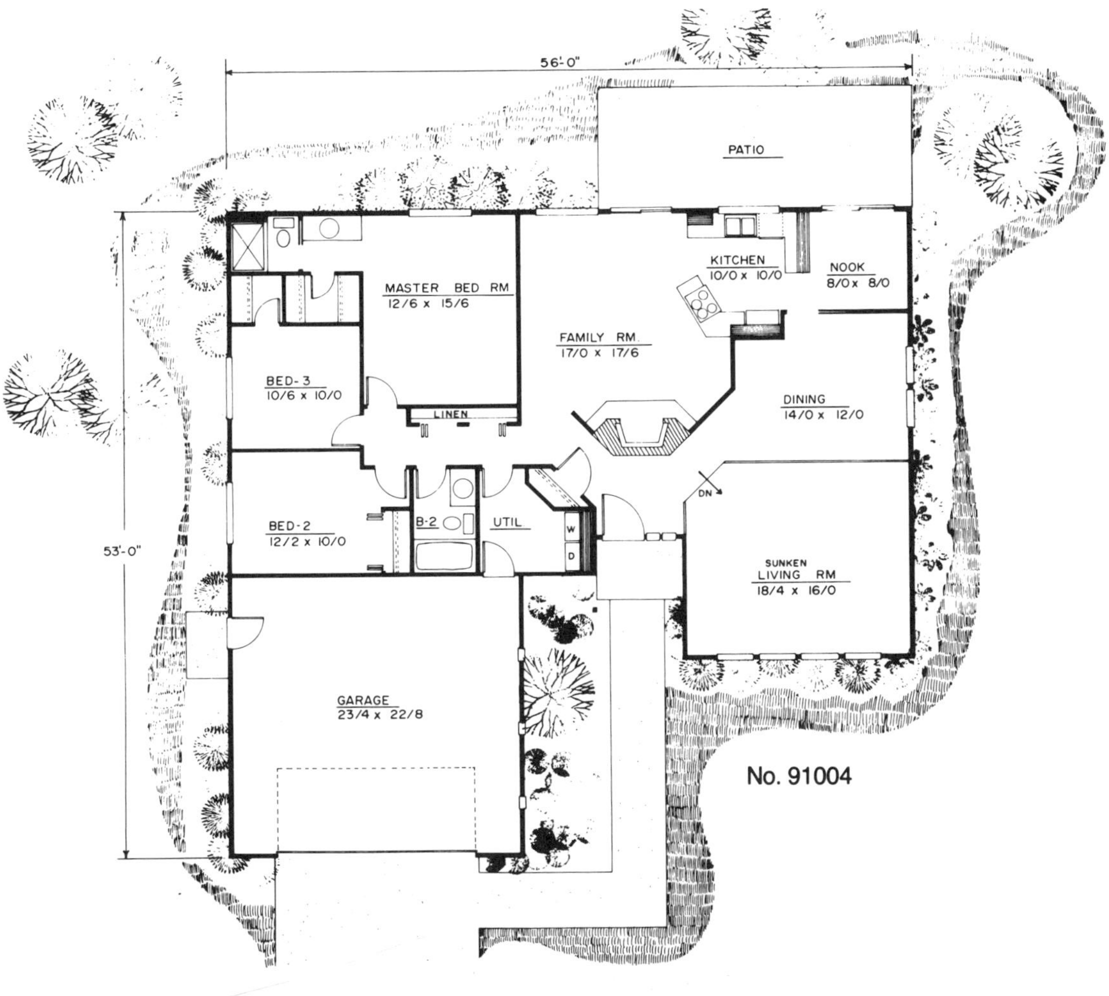

Graceful Porch Enhances Charm

No. 90106

The formal living room which is sheltered by the railed porch may be used only for company because of the multifunctional kitchen, dining and family room which are immediately behind it. This "three rooms in one" design is easily adaptable to any number of lifestyles. Adjacent to the open kitchen with its efficient design and ample counter space is the hobby area that includes laundry facilities. Of the three large bedrooms the master bedroom features a walk-in closet and private bath.

Living Area — 1,643 sq. ft.

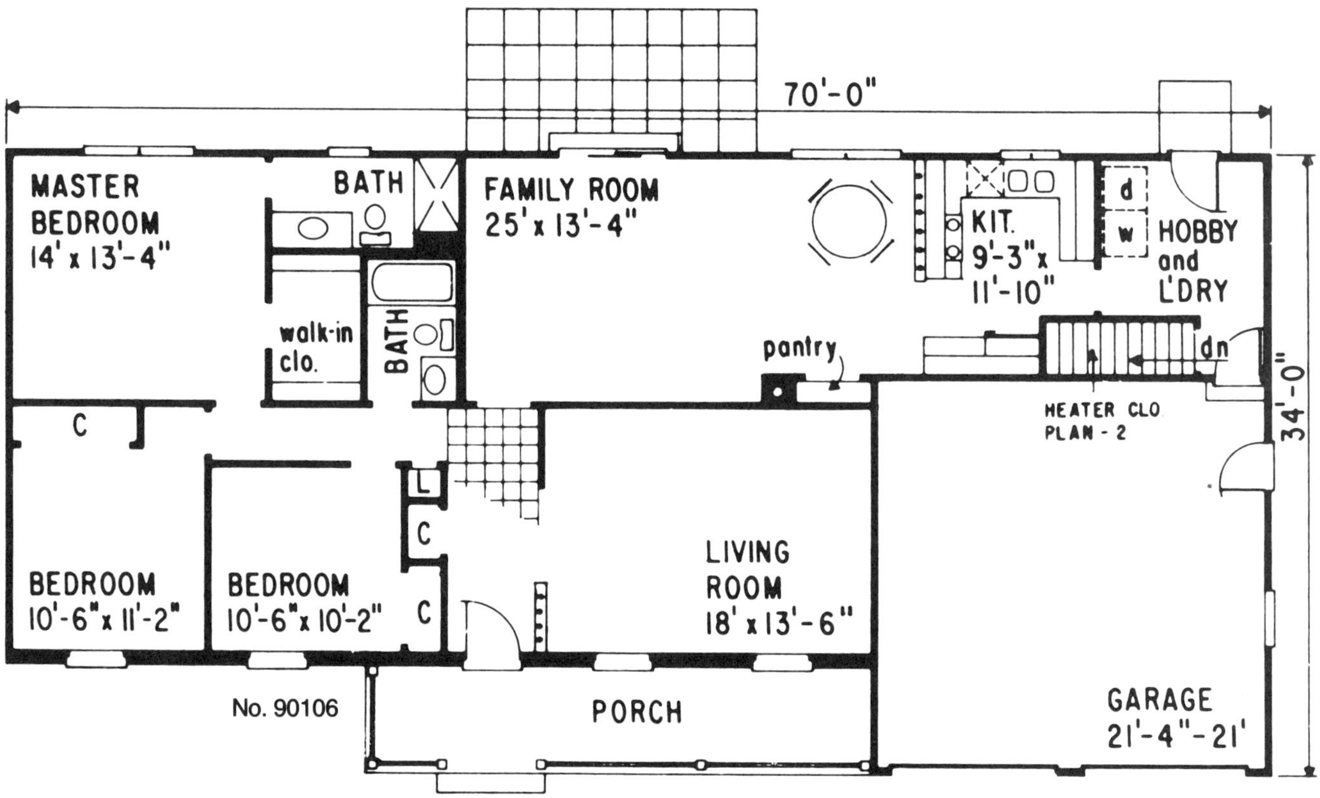

No. 90106

Rustic Vacation House

No. 90004

This compact three-bedroom cabin, designed for vacations and later retirement, would suit many areas. The stone and wood exterior requires little maintenance. Two porches and an outdoor balcony make the most of entertaining, relaxing, or just enjoying a sunset. From the foyer, the spiral stairway in the living room can be seen which leads to a balcony and an upstairs bedroom or studio. A wood fire always seems to make a house warmer and cozier, and this design includes a massive stone fireplace in the living room. The living room also has a pair of floor-to-ceiling windows at the gable end and sliding glass doors to a rear porch. There is a pantry adjoining the eat-in kitchen which has a small bay window over the sink. Off the foyer is a powder room. The design also includes two bedrooms and a bath on the first floor.

First floor — 1,020 sq. ft.
Second floor — 265 sq. ft.

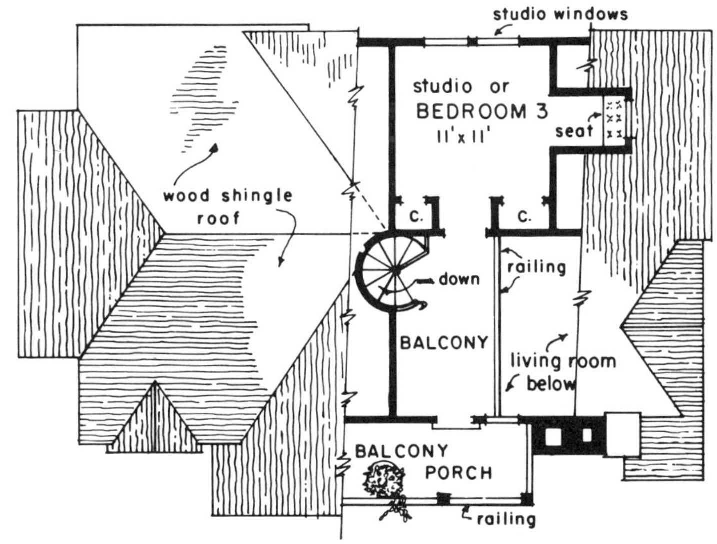

balcony level

No. 90004

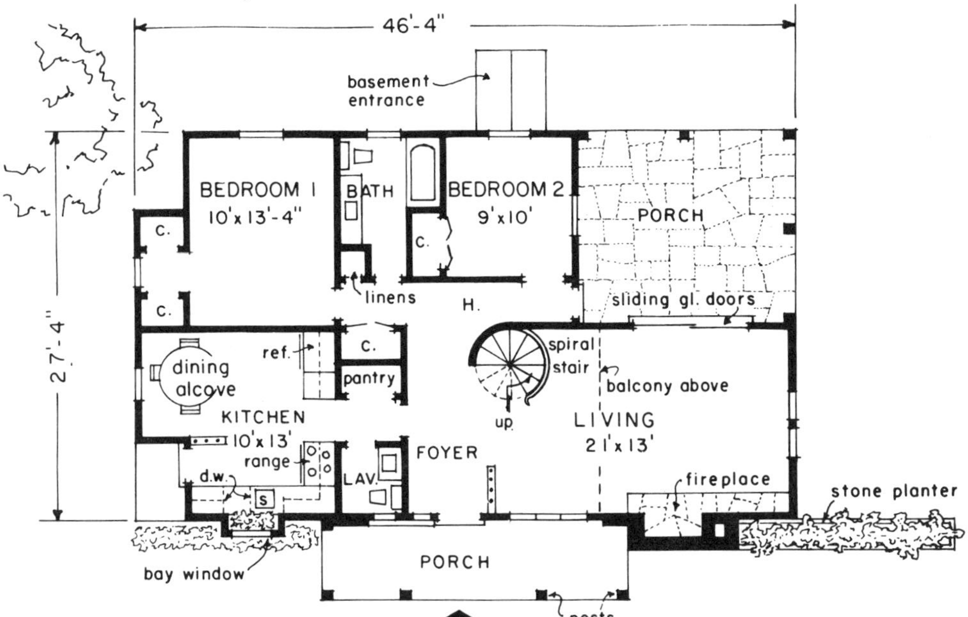

first floor

Clerestory Window Illuminates Entry

No. 91046

There's an obvious Southwestern influence in this distinctive, one-level dwelling. You can see it in the stucco exterior and tile roof, in the open floor plan, and in the graceful arches between living, dining and family rooms. You can almost feel the welcome warmth of the southwestern sun, pouring through generous windows in every room. When night falls, maintain that toasty atmosphere by stoking up the fireplace in the family room. Down the hall, you'll find a cozy bedroom wing, separated from active areas for maximum quiet. Have you always dreamed of a luxurious master suite with your own private sitting room? Look no further. This distinctive room even boasts a walk-in closet and double vanities.

First floor — 1,832 sq. ft.

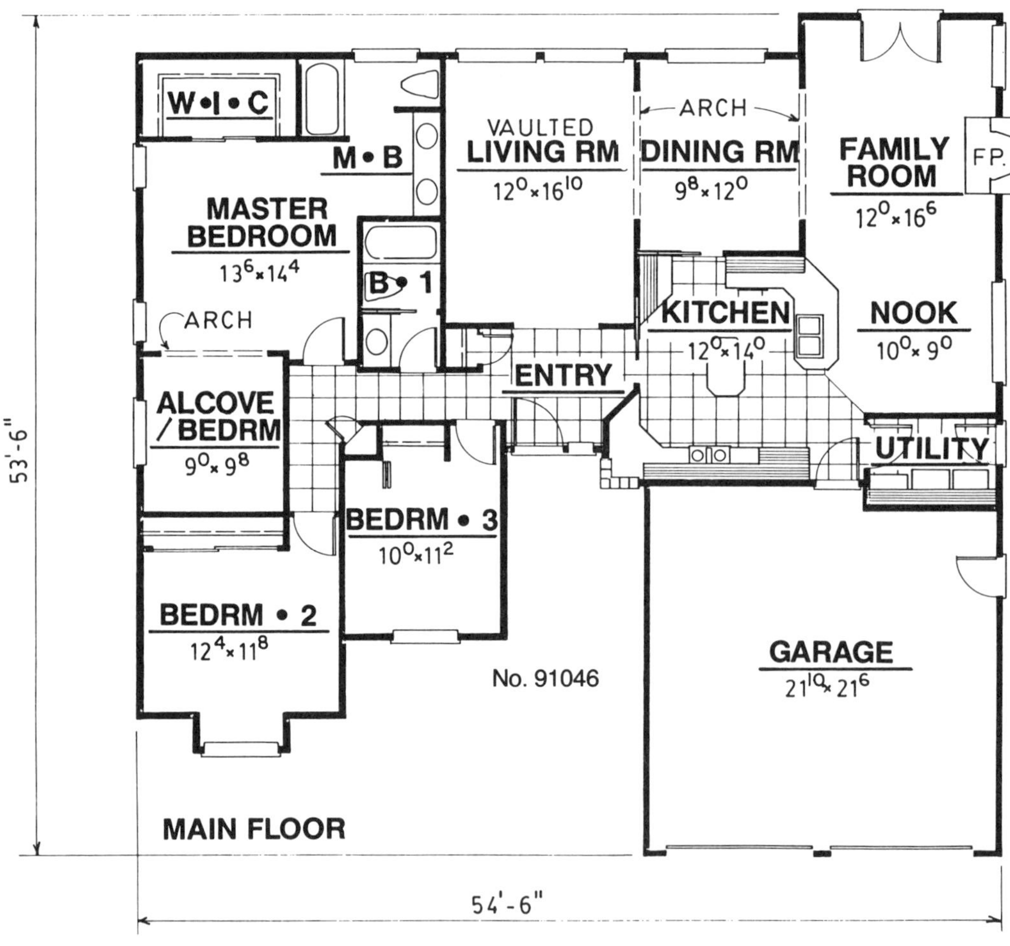

Huge Windows Create Cheerful Atmosphere

No. 91040

Are you looking for a family home that combines a contemporary open plan with a quiet bedroom wing? Here's a one-level gem that fills the bill. The three bedrooms, tucked away from active areas, include a spacious master suite with a private bath and enormous closet. You'll love the easy-care openness of the fireplaced living room, dining nook and kitchen. And, you can expand your outdoor living space through the sliding glass doors to the back... build a patio, porch, or deck to suit your yard.

First floor — 1,206 sq. ft.

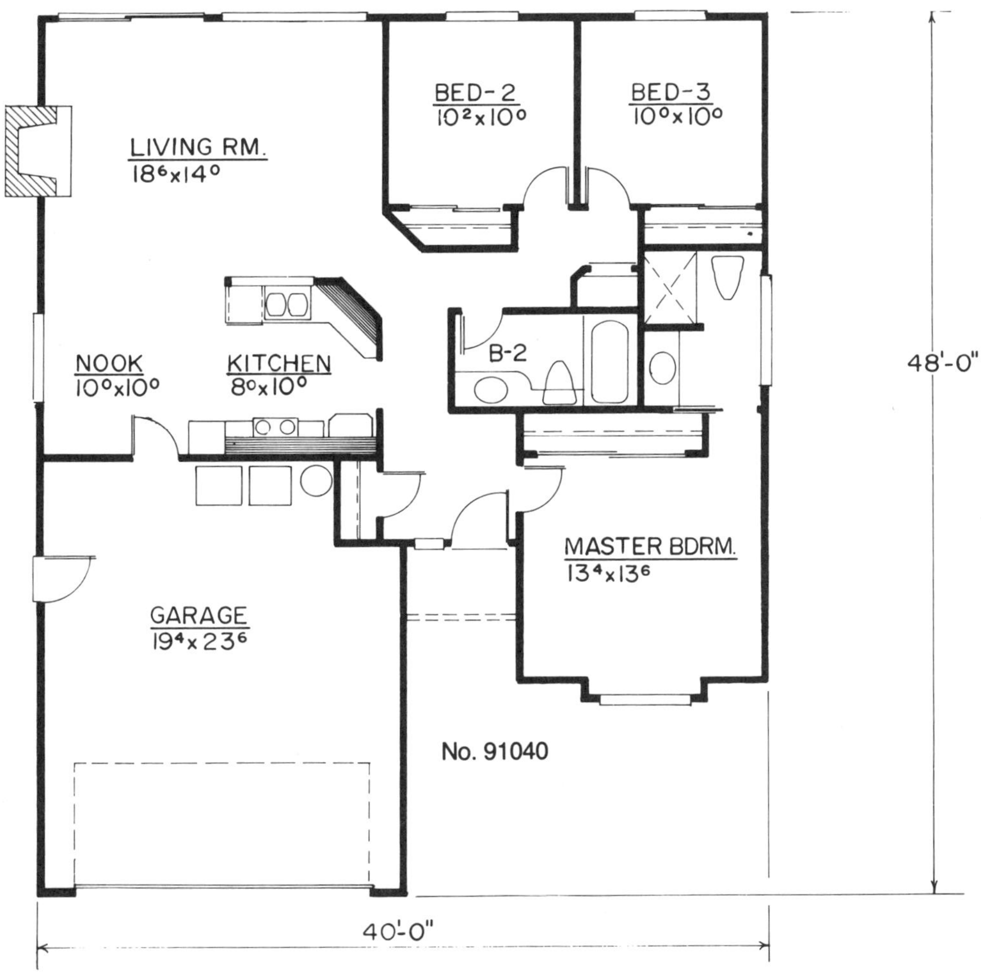

Pamper Yourself

No. 90536

You can build a spectacular home yet stay within your budget with this distinctive family design. Look at the master suite on the second floor. Double vanities, a sunken tub, a walk-in wardrobe and shower, and a private deck are some of the amenities you'll enjoy. The upstairs landing affords a dramatic view of the vaulted living room and entry below. Just off the entry, you'll find a bayed den and nearby powder room. You're sure to appreciate the island kitchen with its convenient location between formal and informal dining rooms. And, you'll love the cozy atmosphere of the sunken family room. The bonus room enjoys an oversized window and awaits you plans for expansion.

First floor — 1,601 sq. ft.
Second floor — 1,047 sq. ft.
Bonus room — 358 sq. ft.

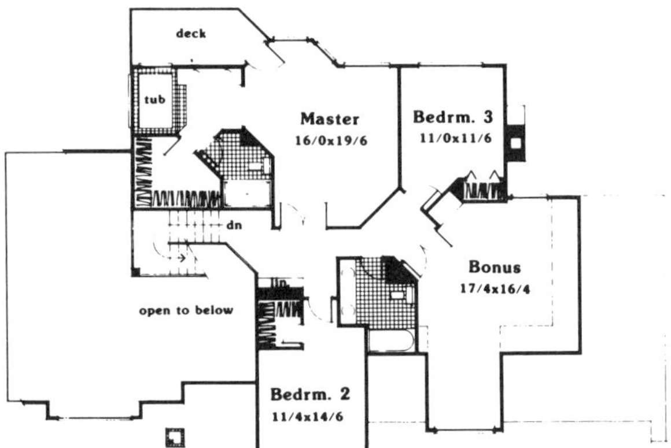

No. 90536

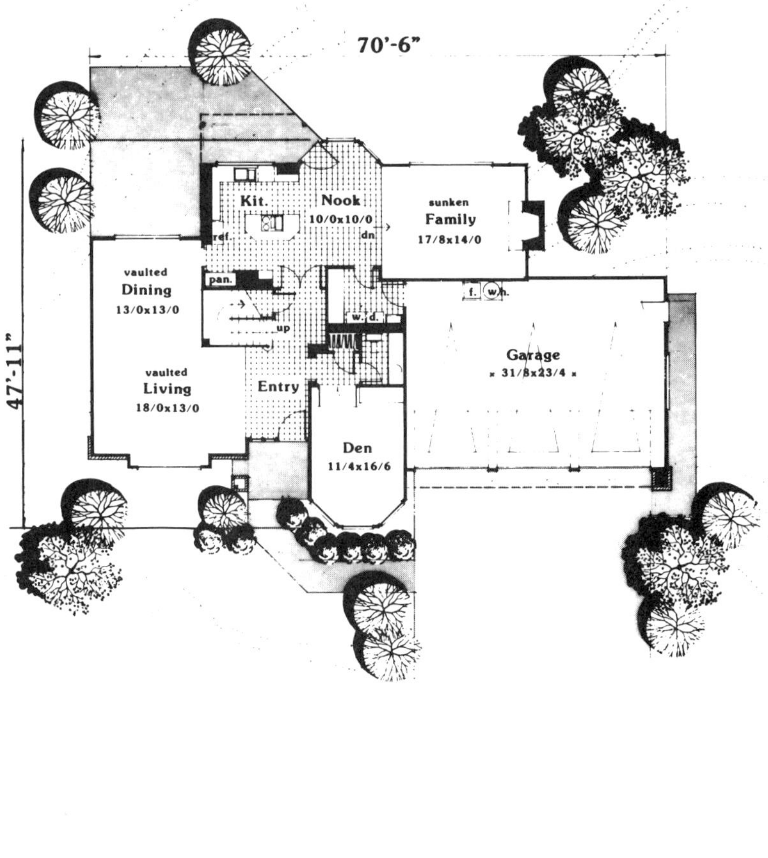

Solarium Design Benefits Both Levels

No. 90647

The traditional exterior styling of this handsome four-bedroom home doesn't even hint at the energy-saving features you'll find inside. An air-lock vestibule maintains the solar-heated atmosphere that's apparent as you enter the foyer. One glance reveals the living room's beamed cathedral ceiling, the dining room with sliders to the rear terrace, the sun-catching solarium, and venting clerestory windows. The nearby kitchen enjoys a two-way view of the back yard. Your needs will dictate whether the first floor bedroom will double as a den, but the adjoining bath makes either possibility tempting. Even the upstairs bedrooms and two baths benefit from the solarium's efficient design.

First floor — 1,028 sq. ft.
Second floor — 770 sq. ft.

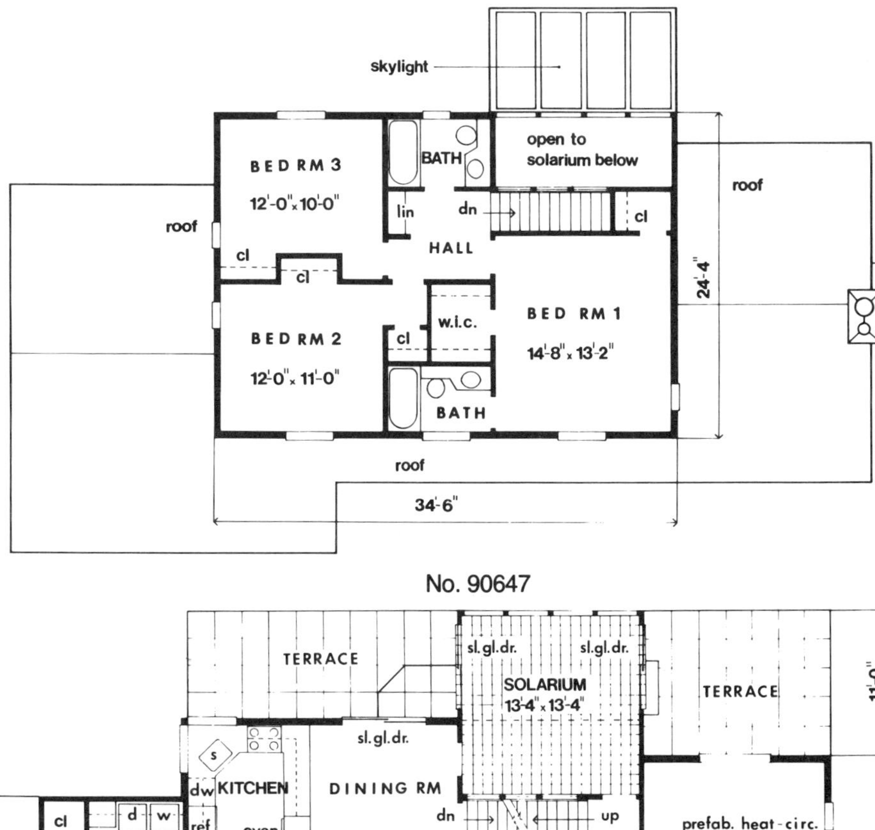

No. 90647

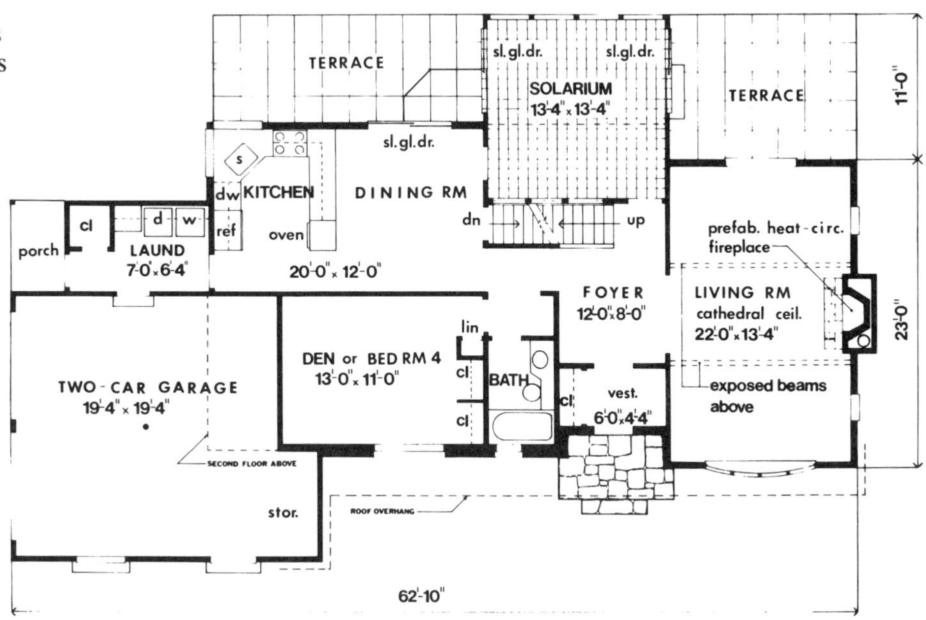

Stately Home Features Formal Courtyard

No. 90014

Gracing the entrance of this elegant home is formal courtyard complete with reflecting pool. The grand foyer leads to the large living room which features a fireplace, window seats and an archway opening onto the dining room. The side terrace is easily reached through the dining room's French doors. The conveniently organized kitchen is located between the dining room and the family room, which is expanded by its French door entrances to both the front courtyard and the more informal porch. The three bedrooms located on the second floor are arranged to make the most efficient use of space.

First floor — 943 sq. ft.
Second floor — 772 sq. ft.

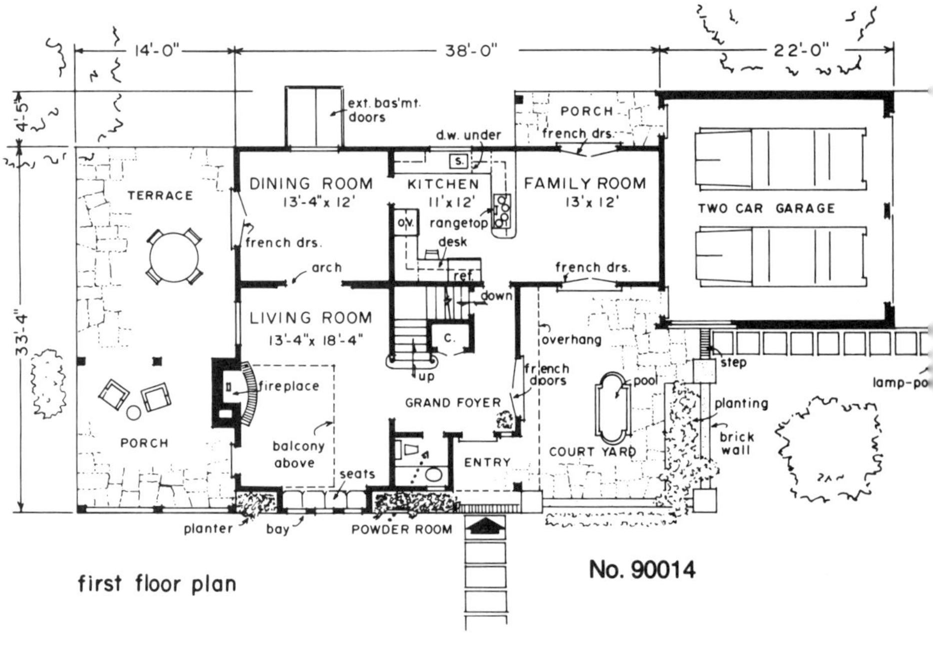

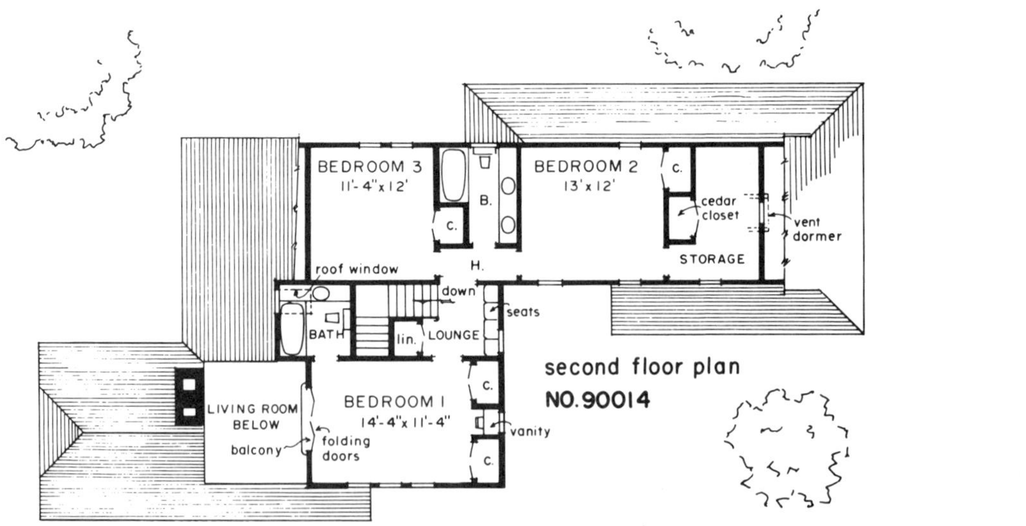

Traditional Looks and Charm

No. 90135

Wherever you build this attractive home, the traditional exterior is sure to please. And inside, there are plenty of livable features, too. The master bedroom boasts a walk-in closet and private bath. The other bedrooms are comfortably arranged with ample closets and convenient access to the second bath. The spacious living areas on the first floor are organized into formal and informal areas. The family room with its sliding glass door to the patio and its imposing fireplace is shielded from the formal areas by the placement of the utility room. The large, eat-in kitchen conveniently serves either the family room or the formal dining room.

First floor — 1,046 sq. ft.
Second floor — 812 sq. ft.

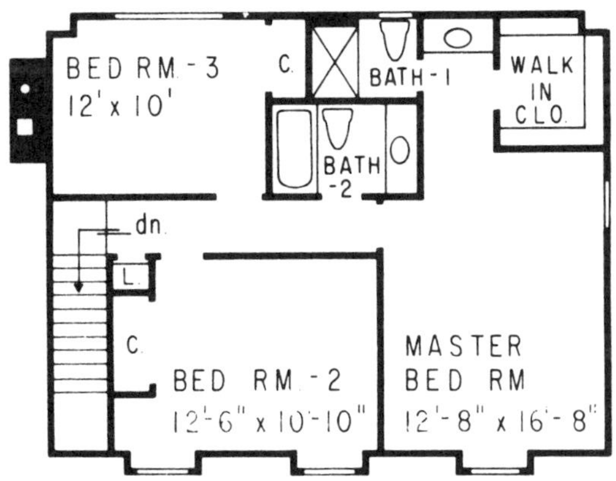

SECOND FLOOR

No. 90135

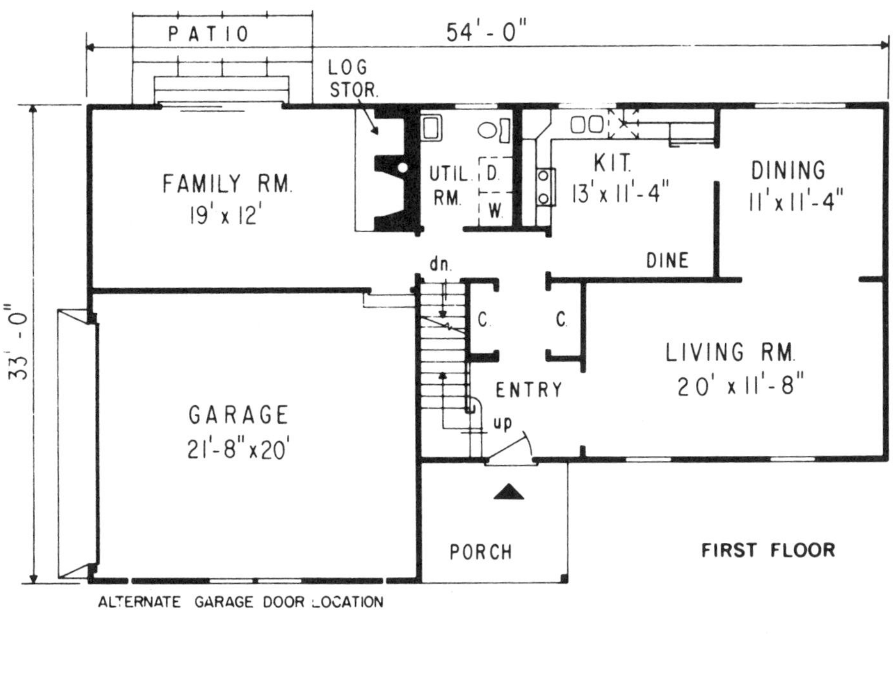

Enjoy the View from the Top

No. 90834

This versatile basement-entry home with a classic flavor will allow you to build now, and best of all, plan for the future. Take the stairs from the roomy, two-story central foyer to main living areas on the second floor. Walk to the right, and you'll find three spacious bedrooms, two full baths, and closets galore. Active areas feature an open plan with expansive windows and sliding glass doors to an outdoor deck. There's plenty of room in the kitchen for family meals. But, if you want a more formal atmosphere, use the dining room, warmed by a fieldstone fireplace in the adjoining living room.

First floor — 751 sq. ft.
Second floor — 1,205 sq. ft.
Garage — 440 sq. ft.

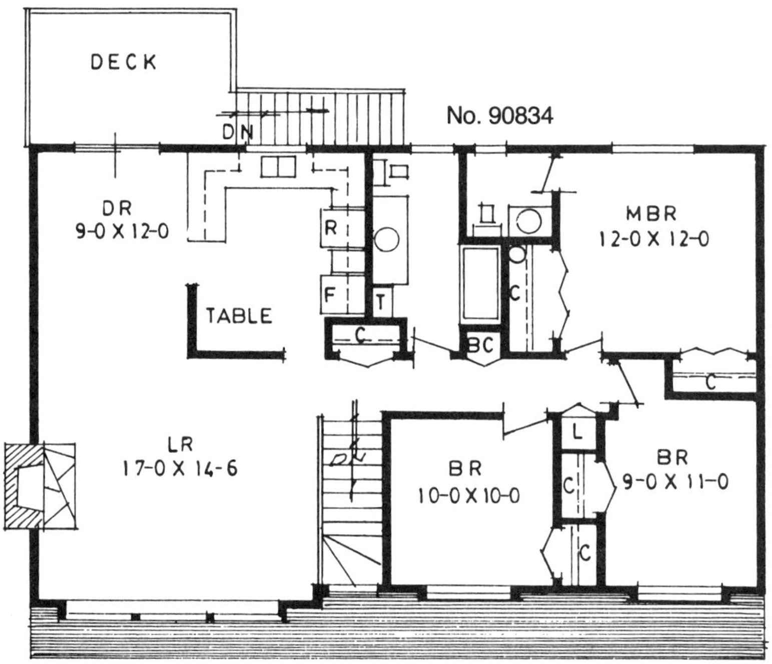

UPPER FLOOR

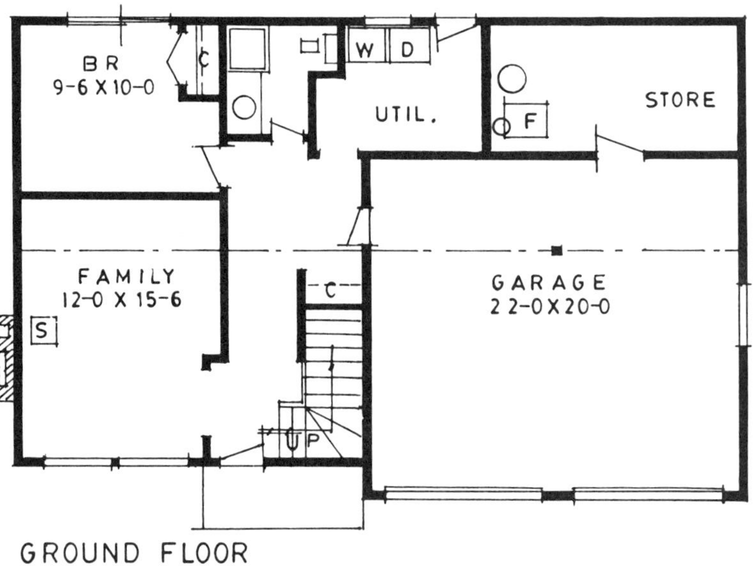

GROUND FLOOR

Right Out of a Gothic Novel

No. 90666

Enjoy the imposing grace of Tudor styling in a surprisingly affordable home. Here's an updated masterpiece just perfect for a dinner party. Show your guests out to the huge terrace that wraps around the house. Can't you imagine candles flickering in the bay windows and sliding glass doors of the dining room? A massive brick fireplace in the living room completes the classic atmosphere. With the expansive counter space, the efficient U-shape of the kitchen, and huge pantry nearby, serving dinner will be a breeze. And, when the last guest has left, you can retire to your luxurious master suite, featuring the tower bath with whirlpool and double sinks, a dressing room with built-in vanity, and a private sitting nook. Three additional bedrooms are served by a roomy bath overlooking the entrance court.

First floor — 1,003 sq. ft.
Second floor — 1,044 sq. ft.

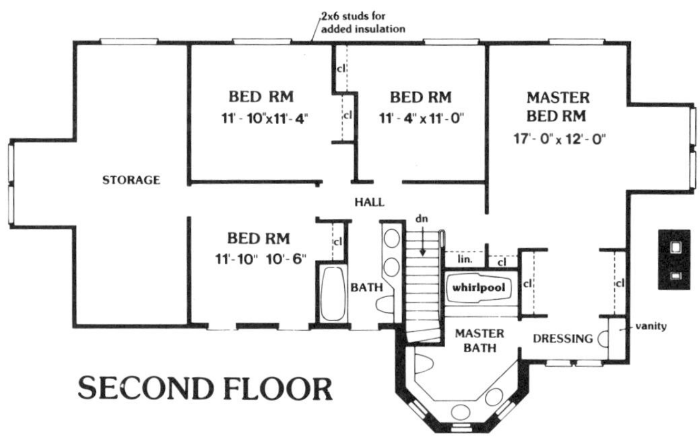

SECOND FLOOR

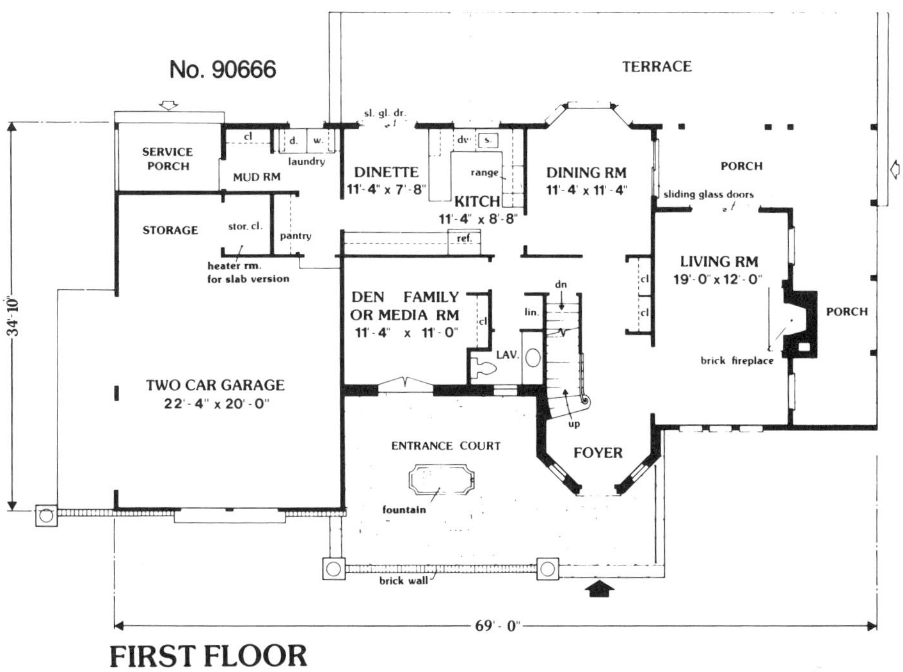

FIRST FLOOR

Soaring Roof Line Hints at Dramatic Interior

No. 90654

Are you a home entertainment buff? There's room for all your equipment in the built-in entertainment center of this stunning, three-bedroom home. High, sloping ceilings studded with skylights combine with window walls to bring a sun-filled atmosphere to active areas. A heat-circulating fireplace kicks in after the sun goes down. When the weather's bad, you'll appreciate the garage entrance that leads past the mud room right into the kitchen. Go ahead and turn up the stereo. A hallway off the foyer and the two full baths act as a buffer to keep the bedrooms quiet.

First floor — 1,560 sq. ft.
Garage and storage — 505 sq. ft.

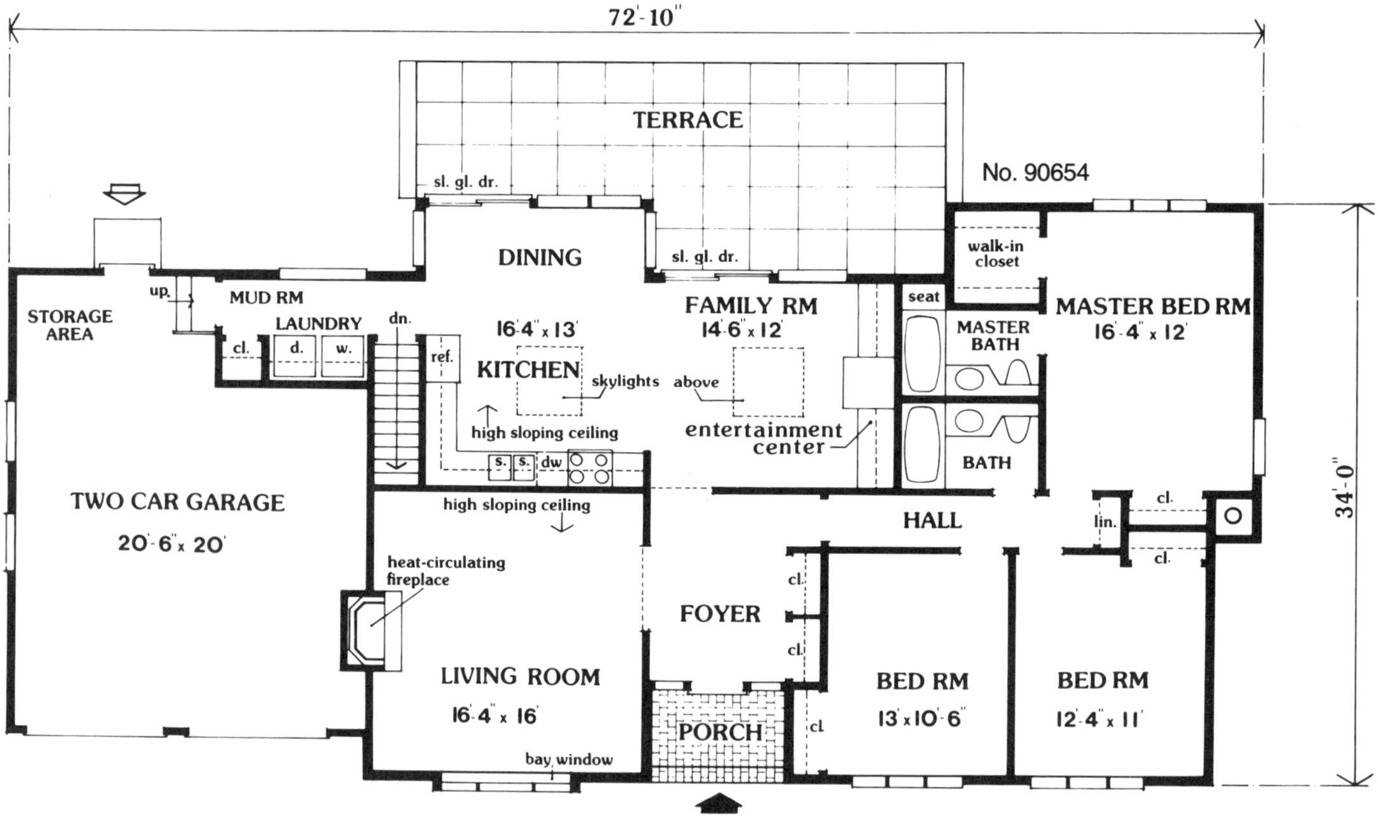

Two-Story Window Creates Breathtaking Stairwell

No. 91043

Wooden columns, stacked bays, and vertical trim accentuate the soaring roof lines of this stately contemporary. Inside, an open plan and massive windows give every room an elegant, sun-filled atmosphere. Look at the adjoining formal areas off the entry, just perfect for entertaining. The handy island kitchen conveniently serves formal and family dining rooms. Upstairs, you'll be rewarded by a magnificent view of the entry below. But, the real payoff is the gracious master suite, which features a cove ceiling, room-sized closet, shower, and raised tub. Across the balcony, two bedrooms, a huge linen closet, a full bath, and a bonus room complete the upper floor.

Main floor — 1,258 sq. ft.
Upper floor — 1,265 sq. ft.

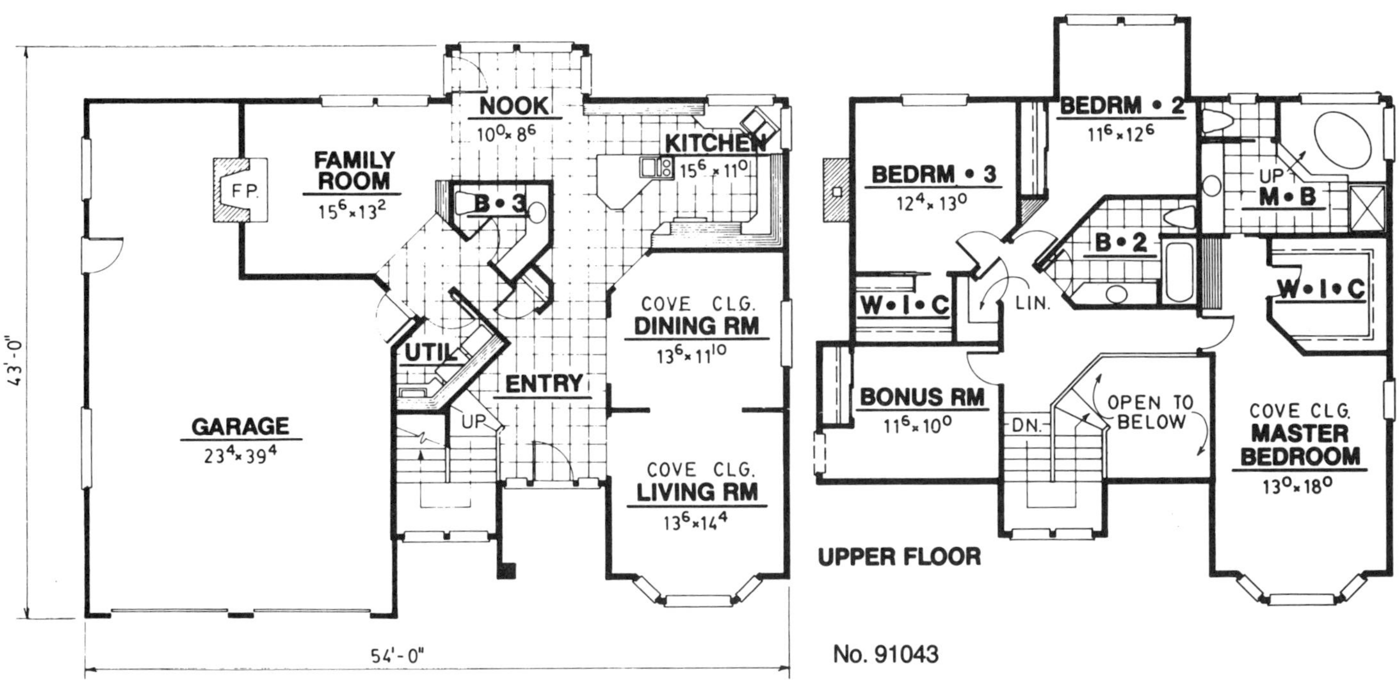

Family Room Doubles as Fourth Bedroom

No. 90648

If you love traditional Tudor styling, here's a gracious home you can adapt to your growing family. The vestibule entry leads to a central foyer, dominated by a stairway to the three second-floor bedrooms. You'll be enthralled with the luxurious master suite, which features a brick fireplace, cathedral ceilings, two closets, and a private bath. Just off the foyer, a fireplace and window seat give the expansive living room a cozy atmosphere. You'll have lots of choices at mealtime. The convenient U-shaped kitchen easily serves the glass-walled dinette, the romantic dining room, and the patio outside.

First floor —1,108 sq. ft.
Second floor — 836 sq. ft.

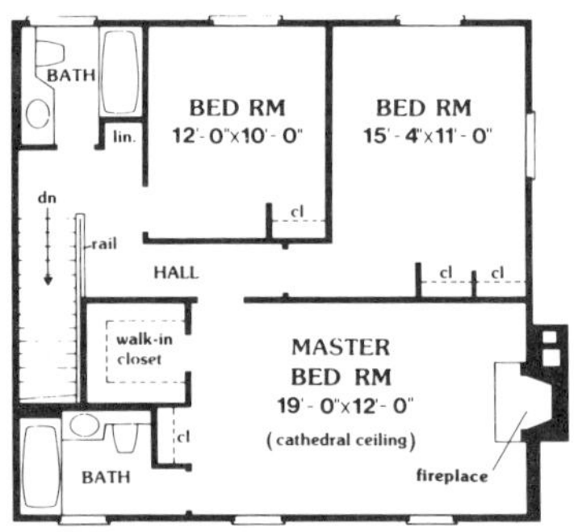

SECOND FLOOR

No. 90648

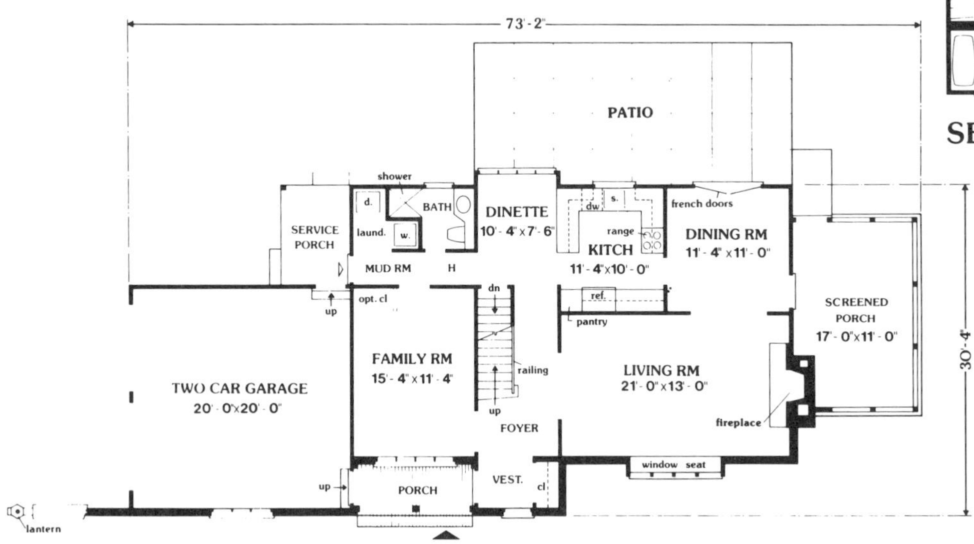

FIRST FLOOR

Open Living Area Plus Traditional Styling

No. 90107

The great room concept in this traditional home combines the kitchen, dining and living areas into one integrated space. Each of the two large bedrooms has its own complete bath. The master bedroom incorporates a spacious walk-in closet. Perfect for adult living and entertaining, this home also features a two car garage with plenty of storage or space for a workshop.

Living Area — 1,092 sq. ft.

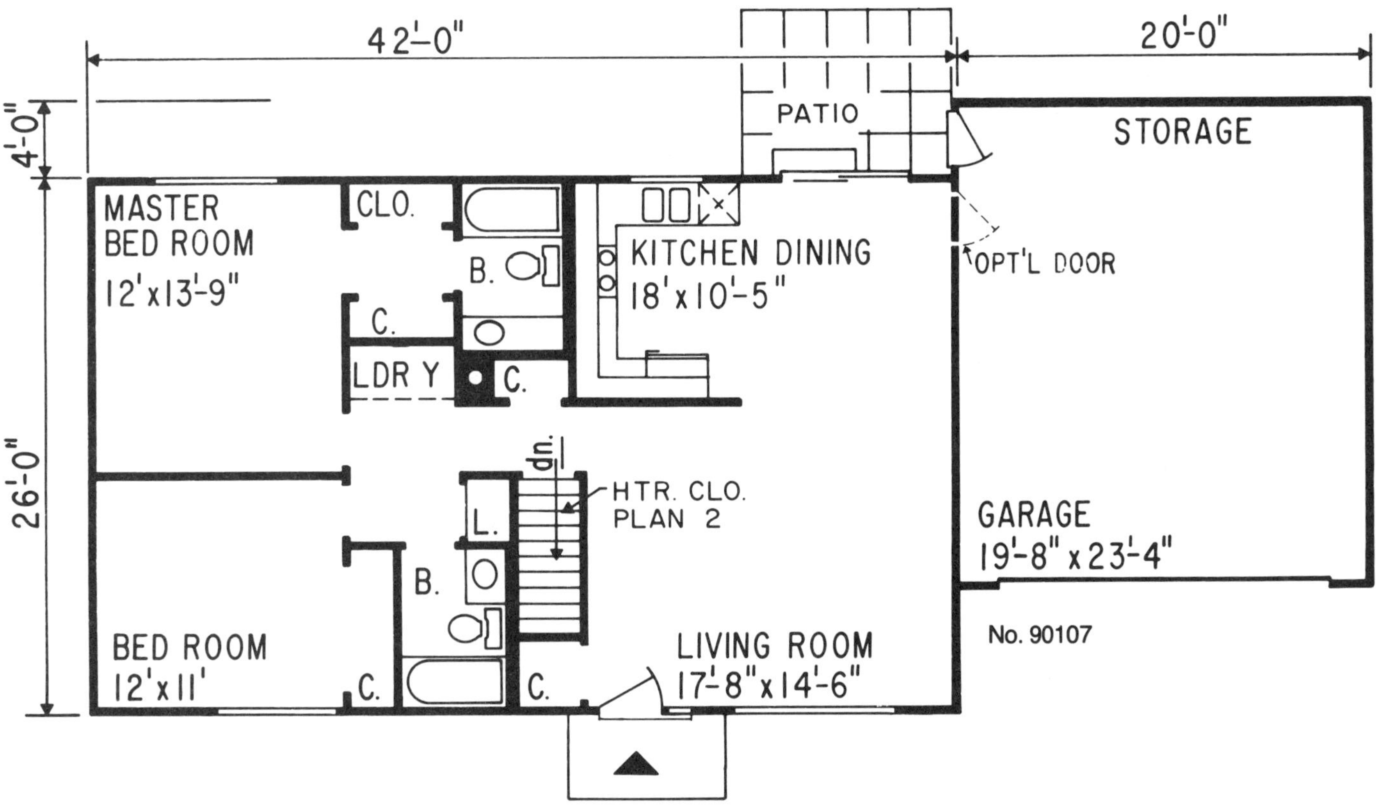

Relax in a Sun-Washed Spa

No. 91009

The luxury of a private spa brightened by a skylight could be enough to convince you that this is your dream house. But, intelligent separation of living and sleeping areas, a sunken living room, and wide-open family area will help you decide that this three-bedroom charmer is made for you. Enjoy the fire in the family room while you dine informally in the nook. The island kitchen makes mealtime a breeze. The den, just off the entry behind double doors, is conveniently located.

Living Area — 1,983 sq. ft.

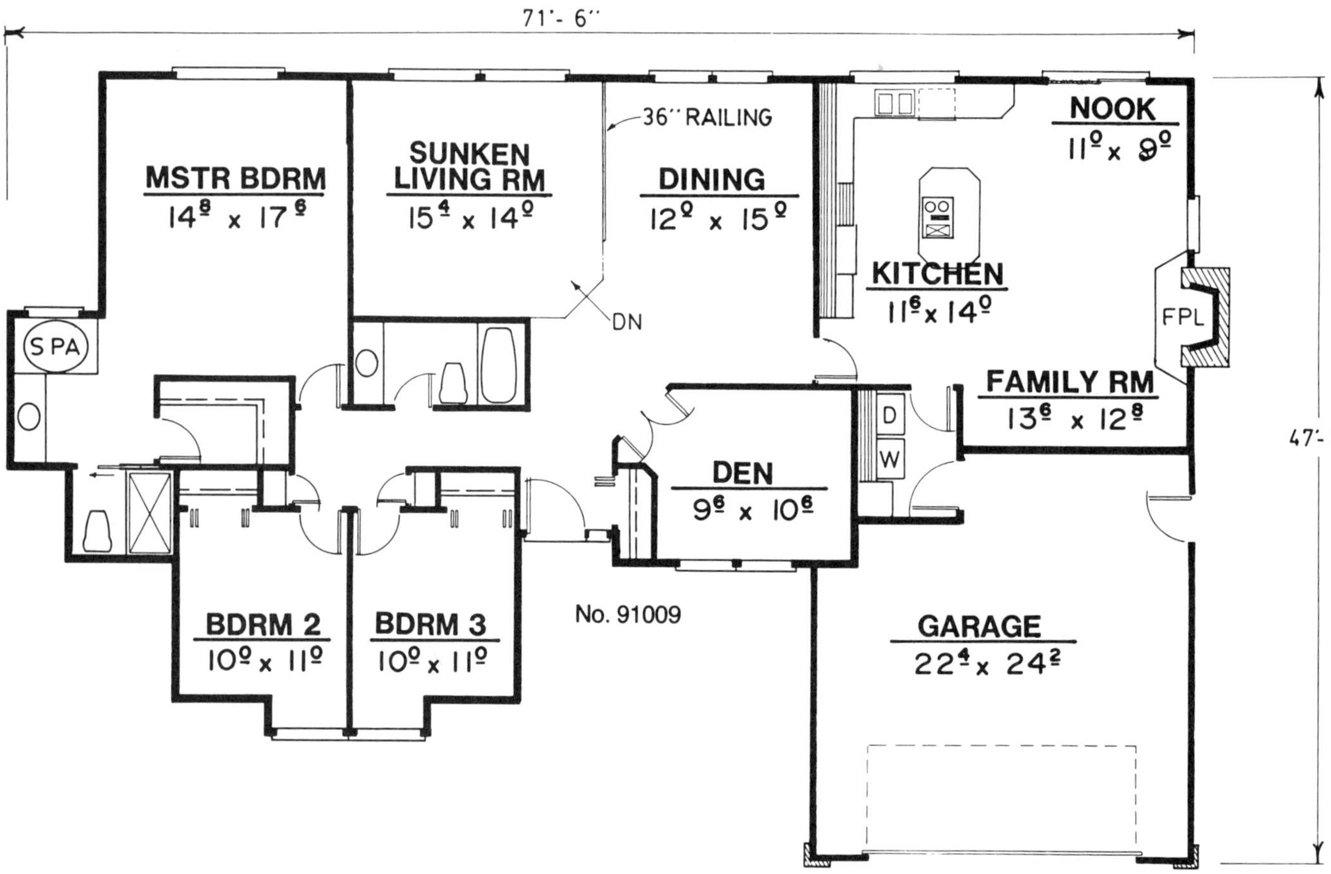

Traditional Elements Combine in Friendly Colonial

No. 90606

Casual living is the theme of this elegant Farmhouse Colonial. A beautiful circular stair ascends from the central foyer, flanked by the formal living and dining rooms. The informal family room, accessible from the foyer, captures the Early American style with exposed beams, wood paneling, and brick fireplace wall. A separate dinette opens to an efficient kitchen. Four bedrooms and a two-basin family bath, arranged around the central hall, occupy the second floor.

First floor — 1,023 sq. ft.
Second floor — 923 sq. ft.
(optional slab construction available)

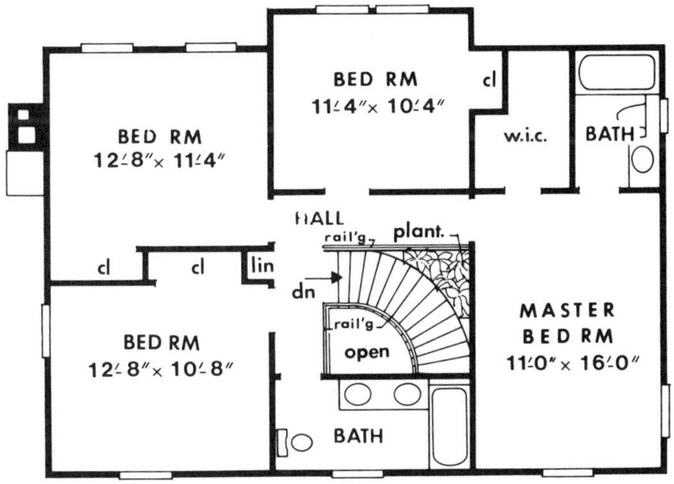

SECOND FLOOR PLAN

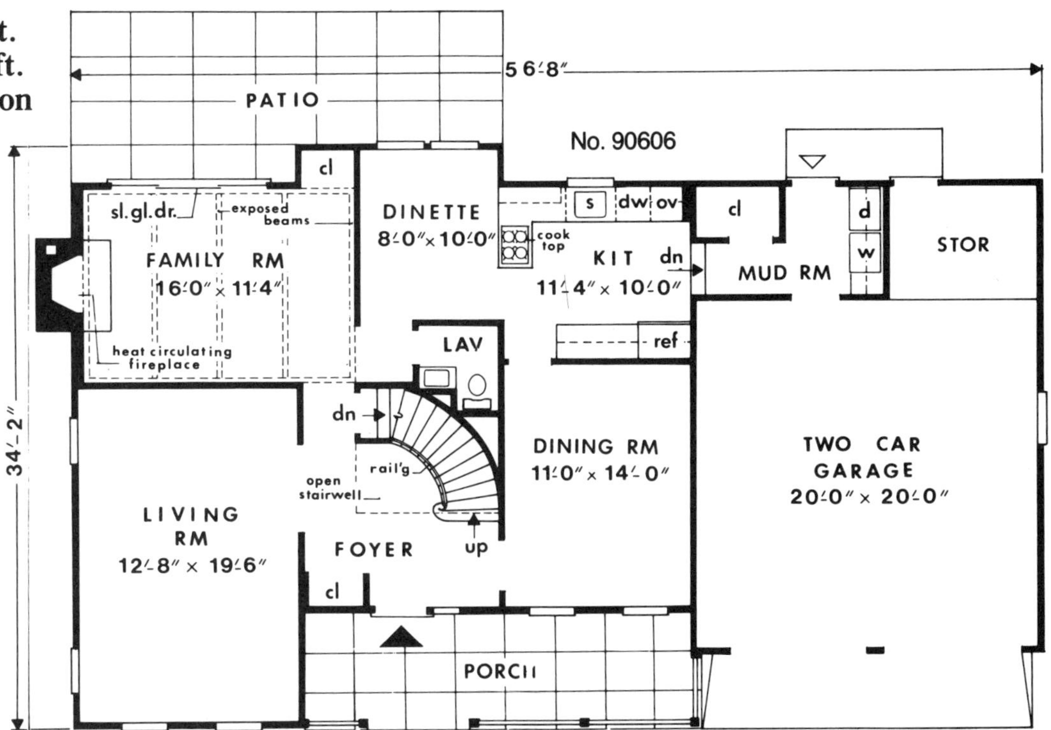

FIRST FLOOR PLAN

Design Portrays Expensive Taste

No. 90040

Inside the front entrance and beyond the foyer, a square reception hall divides traffic to either living or service area. Located here is a powder room for easy guest use. To the left, the 20 x 13 living room —with its 8-foot wide bank of front windows, log burning fireplace and French doors to the connecting porch—provides adequate, comfortable space for entertaining. Its use will continue to be appreciated over years of day-to-day living. The curved staircase to the second floor leads to the sleeping level. To the right is a large storage area. A space to the rear could be finished as a den or office which still would leave plenty of storage. Two baths offer more than adequate service for the three bedrooms. A round master bath is located in the turret.

First floor — 1,069 sq. ft.
Second floor — 948 sq. ft.

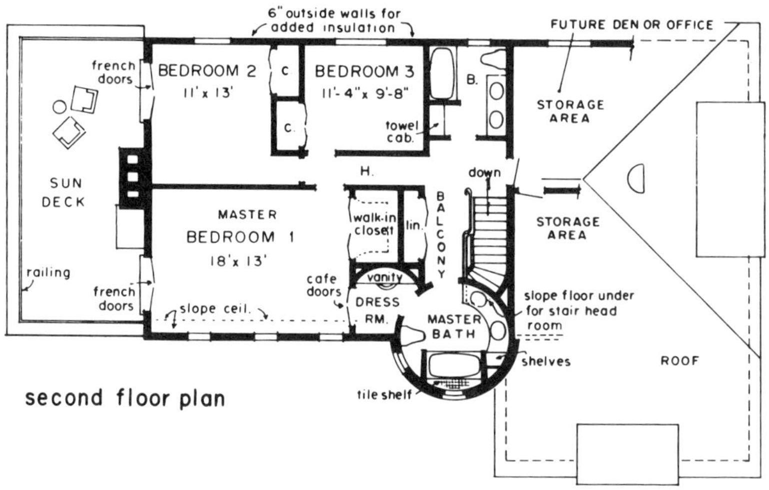

second floor plan

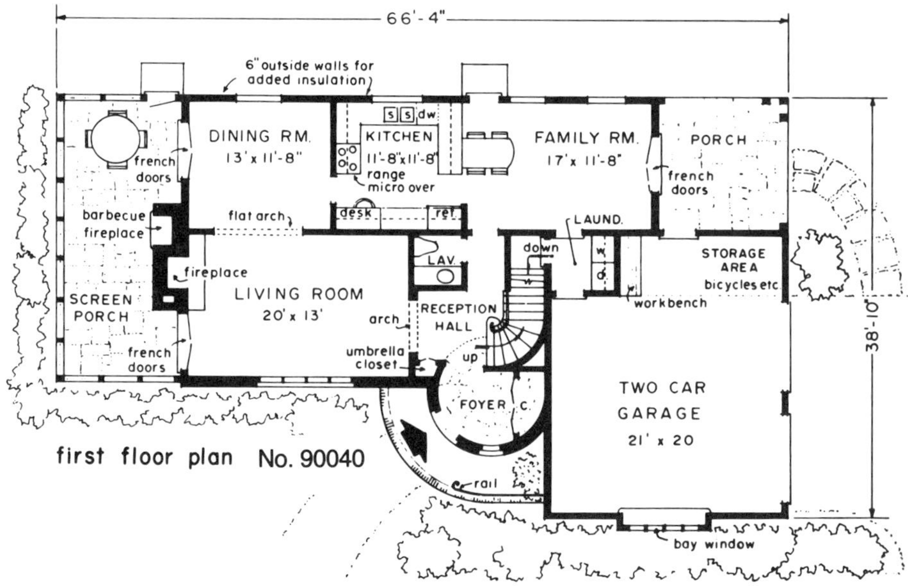

first floor plan No. 90040

Ideal Home for Small Family or Retirement

No. 90114

This well organized home features an efficient design, yet plenty of living space. The L-shaped living and dining area is graced with a fireplace and is easily accessible to the well thought out kitchen and laundry area. With one bedroom and one bath downstairs and the other bath and bedrooms upstairs, the children or guests can have privacy with full accommodations.

First floor — 924 sq. ft.
Second floor — 607 sq. ft.

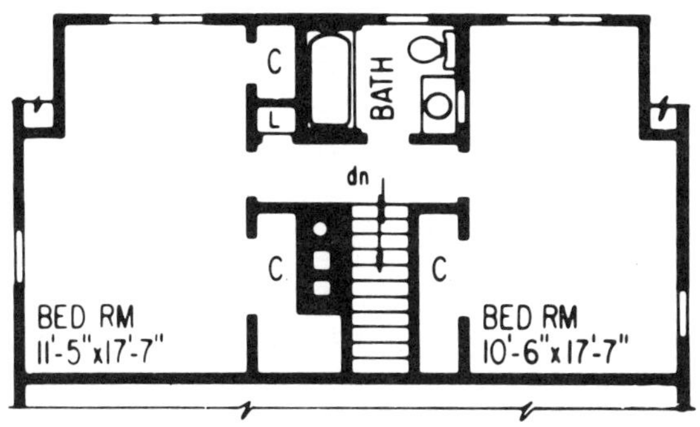

SECOND FLOOR

No. 90114

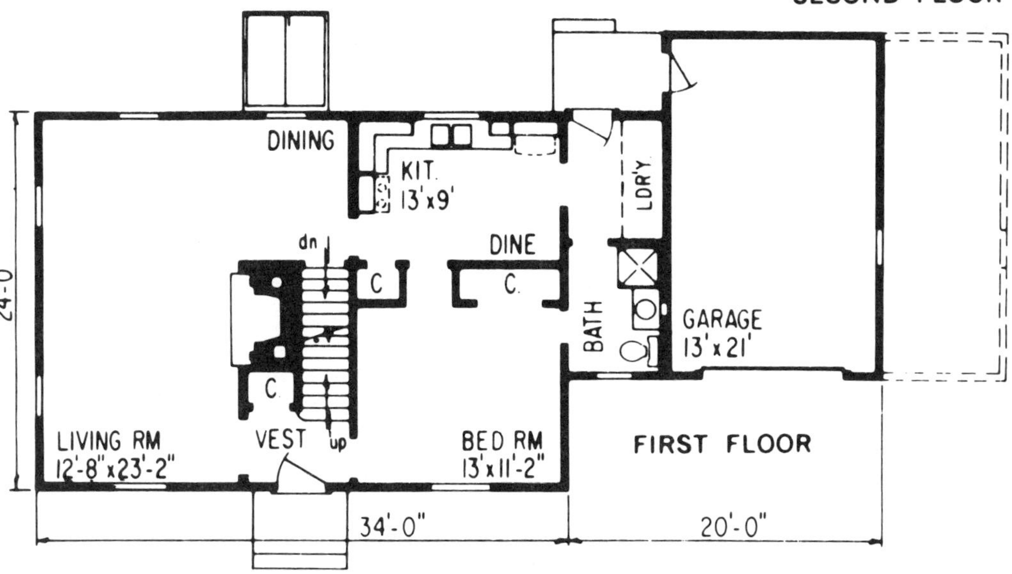

Style and Convenience on a Budget

No. 90540

If you're in an area of high construction costs, get the most for your money. This compact, one-level design squeezes maximum use out of an affordable home. The classic central entry, with coat closet, leads three ways: left into the open living and dining rooms, straight ahead to family living areas, and down a short hall to the bedroom and utility wing. Notice the convenient island that separates the efficient kitchen from the bayed breakfast nook and family room, and the handy pantry for extra groceries. Having the washer and dryer right next to the bedrooms will save steps, as will the nearby garage entrance. You'll really appreciate the master suite, with its skylit bath, double vanities, and expansive wardrobe.

First floor — 1,585 sq. ft.

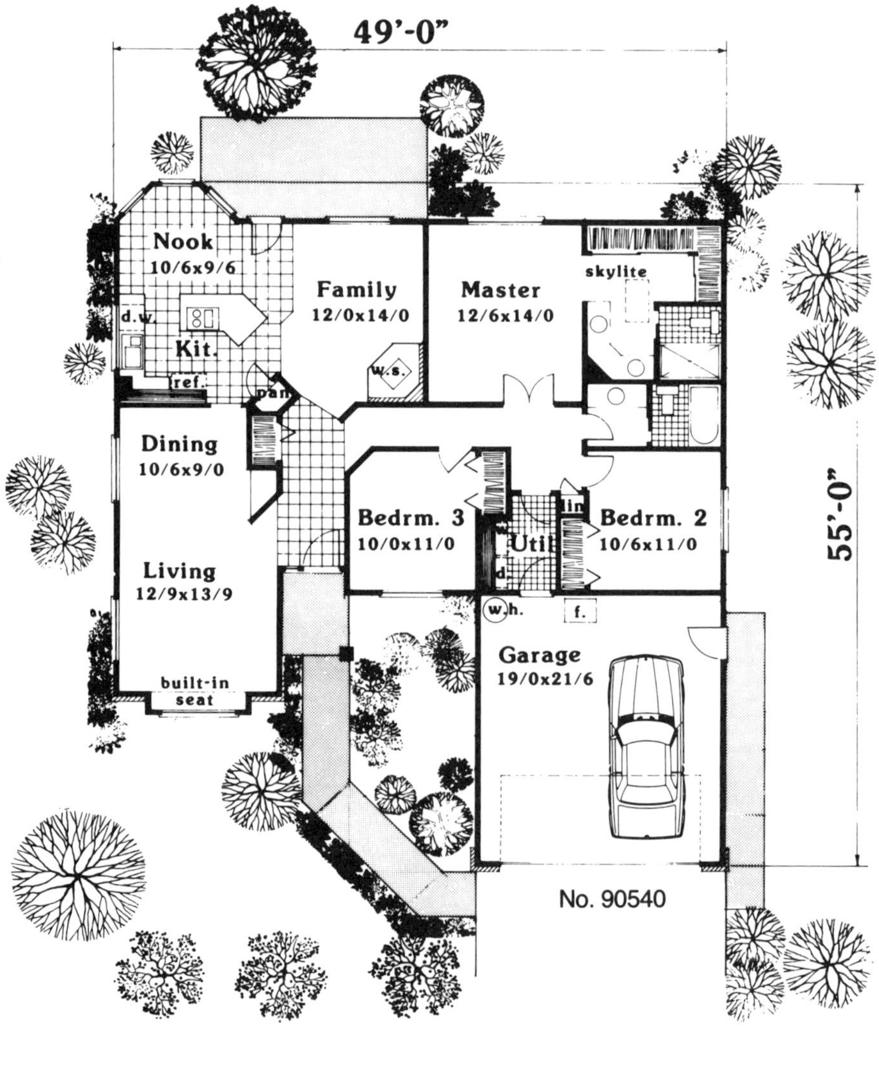

Energy-Saving Cape

No. 90645

This compact cape combines traditional design elements with modern amenities to create a warm, efficient home for your family. The handy, first floor master suite off the foyer features a split bath, double sinks, and three generous closets. Energy-saving features include an air-lock vestibule entry, sun-catching skylights in the dinette, a greenhouse window in the kitchen, and a heat-circulating fireplace in the living room. Sliding glass doors connect the dining and living rooms to the rear terrace. Upstairs, two bedrooms, loaded with closet space, share a full bath.

First floor —1,127 sq. ft.
Second floor — 554 sq. ft.
Basement — 438 sq. ft.

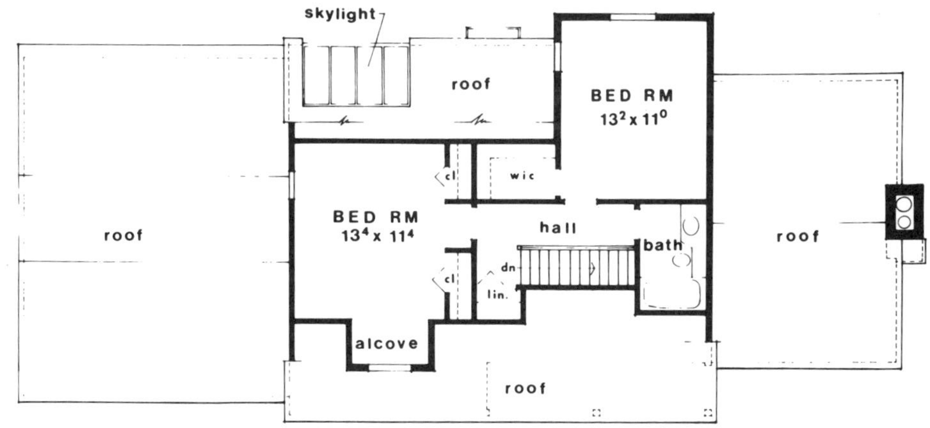

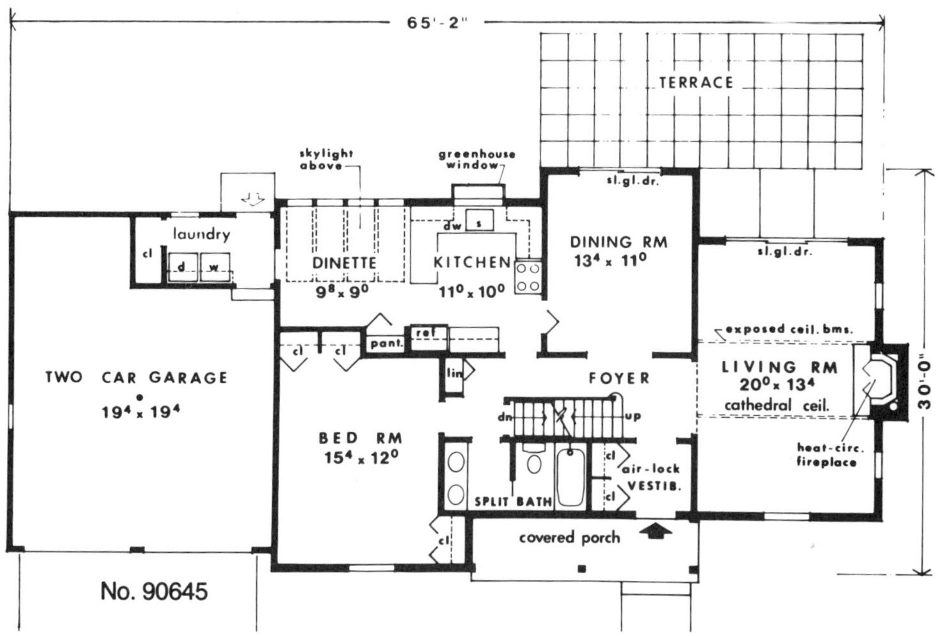

No. 90645

Spacious Master Suite Crowns Plan

No. 90661

Get away from it all in the luxurious master suite of this three-bedroom contemporary. If having your own private retreat isn't enough, the elegantly appointed bath, with double sink, whirlpool, bidet, and walk-in shower should convince you that you deserve this house! And, the first floor is just as spectacular. Cathedral ceilings in the foyer and living room soar to dizzying heights. A wrap around deck, accessible from the living room, doubles your outdoor living space. The dining room, with an attached greenhouse, adjoins the kitchen for an efficient mealtime combination. The first-floor bedrooms share a full bath, and are tucked away at the front of the house.

First floor — 1,286 sq. ft.
Second floor — 463 sq. ft.

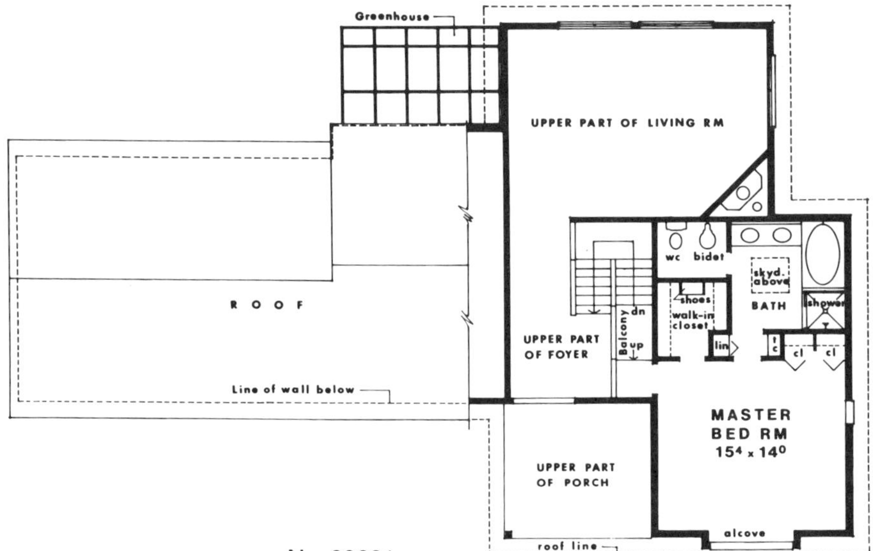

No. 90661

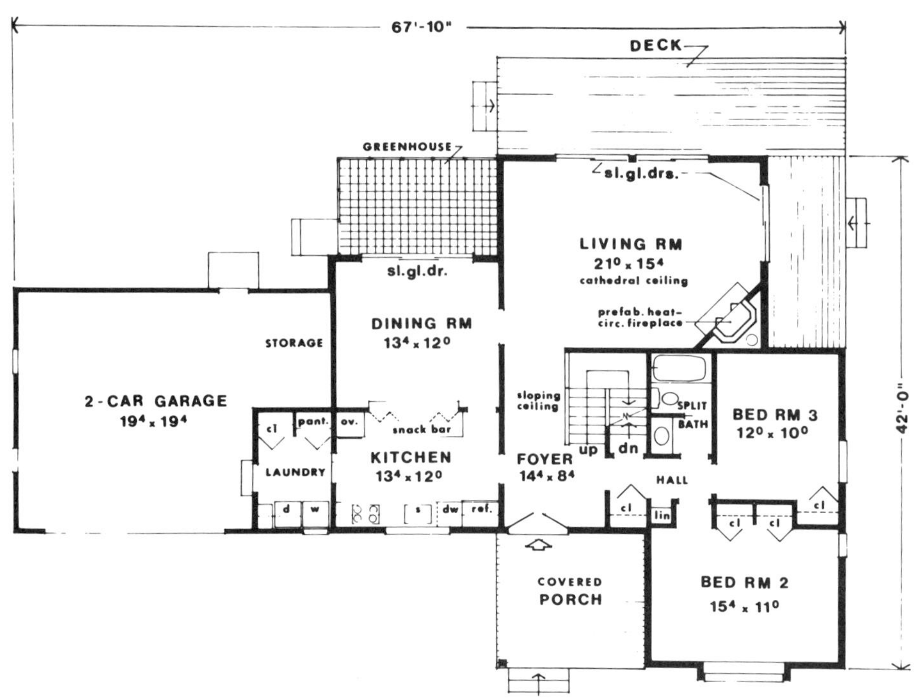

Gentle Curves Soften Every Room

No. 91048

Gracious living, and soaring interior views, characterize this distinctive home. From the foyer, you see the panorama of the living room with its fireside conversation pit, the dining room with french doors to a wraparound deck, and the curved railing of the balcony overhead — in one sweeping glance! Two-story stacked windows flood living areas with sunlight by day, and create a stunning nighttime impression. The first-floor master suite, with double sinks and a luxurious spa, is a convenience you'll appreciate. And up the circular staircase, the manificent, curving balcony leads to two more bedrooms and another full bath.

Main level — 1,938 sq. ft.
Upper level — 962 sq. ft.

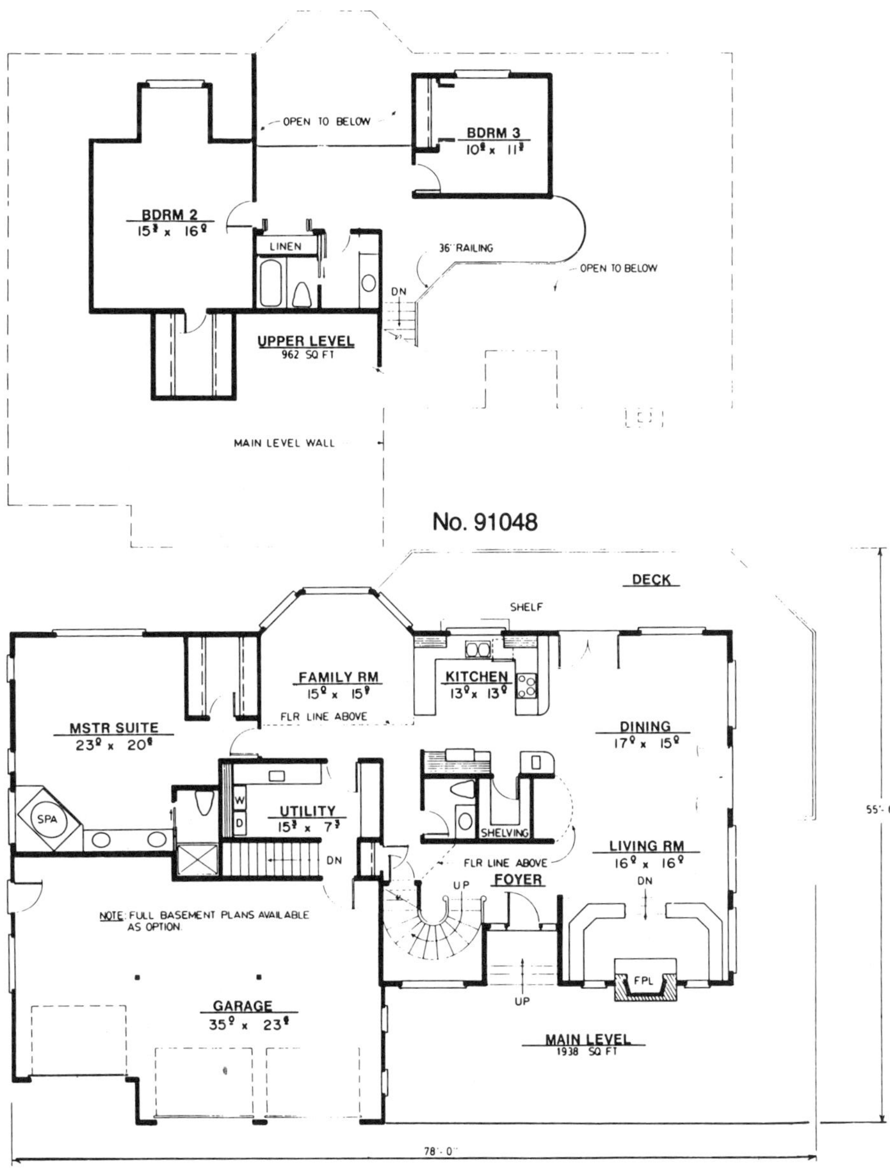

Five-Bedroom French Provincial

No. 90016

Visions of royal living come quickly to mind gazing at this elegant five-bedroom French Provincial. There's royal living inside, too, with spaciousness as the key-note; the room size entrance foyer with circular stair to the secons floor, giant living room with outdoor porch with grill, and the combined family room kitchenette. The grand staircase leads to the five bedrooms on the second floor. The master bedroom has a dressing area with walk-in closet and private bath with tub and stall shower.

First floor — 1,920 sq. ft.
Second floor — 1,780 sq. ft.
Garage — 700 sq. ft.

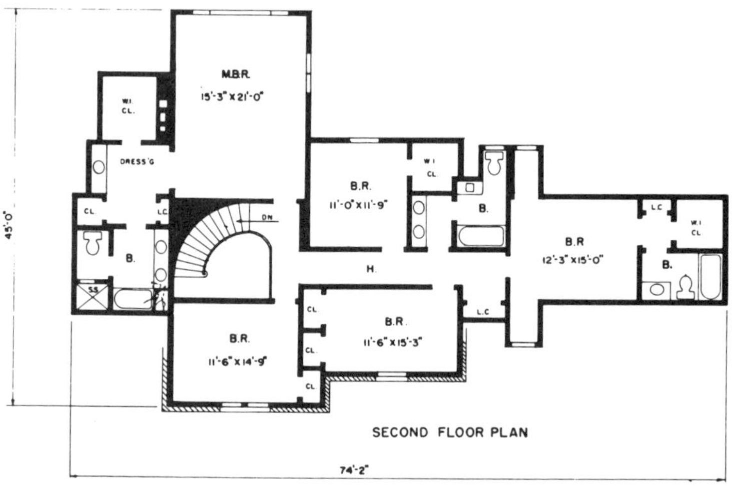

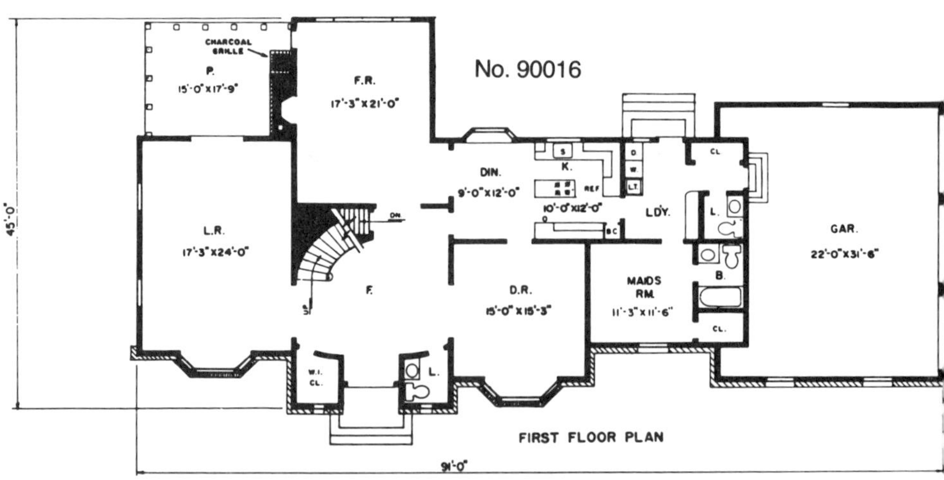

Great Room features Fireplace

No. 90105

Share your family's favorite activities around the fireplace of this spacious great room. It provides a cozy atmosphere that can't be surpassed. The dining area and kitchen with pass-through serving provide easy access to all of the family. Conveniently located adjacent to both the kitchen and the garage, the combination mud room and laundry room make cleaning up a breeze. The recessed entry way gives the front of the house a pleasing, clean line, while the side entrance to the garage lengthens the facade for a more unified look.

Living area — 1,345 sq. ft.

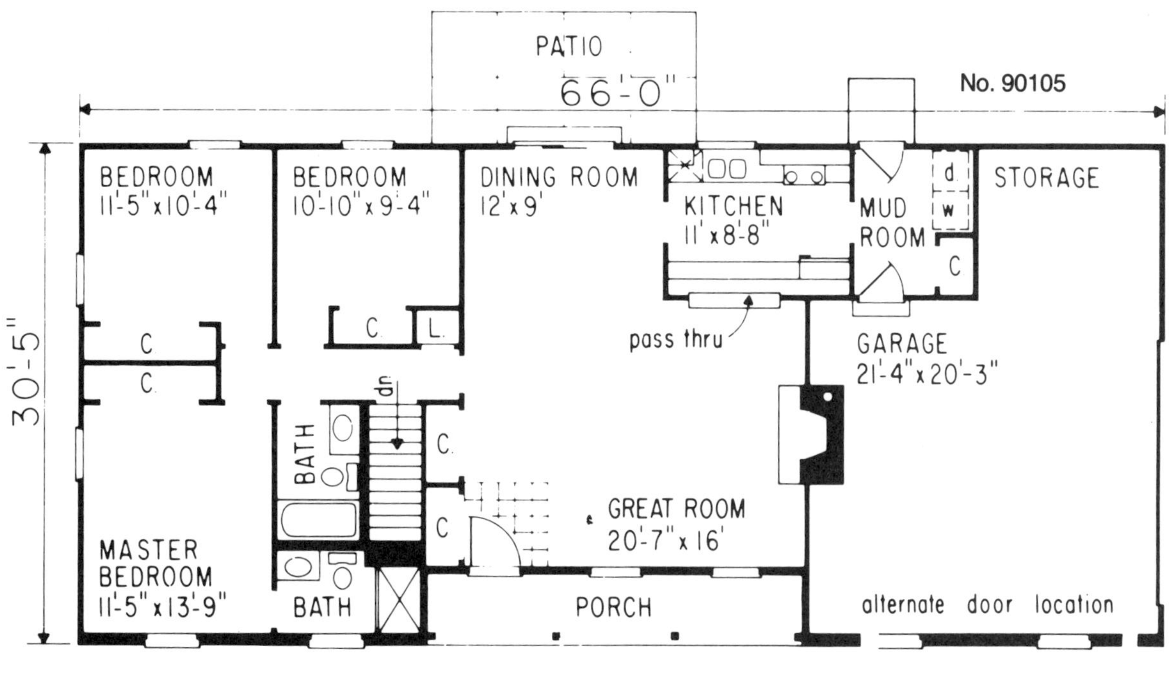

The Timeless Beauty of Brickwork

No. 90532

From the two-story entry and front windows to the passage between formal dining and living rooms, arches adorn exterior and interior spaces throughout this gracious home. At the rear of the home, the island kitchen is conveniently flanked by the formal dining room and breakfast nook. Twin fireplaces warm the adjacent family room and sunken living room. The dramatic angled staircase leads to a view of the open grand entry below. Two bedrooms share a full bath with double sinks. You'll find two sinks in the master suite, too, along with a walk-in shower and spa tub.

First floor - 1,546 sq. ft.
Second floor — 933 sq. ft.

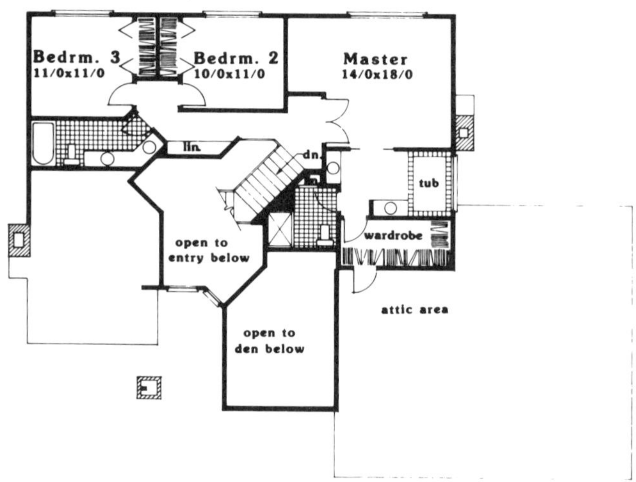

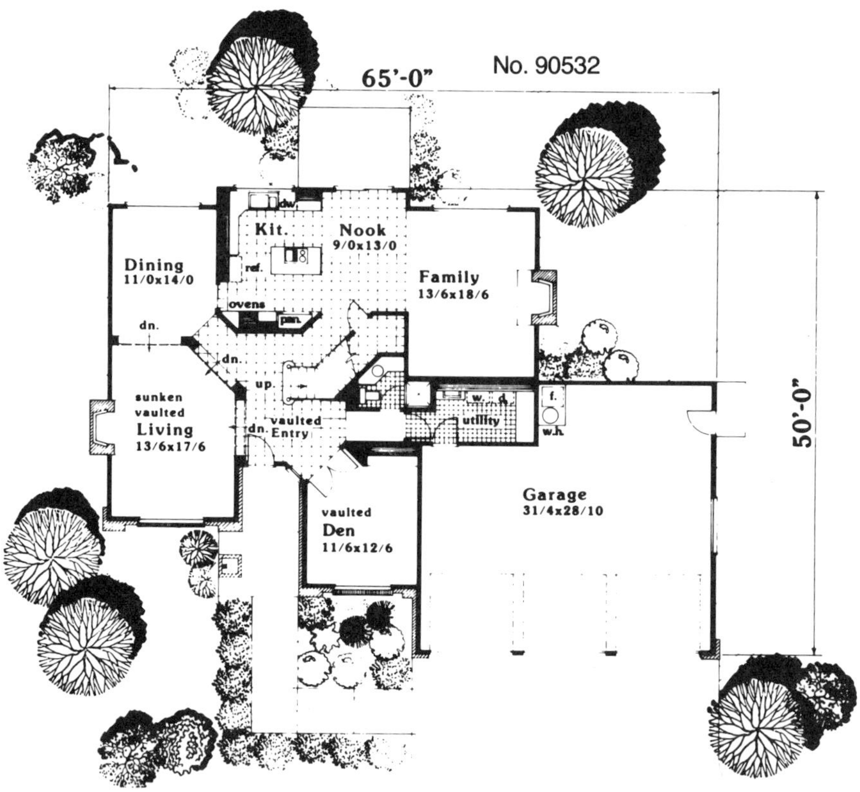

First-Floor Master Suite a Plus

No. 90646

Shuttered windows, a country porch, and flower boxes give a friendly flavor to this beautiful, four-bedroom home. Stepping into the foyer, you'll immediately discover that this classic design boasts some dramatic features. Straight ahead, the living room's sloping ceiling rises two stories. Dominated by the chimney of the heat-circulating fireplace, the room possesses an elegant, ethereal quality, thanks to a huge bow window and skylights. The adjacent dining room is flanked by an optional greenhouse and the handy, eat-in kitchen. Overlooking the foyer and living room, the skylit hall connects the three upstairs bedrooms and full bath.

First floor — 1,135 sq. ft.
Second floor — 827 sq. ft.

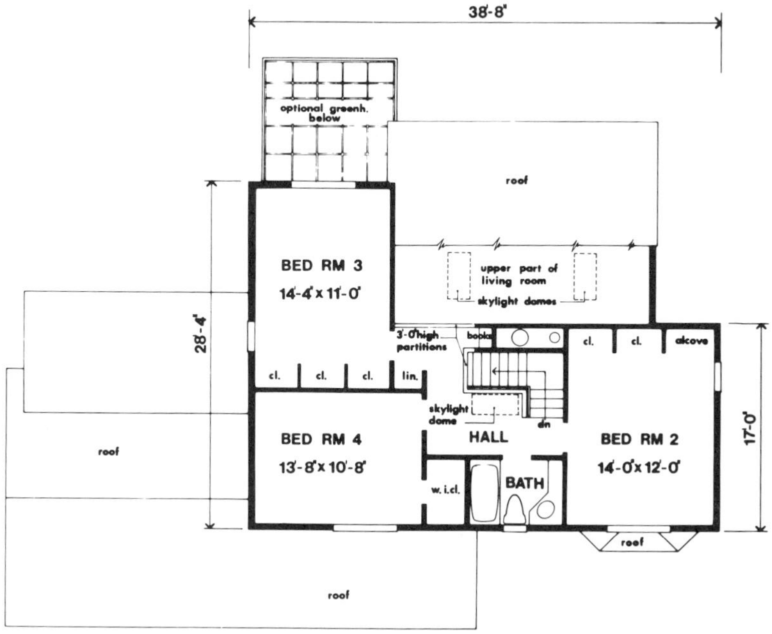

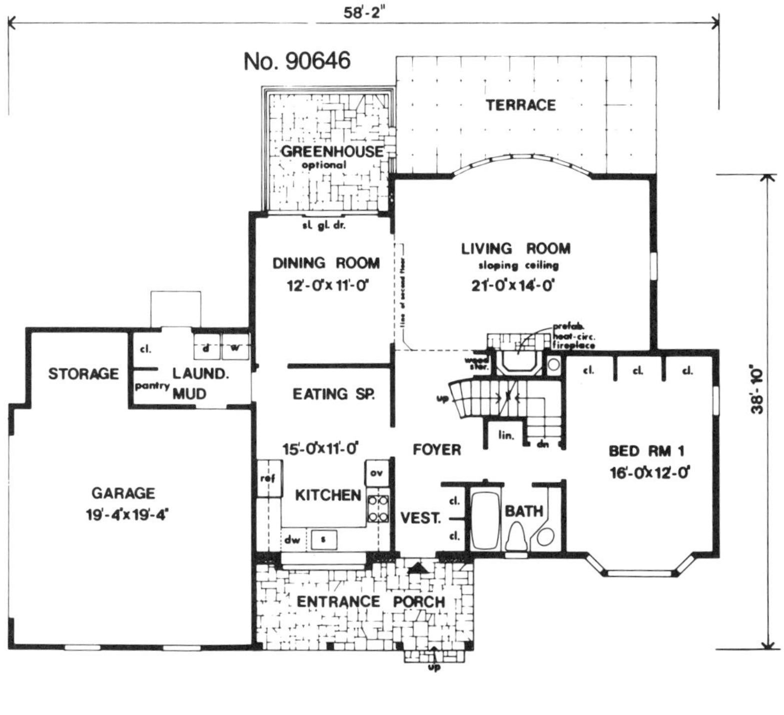

Bays Add Sunny Alcoves

No. 91042

You can reach every room in the house from the entry foyer of this convenient, one-level home. To the left, the quiet area includes two or three bedrooms, depending on your need for a den, office, sewing room, or exercise room. The ample master suite at the rear of the house features a walk-in closet, shower, and private spa tub. To the right off the entry, the great room's massive fireplace, flanked by huge windows, warms the open living areas. The range island keeps the kitchen and living areas separate without isolating the cook. And, just off the sunny, bayed nook, a huge pantry will give you lots of storage space for those extra groceries.

First floor — 1,484 sq. ft.

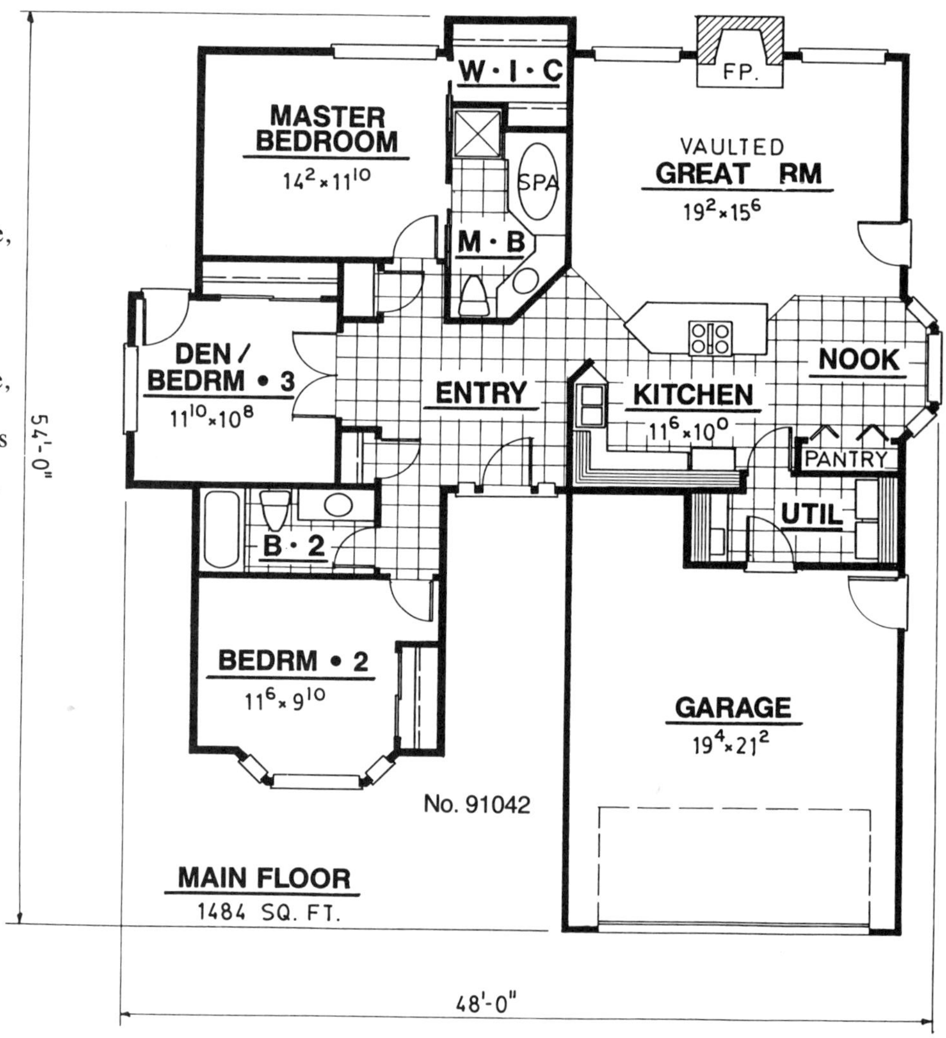

Lovely, Compact Tudor Saves Energy

No. 90641

Brick, stucco, and rough-hewn beams add up to classic Tudor beauty with the convenience of a modern floor plan. The sheltered porch leads into a traditional central foyer with stairs to three roomy bedrooms and two full baths. To the left, you'll find a cozy formal dining room with an expansive bump-out window. Past the coat closet, the living room features a heat-circulating fireplace, rustic beamed ceilings, and a romantic window seat. Sliding glass doors lead to a rear terrace. Build the optional greenhouse off the kitchen and dinette, and you'll be able to enjoy it all year round.

First floor — 893 sq. ft.
Second floor — 812 sq. ft.

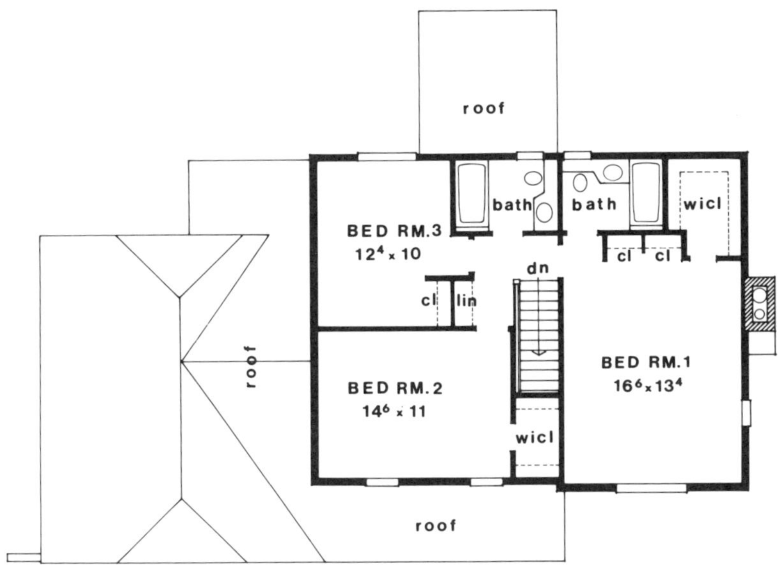

No. 90641

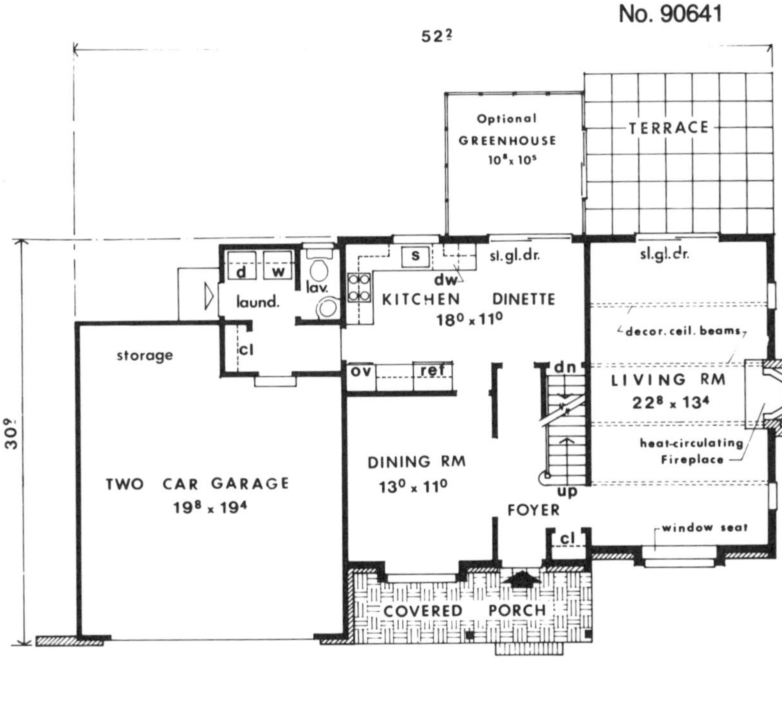

Glass Walls Brighten Living Room

No. 90644

Imagine enjoying the luxury of your own, private whirlpool bath with a built-in planter filled with greenery. That's just one feature of the elegant master suite in this three-bedroom ranch. You'll also appreciate the step-in shower, three closets, and rear window wall. Down the hall, active areas surround the central foyer. Have your morning coffee in the dinette off the kitchen. The formal dining room, with its sliding glass doors that lead to the terrace, is a beautiful room for a special meal. Glass walls give the adjoining living room a greenhouse feeling. And, when the sun goes down, the efficient, heat-circulating fireplace will prove to be more than just a decoration.

Main living area — 1,539 sq. ft.
Basement — 524 sq. ft.

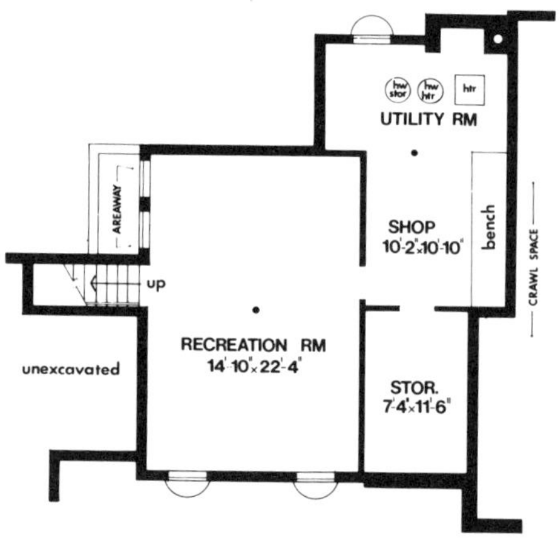

No. 90644

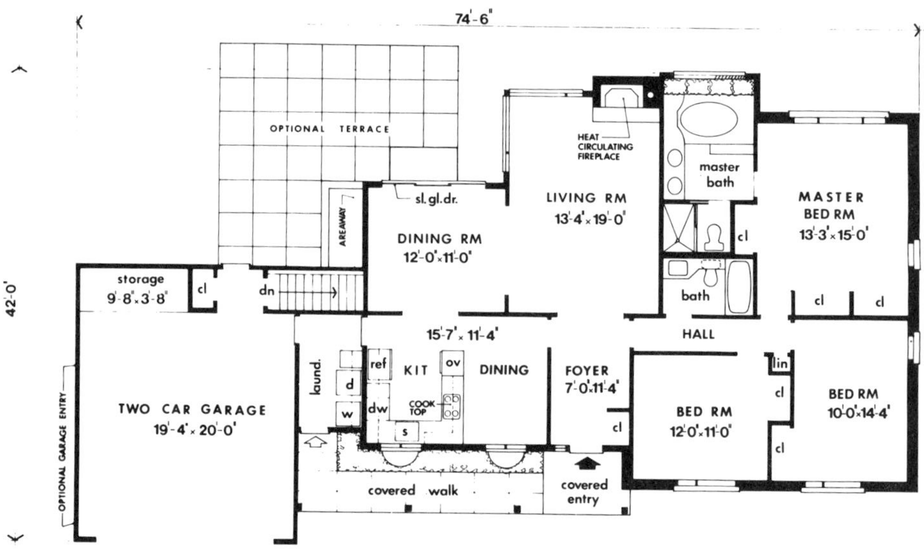

Timeless Design with Contemporary Flair

No. 90533

Brick archways, beautiful bay windows, and vaulted ceilings create a dramatic impression as guests enter this gracious family home. Direct them to the expansive, fireplaced living room with adjoining dining room. Right next door, the efficient kitchen, featuring a cooktop island and walk-in pantry, opens to the breakfast nook, making meal service to both dining areas and the sunken family room a breeze. The den off the entry can double as a fourth bedroom. You'll find the main sleeping area secluded upstairs. A full bath at the head of the stairs is convenient, while the master suite enjoys a lavish bath, complete with walk-in shower, tub, and double vanities.

First floor — 1,864 sq. ft.
Second floor — 1,321 sq. ft.
Bonus space — 336 sq. ft.

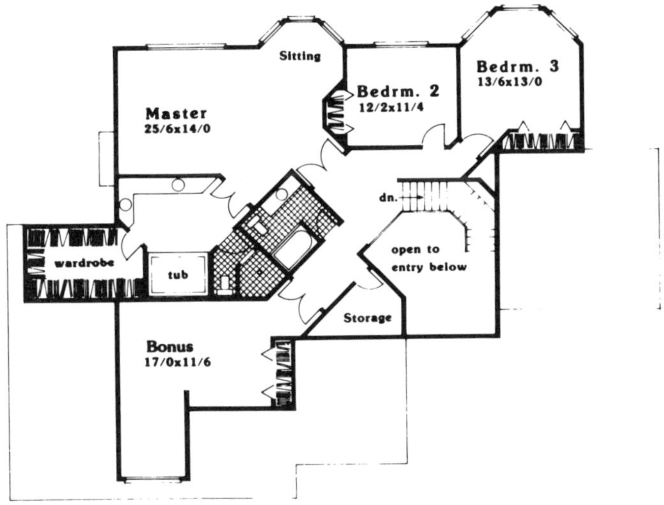

No. 90533

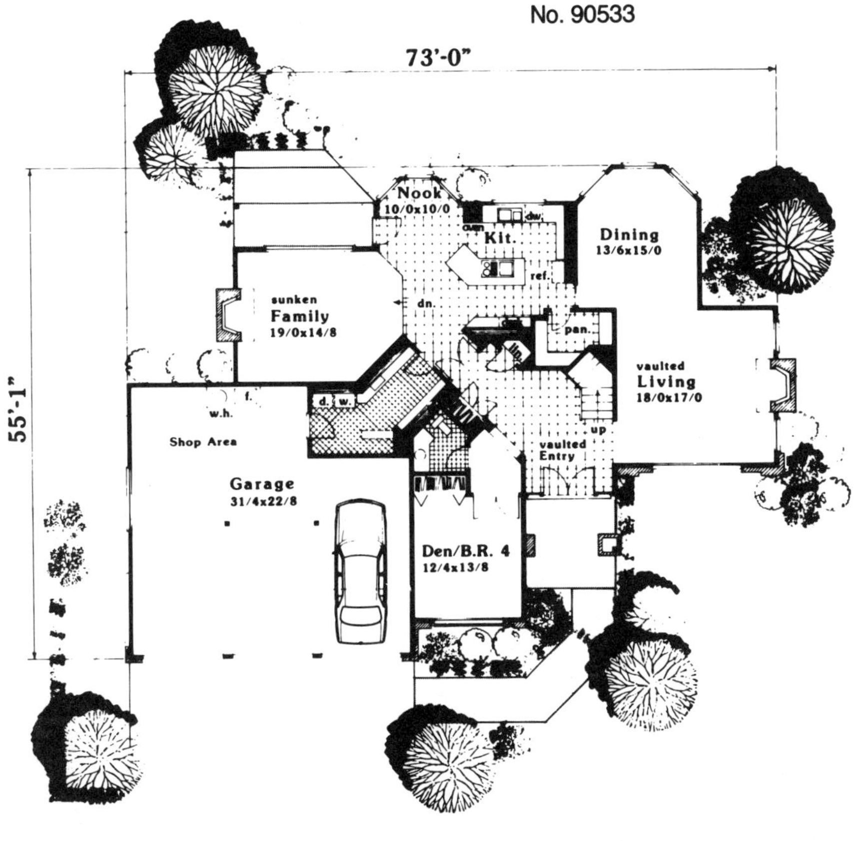

Traditional Styling

No. 90120

The lower level of this traditional home makes a great place for the family to work or play together. Behind the ample family room is a specially designed area that's just perfect for hobbies, crafts, sewing or whatever other activities your family might enjoy. In addition to the bath located on this level, there is also space for two bedrooms or other work areas that you may wish to add in the future. The main level includes three bedrooms separated by a hall from the living, dining and kitchen areas.

Main level — 1,164 sq. ft.
Lower level — 1,108 sq. ft.

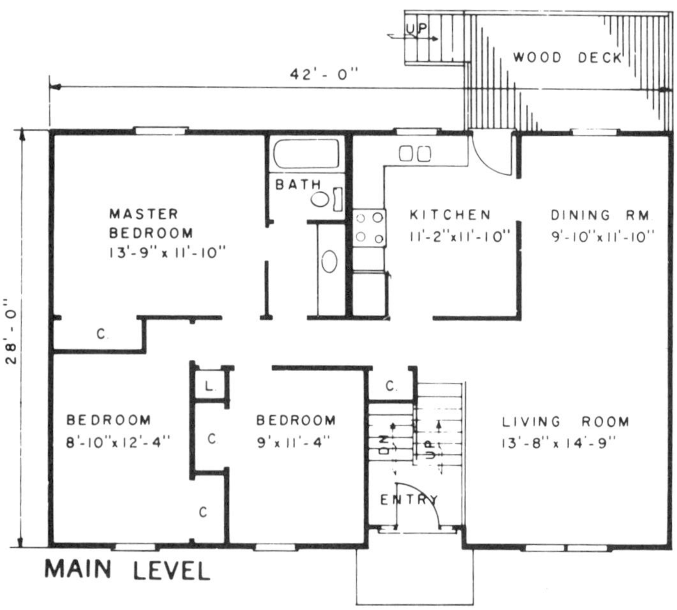

MAIN LEVEL

No. 90120

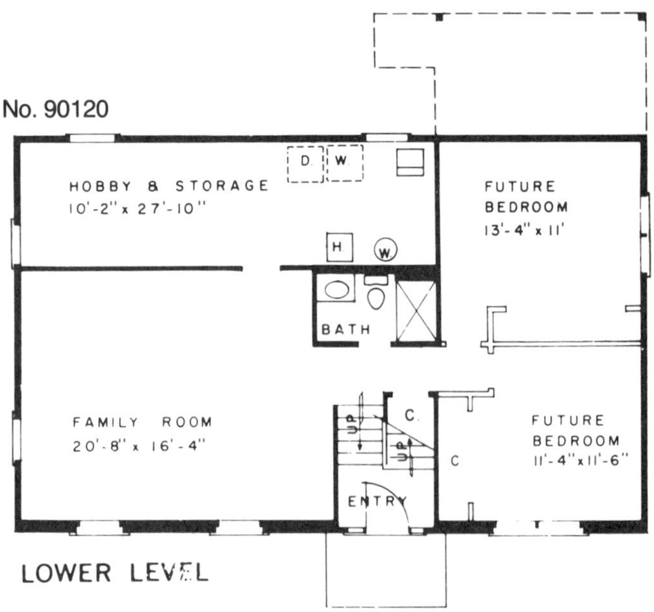

LOWER LEVEL

Romantic French Provincial

No. 90023

The romance of the French Provincial countryside is echoed in the exterior styling of this two-story, four-bedroom plan and should delight families with a taste for continental design. Its eye-catching character is derived from the curved window heads, angular bays, brick quoins at all corners of the brick veneer, steep roofs, and the diamond paned, copper-roofed picture bay over the double-door recessed entrance. The circular staircase with wrought iron railing provides a luxurious access to the four bedrooms on the second floor. You'll enjoy the details which retain the good qualities and hospitality of an earlier era.

First floor — 1,900 sq. ft.
Second floor — 1,692 sq. ft.
Garage — 576 sq. ft.
Basement — 1,725 sq. ft.

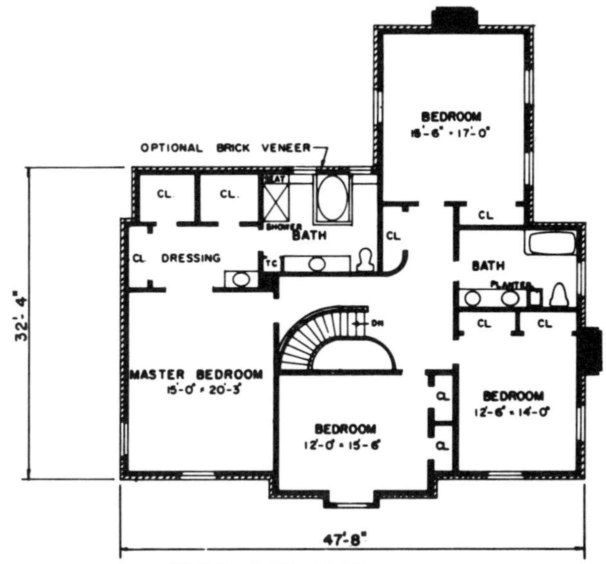

SECOND FLOOR PLAN

No. 90023

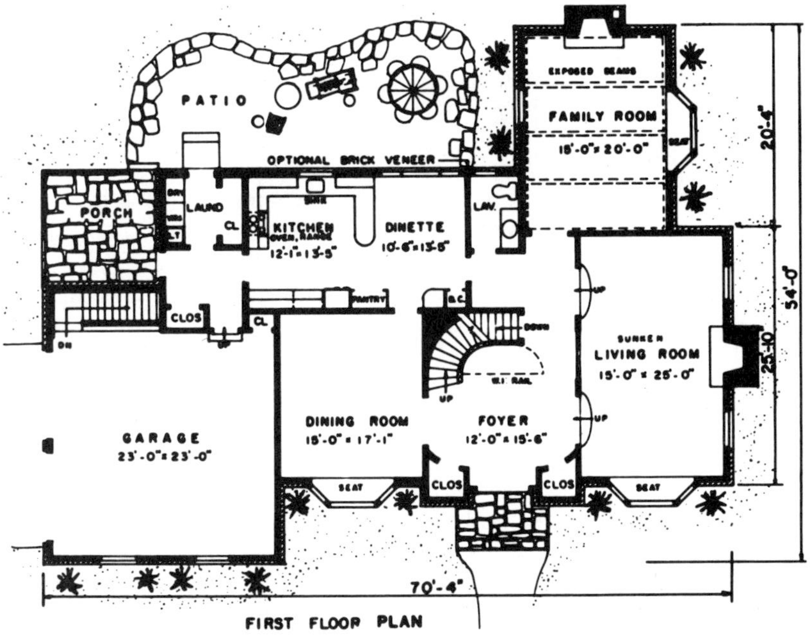

FIRST FLOOR PLAN

To Order Toll Free
1-800-235-5700

Connecticut, Alaska, Hawaii, and foreign residents call 1-203-632-0500

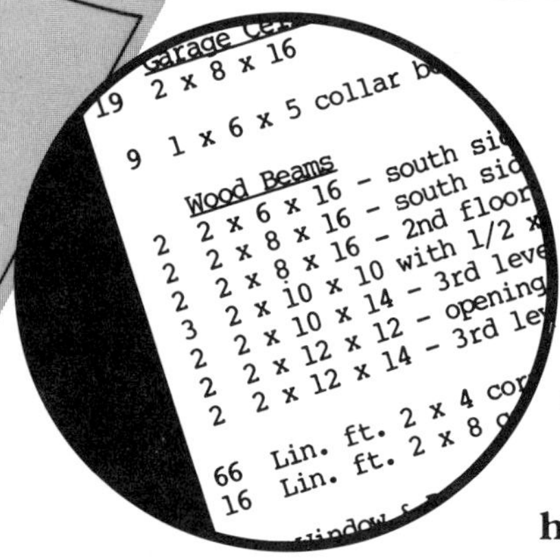

handy materials list available for most home designs

Put Over 80 Years of Experience to Work for You

Get Results Fast

Your complete, accurate Garlinghouse blueprints contain all the information your builder needs to begin construction on your custom home right away. You'll speed every step of the construction of your new home because each detail of construction and materials is already worked out for you and your builder.

Save Time and Money

There's no cheaper way to have the home you've always wanted than our custom blueprints. You pay only a fraction of the original design cost by a respected architect or professional designer. And, our years of experience go into every plan to save you costly mistakes and delays during construction.

Speed Construction, Avoid Delay

You'll speed every step of construction by ordering enough sets of blueprints for the job. Experience shows that 8 sets is best. Once you begin building, everyone seems to need a set. Your lending institution, local building authority, and general contractor each need a set.

And, of course, all the subcontractors will need a set once work is underway . . . the foundation contractor, the framing carpenters, the plumbing contractor, the heating and air conditioning contractor, the electrical contractor, the insulation contractor, the drywall or plastering contractor, the finish carpenters, etc.

While some sets can be handed down as work progresses, you'll avoid delays by having enough sets and eliminate worry about sets being lost or ruined on the job. You'll get faster and better results with the standard 8-set construction package.

Save Even More with a Materials List

Save even more with a materials list for your plan. This helpful list gives the dimensions and specifications of all materials needed to build your home (except for small hardware like nails and screws and the heating/air conditioning, electrical, and plumbing materials which vary according to your local building codes).

With this valuable list, you'll get faster and more accurate bids from your suppliers and avoid paying for unnecessary materials and waste. A materials list is available for most of our plans. Ask when you order.

Here's What You Get

Every set of our complete, accurate blueprints contains everything you need to begin building:

- ***Front, rear, and both side views of the house (elevations)***
- ***Floor plans for all levels***
- ***Foundation plan***
- ***Roof plan***
- ***Typical wall sections (cross sectional slices through the home)***
- ***Kitchen and bathroom cabinet details***
- ***Fireplace details (where applicable)***
- ***Stair details (where applicable)***
- ***Plot plan***
- ***Locations of electrical fixtures and components***
- ***Specifications and contract form***
- ***Energy Conservation Specifications Guide***
- ***Complete materials list (only if ordered and available)***

Add a Personal Touch to Your Home

Your custom dream home can be as wonderful as you want. Easy modifications, such as minor non-structural changes and simple building material substitutions, can be made by any competent builder without the need for blueprint revisions.

However, if you are considering making major changes to

your design, we strongly recommend that you seek the services of an architect or professional designer. Even these expensive professional services will cost less with our complete, detailed plans as a starting point.

Our Custom Design Staff may be able to help you, too, for a very reasonable hourly charge. One advantage of choosing our staff is that we make changes directly to our original drawings and give you a new, complete set of blueprints. Other architects can only attach modified drawings to our originals, which can be more confusing and time consuming for your builder. Call us for more information. Please note that we can make no modifications to #90,000 series plans.

Discover Reverse Plans

You may find that a particular house would suit your taste or fit your lot better if it were "reversed." A reverse plan turns the design end-for-end. That is, if the garage is shown on the left side and the bedrooms on the right, the reverse plan will place the garage on the right side and the bedrooms on the left. To see quickly how a design will look in reverse, hold your book in front of a mirror.

The dimensions and lettering for some Garlinghouse reverse plans are corrected to be right reading on the reversed plan. When this is not the case, one mirror image, reversed set (with "backwards" lettering and dimensions) is provided as a master guide for you and your builder. The remaining sets are then sent as shown in our catalog for ease in reading the lettering and dimensions and marked "REVERSE" with a special stamp to eliminate confusion. (Available only on multiple set orders.)

Price Schedule

One Complete Set of Blueprints	**$110.00**
Minimum Construction Package (5 sets)	**$150.00**
Standard Construction Package (8 sets)	**$175.00**
Each Additional Set Ordered With One of the Above Packages	**$20.00**
Materials List (with plan order only)	**$15.00**

Prices effective 1987.
Prices are subject to change without notice.

International Orders and Shipping

If you are ordering from outside the United States, please note that your check, money order, or international money transfer **must be payable in U.S. currency.**

Also note that due to the extremely long delays involved with surface mail, we ship all international orders via Air Parcel Post. Please refer to the schedule below for the mailing charge on your order and substitute this amount instead of the usual $4.75 mailing charge for domestic orders.

Country	One set	Multiple sets
Canada	**$ 5.75**	**$ 9.75**
Mexico & Caribbean nations	**$16.50**	**$39.50**
All other nations	**$18.50**	**$50.00**

Important Shipping Information

We process and ship your order within 72 hours of receipt, usually via UPS. Then, it normally takes another 5 to 7 working days for delivery. Please allow 10 working days for delivery from the time we receive your order.

Note that UPS will deliver only to street addresses and rural route delivery boxes and not to Post Office Box numbers. Please print your complete street address. If no one is home during the day, you may use your work address to insure prompt delivery.

For fastest service, use your **Visa or Mastercard** and call our Toll Free number. If you are in a special hurry, we offer ultra-fast delivery for an additional charge. Ask for details when you place your order.

for fastest service . . .
Order Toll Free
1-800-235-5700

Connecticut, Alaska, Hawaii, and foreign residents call 1-203-632-0500

Please have your credit card and order form ready when you call

The Garlinghouse Co., P.O. Box 1717, Middletown, CT 06457

Blueprint Order Form

code no. 20008

Please send me:

☐ One Complete Set of Blueprints (**$110.00**)
☐ Minimum Construction Package: five sets (**$150.00**)
☐ Standard Construction Package: eight sets (**$175.00**)

Plan no. ____________ ☐ as shown ☐ reversed

Cost of Blueprints .... $ ________
____ Additional Set(s) $20.00 each .... $ ________
with original order
Materials List ($15.00 per order) ...... $ ________
Mailing Charges .... $ 4.75
Tax* .... $ ________

*Kansas Residents Add 5% Sales Tax
Connecticut Residents Add 7.5% Sales Tax

Total Amount Enclosed .... $ ☐

Purchaser hereby agrees that the home plan construction drawings being purchased will not be used for the construction of more than one single dwelling, and that these drawings will not be reproduced, either in whole or in part, by any means whatsoever.

Charge my Order to: ☐ Mastercard ☐ Visa

Card No. ________________

Exp. Date ______ Signature ________________

Name ________________
(please print)

Address ________________

City & State ________________ Zip ______

Daytime Telephone No. ( ) ________________

GARLINGHOUSE

Send your Check or Money Order to:

The Garlinghouse Company
34 Industrial Park Place, P.O. Box 1717
Middletown, Connecticut 06457

Building Books

2546. Blueprint Reading For Construction This combination text and workbook shows and tells how to read residential, commercial, and light industrial prints. With an abundance of actual drawings from industry, you learn step by step about each component of a set of blueprints, including even cost estimating. 336 pp.; Goodheart-Wilcox (spiral bound) **$18.40**

2570. Modern Masonry Everything you will ever need to know about concrete, masonry and brick is included in this book. Forms construction, concrete reinforcement, proper foundation construction, and bricklaying are among the topics covered in step-by-step detail. An excellent all-round reference and guide. 256 pp.; 700 illus. Goodheart-Willcox **$17.00**

2516. Building Consultant The new home buyer's bible to home construction. This encyclopedia of home building explains in comprehensive detail about all the various elements that go into a completed house. It enables you to deal with the construction of your new home in a meaningful way that will avoid costly errors, whether you use a contractor or build it yourself. 188 pp.; Holland House (paperback) **$9.95**

2504. Architecture, Residential Drawing and Design An excellent text that explains all the fundamentals on how to create a complete set of construction drawings. Specific areas covered include proper design and planning considerations, foundation plans, floor plans, elevations, stairway details, electrical plans, plumbing plans, etc. 492 pp.; over 800 illus. Goodheart-Willcox **$22.00**

The books on this page were written with the professional home builder in mind. They are all comprehensive information sources for contractors or for those beginners who wish to build like contractors.

2508. Modern Plumbing All aspects of plumbing installation, service, and repair are presented here in illustrated, easy-to-follow text. This book contains all the information needed for vocational competence, including the most up-to-date tools, materials, and practices. 300 pp.; over 700 illus. Goodheart-Willcox **$17.60**

2506. House Wiring Simplified This book teaches all the fundamentals of modern house wiring; shows how it's done with easy-to-understand drawings. A thorough guide to the materials and practices for safe, efficient installation of home electrical systems. 176 pp.; 384 illus. Goodheart-Willcox **$9.20**

2510. Modern Carpentry A complete guide to the "nuts and bolts" of building a home. This book explains all about building materials, framing, trim work, insulation, foundations, and much more. A valuable text and reference guide. 492 pp.; over 1400 illus. Goodheart-Willcox **$22.00**

2544. Solar Houses An examination of solar homes from the standpoint of lifestyle. This publication shows you through photographs, interviews, and practical information, what a solar lifestyle involves, how owners react to it, and what the bottom-line economics are. Included are 130 floor plans and diagrams which give you a clear idea of how various "active" and "passive" solar systems work. 160 pp.; 370 illus. Pantheon (paperback) **$9.95**

2586. How to Design & Remodel Kitchens — This book takes you through steps beginning with evaluating your present kitchen and designing a new one to hiring a contractor or doing the work yourself. It offers solid information on the things you need to know to create the kitchen that best fits your needs. Full color charts and illustrations. 96 pp.; Successful (paperback) **$6.95**

2588. **How to Design & Remodel Bathrooms** — This helpful guide shows you step-by-step procedures for designing or remodeling your bathrooms so they suit the needs of your family. Clear charts, illustrations and text present information and techniques necessary for undertaking this immense project. Full color, 96 pp.; Ortho (paperback) **$6.95**

2518. Build Your Own Home An authoritative guide on how to be your own general contractor. This book goes through the step-by-step process of building a house with special emphasis on the business aspects such as financing, scheduling, permits, insurance, and more. Furthermore, it gives you an understanding of what to expect out of your various subcontractors so that you can properly orchestrate their work. 112 pp.; Holland House (paperback) **$9.95**

2602. A Logbuilder's Handbook A marvelously detailed how-to manual that is filled with precise, clear instructions, and sound advice. Packed with 55 illustrations, 126 photos, charts and tables, this handbook details every aspect of log home construction, and explains precisely all of the techniques. Many of the methods shown for hewing and notching logs are innovative and have never been presented until now. There are helpful chapters on making wood shingles, log home economics, site selection, and design, with a well-rounded look at foundation and wood styles and the benefits of different roof shapes. 248 pp.; Rodale Press (paperback) **$9.95**

2604. The Low-Maintenance House — At last, an idea-packed book that will save you thousands of hours on home maintenance. It's an essential planning guide for anyone building a home. Discover new as well as time-tested techniques and products for cutting down the time, and slashing the money, you spend to clean and repair your home...from roof to basement, from front yard to backyard garden. This book will earn its price, and your thanks, over and over again. 314 pp.; Rodale (hardback) **$19.95.**

2598. Alternative Housebuilding This is the most complete and authoritative guide on alternatives to conventional houses. These alternatives include some new and proven building systems based on pole foundations, or rammed-earth sheltering. They also include traditional systems now enjoying widespread revivals — log building, timber framing, and building with adobe, stone or cordwood. Complete with construction details, and step-by-step photos and drawings. 384 pp.; 425 photos; 300 diagrams; Rodale Press **$20.00**

2596. How To Get It Built — No matter how small or how large your construction project is, building will be more cost advantageous with this informative guidebook. This text was prepared especially for people involved in the construction process on a non-professional basis. Guidelines have been carefully prepared to follow step by step construction-cost savings methods and many of the construction problems that can be avoided. Written by an architect/contractor, this book offers home construction owners or investors the planning, construction and cost saving solutions to his own building needs. 238 pp; over 300 illus. Hashagen **$18.00**

2592. **How to Design & Build Decks & Patios** — Learn how to create decks and patios to suit every type of lot and lifestyle. This fully illustrated source book includes detailed information on design and construction as well as special charts on building and paving materials. Full color, 112 pp.; Ortho (paperback) **$6.95**

2514. The Underground House Book For anyone seriously interested in building and living in an underground home, this book tells it all. Aesthetic considerations, building codes, site planning, financing, insurance, planning and decorating considerations, maintenance costs, soil, excavation, landscaping, water considerations, humidity control, and specific case histories are among the many facets of underground living dealt with in this publication. 208 pp.; 140 illus. Garden Way **$10.95**

2562. How To Design and Build Your Own House Illustrated with almost 700 drawings (every step of the way), this complete do-it-yourself manual enables you, the beginner, to design and construct your own house. From putting together your first ideas and translating them into working drawings to figuring out costs and the actual construction of the house. The most complete and best illustrated book on the subject. 384 pp.; Alfred A. Knopf (paperback) **$14.95**

59. 300 Best Selling Home Plans
A unique book that presents the most popular custom home designs and floor plans. These magnificent plans were the highest ranking throughout the United States and Canada. Explore a wide range of acclaimed styles and sizes in one book; from traditional to contemporary, from cozy single level to king-sized multilevel. Each appealing custom design is shown in detail with a description of the features that make it so livable and desirable. 219 pp.; Garlinghouse (paperback) **$6.95**

Building Books order form

Yes! send me the following books:

book order no.		price
	$	
	$	
	$	
	$	
	$	
	$	
Postage & handling (one book only)	$	1.75
Add 50¢ postage & handling for each additional book	$	
Canada add $1.50 per book	$	
Resident sales tax: Kansas (5%) Connecticut (7.5%)	$	
TOTAL ENCLOSED	$	

No C.O.D. orders accepted; U.S. funds only.
prices subject to change without notice

My Shipping Address is:
(please print)

code no. 20009

Name ______________________

Address ______________________

City ______________________

State ______________ Zip ________

Send your order to:

(With check or money order enclosed)

The Garlinghouse Company
34 Industrial Park Place
P.O. Box 1717
Middletown, Connecticut 06457

For Faster Service . . .
CHARGE IT! (203) 632-0500

☐ MasterCard ☐ Visa

Card # ______________________ Exp. Date ________

Signature ______________________

2600. Building Underground This book covers the most current information on underground housing. Information has been compiled on earth sheltered homes, built all over North America — homes that are spacious, attractive and comfortable in every way. Underground houses are heated and cooled for a fraction of the cost of maintaining comfort in above ground houses. Their physical security, low maintenance, low operating costs, and noise and dust control further enhance their attractiveness. 304 pp.; 85 photos; 112 illus.; Rodale Press (paperback) **$14.95**

2542. Designing and Building A Solar House Written by one of America's foremost authorities on solar architecture. It is a practical "how-to" guide that clearly demonstrates the most sensible ways to marry good house design with contemporary solar technology. Included is a thorough discussion of both "active" and "passive" solar systems, and even a listing of today's leading solar homes. 288 pp.; 400 illus.; Garden Way (paperback) **$15.95**

55. Vacation & Leisure Home Plans $2.50

56. Multi-level Hillside & Solar Home Plans $2.95

57. Single-level & Underground Home Plans $2.95

58. Traditional Home Plans $2.95

60. Small Home Plans $2.95

Each of these five books contains over 120 new, innovative home designs from the finest architects and designers all over America. Many full color illustrations, and blueprints are available for all homes. 116 pp.; Garlinghouse (paperback).

71. Project Plans to Build for Children

72. Project Plans for all Around the House

73. Project Plans for Outdoor Living

These idea-packed books contain the most extensive collections of Better Homes & Gardens project plans ever published in a single book or magazine. Each book contains over 125 plans plus full color or black and white photographs of finished projects, diagrams and instructions. In addition to the instructions included in the books, there are order forms for working blueprints and materials lists for selected projects. The three books complement one another and offer many additional ideas for decorating or for future reference when adding on or remodeling. 128 pp.; Garlinghouse (paperback). Each **$3.95**